The Joan Palevsky  Imprint in Classical Literature

In honor of beloved Virgil—

"O degli altri poeti onore e lume..."

—Dante, *Inferno*

The publisher gratefully acknowledges the generous support of
the Classical Literature Endowment Fund of the University of
California Press Foundation, which was established
by a major gift from Joan Palevsky

Melania

CHRISTIANITY IN LATE ANTIQUITY
THE OFFICIAL BOOK SERIES OF THE NORTH AMERICAN
PATRISTICS SOCIETY

Editor: Christopher A. Beeley, Yale University

Associate Editors: Elizabeth A. Clark, Duke University
Robin Darling Young, The Catholic University of America

International Advisory Board:

Lewis Ayres, Durham University • John Behr, St Vladimir's Orthodox Theological Seminary, New York • Brouria Bitton-Ashkelony, Hebrew University of Jerusalem • Marie-Odile Boulnois, École Pratique des Hautes Études, Paris • Kimberly D. Bowes, University of Pennsylvania and the American Academy in Rome • Virginia Burrus, Syracuse University • Stephen Davis, Yale University • Elizabeth DePalma Digeser, University of California Santa Barbara • Mark Edwards, University of Oxford • Susanna Elm, University of California Berkeley • Thomas Graumann, Cambridge University • Sidney H. Griffith, Catholic University of America • David G. Hunter, University of Kentucky • Andrew S. Jacobs, Scripps College • Robin M. Jensen, University of Notre Dame • AnneMarie Luijendijk, Princeton University • Christoph Markschies, Humboldt-Universität zu Berlin • Andrew B. McGowan, Berkeley Divinity School at Yale • Claudia Rapp, Universität Wien • Samuel Rubenson, Lunds Universitet • Rita Lizzi Testa, Università degli Studi di Perugia

1. *Incorruptible Bodies: Christology, Society, and Authority in Late Antiquity,* by Yonatan Moss

2. *Melania: Early Christianity through the Life of One Family,* edited by Catherine M. Chin and Caroline T. Schroeder

Melania

Early Christianity through the Life of One Family

———

Edited by

Catherine Michael Chin and
Caroline T. Schroeder

UNIVERSITY OF CALIFORNIA PRESS

University of California Press, one of the most distinguished university presses in the United States, enriches lives around the world by advancing scholarship in the humanities, social sciences, and natural sciences. Its activities are supported by the UC Press Foundation and by philanthropic contributions from individuals and institutions. For more information, visit www.ucpress.edu.

University of California Press
Oakland, California

© 2017 by The Regents of the University of California

First Paperback Printing 2020

Library of Congress Cataloging-in-Publication Data

Names: Chin, Catherine M., author. | Schroeder, Caroline T., author.
Title: Melania : early Christianity through the life of one family / Catherine M. Chin and Caroline T. Schroeder.
Description: Oakland, California : University of California Press, [2018] |
  Series: Christianity in late antiquity ; 2 | Includes bibliographical references and index. | Description based on print version record and CIP data provided by publisher; resource not viewed.
Identifiers: LCCN 2016020341 (print) | LCCN 2016018264 (ebook) |
  ISBN 9780520965638 () | ISBN 9780520292086 (cloth : alk. paper)
  | ISBN 9780520379213 (pbk. : alk. paper)
  Subjects: LCSH: Melania, the Elder, Saint, 341?–410? | Melania, the Younger, Saint, 385?–439. | Christian women saints. | Women in Christianity—History.
Classification: LCC BR1720.M37 (print) | LCC BR1720.M37 C45 2018 (ebook) | DDC 270.2092/2—dc23
LC record available at https://lccn.loc.gov/2016020341.

for Liz

CONTENTS

Introduction   *1*
Catherine M. Chin and Caroline T. Schroeder

PART ONE. ARISTOCRACY   *15*

1. Apostles and Aristocrats   *19*
   Catherine M. Chin
2. Namesake and Inheritance   *34*
   Christine Luckritz Marquis
3. Exemplary Women   *50*
   Caroline T. Schroeder

PART TWO. BODY AND FAMILY   *67*

4. Holy Households   *71*
   Maria Doerfler
5. Wounded by Divine Love   *86*
   Kristi Upson-Saia

PART THREE. GENDER AND MEMORY   *107*

6. Memories of the Martyrs   *111*
   L. Stephanie Cobb

7. The Memory of Melania   130
Rebecca Krawiec

PART FOUR. WISDOM AND HERESY   149

8. A Life in Letters   153
Robin Darling Young

9. Friends and Heretics   171
Susanna Drake

10. Posthumous Orthodoxy   186
Christine Shepardson

PART FIVE. IN THE HOLY PLACES   203

11. The Lost Generation   207
Andrew S. Jacobs

12. Sing, O Daughter(s) of Zion   222
Stephen J. Shoemaker

PART SIX. MODERNITIES   241

13. Afterlives   245
Michael Penn

14. Monastic Revivals   260
Stephen J. Davis

15. The Future of Sainthood   271
Elizabeth A. Castelli

Afterword   283
Randall Styers

List of Contributors   287
Acknowledgments   291
Bibliography   293
Index   325

Introduction

Catherine M. Chin and Caroline T. Schroeder

The Roman aristocrats Melania the Elder (ca. 341–ca. 410) and her granddaughter Melania the Younger (ca. 385–ca. 439) are startling, glittering, and disturbing figures in the early history of Christianity. From the accounts that have come down to us, they were famous, or notorious, in their own lifetimes for dramatic acts of self-definition and self-denial, acts that sometimes placed them at odds with the expectations of their aristocratic peers but that sometimes fulfilled those expectations so completely that these two women became, in essence, peerless. This book explores the alternation between these oppositions and fulfillments, and between acts and expectations, that historians of early Christianity now see in the careers of the two famous Melanias. They were two of the wealthiest people in human history; they counted monks, miracle workers, bishops, and empresses as their companions; their influence and their property spread across the Mediterranean from Spain to Africa to Turkey. The events that made up the lives of Melania the Elder and Melania the Younger could be used to write many different kinds of stories about the later Roman Empire; in this book we use their lives to survey the dense and surprising landscape that was the early Christian world. Our project is to consider the relationship between the lives and times of two early Christians and the larger social and cultural forces that were at work in the fourth and fifth centuries, which together created the complex sets of artifacts, ideas, and behaviors that we call early Christianity.

The "early Christianity" that we consider in this book takes shape during a period that has come to be defined by scholars since the 1970s as "late antiquity": a set of historical moments between the third and the seventh centuries that was marked by profound novelties in tension with a tenacious traditionalism. New institutions, such as the Christian monastery, erupted onto the scene, where others, such as the Roman Senate, calcified. Still others, including church offices and clerical hierarchies, repeatedly changed: first as Christianity was brought into the public religious landscape by the emperor Constantine (d. 337) and over and over again in the wake of regional power shifts, theological schisms, and the politico-military disruptions sometimes described as the fall of the Roman Empire in the West. Throughout this period, the Christian elite became firmly ensconced in all levels of government, leaving their monumental traces alongside the more modest remains of everyday Christians caught up in the tides of empire. Pilgrims crisscrossed the Mediterranean in new forms of sacred travel, seeking holy people and holy places whose stories fired their imaginations, while others crossed land and sea either to become holy people themselves, in Syria, Palestine, and Egypt, or to fight as soldiers in the Roman army. An abundance of sermons, letters, liturgical books, artifacts, and architectural remains testifies to the hardships and pleasures of this daily life, expressions of lay piety that bubbled to the surface, visible to any historian, archaeologist, or theologian surveying the field. Prayer practices, devotion to the saints, sartorial advice, child-rearing principles, charitable giving, and more all appear in our sources.

Along with these everyday concerns, ardent debates over the very definition of Christianity characterized late antiquity and shaped the Melanias' world. The first Ecumenical Council of Nicaea, in 325 C.E., crafted a creed declaring that the Son of God and God the Father were "of one substance," but late ancient Christians themselves were never of one mind. The Council of Constantinople in 381, which affirmed and expanded upon the creed established at Nicaea, exposed the fissures of belief between clerics and laity alike. Further disagreements over the relationship between Jesus Christ's divinity and humanity quickly spread beyond individual antagonists (such as Cyril, the powerful bishop of Alexandria, and Nestorius, bishop of the imperial capital in Constantinople) and turned into a cluster of disputes known as the Nestorian controversy. The disputed resolutions of these debates in the councils of Ephesus, in 431, and of Chalcedon, in 451, as well as the resulting ecclesiastical divisions, reverberate to this day. Debates about the nature of humanity itself also run through this period. We see Augustine of Hippo refining his argument about original sin and the flawed nature of the human will during what is known as the Pelagian controversy. As fourth- and fifth-century interpreters of the Alexandrian theologian Origen popularized a doctrine that human souls once existed as intellects with God and would eventually return to heaven in a bodiless resurrection, the ensuing Origenist controversy engulfed monk and cleric alike from the deserts of Egypt to the capital cities of Rome and Constantinople. In the midst of all this, such figures as the influential biblical scholar and ascetic Jerome of Stridon (d. 419) worked, networked, and crafted genres of Christian writing that would eventually inspire the humanism of the Renaissance.

Melania the Younger and Melania the Elder moved within this web of institutions, conflicts, and controversies; they were friends, patrons, and sometimes enemies of nearly all the major figures involved in these transformative times. This book positions these women as central figures in the history, religion, and politics of early Christianity and explores how their legacies were crafted and deployed in their historical and literary afterlives. These chapters also consider the systemic constraints on even the most powerful early Christian women in the management of their accomplishments, reputations, and influences. But even more, this book reverses the lens of typical historical investigation. Beyond examining the Melanias in their contexts of gender, religion, and history, the book as a collective volume asks what early Christianity looks like through Melanian lenses. The stakes in this work are high, especially for women. As the chapters demonstrate, from the moments of the Melanias' deaths up to modern times in America and Egypt, male writers have sought to use the Melanias to shape subsequent people's piety and power, particularly women's.

We begin here by setting out some of the issues at stake in writing history as an interaction between individual people and larger social and cultural systems; we then turn to how the different chapters of the book illuminate these issues.

GREAT AND SMALL: THE BOUNDARIES OF HISTORY

For many of us whose understanding of early Christian history comes primarily from texts, the outsized presence of writers like Augustine or Jerome, who hold our attention with their individual voices, can sometimes blind us to how late ancient people functioned not strictly as individuals but as smaller actors within larger sets of relationships. Families, genealogies, cities, religious communities, and friendship networks are only a few of the larger structures within which late ancient people came into being.[1] These individual human figures were temporary, small-scale pinpoints within larger systems as much as they were what we would call, simply, people. Melania the Elder and Melania the Younger occupied specific social, economic, and familial locations, certainly; but by describing late ancient people as being themselves mobile and changeable locations—active locations within a much larger environment, as it were—we can more clearly see the large-scale forces and external entities that allowed them to emerge as the figures that we recognize them to be. We can choose to focus on them as powerful and idiosyncratic individuals, or we can choose to focus on the way that their individual lives are the products and expressions of much larger historical trends and institutions. What would the Melanias have been without the emergence of Christianity? What would they have been without the traditions of the Roman Empire? Within the long history of these larger institutions, the Melanias are small, if colorful, people, stubbornly situated, as all people are, in a limited time and in a particular set of places. In this book, we wish to try to understand how these two extraordinary women were both prominent individual characters in their own worlds and at the same time small representatives of larger historical forces. In order to lay the groundwork for refocusing our historical gaze on the small and the large together, let us tell an outline of the story of the Melanias in a traditional historical sense before considering how they appear, or disappear, in their larger environments.

The main sources for the life of Melania the Elder are Palladius's *Lausiac History* and the bishop and poet Paulinus of Nola's *Letter* 29, along with briefer references from the ascetic writer Jerome.[2] From these a rough outline can be pieced together:[3] Melania the Elder was born around the year 340 or 341 in Spain, into the illustrious *gens Antonia* (making her a very distant relation of Mark Antony); as a sign of her family's political status, her paternal grandfather, Antonius Marcellinus, was consul in 341. Melania married young, probably in her early or mid-teens, as was typical for aristocratic Roman girls, and she married well: it is possible but not certain that her husband was Valerius Maximus, who was urban prefect in Rome in 361–62. Melania was, however, widowed at the age of twenty-one, after having borne three children, two of whom died in childhood. Around 362 Melania relocated to Rome herself, perhaps to secure the public career of her remaining son, Valerius Publicola.[4] In 373 or 374, however, she left Rome to become more engaged with the growing Christian ascetic movement in Egypt and Palestine, and over the next several years, along with the writer and monastic pioneer Rufinus of Aquileia (ca. 345–411), she founded and helped to guide men's and women's ascetic communities on the Mount of Olives, outside Jerusalem. Among the many ascetics whom she supported in this period was the brilliant Evagrius of Pontus (ca. 345–99), who had abandoned a prominent civic career in Constantinople and became the major theoretician of an asceticism steeped in the third-century theology of Origen of Alexandria. Melania's public support for this theology earned her the outspoken ire of Jerome and his anti-Origenist network during the Origenist controversy of the 390s and early 400s. In 400, Melania returned to Rome and, according to Palladius, persuaded her granddaughter Melania the Younger and Melania the Younger's husband, Valerius Pinianus, to take up the ascetic life in their turn; she likely also persuaded them to oppose the anti-Origenists in Rome.[5] Palladius writes that after this, Melania the Elder returned to Jerusalem and "fell asleep at a fine old age";[6] the date of her death is unknown.

The life of Melania the Younger, in turn, is richly narrated in the mid-fifth-century hagiography usually attributed to her follower Gerontius, and Palladius also includes Melania the Younger in his *Lausiac History* after his longer account of her grandmother's career.[7] Melania the Younger was born around 385, the daughter of Melania the Elder's son Valerius Publicola and his wife, Albina, who was in turn the daughter of Ceionius Rufius Albinus, urban prefect in 389–91. According to Gerontius, at a young age Melania resisted the wishes of her parents to marry, but eventually she acquiesced and married Valerius Pinianus (Pinian), who was the son of Valerius Severus, the urban prefect for 382. Melania bore two children who died in infancy, and, Gerontius tells us, the children's deaths served as the turning point at which Melania and Pinian both agreed to take up a life of renunciation.[8] In 408 or 409, Melania and Pinian liquidated much of their property in Italy and traveled to North Africa, where they stayed for seven years; in so doing they left an Italy that was under threat from the Visigoth Alaric's troops, and Gerontius suggests that providence inspired their departure from Rome before the Visigothic sack of the city in 410.[9] While in North Africa, they gave financial support to other refugees from Italy as well as to monastic communities and churches, partly under the guidance of Augustine of Hippo and his fellow North African bishops.[10] After seven years in Africa, they moved on to Palestine and Jerusalem and began to support ascetic communities there. Pinian died in 431 or 432, but Melania the Younger continued a program of support and foundation of ascetic institutions around Jerusalem. In 437, she traveled to the imperial city of Constantinople, ostensibly to convert her maternal uncle, Volusianus, from paganism to Christianity, and she returned to Jerusalem after Volusianus's death. Melania herself died at the end of December, probably in the year 439.

These biographical sketches show the reader two identifiable human beings whose lives were delineated in large part through their own autonomous actions and decisions. There is an attractive simplicity to such stripped-down narratives, stories that, following modern historical conventions, reject what strike modern readers as the more baroque, fantastical, supernatural elements of late ancient hagiography: the miracles performed, the acts of spiritual heroism, the visions seen, the providential coincidences. These two Melanias are, instead, much like us: they are individual actors in a field of human existence in which we as contemporary people also often consider ourselves to be acting. On the human scale, they are born, marry, bear and lose children, travel, give gifts, and so on. The depiction of these figures as recognizably human allows us to identify, and identify with, Melania the Elder and Melania the Younger as beings whom we think of as real, historical people. Yet historiographical trends of the last few decades have alerted students of ancient Christianity to how such identifications are the products of narrative art, the art both of ancient narrators, such as Palladius and Gerontius, and of modern historians.[11] The people with whom we identify are characters in stories that we tell ourselves or in stories that we want to hear told. In many respects, contemporary awareness of the aesthetic and rhetorical effects of history has been fruitful: historians can analyze techniques of late ancient representation to shed light on the larger fields of ideas and language that created narratives of power and possibility for people in the late ancient world. At the same time, our awareness of history as storytelling has limited historians' optimism about the ability of ancient texts to reveal the lives of its subjects directly. The Melanias exist for us in a mediated and elliptical way, simultaneously brought into vivid individual focus by their narrators ancient and modern and yet irretrievably distanced, woven back into larger fields of discourse that themselves come into focus only through the texture of that same narration.

And yet the dual planes created by these stories—stories of people and stories of their larger worlds—can come together for us. In this book we attend to how using multiple focal points, subjects that exist on both small and large scales, ranging from the individual to the city to social class, allows us to explore the history of the early Christian world. In particular, we consider how Melania the Elder and Melania the Younger were simultaneously individual people and small points of intersection amid a variety of much larger historical entities. These larger historical entities were sometimes as concrete as the city of Rome and the assembly of the Roman Senate or as abstract as fourth- or fifth-century medical theories of gender. They were systems of thought and habit, relying on material resources and individual bodies for their expression, like the clothes that aristocratic women were expected to wear or the emotions that they were supposed to hide or display. The Melanias were people located *within* such historical entities, but they also acted as human locations *for* those entities, embodying these systems in recognizable ways and expressing their tangible existence. These historical entities, in turn, were larger than any individual person, but they were nonetheless really existing things, within which, or connected to which, individual persons existed. They were composed of systems of interactions between persons and their material surroundings, and they exerted different kinds of forces than individual persons acting alone.[12] Contemporary theorists of the material networks in which human beings act, writers such as Bruno Latour or Levi Bryant, have emphasized the importance of seeing these networks as true historical agents, with physical properties and effects, assemblages made up of people themselves and the material environments that allow them to be the people that they consider themselves to be.[13] These are the networks in which we place the two Melanias.

How did a large historical entity or assemblage take shape and exert force in the early Christian world? Consider the late Roman senatorial class. In one sense, this was a larger-than-human being because it was composed of multiple people acting together in particularly recognizable ways. Their actions relied on relationships between human beings for success: aristocrats purchased or bequeathed property, held civic office, dressed, spoke, and moved in a manner that distinguished them from members of other classes, and so on.[14] But the senatorial aristocracy was also a larger-than-human being in the sense that in order for its members to act in these recognizable ways, it required the participation of nonhuman collaborators and members: clothing and the pastoral and animal elements that produced it; agricultural land and its production of food; monumental building as well as varieties of domestic architecture. Without the material resources that were brought into the actions that these people undertook, and that structured what kinds of actions were possible, there could not be an aristocracy. The senatorial aristocracy was thus a historical entity made up of multiple human beings along with entire sets of nonhuman things, all of which collaborated on its successful existence in specific times and places. Such large-scale entities have often been discussed as social structures of various kinds, but it is also helpful to recognize them explicitly as historical actors who are in constant interaction both with other large-scale entities and with the smaller-scale beings who live inside them.

In this volume, we have used the following entities to explore the locations of Melania the Elder and Melania the Younger: the senatorial aristocracy; the household; late Roman systems of gendering; heresy and orthodoxy; and place, particularly the places of Rome and Jerusalem. Speaking of these phenomena as historical entities in their own right, rather than simply as hermeneutical categories or discursive fields, helps to describe the complexity of interactions between the Melanias as human individuals and the larger-than-human things that enclosed them and were shaped by them. One famous episode in the life of Melania the Elder, in which she is imprisoned by a corrupt official, may help to illustrate these interactions. Palladius tells the story as follows:[15]

> After this, the prefect of Alexandria sent [the monks] Isidore, Pisimius, Adelphius, Paphnutius, and Pambo, and Ammonius Parotes as well, and twelve bishops and presbyters, into exile in the area around Diocaesarea in Palestine; and she followed them, serving them out of her own possessions. But since they were forbidden to have servants, . . . she put on a slave's cloak and brought them what they needed in the evenings. Once the consul of Palestine discovered this, he wished to fill his pockets and to frighten her; and he arrested her and threw her into prison, not realizing that she was a free woman. But she said to him: "I am this man's daughter and that man's wife; but I am Christ's slave. And do not hold the poverty of my clothing in contempt, for if I want to I can raise myself up; so you can neither frighten me in this way nor can you take what I own. I have told you this so that you will not unwittingly commit any illegal acts: with unperceptive people it is necessary to act proudly, like a hawk." The judge, once he understood the situation, both apologized and honored her, and ordered that she should be able to meet with the holy men freely.

The episode is told with remarkable compression of detail, but although Melania's individual power and agency is emphasized, she is also portrayed as existing within multiple larger entities that have their own potencies and agendas. Melania's paternal and spousal networks, as assemblages that act to elevate and identify her as part of themselves, push Melania toward what would be the expected activity for her, namely dressing aristocratically and using slaves for labor. That is, Melania *with* these other human and nonhuman parts is a different agent, and part of a different system of activity, than she is without them. Although Melania works against these systems in some respects in this story, by dressing as a slave herself and performing labor, she also works within them to manipulate the actions of the Palestinian official and to secure free access to the monks. Her identity is clearly different (she is "Christ's slave") when acting against the potencies of these particular larger entities than it is when acting within them (when she is "this man's daughter and that man's wife"). In turn, the Palestinian official in this story is part of the Roman bureaucratic system, which is made up in this narrative of himself, money, slaves, and prison space. This bureaucratic entity can act to imprison, to extract money, and to restrict or open avenues of movement to those humans within it. In this story, late Roman systems of aristocracy, bureaucracy, piety, wealth, and gender are all exerting different kinds of force on the individuals living within them, who sometimes act against those larger beings and sometimes act along with them. It is, moreover, through the encounter of these larger beings with each other, and with the humans inside them, that Melania's much smaller-scale identity as a person is delineated.

The presence of these larger-than-human historical entities, exercising their own powers and undergoing their own encounters, complicates the narratives of the Melanias as individual persons with which this introduction began. Although historians eschew the supernatural larger-than-human beings on whom their hagiographers rely, we nonetheless return to "big things" as agents who create, shape, challenge, and are challenged by the human individual. In a sense, we have returned to the fantastical, in a way that allows the fantastical to become real according to modern historical norms.[16]

EARLY CHRISTIAN EVOLUTION

This book draws a variety of boundaries around a variety of subjects in order to tell stories about different large historical beings and about two specific persons inside them, Melania the Elder and Melania the Younger. In the second part of this introduction, we turn briefly to how the boundaries that we have chosen to draw are the result of a specific historical evolution over the last forty years.

This book is in part a tribute to the scholarship of Elizabeth A. Clark, who taught and mentored all the contributors either formally or informally. Her work has directed the study of ancient Christianity away from traditional theological readings of the Church Fathers and toward approaches that treat ancient Christianity as a complex social, cultural, and ideological phenomenon. The chapters of this book demonstrate how a single scholar's work on two individuals can evolve over time into a much larger-scale system of analyses and narratives. This is clear even in Clark's own career: in the late 1970s and early 1980s, Clark published a series of works on women in late ancient Christianity, among whom Melania the Elder and Melania the Younger were prominent.[17] In 1984, she published the first full, scholarly English translation and commentary on the *Life of Melania the*

Younger.[18] These works formed part of a project of historical recovery that was necessary for writing women's history as it was conceived in the 1970s and 1980s. They made it possible to create the kinds of narratives of individual human action, women's action, with which we began. Such creations were historically momentous in the context of the late twentieth century, and yet narratively straightforward. As Clark moved away from the delineation of individual women's lives in the late 1980s and early 1990s, however, she began to embed Melania the Elder and Melania the Younger in complex social networks, particularly in her book *The Origenist Controversy: The Cultural Construction of an Early Christian Debate*.[19] In that book, individual characters, including the Melanias, come into and go out of focus as their positions in their social networks shift over time, or shift through different perspectives. Next, the so-called linguistic turn in history introduced historians to the analysis of the construction of subjects and categories of subjectivity through language, a style of analysis that Clark both demonstrated and defended in *Reading Renunciation: Asceticism and Scripture in Early Christianity*,[20] and again in *History, Theory, Text: Historians and the Linguistic Turn*.[21] In these books, the boundaries of the subjects of historical narrative became far broader: the subjects became whole discourses, which enveloped and summoned individual persons, again including the Melanias, into recognizable being. Clark's most recent work, on the reception of early Christian texts in nineteenth-century America,[22] can be understood as an experiment in extending the temporal scale of narratives about discourse. Over the span of one career, then, we can see an evolution in narrative scale that has changed the way that writing the history of early Christianity is possible. The original elements, the outlines and traces of early Christian women as individuals, are not gone but have been extended; the scale of the narrative that contains them has broadened. As Clark writes in the conclusion of her groundbreaking essay "The Lady Vanishes: Dilemmas of a Feminist Historian after the Linguistic Turn": "Has, then, 'the lady vanished'? If this question means, Can we recover her pure and simple from texts? my answer is no. But that is not the last word: she leaves her traces, through whose exploration, as they are imbedded in a larger social-linguistic framework, she lives on."[23]

The contributors to this book take the decision to extend and complicate the narrative scales around Melania the Elder and Melania the Younger as their starting point. They move outward from the Melanias physically, linguistically, and temporally, experimenting with new dimensions around these complicated figures, dimensions that Elizabeth Clark's work has done much to illuminate. The plan of this book is as follows:

In Part I, "Aristocracy," Caroline T. Schroeder, Catherine M. Chin, and Christine Luckritz Marquis explore the relationship between Melania the Elder, Melania the Younger, and the social and physical environment of the late Roman senatorial aristocracy. By focusing on the people, families, and buildings that surrounded the

Melanias, this section paints a picture of an aristocratic class in flux. The social and economic status of their aristocratic family makes demands on these women in terms of everyday behavior and physical practice but also enables them to redirect the resources of aristocracy toward new forms of social hierarchy. We see the late Roman aristocracy working here as an open but durable system that interacts with its constituent parts and can also be changed by them.

In Part II, "Body and Family," Maria Doerfler and Kristi Upson-Saia consider how a strongly delineated individual body—a body recognized as mother and as vulnerable flesh—nonetheless exists within larger systems such as the family, household, medicine, and the civic and ecclesiastical habits that make up Christian doctrine. The complex embeddedness of the Melanias within larger systems is made clear through these scholars' focus on the processes that make these women identifiable as human and female figures: the intimate yet very public complications of childbirth and motherhood, and the susceptibility of the body to injury. These deeply individualized events are structured by and give structure to the large-scale entities in which they occur.

Part III, "Gender and Memory," starts with a wider field of vision, as L. Stephanie Cobb and Rebecca Krawiec examine how readers and audiences in late antiquity remembered both early Christian martyrs and ascetics like the Melanias as gendered persons. Cobb describes how the early third-century martyr stories of Perpetua and Felicitas extended into the later age of the Melanias, and she observes how this extension both prospectively created an identity for fourth- and fifth-century female ascetics and at the same time retrospectively created the stereotype of the earlier Christian female martyr. Krawiec, in turn, focuses on the "genderqueering" of Melania the Elder in the memory of her monastic descendants. Here the temporal extension of Melania as a figure of inspiration from the past to the future becomes an opportunity to blur Melania's physical identity as a gendered person. And yet, the genderqueering of Melania also made possible a much more robust memory of her in a society in which the memory of male figures was always uppermost.

Similarly, in Part IV, "Wisdom and Heresy," Susanna Drake, Christine Shepardson, and Robin Darling Young explore how difficult it is to apply the typical wide-ranging heretical labels—labels like Pelagian, Nestorian, Origenist—to a single human being, since the boundaries of larger social and intellectual entities do not align temporally or socially with the boundaries of the person. Melania the Elder, portrayed positively by Evagrius as belonging to a long tradition of Christian gnostics, will within a few years become an "Origenist" after a new boundary, delineating a different but overlapping intellectual system, has been drawn around the materials and practices that derive from Origen's work. Likewise, Gerontius's attempts to retrospectively construct a "Miaphysite" Melania the Younger, after that category comes to life, illustrates the mismatch between heretical and orthodox intellectual systems and the individual persons who become attached to them. The large scale of the heretical content, and the small scale of the heretical person, means that the boundaries cannot converge.

The physical boundedness of the Melanias is not limited to their bodily shape and size: in Part V, "In the Holy Places," Andrew Jacobs and Steven Shoemaker look at how the geographical locations of the Melanias reconfigured their identities as well as those of the people around them. Jacobs concentrates on the travel of both Melania the Elder and Melania the Younger from Rome to Jerusalem, suggesting that migration serves first to secure the identities of the travelers, pilgrims, and expatriates who moved from the West to the East but that it also constitutes the larger entity that we can describe as a Christian Roman Empire. Shoemaker, in contrast, focuses on the liturgical outlines of Jerusalem, as the Melanias would likely have encountered it. He finds in the set of physical and musical habits there the outline of a different female person, one more powerful than the expected human, namely the Virgin Mary. Here, a dual focus on the place of the human and the larger-than-human reveals how early Christians could see a person as "one of us" and as nearly divine at the same time.

The final section of the volume, "Modernities," Part VI, offers a more explicit analysis of the Melanias as they come into modern view, focusing on their temporal extension beyond late antiquity and into our own age. Michael Penn narrates the early twentieth-century excitement over the manuscript discovery by Cardinal Rampolla that gave us the *Life of Melania the Younger* in the form in which we have it today. Penn details the creation of a mass-media Melania, centuries old, but used to shape the religious and social expectations of the Gilded Age. Stephen J. Davis analyzes the characterization of the Melanias as female exemplars in modern Coptic Orthodox Christianity, in which these extended figures are used to draw distinct and male-sanctioned boundaries for contemporary Coptic women's behavior. Finally, Elizabeth A. Castelli's essay suggests how scholars may fruitfully move away from the habit of outlining Melania the Younger as a woman and toward outlining her as a saint. The productivity of such a new starting point for drawing the boundaries of this subject has yet to be fully realized.

These essays represent a moment in the life of early Christian studies as it has evolved from the late 1970s to the mid-2010s. We believe that it is useful to reflect on that evolution, keeping in view the original materials and narratives that, through their growth, complication, and extension, have become the current state of this historical field. The usefulness of reflecting on such changes in scale is twofold: first, it requires the historical writer to consider carefully what entities can become subjects of history, and how they can become such: How, and for how long, can we recognize the boundaries of complex entities once we have moved beyond the visible limits of the human body? Moving from "Melania" as the subject of history to, say, "heresy" as the subject of history, and keeping Melania in view as a subject within the subject, means that the writer cannot take either "Melania" or "heresy" as an obvious or settled entity. Explicitly shifting between scales thus requires practicing the craft of recognition, outlining subjects provisionally in a given historical narrative. Second, and perhaps more important, reflecting on the scales at which entities act and exist captures an aspect of history that is sometimes lost when narrative is relentlessly humanized. Individual human beings are not the only forces in human history. The larger-than-human beings that invade or envelop us are actors with which humans are in constant negotiation, and whose histories must be told in terms beyond individual human births and deaths. The story of this negotiation is a vital part of what we think of as the past. The interactions and feedback processes involved are what allow complex entities, both physical and social, to emerge and structure human experience. In this book we attempt to describe the processes of negotiation between Melania the Elder, Melania the Younger, and the larger beings whose world they inhabited. We ask our readers to see this as another starting point, an invitation to consider the history of early Christianity from the view of both the great and the small, the old and the new.

NOTES

1. On using family, friendship, and other social networks to understand early Christian history, see especially Elizabeth A. Clark, *The Origenist Controversy: The Cultural Construction of an Early Christian Debate* (Princeton: Princeton University Press, 1992), chapter 1; Clark's work will be discussed further below.

2. Palladius, *Historia Lausiaca*, text and commentary by G. J. M. Bartelink, *Palladio: La Storia lausiaca*, trans. Marino Barchiesi (Milan: Mondadori, 1974); Paulinus of Nola, *Epistulae*, ed. Wilhelm von Hartel and Margit Kamptner, CSEL 29, 2nd ed. (Vienna: Verlag der Österreichischen Akademie der Wissenschaften, 1999); Jerome, *Epistulae*, vol. 1, ed. Isidorus Hilberg, CSEL 54 (Vienna and Leipzig: F. Tempsky and G. Freytag, 1910); Jerome, *Chronicon*, ed. Rudolf Helm, in *Eusebius' Werke*, vol. 7.1, GCS 47, 3rd ed. (Berlin: Akademie-Verlag, 1984).

3. For this rough chronology, I rely primarily on the recent reconstruction of Kevin W. Wilkinson, "The Elder Melania's Missing Decade," *Journal of Late Antiquity* 5.1 (2012): 166–84; but see also Nicole Moine, "Melaniana," *Récherches Augustinennes* 15 (1980): 3–79; E. A. Clark, *Origenist Controversy*, 20–26; F. X. Murphy, "Melania the Elder: A Biographical Note," *Traditio* 5 (1947): 59–77; E. Schwartz, "Palladiana," *Zeitschrift für die Neutestamentliche Wissenschaft und die Kunde der Älteren Kirche* 36.2 (1937): 161–204.

4. Wilkinson, "Elder Melania's Missing Decade," 179–82.

5. E. A. Clark, *Origenist Controversy*, 24.

6. Palladius, *Historia Lausiaca* 54.6.

7. Gerontius, *Vita S. Melaniae Iunioris*: Greek text (with French translation and commentary) ed. and trans. Denys Gorce, *Vie de sainte Mélanie*, SC 90 (Paris: Cerf, 1962); Latin text (with French translation and commentary) ed. and trans. Patrick Laurence, *La vie latine de sainte Mélanie* (Jerusalem: Franciscan Printing Press, 2002); English translation of the Greek text, with commentary, trans. Elizabeth A. Clark, *The Life of Melania the Younger* (Lewiston, N.Y.: Edwin Mellen Press, 1984).

8. It has been much remarked that Gerontius removes Melania the Elder from the story of Melania the Younger's turn to asceticism: see esp. Gerontius, *Life of Melania the Younger*, trans. Elizabeth A. Clark, 85–86, 141–52; and as well Christine Luckritz Marquis's chapter in this volume.

9. *Vita S. Melaniae Iunioris* 19.

10. For a full account of Melania and Pinian's wealth and giving, see now Peter Brown, *Through the Eye of a Needle: Wealth, the Fall of Rome, and the Making of Christianity in the West, 350–550 A.D.* (Princeton: Princeton University Press, 2012), especially chapters 18 and 20. For their complex relationship with Augustine, see Susanna Drake's chapter in this volume.

11. See especially Elizabeth A. Clark, "The Lady Vanishes: Dilemmas of a Feminist Historian after the 'Linguistic Turn,'" *Church History* 67.1 (1998): 1–31.

12. In focusing on the combined historiographical issues of the scale of narrative subjects and the agency of nonhuman entities and assemblages, this chapter relies on theoretical work based in object-oriented ontology and in the related areas of distributed cognition and distributed agency. The most useful discussions of the agency of objects and nonhuman entities for our purposes are in Levi R. Bryant, *Onto-Cartography: An Ontology of Machines and Media* (Edinburgh: Edinburgh University Press, 2014); Ian Bogost, *Alien Phenomenology; or, What It's Like to Be a Thing* (Minneapolis: University of Minnesota Press, 2012); Bruno Latour, *Reassembling the Social: An Introduction to Actor-Network Theory* (Oxford: Oxford University Press, 2005); Jane Bennett, *Vibrant Matter: A Political Ecology of Things* (Durham: Duke University Press, 2010); and on the scale of objects, Timothy Morton, *Hyperobjects: Philosophy and Ecology after the End of the World* (Minneapolis: University of Minnesota Press, 2013).

13. Latour and Bryant (see note 12 above) are influential in the theoretical trend that is sometimes called the New Materialism or the material turn, which draws inspiration from a variety of sources, notably Gilles Deleuze's account of the force of materiality in *Difference and Repetition*, trans. Paul Patton (New York: Columbia University Press, 1994); a useful account of some of the roots of New Materialism is found in Diana Coole and Samantha Frost, "Introducing the New Materialisms," in Coole and Frost, eds., *New Materialisms: Ontology, Agency, and Politics* (Durham: Duke University Press, 2010), 1–43.

14. On the makeup of the late Roman senatorial aristocracy, see the discussion and notes in Chin's chapter in this volume.

15. Palladius, *Historia Lausiaca* 46.3; Chin's translation. For a rich contextualization of this incident, see Sigrid Mratschek-Halfmann, "Melania and the Unknown Governor of Palestine," *Journal of Late Antiquity* 5.2 (2012): 250–68.

16. Bryant, *Onto-Cartography*, 83: "The strange consequence of this hypothesis is that the man who rides the horse and the man-horse-stirrup-lance assemblage are two distinct individuals. It is not that the *man* rides the *horse*, but rather that the man-horse-stirrup-lance assemblage rides. Centaurs really do exist, just not in the sense we thought."

17. The first edition of Elizabeth A. Clark's *Ascetic Piety and Women's Faith* was published in 1979 (Lewiston, N.Y.: Edwin Mellen); with Diane F. Hatch, Clark published *The Golden Bough, the Oaken Cross: The Virgilian Cento of Faltonia Betitia Proba* (Chico, Calif.: Scholars Press) in 1981. The second edition of Clark's *Jerome, Chrysostom and Friends* was published in 1982 (Lewiston, N.Y.: Edwin Mellen). Clark also published selected translations of ancient material on women in early Christianity as *Women in the Early Church* in 1983 (Wilmington, Del.: Michael Glazier).

18. Lewiston, N.Y.: Edwin Mellen, 1984.

19. Princeton: Princeton University Press, 1992.

20. Princeton: Princeton University Press, 1999.

21. Cambridge, Mass.: Harvard University Press, 2004.

22. *Founding the Fathers: Early Church History and Protestant Professors in Nineteenth-Century America* (Philadelphia: University of Pennsylvania Press, 2011).

23. Clark, "Lady Vanishes," 31.

PART ONE

Aristocracy

THE AGE OF THE MELANIAS saw the rise of a new Christian elite: although men and women of means had been part of the earliest Christian communities and reflections on wealth are common in Christian literature of the first through third centuries, it is only in late antiquity that we see Christianity publicly and enthusiastically expounded as appropriate to the senatorial class of the Roman Empire. Melania the Elder and Melania the Younger were among the most spectacular members of this Christian aristocracy, with access not only to vast material wealth but also to social and imperial power. At the same time, both Melanias played major roles in the rise of Christian renunciation through their patronage of ascetic practitioners and their foundation of monastic centers, as well as their own public acts of self-sacrifice. In this section, we consider how Melania the Elder and Melania the Younger negotiated their elite status and the dynamics of inheritance in a way that allowed them both to renounce and to retain their social standing, and to extend their influence to new Christian audiences. The three essays here, by Catherine Chin, Christine Luckritz Marquis, and Caroline Schroeder, point to dramatic moments of redefining elite status in late ancient Christianity, moments in which social hierarchies and family ties are retained but are also used to create new possibilities for social encounter.

In Chin's essay, Melania the Younger is closely tied to the burdens of inherited property. The *Life of Melania* depicts an elite figure summoned into a social position through the claims made on her by the material things that she inherits. The elite heir is expected, above all, to produce children and create a line of human caretakers for the inherited property. Although the *Life* describes Melania's rejection of these claims, it also makes clear that Melania's establishment of monasteries and other church foundations participated in the same traditional elite dynamic: new church buildings also created imagined genealogies, in this case Christian ascetic genealogies, which in turn made claims on the human beings who owned or inhabited these buildings. The same patterns appeared in the Constantinian buildings in Rome, which connected imperial status with the purported golden age of an apostolic past in the city.

Shifting focus back to Melania the Elder, Christine Luckritz Marquis draws attention to the salience of lineage in early Christian literature and explores the constraints that Melania the Elder's legacy placed on her namesake, Melania the Younger. The elder Melania's renunciation looms large, if ambivalently, in literary depictions of her namesake granddaughter's own life and practice. Effaced entirely from *Life of Melania the Younger*, yet held up as the younger Melania's chief inspiration in Palladius's *Lausiac History*, the treatment of the two women's relationship points to the complexities of familial legacies, whether spiritual or material.

For Schroeder, Melania the Younger's excellence is derived from the affective claims made about her in the *Life*. As a woman, she might have been expected to exhibit the traditional feminine emotional weaknesses portrayed in other ancient literature; as an aristocrat, however, Melania is portrayed as transcending this gendered weakness and becoming an emotionally wise Stoic sage. The tension between late Roman gender and wealth distribution reorients Melania in opposition to some gendered stereotypes while at the same time valorizing a conservative view of aristocratic behavioral and emotional ideals. This reorientation, however, also produces a new affective network, connecting Melania as an emotional exemplar to the groups of Christians whom Schroeder analyzes as her "fan base." In this network, the ascetic hero is, to a large extent, separated from her original surroundings and drawn into a much more intimate affective relationship with the audiences of her *Life*, who use her story to negotiate their own emotional and social networks.

The late Roman aristocrat undergoes significant changes in the lives and afterlives of the Melanias, although none of these changes is as simple as a rejection of elite status altogether nor as cosmetic as the creation of a nominally Christian Roman elite that exactly parallels the earlier Roman world. Instead, we see the dynamics of status shifting in order to create new kinds of relationships between the elite figure and her social environment. The Roman aristocracy can become apostolic—and apostles can become Roman aristocrats—while at the same time the audiences for ascetic renunciation, whether in the same family or in a broader emotional network, can use renunciation to navigate the constraints placed on them by elite expectation. The rise of the Christian aristocrat thus opens Roman aristocratic ideals, and Christianity itself, to radically new narrative possibilities.

1

Apostles and Aristocrats

Catherine M. Chin

Roman tradition holds that two of the earliest representatives of Christianity in the city were the apostles Peter and Paul, executed in Rome during the reign of Nero. Inscriptional evidence for the memorialization of Peter and Paul on the Appian Way dates back to the third century; markers of a possible burial place of Peter at the Vatican date to the second. It is tempting to see the establishment of an apostolic genealogy for Roman Christianity as the natural outgrowth of this early tradition, and perhaps for that reason scholarly debate over the apostolic history of the city has largely focused on whether traditional sites of veneration reveal the actual presence of apostolic remains. The idea of Rome as a city with an apostolic past, however, is not solely dependent on the history of first-century martyrdoms or evangelization. Instead, the idea of Rome's apostolic history was constructed in part literally, through the labor of elite building projects in late antiquity. The most spectacular example is the creation of St. Peter's basilica in the early fourth century, but this is not an isolated case. In this chapter, I consider how such building projects contributed to the apostolic past of the city of Rome. The best place to begin, however, is not with the apostolic monuments themselves but with the broader dynamics of building, property, and memorialization among elite Roman families. These dynamics are clearly depicted in the life of one monument builder who left Rome precisely because of the work that elite buildings could do; this is the woman whom her biographer Gerontius introduces simply as "Melania the Roman."

The *Life of Melania the Younger* can tell us a great deal about ideologies of building in late ancient Rome and their complex management of human pasts and futures. In fact, the *Life of Melania* documents an intellectual problem that is clearly observable in late ancient Rome, although not exclusive to it—namely the persistence of large-scale buildings that interact with and make demands on a series of human caretakers over their long life spans. As the art historian Annabel Wharton notes: "Once it is recognized that a building has a life, architectural historians may be less likely to focus their scholarly attention exclusively on a structure's origins and more likely to treat its full biography."[1] Treating the full biography of buildings also entails understanding how these material structures were understood to participate in larger historical narratives, not merely as locations but as actors in their own right. Using this approach, we can try to read at least some late ancient texts as narratives about the demands and agencies of late ancient buildings, and about how those buildings interacted with the desires and agencies of the more fragile human actors to whom they were joined. In this view, the creation of late ancient Christianity becomes a negotiation between human and nonhuman beings that lived on different timescales. From this negotiation were born a variety of human genealogies: in Rome, it produced aristocratic families, past apostles, and future popes. For although Christians in the city venerated Peter and Paul from an early date, the memory of Rome as an apostolic city, with a bishop, emperor, and aristocracy as the caretakers and inheritors of the apostolic presence, is a very striking late antique development. The dynamics of building in the *Life of Melania* can illuminate this development, in dialogue with other texts that describe the interactions between buildings and human beings in late antique Rome.

We will begin with the Roman property of Melania and her husband, Pinian, especially the house that has traditionally been located on the Caelian Hill, and consider how the *Life of Melania* depicts such houses as agents that make genealogical demands on their owners. We will then move slightly farther east on the Caelian Hill and discuss a parallel set of genealogical demands made by the Constantinian basilica complex as depicted in the *Liber Pontificalis*. Finally, we will turn to the *Life of Melania*'s description of Melania's building projects in Jerusalem, to consider briefly how the demands of buildings can also articulate an eschatological future.

THE HOUSE THAT NO ONE COULD AFFORD TO BUY

Early in the *Life of Melania*, first Melania and then her husband, Pinian, decide to lead ascetic lives. The standard approach to Melania and Pinian's decision assumes that the primary conflict in the narrative is between the young ascetic couple and their parents, who are intent on persuading them to have children.[2] As Gerontius explains: "Melania and Pinian suffered much pain since they were unable to take up the yoke of Christ freely because of their parents' compulsion."[3] Yet the rationale that Melania's parents, and indeed Pinian himself, at first supply for the couple's need to reproduce is firmly rooted in the problem of family property. Gerontius has Pinian originally make this argument: "If and when by the ordinance of God we have two children to inherit our possessions, then both of us together shall renounce the world."[4] Further, even after their parents do agree to their ascetic ambitions, the two are still stalled in their ascetic careers by their property, as Melania tells Pinian: "The burden of life is very heavy for us, and we are not competent in these circumstances to take on the light yoke of Christ. Therefore let us quickly lay aside our goods that we may gain Christ."[5] Gerontius describes a long period of property disputes between the couple and Pinian's brother Severus, along with property "schemes" by "every one of their senatorial relatives."[6] In the narrative, these problems are to some extent resolved through the intervention of the empress Serena, who persuades the emperor Honorius to allow the sale of Melania and Pinian's extensive property.[7]

There remains, however, one stubbornly resistant estate in Rome, whose fate Gerontius describes:[8]

> Since none of the senators in Rome had the means to buy the house of the blessed Pinian, they let the empress ... know through the holy bishops that she might buy it. She did not want to do this, however, and said to the intermediaries, "I do not think I have the means to buy the house at its true value." They requested that she at least accept some of the precious statues from the saints as a token of friendship. Serena reluctantly acquiesced, for she did not wish to grieve them any further. The saints were not able to sell the house, and after the barbarian invasion they let it go for less than nothing, since it was burned.

The emphasis on the transfer of property in the *Life,* and on Melania and Pinian's need to liquidate property in order to begin their ascetic careers, suggests that the primary conflict in this part of the *Life* is not between two generations of human actors but between human actors and the material structures that surround them. The villain, in other words, is not the older generation, nor even the abstraction wealth or money.[9] Instead, the hindrances to Melania and Pinian's activity are particular pieces of property, most clearly represented by the house in the city of Rome, a house that demands to be inherited and that refuses to be sold.

The fact that houses and other structures make claims on their owners and inhabitants should not be surprising. Such structures possess a basic physical power to constrain human action.[10] They are, moreover, embodiments of combined human and environmental labor. Architecturally products of human design and construction, their material elements are equally manifestations of geologic formation, forest growth, soil deposit, and so on. These nonhuman activities are masked when we consider buildings to be exclusively passive human products rather than composite beings interacting with humans in complex ways. As Kim Bowes has argued in her work on late Roman houses, it is typical for scholars to treat these structures primarily as vehicles for the owners' displays of status, which of course they were to some extent.[11] At the same time, inhabitants and inheritors of these beings would repeatedly be required to reckon with the strength, condition, and internal dynamics between the original materials of the house, and they would necessarily interact with their property in ways that were genuinely constrained by the matter and arrangement of the house itself. A late Roman senatorial house excavated at Butrint, for example, shows several different stages of construction and renovation from the third through the fifth century.[12] On the one hand, these stages clearly show human beings acting on the house in its renovation, expansion, and redesign. On the other hand, the renovations and changes are constrained, although not completely determined, by the footprint of the original complex as well as its natural setting. We should locate some agency in the house as a nonhuman being and see the process of home renovation as one in which human and nonhuman agents are compelled to act together over time, sometimes in conflict, and not necessarily in ways wholly subordinated to human desires. This is the situation we find in the *Life of Melania*. Even after the human opponents of asceticism are defeated or won over, the physical matter of the house remains unmoved. It can be made to cooperate with Melania and Pinian only after being burned in the Gothic sack of the city.

Up until its damage by fire, however, the power that this property exerts, as with the other properties mentioned in the *Life*, is understood primarily in terms of inheritance. The house, in other words, makes spatial and material claims, and in doing so it also makes temporal and genealogical claims. In fact, in the *Life of Melania*, the claims of property are configured as *primarily* temporal and genealogical. The first claim that property makes in the *Life* is on Melania's chastity, since her body is intended to produce future caretakers for that property: "children to inherit our possessions."[13] The house in Rome may be an extension of its owners in terms of status display, but in genealogical terms the bodies of human owners act simply as extensions of the matter and life of the house. The presumption in the text is that the human actors will disappear before the property does; the only way for humans to adapt to the property's temporal scale is by producing children. Our sense of the genealogical claims that property could make is further sharpened if we recall that membership in the senatorial class in late antiquity was hereditary, but in a somewhat restricted sense: it was also dependent on property, and was subject to what Samuel Barnish has called the "complementary risks of economic and biological failure."[14] The other side of that failure, landed success, could generate largely fictitious genealogies for late ancient families whose property gave them prominence. Thus, for example, in his epitaph on Paula, Jerome links Paula's "palace glittering with gold" to her putative descent from the Gracchi and the Scipios.[15] How far such fantastical claims were believed is questionable.[16] Still, the highly competitive and sometimes unpredictable process of becoming and remaining a senatorial family in late antiquity meant that the genealogical claims of property extended both backward in time and forward.

We see these claims at work in the *Life of Melania*. Gerontius introduces the *Life* as "the story of her senatorial family, and how she entered the angelic life."[17] He then begins the narrative proper with an emphasis on Melania's "senatorial rank" and the statement that "her parents, because they were illustrious members of the Roman Senate and expected that through her they would have a succession of the family line, very forcibly united her in marriage with her blessed husband, Pinian, who was from a consular family."[18] The importance of the property that Melania and Pinian inherit is not restricted to its monetary value but is related specifically to its status as heritable within elite families.[19] The text portrays Melania's parents, and at first Pinian, as motivated by the demands of specific properties to be transferred in inheritance. These demands could be made in two ways. The first is through the force of the materials themselves: although real property could be destroyed or worn down (and some Roman buildings were in desperate need of repair in the fifth century),[20] late ancient builders were also fully aware of the potential longevity of brick, marble, and other materials. They regularly reused these materials as either visible spolia or simply as practical material, acknowledging their basic durability.[21] The potential for duration on a longer-than-human scale invited observers to shift their temporal perspective, from the life span of an individual human being to the lives of both earlier and future humans.[22] Buildings, in other words, had a tendency to press human duration beyond its normal individual boundaries.

The second way that buildings might demand human generation is easier to decipher, in the presence of overt signs of the human past. If we recall that it was common for aristocratic Roman homes to include either genealogical inscriptions or ancestor portraits as part of their physical décor, we can understand the kind of genealogical demand that a house might make, regardless of the wishes of its inhabitants, acting as the embodiment of an ancestral past, while laying claim to a particular kind of future.[23] Other decorative elements within houses might underline these claims. In the *Life of Melania*, for example, statues intensify the claims of property. The house that could not be sold contained "precious statues," some of which were given to the reluctant empress Serena.[24] Not long after Gerontius refers to the burning of the Roman house, statues reappear as part of a diabolical temptation in which the devil recalls to Melania's mind "the variety of statues . . . and the inestimable income" of a different family estate.[25] The temporal claims implied by these materials are, however, rejected in Melania's response, which is framed in explicitly temporal terms: "How can these things that today exist and tomorrow will be destroyed by the barbarians, or by fire, or by time . . . be compared to eternal goods that exist forever?"[26] Melania appeals to the sack of Rome in order to deny the relative longevity of statuary in late antiquity, but it is clear from other sources that statues in late antiquity had many ways of surviving the passage of time. The repeated restrictions in the *Theodosian Code* against repurposing marble artworks from older structures suggest that spoliation and reuse were common.[27] Similarly, portraits and other older figural works might be recut, either to change their subjects entirely or simply to "modernize" or renovate them. These repurposed or reused objects could thus either embody earlier imperial eras or become raw material for different objects that were simultaneously old and new.

The residents of late ancient Rome thus lived within a vast, slow-moving kaleidoscope of ancient, reused materials. The intellectual problems that such surroundings posed are made clear in the *Life of Melania*: in this text, the obstacle to the ascetic life is the fact that brick, concrete, marble, and metal last longer than people do. Their long lives demand a human response. In the first part of the *Life of Melania*, this problem is solved by the destruction that accompanied the sack of Rome in 410, and by Melania and Pinian's spectacular ascetic liquidation, in which property becomes simply money. This refusal of the claims of buildings is not, however, the only early Christian response to the long-lived material fabric of the city of Rome. Rome's apostolic genealogy is established through a very similar dynamic; this will become clear if we take a slight temporal and geographical detour into the Constantinian building projects as they are described in the *Liber Pontificalis*.

THE SAVIOR SEATED ON A CHAIR, FIVE FEET IN SIZE, WEIGHING 120 POUNDS

A few hundred meters away from the site on the Caelian Hill where scholars have traditionally placed Melania and Pinian's recalcitrant house, and where a house belonging to the Valerii once certainly stood, we find the basilica of St. John Lateran, the now mostly seventeenth-century structure that has taken the place of the Basilica Constantiniana. The fourth-century basilica was the first of Constantine's monumental church buildings, probably begun not long after his defeat of Maxentius in 312.[28] Like other Constantinian monuments in Rome, most famously the Arch of Constantine, the Constantinian basilica was constructed and decorated partly with reused and perhaps spoliated earlier materials.[29] For example, the imposing gilt-bronze columns currently in the south transept are from an earlier imperial period and were likely used in the Constantinian building.[30] As Hugo Brandenburg has suggested, given the quantities of gold and silver decoration in the basilica as described in the *Liber Pontificalis*, and extrapolating from Eusebius's descriptions of other Constantinian churches, it is likely that the aesthetic emphasis in the Basilica Constantiniana was on the richness of the collected materials rather than on their stylistic unity.[31] In other words, the Constantinian basilica on the Caelian Hill would have been an appropriate material neighbor to the house that no one in Rome could afford to buy. It will be useful, then, to consider how this basilica was also understood to make genealogical claims.

The Constantinian basilica certainly began in a set of familial claims. As is well known, it was constructed on the site of a former barracks for the *equites singulares,* who had probably been loyal to Maxentius. After Constantine's victory, the site was leveled to make way for the construction of the new monumental basilica.[32] The new structure obviously served as both a political and a religious statement, but Constantine also claimed as his imperial residence a nearby property, the Sessorian Palace, that had been home to several members of the Severan dynasty.[33] Even after the establishment of Constantinople as the Eastern capital, the Sessorian Palace would remain the residence of Constantine's mother, Helena. Thus the Constantinian basilica was not merely the sign of military victory or of a new divine presence in the city, but through its connection to the imperial residence would also have made dynastic claims, connecting Constantine's family to an earlier imperial dynasty, one with its own monumental remains. The basilica's claims would likely have been consistent with those made by Constantine himself; the basilica and its founder would have begun in relative agreement. Yet as we move into the *Liber Pontificalis*'s sixth-century retelling of Constantine's building projects, particularly in its interesting inaccuracies, we can begin to see first the mingling of Constantinian genealogical claims with other genealogical claims, and ultimately the replacement of Constantinian claims with claims that appear to be made by the basilica complex itself. Over the course of the fourth and fifth centuries, the longevity of the building allowed it to generate its own previous history and future.

The text of the *Liber Pontificalis* makes clear how the text's sixth-century compiler conceived of the force of these buildings. Where the previous entries in the list of Roman pontiffs are quite short and provide scant information about the series of bishops claimed for Rome, Constantine's appearance and conversion to Christianity during the pontificate of Sylvester changes the *Liber Pontificalis* radically.[34] The extensive lists of Constantine's churches, and his gifts to these churches, make this entry many times longer than any previous entry. The description of the pontificate of Sylvester establishes a pattern of including donation lists that will recur in the text well into the entries covering the sixth century. The text describes ten different structures, mostly in and around Rome, that it ascribes to Constantine, although it also gives credit to some other members of the Constantinian dynasty. These descriptions follow a basic pattern: first the text notes the establishment of the building and its dedication to Jesus or to apostles or martyrs. Next, the text lists the gifts given for the building's decoration, mostly large quantities of silver and gold; and finally the text presents a list of lands donated to provide ongoing monetary support, with a note on how much money the land would be expected to produce per year.[35] This pattern appeals to three different temporal focal points for each building: first the apostolic or martyrial past, second the imperial present, and third the agricultural or landed future, in which the building will be maintained. Each of these temporal states is tied to the material demands of the building, in its existence (and often its location), its material decoration, and the land dedicated to it. The Roman churches are conceived here as forcefully material, and this materiality makes temporal claims. Like those of the late Roman house, these claims reach both forward and backward in time.

Moreover, these different temporal focal points are not neatly divided. They are all understood to be embodied in the buildings themselves, as complex temporal objects. This can be seen most clearly if we linger on one complex object in particular, the famous *fastigium* in the Constantinian basilica. The actual facts about this object have long been disputed,[36] but for our purposes the description of the object in the text brings out most of its temporal complexity:[37]

> [He placed in the Constantinian basilica] a hammered silver *fastigium*—on the front it has the Saviour seated on a chair, 5 ft. in size, weighing 120 pounds, and 12 apostles each 5 feet and weighing 90 pounds with crowns of finest silver; for someone in the apse looking at it from behind, it has the Saviour sitting on a throne, 5 feet in size, of finest silver weighing 140 pounds, and 4 spear-carrying silver angels, each 5 feet and weighing 105 pounds, with jewels of Alabanda in their eyes; the *fastigium* itself where the angels and apostles stand weighing 2025 pounds of burnished silver; the vault of finest gold; and hanging beneath the *fastigium*, a light of finest gold with 50 dolphins, of finest gold weighing 50 pounds, with chains weighing 25 pounds.

The *fastigium* obviously evokes an apostolic past in the figures of Jesus and the apostles. But by virtue of being Constantine's gift, and in the remarkable weight of silver and gold that is carefully laid out, it equally clearly makes claims to an imperial present and dynastic future, along with the imperial past that its location next to the Sessorian Palace implies. The vivid description of the *fastigium* in the text thus expresses not only the material force of the object but also how material and temporal claims were simultaneously embodied in it.

Throughout the entry on the pontificate of Sylvester, the donation lists and building projects that the *Liber Pontificalis* describes include a mix of appeals to imperial and apostolic genealogies. It is clear that the writer of the text sees a close connection between the buildings as structures dedicated to an apostolic (or martyrial) past and as structures connected to the family of Constantine. The text explicitly connects all these structures to Constantine and many of them also to Constantius, Helena, or Constantia.[38] At the same time, the buildings are clearly meant to make claims for an apostolic Roman past, to which Constantine's family is physically connected through the basilicas themselves. This kind of genealogical mingling in objects has other parallels in late antiquity. One similar example is found in the famous lamp discovered in the house of the Valerii on the Caelian Hill, which shows Paul and Peter in a boat and is inscribed with the words "Dominus legem dat Valerio Severo Eutropi vivas." This "giving of the law" to a Roman aristocrat, possibly Pinian's acquisitive brother Severus or his father, is usually explained simply as a baptismal reference,[39] but most other uses of the *traditio legis* formula in late ancient art refer specifically to a handing on of the law to the apostles.[40] The extension of this lawgiving through the Roman apostles and martyrs Peter and Paul to a Roman aristocrat suggests the mingling of aristocratic genealogical thought with the idea of apostolic tradition. Pinian's family, through baptism or otherwise, can count the apostles as part of their genealogy. Similarly, Constantine's building projects in Rome are simultaneously dynastic and apostolic claims, with first-century figures assuming their places in imperial genealogy.

It is sometimes argued that early Christian building projects that include classical spolia should be read as triumphalist: that is, that the classical elements on display are signs of Christianity's displacement of the classical past.[41] Surely in some cases this is correct. Yet the intermingling of imperial dynastic claims and apostolic claims in Constantine's building projects as described in the *Liber Pontificalis* suggests a less clear-cut distinction between the supposedly classical and the supposedly apostolic. It has been suggested, for example, that the earlier imperial gilt-bronze columns now in the south transept of the basilica were themselves used as the supports for the *fastigium* with the figures of Jesus and the apostles.[42] Rather than being signs of the triumph of a new religion over a classical pagan past, this kind of mingling of claims about the past instead pushes the imperial genealogical claims of the Constantinian dynasty back into the apostolic age—which is of course also the age of Augustus, Tiberius, and Nero. It would, in fact, make sense for this Constantinian monument to make a physical connection to a Julio-Claudian or even Neronian past: as Elizabeth Marlowe has shown, the Arch of Constantine itself was designed to interact visually with the bronze Colossus that originally bore the features of Nero as the sun god, along the triumphal route into the city of Rome.[43] In brief, the statues of Jesus and the apostles in the Constantinian basilica, at least as described in the *Liber Pontificalis*, play the same role as other material that refers to an earlier imperial past. These first-century figures, placed at the top of the Constantinian basilica, play the same role as the Colossus of Nero overlooking the Constantinian arch. All these figures create a genealogical link between an evoked imperial past and an implied present, and they lay claims on that present using the agency of both their materiality and their signification. The apostolic history of Rome becomes materially inseparable from the imperial power of the city.

The power of structures that evoke the past to make additional claims on the future becomes clear if we consider the future of the *fastigium* in the Constantinian basilica as laid out in the later entries of the *Liber Pontificalis*. In the entry on the mid-fifth-century Sixtus III, we learn only in passing that the *fastigium* in the Constantinian basilica had been plundered in the sack of Rome and was later replaced by Valentinian III: "At bishop Xystus' request the emperor Valentinian constructed a silver *fastigium* in the Constantinian basilica—it had been removed by the barbarians."[44] The sixth-century compiler thus had never seen the Constantinian *fastigium* and in the original entry on Sylvester was either describing a fourth-century figural structure of which there were records, or may have been describing and retrojecting Valentinian III's fifth-century replacement, or was describing some combination of Constantinian and later material.[45] The sixth-century compiler, however, emphasizes the Constantinian connection of the *fastigium* and relegates Valentinian III's activity to mere maintenance, even though it may have been a replacement or an entirely new construction. This fact, along with other anachronisms in the account of Constantine and Sylvester, such as the assurance that Sylvester baptized Constantine in the baptistery that Constantine commissioned for his basilica,[46] gives us a strong indication of the genealogical demands that the Constantinian basilica complex did indeed make quite separately from the actual intentions of either Constantine, Sylvester, or Valentinian. After the sack of Rome in 410, the replacement of the Constantinian *fastigium*, possibly with the figural group described in the *Liber Pontificalis*, attests to two such demands. First, that the basilica should continue as a monumental church structure cared for by both the emperor and the bishop of Rome, and second, that its connection to the classical, apostolic, and imperial past should be reinforced, even perhaps fictitiously enhanced. In other words, the basilica successfully drew out human caretakers and inheritors, and it also reasserted its claim to much earlier apostolic and imperial ancestry. The compiler of the *Liber Pontificalis* understood these claims to connect the apostolic *fastigium* to the original Constantinian foundation, but, equally important, he emphatically placed the basilica within the longer-than-human history of imperial and pontifical succession.

The Constantinian basilica complex thus demonstrates in dramatic fashion the genealogical ambitions of aristocratic properties in late antique Rome. In its interactions with its human chroniclers and caretakers, the basilica generates an imperial and apostolic ancestry for itself that may or may not be factual, and also stakes a claim to the care of its future inheritors, both imperial and papal. These are the same kinds of claims to which earlier Roman families were responding when they created fantastic genealogies, with a variety of gods and heroes, to explain their in-fact recent prominence.[47] But the late antique trend toward the reuse of earlier materials in building, especially after the third century, would also have increased the strength of structures' claims to be living on a more-than-human scale. The evocations of the past that such structures could convey were neither simple nostalgia nor triumphalism but a set of claims about ancestry that entailed demands on the future. From the textual response to these structures that we have seen, it seems clear that we should imagine at least some late ancient Romans as intensely aware of themselves as living amid material structures and objects with more-than-human life spans, structures that by virtue of their temporal difference could make demands on the much more transient lives of their human compatriots. In a more positive light, these structures could also provide their inheritors with historical identities and possible futures. The compiler of the *Liber Pontificalis* jumbles together Constantinian and apostolic history and imperial and papal legend in his treatment of the Constantinian basilica. In this text, we can observe the creation of past apostolic and future papal Rome. Both grow out of the demands that property made for human ancestors and inheritors.

CONCLUSION: JERUSALEM

The imperial and pontifical acceptance of the demands of property may at first seem antithetical to the ascetic actions celebrated in the *Life of Melania*. But Melania and Pinian's sale of their Roman property and their departure from Rome, first for Africa and then for Jerusalem, in some ways merely reinforces the nonhuman force of structures in the late ancient imagination. Among the most clearly articulated demands that property continues to place on Melania and Pinian is a demand for maintenance. As they support monasteries in North Africa en route to Jerusalem, Gerontius describes their continued activity selling property but introduces a new development:[48]

> When the blessed ones decided to sell all their property, the most saintly and important bishops of Africa (I mean the blessed Augustine, his brother Alypius, and Aurelius of Carthage) advised them, saying, "The money that you now furnish to monasteries will be used up in a short time. If you wish to have a memorial forever in heaven and on earth, give both a house and an income to each monastery." Melania and Pinian eagerly accepted the excellent counsel of the holy men and did just as they had been advised by them.

The memorial force of Melania and Pinian's charity depends on the physical house as well as the income for its maintenance: the ascetic couple are again confronted with the temporal and physical demands of property, and in this case they decide to take up the responsibilities that such property lays before them.

This acquiescence to the demands of property in order to create a memorial for themselves "in heaven and on earth" leads Melania to a much more extensive set of building projects, which have even greater future ambitions than the house in Rome whose demands were ultimately not met. Gerontius tells us that, like Constantine and other aristocratic predecessors, Melania herself embarked on a building program in Jerusalem, one that made genealogical claims both for the past and for the future. The claims that Melania's buildings in Jerusalem would have made for an apostolic and martyrial past are perhaps obvious. Constantine had begun the process of monumental building in Jerusalem in order to evoke simultaneously an imagined biblical history and an imperial Christian present.[49] Melania's buildings take up the biblical genealogy and extend it into an imagined eschatological future. These buildings centered on the Mount of Olives, near the Church of the Ascension. After the death of Pinian, according to Gerontius, Melania "wished to build a monastery for holy men that they might carry out their nightly and daily psalmody without interruption at the place of the Ascension of the Lord and in the grotto where the Savior talked with his holy disciples about the end of time."[50] Gerontius further claims that at her own death, she prayed to the martyrs whose relics were in the martyrium of Stephen the Protomartyr, at this monastery, so that these martyrs would "be my ambassadors to the God who loves mankind, so that he may receive my soul in peace and guard the monasteries up to the end in the fear of him."[51] The buildings that both memorialize and anticipate the end of time in the *Life of Melania* play a role similar to the Constantinian structures in the *Liber Pontificalis*, which summon both an apostolic past and a pontifical future. The future of the Jerusalem buildings, however, is explicitly eschatological, summoning both the Jerusalem of the gospels and the New Jerusalem of the book of Revelation. Gerontius claims that Melania's last human instruction is for him to take over the care of the monasteries, for which God will reward him "in the age to come."[52] We have returned, in other words, to the beginning of the life of Melania, and to the problem of maintaining property that persists beyond that life. The future that this property claims, however, is not a new generation of children but the age to come, in which, with the verse that Gerontius uses to end the *Life of Melania*: "Eye has not seen, nor ear heard, nor has entered into the heart of man, what God has prepared for those who love him."[53]

The creation of Christianity's history, whether apostolic in Rome or biblical in Jerusalem, is tied to the same kinds of interactions that are responsible for the creation of elite familial traditions in late antiquity more generally. Elite built environments made claims on humans' behalf and in turn demanded of those humans the protection of new caretakers, manipulating human action in ways that aligned human ability with nonhuman duration. Late ancient elites were conscious of the temporal demands placed on them by the ancient things that they inherited, lived among, and at times called into being. They were aware that some of these ancient things would live longer than they would, and that some would not; and so they interacted with these nonhuman things, accepting some of their demands while rejecting others. The *Life of Melania* and the *Liber Pontificalis* describe a few interactions between ancient things and their succession of human caretakers. These texts demonstrate the productivity of these interactions in creating both apostolic genealogies and eschatological futures for the humans who took up the responsibilities of buildings. Melania and Pinian, Constantine and the popes of Rome, created both their pasts and their futures in cooperation with the buildings that they built, maintained, and passed on to others. In this activity of creation and inheritance, we see the greater-than-human summoning of New Jerusalem from the long life of Rome.

NOTES

1. Annabel Wharton, "The Tribune Tower: Spolia as Despoliation," in Richard Brilliant and Dale Kinney, eds., *Reuse Value: Spolia and Appropriation in Art and Architecture from Constantine to Sherrie Levine* (Farnham: Ashgate, 2011), 195.

2. E.g., Elizabeth A. Clark, "Antifamilial Tendencies in Ancient Christianity," *Journal of the History of Sexuality* 5.3 (1995), 372; or Kate Cooper, "The Household and the Desert: Monastic and Biological Communities in the *Lives* of Melania the Younger," in Anneke B. Mulder-Bakker and Jocelyn Wogan-Brown, eds., *Household, Women and Christianities in Late Antiquity and the Middle Ages* (Turnhout: Brepols, 2005), 11–13.

3. Gerontius, *Vita Melaniae Iunioris* 6; throughout, I use the Greek edition of Denys Gorce, *Vie de sainte Mélanie* SC 90 (Paris: Cerf, 1962), and the English translation of Elizabeth A. Clark, *The Life of Melania the Younger: Introduction, Translation and Commentary* (Lewiston, N.Y.: Edwin Mellen, 1984), quotation at SC 90: 138; trans. E. A. Clark, 30. For comparison with the Latin *vita*, I have used the edition of Patrick Laurence, *La vie latine de sainte Mélanie* (Jerusalem: Franciscan Printing, 2002).

4. Gerontius, *Vita Melaniae Iunioris* 1 (SC 90: 132; trans. E. A. Clark, 28). For discussion of inheritance through and to women, see esp. Antti Arjava, *Women and Law in Late Antiquity* (Oxford: Clarendon Press, 1996), 52–73 and 94–110; on the intersection of such laws and women's ascetic renunciation, see Kate Cooper, "Poverty, Obligation and Inheritance: Roman Heiresses and the Varieties of Senatorial Christianity in Fifth-Century Rome," in Cooper and Julia Hillner, eds., *Religion, Dynasty, and Patronage in Early Christian Rome, 300–900* (Cambridge: Cambridge University Press, 2007), 165–89.

5. Gerontius, *Vita Melaniae Iunioris* 15 (SC 90: 158; trans. E. A. Clark, 38–39).

6. Ibid. 12 (SC 90: 152; trans. E. A. Clark, 36).

7. Ibid. For discussion of the practical problems that this kind of asceticism could cause, see Claude Lepelley, "Mélanie la Jeune entre Rome, la Sicile et l'Afrique: Les effets socialement pernicieux d'une forme extrême de l'ascétisme," *Kōkalos* 43–44.1 (1997–98): 15–32.

8. Gerontius, *Vita Melaniae Iunioris* 14 (SC 90: 154–56; trans. E. A. Clark, 38).

9. The distinction between monetary wealth and real property is not often made, either by ancient or modern sources, partly because they were of course closely tied together; for a recent example, see the discussion of Peter Brown, *Through the Eye of a Needle: Wealth, the Fall of Rome, and the Making of Christianity in the West, 350–550 A.D.* (Princeton: Princeton University Press, 2012), who helpfully outlines the relationship between land and wealth (8–21) but does not sustain the distinction in his discussion of Melania and Pinian (291–300).

10. The recent bibliography on the agency and lives of buildings is large, stemming especially from engagement with Alfred Gell's *Art and Agency: An Anthropological Theory* (Oxford: Clarendon Press, 1998).

11. Kimberly Bowes, *Houses and Society in the Later Roman Empire* (London: Duckworth, 2010), especially chapter 3.

12. William Bowden and John Mitchell, "The Triconch Palace at Butrint: The Life and Death of a Late Roman Domus," in Luke Lavan, Lale Özgenel, and Alexander Sarantis, eds., *Housing in Late Antiquity: From Palaces to Shops* (Leiden: Brill, 2007), 455–74; the house is also discussed in Bowes, *Houses and Society*, 45.

13. Gerontius, *Vita Melaniae Iunioris* 1 (SC 90: 132; trans. E. A. Clark, 28).

14. S. J. B. Barnish, "Transformation and Survival in the Western Senatorial Aristocracy, c. A.D. 400–700," *Papers of the British School at Rome* 56 (1988), 140; for discussion of the composition of the senatorial aristocracy, see R. Étienne, "La démographie des familles impériales et sénatoriales au IVe siècle après J.-C.," in A. Alföldi and J. Straub, *Transformation et conflits au quatrième siècle après J.-C.* (Bonn: Habelt, 1978), 133–68; and Michele Salzman, *The Making of a Christian Aristocracy: Social and Religious Change in the Western Roman Empire* (Cambridge, Mass.: Harvard University Press, 2002), 22–24.

15. *Ep.* 108.1-4; CSEL 55: 308.

16. For comparison, see T. P. Wiseman, "Legendary Genealogies in Late-Republican Rome," *Greece and Rome* 21.2 (1974): 153-64.

17. Gerontius, *Vita Melaniae Iunioris*, prol. (SC 90: 124; trans. E. A. Clark, 25).

18. Ibid. 1 (SC 90: 130; trans. E. A. Clark, 27-28).

19. I am not arguing that strict patrilineal inheritance of a familial *domus* was the norm in late ancient aristocratic families; Julia Hillner ("Domus, Family, and Inheritance: The Senatorial Family House in Late Antique Rome," *Journal of Roman Studies* 93 [2003]: 129-45) has rightly questioned that stereotype. Instead, I am asking how the material presence of late Roman aristocratic houses contributed to the idea of genealogy in late antiquity.

20. Bryan Ward-Perkins, *From Classical Antiquity to the Middle Ages: Urban Public Building in Northern and Central Italy, AD 300-850* (Oxford: Oxford University Press, 1984), 38-48.

21. Arnold Esch, "On the Reuse of Antiquity: The Perspectives of the Archaeologist and of the Historian," in Brilliant and Kinney, eds., *Reuse Value*, 13-31.

22. See discussion in Edmund Thomas, *Monumentality and the Roman Empire: Architecture in the Antonine Age* (Oxford: Oxford University Press, 2007), 170.

23. See discussion in Hillner, "Domus," 137-40; and see more generally Harriet Flower, *Ancestor Masks and Aristocratic Power in Roman Culture* (Oxford: Oxford University Press, 1996).

24. On the use of statues and inscribed statue bases to make ancestral claims, see Heike Niquet, *Monumenta virtutum titulique: Senatorische Selbstdarstellung im spätantiken Rom im Spiegel der epigraphischen Denkmäler* (Stuttgart: Steiner, 2000), 15-33. Zosimus (*Hist. Nov.* 5.38) will later tie Serena's death to her impiously taking a necklace from a statue of Rhea Silvia in Rome and wearing it herself.

25. Gerontius, *Vita Melaniae Iunioris* 18 (SC 90: 162; trans. E. A. Clark, 40).

26. Ibid. (SC 90: 162; trans. E. A. Clark, 40-41).

27. For a brief survey, see Dale Kinney, "'Spolia. Damnatio' and 'Renovatio Memoriae,'" *Memoirs of the American Academy in Rome* 42 (1997): 117-48; at greater length, Maria Fabricius Hansen, *The Eloquence of Appropriation: Prolegomena to an Understanding of Spolia in Early Christian Rome* (Rome: L'Erma di Bretschneider, 2003); for a more skeptical view of the ideological import of spolia, see Paolo Liverani, "Reading Spolia in Late Antiquity and Contemporary Perception," in Brilliant and Kinney, eds., *Reuse Value*, 33-51.

28. Richard Krautheimer, Spencer Corbett, and Alfred K. Frazer, eds., *Corpus Basilicarum Christianarum Romae: The Early Christian Basilicas of Rome (IV-IX Cent.)*, vol. 5 (Vatican City: Pontificio Istituto di Archeologia Cristiana, 1980), 10.

29. For a comparison between the use of spolia on the arch and at the Lateran, see Beat Brenk, "Spolia from Constantine to Charlemagne: Aesthetics versus Ideology," *Dumbarton Oaks Papers* 41 (1987): 103-7.

30. Hugo Brandenburg, *Ancient Churches of Rome from the Fourth to the Seventh Century: The Dawn of Christian Architecture in the West*, trans. Andreas Kropp (Turnhout: Brepols, 2005), 26.

31. Ibid.

32. Krautheimer, Corbett, and Frazer, eds., *Corpus Basilicarum* vol. 5, 28-31. For discussion of Constantine's treatment of Maxentian Rome, see John R. Curran, *Pagan City and Christian Capital: Rome in the Fourth Century* (Oxford: Oxford University Press, 2000), chapter 3.

33. Curran, *Pagan City*, 95-96. See also the discussion of Richard Krautheimer in *Three Christian Capitals: Topography and Politics* (Berkeley and Los Angeles: University of California Press, 1983), 18-23.

34. I follow here the school of thought, begun with Louis Duchesne, that holds that the first part of the *Liber Pontificalis* is substantially a very late fifth- or sixth-century work but incorporates textual fragments from earlier traditions. I use the Latin text of Duchesne, ed., *Le Liber pontificalis: Texte, introduction et commentaire*, 3 vols., 2nd ed. (Paris: Boccard, 1955-57). The English here is that of *The*

Book of Pontiffs (Liber Pontificalis): The Ancient Biographies of the First Ninety Roman Bishops to AD 715, trans. Raymond Davis, rev. 2nd ed. (Liverpool: Liverpool University Press, 2000).

35. *Liber Pontificalis* 34.9–33.

36. See the thorough discussion in Sible de Blaauw, *Cultus et Décor: Liturgia e architettura nella Roma tardoantica e medievale—Basilica Salvatoris, Sanctae Mariae, Sancti Petri*, vol. 1 (Vatican City: Biblioteca Apostolica Vaticana, 1994), 117–27.

37. *Liber Pontificalis* 34.9, trans. Davis, 16.

38. According to the *Liber Pontificalis*, the churches built at Constantine's direction are as follows: the Constantinian basilica, dedicated to the Savior; the baptistery of that basilica, where according to the text Constantine was baptized; the basilica of Peter at the Vatican, which included the inscription CONSTANTINE AUGUSTUS AND HELENA AUGUSTA. HE SURROUNDS THIS HOUSE WITH A ROYAL HALL GLEAMING WITH EQUAL SPLENDOR; next, the basilica of Paul outside the walls, which the text ascribes jointly to Constantine and Constantius; the basilica for relics of the cross in the Sessorian Palace, "which today is still called Jerusalem"; the basilica to the martyr Agnes, built at the request of Constantia; the basilica to Lawrence; the basilica to the martyrs Peter and Marcellinus, "where his own blessed mother the empress Helena was buried"; a basilica in Ostia to the apostles Peter and Paul and John the Baptist; a basilica in Capua to the apostles, "which he styled Constantinian," and finally a basilica in Naples: *Liber Pontificalis* 34.9–32; trans. Davis, 19.

39. Mariarosaria Barbera, Sergio Palladino, and Claudia Paterna, "La domus dei Valerii sul Celio alla luce delle recenti scoperte," *Papers of the British School at Rome* 76 (2008): 81, 86.

40. For discussion, see, e.g., J.-M. Spieser, "The Representation of Christ in the Apses of Early Christian Churches," *Gesta* 37.1 (1998): 63–73; on the practical and aesthetic dimensions of the tradition, see Bas Snelders, "The *Traditio Legis* on Early Christian Sarcophagi," *Antiquité Tardive* 13 (2005): 321–33.

41. See especially Hansen, *Eloquence of Appropriation*, 225–44.

42. Brandenburg, *Ancient Churches of Rome*, 26–28.

43. Elizabeth Marlowe, "Framing the Sun: The Arch of Constantine and the Roman Cityscape," *Art Bulletin* 88.2 (2006): 223–42.

44. *Liber Pontificalis* 46.5; trans. Davis, 37.

45. See Herman Geertman, "Il *fastigium* lateranense e l'arredo presbiteriale: Una lunga storia," in Herman Geertman, Sible de Blaauw, and Christina van der Laan, *Hic fecit basilicam: Studi sul Liber Pontificalis e gli edifice ecclesiastici di Roma da Silvestro a Silverio* (Louvain: Peeters, 2004), 133–48.

46. See the excellent discussion of Samuel N. C. Lieu, "Constantine in Legendary Literature," in Noel Lenski, ed., *The Cambridge Companion to the Age of Constantine*, rev. ed. (Cambridge: Cambridge University Press, 2012), 298–303; and Paolo Liverani, "St. Peter's, Leo the Great, and the Leprosy of Constantine," *Papers of the British School in Rome* 76 (2008): 155–72.

47. Wiseman, "Legendary Genealogies," 155–58.

48. Gerontius, *Vita Melaniae Iunioris* 20 (SC 90: 170; trans. E. A. Clark, 43). See also the discussion of Melania and Pinian's time in North Africa in Brown, *Through the Eye of a Needle*, 322–25; and Lepelley, "Mélanie la Jeune," 23–32.

49. Again, the bibliography on early Christian migration to and building in Palestine is vast. For an excellent overview, see Andrew S. Jacobs, *Remains of the Jews: The Holy Land and Christian Empire in Late Antiquity* (Stanford: Stanford University Press, 2003).

50. Gerontius, *Vita Melaniae Iunioris* 49 (SC 90: 220–22; trans. E. A. Clark, 61).

51. Ibid. 64 (SC 90: 258; trans. E. A. Clark, 77).

52. Ibid. 68 (SC 90: 266; trans. E. A. Clark, 80).

53. 1 Cor. 2.9; Gerontius, *Vita Melaniae Iunioris* 70 (SC 90: 270; trans. E. A. Clark, 82).

2

Namesake and Inheritance

Christine Luckritz Marquis

They longed to have their woolen garments, so valuable with their golden embroidery, trodden down beneath her feet or worn away with the rubbing of her rags. For they thought that they were cleansed from the pollution of their riches if they succeeded in gathering some of the dirt from her tawdry clothing or her feet.

—PAULINUS OF NOLA, EP. 29.12

Paulinus of Nola's rich description expresses the deeply etched longing that Melania the Elder's return to the West produced in her family members.[1] He paints an image of striking contrasts between Melania's family and the holy woman herself as the retinue made its entrance into Nola: Melania the Elder, humbly dressed, riding a worthless horse,[2] and the pomp of her family, clothed in lush wools and silks and riding in coaches and carriages with fine horses. This disparity is sketched in order to heighten rhetorically both Melania's holiness ("Look what she has unproblematically forsaken!") and her family's intense joy at being near her and being able to touch and be touched by her. The sumptuousness of their silken garments and finely decorated wools (a mark of their aristocratic status) is ignored, displaced by the sacred friction of her coarse rags.

The scene makes a striking portrait. Of course, the description belongs to Paulinus's imagination more immediately than to the memories of the family members trailing behind the blessed Melania the Elder. For Paulinus is writing to Sulpicius Severus in a bit of friendly competition, so common to Roman relations of *amicitia*.[3] Severus had sent Paulinus his *Life of Martin of Tours*, and here we find Paulinus's epistolary attempt at a brief one-upmanship, or at least an assertion of sacred parity.[4] Severus's Martin is repeatedly described as poorly dressed, the meanness of his clothes serving as a partial reason to resist his ordination as priest,[5] his tattered tunic threads resulting in miracles,[6] while demonic attempts to mislead take the form of a Christ *wrongly* dressed in robes of purple.[7] Thus, we must first recognize in Paulinus's wardrobe contrasts a rendering of Melania through the rhetorical trope of saints in rags, in particular as a response to Martin's tattered clothes.

But even allowing for the liberties that Paulinus takes in his ecphrastically embellished procession, it seems fair to assume that he offers a plausible view of familial devotion to Melania. In particular, attention to the relationship between Melania the Elder and her namesake, Melania the Younger, sheds light on the complicated intersections of generations and their interactions around spiritual and material inheritances (especially the bequeathal of land) that occurred in aristocratic families. The intertwined nature of their legacies highlights a continuity between the aristocratic and the ascetic world, as early Christian institutions, including monasteries, remained heavily reliant on the traditional modes of wealth distribution. The interconnected lives of the Melanias illustrate not only how enmeshed in their familial network they remained but also how indebted they and early Christians in general remained to the logic of inheritance for articulating and enacting financial *and* spiritual matters.

Given the linked nature of the Melanias' legacies, let us return to Paulinus's vignette and begin by imagining how Melania the Younger, roughly sixteen years old, felt in her grandmother's presence. Here, enfleshed before her eyes, was her namesake. Whether one is more inclined to see her desire for virginity as a self-induced yearning (with her biographer)[8] or as a function of her familial heritage (with Palladius),[9] the physical experience of her ascetic grandmother must have been significant. As Caroline Schroeder notes, Melania the Younger, just like her grandmother, would eventually become accustomed to coarse clothing, so much so that any finer garments produced an allergic response.[10] Although these rhetorically constructed Melanias illuminate far more about a given authorial agenda than about any real introspection into either woman's inner life, nevertheless these discursive Melanias must have held a certain truth for their audiences, companions of these women catching glimpses of the Melanias they thought they knew. Thus, this section of this chapter will imaginatively reconstruct, based on late ancient aristocratic social praxes, how Melania the Younger would have been influenced by the financial *and* spiritual patrimony of her grandmother. In particular, Melania the Elder's continued reliance on familial wealth to finance her ascetic lifestyle would have also shaped Melania the Younger's vision of asceticism, especially as she found herself walking in her grandmother's spiritual footsteps, taking up the ascetic life and quite possibly inheriting her grandmother's Jerusalem monastery.

To understand Melania the Elder's financial and spiritual relationship to her family, and therefore her appearance at Nola, we must revisit how she came to stand as a paradigm of asceticism by 400 C.E. What is narrated about Melania the Elder's decision to ascetically reorient her life is primarily found not among Paulinus's letters but in two chapters of Palladius's *Lausiac History*. So, to begin, I argue below for the rehabilitation of Palladius as a reliable source on which to base our picture of Melania the Elder, specifically her continued financial relationship to her son, Publicola. Palladius's first entry describes her lineage and early years as an ascetic, especially how her assistance of the prominent exiled Egyptian abbas led her to Palestine.[11] Of all the figures in the *Lausiac History*, Palladius deemed only Melania the Elder worthy of a supplemental entry. In this additional passage, Palladius recounts Melania's generosity, her later involvement in the escape of her family from Rome, her impressive reading habits, and her prominence in the beginnings of her granddaughter's asceticism.[12] Beyond the Elder's two entries, she also appears in numerous other portrayals, often as the conveyer of stories about a given holy man.[13] In the Coptic version, Melania not only gives money to the monks of Egypt but also builds a church for those at Scetis, a point that will be returned to below.[14] Thus, it would seem that she was the source of some of Palladius's stories. Be that as it may, Palladius is quite explicitly laying claim to her authority to garner his own, painting *his* image of prominent ascetics (and of her) through her witness.[15]

After the publication of Nicole Moine's "Melaniana," scholars have tended to be warier of trusting Palladius as a source.[16] Only recently have some scholars begun to counter this distrust, and I would agree with them that it is a mistake to discount Palladius. As Kevin Wilkinson has argued, it seems that Palladius knew Melania the Elder quite well, perhaps even receiving much of the material for his *Lausiac History* from her.[17] He reasserts a traditional chronology for Melania the Elder's life up to 400 C.E., highlighting the many reasons Palladius's information is reliable.[18] The narrative of her early life as he recounts it is: born in Spain, she married and was widowed at twenty-two, moved to Rome to launch her surviving son's public career, and, having secured his career, began her own ascetic life, eventually establishing her monastery in Jerusalem.[19]

Notably, Paulinus seems to concur with Palladius about the length of Melania's absence and in portraying her son, Publicola, as a devoted Christian—and this despite the fact that he never left the limelight of public, civic life for ascetic retreat. Contrary to harsher portrayals of Melania as mother, often dependent on Jerome's self-serving depiction of her actions,[20] it seems that she abandoned Publicola not as a young child but rather as a teenage boy.[21] Although it may have served Paulinus and Palladius to portray Melania the Elder's asceticism in contrast to her familial background, neither remembrance of Melania would have much benefited from inventing a continued relationship between mother and son. That is, it would seem that Palladius and Paulinus are reflecting something of her actual familial situation, though we can catch only hazy glimpses. The shift in viewing her departure helps make sense of the continued relations between mother and son. According to Palladius, Melania the Elder's family may even have been supportive of her monastic endeavors: "Her own family and son and stewards provided the funds for this."[22] Such a view of the Elder's familial relations also seems much more in keeping with Paulinus's vignette with which we began. Though what precisely these familial exchanges over several years looked like remains unknowable, we need not imagine them as hostile.

Fairly civil if not continually devoted interactions between Publicola and Melania the Elder also help render explicable Publicola's choice to name his only daughter after his mother. Certainly, naming a grandchild after a grandparent was established practice among Roman aristocracy. Yet, had Publicola so banished his mother for her ascetic "madness," could we not imagine that he may have had other nominal options available? Families passed on set names, serving to bolster family identity. Inheritance of a name underscored the intricate networks of wealth, *amicitia*, alliance, and expectation into which one was born. Your name reminded both you and others from which family you hailed and what expectations you could make and have made of you.[23]

The date of Melania the Younger's birth is generally given as roughly around 385 C.E.[24] So, by the time she was made her grandmother's namesake, the Elder had already been well enmeshed in ascetic praxis for about a decade. That Publicola named his daughter for his mother not only indicates that his relations with Melania the Elder were probably amicable but also hints at how ensconced in the aristocratic world Melania the Elder remained. Whether Publicola explicitly imagined his daughter as following in her grandmother's ascetic legacy is difficult to discern, though one suspects he did not. Yet, by naming his daughter for his mother, Publicola placed Melania the Younger in a cultural context ripe for drawing analogical expectations across generations; and as we shall see, his daughter was only too willing to succumb to such pressures.

As just noted, the Palladian Melania the Elder was repeatedly offered fiscal support for her ascetic lifestyle in Palestine by her son, Publicola. Thus, during Melania the Younger's childhood, we can imagine that her grandmother must have stood as an imposing and ambiguous figure. Whether she heard numerous stories of her grandmother or only caught rare snippets, the prestige that her grandmother retained among Roman aristocrats and the respect that the Elder garnered among those who sought a life of retreat would no doubt have left an impression on her childhood. As the evidence indicates, not a few young Roman women (for reasons it is sometimes difficult to discern) were quite enamored with becoming Christian virgins.[25] So the general cultural cachet of being a virgin among these wealthy young women would have easily been enhanced for Melania the Younger by her grandmother's prominence in ascetic circles.

To claim that Melania the Elder influenced her granddaughter is not a bold, new suggestion, but it is an important one to reassert, as it is all too easy in studies of Melania the Younger to forget what an impact her grandmother must have had. Although Palladius offers a short description of the granddaughter of his prominent friend, the primary witness to Melania the Younger remains her biography. As with her grandmother, both images of Melania the Younger are not straightforward retellings of her life nor, especially, her turn to asceticism. Both Palladius and her biographer (generally believed to be Gerontius, her successor) have strong agendas for which Melania the Younger's narrative is deployed. As Elizabeth Clark notes in her translation of Melania's life, the striking absence of her grandmother seems a conscious decision on Gerontius's part.[26] Clark posits that this *damnatio memoriae* may have been the result of Melania the Elder's strong Origenist leanings.

Depending on whose Melania one considers, the narration of her turn to the ascetic life shifts. For Palladius, Melania the Younger *is* drawn into the vortex of Melania the Elder's ascetic presence (and therefore into her Origenist circle) from an early age. He asserts that Melania the Younger was "continually stung by the stories about her grandmother."[27] Here, the term translated as "stung" is *nyttomenē*, a term that in more literal contexts can also mean "pierce." Thus, Palladius would have us imagine Melania's person as deeply *pierced* by tellings of her grandmother, the resulting wound drawing a strong tie between Melania the Elder and her namesake. But it is only with the death of both of Melania the Younger's children, when she is twenty (two years younger than her grandmother had been when she lost her own two children), that Palladius depicts her officially taking up the yoke of asceticism, giving away her silken clothes as the first outward symbol of her new life.[28] Recall that it was precisely her silk-clad body, among the others of her family, that Paulinus had put to such good use in his portrayal of her grandmother. Now, suddenly, we find Melania the namesake replacing her "worldly" clothing with rags and stepping into her grandmother's dusty footprints. But this is also our first indication that Palladius's chronology of Melania the Younger's turn to the ascetic life may not be very precise. Rather, he seems to be deploying the costume change as a renunciatory trope, a visual marker for her newfound asceticism. For Palladius also claims that Melania the Elder returned to Rome after she heard that her granddaughter had "elected to leave the world," another clear euphemism for her ascetic turn.[29] It is precisely this return West around 400 that Paulinus narrates, the Elder's family all decked out in their finery to greet her. Of course, as acknowledged above, Paulinus's Melania the Elder is competing with Severus's Martin, so the starker the contrasts he presents, the more impressive a figure of Melania he draws. Yet, Paulinus is more than happy in later correspondence to note the ascetic zeal of the junior Melania. Can we not imagine that had Melania the Younger been dressed in poorer clothes, Paulinus would have used her as a model of the converts whom the Elder drew to her community just as Martin did to his? That is, if Melania the Younger was contemplating the ascetic life, nothing about her outward appearance seems to have caught the eye of Paulinus. He recognizes her impulse only at a later date.

In contrast to the Palladian Melania the Younger, who continued to follow in her grandmother's footsteps, Gerontius locates Melania's ascetic impulse in her own innate holiness, since "she had from her earliest youth yearned for Christ, had longed for bodily chastity."[30] By erasing her spiritual legacy from her Origenist grandmother, he frees Melania the Younger to stand always on the side of orthodoxy (so her anti-Nestorian lectures but also Gerontius's own presumed non-Chalcedonianism).[31] But he seems, in fact, keenly aware of where he places her feet, for in the opening lines of her *vita* he uses the image of her "putting underfoot all the pride of worldly glory" in order to indicate her success in ascetic pursuits.[32] If one follows those scholars who see Gerontius as reliant on Palladius's narrative, then it should not be surprising that both authors agree that Melania came to asceticism only after her marriage. That is, the presence of Pinianus remained one relic of her life that was harder to wipe away.

In comparing these portrayals, a fascinating aspect of the competition between these two authors for Melania the Younger's legacy emerges: her legacy was not solely her own, for she also bore the spiritual legacy of her grandmother. As discussed earlier, the cultural logic of namesakes meant that Melania the Younger inherited a legacy from her family, especially her grandmother. While we could only conjecture above *what* Melania the Younger may have known about or felt toward her paternal grandmother, the larger cultural (and specifically financial) expectations of her, especially once she became an ascetic, may still be traceable.

Palladius offers a straightforward rendering of this social logic in his portrayal of her wealth and his use of the language of inheritance. Recall that in his earlier description of Melania the Elder Palladius had pointed to the location of her material sustenance: her family, Publicola, and her steward. Especially if one believes Palladian portrayals of her, she came to the ascetic life with a rather haughty attitude about money. Her expectation of praise and honor for her "donation" to Abba Pambo was quickly inverted, as he pulled spiritual rank on her.[33] She did not merely proffer coinage but also left a more permanent mark on the desert landscape: the church for Abba Isidore at Scetis.[34] Her building of a church with her funds for these Egyptian abbas smacks of precisely the type of estate-church building documented as occurring elsewhere in late antiquity.[35] As Kimberly Bowes has shown, in a villa-*cum*-monastery such as that of Paulinus of Nola, building was not done to attract converts from the local peasantry, but rather to construct, manipulate, and advertise his own aristocratic identity. Such architectural and decorative work was intended to "speak" to family and friends on the estate as well as to other *amici* who might occasionally visit, just as Melania the Elder and her family had at Paulinus's villa.[36] Thus, buildings served as an extension of a patron or matron's power.

Activating such cultural making of meaning, Palladius portrays Melania not only as receiving relics from several prominent Egyptian abbas (a reception of powerful items from holy men)[37] but also as leaving an architectural memorial on the desert landscape (a physical marker of her own power). If Melania the Elder did build a church at Scetis, especially shortly after Abba Pambo's rebuke, we should envision her building project as her aristocratically styled counter to Pambo's dismissal. The structure functioned as Melania's attempt to articulate to the abbas the ascetic identity with which she wanted to be honored, while simultaneously serving as an imposing reminder of her social status vis-à-vis the monks. But as no archaeological evidence has been found and the reference is only present in the Coptic version, the actual existence of the church remains debated. If it was not built, this narrative stands as an interesting inverse of Catherine Chin's point: to understand Melania the Elder's influence cultural logic demanded a building even where there was not one. That is, whether or not Melania actually built the church, that the author places it in the imagined heart of asceticism says much about how her impact in Egypt was interpreted by at least some of its inhabitants.[38]

Though the Elder certainly handed out her wealth quite generously, her coffers likely stayed full by means of money channeled from her familial wealth. This fiscal flow is important to note because, as mentioned several times now, it is indicative of Melania's relationship to her family, and in particular of her self-understanding of her asceticism vis-à-vis her own aristocratic heritage. As part of his reassertion of Melania's traditional chronology before 400 C.E., Wilkinson makes the case that Melania spent her time as a new widow in Rome preparing her son's civic future. Shortly after their arrival in Rome, Melania quite quickly secured Publicola's position in the queue to be urban praetor, an event that would have taken her entire ten-year tenure in Rome to prepare for and that would have set him on course for a successful imperial career.[39] That when she left Rome on her ascetic voyage she left him in the care of a guardian would not contradict this scenario and certainly would have helped ensure her access to familial wealth for the next decade: that is, until Publicola came of full legal age. Once he did reach full inheritance, and therefore legal control of his wealth, it seems he continued to fund her (and certainly named his daughter after her). By then her largest ascetic endeavor, her and Rufinus's dual monasteries, would already have been well established. Again, given Palladius's intimate friendship with Melania the Elder, there is no reason to assume that he has got his narrative entirely wrong. But even if it is all only so much rhetorical creation many years after her death, Palladius certainly wants to frame Melania as a rather traditional Roman aristocratic mother despite her decades of asceticism. Thus, when Palladius has Melania return to Rome on her granddaughter's behalf, we find her quite easily stepping into a matriarchal role that she had never fully abandoned.

Here we now return to the question with which we began: How significant must Melania the Elder's influence have been on her namesake? That Melania the Younger's attempt to forsake her aristocratic life in Rome for a new ascetic way of being was resisted is something that both Palladius and Gerontius describe.[40] And, in particular, it is her and Pinianus's immense familial inheritance that prevented an easy escape. As Catherine Chin highlights, some of Melania the Younger's buildings resisted dismissal, her family house on the Caelian Hill being the ultimate example.[41] Even when Melania could liquidate an asset, under the pressure of Alaric's escalating extortion of money from the people of Rome, many among the senatorial, upper classes would have frowned on Melania the Younger's desire to take her money and run.[42] Gerontius plays up Melania the Younger's difficulties with her own family, conveying that even her father initially resisted her call to asceticism.[43] As others have noted, Gerontius's portrayal is rooted in a desire to displace Melania's biological family with a new ascetic one.[44] He continually paints Melania as uninterested in her family, except perhaps for Pinianus and her mother, Albina, whose ascetic endeavors result in an overlay of the ascetical upon the biological. It is Gerontius's Melania the Younger who seems to rejoice in the death of her children, finally free from the burden that they presented.[45]

Palladius, too, has Melania the Younger confront strong resistance to her new life choice, but he paints the difficulties as arising from within the senatorial class, who desired to keep her immense financial resources at hand to soothe Alaric. Quite explicitly, Palladius praises Melania the Younger for saving her money from Alaric's clutches, that it might yet be put to good use among her fellow Christians.[46] Where the Palladian Melania the Younger differs is in her relationship to her family. His Melania does not praise God for her children's death but rather recognizes in their fate her own: God has taken her children early so that she may take up renunciations earlier in life.[47] That is, Palladius's junior Melania seems to have been originally set to follow in her grandmother's footsteps, procreating and thus continuing the family line before turning herself over to renunciation. Thus, we can imagine that the death of Melania's children may actually have proved a stumbling block in her expectations for her life. Palladius certainly indicates that a different route had to be imagined for her. And so, Melania the Elder reenters the Western scene.

Here again, Palladius's depiction of Melania rings more *truthful* (if not true) than Gerontius's. Even in his own narrative, Gerontius is hard pressed to walk the delicate line between appreciation and praise for certain members of Melania's family (her mother and husband) and disparagement or erasure of the presence of others (her father, children, and grandmother). The case of Melania's grandmother has been of particular interest among scholars, for it is a noted lacuna in Gerontius's life that the woman for whom Melania the Younger was named never registers in the narrative. As mentioned above, Clark is undoubtedly correct when she points to Melania the Elder's Origenist tendencies as part of Gerontius's motivation.[48] The role that Origenism's erasure plays in modern interpretations of Melania the Younger is not to be downplayed. When Gerontius removes Melania the Elder and her Origenism from Melania the Younger's past, he obscures not only the relationship between grandmother and granddaughter but also the much larger network of patronage and *amicitia* in which Melania the Younger is purported to have circulated as she began her ascetic life: close interactions with Paulinus, Palladius, and (perhaps most troubling from a later, anti-Origenist viewpoint) Rufinus.

The passage from Palladius so crucial for imagining Melania the Elder's concern that her granddaughter might end up among the anti-Origenists is: "A long time afterwards she heard how her granddaughter was doing, how she had married and then elected to leave the world. She feared that they might be utterly destroyed by bad teaching or heresy or bad living."[49] Clark convincingly argues that the "bad teaching or heresy" that Melania feared around 400 C.E. could be nothing other than the theological debate surrounding Origen, in which she herself was embroiled.[50] Palladius undoubtedly had this issue in mind, as he himself was a strong spokesman for those condemned as Origenists, especially John Chrysostom.

But it is not *only* "bad teaching and heresy" that Melania feared for her namesake. She also worried that Melania and Pinianus might fall into "bad living." The Greek word here, *kakozōia*, occurs only one other time in Palladius's works. Writing in defense of Chrysostom, Palladius uses this term to describe how John rightly condemned as living badly those clergy who chose to live with "introduced" (*syneisaktoi*) women.[51] Although these individuals were ideally a man and woman living together chastely, Chrysostom repeatedly railed against the dangers of such intimate living arrangements.[52] Given the meaning of this term for Palladius already in his defense of Chrysostom, we should imagine that when he deploys the term again roughly a decade and a half later he means to signal the same sort of living arrangement. Melania the Elder returned in order to ensure that her namesake was not living in a chaste marriage with Pinianus but rather that both young ascetics would live in separate, companion monasteries, as she and Rufinus had. Perhaps she even hoped that her granddaughter would join her community at Jerusalem, and Pinianus Rufinus's. That is, Palladius would have his readers believe that part of what spurred Melania the Elder's trip back to Rome was concern that her granddaughter was at risk for "subintroductory" living.

Thus, Palladius would have us envision Melania the Elder as worried about her legacy as embodied by her granddaughter's ascetic choices and theological convictions. But, given that Melania the Elder (at least in Palladius's rendering) was still very much a prominent matriarch in the family, who had continued to tap the familial coffers, we may also imagine that Melania the Elder was concerned for the financial legacy of her family (meaning both her biological family and her ascetic family). Thus, she may have felt pressed to come and direct her granddaughter in person in the more financially savvy ways to perpetuate an ascetic agenda.[53] As just noted, Palladius foregrounds another explanation for Melania the Elder's visit: fears of bad teaching, heresy, or wrong living.[54] Yet, even as he does so, his main description concerns the Elder's struggle against and chastising of the senatorial families for attempting to prevent her granddaughter from renunciation (resistance that was clearly based on issues of financial responsibility). In particular, he states that as part of her "moral support" of Melania the Younger, Pinianus, and Albina, Melania the Elder "induced them to sell their goods and led them away from Rome."[55] Palladius interprets her actions through scriptural allusion to 1 Corinthians 15:32, constructing Melania's battles with the Senate as similar to persecution faced by the apostle Paul. But, as Melania attempted to shame these senatorial combatants, financial issues surrounding familial inheritance once more surfaced as the pressing concern. She warns them: "Beware lest the days of the anti-Christ overtake you and you not enjoy your wealth and your ancestral property."[56] Palladius's Melania the Elder does not demonize wealth, nor does she deny its usefulness; rather, she seems to recommend an attitude toward familial wealth that acknowledges that such money is temporal and best spent on Christian causes, especially her monastery at Jerusalem. In this way, she invokes an eschatological end view that makes the concerns of continuity among the aristocracy of Rome seem misguided. The eschatological reorientation that Melania the Elder recommends bears a striking resemblance to the eschatological worldview that, Chin argues, informs Melania the Younger's bequeathing of her properties to Gerontius.[57] Melania the Elder, having "freed" her family members from the grip of Roman greed and introduced them to the ascetic life, goes on to sell "everything which remained."[58] She then takes *her* newfound funds and returns to Jerusalem, distributing some and presumably establishing the rest as an endowment for her monastery. Thus, Melania the Elder's return to Rome was heavily concerned with modeling proper fiscal behavior for her granddaughter while also financially shoring up her own ascetic legacy, one embodied in her monastery.

Palladius, likewise, devotes a lengthy portion of his description of Melania the Younger to her distribution of her own wealth. Palladius makes clear that his audience is supposed to interpret Melania the Younger's asceticism through that of her grandmother. Shortly before he discusses the disbursement of her riches, Palladius frames Melania's ascetic reorientation with the language of inheritance. Speaking to her husband, Pinianus, the Palladian junior Melania asserts that if Pinianus will not join her in renunciation she is willing to make a deal: "If this seems too hard for you, for you are a young man, take what is mine, but set my body free so that I may fulfill my will to God and enter into the inheritance of the zeal of my grandmother whose name I bear."[59]

Multiple issues are gathered in this single utterance. First, not only is Palladius's Melania pierced by the stories of her grandmother,[60] but here she makes clear that being her grandmother's namesake carries with it an inheritance. The inheritance of her grandmother's name signifies the larger inheritance that she has received from Melania the Elder. What she has been bequeathed of value is not her riches (Pinianus may take those), but rather her grandmother's zeal is what is precious. (It was precisely her grandmother's zealousness, according to Palladius, that would help her escape Rome on the eve of its sack.)[61] We should note that Pinianus presumably would *not* have been privy to the wealth allocated for Melania the Elder, and so Melania the Younger in joining her grandmother would hardly have been left destitute. But as Palladius then relates, Pinianus joins her in renunciation, and so she gets to retain her wealth. She is then left to distribute her bounty, and as Palladius tells it, she does so wisely. Her donations of money to various locales well known for ascetic enterprises are noteworthy. Whereas those in Egypt and the Thebaid, those in Antioch, and those of the island regions all received ten thousand pieces, only Palestine, home of her grandmother's monastery, received fifteen thousand pieces.[62] And though she freed or donated to her brother many of her slaves, we should imagine that she did keep those who worked on the estates she retained in Sicily, Campania, and Africa. Palladius claims her purpose for keeping the properties was as an "endowment of the monasteries."[63] Such actions would reflect that Melania the Younger has learned something from her grandmother's own precarious financial situation, making sure that she has continual funds from which to care for her monastic endeavors.[64]

Although this section has concentrated more intensely on Melania the Younger's life through Palladius's eyes rather than Gerontius's, both authors make clear that her life would have been interpreted for those around her (and perhaps the woman herself) only in reference to her grandmother Melania the Elder. Melania the Younger's life, both in the presence (Palladius) and absence (Gerontius) of Melania the Elder, is made meaningful through visions of her grandmother. For Palladius, the Elder stands as the ascetic model par excellence on which the junior Melania would base her new life, her grandmother explicitly slipping her feet back into the shoes of family matriarch to direct not only her granddaughter but her daughter- and grandson-in-law as well. By contrast, Gerontius intentionally erases the presence and influence of Melania the Elder, a scrubbing that we must imagine was no easy task given how influential an aristocrat she was. Perhaps we should see in this erasure an attempt by Gerontius to claim more autonomy for his heroine, Melania the Younger. It would not be the only time in the *Life* he did so, for his portrayal of Melania's relations with the empress Eudocia indicates that Melania the Younger (or more correctly Gerontius) also found herself (himself) in "friendly" competition with the empress's largess (as portrayed by John Rufus in his *Life of Peter the Iberian*).[65]

Viewing Gerontius's *damnatio memoriae* of Melania the Elder as located not just in anxiety over Origenism but also in what he felt was a competition between the elder aristocrat and her namesake, his heroine, may prove productive. In this light, should we imagine that Melania the Younger really built brand-new, dual monasteries on the Mount of Olives? Scholars have long accepted that Melania the Elder's monasteries may well have vanished by the time her granddaughter arrived in Palestine, many years after her grandmother's death. The explanation most often given is that Melania the Elder did not properly endow her monasteries. Yet such a claim stands in stark contrast to the greater longevity that Chin has illustrated aristocratic buildings had.[66] It also contradicts information gleaned from Palladius. First, recall that Melania the Elder is said to have taken her portion of the money liquidated during her last trip to Rome and left some of it to fund her monastery at Jerusalem.[67] Similarly, we may reconsider precisely *which* monasteries Palladius was referring to when he asserted that Melania the Younger kept her estates in Sicily, Campania, and Africa "for endowment of the monasteries."[68] Here he does not seem to gesture to monasteries generically but perhaps assumes that his audience knows *the* monasteries to which Melania the Younger would be most tightly linked, those on the Mount of Olives. Moreover, Palladius has Melania the Younger donate fifteen thousand pieces to monasteries in Palestine. It hardly seems possible that none of that money went to the Elder and Rufinus's ascetic family.

As noted earlier, it is worth remembering that senatorial families often used their homes as visual, architectural embodiments of their legacies. As both Richard Saller and Julia Hillner note, aristocratic houses might symbolize continuity in familial power;[69] and as Chin has shown, such buildings with their furnishings made demands upon their owners.[70] Though the dynamics of the Roman imperial family certainly changed vis-à-vis asceticism, there was also much that remained traditional.[71] Melania the Elder may have participated in estate building first at Scetis and certainly did so at Jerusalem. Stories of such figures as Evagrius of Pontus visiting make clear that Melania and Rufinus's monasteries functioned as places of retreat for *amici* just as villas did. Given the demands that such buildings made on their inheritors, Melania the Younger must have grappled with the gift of Melania the Elder's monastery after her grandmother's death. The most culturally plausible response for Melania the Younger would have been to rehabilitate (and possibly expand) her grandmother's properties rather than build from scratch. Modern scholars are perhaps seduced by Gerontius's rhetoric (and in particular his anti-Origenism) when we too eagerly accept his claims that Melania the Younger built herself new monasteries on the Mount of Olives. There can be little doubt that he intentionally excludes Melania the Elder from his narration of her granddaughter's life. He explicitly seeks to undo the image that Palladius has painted of Melania the Younger retracing the footsteps of her grandmother as she takes up the ascetic life.[72] It would follow that he could never allow the possibility that his heroine had architecturally expanded or restored her grandmother's property, the far more common late ancient practice with regard to inherited buildings. To acknowledge her reuse of the land would produce a topographical link between grandmother and granddaughter, diminishing Melania the Younger's ascetic endeavors and instead tainting her feet with Origenist dust. Gerontius's new monasteries reflect less an actual structure and more his rhetorical construction of a new, independent legacy for the younger Melania.

Reassessing the Melanias' monastic construction projects highlights how intertwined Melania the Younger's legacy was with her grandmother's. While Melania the Elder is largely inaccessible as a historical subject except through the remembrances and imagination of Palladius, her granddaughter is doubly so. She was rhetorically constructed not only by male authors but also through the discursive appropriation or denial of her grandmother's spiritual legacy. Attention to the material and financial aspects of inheritance indicates how dependent early Christian institutions such as monasteries were upon traditional channels of aristocratic wealth. As aristocrats entered the ascetic life, they brought with them the cultural logic of their social networks as well as the actual *amici* who made up such networks. In an ascetic context, such friends and practices were inscribed with a new spiritual competitiveness. Reconsideration of the lives of Melania the Elder and her namesake, as imagined by male authors, brings to light the unstable delineation of material and spiritual inheritance that arose more broadly as aristocrats joined the monastic milieu in the fourth and fifth centuries.

NOTES

1. The epigraph to this chapter: Paulinus of Nola, *Ep.* 29.12 (CSEL 29: 259–60). Here I largely follow the English translation found in *The Letters of Paulinus of Nola*, vol. 2, trans. P. G. Walsh (Westminster, Md.: Newman Press, 1967).

2. Here it is worth noting that Paulinus describes her horse as worth less than a donkey. This distinction suggests that he also intended to summon a scriptural allusion to Jesus's entry into Jerusalem on an ass.

3. As Sigrid H. Mratschek-Halfmann has argued, continued use of the practices of *amicitia* and *hospitium* were important to Paulinus's new self-fashioning as an ascetic ("*Multis enim notissima est sanctitas loci*: Paulinus and the Gradual Rise of Nola as a Center of Christian Hospitality," *Journal of Early Christian Studies* 9.4 [2001]: 511–53).

4. Paulinus, *Ep.* 29.6 (CSEL 29: 251–52) himself acknowledges that his portrayal of Melania the Elder is to be read as a response to Sulpicius Severus's recent gift of the *Life of Saint Martin*. Here, Paulinus suggests he offers his description as a debt owed to a friend who has given him so much in the figure of Martin. Of course, this is undoubtedly true, but it is also perhaps an indication that old habits die hard and that Paulinus was still very much a practitioner of literary competitiveness, even if his dialogue partners were now of a more ascetic bent.

5. Sulpicius Severus, *Vita Sancti Martini* 9.3 (SC 133: 270, 272).

6. Ibid. 18.4–5 (SC 133: 292).

7. Ibid. 24.4. (SC 133: 306, 308).

8. Gerontius, *Vita Melaniae Iunioris* 1 (SC 90: 130). English translation: Elizabeth A. Clark, ed. and trans., *The Life of Melania the Younger: Introduction, Translation, and Commentary* (Lewiston, N.Y.: E. Mellen Press, 1984), 27.

9. Palladius, *Historia Lausiaca* 61.1–2. Greek text: Cuthbert Butler, ed., *The Lausiac History of Palladius: A Critical Discussion Together with Notes on Early Egyptian Monachism* (Cambridge: Cambridge University Press, 1898–1904; reprint, Hildesheim: Georg Olms, 1967), 155.

10. C. Schroeder, "Exemplary Women," this volume.

11. Palladius, *Historia Lausiaca* 46 (ed. C. Butler, 134–36).

12. Ibid. 54–55 (ed. C. Butler, 146–49).

13. Ibid. 9, 10, 18, 38 (ed. C. Butler, 29, 29–32, 47–58, 116–23).

14. *Vita Pambo* 5 (É. Amélineau, ed., "De *Historia Lausiaca* Quaenam Sit Huius ad Monachorum Aegyptiorum Historiam Scribendam Utilitas" [Ph.D. dissertation, University of Paris (Paris : E. Leroux, 1887)], 96). A French translation of the amended Coptic is found in Gabriel Bunge, ed., and Adalbert de Vogüé, trans., *Quatre ermites égyptiens: D'après les fragments coptes de l'Histoire lausiaque*, Spiritualité Orientale 60 (Bégrolles-en-Mauges: Abbaye de Bellefontaine, 1994). I have compared this French translation with Amélineau's text as no collated version of all the Coptic manuscripts exists.

15. Robin Darling Young explores Palladius's representation of Melania the Elder, her relationship with Melania the Younger, and Evagrius's relationship with her in more depth in her chapter, "A Life in Letters," in this volume.

16. Nicole Moine, "Melaniana," *Recherches Augustiniennes* 15 (1980): 1–79.

17. Kevin W. Wilkinson, "The Elder Melania's Missing Decade," *Journal of Late Antiquity* 5.1 (2012): 168. See also Young's assessment of Wilkinson in "A Life in Letters," in this volume.

18. He is largely suggesting a return to the chronology and explanation of F. X. Murphy, though with some emendations: Francis X. Murphy, "Melania the Elder: A Biographical Note" *Traditio* 5 (1947): 59–77.

19. Wilkinson, "Elder Melania's Missing Decade," 177.

20. Jerome, *Ep.* 39.5 (CSEL 54: 305).

21. Wilkinson, "Elder Melania's Missing Decade," 180–82. As Wilkinson notes, this process of promoting her son's praetorship may even help explain her commissioning a bath-house epigram on one of her estates (184). On the epigram, see also Alan Cameron, "Filocalus and Melania," *Classical Philology* 87.2 (1992): 140–44.

22. Palladius, *Historia Lausiaca* 54.2 (ed. C. Butler, 146).

23. Such familial continuity and inheritance was also often embodied in the architecture of the home, for a good discussion of which, see Julia Hillner, "Domus, Family, and Inheritance: The Senatorial Family House in Late Antique Rome," *Journal of Roman Studies* 93 (2003): 129–45; and Chin, "Apostles and Aristocrats," this volume.

24. E. A. Clark, *Life of Melania*, 84.

25. Susanna Elm's explanation of the complicated situation among female late ancient virgins remains among one of the most nuanced and helpful views (*Virgins of God: The Making of Asceticism in Late Antiquity* [Oxford: Oxford University Press, 1994; reprinted 2000]).

26. E. A. Clark, *Life of Melania*, 148–51.

27. Palladius, *Historia Lausiaca* 61.1 (ed. C. Butler, 155).

28. Ibid. 61.3 (ed. C. Butler, 155–56). Gerontius also makes much throughout his *Life of Melania* about the various clothing changes Melania the Younger gradually makes. For a good discussion of the meaning of these wardrobe changes, see R. Krawiec, "'Garments of Salvation': Representations of Monastic Clothing in Late Antiquity," *Journal of Early Christian Studies* 17.1 (2009): 125–50, especially 137–39.

29. Palladius, *Historia Lausiaca* 54.3 (ed. C. Butler, 147).

30. Gerontius, *Vita Melaniae Iunioris* 1 (SC 90: 130).

31. Ibid. 54 (SC 90: 232; anti-Nestorianism). On Gerontius's Miaphysitism, see E. A. Clark, *Life of Melania*, 18–22.

32. Gerontius, *Vita Melaniae Iunioris*, prol. (SC 90: 124).

33. Palladius, *Historia Lausiaca* 10.3–4 (ed. C. Butler, 30).

34. *Vita Pambo* 5 (ed. Amélineau, 96).

35. For a good recent discussion of such building activities, see Kimberly Bowes, *Private Worship, Public Values, and Religious Change in Late Antiquity* (Cambridge: Cambridge University Press, 2008).

36. Bowes, *Private Worship*, 179–82.

37. So, for example, Palladius, *Historia Lausiaca* 10.5 (ed. C. Butler, 30), where she receives a basket from Abba Pambo.

38. Chin, "Apostles and Aristocrats," this volume. One can only speculate what the (real or imagined) presence of this church may have come to symbolize for those of an Origenist inclination, such as Palladius and his audience, who had been exiled from the Egyptian desert.

39. Wilkinson, "Elder Melania's Missing Decade," 181–82.

40. Palladius, *Historia Lausiaca* 54.5, 61.1 (ed. C. Butler, 148, 155); Gerontius, *Vita Melaniae Iunioris* 12 (SC 90: 150, 152).

41. Chin, "Apostles and Aristocrats," this volume.

42. So notes E. A. Clark, among others: *Life of Melania*, 100–108.

43. Gerontius, *Vita Melaniae Iunioris* 12 (SC 90: 150, 152).

44. K. Cooper, "The Household and the Desert: Monastic and Biological Communities in the *Lives* of Melania the Younger," in *Household, Women, and Christianities*, ed. Anneke B. Mulder-Bakker and Jocelyn Wogan-Browne (Turnhout: Brepols, 2005), 11–35.

45. Gerontius, *Vita Melaniae Iunioris* 5–6 (SC 90: 134, 136, 138).

46. Palladius, *Historia Lausiaca* 61.5 (ed. C. Butler, 156).

47. Ibid. 61.3 (ed. C. Butler, 155–56).

48. E. A. Clark, *Life of Melania*, 148–51.

49. Palladius, *Historia Lausiaca* 54.3 (ed. C. Butler, 146).

50. E. A. Clark, *The Origenist Controversy: The Cultural Construction of an Early Christian Debate* (Princeton: Princeton University Press, 1992), 24.

51. Palladius, *Dialogue concerning the Life of John Chrysostom* 5 (SC 341–42: 118).

52. For a thorough discussion of Chrysostom on the issue, with relevant citations from his various writings, see E. A. Clark, "John Chrysostom and the 'Subintroductae,'" *Church History* 46.2 (1977): 171–85.

53. It is worth noting that at the time of Melania the Elder's interventions, it is unclear whether Publicola remained alive. Most scholars date Publicola's death ca. 408 C.E., based on evidence from Paulinus's *Ep.* 45 (see D. Forie, Gerontius, *Vita Melaniae Iunioris* [SC 90: 37 n. 2]). This is important because Paulinus's correspondence also anchors the arrival of Melania back in the West: 400. The calculation is based on a reference to Nicetas's visit as well in *Ep.* 29. In a celebratory poem for St. Felix's feast day some four years later, Nicetas is said to stay once more in Nola. It is the date for Felix's celebration that is most discernible; scholars then counting back four years assume the letter was written in 400 C.E. (On this process of dating, see Alan D. Booth, "Quelques dates hagiographiques: Mélanie l'Ancienne, saint Martin, Mélanie la Jeune," *Phoenix* 37.2 [1983]: 144–47.) Scholars tend to date Melania the Younger's abandonment of Rome to late 408 or early 409 C.E. What is striking in these chronological issues is that Palladius does speak well of Publicola as he begins his explanation of Melania the Elder's return voyage but then never again mentions Publicola's role in the escape from Rome. Neither is he placed on the side of the senatorial "beasts," nor is he found fleeing with his wife, daughter, and son-in-law. Moreover, had Publicola been present, it seems unlikely that Melania the Younger would have needed her grandmother to advocate on her behalf. Although it is beyond the scope of the current paper, the muddled extant evidence should indicate how incredibly confused the chronology of Melania the Elder's life (and with it the actions of her granddaughter) becomes after 400 C.E.

54. Palladius, *Historia Lausiaca* 54.3 (ed. C. Butler, 146).

55. Ibid. 54.4 (ed. C. Butler, 147).

56. Ibid. 54.5 (ed. C. Butler, 147). Anne Yarbrough ("Christianization in the Fourth Century: The Example of Roman Women," *Church History* 45.2 [1976]: 156) rightly highlights how threatening and socially disruptive Melania and Pinianus's actions would have seemed. Their choice to take their wealth and disburse it as they saw fit meant that their money (quite a substantial amount) was permanently exiting the small loop of exchange among aristocratic families.

57. Chin, "Apostles and Aristocrats," this volume.

58. Palladius, *Historia Lausiaca* 54.6 (ed. C. Butler, 147).

59. Ibid. 61.2 (ed. C. Butler, 155).

60. Ibid. 61.1 (ed. C. Butler, 155).

61. Ibid. 54.7 (ed. C. Butler, 148).

62. Ibid. 61.4 (ed. C. Butler, 156).

63. On the vastness of Melania the Younger's wealth, see E. A. Clark, "Antifamilial Tendencies in Ancient Christianity," *Journal of the History of Sexuality* 5.3 (1995): 374.

64. Palladius's Melania the Younger, so full of fiscal wisdom regarding the distribution of her wealth, stands in some contrast to the image painted in Augustine's correspondence with the family, in particular with her mother, Albina. Augustine's interactions with the family are described in *Ep.* 124–26. *Ep.* 124 is to Melania, Pinianus, and Albina, whereas *Ep.* 126 addresses only Albina. The intervening letter, *Ep.* 125, is written to Augustine's fellow bishop, Alypius, detailing the troubles that he has had with Melania and her family. (CSEL 44: 178–94). For an explanation of how Melania and Pinianus's liquidation of certain properties and their gift giving may have been received, see K. Cooper, "Poverty, Obligation, and Inheritance: Roman Heiresses and the Varieties of Senatorial Christianity in Fifth-Century Rome," in *Religion, Dynasty, and Patronage in Early Christian Rome, 300–900,* ed. Kate Cooper and Julia Hillner (Cambridge: Cambridge University Press, 2007), 165–89.

65. On the competing legacies of Melania the Younger and Eudocia regarding St. Stephen's relics, see E. A. Clark, "Claims on the Bones of Saint Stephen: The Partisans of Melania and Eudocia," *Church History* 51.2 (1982): 141–56.

66. Chin, "Apostles and Aristocrats," this volume.

67. Palladius, *Historia Lausiaca* 54.6 (ed. C. Butler, 147).

68. Ibid. 61.5 (ed. C. Butler, 156).

69. R. Saller, *Patriarchy, Property, and Death in the Roman Family* (Cambridge: Cambridge University Press, 1994), 163–64; Hillner, "Domus," 130–31.

70. See Chin, "Apostles and Aristocrats," this volume.

71. Cooper, "Household," 26–27.

72. This is especially true if one accepts Rampolla and Butler's claims, as Clark does, that Gerontius had access to a copy of Palladius's *Historia Lausiaca* when he wrote his *Life*: E. A. Clark, *Life of Melania*, 148–49.

3

Exemplary Women

Caroline T. Schroeder

The *Life of Melania the Younger* is replete with emotional language and emotionally charged interactions between characters. Desire, zeal, grief, distress, and other feelings paradoxically drive events in a narrative about a woman exceedingly successful in the art of self-control. Emotions are even vehicles for implementing the Lord's work here on earth. This chapter examines the function of emotions at the intersection of gender, class, and religion in the *Life of Melania the Younger* within the context of late antique hagiography, which typically privileged desire, grief, and maternal love as the standard feminine emotional repertoire. From Cicero to Plutarch and beyond, emotional exchanges in ancient texts often functioned as signs of intimacy; the language of affect could express affection for the audience, drawing it in to the world of the author's or orator's relationship with the person about whom he wrote (and that author or orator was almost always male).[1] Broaching the feeling—whether love, joy, grief, or some other emotion—opened up a space for intimacy and exchange between author and reader, orator and audience. It reinforced bonds between already intimate parties or wove new threads between previously unknown dialogue partners.

The prominence of emotional exchanges and expression in saints' lives like the *Life of Melania the Younger* led some to compare hagiography to the ancient romance. As Elizabeth A. Clark has noted in her commentary on the *Life*, early Christian hagiography's explicitly instructional nature differentiates it from the genre of the ancient novel, no matter how many romantic tropes they share.[2] The *Life*, in fact, provides a handbook of elite emotional behavior for the emerging Christian ascetic set. Through the figure of Melania, the *Life* presents a woman deft at the art of public and private self-fashioning, strategically managing her own emotions while eliciting the desired emotional response among the people she encounters.

Melania the woman proves to her audience that the ascetic life of renunciation remains nonetheless a life of deep affect. Moreover, given the gender conventions in ancient emotional theories, in which elite male patrons were allowed a different range of emotional expression than were women, the *Life* presents an expansive emotional world for elite ascetic women. Melania has access to the persuasive powers of both feminine and masculine emotional expression and deploys them as one would expect of an ancient sage or hero. As literary protagonist, she also serves as a role model for her female readers and admirers to imitate. What emerges from the *Life* is an aristocratic hero, created in part out of her own very particular circumstances but nonetheless a paragon of virtue for women to come.

MELANIA AND MASCULINITY

To understand emotions and their role in the *Life*, we must first understand the intersection of gender with the other subject positions that Melania occupied, since the relationship between affect and virtue in late antiquity depended on a person's gender, education, and class. Sociological theory refers to the interlocking aspects of identity (such as race, class, and gender) experienced by one individual as "intersectionality." In her seminal article on the concept, Kimberlé Crenshaw argued that late twentieth-century identity politics "frequently conflates or ignores intragroup differences," especially differences among women that are inflected by class and race.[3] Crenshaw's work is dedicated to understanding the compounding effects of intersectionality on the oppression of women of color in modern America, and her research examines violence against women of color. A study of Melania the Younger must of course look at the reverse side of this coin: the way class and other forms of identity (such as family legacy) accord her privileges unavailable to all women (and result in the exploitation of other women, such as her slaves).[4] Following Crenshaw, we cannot comprehend a person's identity in his or her culture in singular terms; our understandings of ourselves, and the individual and institutional interactions that we experience, result from an intersection of multiple modern identities: gender, sexual orientation, race, ethnicity, religion, and so forth. Likewise, late antique identities were constituted by multiple factors, and Melania the Younger stood squarely at the intersections of class (extreme wealth), gender, status (itself an intersection of multiple categories: free, citizen, senatorial family), and religious identity (Christian). As Clark has argued, late antique ascetic women pushed against the constraints imposed on their gender by renouncing many of the socially constructed trappings of womanhood, particularly marriage (which brought with it wifely obedience) and motherhood (which tied women down physically, economically, and socially).[5] The *Life* represents

Melania the Younger as leveraging her wealthy status to shift the terms of another aspect of her identity: her gender. As chapters in this volume by Catherine Chin and Andrew Jacobs attest, Melania's family was among the richest of the ancient Roman elite, if not *the* richest.[6]

According to the *Life*, Melania's wealth, including her *renunciation* of her wealth, was linked both to her identity as an elite wife and mother and to her ability speak and act in ways often reserved for men. Such behavior included the gendered expectations for both expressing feelings and eliciting emotions. As Clark notes in her study of Melania and her ascetic compatriots: "The fact that these women lived in a fashion similar to that of male monastics gave them freedom to pursue activities that would not have been considered entirely proper for Christian matrons in the world, activities that were for the ascetic women not only permitted, but sanctioned, by churchmen."[7] Women like Melania were "manly," shrugging off the trappings of womanhood for more masculine qualities.[8] Even the narrator of the *Life* praises the "manly deeds of this blessed woman" (*ta tēs makarias tautēs andragathēmata*), including her "zeal" (*ton zēlon*) for orthodoxy, enthusiasm for bodily scourging and self-flagellation, humility, cheap clothing, and temperance.[9] Wealth enabled Melania's gender-bending by giving her the resources to travel, to request audiences with influential people, and to establish her monastery. Wealth intersected with gender and status to her advantage. But it also provided a very gendered temptation to renounce. According to the *Life*, when Melania donned an expensive dress, she broke out in inflammation from the embroidery.[10] Through her asceticism, she had become simply allergic to wealth!

Melania thus straddles the identities of late antique matron *and* patron. Melania's money and her renunciation of it in service to the church (i.e., giving copious resources for churches and other "religious projects") "gave voice" to one "rich in funds but poor in other status determinants"—namely gender. Ascetic women's renunciation of their femininity—and especially their *elite* femininity—opened some doors typically labeled "men only," but not the door to the priesthood. Ascetic matrons like Melania became "patrons, not priests," eclipsing in authority and influence their poorer sisters as well as their class-compatriots who remained traditionally married matrons.[11]

Even the empress praises Melania's scorning of privilege, placing her on the golden throne and exhorting an audience: "She has rather even bridled nature itself and delivered herself to death daily, demonstrating to everyone by her very deeds that before God, woman is not surpassed by man in anything that pertains to virtue, if her decision is strong."[12] The empress, the very pinnacle of elite womanhood—and quite possibly the only one among Melania's contemporaries to surpass her in wealth and influence—praises the matron for transcending her femininity. Though in doing so, she simultaneously naturalizes women's inferiority to men, by characterizing Melania's virtue as containing and taming "nature itself" (*tēn physin autēn*). (Gerontius, the narrator, perhaps takes a page from Palladius's *Lausiac History*, which famously describes her grandmother Melania the Elder as a "female man of God.")[13]

In her ascetic discipline, especially, Melania represented the very model of premodern masculinity, honing spirit and body in constant "combats" against temptation and the devil. The *Life* repeatedly describes her and her husband Pinian's renunciation as a "combat" or "contest," evoking the image of the athlete or even martyr in the arena.[14] The heroes of those contests were often coded as masculine even if they had been born female, as L. Stephanie Cobb has demonstrated.[15] Gerontius carefully depicts his heroine as a manly heir to the martyrs. In her Jerusalem monastery, she "shut herself up in a tiny cell" in order to pursue "even greater contests" than she could among the general monastic population.[16] This withdrawal seems a variation on the *Life of Antony*, in which the Egyptian monk repeatedly withdrew ever deeper into the desert—at one point walling himself up in a tomb, and at another barricading himself in a desert fortress for twenty years.[17] For like Antony, Melania could not isolate herself completely, because her fellow monastics continued to seek her out for her teachings. In her fights against the devil, writes Gerontius, she "clothed herself in virtues as a garment" so that "the hostile powers did not trouble her, for they were able to find nothing of their own in her." She had imitated the angels, who welcomed her, as well as the prophets and apostles, but especially the martyrs, "whose combats she had voluntarily endured."[18] Melania's husband, Pinian, too is portrayed as a combatant who waged the good fight as an ascetic before expiring; his death spurred his widow on to "contesting even more."[19] Her "combats" then provide inspiration to her male narrator; remembering her valiance, seeking to imitate it, and calling upon her in prayer gives Gerontius the strength for his own battles.[20]

Even Melania's acts as a patron constitute individual battles in a larger war waged against the devil. Divesting herself of her wealth (in the service of the church) requires repeated contests with Satan, to the point where she even reportedly yells at him about a coastal bath she owns.[21] The devil is so envious of her "spiritual love" that he attacks her ally, the empress, by causing Eudoxia to twist her foot. Melania prays and fasts with the virgins in her community until the pain recedes; emboldened, she then continues "fighting" against the devil.[22] Her strength in combat ultimately overcomes even nature itself. On a trip home during a harsh winter, her prayer is the "very strong weapon" that overcomes the winter elements threatening the travelers and their voyage.[23] Eventually, she successfully fends off a sin to which prominent ascetics are especially susceptible—that of arrogance, a sin that the *Life* equates to the devil himself.[24] Even her conversion of her pagan uncle to Christianity becomes part of this narrative of lifelong combat, one of many "other battles" that subsequently "fell to her, greater than the earlier labors."[25] Masculinity itself—even for men—was not a stable characteristic but rather something achieved through contest and competition; masculinity was constantly made and remade, attained and reattained in the public view. As Maud Gleason has argued: "Manliness was not a birthright. It was something that had to be won."[26] Melania proved a champion over and over.

Her manly mettle as a soldier for Christ appears nowhere more clearly than at her death. The bishop and anchorites who assemble at her deathbed praise her for her heroic strength over the years. "You have fought the good fight on earth," they recite. "Go with joy to the Lord, as all the angels rejoice."[27] This lifetime of "fighting the good fight" thus culminates in the *vita* with an account of what in antiquity was known as a "good death."[28] According to the narrator, Melania faces her impending demise with strength, not weakness; with understanding, not fear; with wisdom, not shock. And throughout the account of her steady progress toward death, the female saint outmans her male narrator and the male clerics and monks who attend her final moments. Though "severe pain gripped her body," she remained "a truly noble woman" (*hē alēthōs gennaia, kai tauta tōn chalepōn ekeinōn odynōn haptomenōn autēs tou sōmatos*) of "undoubting heart" (*adistaktō kardia*).[29] In these last days, Melania exhibits masculine virtue in imitation of the martyrs, whose perseverance and power Cobb has described as follows: "Having made the choice to die, Christians had only to persevere in the good death to embody masculine *virtus*.... When the martyrs 'received the fury of the adversary' and 'beheld the passion of the enemy,' they responded like noble athletes and gladiators, models of masculinity: they focused on dying with honor."[30] Candida Moss concurs, observing about the classical Greek and Roman notions of virtue: "The good death also provided an opportunity to prove, decisively, one's worth and manliness. Dying well with dignified self-control was long considered the mark of a good soldier."[31]

It was not only men who laid claim to the classical tradition of the noble death. Women, too, shared in this heritage, albeit with some disturbing wrinkles. As Moss argues, women's deaths in ancient literature typically served two very gendered social logics. They often died a "good death" in the face of victimization, whether gendered or sexual, or both—the most famous of these being of course Lucretia, who committed suicide after her rape. Or a woman's virtuous death shamed (and brought to light) the less virtuous behavior of men in her narrative.[32] Rather than heroes in their own right, such women served (and died to serve) primarily as foils for unheroic men. Although no Lucretia, Melania the Younger certainly functions as a foil to the men in the story. Although ill and nearing death, Melania nonetheless attends the morning liturgies, mustering the strength to remain standing throughout the chanting of the hymns; Gerontius, however, tells us *he* stands in anguish and distress, worried about the living saint.[33] Learning of the severity of her sickness, the bishop of Jerusalem, accompanied by various clergy, visits her on her last day, and Melania receives the Eucharist from him. Whereas he is troubled and distressed, she perseveres.[34] And then in the moments before her death, when the bishop and monks praise her "good fight," she expresses acceptance, dying "gently and peaceably, in joy and exaltation," as they confess their anxiety: "But we are greatly distressed that we will be separated from your beneficient presence."[35] Gerontius at one point compares her perseverance to that of an "expert runner who having come round the stadium desires the trophy."[36] Melania, the manly fighter and competitor for Christ in her activities in life, remains so to the end, a model of discipline and virtue who outstrips her male contemporaries in these qualities.

EMOTIONS

Melania's self-control at the end of her life—in the face of physical pain, personal loss, and death—exemplifies the ideals of emotional expression ascribed to the elites of the ancient world. A person's character was revealed in the way he or she faced and reacted to adversity. The *Life* portrays a Melania whose responses are steeped in Stoic notions of virtue and proper affect, and—what is more interesting—responses expected from both men and women. As Maria Doerfler's chapter in this volume argues, Melania serves some social roles coded distinctly as feminine in the ancient world. Indeed, in the *Life,* she reacts to events as both man and woman, exposing a range of emotional expression not usually expected of or allotted to women, especially in hagiography.

The *Life of Melania the Younger* draws broadly on ancient emotional theories, but especially on those most commonly categorized as Stoic. The saint often (and especially at her death) epitomizes the sage, a model of virtue that is aspirational even if not always achieved—as Margaret S. Graver describes it: "Courage, intelligence, fairness, and self-control are possibilities inherent in our rational nature, even if we in our current condition do not properly exemplify them."[37] Melania performs the ideal, while the monks and clerics around her are the "we" who fail to embody full virtue. The Stoic theories of emotions hinged on a distinction between feeling or affect and emotions, the latter involving judgments in response to perceived events. Feelings could be involuntary and natural (such as the sense of loss upon the death of a loved one) and thus were not necessarily inappropriate. Emotions, however, were regarded as volitional—one assents to certain responses and feelings with a judgment. Emotions (*pathē*) were viewed as inappropriate responses to circumstances: anger, for example, is a dangerous and destructive emotion because it overrides a person's rational responses. Anger is volitional, and people can train themselves to respond without anger.[38] *Eupatheiai*, in contrast, were desirable affective responses, such as friendship and some forms of love, expressed as a result of good judgment.[39] An examination of zeal, desire, love, distress, and grief and sadness in the *Life* demonstrates that Melania's regulation of her affective responses positions her as a sage.

The gender dimensions of a courageous, wise, just, and disciplined sage are complex. As Margaret Graver and Martha Nussbaum have argued, Stoic *theory* posits a philosophical school and way of life open to men and women; the female sage was not an oxymoron.[40] As in so many cases, however, practice does not always live up to its theoretical principles.[41] As Gretchen Reydams-Schils has argued, for example: "According to Seneca, women are by nature more prone to lack of self-control, to moral weakness, and to the passions in general: they are more easily broken by excessive grief (*Cons. Marc.* 7.3); they get carried away by anger (*Clem.* 1.5.5); they are too soft in compassion (*Clem.* 2.5.1); they are incontinent in luxury and debauchery, and manipulative in trying to realize misguided ambitions."[42] Melania, most notably, embodies none of these feminine failings. A particularly "womanly" virtue is "chastity and restraint" (*pudicitia*), which Melania *does* possess in spades.[43] The regulation of the self in public, in terms of rhetoric, body language, and feelings, is part of the performance of a civic identity and status, one that is bound up in expectations for men and their manhood, as Gleason has argued.[44] Melania, while a monastic, is a public patron for the church, and thus she performs a very *masculine* identity at times, even while maintaining her very feminine identity as a woman.

Melania the Younger's typical emotional state is one of equilibrium, albeit occasionally punctuated by more extreme expressions. As we discovered when examining her death, Melania's self-control usually appears as a foil to other characters' distress—or rather, their distress functions as a foil to her equanimity, highlighting her saintly discipline. The ancients regarded distress among the negative passions, *pathē*.[45] Occasionally, however, Melania herself experiences it, usually in the context of her ascetic renunciation of wealth, and it is always tempered by some contextual justification, or the saint's subsequent maturity in virtue, or both. For example, as a young woman, Melania becomes "distressed" (*hē de pany lypētheisa*) when people discover that she has secretly been wearing a "coarse woolen garment" under her silk dress.[46] Similarly, the narrator describes Melania and Pinian's struggle to divest themselves of their substantial property as a "battle" against the devil himself, who is tempting them with wealth. They were "vexed and distressed" (*dysphorountes te kai thlibomenoi*) as well as extremely "upset" (*lypoumenoi sphodra*) by this combat; ultimately, however, the distress gives way to "great relief and ineffable joy" over the "future repose" that God promises them upon their renunciation of so much of their riches.[47] Although Melania exhibits emotions that Cicero might disdain (such as *lypē*), these tests build her virtue and strength.[48] Moreover, she also experiences one of the most cherished of *eupatheiai*, joy.[49] Likewise, soon after, the *Life* describes her as "upset" (*edysphoroun*) during her fight against the devil, but she then runs "sober-minded" (*nēpsasa eutheōs edramon*) for help from God through prayer.[50] These accounts portray a Melania who experienced distress *before* the establishment of her monastery in Jerusalem but then continued to grow in virtue. The founding of an ascetic community seems a milestone in her journey toward sagelike perfection; she experiences few negative emotions after this point.

On one notable occasion Melania feels passions associated with anger or distress after founding her monastery: when she is traveling through North Africa. Upon leaving Tripoli, she becomes "very upset" (*sphodra ek toutou lypētheisa*) to learn that an official will not release her animals for travel. Her status, however, is soon recovered, for the official catches up to her party seven miles out of town to apologize; he lowers himself to his knees, embraces her feet, and "amid many tears" asks for her forgiveness.[51] Melania's fit of pique over her travel inconvenience, thus, is soon overshadowed by a more dramatic scene in which gender performance is reversed in a display of the maintenance of late antique status: the man prostrates himself tearfully before the wealthy female patron. Class trumps gender. With the final episode as the exception, the *Life* describes these moments of inappropriate or uncontrolled emotion as occurring *before* she moves to Jerusalem and establishes her monastery—before she matures in her role as ascetic sage.

This pattern holds for other emotional outbursts, as well, particularly those of grief. Early in the *Life*, Melania pleads with her husband, Pinian, to release her from her marriage vows in order that she can live a celibate life. The narrator describes her as "beg(ging) her husband with much piteous wailing," signaling an emotional constellation of grief, sadness, and remorse—remorse for having lost her virginity in the first place.[52] This "piteous wailing" is coded as feminine both in its substance and in its context; wailing and excessive grief are hallmarks of womanly lament.[53] The exceptions in the Christian tradition, of course, are male biblical exemplars who wail in lament. The context of Melania's wailing—her sexuality—underscores the feminine nature of this act in her *vita*. As an ascetic woman, Melania seeks to pursue the virtue of *pudicitia* to its furthest limit, and laments her loss of virginity. The Stoic sage, however, does not indulge in such expressions of remorse: the sage judges that nothing can be done to reverse a past action, and thus does not feel regret. The average person, however, could and should experience remorse. In Graver's estimation, "One would expect that remorse would be a very frequent experience for the nonwise, provided they see their situation with some degree of accuracy. From the standpoint of theory, the ordinary person is always in line for remorse, since everything ordinary people do is an expression of our flawed epistemic state."[54] Remorse, therefore, may be an *appropriate* feeling for the average person, but its presence is also a sign that such a person is not yet a sage.[55] The Platonists, in contrast, found remorse followed by repentance a useful tool for training the character.[56] Melania's wailing over her lost virginity is appropriate in both philosophical contexts; her regret proves she has not yet reached ascetic perfection and can cultivate her virtue along the way. Moreover, Melania's remorse works in multiple registers. She cannot undo the past, but her audience can (and should) benefit from her emotionality in order to learn not to repeat her mistake; the audience learns the proper choices on the path to ascetic perfection or (if already consecrated virgins) sees in her regret a validation of their decision.

At two other key moments, the young Melania grieves. In the Latin Stoic tradition, grief and, especially, tears are not in and of themselves negative. Seneca and Cicero agree that upon the loss of a loved one the wise person will experience tears, an involuntary bodily movement as a result of a wholly natural feeling (not a judgment leading to an emotion); Seneca argued that the sage weeps voluntary tears, ones that are controlled, mixed with joy, conscious, and willful.[57] Upon the death of her mother, Melania spends a year fasting and mourning, which seems both controlled and volitional as well as culturally appropriate for a daughter. When Pinian dies, in contrast, Melania succumbs to what may seem extreme grief, "wearing herself out in fasting, vigils, and intense sorrow" for four years.[58] These years of sadness prove to be a stage in her journey toward perfect virtue; they end when she is "aroused by divine zeal" (*theiō zēlō kinētheisa epethymēsen*) and is inspired to establish her ascetic community in Jerusalem. Divine intervention transitions her into the sage, who then spends much of her life consoling *others* in their grief (including grief over her own impending demise).[59] Her mourning straddles two ancient definitions of elite decorum. Even people who do not count themselves among the Stoics might find four years excessive, yet that extensive grief fulfilled her wifely duty of devotion to her dead husband.

Melania the monastic also serves as a hagiographic model for expressing *eupatheiai,* good feelings. Her otherwise controlled demeanor is regularly punctuated by moments of zeal, desire, and joy, which are almost always coded as virtuous. While she and Pinian early on struggle to keep from "surrender(ing) [them]selves to sensuality" and sexual desire, their "burning desire" for God so swells that the devil himself becomes jealous of them.[60] According to Gerontius, the saint reoriented her desire from wealth and physical love to more appropriate objects. She displayed "zeal" for orthodoxy while her heart "burned even more strongly with the divine fire." She distributed her wealth to charity "eagerly" and felt ardor for God.[61] Her love might be "overwhelming," but it was reserved for "learning," God, and the spiritual welfare of others.[62] It was also love as *agapē, philos,* and *prothymia.*[63] Reverence for the gods, which Christian literature often codes as fear of God, and love (love, at least, toward friends and family, and even *erōs* directed toward beauty) both count among the *eupatheiai* for the ancients.[64] Melania's "zeal" (*zēlos,* typically a negative feeling, in the ancient world) wanes in favor of these other more virtuous expressions of love. And here *The Life of Melania*'s emotional world conforms clearly to ancient theories of affect: the valence of feelings as virtuous or not depends on their object and the judgment made about that object, the judgment inherent in the feeling triggered by it.[65] Gerontius's understanding of Melania's own virtue, and her status as a model for imitation, stems in no small part from what he regards as her superior judgment. The objects of his sage's affections are Christian beauty: God, orthodoxy, and virtue itself. Although zeal is a feeling of some ambivalence in the ancient world, containing within it a sense of excess that makes it in its very nature inappropriate, Melania's channeling of zeal toward its only appropriate objects—God and his will—makes zeal instead a sign of Christian self-control and volitional virtue.

Melania, of course, does not always model perfection for her audience. As a young woman, she burns with the passion of youth, and she becomes "vexed and distressed" in the battle against Satan over relinquishing her wealth.[66] These moments typically occur, however, during her earlier years, and so these moments of imperfection plot the progress of the sage. She models for her audience the path to perfection.

MELANIA AND HER SAINTLY SISTERS

Melania's self-fashioning (or rather, Gerontius's fashioning of Melania) as both feminine and masculine opens up a range of representations often not allowed to female saints, particularly in the realm of feeling, emotion, and affect. Some of the best-known lives of holy women are those of repentant harlots, Pelagia, Mary of Egypt, and Mary niece of Abraham. Mary and Pelagia, in particular, perform remarkable feats of asceticism: Pelagia's reputation for her numerous "virtuous deeds" and fame as a monk "perfect in his service" spread widely; Mary of Egypt's sanctity enabled her to imitate Christ and walk on water.[67] These feats come at some expense, however. These women are paragons of the "extremes of sinfulness and sanctity" seen in much hagiography about women, especially the penitent harlots who experience lives of utter holiness only after extricating themselves from the depths of sin.[68] Melania's *Life*, however, complicates this trajectory and instead presents a woman whose holiness and perfection are not solely predicated on a rejection of her past. Melania as sage is patron and matron, an elite woman who won the battle with the demons of wealth without actually living in extreme poverty and renunciation. Virginia Burrus's work on the hagiography of harlotry has exploded the binary of sin and sanctification, and has challenged interpretations of the penitent harlots' hagiography that plot them exclusively on a linear continuum from extreme depravity to holy renunciation. What marks the harlots in both their "before" and "after" portraits, she argues, is their desire and seduction.[69]

Melania's journey from wife and mother to monastic is indeed marked by renunciation and deprivation alongside desire and zeal. But unlike the harlots' journey, it is marked by tears issued most often not out of regret, which is an emotion steeped in a sense of wrongdoing and irreconcilable error; though the harlots' sanctification peaks along with their desire for God (as witnessed by Mary of Egypt's ability to walk on water, for example), their bodies continue to bear witness to their mistakes, whether that testimony is through tears, emaciation, or a gender disguise. Burrus observes that their passion burns their entire lives, and so too do their mistakes live on with them despite this arc of repentance. Neither they nor the reader can ever be allowed to forget that they are deeply flawed, and this memory is reinforced through their range of emotional expressions. Melania's tears flow from a grief that is no flaw in her character. Even her lamentation for her own loss of virginity appears as a cameo in the story of her life, something easily recognized by the audience the moment it appears but fundamentally an ornamentation on the narrative, not its central character. Melania exhibits self-control but not a life free of affect. As a sage, she has wide range of affective feelings, in some ways perhaps wider than the emotionally expressive harlots, whose particular desire and regretful grief burn so brightly as to blind them and the reader to other emotions. Love, zeal, grief, humility, fear, desire, and even distress are all open to Melania. She models for her readers not self-control's extinguishing of affect but instead its virtuous deployment of affect.

Melania's emotional life seems positively effusive when compared with that of another famous female saint, Macrina, sister of the Cappadocian Fathers Basil and Gregory of Nyssa. In fact, Melania may be more fairly matched with Macrina for a comparison than with the penitent harlots, since Macrina also was born to a wealthy, politically influential family. Macrina is the saint most commonly seen as a female sage, in the *vita* penned by her brother but even more so in his treatise *On the Soul and the Resurrection*. Like Diotoma schooling Socrates, Macrina imparts wisdom to her male companions in the latter text.[70] And like Melania, Macrina often expresses a very distinctively masculine subjectivity alongside her feminized philosophical fecundity.[71] Her characterization is so stylized that Clark has questioned whether we learn much about the authentic Macrina from either text.[72]

The representation of Macrina as sage in the *Life* does not position her as teacher to a symposium of philosophers, but her sagelike persona persists nonetheless, perhaps even rising to the status of a Stoic stereotype or caricature. The Macrina of the *Life* rarely expresses feelings of any stripe, much less the eschewed *pathē* of sadness, excessive lamentation, or inappropriate desire. Only upon her deathbed (where she dies a good death, like Melania) does she feel the love of God as "bridegroom" for her and in her turn voice a love for God herself. She shows eagerness and desire only for the Lord and only at this moment. But even then, when her heart is "hurrying" toward what she "desired," the *vita* frames her feelings as a quest for virtue: "For in very truth her course was directed towards virtue, and nothing else could divert her attention."[73] When her brother Naucratis dies, she teaches her own mother to be "brave" rather than to succumb to the "abyss of grief." The model of "steadfastness and imperturbability," Macrina understandably has a "natural affection" for her brother but nonetheless "conquer[s] nature" and becomes "superior to her sorrow," exhibiting a "rational spirit." With Macrina's support, and with her example to follow, "her mother was not overwhelmed by the affliction (*pros to pathos*), nor did she behave in any ignoble and womanish way, so as to cry out at the calamity, or tear her dress, or lament over the trouble, or strike up funeral chants with mournful melodies. On the contrary, she resisted the impulses of nature."[74] Indeed, Macrina's entire ascetic practice is based upon the extinction of emotions, and so she instructed the virgins in her charge: "For no anger or jealousy, no hatred or pride, was observed in their midst, nor anything else of this nature, since they had cast away all vain desires for honour and glory, all vanity, arrogance and the like. Continence was their luxury, and obscurity their glory."[75]

CONCLUSION: MELANIA'S AUDIENCE

Melania thus emerges from her *Life* as a woman who has mastered *sōphrosynē* without sacrificing a life of affect and affectionate connections with others. Her complicated performance of gender, class, and emotion comes in the context of hagiography—the readers and listeners are her audience, and hagiography is, of course, instructional and mimetic. The text functions as a handbook for the ascetic set, especially the women who may be reading or hearing the hagiography in their own ascetic communities. And while her *vita* traffics in some traditional tropes seen in the other lives of ascetic women, it also offers ascetic women a distinctive model of a range of virtuous emotions, one in which affective expression is not incongruous with the perfection, wisdom, and virtue they seek to achieve.

Imagining the Melania of the *Life* as a role model for others is tricky, however. Even among other elite women, Melania the Younger stood out. She was not among what we in the early twenty-first century may call the "one percent"; her status was even more rarified, with stratospheric wealth perhaps surpassed only by the imperial house. In that way, Melania is the Angelina Jolie of the ancient world—a finely wrapped package of femininity, wealth, and influence completely out of reach for the average woman, even the average ascetic woman. Like Jolie, Melania at times transgressed gender norms, and yet she also represented the ideal Roman matron at the same time, and her fame reached across the empire centuries before the phenomenon of mass media.[76]

Contemporary studies of the relationships between female fans and women media celebrities may be helpful for understanding the way that Melania's hagiographical representation affected the ascetic women who read her *Life*, despite the obvious differences between late antiquity and our digital, consumerist age. For we have little access to the female audience who read, listened to, and discussed together the account of their more famous and widely revered ascetic sister. Did they identify with her despite vast differences in social status? Did reading her *Life* affect their perceptions of the range of possibilities for their own lives?

Recent scholarship on media consumption and celebrity-fan culture suggests the answer to both questions is yes. In their study of movie consumers watching film clips that depicted stereotypically "attractive" and "unattractive" actresses acting in ways culturally coded as aggressive or masculine, Laramie D. Taylor and Tiffanie Setters concluded: "Watching a female protagonist behave aggressively was found to activate stereotypically masculine gender role expectations for women, but only when the protagonist was stereotypically physically attractive." In other words, this combination of aggression with traditional attractiveness increased women's acceptance of other women taking on both masculine and feminine "gender role expectations." Moreover, they state: "The effect on endorsement of stereotypically masculine expectations was partially mediated by the perception that the protagonist was a good role model for women."[77] Melania the Younger, of course, does not dress like Angelina Jolie in *Tomb Raider* (rather the opposite, in fact), nor does she "aggressively" carry a physical weapon. She is, however, a "good role model for women" who also acts in ways that are not passive, and not uniformly culturally coded as stereotypically feminine, such as when she lives among the monks of Nitria as a man would.[78] At times she even acts "aggressively," as in her repeated combats against the devil or even when she insists that a monk accept her donation of gold after he has resolutely refused.[79] Her prayer is her "very strong weapon," powerful enough to defeat even nature itself.[80] Therefore, this study is suggestive that the "effects of exposure" to women who are simultaneously culturally "attractive" and actively transgressing some of their culture's gender stereotypes indeed affects women's views on how it is and is not appropriate for them to behave in society.

In addition, the work of Melissa Click and her coauthors Hyunji Lee and Holly Holladay on the fan-celebrity relationship between Lady Gaga and her "Little Monsters" argues that these relationships are formative for the media "consumers'" self-identity and self-fashioning. Summarizing recent scholarship on multimedia, they write: "Fans use objects or texts (like books, television shows, or celebrities) for self-reflection, essentially fashioning them into mirrors. Fans both mimic and see themselves in such objects."[81] Click, Lee, and Holladay follow the work of Jackie Stacey, whose book *Star Gazing: Hollywood Cinema and Female Spectatorship* argued that women spectators of 1940s and 1950s films acknowledged the differences between themselves and the female movie stars they followed, and that their perceived connection with these celebrities involved a constant negotiation of these differences, a negotiation between self and Other that at times led to women feeling as though they could escape or transcend their own situations and at other times identify with the celebrity to mobilize their own behavior.[82] The research of Click and her coauthors confirms this interplay between spectator and media figure on the part of the media consumer; Lady Gaga fans' identification with their socially and politically provocative celebrity idol generated material, political benefits. It "helped them survive the regular bullying and marginalization that they have experienced and endured because they were seen as different."[83] Social media "amplifies" the relationship of "reciprocity" in the imagined relationship with the celebrity, since Lady Gaga can communicate directly with her Little Monsters through Twitter, YouTube, and other interactive vehicles of digital communications. Yet, the authors note, this is an amplification of a trend seen in other media, even in other cultures besides the North American.[84]

We therefore may imagine late antique ascetic women reading the *Life of Melania*, identifying with its protagonist, recognizing the class differences, and nonetheless finding validation in her for their *own* behavior and emotional expression that might not conform to feminine gender norms. What is more, as a didactic and mimetic text, the *Life* provides a guide to women for navigating the emotional landscape of the ascetic life. Melania provides both a beacon to women seeking to achieve her sage status and also, especially in her earlier years, glimpses into alternative emotional paths that other ascetics can learn to avoid or, following Melania's ultimate success, learn to overcome. Melania the Younger was one of a kind, both in her life and in her hagiographic representation. Yet she likely served as a paragon of masculine and feminine virtue for a much wider population of ascetic women.

NOTES

I would like to express my appreciation to Catherine M. Chin and L. Stephanie Cobb, whose comments have greatly improved this piece.

1. Susan Treggiari, *Terentia, Tullia and Publilia: The Women of Cicero's Family* (New York: Routledge, 2007), 136–39, 161–62; Plutarch, *Consolatio ad Uxorem*, in *Moralia* vol. 7, Loeb Classical Library 405 (Cambridge, Mass.: Harvard University Press, 1959).

2. Elizabeth A. Clark, *The Life of Melania the Younger: Introduction, Translation, and Commentary* (Lewiston, N.Y.: Edwin Mellen Press, 1984), 153–70.

3. Kimberlé Crenshaw, "Mapping the Margins: Intersectionality, Identity Politics, and Violence against Women of Color," *Stanford Law Review* 43.6 (1991): 1242.

4. See the important corrective to white feminists (mis)appropriating Crenshaw's work by Terese Jonsson, "Some Thoughts on Intersectionality and Class," *Between the lines* (blog), May 26, 2012, http://researchingbetweenthelines.wordpress.com/2012/05/26/some-thoughts-on-intersectionality-and-class/.

5. Elizabeth A. Clark, "Ascetic Renunciation and Feminine Advancement: A Paradox of Late Ancient Christianity," *Anglican Theological Review* 63 (1981): 240–57.

6. Catherine M. Chin, "Apostles and Aristocrats," and Andrew S. Jacobs, "The Lost Generation," both in this volume.

7. E. A. Clark, "Ascetic Renunciation and Feminine Advancement: A Paradox of Late Ancient Christianity," reprinted in *Ascetic Piety and Women's Faith: Essays on Late Ancient Christianity* (Lewiston, N.Y.: Edwin Mellen Press, 1986), 186.

8. Ibid.; see also Gillian Cloke, *This Female Man of God: Women and Spiritual Power in the Patristic Age, AD 350–450* (New York: Routledge, 1995).

9. Gerontius, *Vita Sanctae Melaniae Iunioris*, prol., in Denys Gorce, ed. and trans., *Vie de sainte Mélanie: Texte grec, introduction, traduction et notes*, Sources Chrétiennes 90 (Paris: Cerf, 1962), 126; trans. E. A. Clark, *Life of Melania*, 25–26.

10. Gerontius, *Vita Sanctae Melaniae Iunioris* 31 (SC 90:186–88; trans. E. A. Clark, 48).

11. Elizabeth A. Clark, "Patrons, Not Priests: Gender and Power in Late Ancient Christianity," *Gender & History* 2.3 (1990): 253, 263.

12. Gerontius, *Vita Sanctae Melaniae Iunioris* 12 (SC 90:150; trans. E. A. Clark, 35).

13. Palladius, *Lausiac History* 9.1 in *Palladius: The Lausiac History*, ed. and trans. Robert T. Meyer (Westminster, Md: Newman Press, 1965). See also the essay by Robin Darling Young, "A Life in Letters," in this volume.

14. Gerontius, *Vita Sanctae Melaniae Iunioris* 49, 63 (SC 90: 220–22, 252–54; trans. E. A. Clark, 61, 75).

15. L. Stephanie Cobb, *Dying to Be Men: Gender and Language in Early Christian Martyr Texts* (New York: Columbia University Press, 2008).

16. Gerontius, *Vita Sanctae Melaniae Iunioris* 32 (SC 90: 188; trans. E. A. Clark, 49).

17. Athanasius, *Life of Antony* 8, 14 in G. J. M. Bartelink, ed., *Vie d'Antoine,* Sources Chrétiennes 400 (Paris: Cerf, 1994), 156–58, 172–74; Engl. trans. in *Athanasius: The Life of Antony and the Letter to Marcellinus,* trans. Robert C. Gregg (New York: Paulist Press, 1980), 37, 42.

18. Gerontius, *Vita Sanctae Melaniae Iunioris* 70 (SC 90: 270; trans. E. A. Clark, 82). As Kristi Upson-Saia argues (*Early Christian Dress: Gender, Virtue, and Authority* [London: Routledge, 2011], 14, 35, 52–53), the connection between virtue and clothing cuts both ways. Melania clothes herself in virtue *in contrast to* traditional (and material) elite women's dress, which would signal attachment to wealth. The materiality of ascetic women's dress (as in the case of Melania's rash) also signaled their inner virtue.

19. Gerontius, *Vita Sanctae Melaniae Iunioris* 49 (SC 90: 220–22; trans. E. A. Clark, 61).

20. Ibid., prol. (SC 90: 126–28; trans. E. A. Clark, 27).

21. Ibid. 15–19 (SC 90: 156–66; trans. E. A. Clark, 38–41).

22. Ibid. 59 (SC 90: 244–46; trans. E. A. Clark, 71).

23. Ibid. 56 (SC 90: 238–40; trans. E. A. Clark, 68–69).

24. Ibid. 62 (SC 90: 250–52; trans. E. A. Clark, 73–75).

25. Ibid. 50 (SC 90: 224; trans. E. A. Clark, 62).

26. Maud W. Gleason, *Making Men: Sophists and Self-Presentation in Ancient Rome* (Princeton: Princeton University Press, 1994), 159.

27. Gerontius, *Vita Sanctae Melaniae Iunioris* 68 (SC 90: 266; trans. E. A. Clark, 81).

28. On this phenomenon more generally in Roman society, see Catharine Edwards, *Death in Ancient Rome* (New Haven: Yale University Press, 2007).

29. Gerontius, *Vita Sanctae Melaniae Iunioris* 68 (SC 90: 264; trans. E. A. Clark, 80 [modified]).

30. Cobb, *Dying to Be Men,* 58.

31. Candida R. Moss, *Ancient Christian Martyrdom: Diverse Practices, Theologies, and Traditions* (New Haven: Yale University Press, 2012), 28.

32. Ibid., 30–32.

33. Gerontius, *Vita Sanctae Melaniae Iunioris* 64 (SC 90: 260; trans. E. A. Clark, 78).

34. Ibid. 64–66 (SC 90: 254–64; trans. E. A. Clark, 77–79).

35. Ibid. 68 (SC 90: 266–68; trans. E. A. Clark, 81).

36. Ibid. 63 (SC 90: 252–54; trans. E. A. Clark, 75).

37. Margaret R. Graver, *Stoicism and Emotion* (Chicago: University of Chicago Press, 2007), 51.

38. Ibid., 109–32.

39. Ibid., 4.

40. Martha Craven Nussbaum, *The Therapy of Desire: Theory and Practice in Hellenistic Ethics,* 2nd ed. (Princeton: Princeton University Press, 2009), 322–28, 334; Graver, *Stoicism and Emotion,* 164.

41. Martha Craven Nussbaum, "The Incomplete Feminism of Musonius Rufus: Platonist, Stoic, and Roman," in Martha Craven Nussbaum and Juha Sihvola, *The Sleep of Reason: Erotic Experience and Sexual Ethics in Ancient Greece and Rome* (Chicago: University of Chicago Press, 2002), 283–326; L. Hill, "The First Wave of Feminism: Were the Stoics Feminists?" *History of Political Thought* 22.1 (2001): 13–40.

42. Gretchen Reydams-Schils, *The Roman Stoics: Self, Responsibility, and Affection* (University of Chicago Press, 2005), 168.
43. Ibid.
44. Gleason, *Making Men*.
45. Graver, *Stoicism and Emotion*, 93; Reydams-Schils, *The Roman Stoics*, 25, 49–50.
46. Gerontius, *Vita Sanctae Melaniae Iunioris* 4 (SC 90: 134); trans. E. A. Clark, 29).
47. Ibid. 16 (SC 90: 158–60; trans. E. A. Clark, 39).
48. Graver, *Stoicism and Emotion*, 93.
49. Reydams-Schils, *The Roman Stoics*, 49–50, 141; Graver, *Stoicism and Emotion*, 52–53, 58.
50. Gerontius, *Vita Sanctae Melaniae Iunioris* 17 (SC 90: 160; trans. E. A. Clark, 40).
51. Ibid. 52 (SC 90: 226–28; trans. E. A. Clark, 63–64).
52. Ibid. 1 (SC 90: 130; trans. E. A. Clark, 28).
53. Reydams-Schils, *The Roman Stoics*, 168; Antigone Samellas, *Death in the Eastern Mediterranean (50–600 A.D.): The Christianization of the East—An Interpretation* (Tübingen: Mohr Siebeck, 2002), 75–76 note 13; for more on lament, see also Gail Holst-Warhaft, *Dangerous Voices: Women's Laments and Greek Literature* (New York: Routledge, 1992).
54. Graver, *Stoicism and Emotion*, 194.
55. Ibid., 194–96.
56. Ibid., 206–7.
57. Ibid., 78, 91–93, 101; Reydams-Schils, *The Roman Stoics*, 140–41.
58. Gerontius, *Vita Sanctae Melaniae Iunioris* 49 (SC 90: 220; trans. E. A. Clark, 61 [modified]).
59. Ibid. 49, 64, 65–66 (SC 90: 220, 254–56, 260–64; trans. E. A. Clark, 61, 76, 79–80).
60. φθονήσας γὰρ τῇ τοσαύτῃ κατὰ θεὸν πυρώσει τῶν νέων; Gerontius, *Vita Sanctae Melaniae Iunioris* 9–10 (SC 90: 142–46; trans. E. A. Clark, 32–33).
61. Ibid., prol. (τὸν ζῆλον), 2 (τῷ θείῳ πυρὶ κατεφλέγετο), 15 (προθύμως), 47 (πλέον πάντων σπουδάζειν), 48 (τὴν προθυμίαν) (SC 90: 126, 132, 158, 216, 218; trans. E. A. Clark, 26, 28, 38, 60). Clark translates forms of προθυμία as "zeal," an English phrasing I reserve for the Greek ζῆλος.
62. Ibid. 26, 43, 65 (SC 90: 180, 208, 260; trans. E. A. Clark, 46, 56, 78).
63. For another reference to *prothymia*, see ibid. 40, 48 (SC 90: 202, 218).
64. Nussbaum, *Therapy of Desire*, 91–98, 501; Graver, *Stoicism and Emotion*, 4, 8, 58. Nussbaum in particular traces the complexities of ancient emotional theories on love, friendship, and *eros*.
65. Ibid., 4–8; Martha Craven Nussbaum, *Upheavals of Thought: The Intelligence of Emotions* (Cambridge: Cambridge University Press, 2001), 3–4, 19–55.
66. Gerontius, *Vita Sanctae Melaniae Iunioris* 1, 16 (SC 90: 130–32, 158; trans. E. A. Clark, 28, 39).
67. *Life of Pelagia* 43, 47, in Sebastian P. Brock and Susan Ashbrook Harvey, *Holy Women of the Syrian Orient* (Berkeley and Los Angeles: University of California Press, 1998), 59, 61; *Life of Mary of Egypt* 12, in Benedicta Ward, *Harlots of the Desert: A Study of Repentance in Early Monastic Sources* (Kalamazoo: Cistercian Publications, 1987), 53.
68. Brock and Harvey, *Holy Women of the Syrian Orient*, 25; see Virginia Burrus's challenge to viewing the penitent harlots purely on this spectrum: Virginia Burrus, *The Sex Lives of Saints: An Erotics of Ancient Hagiography* (Philadelphia: University of Pennsylvania Press, 2004), 129–30.
69. Ibid., 131.
70. The definitive treatment is in Elizabeth A. Clark, "The Lady Vanishes: Dilemmas of a Feminist Historian after the 'Linguistic Turn,'" *Church History* 67.1 (1998): 1–31; see also Virginia Burrus, *"Begotten, Not Made": Conceiving Manhood in Late Antiquity* (Stanford: Stanford University Press, 2000), 113–23.
71. Ibid., 120.
72. Clark, "The Lady Vanishes," esp. 24.
73. Gregory of Nyssa, *Vita Sanctae Macrinae*, in *Gregorii Nysseni Opera Ascetica*, ed. Werner Wilhelm Jaeger, John Peter Cavarnos, and Virginia Woods Callahan (Leiden: Brill, 1952), 396; trans. W. K.

Lowther Clarke, *St. Gregory of Nyssa: The Life of St. Macrina* (London: Society for Promoting Christian Knowledge, 1916), 53–54.

74. Gregory of Nyssa, *Vita Sanctae Macrinae*, 380–81; trans. Clarke, *St. Gregory of Nyssa*, 32–33.

75. Ibid., 382; trans. Clarke, *St. Gregory of Nyssa*, 35.

76. On Angelina Jolie's transgressive gender identity, see Cristina Stasia, "Butch-Femme Interrupted," *Journal of Bisexuality* 3.3–4 (2003): 181–201; Laramie D. Taylor and Tiffany Setters, "Watching Aggressive, Attractive, Female Protagonists Shapes Gender Roles for Women among Male and Female Undergraduate Viewers," *Sex Roles* 65.1–2 (2011): 35–46.

77. Ibid., 35, 43.

78. Gerontius, *Vita Sanctae Melaniae Iunioris* 39 (SC 90: 200–202; trans. E. A. Clark, 53–54).

79. On combats and battles, see above, notes 16, 21, 23, 26–28, 50. On the gold: Gerontius, *Vita Sanctae Melaniae Iunioris* 38 (SC 90: 198; trans. E. A. Clark, 52–53).

80. Ibid. 56 (SC 90: 238–40; trans. E. A. Clark, 68–69).

81. Melissa A. Click, Hyunji Lee, and Holly Willson Holladay, "Making Monsters: Lady Gaga, Fan Identification, and Social Media," *Popular Music and Society* 36.3 (2013): 363.

82. Jackie Stacey, *Star Gazing: Hollywood Cinema and Female Spectatorship* (New York: Routledge, 1994), esp. chapter 5.

83. Click, Lee, and Holladay, "Making Monsters," 377.

84. See, for example, the discussion of "Chinese Cantopop Diva FayeWong," ibid., 364.

PART TWO

Body and Family

AS WE SAW IN THE previous section, Christians like the Melanias, who renounced physical comfort and voluntarily embraced a practice of extreme physical self-denial, could become wildly famous and sought-after figures in late antiquity. Yet this denial, and the popular descriptions of it, introduce a fundamental paradox: explaining what it meant to deny the importance of the body often also meant indulging in long, lingering descriptions of bodies that had undergone the rigors of denial. Descriptions of illness untreated, injuries left to fester, near-deaths ignored, desires cut off completely—all are staples of early Christian ascetic literature. Ascetic writing dwells on the frail, desiring body and its meanings at the same time as it attempts to see the human body as both the location of, and the opportunity for, spiritual transformation. The two essays in this section describe two ways in which early Christians thought about the bodies of the Melanias in deeply physical and deeply spiritual ways. First, they introduce us to some of the hard facts of physical life in the early Christian world, and they ask: What did it mean to practice "renunciation" of the body in a world in which mortality rates were, by our standards, incomprehensibly high? At a time when modern medicine simply did not exist? When pain and discomfort were constant facts of daily life for the entire population, not just for the poor or disenfranchised? Second, they consider how the Melanias, and people like them, tried to translate the hardships and dangers of physical life into valued spiritual realities. What might it mean, and how would it feel, to have "spiritual children" rather than physical ones? To pursue "spiritual health" rather than physical? These chapters examine how bodily frailty in the time of the Melanias could become a way to imagine spiritual power but could also be seen as a sign of interior spiritual weakness.

First, Maria Doerfler asks how the social role of the mother was reimagined in the ascetic context. Motherhood had long been among the essential roles for elite Roman women, and both Melania the Elder and Melania the Younger themselves felt the expectation that they would experience childbirth and motherhood. Their interactions with other women are repeatedly described by their biographers as contributions to households and families, although the definitions of household and family in these Melanian texts are complex. Asceticism's call to renunciation threatened to undermine or devalue the function of maternity, or at least its natural, biological manifestation. Doerfler argues that, by describing female ascetics' relationships, particularly with other women, in terms of spiritual motherhood, and the creation of spiritual households, late ancient writers attempted to salvage a well-established cultural ideal, the ideal of the Roman mother, for new paths of Christian thought.

Next, Kristi Upson-Saia examines how the idea of wounds and wounding, and the roles of physician and patient, shaped early Christian relationships. In a social context in which illness and injuries were the norm, and in which medical interventions were prized, wounding and healing provided an effective set of symbols for articulating the spiritual injuries of sin and heresy, as well as the spiritual remedies of contrition, repentance, and church discipline. The concepts of sin and heresy were structured on the qualities of the wound—painful, ugly, smelly; disordering mind and body; threatening to spread; and leading to mortification and death. These qualities were recalled in order to generate a similar abhorrence for behaviors and ideas proscribed by the church. Further, Christians were exhorted to endure painful healing processes (framed as similar to the painful medical treatments of wounds) in order to restore the individual, as well as the fractured community, to full health and unity. The idea of the ascetic figure, like Melania, as "wounded by divine love" provides a double-edged metaphor for describing both the literal, physical hardships of the renunciant, and the spiritual injuries that she must overcome to be fully transformed.

These chapters bring to light how fundamental physical differences between the late ancient world and our own could structure the pursuit of an ascetic lifestyle that often seems strange and outlandish to modern eyes. The Melanias were extraordinary figures, but they were figures whose spiritual heroism was understood in terms of an ancient way of life that is hard for us to grasp completely. Modern understandings of pain, parenthood, illness, death, and grief do not translate easily into the lives of ancient Christians. Instead, to understand how early Christians understood their bodies, and how their bodies could become holy, we must expand our view to include the very different medical, biological, and familial expectations that formed the backdrop of the early Christian world.

4

Holy Households

Maria Doerfler

MELANIA AND THE LIBERATED WOMAN

The *Vita Melaniae Iunioris*, in the course of narrating a number of its protagonist's choice miracles, recounts Melania's healing of a woman literally caught in childbirth. In the process of a difficult labor, the infant had died in the mother's womb. Rather than relinquishing the dead child, however, the woman's body clung to the fetus, leaving the woman, in the words of the Greek *vita*, "neither able to live or die."[1] Once the news of the woman's plight reaches Melania, the saint is moved by sympathy and an apparent desire to seize a teachable moment. Upon leading her company of virgins to the woman's sickbed, Melania prays over her and places her belt upon the woman's stomach. The garment, a gift from a holy man and infused with his prayers, as Melania piously reminds her audience, works its wonders: at long last, the dead fetus is expelled, the woman liberated, and the attending crowds amazed.

The miraculous delivery, while evidently among the tokens of Melania's saintliness in the eyes of the *vita*'s author and translator, nevertheless strikes modern readers as oddly incomplete. Melania's intervention saves the life of the pregnant woman, yet there is no concomitant healing for the child in her womb. The *vita* does not depict Melania as offering prayers on the infant's behalf, and after the body's expulsion, the child's death is passed over amid the crowd's rejoicing over the mother's being freed of its body. Neither does Gerontius offer any apologies for the child's fate; for the *vita*'s original audience, the stillbirth evidently signaled neither a limitation of divine power nor callousness on Melania's part, as it may for contemporary readers. By its very incongruity—the disconnect between ancient and modern expectations of what may constitute a proper miracle in this context—the incident allows readers a glimpse into late ancient thought about children, their lives and deaths, and perhaps even their place in the lives of "holy women" like the Melanias and their famous ascetic contemporaries.

On the one hand, the story thus attests to the harsh realities of late ancient Roman life expectancies. Although exact data are for obvious reasons inaccessible, conservative estimates suggest infant- and childhood-mortality rates of roughly one-third of all births, with many of the deaths occurring at birth or during the child's first few days of life.[2] Not only were these first moments of life precarious for the infants in question, mothers' lives, too, were in acute danger. Gregory of Nyssa memorably describes the approaching birth as follows: "Assume the moment of childbirth is at hand; it is not the birth of the child but the presence of death that is thought of, and the death of the mother anticipated. Often, the sad prophecy is fulfilled and before the birth is celebrated, before any of the anticipated goods are tasted, joy is exchanged for lamentation."[3] Gregory writes with both literary flair and ascetic bias—the aim of his treatise is, after all, to convince virgins that the way of life they have chosen for themselves is infinitely preferable to a life burdened by the cares of marriage and motherhood. Yet late ancient medical sources paint a similar picture. The majority of the fourth book of Soranus's *Gynaecology* is thus dedicated to difficulties in childbirth, including scenarios in which the fetus's extraction required the use of hooks or embryotomy.[4] Little wonder, then, that the Greek *Vita Melaniae*, likely the earliest version of the text, does not elaborate on the cause of the woman's predicament: death in childbirth was common for both mothers and infants, and required no special explanation, even if such deaths were no less grievous for that reason.[5]

The *vita*'s account of the nearly fatal pregnancy and its miraculous resolution nevertheless also suggests itself as a metaphor for the fraught experience of motherhood among late ancient ascetics. For Melania's patient, the struggle to rid herself of the child in her womb threatens her own life. Able to "neither live nor die" as long as the fetus remains within her, it is only through the intervention of the saints that the woman is able to relinquish the infant and draw back from the brink of death herself. Many women in late antiquity might face and perhaps survive such struggles on the physical plane. Ascetic writings suggest, however, that female renunciants confronted a similar battle between attachment to offspring and family, and the fullness of life in Christ on the spiritual level as well. Dedication to ascetic practice, including the sexual renunciation that it entailed, was thus one of the few ways by which late ancient women could escape the challenges of marriage and motherhood, and expand the palette of roles available to them in society.[6] Yet for women of Melania's class, renunciation frequently entailed compromises. As the *vita* acknowledges, Melania herself had given birth to two children prior to being able to persuade her husband to abandon marital relations in favor of a spiritual, that is to say: sexless, union.

Melania's example is both common and instructive: even situations in which the would-be ascetic's spouse was sympathetic to her project,[7] a token effort at procreation was frequently required. By comparison to her peers, moreover, Melania entered the longed-for monastic life quite early. Her saintly grandmother, the elder Melania, had given birth to three children before the death of her husband and two of her offspring created the opportunity for her to set sail for the Holy Land. Similarly, Paula, the elder Melania's rough contemporary and, like her, a convert to Christian asceticism, withdrew from Rome after her husband's death. Relinquishing hopes of remarriage, she left behind her own, still-young—and, if Jerome's account is to be trusted, pitifully weeping—children in the process.

In choosing asceticism, these women, late ancient sources claimed, had bravely and happily chosen against their offspring and families. Such antifamilial decisions, however, did not necessarily change the rhetorical characterization of ascetic women in Christian sources. Instead, female renunciation resulted in the rescripting of one of the most central aspects of Roman women's existence: motherhood. The loss, avoidance, or abandonment of biological offspring for these women needed not entail the rejection of the motherly role, late ancient writers argued. Instead, it was precisely such ascetics who could be better and truer mothers to large numbers of spiritual children than their more conventionally maternal counterparts. At times, this new construction of motherhood even allowed for a readoption of an ascetic's biological offspring—if, and only if, they were prepared to follow her along the path to renunciation. The following chapter explores the different configurations of motherhood—biological, spiritual, and, above all, rhetorically scripted—in the lives of the Melanias and their late ancient peers.

PHYSICAL MOTHERS AND BIOLOGICAL CHILDREN

Asceticism, late ancient Christians knew, might be a prescription against the death of the soul but did not ward against bodily death—indeed, at times severe renunciation even hastened death's arrival. Such had been the case for Blesilla, a young Roman widow who under Jerome's tutelage had embraced a harsh ascetic regime. The latter had, so her outraged contemporaries argued, claimed her life before she had reached the age of twenty. Blesilla's death was a public-relations disaster from the perspective of ascetic writers.[8] Jerome himself was forced to leave Rome in the its aftermath and took to exhorting from afar Blesilla's mother, Paula, to temper her mourning, lest public displays of her grief call Christianity, and particularly its more ascetic manifestations, further into question. To this end, Jerome conjured up for Paula's benefit the stolid bravery of various biblical mothers, before concluding with an example closer to Paula's own experience:[9]

Why repeat old tales? Follow a contemporary model. The holy Melania, who is among Christians of our era of true nobility (May the Lord grant that you and I may partake with her in His day!), while her husband's body was still warm and yet unburied, lost two of her sons at the same time. What I tell you is incredible, but, as Christ is my witness, not untrue. Who would not have believed her then to appear in a frenzy, with disheveled hair, torn clothes, a pierced breast? She shed not a single teardrop! She stood motionless, and casting herself at Christ's feet, she smiled, as if she were holding him. "I am prepared," she said, "to serve you, Lord, for you have freed me from such a burden."

In later years, Jerome would grow to hate and malign the subject of his present exhortation: Melania the Elder, the namesake of her wonder-working granddaughter, and chief supporter of Jerome's former friend Rufinus. In the 380s C.E., however, Jerome could deploy her supposedly Stoic response in the face of overwhelming grief to illumine the posture appropriate to a Christian woman. The dead, after all, could be safely assumed to have entered a blissful afterlife, especially when the deceased was a young child or a practicing ascetic. By contrast, for the bereaved, God had created by their death an opportunity for a new, better life of superior spirituality. Released from her roles as wife to an ordinary (if highborn) man and mother to biological children, such a one could now embrace an existence as Christ's beloved and spiritual parent to many.

While Jerome's depiction of the elder Melania bears traces of his characteristic shrillness, other contemporaneous accounts nevertheless echo the underlying story. Both the *Lausiac History* and Paulinus of Nola's epistolary biography of her offer similar accounts of a saintly woman empowered to embrace a life of renunciation, following in Jesus' and Mary's footsteps, in the aftermath of her loved ones' deaths.[10] Neither text goes so far as Jerome in naming God as Melania's liberator; all alike, however, emphasize the redemptive quality of Melania's ascetic existence, a fate far superior to that of an ordinary wife and mother. "Through the loss of her human love," Paulinus argues, "[the elder Melania] conceived a love for God. She was made wretched to become blessed; she was afflicted to be healed."[11]

Nor was the elder Melania the only female ascetic whose biographers construed the death of a child as a show of divine favor. The *vita* of her granddaughter, the younger Melania, depicts a similar show of "grace from on high" in the form of a divinely severed bond between mother and biological offspring.[12] Just before giving birth to her second child, Melania thus tearfully "prayed to God that she might be freed from the world and spend the rest of her days in the solitary life, for this is what she had yearned for from the beginning."[13] Her prayers are answered promptly: upon returning from church, Melania goes into premature labor, giving birth to a child who lives just long enough to receive baptism. The infant's death prompts her husband's assent to live together in chastity thenceforth, the *vita* claims, with the death of their older child soon thereafter further uniting the couple in their decision to embrace asceticism.

These stories tell readers little about how late ancient women with ascetic aspirations actually felt about the deaths of their children. They do, however, provide a glimpse at the rhetorical culture that had sprung up around the ubiquitous tragedies of infant mortality and parental bereavement. Such accounts may have been read through the lens of ascetic excess or divine chastisement—and were no doubt read in this way by many contemporaries. By crafting rival narratives of liberation and empowerment, Gerontius, Jerome, and other champions of late ancient renunciation not only offered an apologia for ascetic practice but created role models for other elite women sympathetic to spiritual pursuits and afflicted by personal grief.

Jerome's exhortation to Paula to temper her mourning for her daughter thus evidently proved persuasive. Soon after Blesilla's death, Paula removed herself to Jerusalem, where she founded and oversaw a monastery for women alongside Jerome's. In the process, she left behind in Rome not only her deceased daughter but also several other children. To them, in Jerome's words, "she did not know herself to be a mother, that she might prove herself to be a handmaid of Christ."[14] Not all occasions of Roman women's relinquishing a child in favor of an ascetic vocation thus required the promptings of death and tragedy. Stories of youngsters thrust from their mothers' breasts and left weeping at the harbor may strike contemporary readers as the height of maternal irresponsibility; by late ancient standards, however, ascetic heroines of Paula's caliber acquitted themselves of their responsibilities in entirely socially appropriate ways, appointing guardians and providing financial support for children who had not yet reached the age of majority.

Paulinus of Nola, for example, likens the elder Melania, who similarly left behind her remaining child to pursue an ascetic vocation, to both the prophet Samuel and Samuel's mother, Anna (1 Samuel 1). By dedicating herself to divine service, Paulinus claims, Melania in her own person fulfilled the vow that Anna made on Samuel's behalf. Her "sacrifice" of her sole surviving son nevertheless qualifies her for Anna's position: while the young man, as Paulinus writes, "enjoys the riches and distinctions of the world," "once Melania had torn her one son from her breast and set him in Christ's bosom so that the Lord might nourish him, she bestowed no subsequent personal care on him, for she thought it a sin of distrust to give her own attention to one whom she had entrusted to Christ."[15] Melania's sacrifice lies in her trustful abandonment of her son to divine care. In Paulinus's words, "she loved the child by neglecting him and kept him by relinquishing him."[16]

Consistent throughout these narratives is the theme of the necessary separation between mothers and their biological children to facilitate full ascetic engagement. An ascetic woman might be "relieved" of her child by divine fiat or by her own strength of faith and character. To enter the life of renunciation, these narratives suggest, nevertheless required the severing of familial ties; only by removing themselves from the households that had determined their social loci thus far could a renunciant enter the household of God—or so late ancient Christian writers claimed.[17] Yet even though consecrated virgins, holy widows, and chaste wives had to relinquish both their connection with existing offspring and their hopes for additional births, their status as mothers nevertheless remained intact—indeed, it could even greatly expand by virtue of their adoption of spiritual children.

SPIRITUAL MOTHERS AND SPIRITUAL CHILDREN

Melania the Younger's visit to Constantinople, by all accounts, could be considered a family reunion. Not only was the saint able to convert her ailing uncle, Volusianus, to the Christian faith; she also persuaded Theodosius II to permit his wife, the empress Eudocia, to travel to Jerusalem and worship at the "Holy Places." There, Melania arranged to meet Eudocia at Sidon, where the latter "fittingly received her with every honor, as Melania was a true spiritual mother [to her]."[18] When exhorted to continue in her good works, the empress informed Melania that she was fulfilling a "double vow to the Lord, to worship at the Holy Places and to see my mother, for I have wished to be worthy of Your Holiness while you still serve the Lord in the flesh."[19] Indeed, Gerontius depicts the filial tie between Melania and Eudocia as sufficiently firm that even the ascetic's other daughters become Eudocia's kin: the empress is thus said to regard the virgins of Melania's monastery "as if they were her own sisters."[20]

Spiritual motherhood to the Roman emperor's wife may seem like a tall order even for a highborn renunciant. Yet this was a role for which the younger Melania had arguably prepared her whole life. Upon the death of her own mother, Albina, Melania had gathered around herself virgins whose every need she promised to supply, just as long as the women agreed to keep away from men. Out of humility, Gerontius reports, Melania did not choose for herself the title of mother superior of the group, instead appointing another woman to this office. Her tireless activity behind the scenes, including extensive instruction and setting the liturgical schedule for the group, nevertheless must have placed Melania very firmly at the head of this *monasterium*.[21] Indeed, spiritual motherhood was a trope commonly invoked for female heads of monasteries. Both Jerome and Augustine designate the supervisors of monastic houses the mother (*mater*) of the virgins dwelling there.[22] At times such mother-daughter relationships between a monastic leader and her retinue were more than merely metaphorical. Gregory of Nyssa's account of his sister Macrina's death thus describes the women who had lived under her care as mourning her as their mother and nurse. These, Gregory writes, "were those whom she had taken up when they had been thrown along the roads in time of famine and tended and fostered and led by the hand to the holy and spotless life."[23] Somewhat ironically, then, Macrina's *monasterium* was populated in part by virgins whom she had rescued as infants from abandonment by their biological families.

By the same token, relations of spiritual mentorship, particularly in cases in which all parties involved were women, could be couched in maternal terms as well. Marcella, a member of the *gens Caeonia* and as such one of the wealthiest women in the Roman Empire, evidently sought to cultivate such relationships with like-minded women in her circle. Unlike Paula or the Melanias, Marcella remained in Rome after embarking upon the ascetic life as a young widow, wherein she cultivated the kind of household monasticism that straddled the spheres of elite Roman society and refined Christian asceticism. Marcella's failure to succumb to the allure of the desert as some of her contemporaries had done evidently frustrated Jerome. Writing ostensibly on behalf of Paula and her daughter Eustochium, both of whom he had first encountered as part of Marcella's circle, he exhorted Marcella to join their party: "You were the first to spark our tinder, the first to urge us to this [way of life], by teaching and example; like a hen you gathered us, your chicks, under your wing. And will you now permit us to fly with no mother near us?"[24] Marcella proved unresponsive to such pleas; even in Rome, however, she continued to cultivate a circle of spiritual daughters, that included, *inter alias*, Principia, another of Jerome's correspondents, who, he readily conceded, "had found a mother in [Marcella] and she a daughter in you."[25]

Discourses concerning spiritual mentorship as motherhood thrived on late ancient rhetoric about the role of the mother in the Christian household. In theory and in Roman law, even in late antiquity fathers continued to reign supreme over their households. In practice, however, both parents were owed *pietas*—filial devotion—in equal measure,[26] and mothers were expected to take an active—even *the* active—role in children's upbringing and education. The latter was certainly the case until at least the age of seven for the children of elite families, after which time male children were frequently educated outside the home, whereas girls remained under the auspices of their mothers until they married, typically less than a decade later.

One of the most fulsome exemplars of instructions on the topic of childrearing comes, somewhat ironically, from Jerome, champion extraordinaire of sexual renunciation, in his letter to Laeta, Paula's married daughter, concerning the upbringing and education of her child, a girl named after her saintly grandmother. The "little Paula" had been dedicated to the monastic life from an early age—no doubt the primary reason Jerome took an interest in her development.[27] In *Epistle* 107, he recommends a challenging educational program for the girl, alongside detailed instructions about the comportment that could be expected from a budding ascetic. Both parents had responsibilities vis-à-vis their offspring—Jerome notes, for example, that neither mother nor father was to teach her by example those kinds of behavior that they would not have her emulate. Laeta's role, however, predominates throughout the letter, both in her ability to control access to her daughter, for example by facilitating her instruction by experienced teachers or removing her from the temptations of the familial table, and in her role as the younger Paula's chief instructor in spiritual matters.[28]

The program here set out by Jerome or, in even greater depth, by John Chrysostom for male children with no particular ascetic vocation among his community, combines classical and Christian sensibilities about education and parents' role therein. Parents and, in the case of daughters, particularly mothers molded the soft wax of a child's character lest it take on shameful or destructive form. For ascetics, however, the process of spiritual formation was not limited to childhood or youth. Virgins, widows, and their fellow renunciants required the sustained attentions of a household dedicated to their virtue and education. Women's monasteries provided such a setting, as did the kind of fellowships that ascetics from the elite strata of Roman society on occasion gathered around themselves. While abbots and bishops readily assumed the role of paterfamilias vis-à-vis their male charges, in women's communities spiritual mothers reigned at least qualifiedly supreme.[29] In these settings, at times even biological children could be reunited with their birth mothers—the filial bond between them now renewed and strengthened by their shared ascetic devotion.

SPIRITUAL MOTHERS AND BIOLOGICAL CHILDREN

Part of Jerome's instructions for the younger Paula's upbringing concerns the girl's relations with those among her family who had gone before her in choosing the ascetic life: "Let her learn at once also of her other grandmother and her aunt"—Jerome's companion Paula and her virginal daughter Eustochium—"and for what emperor, for what army she is being raised as a soldier."[30] Pledged from birth to a life of asceticism, little Paula was to know herself the product of a doubly noble lineage, a member of the elite by the standards of both Roman society and Christian monastic practice. If Laeta did not feel equal to implementing the demanding program that he had set out for her daughter amid the busy life of Roman high society, Jerome suggests, she ought to dispatch the girl to Jerusalem's monasteries, where her own relatives would rear her more ably than her own mother:[31]

> Hand the little one, whose every cry is a prayer to you, over to Eustochium. Hand her a companion in holiness, a future heir. . . . Let her sit in her grandmother's lap, and let her repeat to her granddaughter what she once before imparted to the daughter. She, who has been taught by long practice how to care for, preserve, and instruct virgins; in whose crown is daily woven the hundredfold reward of chastity.

Though Jerome no doubt would have rejoiced over any highborn girl dedicated to a life of permanent virginity, the kinship that tied the younger Paula to his great ascetic friends both sweetened the deal and heightened the stakes. As Rebecca Krawiec has noted, late ancient asceticism was seldom entirely antifamilial, and the evidently tension-riddled discourse surrounding monastic and biological family ties rarely went so far as to affirm one to the exclusion of the other.[32] That even Jerome, perhaps the most uncompromising champion of sexual renunciation, should demonstrate an investment in ascetic genealogies forged not merely by shared faith and practice but by blood relation is therefore not surprising. Virgins in theory left their native households to join the larger family of God—allowing Jerome on another occasion to tactlessly promise to the mother of one such virgin status as mother-in-law to the divine. Yet where renunciants' familial pedigree gave cause for celebration, ascetic authors did not hesitate to dwell upon it.[33]

As a married woman, Laeta, as Jerome acknowledged, was not at liberty to leave her husband and her social obligations in pursuit of a life amid the physical remnants of Jesus's ministry in the company of her saintly relatives. By contrast, Laeta's daughter, the young Paula, could do so, and in the process could join an alternative but even nobler genealogy. Jerome sketches an ascetic family tree that excludes precisely those members of Paula's family—her son, Toxotius, and his wife, Laeta—who by Roman (and, no doubt, many Christians') standards conducted their lives in appropriate dedication to the familial ideal. By contrast, renunciants, virgins, monks, and widows, who by most standards represented procreative dead ends for their families, in these genealogies become the vital, fruit-bearing branches.

Late ancient sources attribute a similar (and arguably still more successful) attempt at reclaiming her biological family as her spiritual kin to Melania the Elder. Paulinus of Nola, writing to Sulpicius Severus, describes with no little irony the elder Melania's arrival in Italy. Sixty years old, worn out by the demands of the ascetic life and extravagant in her humility, she is met by her children and grandchildren.[34] The latter are dressed in silk, traveling in grand style, but sufficiently cowed by the long-absent matriarch's example to assent to accommodation in Paulinus's "hut" (*tugurium*), his humble *monasterium*.[35] By the time of her departure, the *Lausiac History* claims, both her daughter-in-law, Albina, and the younger Melania and Pinianus had come to embrace lives of asceticism, with the elder Melania "[leading] them out of Rome and [bringing] them into the holy and calm harbor of the [religious] life."[36] In this fashion, the younger Melania demonstrates the true family resemblance between herself and her grandmother: Palladius depicts her as pleading with her husband to "set my body free, that I may fulfill my desire toward God and become heir of the zeal of my grandmother, whose name I also bear."[37]

Yet the prayers and attentions of even the saintliest of women could not win all her children for the ascetic life and in the process repopulate her ascetic family tree with members of their native household. When Jerome thus at long last crafted an epitaph for Paula, he named her ancestors in considerable detail but deprived his departed friend of all but one of her children. Forgotten were Toxotius, father of Paula's namesake, Paulina, Rufina, and even the long-dead Blesilla. In death as in life, Paula's only companion—and only true daughter—would be the virginal Eustochium, who had followed her mother to Bethlehem.[38]

CONCLUSION: MOTHERS BETWEEN TEXTS AND HOUSEHOLDS

Late antiquity provided few roles for even the highest-born of women and, similarly, few scripts by which to make sense of their existence and place in society. Christianity, particularly its most ascetic variants, held the potential to enhance such women's autonomy and to move them from the periphery of their own lives' stories closer to the center. These opportunities, however, came at considerable cost, not only in terms of material resources and physical pleasure but also by threatening to deprive female renunciants of some of the trenchant roles that they had played or could have been expected to play within their own households: those of wife and mother. Christian writers accordingly labored to rescript women's experiences of renunciation. A consecrated virgin might never marry a human husband but could know herself to be betrothed to Christ; similarly, a widow might never bear a child (or another child), but she could aspire to become spiritual mother to many.[39]

The *Vita Melaniae* reflects these concerns in crafting a new kind of maternal existence in the text's depiction of its protagonist. Throughout the narrative, Melania is portrayed as profoundly maternal. She shows, for example, a curious preoccupation with feeding and nurturing others, particularly the women under her care. As the de facto—if, out of humility, not de iure—head of a monastery, Melania thus provides for the physical as well as the spiritual needs of her virgin companions, sneaking additional food into the rooms of those women least able to withstand the rigors of ascetic fasting.[40] Her miracles, too, display her as a prototypically motherly and mothering figure. Melania thus heals two women whose lips have been sealed by demons, miraculously imparting food to them.[41] Similarly, the woman caught in childbirth with whom we began this essay is not released from Melania's care until the saint has fed her, nursing the woman back to health. Here Melania's actions both perfect the healing and bring into focus the contrast between the two kinds of motherhood involved: the one corporeal, painful, ultimately producing nothing but death; the other spiritual, joyful, and genuinely life-giving. By renouncing the former, the *vita* suggests, Melania has been set free to assume the latter role, in the process serving, nourishing, and reviving many.

Most Roman women no doubt never faced a choice between these different constructions of motherhood. Even among elite Christians of an ascetic bent—a small sample indeed—many saw no necessary contradiction between the life of the Roman household and the practice of the faith.[42] The latter could even be employed in the service of the former: as Ville Vuolante has argued, for example, dedicating a child to the ascetic life could be an investment in estate planning for parents.[43] Still less can we assume that ascetics who *did* renounce traditional roles and their positions within elite households understood themselves to be reassuming these roles in a spiritualized guise. Narratives involving holy women casting away offspring and hopes of offspring in favor of spiritual lives and spiritual children are nevertheless sufficiently pervasive in late ancient literature to suggest that they had captured the attention of their contemporaries—even if the only group whose fascination with the trope is clearly apparent are those male ascetics who composed, translated, and copied these texts.

These writers, as a rule, were preoccupied less with ordinary households, women, and mothers than with their expediency as metaphors and their usefulness in theological debates. The prototypical mother for late ancient writers was thus either the church, whose spiritual nature could be deployed to good effect against the fleshliness of the synagogue,[44] or the Blessed Virgin Mary, the celebrated glory of mothers, whose virginity remained uncompromised even after Jesus's birth. Both entailed potential for empowering ascetics intent on transgressing the strictures of family life in the Roman Empire while simultaneously limiting the scope of such transgressions. Late ancient women, including those who, like the Melanias, became the subjects of literary attention, had to negotiate their existence between experience and metaphor, their roles both defined and circumscribed within a male framework of textuality.[45]

NOTES

1. Gerontius, *Vita Melaniae Iunioris* 61. Unless otherwise indicated, all translations are taken from Elizabeth A. Clark, *The Life of Melania the Younger: Introduction, Translation, and Commentary* (Lewiston, N.Y.: Edwin Mellen Press, 1984), here at 73. The Latin version of the *vita* is even more explicit concerning the woman's long-suffering: for three days already had she been near death, and that despite the best efforts of the obstetricians to free her from the child (Mariano Rampolla del Tindaro, *Santa Melania giuniore, senatrice romana: Documenti contemporanei e note* [Rome: Tipografia Vaticana, 1905], 34–35).

2. For a discussion of infant mortality rates in late antiquity and their impact upon popular life expectancy, see, e.g., Thomas Wiedemann, *Adults and Children in the Roman Empire* (New Haven: Yale University Press, 1989), 12; Tim G. Parkin, *Demography and Roman Society* (Baltimore: The Johns Hopkins University Press, 1992), 93; Geoffrey S. Nathan, *The Family in Late Antiquity: The Rise of Christianity and the Endurance of Tradition* (New York: Routledge, 2000), 139–40.

3. *De Virginitate* γ, in Werner Wilhelm Jaeger, John Peter Cavarnos, and Virginia Woods Callahan, eds., *Gregorii Nysseni Opera Ascetica*, (Leiden: Brill 1952), 261; trans. in *On Virginity*, in *St. Gregory: Ascetical Works*, trans. Virginia Wood Callahan (Washington, D.C.: Catholic University of America Press), 15–16.

4. Soranus, *Gynaecology* 4.3(19).9(61)–13(65), in *Soranus' Gynecology*, trans. Owsei Temkin (Baltimore: The Johns Hopkins University Press, 1991), 189–96. In Keith Bradley's assessment, ancient writings about the treatment of childhood ailments showed "evidence here of an intellectual effort to understand a medical condition, . . . but there is also evidence of the massive ignorance that characterized all

medical science before the modern era" ("The Roman Child in Sickness and Health," in *The Roman Family in the Empire: Rome, Italy, and Beyond*, ed. Michele George [Oxford: Oxford University Press, 2005], 70).

5. The Latin, by contrast, attributes the difficult birth to demonic influence: "Nec non et quemdam virum a daemone horribiliter correptum sanavit" (Rampalla, *Santa Melania*, 34). This characterization is in keeping with the Latin *vita*'s theological aims in this passage. For a discussion in greater depth, see E. A. Clark, *Life of Melania*, 147–48. Given the pervasiveness of threat to the life of mother and infant, late ancient parents and would-be parents frequently turned to spiritual remedies alongside more mundane medical means. The use of amulets—both Christian and not—designed to protect children is well documented in late antiquity, and children's health was evidently a prominent subject for prayer among parents of all religious affiliations. Marcus Aurelius, himself well acquainted with the grief of a child's death, acknowledges this practice in his *Meditations:* "Another prays: 'How I may not lose my little child', but you must pray: 'How I may not be afraid to lose him'" (*Meditations* 9.40.1; in Jan Hendrik Leopold, ed., *M. Antonius Imperator ad Se Ipsum* [Leipzig: Teubner, 1908], 120. No doubt only the most philosophically inclined joined him in such prayers. While the historical basis for much of the *Vita Melaniae Iunioris* is not free from suspicion, there is nevertheless nothing inherently improbable about a well-known local noblewoman, perhaps known to be sympathetic to "women's issues" and no doubt with a particular reputation for saintliness, being consulted to intervene in the case of a pregnancy that had proved beyond the midwives' and obstetricians' efforts.

6. Cf., e.g., Elizabeth A. Clark, "Ascetic Renunciation and Feminine Advancement: A Paradox of Late Ancient Christianity," *Anglican Theological Review* 63 (1981): 240–57.

7. Hagiographic literature surrounding women's renunciation frequently depicts such a move toward celibacy and chastity or, in the case of a virginal daughter's rejection of marriage, as originating from the woman herself rather than from a spouse or parent. Such womanly initiative does not necessarily reflect the historical record, however; rather, the valorization of women, even very young women, as initiators of the ascetic lifestyle was a rhetorical trope useful for shaming men or enhancing the female ascetic's standing. For a discussion of this trope with regard to elite women, see Michele Renee Salzman, "Aristocratic Women: Conductors of Christianity in the Fourth Century," *Helios* 16 (1989), 207–20; for the exploration of a similar theme with regard to intrafamilial conflict surrounding children's renunciation, see Ville Vuolanto, "Choosing Asceticism: Children and Parents, Vows and Conflicts," in *Children in Late Ancient Christianity*, ed. Cornelia B. Horn and Robert R. Phenix, Jr. (Tübingen: Mohr Siebeck, 2009), 255–91.

8. Jerome himself writes to both Paula (*Ep.* 39) and Marcella (*Ep.* 38) about his part in Blesilla's renunciation and death, his strongly avowed innocence for the latter, and the persecution he nevertheless experienced at the hands of the "mob" in conjunction with it. Cf. also Andrew Cain, *The Letters of Jerome: Asceticism, Biblical Exegesis, and the Construction of Authority in Late Antiquity* (Oxford: Oxford University Press, 2009), 102–5.

9. *Ep.* 39.5 (CSEL 54: 305). Jerome's depiction here echoes descriptions of other famously heroic mothers from both the Roman and the Jewish traditions. Plutarch, for example, depicts Cornelia, the mother of the Gracchi, as speaking of her untimely deceased sons "without grief or tears" (ἀπενθὴς καὶ ἀδάκρυτος; Plutarch, *Lives: Tiberius Gracchus* 40.1.2, in Konrat Ziegler, ed., *Plutarchos: Tiberius und Gaius Gracchus* [Heidelberg: Winter, 1911], 51. Similarly, 4 Maccabees 14 and 15 depict the mother of the Maccabean martyrs as displaying calmness and fortitude even in the face of extreme grief, emboldened by "devout reason" (15.23).

10. The *Lausiac History* is the briefest of the three, noting merely that in the aftermath of Melania's husband's death, she journeyed to the Holy Land on a ship that carried other highborn women and children also (Palladius, *Lausiac History* 46.1;Cuthbert Butler, ed., *The Lausiac History of Palladius Together with Notes on Early Egyptian Monachism*, vol. 2 [Cambridge: Cambridge University Press, 1904], 134). Paulinus of Nola's letter, the earliest of the three texts, goes into still greater depth and once

again increases Melania's woes as well as her emotional response thereto: at the time of the death of Melania's husband and sons, she had already suffered two prior miscarriages, leaving her one remaining child a mere bitter reminder to the grieving widow of the others that had gone before him (*Ep.* 29.8 [CSEL 29: 252–54]).

11. Ibid. (CSEL 29: 254). All translations, unless otherwise indicated, are from *The Letters of St. Paulinus of Nola*, vol. 2, *Letters 23–51*, trans. and annot. P. G. Walsh (Westminster, Md.: The Newman Press, 1967), 109. Paulinus's depiction of Melania similarly echoes contemporary expositions of the mother of the Maccabean martyrs. Augustine, for example, in a sermon on the Maccabean martyrs' feast day places the following reassurance in the character's mouth: "If you seem to desert me, then you are not deserting me. There I will have you, where I will not be afraid of ever losing you again" (*Sermo* 300.7 [ed. *PL* 38: 1380]).

12. Gerontius, *Vita Melaniae Iunioris* 6 (SC 90: 136–38; trans. E. A. Clark, 30).

13. Ibid. 5 (SC 90: 134–36; trans. E. A. Clark, 29).

14. *Ep.* 108.6 (CSEL 55: 33).

15. *Ep.* 29.9 (CSEL 29: 256; trans. Walsh, 110–11).

16. Ibid. Such a logic of "parental exchange" is already at work in late ancient martyr narratives and may have even originated there. As Susan Holman has recently noted ("Martyr-Saints and the Demon of Infant Mortality: Folk Healing in Early Christian Pediatric Medicine," in *Children and Family in Late Antiquity: Life, Death and Interaction*, ed. Christian Laes, Katariina Mustakallio, and Ville Vuolanto [Louvain: Peeters, 2015], 235–56), in the third-century *Martyrdom of Perpetua and Felicitas*, Perpetua's martyrdom purchases not only her own salvation but the health and well-being of three children. Her already deceased younger brother, and her son and daughter, both at vulnerable ages and, in the case of the former, still dependent upon her ability to nurse him, are thus restored—to physical survival, in the case of the children, and to spiritual health, in the case of the dead.

The elder Melania, of course, does not face physical martyrdom. Paulinus, however, strongly suggests that the sacrifice of her child and her maternal relationship with him constitutes a spiritual martyrdom—a neglectful love, by which Melania purchased, among other things, her son's spiritual and physical well-being. We are, of course, unable to discern whether Melania herself interpreted her relinquishment in these terms. Cornelia B. Horn has suggested nevertheless that martyr narratives involving children (and, presumably, other figures) were consciously crafted and deployed to allow ascetics of later centuries to interpret their own actions in light of their heroic predecessors' stories ("Raising Martyrs and Ascetics: A Diachronic Comparison of Educational Role-Models for Early Christian Children," in *Children in Late Ancient Christianity*, 293–316).

17. Such rhetoric of separation contrasts sharply with evidence for the existence of domestic monastic arrangements from this era, in which widows and virgins gathered around themselves like-minded relatives and friends. For a more in-depth discussion of the tensions between rhetorical construction and the historical record, see below, pp. 80–81.

18. Gerontius, *Vita Melaniae Iunioris* 58 (SC 90: 242; trans. E. A. Clark, 70).

19. Ibid. 58 (SC 90: 242–44; trans. E. A. Clark, 70–71).

20. Ibid. (SC 90: 244; trans. E. A. Clark, 71).

21. For a further discussion of Melania's depiction as mother in the *Vita Melaniae Iunioris*, see below, p. 80.

22. Cf. Jerome, *Ep.* 108.19 (CSEL 55: 332–34).

23. Gregory of Nyssa, *Vita Macrinae* 26.30 (SC 178: 232). For a more in-depth discussion of Christian ascetics' adoption of children, see, e.g., Judith Evans Grubbs, "Church, State, and Children: Christian and Imperial Attitudes toward Infant Exposure in Late Antiquity," in *The Power of Religion in Late* Antiquity, ed. Andrew Cain and Noel Lenski (Farnham: Ashgate, 2009), 119–31.

24. *Ep.* 46.1 (CSEL 54: 329).

25. *Ep.* 127.8 (CSEL 56.1: 151).

26. For a discussion of *pietas* and what it entailed, see Richard P. Saller, *Patriarchy, Property and Death in the Roman Family* (Cambridge: Cambridge University Press, 1994), 110, 131.

27. Such dedications were not binding upon the child, as, for example, Ambrose's *Exhortation to Virginity* suggests, directed to four children whose parents had already vowed them to the religious life. Similarly, Gregory of Nazianzus claimed to have been promised to divine service prior to his own birth by his mother—a vow he fulfilled after a nearly fatal accident as a young adult (*Or.* 2.77; discussed in Vuolanto, "Choosing Asceticism," 56–57). Nor did the younger Paula's embrace of the ascetic life necessarily require her to leave her ancestral home, still less to join Jerome and her extended family in Jerusalem. For elite ascetics, whether virgins or widows, domestic forms of monasticism that never required a woman to leave her household were still a popular option at the turn of the fifth century. As such, asceticism could become and frequently was, in Vuolanto's apt expression, an "intergenerational effort" (Vuolanto, "Choosing Asceticism," passim). Jerome's pointed suggestions that Laeta might find the proper training of a Christian virgin to be impossible in her own home thus reflect his evident anxiety to move the girl to Jerusalem rather than an antiascetic environmental bias.

28. Geoffrey Nathan has argued on this basis that "motherhood ... placed a great responsibility on a woman: she was in large part to blame for a son or daughter's spiritual and religious failings. In that sense, her importance far outweighed that of a father" (*The Family in Late Antiquity*, 151). A somewhat different picture emerges, however, if one consults texts addressing the formation of sons rather than, in the case of *Ep.* 107, that of a daughter. John Chrysostom's treatise *On Vainglory and the Right Way for Parents to Bring Up Their Children*, by contrast, focuses on the education of boys and devotes a concomitantly greater part of the text to the duties of fathers. For a discussion of the treatise, its contents, and its context in late ancient parenting, see Cornelia B. Horn and John W. Martens, *"Let the Little Children Come to Me": Childhood and Children in Early Christianity* (Washington, D.C.: The Catholic University of America Press, 2009), 149–59.

29. For a discussion of the bishop as paterfamilias in the Latin West during a slightly later period of late antiquity, see Kristina Sessa, *The Formation of Papal Authority in Late Antique Italy: Roman Bishops and the Domestic Sphere* (Cambridge: Cambridge University Press, 2011).

30. *Ep.* 107.4 (CSEL 55: 296).

31. Ibid. 13 (CSEL 55: 304).

32. Rebecca Krawiec, "'From the Womb of the Church': Monastic Families," *Journal of Early Christian Studies* 11.3 (2003), 283–307. See, however, Elizabeth A. Clark, "Antifamilial Tendencies in Ancient Christianity," *Journal of the History of Sexuality* 5.3 (1995): 356–80.

33. See, for example, Paulinus's lengthy introduction of Melania's ancestors—as well as his self-consciously biblical justification for the relevance of the latter (*Ep.* 29.7–8 [CSEL 29: 252–54]). Similarly, Gregory of Nazianzus's funerary oration for his friend Basil dwells not only upon the faith and virtue of the latter's ancestors but also on their noble rank (*Or.* 43.3–10).

34. Skeb surmises that the terms refer to Melania's spiritual progeny ("ihre geistliche Nachkommenschaft": Paulinus of Nola, *Epistulae*, 708 note 17). In context, however, the interpretation proffered by, e.g., Walsh, that the children in question are Albina and Publicola, with Melania the Younger, her husband, Pinianus, and perhaps Melania's unnamed brother as the requisite grandchildren makes better sense (*Letters of Paulinus of Nola*, vol. 2: 325).

35. *Ep.* 29.13 (CSEL 29: 260).

36. Palladius, *Lausiac History* 54.4 (ed. C. Butler, 148). The *Vita Melaniae Iunioris* presents a rather different picture—in that it surprisingly omits any reference to its subject's famous grandmother, even where Gerontius cites dialogue from the *Lausiac History* in which Palladius has the younger Melania name her grandmother as the impetus for her renunciation. Cf. Palladius, *Lausiac History* 61.2 (ed. C. Butler, 155). This curious omission on Gerontius's part is unlikely to be accidental but rather may reflect the perceived taint of heresy that attached to the elder Melania by virtue of her association with Evagrius and other so-called Origenists. Cf. E. A. Clark, *Life of Melania*, 148.

37. Palladius, *Lausiac History* 61.2 (ed. C. Butler, 155).

38. *Ep.* 108.34 (CSEL 55: 351).

39. Such negotiations were not limited to mothers, nor even to women. Mathew Kuefler has argued, for example, that one of ascetic authors' primary concerns was the rescripting of Roman notions of masculinity to include or even privilege monks and clergy, who lacked some of the most visible trappings of Roman manhood (*The Manly Eunuch: Masculinity, Gender Ambiguity, and Christian Ideology in Late Antiquity* [Chicago: University of Chicago Press, 2001]).

40. Cf. Gerontius, *Vita Melaniae Iunioris* 41 (SC 90: 204–6; trans. E. A. Clark, 54–55).

41. Ibid. 60 (SC 90: 246; trans. E. A. Clark, 72).

42. As Averil Cameron has observed, "the very urgency of [Jerome's] persuasion towards asceticism shows perhaps that it was not really very common" ("Virginity as Metaphor: Women and the Rhetoric of Early Christianity," in *History as Text: The Writing of Ancient History*, ed. Averil Cameron [London: Duckworth, 1989], 195).

43. Vuolanto, "Choosing Asceticism," 269–74.

44. Both Jerome and Augustine thus offer interpretations of the Judgment of Solomon (1 Kings 3:16–28), which cast the two mothers as the church and the synagogue, with the latter falsely attempting to lay claim to the former's true children. (Cf. Jerome, *Ep.* 74 [CSEL 55: 23–29]; Augustine, *Sermo* 10 [CCL 41: 152–59]).

45. I have borrowed this apt expression from Averil Cameron's perspicacious reflections on this subject nearly twenty-five years ago: "Virginity as Metaphor," 184.

5

Wounded by Divine Love

Kristi Upson-Saia

In the opening chapters of his *Life of Melania the Younger,* Gerontius describes the young Melania's intense longing for an ascetic life, a longing that would remain unfulfilled for years. Thwarted by her parents, who wished her to continue the illustrious family line, Melania was instead forced into marriage. Yet Melania continued to yearn for a life of renunciation, because as Gerontius tells us, she had been "wounded by divine love."[1] This metaphor, which would become commonplace in ascetic literature from the fourth century onward, derives from the Septuagint translation of Song of Songs 2:5.[2] The expression likely drew meaning from notions of sexual intimacy; that is, the agonized emotions associated with human love were transferred to an ascetic's feelings toward her divine lover.[3] The expression not only described but also promoted an ascetic subjectivity characterized by passion and devotion for God and motivated the ascetic to comport herself like an ideal lover or betrothed: in full subjection to God.[4]

Although notions of intimate love certainly informed the meaning drawn from this expression, my research has revealed that it also builds from wound metaphors pervasive in earlier Christian writings. Gerontius's *Life of Melania*—to my knowledge, the earliest use of the metaphor "wounded by divine love" in the ascetic context[5]—marks a new phase in the early Christian language of wounds and wounding. Hitherto, from the second century C.E., early Christians used wound and wounding metaphors almost exclusively to describe sin and heresy. Studying these earlier expressions, I argue, enables us to better understand the layered meanings expressed by wound metaphors as they moved into the ascetic context and, further, to better understand the layered notions of ascetic piety to which the metaphors referred.

In the ancient Mediterranean world, at any given moment, nearly everyone was enduring some injury, ailment, or illness.[6] Thus, wounds and wounding provided a widely recognizable conceptual frame and an immediately meaningful linguistic device. In this chapter, I first discuss the cognitive linguistic theory that shapes my analysis of early Christian metaphors. Next, I explain how early Christian wound metaphors in particular activated the qualities and affordances of being wounded in order to structure the conceptualizations of sin and heresy. I describe how these metaphors also mobilized the roles of physician and patient in order to motivate the actions of lay Christians, priests, bishops, and of sinners and heretics as well.[7] In short, I demonstrate how this early set of wound metaphors constructed a thoroughly medicalized notion of Christian piety. Finally, I trace how ascetics assimilated and built on these earlier concepts of piety—and the figurative language employed to communicate such concepts—when they rendered ascetic bodies injured or healthy and when they described ascetics as "wounded by divine love."

METAPHOR, MEANING, AND BODILY EXPERIENCE

Elizabeth A. Clark has helped scholars better understand how early Christian metaphors of the virgin bride or celibate bride drew meaning from "forms of everyday life."[8] Clark explains that elements of a bride's identity were transferred to the ascetic context to construct the identity of Christian ascetics: specifically, the ascetic who considered herself the bride of Christ cultivated the submission and devotion characteristic of a good wife and was ignited with the passion and desire characteristic of a lover. Further, the Christian ascetic guarded her purity and bodily integrity in order to be counted worthy of her impending union with her divine spouse.[9] Although when taken too far the correspondence between the bride and the ascetic posed potential problems, the usefulness of the celibate-bride metaphor in motivating ascetic behavior outweighed its potential misuse, and thus it enjoyed a popular place in early Christian ascetic discourse.

My analysis in this chapter takes its cue from Clark. I am also interested in the connection between early Christians' figurative language and their experiences from everyday life. Whereas Clark investigates how figurations of marriage and intimacy between spouses were imported into the realm of Christian renunciants, I endeavor to explore how the experience of being wounded became a metaphoric frame through which early Christians conceived of piety.

In so doing, I lean heavily on cognitive linguistic theory. In the past few decades, linguistic theorists and cognitive scientists have argued that the structure of conceptual and linguistic meaning—especially in the case of metaphors—is scaffolded on the properties, affordances, and qualities of people's ordinary kinesthetic experience.[10] For example, in the American context, the concept of love is structured on the experience of a journey, evident in the language of road, rail, and sea travel that we use to describe stages of a relationship (e.g., hitting a "bumpy road" or "dead end"; coming to a "crossroads"; going "off the tracks" or being "on the rocks"), as well as the language that we use to communicate a relationship's progress (e.g., "look how far we've come"; "it's too late to turn back now"; "it's time to go our separate ways").[11] Through examples like this, cognitive linguists argue that the conceptualization and linguistic expression of the love concept correspond systematically to "people's ordinary, felt sensations of their bodies in action," specifically with respect to a journey.[12] From this scholarship, we understand that meaning is—or, more precisely, *structures* of meaning are—deeply corporeal. As the cognitive linguist Mark Johnson succinctly writes, conceptual meaning is "shaped by the patterns of our bodily movement, the contours of our spatial and temporal orientation, and the forms of our interaction with objects. [Meaning] is never merely a matter of abstract conceptualizations and propositional judgments."[13]

In line with this view, I suggest that metaphorical wounds of sin and heresy in late antiquity were not merely linguistic flourishes but that the bodily experience of being wounded structured early Christians' concepts of sin and heresy. In other words, the figurative device and the bodily grounding of the concepts are indivisibly linked; the ordinary meanings of sin and heresy emerged from the physical *properties* and *affordances* of being wounded.[14] Early Christian discourse on the wounds of sin and heresy activated and harnessed cognitive associations, as well as a rich set of affective associations, with the experience of being wounded.[15]

Yet injuries and wounds could be a governing figure for conceptions of sin and heresy only if the experience of wounding was relatively uniform; that is, if people understood wounding to contain a stable set of properties and affordances that could be meaningfully exported to the conceptual categories of sin and heresy. Some cognitive linguists argue that there are kinesthetic experiences that are experientially constant, offering as evidence similar metaphorical language that exists across cultures that otherwise possess different linguistic and cultural trajectories (e.g., the kinesthetically uniform experiences of *hunger* that serve as a structural basis for the concept and language of *desire*).[16] Other scholars argue that a standardization of embodied experiences is at least in part mediated by culture.[17] With this latter group of scholars, I wish to argue that the bodily experience of being wounded in antiquity was constrained by the emerging discipline of medicine, which consolidated and standardized disparate experiences. Specifically, medical theories and writings shaped ancient notions about, perceptions of, and practices related to wounds and wound treatment, in turn creating a stylized experience of being wounded that was broadly shared no matter how idiosyncratic each individual event may have been. I contend that Christian wound metaphors drew from this stylized experience and from a controlled set of perceptions and meanings related thereto.

Relying on the theoretical insights described above, in the next two sections I investigate how early Christian authors leveraged dimensions of the experience of being wounded as they constructed theological concepts of impiety and piety, as they disciplined right relations between members of the Christian community, and as they sought to stimulate pious behavior among lay Christians and especially among ascetics. From this work, I suggest, we gain a finer understanding of early Christians' embodied social logic; or, in the words of the cognitive linguist Mark Johnson, of how the ancient body "worked its way up into the mind."[18]

WOUNDS AND WOUND TREATMENT IN ANCIENT MEDICAL LITERATURE

Ancient medical writers discuss wounds in case studies and in treatises devoted exclusively to wound treatment.[19] From this literature, we discover that medical writers presumed two types of wounds: the first were the harmful, malevolent wounds, ulcers, and sores incurred by some accident in daily life, on the battlefield, or in the throes of illness or disease. The second type included the salutary cutting and probing incurred at the hands of the physician who toiled to bring his patient back to full health.

Within the first type of wound, some were more serious than others. Medical writers were not very concerned about flesh wounds (i.e., cuts or bruises that barely breached the epidermis). Rather, they concentrated their attention on contusions that severely bruised the flesh, deep wounds that tore the muscle and fractured or splintered the bone underneath, or wounds with embedded foreign objects (e.g., arrowheads or spear tips). In these cases, physicians expected the wound to become infected as the crushed tissue around the wound or the copious blood flowing to the wound rotted and turned to pus.[20] They became especially concerned when the wound was not adequately purged, because the rotting blood, humours, and tissue caused painful inflammation and spread putrefaction to the surrounding flesh or organs, leading to life-threatening gangrene and sepsis.[21] The physician could surmise the onset of gangrene by the constitution of the pus drained from the wound: "pure," "clean," "white," and "odorless" pus meant that the wound was healing properly, whereas "thick," "yolk-colored," and "stinking" pus was a sure sign of trouble.[22] When the wound turned black and the patient lost sensation in the infected area, the physician knew that it was too late for treatment.[23]

To avoid this outcome, physicians recommended that, as soon as it was incurred, the wound should be allowed to bleed dry. Bleeding limited the amount of blood that lay stagnant under the skin's surface, in turn limiting the potential for putrefaction. Then, a few days after the wound had scabbed over, physicians used a scalpel to cut an opening in it—sometimes inserting a tin drain—in order to extract any rotting blood or flesh that had turned into pus.[24] The timing of these interventions was crucial: at the time of the injury, the wound must bleed long enough to ensure that as little blood as possible pooled (and rotted) under the scab, and then the physician must wait the right amount of time to make sure that the decomposed blood and flesh had fully converted into pus before purging (i.e., lest they would have to rewound the patient again for additional suppurations).[25] If he did not treat the patient correctly, and gangrene set in, a surgeon was to make deep incisions (down to the bone) around the margins of the wound, cutting out and removing the rotten flesh from the healthy flesh.[26]

In addition to making incisions to drain wounds or to cut away gangrenous flesh, physicians also cut wounds wider as part of their diagnostic process. For instance, if the patient's wound was deep enough to injure an organ or bone, the physician might enlarge the wound in order to inspect the organs or to check for bone fractures or breakage. If he concluded that an operation on the organ or bone was necessary, he might widen the wound even further in order to perform surgery.[27]

Physicians cut open wounds to probe for, dislodge, and extract arrowheads and spear tips.[28] And physicians also made incisions to enable wounds to close and scar properly. Some wounds could not close on their own because the flesh surrounding the wound was too moist or flimsy or because the shape of the wound was uneven. Physicians thus cut around the edges of the wound to allow the thicker, healthy flesh to be drawn together and sutured closed.[29]

As we can see from this brief survey of the medical literature, there were many instances in which the physician was called to wound in order to heal. Yet because these medical treatments were painful—sometimes more painful than simply leaving the wound untreated—they were greatly feared. Some called them "cruel," or "wicked torture," and some patients refused to submit to them.[30]

To address this resistance, medical writers cultivated notions of the good physician, of the good patient, and of a right relationship between the pair. On the one hand, the ideal physician was to be resolved to bring his patient back to health, no matter what it required. If the patient was fearful of the necessary treatment, the physician was to encourage him by whatever means necessary: "sometimes reproving sharply and emphatically and sometimes comforting with solicitude and attention."[31] The best physicians were those who modulated their behavior to suit their patients' individual temperaments and those who possessed the sharp rhetorical skills and easy bedside manner that enabled them to convince any patient to "submit to the surgeon's knife."[32] Finally, the physician himself was to possess the fortitude necessary to perform the procedures. He was to be "unmoved by the cries of his patient . . . as if the cries of pain cause[d] him no emotion," and, above all, he must never "cut less than [was] necessary" because swayed by his patient's fear or pleas.[33]

On the other hand, the ideal patient should submit wholly to the physician's treatment. Knowing that fever and delirium commonly accompanied septic wounds, the good patient was to distrust his own judgment and give himself over wholly to the treatment prescribed by a physician who was in full possession of his reason.[34] Further, acknowledging that the pain of surgery might be necessary for a healthful outcome, the good patient should muster the courage and fortitude necessary to endure painful procedures without flinching or groaning. In fact, the ideal patient even positions himself in such a way as to "assist the surgeon" in his operation.[35] Only when both physician and patient acted according to their roles would treatment be successful.

TREATING THE PUTRID WOUNDS OF SIN AND HERESY

Some early Christian writers had medical training themselves or had friends or family who were physicians; thus their familiarity with medical treatments informed the medicalized language that they employed in their writing and preaching.[36] That said, given that nearly everyone in antiquity experienced debilitating injuries or illnesses, Christian writers and preachers did not need to be highly trained in medicine in order to draw on rudimentary precepts and practices that were well known through experience.[37] In this section, I describe how early Christian writers and preachers from the second century C.E. on defined the concepts of sin and heresy according to the qualities, properties, and affordances of a gangrenous or septic wound.[38] I further discuss how they leveraged the medical taxonomy of harmful and healthful woundings to contrast the dangerous wounds of sin and heresy with the salutary wounds of chastisement and ecclesial discipline.[39] Both types of wounds were painful, but whereas the former led to a putrefied and rotten soul, the latter restored health to the individual and to the social body. Finally, I show how early Christians marshaled the roles of patient and physician to serve as a frame through which Christians disciplined their relationships with one another.

Conceptualizing Sin and Heresy as Wounds of the Soul

Early Christians understood sin and heresy, like physical wounds, to derive from a range of situations. According to some, each time that humans chose to indulge their vices they rewounded their souls.[40] Others argued that Satan seizes upon openings already made in the soul by sin and vice; into these openings he "hurls his flaming arrows,"[41] or he "injects heretical venoms" that exacerbate existing wounds of the soul.[42] Still others believed that sin and heresy were evidence that human nature had fallen into a mortified, rotten state.[43] Whatever the origin, the constituent feature of sin and heresy was a corruption and putrefaction of the soul (or mind) that was likened to a gangrenous, septic wound.

Moreover, the symptoms that attended sin and heresy were like those exhibited by someone who was physically wounded. Clement of Alexandria and Ambrose both emphasized pain as an accompaniment of sin. Those who indulged the vice of heavy drinking, for example, experienced not only painful deterioration of their bodies but also shame that pained their souls. This pain, they argued, should prompt sinners to seek treatment like those pained by physical wounds.[44] For Augustine, the symptom that prompted sinners to reform was not pain but rather the horrifying appearance of one's sin. Describing his own rehabilitation, Augustine writes: "You, Lord, turned me toward myself, ... setting me before my own eyes so that I could see how sordid I was, how deformed and squalid, how tainted with wounds and sores. I saw it all and stood aghast."[45] Whether because of their pain or their unsightly appearance, sinners ought to regard these symptoms of sin as reasons to seek help.

Yet when a sinner's abscessed soul has progressed to a certain point, Origen remarks, he can no longer perceive its festering: like a gangrenous wound, his soul "lacks natural senses.... We cannot feel the extent of the wounds or the extent of the grief we are bringing on our soul by [continuing to] sin."[46] Similarly, as Tertullian describes heretics' disordered minds, he recalls the fevers and delirium that accompany septic wounds in order to explain why "all the normal senses become sluggish" and heretics' perception of orthodoxy becomes dull.[47]

Finally, the outcome of an untreated wound of the soul was fashioned like an untreated gangrenous wound of the body: the soul or mind would become putrid, eventually leading to death.[48] But whereas a gangrenous sore deadened only an individual's limb or organ, the gangrene of sin and heresy threatened to spread and to mortify the entire community, the social body.[49] Sin and heresy could even sever the relationship between humans and their creator, a separation that the desert ascetic Antony called the "great wound."[50]

Early Christian conceptions of sin and heresy were organized according to the affordances of physical wounds: painful, ugly, stinking, and abhorrent, disordering mind and body, threatening to spread, leading to mortification and death. Further, wound metaphors for sin and heresy culled the palpable, somatic sensations of being wounded.[51] As Susan Ashbrook Harvey has demonstrated, early Christian wound metaphors elicited the foul and repellent stench of putrefied flesh.[52] I would add that early Christian moralists and heresiologists evoked the full range of an audience's sensibilities in order to associate fear, horror, and disgust with the vices and heretical ideas that they rebuffed. To this end, they described the wounds of sin and heresy in lurid detail: oozing pus and blood, ridden with worms or maggots, and exuding a noxious stink.[53] Conjuring the feelings, sights, smells, and anxiety attendant with physical wounds was a particularly effective way to stimulate Christians' moral and theological compliance, "a powerful instrument of moral suasion" that helped Christian moralists and heresiologists activate an embodied understanding of and revulsion for sin and heresy.[54]

Advising Treatment: Salutary Wounding by Christian "Physicians"

As in medical writings, early Christian moralists and heresiologists distinguished two types of wounds: some that were harmful and others that were healthful. Whereas they structured their conceptualizations of sin and heresy on dangerous, gangrenous wounds, they structured an understanding of beneficent chastisement and ecclesial discipline on the physicians' rewounding treatments. Moreover, early Christians also construed right relations among members of the community according to the idealized interaction between patient and physician.

On occasion, moralists and heresiologists figured God as a good physician who treated the wayward Christian. According to Origen, God may abandon heretics for a time, allowing their wounds to fester until treatment is most advantageous. Should God treat them too soon, the healing would be only superficial, and even if the visible wound scarred over, the putrefaction underlying the wound would persist. God is like physicians who[55]

> know that it is preferable to allow wounds to fester for a time, in order that the malignant humour could flow out completely, rather than to hasten a superficial cure, shutting up within the veins the inflamed and poisonous matter that, when cut off from its usual outlets, will undoubtedly creep into the interior of the body and penetrate to the vital parts themselves, bringing on not merely bodily disease but indeed loss of life.

At times, God's treatment might be as severe and painful as surgery.[56] And just as some patients railed against the painful treatments of physicians, some Christians wondered if God's treatments were too harsh. Basil defended God through a well-worn justification of physicians: "You do not accuse the physician of any wrong in his cuttings and burnings and complete mutilations of the body; but rather you probably pay him money and you call him a savior since he has wounded a small part of the body to prevent the suffering from spreading throughout the whole of it."[57] At other times, though, God's treatments were figured as more gentle and staged. When sin is like an embedded thistle, prickly on every side, Chrysostom explains, the divine physician has to gauge just how much to extract at any one time lest he introduce too much new wounding, which would leave his patient lifeless from the pain.[58] Regardless of how harsh or measured his method, God is repeatedly cast as the true physician, who—echoing the words of the Deuteronomic author—wounds in order that he may heal (Deut. 32:39).[59]

On other occasions, moralists and heresiologists called upon clerics and lay Christians to act as physicians and to deliver treatment in the form of rebuke or ecclesial discipline: "For indeed the church is an admirable surgeon, though the surgery is not for bodies, but for souls. For it is spiritual, and sets right not fleshly wounds, but errors of the mind."[60] Early Christians were not to be "negligent and despairing" of their friends' wounded souls, but even if the chastisement and discipline were painful, they were called to heal one another.[61] Again, some Christians hesitated to rebuke their friends, because this seemed to intensify pain and "make the wound greater"; they regarded reprimand and punishment as cruel or even evil. Those who were hesitant were reminded of the salutary pain, wounding, and incisions made by surgeons. Chastisement would indeed exacerbate pain, Augustine explains, because a putrefied wound has lost its sense of feeling; when "the knife or leech comes, the wound now hurts.... It hurts more under the healing operation than it would if it were not operated upon." Yet Augustine reminds his audience of their ultimate goal: "that [the wound] may never hurt again once healing is effected."[62] Taking a stronger position, Gregory the Great likens the cleric who refuses to rebuke a parishioner to a worthless physician: "If persons by no means ignorant of the medicinal art were to see a sore that required lancing, and yet refused to lance it, certainly by their mere inactivity they would be guilty of a brother's death. Let [clerics] see, then, how much guilt they accrue when, knowing the sores of the soul, they neglect to cure [the spiritually wounded] with the lancing of words."[63]

Urging Christians to adopt the idealized comportment of a skilled surgeon, Gregory of Nazianzus exhorts his audience to do what is healthful regardless of the objections raised by patients.[64] If necessary, Augustine presses Christians to steel themselves and, "out of compassion, turn a deaf ear to the many cries" of those being punished or rebuked.[65] Echoing this sentiment, Chrysostom warns Christians to be prepared to be yelled at or even struck by those incurring the pain of chastisement and reproof. Chrysostom urges his community to remember that "those who are cut by surgeons utter numberless cries against those who are cutting them," and yet he urges them to mimic the behavior of "the surgeon [who] heeds none of these things, but [has in mind] only the health of the patients."[66]

Elsewhere, Chrysostom modeled Christian reproof on a physician's gentle persuasion and comforting bedside manner.[67] He insists that sometimes mildness is necessary in order to[68]

> persuade [your friend] to bear the cutting. Do you not see how surgeons, even when they burn and cut, apply their treatment with great gentleness? Much more ought those who reprove others act. For reproof is sharper than fire and knife and makes men flinch. On this account surgeons take great pains to make them bear the cutting quietly and apply it as tenderly as possible, even allowing time [between cuts] to take a breath. So ought we also to offer reproofs that the reproved may not start away.

Addressing patients' fear, anxiety, and pain, Chrysostom adds that physicians sometimes prefer to stage their treatments—"Wise physicians do not cure those who have fallen into a long sickness all at once, but [treat] little by little, lest [the patient] should faint and die"—and he urges Christians likewise to stage their rebukes of some sinners in their communities.[69]

Chrysostom ultimately concludes that Christians must calibrate the degree of their chastisement according to sinners' and heretics' ability to endure it. They must model their approach on physicians' practice of sizing up the constitution of each patient and adjusting their treatments accordingly. For instance, Chrysostom asks:[70]

> What then is one to do? For if you deal too gently with him who needs a severe application of the knife, and do not cut deeply into one who requires such treatment, you remove one part of the sore but leave another part. If, on the other hand, you make the incision unsparingly, the patient, driven to desperation by his sufferings, will fling away at once both the remedy and the bandage and throw himself down headlong.

Chrysostom thus advocates rebuke and punishment that correspond not to the offense but rather to the temperament of the sinner.

Whatever the manner of treatment, timeliness mattered. Clerics and lay Christians needed to correct their parishioners and friends on small matters—mere flesh wounds—before their vice or false ideas progressed into full-blown sepsis. Just as minor wounds eventually led to greater trouble, so too would isolated indecencies turn into sinful habits or slight perversions of Christian doctrine turn into heresy.[71] Moreover, those who are mostly healthy endure the surgeon's knife and have better results from surgery than those who are so riddled with sin and heresy that even minor incisions "irritate" existing sores.[72] Like good physicians, Christians must act quickly, but clerics must also be able to discern the point at which the sin or heresy has become so firmly entrenched—like a poison that has entered the bloodstream or gangrene that has fully consumed a limb or organ—that the sinner or heretic is incurable.[73] At that point, the community can no longer force contrition and penance; they have no other option but to "cut off that putrefied member so that it does not corrupt the whole body."[74]

Whereas the cleric or lay person was to structure Christian discipline on the comportment and approach of a skilled physician, the sinner or heretic was to frame his attitude and behavior according to an idealized—that is, humble, submissive, and compliant—patient.[75] Aphrahat urges his readers to take their sins as seriously as gangrenous wounds; just as one would seek immediate help from a physician in that case, so too should those wounded by sin confess their sins, seek treatment, and submit to the discipline of the community.[76] Basil calls his readers to emulate the posture of a good patient as they endure reproof: "Just as we endure cuttings and cauterizations and the taking of bitter drugs for the cure of the body, so also in this way we must accept the cutting effects of the word that exposes and the bitter drugs of penalties for the cure of the soul."[77] Even if they do not perceive themselves as in need of treatment, sinners and heretics ought to acknowledge that they may not possess their senses or be in their right minds; thus, when chastised by the community, they should, even against their own judgment, humbly submit to the community's discipline.

Early Christian writers tapped into the medicalized experience of being wounded to structure the concepts of sin and heresy, as well as to charge them with affective and somatic meaning. The wounds of sin and wounds of heresy metaphors served to repel Christians from sinful behavior and heretical ideas, and the physician-patient relationship organized the policing of such behavior and ideas. In short, these earliest Christian wound metaphors helped to construct medicalized notions of piety and to catalyze behavior that conformed to these notions.

WOUNDS AND MEDICAL LOGIC IN EARLY CHRISTIAN ASCETICISM AND IN THE MELANIAN LITERATURE

Although in Gerontius's *Life* Melania the Younger insists that "our battle is not against flesh and blood, but . . . against the world rulers of this realm of darkness," throughout ascetic literature we find waywardness, sin, and heresy *manifesting physically* in the bodies of the Melanias and of their companions, suggesting that the divide between the bodily and the spiritual was not so clean as Melania makes it out to be.[78] Descriptions of ascetics' bodily afflictions—afflictions that are interpreted as evidence of or punishment for sin or vice—make visible the embodied foundations of the theological concepts discussed in the previous section. In other words, because the ordinary theological meaning of sin and likewise the ordinary theological meanings of contrition and repentance were conceived with respect to embodied experiences of injury and wounding, it is not surprising that we find the sinful and repentant dispositions of ascetics rendered physical and bodily with illness, injury, wounds, and pain that accompanies impiety, and full health being restored to the contrite and repentant.

For example, in a particularly striking scene in Palladius's *Lausiac History*, Evagrius received a warning in a dream to quit his sexual relationship and, once and for all, make a firm commitment to the ascetic life. Having done so, Evagrius moved to Jerusalem, where he soon lapsed. For this, God sent a "bout of fever" and "a long illness lasting six months."[79] Doctors could "find no treatment to cure him," but Melania the Elder summoned from him a confession and offered to pray on his behalf.[80] In this scene, Evagrius's illness is construed as a physical eruption or materialization of his disordered and sinful soul (presumably this is why doctors could not help the monk); it is also regarded as the salutary treatment sent by the Good Physician to elicit contrition and penance. Thus Evagrius's illness collapses the two types of wound—the harmful and the healthful—found in the medical taxonomy.

The connection between sin, physical distress, and treatment is also apparent in Palladius's account of the seasoned monk Stephen, who developed a terrible wound that was eating away his flesh. When the brothers around him became upset that a man of his holiness should succumb to such a dreadful ailment,

Stephen insisted that their good God would send the affliction only if he himself deserved punishment. Interpreting his wound as a painful yet salutary correction of his sin, Stephen further remarks that it is "better to pay the penalty here than after I have left the arena."[81]

Such examples as these demonstrate how the concepts of sin and repentance—concepts premised on medicalized bodily experiences—emerge in ascetic literature as physical afflictions and healing, and they also exhibit how the behavior of idealized patients organized ascetics' responses to bodily and spiritual afflictions. The humble and obedient posture of a good patient and of the repentant collapse into one, and those who adopt this posture are healed physically and spiritually. To be more specific: when his untreated wound became gangrenous and ultimately required surgery, Stephen exhibited the remarkable composure and unflinching endurance of a model patient. As the surgeon cut away Stephen's corrupt flesh, the monk conducted his daily task of weaving palm leaves, acting "as though it were someone else who was undergoing the knife. While his members were being cut away like locks of hair, he showed no sign whatsoever of pain."[82] The ability to withstand bodily pain and suffering—with courage and steadfastness—marked a good ascetic just as it marked a repentant sinner, both premised on the idealized behavior of a good patient.[83]

Let us return finally to Gerontius's metaphorical description of Melania being wounded by divine love. As mentioned above, in the opening chapters of the *Life*, the metaphor is used to describe the passion and fervor that Melania possesses for a life of renunciation. As such, the metaphor seems to position Melania as an ideal lover or betrothed, enflamed with desire for and in ready subjection to God. Later in the narrative, though, Gerontius again uses the expression as he recalls this earlier moment. Gerontius notes that the young girl was "still wearing worldly clothes" and recounts an incident when the young Melania developed an inflammation from her embroidered garments. Directly after this story, he reports that Melania had been wounded by divine love and that "she could not bear to live the same life any longer, but prepared herself to contend in even greater contests."[84] I suggest that, in this instance in the *Life*, the new ascetic metaphor enfolds earlier expressions of theological and heresiological piety into a conception of ascetic piety. Here we may read the sore caused by Melania's clothing as a corporeal wound inflicted by the Great Physician, a wound that mirrors or manifests the wounding of Melania's soul.[85] Again, collapsing together the two types of wounds found in medical taxonomy, the sore arises from clothing considered impious (thus manifesting sinfulness in the body), yet the sore also stimulates Melania's repentance. Just as God, fellow lay Christians, and clergy are to cut the hearts, minds, and souls of those who need to repent and to commence a new life of piety and orthodoxy, here too wounds—both physical and spiritual—precede Melania's adoption of a more rigorous form of asceticism, a more healthful life.[86] Thus, here the expression of being wounded by divine love draws meaning from the experience of physicians' harming in order to heal and builds from Christians' theological understanding of the relationship between wounds and piety.[87]

...

In this chapter, I have aimed to demonstrate how embodied experiences of wounds and wound treatment structured early Christians' conceptualization of sin, heresy, contrition, and repentance, and conditioned a notion of Christian piety based on and emerging through physical bodies. Once the connections between embodied experience, theological notions, and piety become clear, we are better able to surmise the polyvalent meanings of wounding metaphors across contexts and across time, including how they underwrote notions of ascetic piety. Further, by reflecting on the embodied foundation of early Christian concepts and metaphors, we heed the call of Laurence Kirmayer to "give due weight to the primacy of the body not only as an object of thought but as itself a vehicle for thinking, feeling, and acting."[88]

NOTES

The research for this chapter was supported by the Arnold L. and Lois S. Graves Award in the Humanities. I am grateful to the following individuals, who provided instructive feedback on drafts: Catherine Chin, Carrie Schroeder, Maria Doerfler, Christine Luckritz Marquis, Clair Morrissey, Amy Lyford, and the anonymous reviewer for the University of California Press. I dedicate this chapter to Liz Clark, whose scholarship and mentoring serve as a model of the professional life that I strive to emulate.

1. Gerontius, *Life of Melania* 1, 32 (SC 90: 132, 188; trans. E. A. Clark, 27, 49).
2. Septuagint: "I am wounded with divine love" (τετρωμένη ἀγάπης ἐγώ). Compare the Latin Vulgate: "I languish with love" (*amore langueo*).
3. As such, the metaphor participated in an eroticism that pervaded early Christian asceticism.
4. See, for example, Gerontius, *Life of Melania* 1, 2; cf. 29, 42, 43, 49 (SC 90: 132–34, 182, 206–10, 220–22; trans. E. A. Clark, 27–29; cf. 47, 56–57, 61).
5. Though the expression becomes commonplace in late ancient ascetic sources. See, for example, Jerome, *Ep*. 22.25 (*Sancti Eusebii Hieronymi Epistulae*, ed. Isidorus Hilberg, CSEL 54: 178–80).
6. Although only the wealthy had access to professional physicians, rudimentary medical knowledge and treatments were widespread (Robert Garland, *The Eye of the Beholder: Deformity and Disability in the Graeco-Roman World*, 2nd ed. [London: Bristol Classical Press, 2010], 11, 18–23, 26–27; Valerie M. Hope, *Roman Death: The Dying and the Dead in Ancient Rome* [London: Continuum, 2009], 42–46).
7. Scholars of early Christianity have addressed issues of illness, disability, and medicine from several perspectives: studying early Christians' role in health care, how early Christians made sense of illness and suffering, and the use of medical language or motifs in early Christian discourse. For a comprehensive survey of the state of the field, see Heidi Marx-Wolf and Kristi Upson-Saia, "State of the Question: Religion, Medicine, Disability, and Health in Late Antiquity," *Journal of Late Antiquity* 8.2 (2015): 257–72 and the bibliography at the end of this special issue.
8. Elizabeth A. Clark, "The Celibate Bridegroom and His Virginal Brides: Metaphor and the Marriage of Jesus in Early Christian Ascetic Exegesis," *Church History* 77.1 (2008): 2.

9. The metaphor also aligned ascetics with domestic roles and values, dampening pagan neighbors' scorn for Christian ascetics who refused marriage, by "imagining them as *someone's* wife" (E. A. Clark, "Celibate Bridegroom," 2; emphasis original).

10. George Lakoff and Mark Johnson, *Metaphors We Live By* (Chicago: University of Chicago Press, 1980); Mark Johnson, *The Body in the Mind: The Bodily Basis of Meaning, Imagination, and Reason* (Chicago: University of Chicago Press, 1987); Brian MacWhinney, "The Emergence of Language from Embodiment," in *The Emergence of Language*, ed. Brian MacWhinney (Mahwah, N.J.: Lawrence Erlbaum Associates, 1999), 213-56; Raymond W. Gibbs, "Embodied Experience and Linguistic Meaning," *Brain and Language* 84.1 (2003): 1-15.

11. Lakoff and Johnson, *Metaphors We Live By*, 44-45.

12. Raymond W. Gibbs, Paula Lenz Costa Lima, and Edson Francozo, "Metaphor Is Grounded in Embodied Experience," *Journal of Pragmatics* 36.7 (2004): 1190. Cognitive linguists acknowledge that, as lifestyles change, the experiential origins of conceptual and linguistic meaning may become oblique and difficult to perceive. At this point the metaphor becomes dead (Gibbs, "Embodied Experience," 7; Gibbs, Costa Lima, and Francozo, "Metaphor," 1191). Yet scholars nonetheless conclude that conceptual meaning and linguistic expressions were originally grounded within the parameters of embodied experience and orientation. See Eve Sweetser, *From Etymology to Pragmatics: Metaphorical and Cultural Aspects of Semantic Structure* (Cambridge: Cambridge University Press, 1990); Raymond W. Gibbs, *The Poetics of Mind: Figurative Thought, Language, and Understanding* (Cambridge: Cambridge University Press, 1994); Lynne Cameron and Graham Low, eds., *Researching and Applying Metaphor* (Cambridge: Cambridge University Press, 1999); Raymond W. Gibbs and Gerard Steen, eds., *Metaphor in Cognitive Linguistics: Selected Papers from the Fifth International Cognitive Linguistics Conference, Amsterdam, July 1997* (Amsterdam: John Benjamins, 1999); Gibbs, Costa Lima, and Francozo, "Metaphor," 1189-210.

13. Johnson, *Body in the Mind*, xix.

14. My discussion below maps the qualities and affordance of being physically wounded onto early Christian concepts of sin and heresy as if this can be done cleanly and neatly. That said, I acknowledge Laurence Kirmayer's insistence that "the body provides a structure to thought that is, in part, extrarational and disorderly" ("The Body's Insistence on Meaning: Metaphor as Presentation and Representation in Illness Experience," *Medical Anthropology Quarterly* 6.4 [1992]: 325).

15. On the role of emotion in metaphoric meaning-making, see Zoltan Kövecses, *Metaphor and Emotion: Language, Culture and Body in Human Feeling* (Cambridge: Cambridge University Press, 2000); Kirmayer, "The Body's Insistence on Meaning," 332, 334, 336, 337.

16. Gibbs, Costa Lima, and Francozo, "Metaphor."

17. Lakoff and Johnson, *Metaphors We Live By*, 57, 63-64, 233-35; Johnson, *Body in the Mind*, 20-23.

18. Ibid., xxxvi-xxxvii.

19. Hippocratic texts that address instances of wound diagnosis and treatment are *Epidemics, Aphorisms, On Diseases, On Affections, On Fractures, Surgery*, and *The Physician*. See also scattered discussions in Celsus, *On Medicine*, and Galen, *On Swelling*. Hippocratic treatises that provide expanded discussion of wound treatment are *On Wounds of the Head* and *On Wounds* (alternatively titled *On Ulcers*). We know of several other texts, no longer extant, that also focused on wound treatment; for a discussion of the lost works, see Christine F. Salazar, "Fragments of Lost Hippocratic Writings in Galen's Glossary," *Classical Quarterly* 47.2 (1997): 543-47.

20. On the conversion of rotting blood and tissue to pus, see: Hippocrates, *On Wounds* 1, 10 (LCL 482: 344, 350); idem, *On Wounds of the Head* 11 (LCL 149: 24); id., *On Diseases* 1.14, 15, 17; 4.19 (LCL 472: 124-26, 132, 136; LCL 520: 146-50); id., *Epidemics* 5.28, 41 (LCL 477: 178-80, 184); Celsus, *On Medicine* 5.26.23 (LCL 304: 84); Galen, *On Swelling* 3.715, 4.717 (Jeremiah Reedy, "Galen, *De Tumoribus praeter Naturam*: A Critical Edition with Translation and Indices" [Ph.D.dissertation, University of Michigan, 1968], 36-38). On other humours, such as phlegm, putrefying and turning into pus, see Hippocrates, *On Diseases* 1.15, 17 (LCL 472: 128-30, 136). On the presumption that the purification of blood, humours,

and tissue was part of the normal course of healing, see idem, *On Wounds of the Head* 15 (LCL 149: 38); id., *On Fractures* 26 (LCL 149: 156). On the timing of the festering, see id., *On Fractures* 31 (LCL 149: 170).

21. Idem, *On Diseases* 1.17–18 (LCL 472: 136–40); Galen, *On Swelling* 8.720 (trans. Reedy, 41); cf. Hippocrates, *Epidemics* 5.26 (LCL 477: 176–78). The understanding that excess blood or pus led to putrefaction was grounded in the more general idea that "dryness is nearer to health, and moistness to unhealthiness; a wound is moist, but healthy tissue is dry" (idem, *On Wounds* 1; cf. 4, 12 [LCL 482: 342; cf. 346–48, 356]). Thus the physician ought to "employ a regimen that will make [the wounded patient] as dry and bloodless as possible" (id., *On Diseases* 1.14 [LCL 472: 128]; cf. Celsus, *On Medicine* 5.26.29 [LCL 304: 96]).

22. Hippocrates, *Aphorisms* 7.44–45 (LCL 150: 202); idem, *On Diseases* 2.47 (LCL 472: 274–76); Celsus, *On Medicine* 5.26.20; 7.1.2 (LCL 304: 78; LCL 336: 304).

23. Ibid. 5.26.31 (LCL 304: 100); cf. Hippocrates, *Epidemics* 4.39 (LCL 477: 134); idem, *Instruments of Reduction* 35 (LCL 149: 432); id., *On Joints* 59 (LCL 149: 360–66); id., *On Fractures* 11 (LCL 149: 122); Galen, *On Swelling* 6.719–20, 8.720–21, 11.726, 13.727 (trans. Reedy, 40–41, 45–46).

24. On bleeding and suppurating, see Hippocrates, *On Wounds* 2, 24, 25 (LCL 482: 344–46, 370, 372); idem, *Epidemics* 5.7 (LCL 477: 158); id., *On Diseases* 1.14, 2.47 (LCL 472: 126–28, 272–74); id., *Aphorisms* 2.20 (LCL 150: 184); id., *On Fractures* 31 (LCL 149: 174); Celsus, *On Medicine* 5.26.20, 22–23; 7.1.2 (LCL 304: 78, 82, 86; LCL 336: 298–304). Galen argued that the body naturally purges putrefied matter through pores or ducts. When that is not enough, the physician must lend a hand by cutting a wider opening (*On Swelling* 3.715 [Reedy, 37]).

25. Hippocrates, *On Wounds of the Head* 15 (LCL 149: 38); idem, *On Fractures* 26 (LCL 149: 156). On the delicate balance between healthful bleeding and the imminent danger of hemorrhaging, see id., *On Wounds* 26–27 (LCL 482: 372–74); Celsus, *On Medicine* 5.26.21 (LCL 304: 80).

26. Ibid. 5.26.32, 34; 7.31.33 (LCL 304: 100, 106; LCL 336: 468–70). In order to avoid "use of the scalpel," the wound could be cauterized or plastered (ibid. 5.26.32, 33–34 [LCL 304: 102, 104]). Similarly, when confronted with the bite of a dog, snake, or spider, or a scorpion sting, the physician was to "make incisions with a scalpel around the wound" and then to cup or suck out the toxins (ibid. 5.27.3; cf. 5, 9 [LCL 304: 114; cf. 118, 120]).

27. Hippocrates, *On Wounds of the Head* 14 (LCL 149: 32–34); cf. idem, *On Fractures* 31 (LCL 149: 170); id., *Physician* 14 (LCL 482: 314).

28. Celsus, *On Medicine* 7.5.1–4 (LCL 336: 314–23); Paul of Aegina, *Medical Compendium* 6.88.3–9 (ed. I. L. Heiberg, Corpus Medicorum Graecorum [Berlin: Akademie-Verlag, 1924], 9.2: 130–35); Quintus Curtius, *History of Alexander* 9.5.23–28 (LCL 369: 410–12). For a discussion, see Christine F. Salazar, *The Treatment of War Wounds in Graeco-Roman Antiquity* (Leiden: Brill, 2000), 46–50.

29. Hippocrates, *On Wounds* 8, 10 (LCL 482: 348, 350). On stitches and sutures in general, see Celsus, *On Medicine* 5.26.23 (LCL 304: 82–86).

30. See, for example, Martial, *Epigram* 1.47 (LCL 95: 58); Hippolytus, *Omnium Haeresium Refutatio*, 9.10 (*PG* 16.3: 3375); and Augustine, *De Civitate Dei* 22.8 (CCL 48.2: 567–68). On the general distrust of physicians, see Ralph Jackson, *Doctors and Diseases in the Roman Empire* (Norman: University of Oklahoma Press, 1988), 10, 57–60.

31. Hippocrates, *Decorum* 16 (LCL 148: 296–98).

32. See, for example, Plato, *Gorgias* 456b. On blaming patients for obstructing treatments, see Hippocrates, *Art of Medicine* 7 (LCL 148: 200).

33. Celsus, *On Medicine* 7, prooem. (LCL 336: 296).

34. Ibid. 5.26.26 (LCL 304: 90); on fevers accompanying severe wounds, see Hippocrates, *Epidemics* 5.65, 97 (LCL 477: 198, 212).

35. See the examples of Marius (Plutarch, *Lives: Life of Marius* 6.3 [LCL 101: 476–77]), Alexander (Quintus Curtius, *History of Alexander* 9.5.27–28 [LCL 369: 412–13]), and Epaminondas (Cicero, *Tusculan*

Disputations 2.24 [LCL 141: 212]). On how this ideal was also reflected in artistic representations, see Salazar, *Treatment*, 245-46.

36. For example, Gregory of Nazianzus and Augustine (Susan B. Griffith, "*Iatros* and *Medicus:* The Physician in Gregory Nazianzen and Augustine," in *Orientalia: Clement, Origen, Athanasius, the Cappadocians, Chrysostom*, ed. F. Young, M. Edwards, and P. Parvis [Louvain: Peeters, 2006], 323-24).

37. See Marx-Wolf and Upson-Saia, "State of the Question," 257-72.

38. As I set out to research dozens of early Christian texts that employed the metaphors "wounds of sin" or "wounds of heresy," I was interested in how early Christian authors used wounds as their chief metaphor for sin and heresy and why this rhetorical strategy was able to consolidate orthodox beliefs and practices. Although the discourses of sin and heresy should not be conflated entirely, early Christian moralists and heresiologists used remarkably consistent figures to conceptualize, describe, and police sin and heresy. Thus, for the purposes of this paper, I will merge the discourses when early Christians' figurative language in them overlaps. Given my interest in broad structures of language, my discussion proceeds on a rather general level. More work needs to be done to investigate the nuanced ways in which wound metaphors were deployed in specific contexts.

39. In this section, I draw examples of passages from a range of primary sources, but we should also recall the titles of two famous heresiological texts: Epiphanius's *Panarion* (Medicine Chest) and Theodoret's *Graecarum Affectionum Curatio* (Treatment for Greek [i.e., pagan] Illnesses).

40. Origen writes: "As often as the soul sins, just so often it is wounded ... [like] someone repeatedly wounded in the same spot" (*In Numeros Homilia 8* [SC 415: 212-14; trans. Thomas P. Scheck, *Origen: Homilies on Numbers* [Downers Grove, Ill.: InterVarsity Press, 2009], 34). Cf. Clement of Alexandria, *Christ the Educator* 2.2 (*Paedagogus*, ed. M. Marcovich, Supplements to Vigiliae Christianae 61: 80); John Chrysostom, *Homilia 31 in Epistolam Primam ad Corinthios* (PG 61: 264); idem, *Homilia 6.4 in Epistolam Secundam ad Timotheum* (PG 62: 634); Jerome, *Dialogus adversus Pelagianos* 3.11 (CCL 80: 111); Augustine, *Confessions* 3.2, 6.15 (PL 32: 683, 731-32); idem, *In Iohannis Evangelium Tractatus* 25.16 (CCL 36: 256-57); Ps.-Athanasius, *Vita S. Syncleticae* 51 (PG 28: 1517).

41. Origen, *De Principiis* 3.2.4 (SC 268: 172-74; trans. G. W. Butterworth, *Origen: On First Principles* [Gloucester, Mass.: Peter Smith, 1973], 218); cf. Hippolytus, *In Susannam* 10 (PG 10: 691); Origen, *In Numeros Homilia 8* (SC 415: 212-14); idem, *In Numeros Homilia 20* (SC 461: 20); Ephrem the Syrian, *Hymnus 22.17 de Nativitate* (*Des heiligen Ephraem des Syrers Hymnen de Nativitate*, ed. and trans. Edmund Beck, CSCO 186: 112); Epiphanius, *Panarion* 1.25 (GCS 25, Epiphanius 1: 267); Ps.-Athanasius, *Vita S. Syncleticae* 49, 65 (PG 28: 1516-17, 1525).

42. Tertullian, *Scorpiace* 1.5, 9-10 (CCL 2: 1069-70; trans. Geoffrey D. Dunn, *Tertullian* [New York: Routledge, 2004], 108-9); cf. Irenaeus, *Adversus Haereses* 4, pref. (SC 100: 386-90); Cyprian, *Ep.* 30.7 (*Epistulae 1-57*, ed. G. Diercks, CCL 3B: 148-49); Ephrem the Syrian, *Hymnus 1.3 de Virginitate* (*Des heiligen Ephraem des Syrers Hymnen de Virginitate*, ed. and trans. Edmund Beck, CSCO 223: 2); Leo the Great, *Homily 16 on the Fast of the Tenth Month* (*Tractatus*, ed. Antoine Chavasse, CCL 138: 63).

43. Augustine, *In Iohannis Evangelium Tractatus* 25.16 (CCL 36: 256-57). For a combination of all three causes, see Antony, *Ep.* 1.49-72 (Samuel Rubenson, *The Letters of St. Antony: Monasticism and the Making of a Saint* [Minneapolis: Fortress Press, 1990], 200-202).

44. Clement of Alexandria, *Christ the Educator* 2.2 (*Paedagogus*, ed. Marcovich, Supplements to Vigiliae Christianae 61: 80).

45. Augustine, *Confessions* 8.7 (PL 32: 756; trans. Maria Boulding, *The Confessions*, part 1, vol. 1 of *The Works of Saint Augustine: A Translation for the Twenty-First Century* [Hyde Park, N.Y.: New City Press, 1997], 169); cf. Ephrem the Syrian, *Hymnus 5.19 de Fide* (*Des heiligen Ephraem des Syrers Hymnen de Fide*, ed. and trans. Edmund Beck, CSCO 154: 23).

46. Origen, *In Numeros Homilia 8* (SC 415: 214; trans. Scheck, *Homilies on Numbers*, 34); cf. Ephrem the Syrian, *Hymnus 1.9 contra Julianum* (*Des heiligen Ephraem des Syrers Hymnen de Paradiso und contra Julianum*, ed. and trans. Edmund Beck, 174:73).

47. Tertullian, *Scorpiace* 1.10 (CCL 2: 1070; trans. Dunn, *Tertullian*, 109, amended); cf. John Chrysostom, *Commentarius in Epistolam ad Galatas* 1 (PG 61: 622).

48. Irenaeus, *Adversus Haereses* 4, pref. (SC 100: 386–90); Tertullian, *Scorpiace* 1.5, 9 (CCL 2: 1069–70); Cyprian, *Ep.* 30.7 (*Epistulae 1–57*, ed. Diercks, CCL 3B: 148–49); Ambrose, *De Fide*, 3.16.132 (CSEL 78: 154–55); Leo the Great, *Homily 16 on the Fast of the Tenth Month* 3 (*Tractatus*, ed. Chavasse, CCL 138: 63).

49. Aphrahat, *Demonstrationes* 7.24 (PS 1: 353); Irenaeus, *Adversus Haereses* 4, pref. (SC 100: 386–90); Athanasius, *Epistola ad Episcopos Aegypti et Libyae* 1.5 (*Athanasius: Werke* 1.1.1, ed. K. Metzler [Berlin: de Gruyter, 1996], 40–41); Basil of Caesarea, *Quod Deus Non Est Auctor Malorum* 3 (PG 31: 333); Ambrose, *De Fide*, 3.16.132 (CSEL 78: 154–55); John Chrysostom, *Homilia 12 in Acta Apostolorum* (PG 60: 101); Leo the Great, *Homily 16.3 on the Fast of the Tenth Month* 3 (*Tractatus*, ed. Chavasse, CCL 138: 63); *Life of John the Nazirite* (John of Ephesus, *Lives of the Eastern Saints* 3, PO 17: 55).

50. Antony, *Ep.* 2.9–15; 3.20–21; 5.18–23; 6.7–12, 87–91; 7.26–29 (Rubenson, *Letters of St. Antony*, 203–4, 207, 213, 216, 222, 227). For a discussion of this motif in Antony's letters, see Andrew T. Crislip, *Thorns in the Flesh: Illness and Sanctity in Late Ancient Christianity* (Philadelphia: University of Pennsylvania Press, 2013), 51–54.

51. On the relationship between embodiment, concepts, and affect, see the references cited in note 15 above.

52. Susan Ashbrook Harvey, *Scenting Salvation: Ancient Christianity and the Olfactory Imagination* (Berkeley and Los Angeles: University of California Press, 2006), 207–10. The words of the Psalmist—"My wounds stink and are corrupt because of my foolishness" (Psalm 38:5)—were an apt exclamation to be uttered by sinners and heretics. On the use of this psalm, see John Chrysostom, *Homilia 2 in Epistolam Secundam ad Timotheum* (PG 62: 514); idem, *Homilia 44 in Epistolam Primam ad Corinthios* (PG 61: 378); Augustine, *Confessions* 6.15 (PL 32: 731–32).

53. See, for instance, Epiphanius, *Panarion* 1.26 (GCS 25, Epiphanius 1: 275); Jerome, *Commentary on Micah* 2.7 (*Commentarii in Prophetas Minores*, ed. M. Adriaen, CCL 76: 505); *Life of John the Nazirite* (John of Ephesus, *Lives of the Eastern Saints* 3, PO 17: 50–55); Simon of Ṭaibūtheh, *Medico-Mystical Work* 200b (*Early Christian Mystics*, ed. and trans. A. Mingana [Cambridge: W. Heffer and Sons, 1934], 68); John Chrysostom, *Ad Eos Qui Scandalizati Sunt*, prol. (SC 79: 52–54).

54. Harvey, *Scenting Salvation*, 210.

55. Origen, *De Principiis* 3.1.13 (SC 268: 76–80; trans. Butterworth, *Origen: On First Principles*, 181–82, amended).

56. John Chrysostom, *Homilia 6 de Statuis ad Populum Antiochenum* (PG 49: 89; *St. Chrysostom: On the Priesthood, Ascetic Treatises, Select Homilies and Letters, Homilies on the Statues*, trans. W. R. W. Stephens, R. Blackburn, and T. P. Brandram, NPNF, ser. 1, 9: 387).

57. Basil of Caesarea, *Quod Deus Non Est Auctor Malorum* 3 (PG 31: 333; *St. Basil: On the Human Condition*, trans. Verna Harrison [Crestwood, N.Y.: St. Vladimir's Seminary Press, 2005], 68); cf. Tertullian, *De Paenitentia* 10 (CCL 1: 337–38); idem, *Adversus Marcionem* 2.16 (CCL 1: 492–93); Origen, *Contra Celsum* 6.56 (SC 147: 318–320); John Chrysostom, *Homilia 1 de Imbecillitate Diaboli* (PG 49: 251–52); Augustine, *Sermo 77.3 in Matthaeum* 15:21 (*Sermones de Scripturis*, PL 38: 484).

58. John Chrysostom, *Homilia 10 in Epistolam ad Hebraeos* (PG 63: 84–85); cf. Ephrem the Syrian, *Hymnus 3.20 de Nativitate* (*Des heiligen Ephraem des Syrers Hymnen de Nativitate*, ed. and trans. Beck, CSCO 186: 24).

59. Augustine, *Sermo 77.3 in Matthaeum* 15:21 (*Sermones de Scripturis*, PL 38: 484). Thus sinners are to show their wounds to God with a contrite and penitent heart (Ambrose, *De Poenitentia* 1.7.31, 2.8.66 [SC 179: 80, 174–76]).

60. John Chrysostom, *Hom. against Publishing the Errors of the Brethren* 1 (*St. Chrysostom: On the Priesthood, Ascetic Treatises, Select Homilies and Letters, Homilies on the Statues*, trans. W. R. W. Stephens, R. Blackburn, and T. P. Brandram, NPNF, ser. 1, 9: 235). See also Anonymous, *Treatise against*

Novatian 6 (CCL 4: 141–42). Should they refuse to offer such aid, they are ignoring Jesus's call to tend to the wounded like the good Samaritan in Luke 10:30–37 (ibid. 1 [CCL 4: 137]). On the special obligation of clerics and bishops to tend to the wounds of their brethren, see Ambrose, *De Officiis Ministrorum* 2.27 (CCL 15: 145–46).

    61. John Chrysostom, *Ad Theodorum Lapsum* 1.15 (16) (SC 117: 176; trans. NPNF, ser. 1, 9: 105); cf. *Didascalia Apostolorum* 10 (CSCO 401: 121); Ephrem the Syrian, *II Sermo* 1.715–22 (*Des heiligen Ephraem des Syrers Sermones*, ed. and trans. Edmund Beck, CSCO 311: 14); Ambrose, *De Officiis Ministrorum* 3.22 (CCL 15: 200–204); idem, *Ep.* 41.4 (*Epistulae et Acta*, ed. O. Faller and M. Zelzer, CSEL 82.3: 146–47); John Chrysostom, *Homilia 4 in Epistolam Secundam ad Corinthios* (PG 61: 421); idem, *Homilia 44 in Epistolam Primam ad Corinthios* (PG 61: 377); Jerome, *Commentary on Micah* 2.7 (*Commentarii in Prophetas Minores*, CCL 76: 50); Augustine, *Sermo 83.8 in Matthaeum 17:21* (*Sermones de Scripturis*, PL 38: 518).

    Ambrose and John Chrysostom further justify rebuke as a constituent feature of friendship by appealing to Proverbs 27:6: "The wounds of a friend are better than the kisses of flatterers" (Ambrose, *De Officiis Ministrorum* 1.34, 3.22 [CCL 15: 63, 201]; idem, *Ep.* 41.4 to Marcellina [PL 16: 1161]; John Chrysostom, *In Eutropium Homilia 1* [PG 52: 392]).

    62. Augustine, *In Epistolam Joannis ad Parthos Tractatus* 9.4 (SC 75: 386); also *St. Augustine: Homilies on the Gospel of John, Homilies on the First Epistle of John, Soliloquies*, trans. John Gibb, H. Browne, and C. C. Starbuck, NPNF, ser. 1, 7: 515–16).

    63. Gregory the Great, *Pastoral Rule* 3.25 (*Règle pastorale*, ed. Bruno Judic and Floribert Rommel, trans. Charles Morel, SC 382: 430); also *Leo the Great, Letters and Sermons; Gregory the Great, The Book of Pastoral Rule and Selected Epistles*, trans. Charles Lett Feltoe and James Barmby, NPNF, ser. 2, 12: 53); cf. Aphrahat, *Demonstrationes* 7.4 (PS 1: 317–20); John Chrysostom, *Homilia 14 in Epistolam Secundam ad Corinthios* (PG 61: 501).

    64. Gregory of Nazianzus, *Oratio* 2.18 (*Discours 1–3*, ed. Jean Bernardi, SC 247: 114).

    65. Augustine, *Ep. 104.2 to Nectarius* (CSEL 34.2: 587; trans. J. G. Cunningham, *The Confessions and Letters of St. Augustine*, NPNF, ser. 1, 1: 429); idem, *Sermo 83.8 in Matthaeum 17:21* (*Sermones de Scripturis*, PL 38: 518); cf. Ambrose, *De Officiis Ministrorum* 1.34, 2.27, 3.22 (CCL 15: 64, 145, 201); idem, *Ep.* 41.4 (*Epistulae et Acta*, ed. Faller and Zelzer, CSEL 82.3: 146–47). On the treatment necessary to heal not only the visible symptoms but the source of the sin, see Augustine, *in Iohannis Evangelium Tractatus* 25.16 (CCL 36: 256–57).

    66. John Chrysostom, *Homilia 30 in Epistolam ad Hebraeos* (PG 63: 212; also *St. Chrysostom: Homilies on the Gospel of St. John and the Epistle to the Hebrews*, trans. Frederic Gardiner, NPNF, ser. 1, 14: 505).

    67. See medical writers' advice on bedside manner in Hippocrates, *Decorum* 3, 7, 12, 16 (LCL 148: 280–82, 290, 294, 296–98).

    68. John Chrysostom, *Homilia 30 in Epistolam ad Hebraeos* (PG 63: 212; trans. Gardiner, NPNF, ser. 1, 14: 505).

    69. John Chrysostom, *Commentarius in Epistolam ad Galatas* 4 (PG 61: 660; also *St. Chrysostom: Homilies on Galatians, Ephesians, Philippians, Colossians, Thessalonians, Timothy, Titus, and Philemon*, trans. Gross Alexander and John A. Broadus, NPNF, ser. 1, 13: 33); cf. idem, *Homilia 13 in Epistolam Primam ad Corinthios* (PG 61: 109); idem, *Homily against Publishing the Errors of the Brethren* 3–4 (*St. Chrysostom: On the Priesthood, Ascetic Treatises, Select Homilies and Letters, Homilies on the Statues*, trans. W. R. W. Stephens, R. Blackburn, and T. P. Brandram, NPNF, ser. 1, 9: 236–37).

    70. Idem, *De Sacerdotio* 2.4 (SC 272: 112–14; also *St. Chrysostom: On the Priesthood, Ascetic Treatises, Select Homilies and Letters, Homilies on the Statues*, trans. W. R. W. Stephens, R. Blackburn, and T. P. Brandram, NPNF, ser. 1, 9: 41); cf. id., *Homilia 6.2 in Epistolam Secundam ad Timotheum* (PG 62: 632). Canon 102 of Council of Trullo directs clergy to assess "the disposition of him who has sinned"—namely whether he welcomes or resists treatment—before prescribing a gentle or harsh treatment for

"the ulcer of the soul" (*Conciliorum Oecumenicorum Generaliumque Decreta* 1: 292–93; also *The Seven Ecumenical Councils*, ed. and trans. Henry R. Percival, NPNF, ser. 2, 14: 408). See also Origen, *In Numeros Homilia 8* (SC 415: 212–14).

71. John Chrysostom, *Commentarius in Epistolam ad Galatas* 1 (PG 61: 622).

72. Idem, *In Eutropium Homilia 1* (PG 52: 393).

73. *Didascalia Apostolorum* 10 (CSCO 401: 121); Ambrose, *De Officiis Ministrorum* 2.27 (CCL 15: 145); John Chrysostom, *Homilia 31 in Epistolam Primam ad Corinthios* (PG 61: 264); idem, *Homilia 6.3 in Epistolam Secundam ad Timotheum* (PG 62: 633); Augustine, *Confessions* 6.15 (PL 32.731–32).

74. *Didascalia Apostolorum* 10 (CSCO 401: 121; trans. Vööbus, CSCO 402: 115); cf. Cyprian, *De Lapsis* 15 (CCL 3: 229); Aphrahat, *Demonstrationes* 7.24 (PS 1: 353); Basil of Caesarea, *Homilia Quod Deus Non Est Auctor Malorum* 3 (PG 31: 333); Ambrose, *De Fide* 3.16.132 (CSEL 78: 154–55); John Chrysostom, *Homilia 12 in Acta Apostolorum* (PG 60: 101). Taking a contrary position, Gregory and John Chrysostom argue that, unlike some bodily wounds that are deemed untreatable by medical science (Hippocrates, *Art of Medicine* 8 [LCL 148: 202–4]), the wounds of the soul—if caught early enough and treated properly—are always curable (John Chrysostom, *Ad Theodorum Lapsum* 1.15 (16) [SC 117: 176]; NPNF, ser. 1, 9105]; cf. Gregory the Great, *Pastoral Rule*, 3.25 [*Règle pastorale*, ed. Judic and Rommel, trans. Morel, SC 382: 430]).

75. The patient-physician relationship also structured the compliance and obedience that lay people showed to rabbis. See Mira Balberg, "Rabbinic Authority, Medical Rhetoric and Body Hermeneutics in Mishnah Nega'im," *AJS Review* 35.2 (2011): 323–46.

76. Aphrahat, *Demonstrationes* 7.3 (PS 1: 317); cf. *Life of John the Nazirite* (John of Ephesus, *Lives of the Eastern Saints* 3, PO 17: 49, 52–55). Contrast the one who does not seek the necessary treatment (Aphrahat, *Demonstrationes* 7.5 [PS 1: 320–21]).

77. Basil, *Longer Responses* 55.3 (trans. Anna Silvas, *The Asketikon of St. Basil the Great* [Oxford: Oxford University Press, 2005], 266); cf. Ephrem the Syrian, *Hymnus 3.10 de Virginitate* (*Des heiligen Ephraem des Syrers Hymnen de Virginitate*, ed. and trans. Beck, CSCO 223: 11); Gregory of Nazianzus, *Oratio* 33.6 (*Discours*, ed. Bernardi, SC 318: 168–70).

78. Alluding to Eph. 6:12; Gerontius, *Life of Melania* 16 (SC 90: 158; trans. E. A. Clark, 39).

79. Palladius, *Lausiac History* 38.8 (ed. Cuthbert Butler, *The Lausiac History of Palladius: A Critical Discussion Together with Notes on Early Egyptian Monachism* [Cambridge: Cambridge University Press, 1898; reprint, Hildesheim: Georg Olms, 1967], 119).

80. Palladius, *Lausiac History* 38.9 (ed. C. Butler, 119–20).

81. Ibid. 24.2–3 (ed. C. Butler, 78; trans. Robert T. Meyer, *Palladius: The Lausiac History* [Westminster, Md.: Newman Press, 1965], 84); cf. Sozomen, *Historia Ecclesiastica* 6.29 (PG 67: 1380–81).

82. Palladius, *Lausiac History* 24.2 (ed. C. Butler, 78, trans. Meyer, 83–84). In like manner, Aaron "bore the distress [of gangrenous loins] with great devoutness. . . . [He] stoutly endured" (*Life of Aaron* [John of Ephesus, *Lives of the Eastern Saints*, PO 18: 643]). Compare also Theodoret's description of Symeon's endurance of a severe wound, "one that a great quantity of pus oozed from continually," in *Religious History* 26.23 (*Histoire des moines de Syrie: Histoire Philothée*, ed. and trans. Pierre Canivet and Alice Leroy-Molinghen, SC 257: 206).

83. The ideal comportment of an ascetic lines up with that of a patient even in scenes that do not involve bodily afflictions. For instance, when Melania the Younger offers advice on fasting in particular and on ascetic contests in general, she recommends that ascetics endure these hardships with "patience and long-suffering" (Gerontius, *Life of Melania* 45 [SC 90: 214; trans. E. A. Clark, 59]). Offering a different logic, Syncletica explains that the pain that accompanies bodily injuries sometimes distracts the ascetic from the passions of the body; thus they should be considered treatments that "bring health to the inner person" (Ps.-Athanasius, *Vita S. Syncleticae* 99 [PG 28: 1549]).

84. Gerontius seems to have jumped forward in time; he explains that Melania's divine wound led her to *intensify* her ascetic regime, implying that she had already made her vow (*Life of Melania* 31–32

[SC 90: 186–88; trans. E. A. Clark, 48–49]). Gerontius suggests that God enabled the young Melania—whose delicate skin was irritated even by the finest clothing—to withstand pain and irritation when she donned far harsher garments, such as a hood of haircloth.

85. We should not ignore the placement of the metaphor immediately after this scene. In fact, we may wonder if the modern chapter divisions inappropriately separate and thus occlude the connection between Melania's being wounded by divine love and the story about her physical wound.

86. In another scene, Melania (and with her Pinian) "suffered much pain" when she was prohibited from taking a vow and forced to live what she considered a sinful life (Gerontius, *Life of Melania* 6; cf. 7, 12 [SC 90: 138, cf. 140, 150; trans. E. A. Clark, 30; 31, 35–36]). When her parents and husband finally acceded to her wishes and Melania was able to live the ascetic life that she desired, "she got better and completely regained her health" (Gerontius, *Life of Melania* 6 [SC 90: 136; trans. E. A. Clark, 30]).

87. Medical notions of wounds may be operating in the first few chapters as well. After Melania's failed attempt to convince her husband to renounce sexuality, Gerontius writes that Melania's "heart burned even more strongly with divine fire," perhaps an indication that Melania's contrition had reached a fever pitch (*Life of Melania* 2 [SC 90: 132; trans. E. A. Clark, 28]).

88. Kirmayer, "The Body's Insistence on Meaning," 325.

PART THREE

Gender and Memory

BEYOND THEIR SHARED ARISTOCRATIC wealth and their simple human frailty, Melania the Elder and Melania the Younger also navigated a world that was sharply defined by gender roles. To some extent, as we have already seen, these roles could take different forms in contexts of wealth or poverty, sickness or health. But the limited range of gender roles available to women in this period also determined how the Melanias could fit into, or fight against, previously established patterns of female behavior, and how they could be remembered by their male followers. The celebrated female ascetic was a new role that Christianity made possible, and yet this role interacted uneasily with earlier stories about women. Melania the Elder and Melania the Younger were ascetic women who challenged traditional Roman notions of gender, but they were not the only ones who did so. All these women had their status as women questioned, as when Paulinus of Nola exclaims about Melania the Elder that he is not certain that he can call someone with such manly virtues a woman. The discrepancy lay in a dichotomy between ancient notions of nature and body. Thus Palladius likewise says about another female ascetic, Olympias, that she cannot be called a woman, since she is a man despite her body. What is more, women could make similar claims about themselves, echoing this gender hierarchy of masculine superiority that some women, usually through asceticism and its attendant manly virtues, could attain. The Egyptian hermit Amma Sarah of the Desert famously denied being female in nature, though still female in body, and in another saying she switched gender with inferior ascetic men, making herself the man and them the women. Over and over again, these women were able to perform masculinity, sometimes in male dress, to a degree that overcame their bodily categorization.

There is, of course, an element of mythmaking in the literary depictions of these women. The linguistic turn in history, which calls our attention to how historical writing shapes our understanding of the past through literary means, calls into question the agency and autonomy of such ancient women—and at times even their real existence. Thus, even as young female ascetics seemingly exercise their autonomy to refuse marriage, or others are able to resist the pressures to remarry, each does so in a way that clearly reinforces the larger ecclesiastical concerns of the male writers who tell their stories. Witty rejoinders, philosophical speeches, and even biblical exegesis lend these women voices of authority, but the holy words are not necessarily their own. The purpose of these words, moreover, often lies in educating, or shaming, a predominantly male audience. Yet, as with myths, early Christian audiences would have experienced these figures—even those whose historicity may be questioned—as real. They served as examples of what was possible through the transformative aspects of Christianity, or more specifically through the transformative power of Christ: a space between this world—and its social conventions of gender—and the next, the eschatological expectation of a world in which there was neither male nor female. In this section, both essays address the construction of women through the lens of memory or tradition. Stephanie Cobb asks how stories of the female martyrs Perpetua and Felicitas lived on, in altered form, in fourth-century accounts, and how these stories intersected with the lives of women in the age of the Melanias. She argues that some elements of the third-century narrative are emphasized, magnified, and even fabricated to align with the ascetic ideals of the later age. These changes in emphasis and development of tradition lay bare the process by which shifting social and theological concerns create new versions of womanhood. Rebecca Krawiec looks at one of the Melanias herself, the Elder, in relationship to monastic memory. Melania's long-recognized status as a masculinized woman receives a new treatment through examining how she remembers, as well as how she is remembered in Palladius's *Lausiac History*. Both pieces engage the theoretical challenges of studying gender in the age of the Melanias and propose that, although the real women may be beyond recovery, their gendered selves remain.

6

Memories of the Martyrs

L. Stephanie Cobb

In her article "The Lady Vanishes: Dilemmas of a Feminist Historian after the 'Linguistic Turn,'" Elizabeth A. Clark asks how attention to the issues raised by literary theory may cause us to read texts differently.[1] She focuses especially on women's history: "The desire of many feminists to uncover 'real women,' to hear 'real female voices,' is often thwarted when these texts are subjected to theoretical critique."[2] Even as Clark acknowledges the importance of quests for historical women—it is a desire that we should not dismiss even if it is more complex than we once hoped—she proposes that we move toward Gabrielle Spiegel's notion of the "social logic" of a text in order to notice "interesting themes that prompt different explorations of these texts in their cultural milieu and relate them to other texts of the period."[3] The social logic of the early Christian texts that Clark goes on to explore has less to do with real women than with elaborating theological issues relevant for an author's audience.

The Life of Melania the Younger serves as an example for Clark. Although the *vita* is ostensibly about the female ascetic Melania, much of Clark's work examines how the figure of Melania is put to work by her hagiographer. For instance, although the historical Melania seems to have associated with heterodox figures, the *vita* places her squarely in orthodox camps, even going so far as to erase the memory of Melania's grandmother, who was associated with the Origenist controversy.[4] Thus Clark demonstrates how the *Life of Melania the Younger* was used to further fifth-century ecclesiastical interests in asceticism and orthodoxy.

The *vita* also stands as an important witness to dramatic shifts in ecclesiastical interest between the third and the fifth century—from a discourse of martyrdom to a discourse of asceticism. Although the age of the martyrs may seem like a distant—or at least discrete—era from the height of asceticism, Gillian Clark reminds us of their temporal proximity: "The ascetics of the late fourth century were only half a century away from victims of persecution under Diocletian."[5] Public torture and execution—identical to the experiences of the martyrs—continued to be part of Late Roman penal codes, and thus they served as reminders of martyrs' faithfulness in the face of physical assault.[6] Martyr stories, moreover, were read and expounded not only in basilicas on feast days but also in the growing web of shrines outside city centers where large groups of Christians might gather to remember—and benefit from—the martyrs.[7] Thus the rise of the relic cult and the popular piety practiced at martyria across the empire made the martyrs' faith ever-present to late ancient Christians.

The continued importance of martyrs may also be seen in ascetic *vitae*, which, as scholars note, appropriated discourses of martyrdom. Elizabeth Clark, for instance, explains that "the church fathers frequently asserted that asceticism was a new form of martyrdom, one in which we could be martyred daily."[8] Comparisons between martyrdom and asceticism may be dated as early as Cyprian, who equated the crowns received by suffering (red) with those that were a product of "labors" (white).[9] Gregory the Great asserted that martyrdom is earned equally by public or secret suffering; even without experiencing external persecution, that is, the individual who desires suffering may be considered a martyr.[10] Isabelle Kinnard argues that by the late sixth century, the "linkage is . . . seamless" between ascetics and martyrs: ascetic discourse so fully appropriated martyrdom that ascetics *were* martyrs.[11] Similarly, as Sebastian Brock notes, "the ascetic is in many ways the successor of the martyr. To the early church the martyr represented an ideal, and after the end of the persecutions, when this ideal was no longer attainable, it was replaced by that of the ascetic, whose whole life was in fact often regarded in terms of a martyrdom."[12] Indeed, on occasion the sufferings of the ascetic were claimed to be even more significant than those of the martyr.[13]

The ideal Christians of ascetic *vitae* are often described in terms reminiscent of martyrs: they are athletes or soldiers whose endurance of contests and sufferings has earned them the crowns and laurels of victors. Such language is ubiquitous in the *Life of Melania the Younger*. Gerontius, for instance, voices concern about his ability to relate Melania's "great contests" (*agōnōn*: prol.). Nonetheless, he describes them, confident that Melania's story will glorify even those who "have contested [*agōnisamenōn*] up to the very point of death" (prol.).[14] Melania taught that those who "endure [*hypomeinate*] a little" will be "crowned with the wreath of righteousness" (45). The empress Serena describes Melania and Pinian as having "suffered [*peponthasin*] in their renunciation" (12). Melania, moreover, is said to have "delivered herself to death daily," and she was "persecuted" by her father (*ediōchthēsan*: 12). Her renunciations are described as a "battle" (*palē*: 16) and a "contest" (*agōsin*: 32). Melania related a dream in which she and Pinian passed through a narrow opening in a wall and "came through that pain with great suffering." The dream signaled to Melania the promise of future reward in return for present suffering (16; cf. 34). The saint "prepared herself to contend in even greater contests" by shutting herself in a small cell and devoting herself to prayer and fasting (32); she even had prepared for herself a "wooden chest" that did not allow for physical movement when she was lying in it (32). The language of endurance (*hypomenō*), so typical of martyr narratives, is also used of Melania (34). In addition, the text—like martyr narratives preceding it—appropriates athletic language: Melania is described as a runner who comes to the stadium desiring the trophy (63), and Pinian is described as being "crowned with a wreath" at his death in reward for "having fought the good fight" (49). Perhaps the most overt appropriation of martyr language and imagery within the *vita* is Albina's comparison of herself to the Maccabean mother, which simultaneously implies a correlation between Melania and the Jewish martyrs (33). Thus *The Life of Melania the Younger* offers one—certainly not unique—example of how ascetic discourse appropriates the language of martyrdom.

Terminology is not the only way that the *vita* recalls martyrdom. The cult of the martyrs also plays a significant role in the author's construction of Melania's piety.[15] It is, after all, at a martyrium that Melania's desire for continence is granted: after her vigil observing St. Lawrence's feast day, Melania prematurely gives birth to a son who dies soon thereafter. The toll that the difficult birth takes on Melania (perhaps a consequence, as Gillian Clark surmises, of Melania's all-night vigil) convinces Pinian to agree to a life of continence (5–6).[16] Later, when in the Holy Land, Melania arranges for the relics of Zechariah, Stephen, the Forty Martyrs of Sebaste, and others to be placed in the oratory of the monastery that she built in Jerusalem (48). Indeed, Clark has demonstrated that Gerontius constructs Melania's piety, in part, by assigning to her the possession of Stephen's relics.[17] Her journey to Constantinople begins a cycle of stories centering on martyr shrines: she and her group first stay at the martyrium of St. Leontius and receive the aid of the martyr in obtaining the release of their animals (52); before entering Constantinople, the group stops at the martyrium of St. Euphemia in Chalcedon, where an anxious Melania receives comfort from the saint (53). Toward the end of the *vita* Gerontius relates a number of miracles performed by Melania, many of which involve the appropriation of saints' power via relics. Melania, for instance, heals a possessed woman by applying to the woman's mouth consecrated oil from martyrs' relics (60), and she helps a woman whose fetus has died in utero by binding about the woman the belt of a saint (61). Melania's death is recounted in relationship to her visit to the martyrium of St. Stephen and the celebration of his feast day (64). Her final prayers repeatedly invoke the martyrs, both relating their faithfulness and pleading for their intercession (64). After her death, she is clothed in various garments and belongings of saints, "for it was fitting that she be buried in the garments of those whose virtues she had acquired while she was living" (69). Thus the story of the famous ascetic Melania is infused at numerous levels with the discourse of martyrdom; it clearly draws inspiration from earlier *passiones* and is filled with their language, making claims to their memories.

Ascetic authors, however, did not merely borrow the language of martyrdom; they also *reconstituted* martyrdom. Since the interest in linking asceticism and martyrdom appears to have developed in the fourth century, the *Acta Perpetuae et Felicitatis* offer an opportunity to trace this discursive appropriation. In what follows, then, I hope to shed light on some ways that the *Acta* recount but also rework and, I suggest, reclaim the exemplary lives and deaths of two North African martyrs, Perpetua and Felicitas. I will argue that the fourth-century *Acta* reconceptualize the third-century *Passio* by placing the martyrs in the service of developing ascetic interests. Although the memories of the martyrs were certainly not fading when Melania undertook her travels, certain of their stories were being revisited, refreshed, and reappropriated to exemplify new constructions of Christian piety and, perhaps, to offer models of ascetic life to women like Melania.

By focusing on the social logic of the *Acta*, this chapter asks a different set of questions than typically have been asked of these texts.[18] When scholars discuss the *Acta* and other retellings of Perpetua's and Felicitas's story, their concerns are often with the texts' derivative status and misogynistic nature.[19] But if we read these later accounts as contributions to an ascetic discourse—rather than as distortions of Perpetua's real words—we may better appreciate their social function.[20] Shifting our focus from questions of historicity to questions about the discourses in which these texts participate allows us to read the *Acta* as sharing in a larger collection of reflections on an earlier martyrological tradition. Furthermore, I propose that reading these texts as products of a new political and ecclesiastical milieu—namely as texts emerging from a postpersecution church that demonstrate affinities with the ascetic movement—may offer new insights into the differences among the stories. From this perspective, the social logic of the *Acta* has less to do with a misogynistic Christian impulse and more to do with appropriating stories about exemplary martyrs to make them relevant for the church in a new age.

ACTA

The fourth-century *Acta* are extant in two Latin versions, which may have been created to meet liturgical needs for brief accounts of the martyrdoms.[21] Three trends in the *Acta* may offer clues to the authors' ascetic interests: the texts highlight the theme of renunciation; they relate the events to communal rather than individual concerns; there is a narrative emphasis on the Fall and the relationship between asceticism and the restoration of humanity.

Renunciation

Both *Acta* begin with a cursory interrogation scene in which the proconsul Minutius commands the Christians to sacrifice; after their refusal, they are returned to prison (I.1.1–3, II.1.1–3). The next scene in *Acta* I is reminiscent of the *Passio:* Perpetua explains to her father that as a vase can go by no other name, so she cannot be called anything other than "Christian" (I.1.2). Her father's response is to lunge at her, determined to "dig out her eyes" (I.2.3). This interaction is markedly different in *Acta* II: in this version, Perpetua's father expresses the shame that her imprisonment has brought on the family. Perpetua responds: "If you want your daughter to be perpetual, the perpetual and blessed life is not able to be obtained without confession of Christ and the contempt [*contemptum*] of the present world" (II.2.2). In both versions—albeit in different ways—the theme of renouncing the world is underscored by the introductory scenes. *Acta* I focuses on naming: Perpetua renounces all forms of identity other than Christian; *Acta* II articulates a larger renunciation of the present world.

The next notable example of the theme of renunciation comes in *Acta* I.5. The proconsul calls the women before him and begins interrogating Felicitas. The proconsul asks if she has a husband, which gives Felicitas the opportunity to reject out of hand the institution of marriage: "I have, whom I now despise [*contemno*]" (I.5.3).[22] The proconsul pushes for information on her husband's whereabouts, to which she simply responds: "He is not here" (I.5.4). Felicitas is pressed yet further for information about other possible authority figures, presumably to whom the proconsul might appeal. She informs him that she does not have parents, allying herself only with her fellow Christian and brother Revocatus. Finally, Felicitas is urged to take pity on her unborn child.[23] In response, she asserts: "It is commanded to me to despise [*contemnere*] all things on account of God" (I.5.7). This short interview covers important ground: Felicitas is depicted as independent of all pagan male authority—though it is important that she acknowledges her brother Revocatus, who is also imprisoned as a Christian.[24] Furthermore, she "despises" the two family members who would most likely serve as emotional hindrances to her goal: husband and child. Renunciation of worldly attachments is an important theme in this episode, though the narrative does not subvert intra-Christian hierarchical interests, since Felicitas allies herself with her *congermanus* Revocatus.[25]

The narrative of *Acta* I then turns to the proconsul's much shorter interrogation of Perpetua. In a rhetorical flourish, Perpetua puns on her own name when asked if she will sacrifice: "I am a Christian and I follow the command of my name, to be perpetual" (I.5.10; cf. II.5.4).[26] The proconsul also asks Perpetua if she has parents, to which the soon-to-be-martyr replies simply yes. The narrative shifts at this point to Perpetua's family's arrival at court. Both *Acta* inform us that her parents, her brothers, and her husband, together with his child, came as soon as they heard of her arrest.[27] *Acta* II alone specifies the family's motive for coming: they were "endeavoring to soften the constancy of her faith" (II.6.1). *Acta* I recounts Perpetua's father's words in ways reminiscent of the *Passio*: he begs Perpetua—"now not daughter but woman"—to have pity on him, on her mother, on her brothers, on "this unfortunate husband of yours," and, finally, on her child, "who will not be able to live without" her (I.6.2). In the end, Perpetua does not pity her family members, countering her father's words with a (witty) plea and a promise: "Father, do not be afraid: if you do not stand in the way of your daughter Perpetua, you will possess a perpetual daughter" (I.6.3). The proconsul further suggests that Perpetua's parents' tears—or, at least, the cry of her child—should move her, but it is a proposition that she rejects: tears would move her only if she were found "apart from the sight of God and the fellowship of the saints" (I.6.4).

In the final act of the interrogation scene, Perpetua's father throws (*jactans*) her child at her neck, while he, her mother, and her husband beg her: "Have pity on us" (I.6.5). Readers familiar with the complexity of feelings related by the *Passio* may be surprised at Perpetua's single-minded response here.[28] Without signs of hesitation or sadness, Perpetua throws down (*proiciens*) the infant and drives back (*repellens*) her family members with a Gospel quotation: "Depart from me, workers of iniquity, for I do not know you" (I.6.6; II.6.6). It is, she asserts, not because of them but "on account of God" that she is able "to do greater and better things" (I.6.6). The interrogation scenes in the *Acta*, therefore, focus on the renunciation of marriage and family attachments. Both martyrs have contempt for their husbands, and both reject natal family in favor of their Christian family, an alliance that allows them to achieve "greater and better things."

Brent Shaw has characterized the author's presentation of the women in the *Acta* as "schizoid": on the one hand, "the women are to be praised—after all they *were* martyrs to the Christian faith. On the other hand, their actions are so unnatural, from the standpoint of male cultural expectations, that they are portrayed in an extreme and rather unlikeable manner."[29] Perpetua's actions, Shaw argues, "would be bound to elicit a negative reaction from (at least) the male listeners of the *Acta*."[30] Conversely, Rex Butler has argued that the author of the *Acta*, working against Montanist interests in the *Passio*, normalizes Perpetua's marital situation: "The redactor's inclusion of the husband restored the heroine to an orthodox family circle."[31] Butler argues that traditions about the Montanist prophets' rejection of their husbands influenced the portrayal of Perpetua in the *Passio*, and thus the introduction of Perpetua's husband in the *Acta* is a means of taming an otherwise socially subversive text.

Certainly there is ample evidence for growing concerns about women's power in the early church, as Shaw's and Butler's arguments suggest. But the trends in the *Acta* may be better understood as reflecting interests associated with the rise of the ascetic movement in North Africa rather than as serving primarily to indicate growing unease with Perpetua's words and her power. First, we should note that Perpetua's "own words"[32] are not excised in this narrative. If the *Acta* are read as digests of the *Passio* (as both Shaw and Butler do), and if we assume—again, with Shaw and Butler—that the *Passio* preserves historically reliable textual traditions originating with Perpetua—then it is true that *some* of Perpetua's words have been omitted, and that some words have been replaced by others. But, it is not the case that the *Acta* represent a silencing of the female martyr's voice. In fact, the inclusion of Felicitas's interrogation argues against an agenda focused primarily on silencing women. As in the *Passio*, the women's roles in the *Acta* are larger and more pronounced than the men's, and their witness is more complete: whereas each male martyr is given two sentences of testimony—one individual and one collective—Felicitas and Perpetua are given much more.

The presence of Perpetua's and Felicitas's husbands in the *Acta* may offer clues to understanding the social context within which to place these texts. Because Shaw and Butler—in different ways—approach the *Acta* as derivative texts, as texts that alter a historical, original witness, they interpret the differences between the *Passio* and the *Acta* in negative terms: the authors of the *Acta* have distorted the authentic text. When we shift our interests to inquiring how the characters function in narratives produced by and for fourth-century communities, another interpretation becomes possible. From this perspective we may focus on how communities *adapt* texts to new situations. On the one hand, perhaps we may assume an ancient audience had the same questions that modern audiences often have: Why are the saints' husbands absent from the narrative?[33] If Perpetua was "properly married" (*matronaliter nupta*: *Passio* 2.1), where is her husband? Why doesn't he make a claim for his child, as was his legal right?[34] The silence of the *Passio* may simply have demanded an answer. Indeed, Jacqueline Amat surmises that the author of the *Acta* supplied a husband for Perpetua "sans doute parce que son absence a étonné le rédacteur."[35]

On the other hand, the *Acta*s' explicit introduction of the husbands into the narratives—whom the martyrs immediately and categorically reject—aligns the women with contemporary interests in celibacy. Melania, for instance, repeatedly begs her husband, Pinian, to live with her in continence. And although Melania does not reject her husband outright—as Perpetua and Felicitas do—she clearly wishes to reject marriage as an institution: she asks Pinian to allow her to live in continence (*Vita* 1), she continually tries to flee (*Vita* 4) until, eventually, he agrees to live as "her brother in the Lord" (*Vita* 8). Within the confines of an ascetic discourse, Perpetua's rejection of her husband and child may have seemed not "unnatural," "extreme," "unlikeable," or even "harsh," but, rather, exemplary.[36] Although contemporaneous non-Christians, or nonascetic Christians, might react to the *Acta*s' portrayal of Perpetua and Felicitas negatively, an audience receptive to an ascetic form of Christianity likely would not. Christians of this ideological persuasion would presumably find nothing offensive about Perpetua's actions. In the *Acta*, then, the husbands may be introduced precisely in order to allow the saints to renounce them, thereby aligning the women with ascetic ideals and casting the martyrs as models of ascetic piety.

Renunciation is not a surprising theme to find in a martyr narrative. It is certainly present, as a matter of course, in all early Christian martyr texts.[37] The interrogation scenes, however—unique to the *Acta*—underscore the extent of the female martryrs' renunciation of natal family, husbands, and, indeed, of the present world. The authors of the *Acta* may have been constrained by the preexistent tradition that associated the female martyrs with marriage and children, and thus they may not have been free to omit these elements altogether. Apparently, however, they were free to recast the traditional martyr story as an ascetic story, thereby narratively reconstituting the parameters of martyrdom after the fact. The married mother martyrs are, in the hands of the authors of the *Acta*, models for the renunciation of this present world. They serve as an important reminder that lifelong celibacy was not the only route to an ascetic life. Indeed, it is the story of Perpetua and Felicitas—not one like that of the virgin martyr Agnes—that would serve as a particularly apt example of asceticism for women like Melania the Younger, who met social obligations for marriage and childbirth before committing to continence.

Community

The *Acta* display a marked concern for the Christian community and, especially, the relevance of an individual's experience for the larger group. This narrative interest may reflect a desire to make an earlier martyr account applicable, more broadly, to later Christian congregations. The second theme I wish to explore, then, is the texts' interest in the communal over the individual. One iteration of this theme is closely tied to renunciation: the fourth-century texts privilege Christian communal ties over ties to biological families; the second way that the theme can be traced in the *Acta* is through an analysis of Perpetua's visions, which, as opposed to the *Passio*, assert the relevance of the visions for all Christians, not just for Perpetua herself. The victory imagined, therefore, is not that of an individual but that of the entire Christian community; this victory, furthermore, is—as we shall see—not merely a victory over this-worldly persecutors but over cosmic powers that enslave humans.

When the author of *Acta* I introduces the Christians who were arrested in Thuburbo, he highlights their relationships to one another: Saturus and Saturninus were brothers, and Revocatus and Felicitas were brother and sister (*congermanus*: I.1.1). In this small Christian group, we see a merging of natal and Christian families: biological brothers and sisters are also brothers and sisters in faith who were arrested together and who will die together. Felicitas, as we have already seen, acknowledges only Revocatus when the proconsul asks about her family (I.5.6).

She states that she is "not able to have more important relatives" than her fellow Christians (I.5.6). If the author of *Acta* I was familiar with the introductory portion of the *Passio*, he has strengthened family ties among the Christians, since the *Passio* does not relate the arrested Christians to one another biologically. (Cf. *Passio* 2.1.)

Perpetua alone in *Acta* I is unrelated to any other Christian arrested. The author—like the author of the *Passio*—explicitly connects her to her natal family instead: Perpetua "was of noble birth and had a father and mother and two brothers and a child at the breast" (I.1.1). It is of interest that, according to the *Passio*, one of Perpetua's brothers was a catechumen, but the author of *Acta* I does not relate this connection to Christianity. Thus one difference between the *Passio* and *Acta* I is the heightened opposition that Perpetua experiences from her family as a whole; none of her natal family is allied to her spiritually. In this text, then, the first encounter between Perpetua and her father takes on added significance, since she rejects her noble birth and her entire family, claiming only the name "Christian" (2.2).

Elements of *Acta* II also highlight tensions between natal and Christian families. In his prefatory remarks, the author refers to Perpetua as Felicitas's sister, thus invoking a Christian family for Perpetua that will be contrasted to her birth family. And although Perpetua's earthly father's family is noble, having confessed Christ, she is now a daughter of God (II.1.1). The concerns of the two families—Christian and biological—are markedly different. *Acta* II emphasizes the shame that Perpetua's family feels at her arrest (II.2.1, II.6.2; cf. I.2.1). Her father sees her actions as bringing dishonor, but Perpetua considers him foreign (*alienos*) to her, since he is "separated from the redemption of Christ" (II.6.6). Perhaps the Christian group that produced this version of the martyr account struggled with the social consequences of adherence to the Christian life and, in response, heightened the tension between believers and nonbelievers in an effort to emphasize the family of faith.

Another aspect of the emphasis on communal versus individual in the *Acta* is apparent in the visionary episodes. Both texts relate two visions received by Perpetua, one of a ladder extending up to heaven (I.3.1–8, II.3.1–8) and one of a contest against an Egyptian (I.7.1–3, II.7.1–3). Readers familiar with the *Passio* may detect subtle yet important differences in these visions. In the *Actas*' first vision, Perpetua saw a bronze ladder extending up to heaven. Hanging from the ladder were knives and weapons, and at the base was a terrifying dragon. She saw Saturus ascending the ladder, and when he looked back, he said to all the martyrs (*ad nos*: I.3.5)—not just to Perpetua (cf. *dixit mihi*: *Passio* 4.6)—that they should not fear the serpent. Here we see the community incorporated into Perpetua's vision: Saturus promises all Christians that, strengthened in the grace of Christ, they will share his fate (I.3.5).[38] Perpetua then saw a shepherd milking sheep in a garden; the shepherd called to the martyrs and gave them the milk, which they ate.

The presence of the group in this vision is striking. In the *Passio*, the pronouns are singular: Saturus speaks to Perpetua, and the shepherd calls to her and gives her milk. In the *Acta*, though, what was once an individual visionary experience has now become a communal one.

Similarly, in the only other vision related by the *Acta*, Perpetua sees an Egyptian. This vision is notably shorter than the version found in the *Passio*. The authors of the later texts simply report that Perpetua saw an Egyptian, "rolling under their feet" ("volutantem se sub pedibus eorum," I.7.2; "sub eorum pedibus volutantem," II.7.2). In the *Passio*, this vision centers on Perpetua's masculinizing transformation and her singular victory: she alone defeats the Egyptian, understood to be the devil. In the *Acta*, however, the individual experience becomes a communal one: all the martyrs are envisioned as contributing to and benefiting from the Egyptian's defeat.

In both visions, what was once (i.e., in the *Passio*) an individual experience has become a collective experience. Perpetua is not alone in her visions; the community is with her and is the beneficiary of the victory related through them. Although the *Passio* does suggest that the first vision is meaningful for all the imprisoned Christians ("we realized that we would have to suffer," 4.10), the last vision—of the Egyptian—is not. It is Perpetua who fights the Egyptian, and the victory (both in the vision and in reality) is hers alone: "I realized it was not with wild animals that I would fight but with the Devil, but I knew that I would win the victory" (10.14). The *Passio* emphasizes the singular, the individual, whereas the *Acta* apply the visions' lessons to all Christians.

What shall we make of this emphasis on collectivity? In a period of persecution, the individuality of the visionary experience was surely powerful. Christian audiences were invited to marvel at Perpetua's strength and resolve and to imagine doing the same as she had done. The individual nature of the contest was obvious. After the age of persecution, though, martyr narratives might be appropriated to meet new ecclesiastical needs. As Joyce Salisbury has noted: "Many of the acts of the martyrs were rewritten to make them more consistent with prevailing church doctrine, or to put it another way, to bring them up-to-date and make them relevant to the experiences of Christians at any given time."[39] In a postpersecution world, communities might appropriate martyr texts to quite different ends. In the case of the *Acta*, fourth-century communities appear to be claiming the female martyrs for a new ecclesiastical moment. The emphasis on renunciation, on communal interests, and—as we shall see next—on the reversal of the Fall work together to suggest asceticism as a discourse to which these texts contribute. Perpetua and Felicitas, in the hands of these authors, remain noble martyrs, but their example extends further. The *Acta* appropriate the *Passio* to make the martyrs' witness relevant to a new community: these female martyrs become exemplary ascetic Christians, whose victory over Satan is enjoyed by all the faithful.

Reversal of the Fall

Rebecca Krawiec observes: "For Christianity, asceticism does not negate the body and the goods associated with it, but changes the body from its fallen state to one that anticipates the heavenly state, either of the resurrected body or of the angelic body."[40] Understanding this ascetic interest in "anticipat[ing] the heavenly state" helps us isolate and explain the *Actas*' emphasis on the defeat of Satan. This theme may be illustrated in two ways: first, the overthrow of the cosmic enemy of God; and second, the restoration of humanity to a pre-Fall state.

Like the *Passio*, the *Acta* interpret Perpetua's vision of the Egyptian as a defeat of the devil. Upon hearing about the vision, the Christians were "moved with gratitude for God," because "the enemy of the human race having been overthrown, made them worthy of the glory of martyrdom" (I.7.1–1. II.7.1–3). But the *Acta* relate the defeat of the devil by means of a more theologically laden statement than that found in the *Passio*: the devil is identified as "the enemy of the human race," who, having power at one time, has now been "overthrown." The *Acta* may also imagine a more expansive defeat: whereas in the *Passio*, Perpetua understands that *she* will defeat the devil and thus attain personal victory over him, the *Acta* imply a more thorough—or final—overthrow of the cosmic opponent of God.[41]

If the *Acta* imagine Satan's power to have ended—at least within the Christian community—do they also imagine an accompanying anthropological change? Does the overthrow of Satan, in other words, make a difference in the way human existence is imagined in these texts? I suggest that it does, and to demonstrate the point, we must turn to a perpetually understudied character: Felicitas. The lack of attention to Felicitas is regrettable, since later authors invest her with much revealing theological baggage. In particular, late ancient Christians seem especially interested in her labor and in what the scene can reveal about sin and salvation.

The *Passio* and the *Acta* relate that Felicitas was pregnant when she was arrested. Her fellow Christians pray for her to go into labor so that she can die with them. At this point the *Passio* and *Acta* I narrate a story that is different from that of *Acta* II. The former record a verbal sparring between Felicitas and her prison guard. The guard asks her how she will bear the pain of the amphitheater if she is experiencing so much pain in labor. In both texts Felicitas distinguishes what she experiences alone (i.e., labor) with what the Lord will experience for her (i.e., martyrdom; cf. *Passio* 15.6, *Acta* I.8.2).

Acta II, uniquely among these early accounts, associates Felicitas's labor with the curse of Genesis 3:16.[42] Curiously, this text does not relate the interaction between the martyr and the prison guard, in which the fiery Felicitas bests her opponent in verbal repartee. On the one hand, the absence is odd, given this author's interest in contrasting the martyrs to their diabolical persecutors. On the other hand, however, the absence makes sense when we note the author's description of Felicitas: "Desiring Christ and loving martyrdom, she neither asked for a midwife, nor felt the pain of childbirth ["nec partus sensit iniuriam"]" (II.9.2). This description of Felicitas is as important as it is stunning. Earlier martyr texts assume that *in their deaths* the martyrs defeated the powers of Satan and attained the immortal crown. But here, in this ascetically influenced martyr account, Felicitas seems to have defeated Satan, to have reversed the curse of Eve, and to have attained the physical benefits of a prelapsarian body before her death. She is not, it seems, an heir to Eve, but rather she is a new Eve.

A difference between the *Acta* and the *Passio* in the first vision also implies the possibility of Christians attaining the benefits of the prelapsarian life. In the *Passio*, the garden that Perpetua enters is at the top of the ladder (4.8). One must not merely defeat the dragon but also successfully scale the ladder—avoiding its instruments of torture—in order to enter this Edenic paradise in the heavens. Only those who have died may partake of the garden's offerings. In the *Acta*, the location of the garden is "near" [*iuxta*] the base of the ladder (I.3.6, II.3.6), not in the heavens above. Thus, in the *Acta*, the paradisical garden is available to Christians, it seems, even before death and apart from amphitheatrical contests.[43]

Narrative interest in the overthrow of Satan and the ways that Perpetua and Felicitas claim victory over this cosmic power shed light on some aspects of the texts that have been discussed above. Together, the *Actas*' interest in renunciation, community, and defeat of Satan make a text relevant anew to a Christian community concerned not with pagan persecution but Satanic domination. Perpetua and Felicitas are no longer merely models of ideal witnesses in the face of Roman persecution. They are also exemplars of the ascetic life and its tangible, this-worldly benefits: their choice of the ascetic life enacts the reversal of the Fall.

PERPETUAL FELICITY IN MELANIA'S WORLD

For historians interested in the social logic of the texts, the most important aspect of the Perpetua tradition may not be the historical details of the martyrs' deaths but, rather, how subsequent authors worked to keep the tradition alive. But alive for whom? I have posited authors (and an audience) with ascetic interests and suggested ways in which Melania the Younger—or someone like her—could stand for the ideal audience. Although there is no direct evidence that Melania was familiar with the story of Perpetua and Felicitas—much less, which version of the story she may have known—the popularity of the martyrs and their veneration throughout the empire suggests that a literate and well-traveled Christian like Melania would have encountered the stories of the Carthaginian martyrs. I wish to trace the ascetic afterlife of Perpetua and Felicitas further—into the world inhabited by Melania—even if firm connections to Melania herself elude our grasp.

Perpetua and Felicitas were, along with Cyprian, the most venerated of the African martyrs.[44] Ross Kraemer and Shira Lander observe that "by the fourth century,

Perpetua's fame had spread beyond Carthage."⁴⁵ The women's witness would be remembered, of course, through the celebration of their *dies natalis* at the place of their burial in Carthage. But the rites associated with the martyr shrine were not the only ways that these martyrs were remembered. Their story was regularly invoked in North African literature dating from soon after their deaths until well into the fifth century. Tertullian, writing in Carthage a few years after their deaths, appears confident that his audience will understand a passing reference to the *Passio*.⁴⁶ Augustine indicates that the story of Perpetua and Felicitas was treated by some as authoritative scripture.⁴⁷ Their story was also popular enough to become a model for subsequent martyr stories: it influenced at least two other North African martyr stories, the *Martyrdom of Marian and James* (set in Numidia around 300 C.E.) and the *Martyrdom of Montanus and Lucius* (set in Carthage in the mid-third century).⁴⁸ Augustine and Quodvultdeus, as we shall see, mention the women in their sermons. Further evidence of the widespread popularity of the stories of Perpetua and Felicitas may be found in their commemoration in calendars in Rome and Antioch.⁴⁹ Scholars have suggested that a fresco in the fourth-century catacombs of Saints Marcus and Marcellianus in Rome draws on Perpetua's first vision.⁵⁰ A late fifth-century mosaic in Ravenna and a sixth-century mosaic at the Eufrasiana Basilica in Porec serve as further testimony to the widespread veneration of these martyrs.⁵¹ Manuscript data may reflect the popularity of the *Acta* over the *Passio*: the latter is preserved in only ten manuscripts, whereas the former is preserved in forty-one.⁵² The inscription at the Basilica Maiorum, furthermore, may reflect familiarity with—and even a type of canonicity of—the *Acta*, since the inscription preserves the martyrs' names in the same order as is found in the *Acta*.

At least by the fourth century, there was a church dedicated to the memory of Perpetua and Felicitas in Carthage.⁵³ Although we have no direct evidence that Melania visited Carthage or the martyrs' burial place, the Basilica Maiorum, during her seven-year stay in North Africa, given Melania's interest in martyr veneration and relics, it is possible that the saint traveled to Carthage to honor the martyrs.⁵⁴ One interesting and somewhat more firm connection between Melania the Younger and the Perpetua tradition lies in Rome: the Codex-Calendar of 354 contains a list of martyrs commemorated by the church in Rome.⁵⁵ Although most of the martyrs listed were associated with Rome itself, three North African martyrs are included: Cyprian, Perpetua, and Felicitas. The inclusion of the Carthaginian women surely suggests their popularity across the empire by the mid-fourth century. The Codex-Calendar was produced—and perhaps donated by—a famous calligrapher named Filocalus who knew Melania's family.⁵⁶ Thus the feast of St. Perpetua was observed by the Roman church at least by 354, a celebration in which pious Christians like the Melanias would likely have participated. Another interesting connection between Melania the Younger and the *Acta*, in particular, is Augustine. The discovery of *Sermo* 282auct, which is a longer form of the previously known *Sermo* 282, has led scholars to the conclusion that Augustine knew not only the *Passio* but also some form of *Acta* II.[57] This suggests that the *Acta* were used alongside the *Passio* by the North African church and, thus, may have been available to Melania.[58]

The impulse to appropriate the memory of Perpetua and Felicitas for new ends was not unique to the *Acta*. Similar motives may be identified in the homiletical traditions of both Augustine and Quodvultdeus, contemporaries of Melania the Younger.[59] Both bishops, for instance, demonstrate asceticizing interests in their homilies on the female martyrs by underscoring the renunciations—of sex, gender, family, and this world—made by Perpetua and Felicitas. Augustine appears to align Perpetua with the ascetic movement when he explains that the devil did not try to overcome her through her husband, because she "was already, in her exaltation of spirit, living in heaven, and the slightest suspicion of carnal desire would make her, for very shame, all the stronger" (*Sermo* 281.2). Here, Augustine implies that Perpetua is proleptically participating in the promises of the resurrected and perfected body because of her continence. Quodvultdeus explains that the milk Perpetua received from the shepherd in her vision strengthened her to renounce family and world: "The sweetness of perpetual felicity [*felicitates perpetuae*] enabled her to contemn [*contemnere*] her son, despise [*spernere*] her father, to let go the world [*non haerere mundo*], and to lose her life for Christ [*perdere animam pro Christo*]" (*De Temp.* I.V).

The move from individual to communal—primarily seen in the argument that "perpetual felicity" is a reward that all Christians may claim—can also be found in Augustine's and Quodvultdeus's sermons. Augustine, for instance, tells his congregation that "these women were called [i.e., "Perpetua," "Felicitas"] what everyone is called to [i.e., perpetual felicity]" (281.3); on another occasion, he asserts that "by their names they have been witness to the indivisible gift we are going to receive" (282.1). Quodvultdeus tells his congregation that "perpetual felicity is at hand for all of us" (*De Temp.* II.12). He also warns his congregation against attachment to "the passing felicity of this world," reminding them that "if all the saints loved that worldly felicity, they would not have the 'Perpetual Felicity' of the church" (*De Temp.* II.12).[60] These sermons argue that all Christians may claim the reward of the martyrs. We could interpret these shifts from individuality to universality as reflective of a misogynistic impulse aimed at diminishing the testimony of two North African women. But such an interpretation may be unnecessarily limiting. Even if these texts restrict the power of the female martyrs, they simultaneously perform constructive work for the community by applying the women's example to new circumstances.

Finally, the later traditions exhibit interest in the restoration of humanity, especially by allusion to the reversal of the curse of Genesis 3:16. In *Sermo* 280.1, for instance, Augustine adds an explicit reference to Genesis in his discussion of

Perpetua's vision: "Thus the head of the ancient serpent, which had been the ruin of woman as she fell, was made into a step for woman as she ascended."[61] Quodvultdeus also compares the martyrs to Eve. The grace of Christ "has restored [*reparavit*] the female sex," he asserts. "Perpetua and Felicity trod underfoot the serpent's head, which Eve admitted into her heart." Although the devil was able to overcome Eve in the garden, he could not conquer Perpetua and Felicitas, "even when they were under the power of such mighty enemies" (*De Temp.* I.V). Thus, both Augustine and Quodvultdeus imagine Perpetua and Felicitas as new Eves, as women who face temptation but do not succumb to it. In Perpetua and Felicitas, we see what could have been; we see that humanity can be restored through ascetic forms of Christian piety.

CONCLUSION

The work that has been done in the recent past to write women's history and interpret women's absences has been vital work for the scholarship of late antiquity. The literary turn, however, gives new opportunities for interpreting texts apart from their historicity (or lack thereof). Indeed, it allows scholars to circumvent the problematic categories of "original" or "unmediated" texts in favor of readings that focus on how texts are adapted to meet particular social circumstances. Texts that have been undervalued because of their perceived derivative status may now be embraced as literary creations that seek to make earlier events and characters relevant to new situations and congregations. Rather than focusing on what the *Acta* are not—namely Perpetua's words—we do better to follow Elizabeth Clark's call to focus on the social logic of a text, seeking to understand the work that the *Acta* do within their communities, communities for which the age of persecution was past but that wished to claim new relevance for past heroines. Through this lens we see that ascetic literature not only appropriates martyrological language; it also engages in a project that rewrites the martyrs' histories in order to make them relevant to later Christians in need of new guidance and inspiration.

If the *Passio* was outdated and a relic of a past age, focused as it was on crises that had been resolved, the *Acta* and other exegetical traditions suggest that the early church was not done with Perpetua and Felicitas. Rather than discarding the traditions about their martyrdoms once imperial opposition to Christianity had passed, the *Acta* illustrate concerted efforts to remake the martyrs as ascetics whose model could endure beyond the age of persecution. Scholars regularly comment on the appropriation of martyrological imagery and language in ascetic discourse, but the *Acta* illustrate that a more complex literary relationship was taking place. Ascetic literature not only borrows from martyr literature; it also remakes that literature in its own image.

NOTES

1. Elizabeth A. Clark, "The Lady Vanishes: Dilemmas of a Feminist Historian after the 'Linguistic Turn,'" *Church History* 67 (1998): 1–31.
2. Ibid., 15.
3. Ibid. See Gabrielle Spiegel, "History, Historicism, and the Social Logic of the Text in the Middle Ages," *Speculum* 65 (1990): 59–86.
4. See Elizabeth A. Clark, *Life of Melania the Younger* (New York: Edwin Mellen Press, 1985), 166; eadem, "Piety, Propaganda, and Politics in the *Life of Melania the Younger*," *Studia Patristica* 18 (1989): 167–83; Luckritz Marquis, "Namesake and Inheritance," this volume.
5. Gillian Clark, "Women and Asceticism in Late Antiquity: The Refusal of Status and Gender," in *Asceticism*, ed. Vincent Wimbush and Richard Valantasis (New York: Oxford University Press, 1995), 43.
6. Ibid.
7. Ramsay MacMullen, *The Second Church: Popular Christianity A.D. 200–400* (Atlanta: Society of Biblical Literature, 2009), esp. 25–26. See also Peter Brown, *The Cult of the Saints: Its Rise and Function in Latin Christianity* (Chicago: University of Chicago Press, 1981).
8. Elizabeth A. Clark, "Devil's Gateway and the Brides of Christ: Women in the Early Christian World," in *Ascetic Piety and Women's Faith: Essays on Late Ancient Christianity* (Lewiston, N.Y.: Edwin Mellen Press, 1986), 45.
9. Cyprian, *Ep.* 8 (*Epistulae 1–57*, ed. G. Diercks, CCL 3B: 40–43).
10. Gregory the Great, *Dialogues* 3.26.7–8 (SC 260: 370–72).
11. Isabelle Kinnard, "*Imitatio Christi* in Christian Martyrdom and Asceticism: A Critical Dialogue," in *Asceticism and Its Critics: Historical Accounts and Comparative Perspectives*, ed. Oliver Freiberger (New York: Oxford University Press, 2006), 131.
12. Sebastian P. Brock, "Early Syrian Asceticism," *Numen* 20 (1973): 2. See also G. Clark, "Women and Asceticism in Late Antiquity"; Kinnard, "*Imitatio Christi*"; Rebecca Krawiec, "Asceticism," in *The Oxford Handbook of Early Christian Studies*, ed. Susan Ashbrook Harvey and David G. Hunter (Oxford: Oxford University Press, 2008), 769; Elizabeth Castelli, "Virginity and Its Meaning for Women's Sexuality in Early Christianity," *Journal of Feminist Studies in Religion* 2 (1986): 67–68; Monique Alexandre, "Les nouveaux martyrs: Motifs martyrologiques dans la vie des saints et thèmes hagiographiques dans l'éloge des martyrs chez Grégoire de Nysse," in *The Biographical Works of Gregory of Nyssa: Proceedings of the Fifth International Colloquium on Gregory of Nyssa, Mainz, 6–10 September 1982*, ed. Andreas Spira (Cambridge, Mass: Philadelphia Patristic Foundation, 1984), 33–70. Elizabeth Clark and Elizabeth Castelli argue, however, that we need not claim that the end of persecution wholly explains the rise of asceticism in order to acknowledge the ways that the discourse of asceticism appropriates the language of martyrdom (Castelli, "Virginity," 67; Elizabeth A. Clark, *Reading Renunciation: Asceticism and Scripture in Early Christianity* [Princeton: Princeton University Press, 1999], 23).
13. Pseudo-Athanasius, *Vita Syncleticae* 8 (*PG* 28: 1492), surmises that "the gentler sufferings" belong to Thecla—not Syncletica—since she was attacked externally rather than internally through "opposing and destructive thoughts." See Elizabeth Castelli, "The Life and Activity of the Holy and Blessed Teacher Syncletica," in *Ascetic Behavior in Greco-Roman Antiquity: A Sourcebook*, ed. Vincent L. Wimbush (Minneapolis: Fortress, 1990), 269–70.
14. English translations of *The Life of Melania* are from E. A. Clark, *The Life of Melania the Younger*. I follow Clark in assuming the priority of the Greek over the Latin recensions of the *vita*. In what follows, the Greek text is from Gerontius, *Vie de sainte Mélanie: Texte grec, introduction, traduction et notes*, ed. Denys Gorce, SC 90 (Paris: Cerf, 1962).
15. E. A. Clark, *Life of Melania*, 135–36.
16. G. Clark, "Women and Asceticism," 35.

17. Elizabeth A. Clark, "Claims on the Bones of Saint Stephen: The Partisans of Melania and Eudocia," *Church History* 51 (1982): 141–56.

18. Krawiec's observation regarding ascetic discourse is relevant here: "An assessment of 'sources' for asceticism involves an examination of *how* to read particular texts, rather than what to read" ("Asceticism," 770).

19. Brent Shaw ("The Passion of Perpetua," *Past and Present* 139 [1993]: 45) discusses how Perpetua's "unmediated self-perception, her reality" was co-opted by later male authors to better fit a male-dominated culture. See also Rex D. Butler, *The New Prophecy and "New Visions": Evidence of Montanism in the Passion of Perpetua and Felicitas* {Washington, D.C.: Catholic University of America Press, 2006); Joyce Salisbury, *Perpetua's Passion: The Death and Memory of a Young Roman Woman* [New York: Routledge, 1997]).

20. Shaw implies that the later reworkings of the martyrological tradition were deliberate distortions of the text ("Passion," 21).

21. I have followed Jacqueline Amat's text in *Passion de Perpétue et de Félicité suivi des Actes*, SC 417 (Paris: Cerf, 1996). On the production of the *Acta* for liturgical purposes, see Shaw, "Passion," 36; Thomas J. Heffernan, *The Passion of Perpetua and Felicity* (New York: Oxford University Press, 2012), 81, 442; J. Armitage Robinson, *The Passion of S. Perpetua* (Cambridge: Cambridge University Press, 1891), 15. Most analyses assume a literary relationship between the *Passio* and the *Acta*. Important exceptions to the assumption of literary dependency are James Halporn, "Literary History and Generic Expectations in the *Passio* and *Acta Perpetuae*," *Vigiliae Christianae* 45 (1991): 223–41; and Ross Kraemer and Shira Lander, "Perpetua and Felicitas," in *The Early Christian World*, ed. Philip Francis Esler, vol. 2 (London: Routledge, 2000): 1048–68.

22. See Elizabeth A. Clark, "Antifamilial Tendencies in Ancient Christianity," *Journal of the History of Sexuality* 5 (1995): 356–80.

23. See L. Stephanie Cobb, *Dying to Be Men: Gender and Language in Early Christian Martyr Texts* (New York: Columbia University Press, 2008), 92–123.

24. It is unclear whether *congermanus* signals legal authority.

25. See Cobb, *Dying*, 92–123.

26. See Augustine, *Sermons*, ed. John E. Rotelle, trans. Edmund Hill, 280.1, 281.3, 282.1.

27. See Kate Cooper, "A Father, A Daughter, and A Procurator: Authority and Resistance in the Prison Memoir of Perpetua of Carthage," *Gender and History* 23 (2011): 685–702. If Cooper is correct that the introductory notice to the *Passio* is late, then the *Acta* may represent early attempts at reframing Perpetua's status from concubine to *matrona* and, ultimately, to ascetic.

28. See Cobb, *Dying*, 94–111; Shaw, "Passion," 36.

29. Ibid.

30. Ibid.

31. Rex Butler, *New Prophecy*, 101.

32. Shaw, "Passion," 36.

33. See Carolyn Osiek, "Perpetua's Husband," *Journal of Early Christian Studies* 10 (2002): 287–90; *Passion de Perpétue et de Félicité*, ed. and trans. Amat, 31; Cooper, "A Father, A Daughter"; Stuart Hall, "Women among the Early Martyrs," in Diana Wood, ed. *Martyrs and Martyrologies: Papers Read at the 1992 Summer Meeting and the 1993 Winter Meeting of the Ecclesiastical History Society*, (Oxford: Blackwell, 1993), 6–7.

34. On legal custody, see Cooper, "A Father, A Daughter," 688–90.

35. *Passion de Perpétue et de Félicité*, ed. and trans. Amat, 193.

36. Shaw, "Passion," 36.

37. See Danny Praet, "'*Meliore cupiditate detentus*': Christian Self-Definition and the Rejection of Marriage in the Early Acts of the Martyrs," *Euphrosyne* 31 (2003): 457–73.

38. The plural verbs in *Acta* II.3.5 indicate that the vision there, too, is incorporating the larger community.

39. Salisbury, *Perpetua's Passion*, 171.

40. Krawiec, "Asceticism," 774-75.

41. If these texts imagine Satan as fully overthrown, then they diverge from dominant ascetic discourse, which teaches the need for vigilance in guarding against Satan's influence. See David Brakke, *Demons and the Making of the Monk: Spiritual Combat in Early Christianity* (Cambridge, Mass.: Harvard University Press, 2006); *Evagrius of Pontus: Talking Back: A Monastic Handbook for Combating Demons* (Trappist, Ky.: Cistercian Publications, 2009).

42. *De Natale Sanctarum Perpetuae et Felicitatis*, once attributed to Quodvultdeus, also relates Felicitas's labor to Genesis 3:16. See *De Natale* 3.

43. This is evidenced by the fact that in the *Acta* Perpetua observes Saturus scaling the ladder, but she herself does not do so. She does, however, enter into the garden, where she is given milk by the shepherd.

44. Augustine, *Sermons III/8 (273-305A): On the Saints*, trans. Edmund Hill (Hyde Park, N.Y.: New City Press, 1994), 76.

45. Kraemer and Lander, "Perpetua and Felicitas," 1063. Amat argues that the *Passio* enjoyed almost immediate popularity across Africa, which led to the shorter editions of the *Acta* (*Passion de Perpétue et de Félicité*, ed. and trans. Amat, 79, 82-83).

46. Tertullian, *De Anima* 55.

47. Augustine, *De Natura et Origine Animae* 1.10.12.

48. See *Passion de Perpétue et de Félicité*, ed. and trans. Amat, 82; Maureen A. Tilley, *Donatist Martyr Stories: The Church in Conflict in Roman North Africa* (Liverpool: Liverpool University Press, 1996), 16; *The Acts of the Christian Martyrs*, ed. and trans. Herbert Musurillo (Oxford: Oxford University Press, 2000), xxxiii.

49. Timothy D. Barnes, *Tertullian: A Historical and Literary Study* (Oxford: Clarendon Press, 1971), 79.

50. Stephen B. Luce, "Archaeological News and Discussions: Early Christian and Byzantine," *American Journal of Archaeology* 47 (1943): 120; Gail P. C. Streete, *Redeemed Bodies: Women Martyrs in Early Christianity*, (Louisville: Westminster John Knox Press, 2009), 57-58.

51. See Deborah Mauskopf Deliyannis, *Ravenna in Late Antiquity* (Cambridge: Cambridge University Press, 2010), 194; Ormonde Maddock Dalton, *Byzantine Art and Archaeology* (Oxford: Clarendon Press, 1911), 373.

52. Heffernan, *Passion*, 442.

53. Barnes, *Tertullian*, 79.

54. Elizabeth Clark suggests that the lack of detail in narrating the African journeys of Melania may arise because Gerontius was not an eyewitness to these events (*Life of Melania*, 112-14). Victor Vitensis lists the Basilica Maiorum as the place of burial (*Historia Persecutionis Africanae Provinciae* 1.3.9).

55. Michele Renee Salzman, *On Roman Time: The Codex-Calendar of 354 and the Rhythms of Urban Life in Late Antiquity* (Berkeley and Los Angeles: University of California Press, 1990), 42.

56. See ibid., xxi, 3, 202-3; Alan Cameron, "Filocalus and Melania," *Classical Philology* 87 (1992): 140-44.

57. See Jan Bremmer and Marco Formisano, "Perpetua's Passions: A Brief Introduction," in Jan N. Bremmer and Marco Formisano, eds. *Perpetua's Passions: Multidisciplinary Approaches to the Passio Perpetuae et Felicitatis* (Oxford: Oxford University Press, 2012), 5; Dorothee Elm von der Osten, "Perpetua Felicitas: Die Predigten des Augustinus zur Passio Perpetuae et Felicitatis (s. 280-282)," in Therese Fuhrer, ed. *Die christlich-philosophischen Diskurse der Spätantike: Texte, Personen, Institutionen—Akten der Tagung vom 22.-25. Februar 2006 am Zentrum für Antike und Moderne der Albert-Ludwigs-Universität Freiburg* (Stuttgart: Franz Steiner Verlag, 2008), 275-98.

58. The story of Perpetua was well known enough for Augustine to reference it even in treatises not related to the martyrs' feast day: see *De Natura et Origine Animae* 4.18.26.

59. Translations of Augustine are from Hill, *Sermons III/8*. Translations of Quodvultdeus are from Richard Kalkman, "Two Sermons: *De tempore barbarico* Attributed to St. Quodvultdeus, Bishop of Carthage—A Study of Text and Attribution with Translation and Commentary" (Ph.D. dissertation, The Catholic University of America, 1963).

60. Quodvultdeus's sermons are not primarily about Perpetua and Felicitas, and although they were given shortly after the martyrs' feast day, they do not appear to be feast-day sermons. See Kalkman, "Two Sermons."

61. For other allusions to Genesis in Augustine's sermons on Perpetua and Felicitas, see *Sermons*, ed. Rotelle, trans. Hill, 281.1, 3; 282.2.

7

The Memory of Melania

Rebecca Krawiec

MELANIA AND GENDERED HISTORY

In the prologue to his *Lausiac History*, Palladius repeatedly addresses his dedicatee, whom Demetrios Katos has argued was a eunuch in the imperial court at Constantinople,[1] with the command to "act the man," (*andrizou*).[2] At one point, this is a call specifically to a renunciation of wealth, the main model for which is a woman, although a "gender-bent" one: Melania the Elder.[3] This moment sets the tone for gender ambiguity in this work, a topic that earlier scholarship on Palladius's view of ascetic women debated in binary-gender terms. This discussion, predominantly in the 1990s, was divided: some argued that women in Palladius were equal to men only if the feminine was escaped in favor of a masculinized self; this view drew on references to women's having been made male, usually through asceticism, and particularly through sexual renunciation.[4] In contrast, others argued that Palladius favored a common humanity over modern scholars' division "of human identity into cultural fragments."[5] This latter argument maintained that Palladius, as well as other ancient writers, saw women and men as equal in their (fallen) humanity. This argument has often centered on Melania the Elder largely because of her famous epithet—"female man of God"—but also because of her centrality to the *Lausiac History* as a whole. Her role in the text, in turn, is due to her ability to be in social contact with many male monks because of what Elizabeth Clark argues is an Origenist view of fluidity of the body.[6] Thus, Melania's gender-bent status in later scholarship acknowledged the tension between these two positions: Melania is female but not like other women. This emphasis is often more on her gender and less on issues of asceticism and its effects on sexuality.[7]

I will extend this debate to argue that Melania, in Palladius's account, is a transgressive figure in terms both of gender and of sexuality, most significantly because of her relationship to monastic memory. Elizabeth Castelli, in this volume, explores how the introduction of gender as a category questioned the role of women in our sources as historical agents, especially when the sources are hagiographical and so not particularly suited for questions of social history.[8] Rather than limiting Melania to this category, or moving her to its opposite, her transgressiveness requires a concept that challenges the very notion of category—namely queer. Using this noncategory allows an extension in understanding Melania's position in the text. Even though Palladius remains silent on Melania's sexual status in her interactions with other figures male and female, her fluidity is made possible because she is queer. Both Virginia Burrus and Amy Hollywood have argued for queerness being based less in a social history of gays and lesbians, and more in challenges to normative discourses of sexuality, and so of gender.[9] Simply put, Melania can interact with men throughout the text because, although a woman, she has a nonnormative female sexuality: she is never the object or source of desire for the monastic men around her. Rather, in at least one interaction with a monastic woman, she is a conduit of desire for the reader, and later she is able to teach a male figure how to control his own heterosexuality.

Further, these interactions all provide Melania with a voice, the voice of memory; she is not just a "female man of God" but a rare female voice in a male text—yet she does not provide what, in social-historical terms, we may regard as a female view. The text remains male-authored, but both who remembers and who is remembered create a social memory of gender. Part of Melania's gender ambiguity in Palladius's *Lausiac History* is that she is aligned with the predominantly male activity of remembering others. Further, her memory is both of women (as other women remember) and of men (as otherwise only men remember). Thus, alongside the notion that she is queer, we should also include the concept of genderqueer, a refusal of gender assignment, since Palladius ascribes to her roles and actions that in the ancient world were primarily allowed to men even as he continues to identify her as a woman.[10] Patrica Cox Miller has pointed out the dilemma for male writers of combining the categories holy and woman.[11] In the *Lausiac History*, there are monastic (or holy) women, but by and large Melania is not in that category; she is a monk among men, but repeatedly labeled a woman. How Palladius remembers her challenges, and so queers, these binary choices. She is both fully female—a Roman matron who is the head of a female monastery—*and* male, in terms of a variety of roles she plays in civic locations such as Rome and Jerusalem.

This social memory of gender becomes contested in Palladius's and Jerome's competing accounts of monastic women. Here gender and memory take on an eschatological extension as part of the Origenist debate that both authors waged.

Palladius's genderqueer memory of Melania makes her an alternative to the properly gendered ascetic women associated with Jerome. Jerome's memory of Marcella, when contrasted with Palladius's account of Paula, reveals the gender dynamic of their memorials. Within that debate, in terms of memory, Melania is not made male, nor is she a female "person" (which in antiquity implied maleness) appearing as a female alternative to a male model.[12] Rather, Palladius presents her as having what Judith Halberstam terms a "female masculinity," whose existence challenges the binary of male/female, a queer (Origenist) alternative to the dominant femininity that Jerome made a necessary aspect of anti-Origenism.[13]

MELANIA IN THE *LAUSIAC HISTORY*: A QUEER MONASTIC MEMORY

The *Lausiac History* is constructed through a collective monastic memory. Though Palladius, typically for an ancient author, offers his text as a response to his patron's "command" to write it, he nevertheless presents it as a "holy reminder" both to Lausius and, by extension, to his other readers;[14] that is, it provides memories in order to teach readers how to remember their own virtues.[15] The source for these reminders is, further, a collective memory: although Palladius tells Lausius that his work is an "account of my entire experience" totaling some thirty-three years "in the company of the brethren and my own solitary life," he also explicitly draws on stories of others, "those I had seen and those I had heard about."[16] Both sets of memories, individual and collective, are, as memory theory has shown, shaped through the interactions with others who are part of the social movement.[17] The characters in this work, including Palladius, are monastic because they exemplify the monasticism that is "enacted through appeals to [monastic] memory."[18] As a result, Palladius creates a social cohesion for diverse forms of monastic practice over and against the social contestations about monasticism that were taking place as part of the larger Origenist controversy at the time.[19]

Part of that social cohesion is gender roles in memory; monastic memory, in the *Lausiac History*, is primarily male, whether men or women are being remembered. The collective reporting is men remembering men; reports about women are often based on Palladius's memory, though he at times includes their voices about their own experiences. In the terms that Sue Campell uses to describe a process of remembering, Palladius tries to present both a first voice, the one remembering, as he puts himself into the second voice, the listener who prompts the memories (or voices) of others, thus providing "certain ways of remembering the past."[20] Palladius remembers some women remembering—primarily a male activity—just as some women are remembered practicing asceticism and monasticism, as defined in male terms.[21] This asceticism can, at times, masculinize women, as Palladius suggests at the beginning of his chapter on ascetic women: "I must also commemorate in this book the manly women to whom God granted struggles equal to those of men so that no one can plead as an excuse that women are too weak to practice virtue successfully."[22] Thus here there are masculine women (a female masculinity) stemming from asceticism, but the result for Palladius is that they are worthy of being included in monastic memory alongside the memory of men.

Memory theory, once gendered, thus allows one answer to the challenge of the linguistic turn. This approach acknowledges that Palladius is writing these women and their voices or memories;[23] but it also pays attention to the role of women. They occasionally can be part of the collective monastic memory, as Palladius records it, but only when they talk about themselves or, at most, other women. Otherwise the memories of women come from Palladius and his knowledge. The main exception to this gendered aspect of monastic memory is Melania the Elder—for her, memory is not just gendered but queered. Unlike other women, and like men, Melania participates in the memory, and so the authorizing, of stories about other monks, female and male. She is not just part of memory. She remembers, both on her own and as specifically included in a male-monastic collective memory. Just as Burrus has argued that the married Gregory of Nyssa is a "queer ascetic" because "his asceticism fails to conform to expectations," so too the female Melania has a queer memory, because hers challenges the gender norms for memory in this history.[24]

Three accounts in the opening chapters of the *Lausiac History* reveal Melania's gender ambiguity in relation to memory. First, in the fifth chapter, Palladius gives a description of a woman who leaves Alexandria to entomb herself. Though it is Palladius who was told about this woman, Alexandra, by Didymus, it is Melania who reports the reason for her isolation and how she is able to live such a life, because it was Melania who questioned her directly and so remembers the conversation.[25] However, this exchange was not made possible, as we may assume, because of their shared gender, since Alexandra specifically did not meet face-to-face with either men or women once entombed—not even with the woman who brought her supplies.[26] Melania confirms that, during their conversation near the window, she "did not see her face." She does, however, speak with her, something Alexandra seemingly does not do with any other person, man or woman. As a result, the reader learns from Melania the reason for Alexandra's confinement: she showed proper female sexual shame by hiding her body after it caused male heterosexual desire.[27] This desirability is then queered when she hides her face from everyone, men and women, with the implication that everyone needs to be protected from the lust her body can elicit.

Yet the very existence of this desirable female body, the ability to imagine it, is available to the reader only because Melania reports it: that is, here Melania serves as the second voice who prompts the memory of the event that led Alexandra to the tomb and shapes how readers remember Alexandra. Melania, like everyone else, avoids looking at this desirable female body; yet her monastic memory queers her role in this story. Melania, ostensibly a heterosexual Roman widow, has a memory voice that serves in place of the male gaze; she records Alexandra's desirability, even as she (and others) cannot look at it. This position, however, does not make her male but rather provides her with an ancient textual equivalent to Halberstam's description of a butch gaze. A 1993 *Vanity Fair* cover with Cindy Crawford and k.d. lang, says Halberstam, requires heterosexual men to place themselves in the position of lang, the butch, to be able to desire Crawford.[28] In Palladius's text, in order for (male) readers to envision the desirable female body, they have to listen to Melania's memory of their conversation. In other words, as the source of memory, Melania, to quote Eve Sedgwick, "criss-crosses the lines of identity and desire," since any desire for Alexandra or, indeed, desirability itself has to be experienced through Melania's memory.[29]

Four chapters later, the narrative has moved to Nitria, where Palladius relies on the collective memory of the brotherhood (*adelphotēs*) to attest to the virtues of Or, a now-deceased monk whom Palladius never met. Among this *adelphotēs* is Melania, here with her well-known soubriquet, *hē anthrōpos* of God.[30] The Greek term for the brotherhood that serves as the authenticator of memory is important, since Daniel Stramara has shown that Palladius also uses it to describe double monasticism, an "*adelphotēs* of men and women."[31] In this other *adelphotēs*, there is a male monk, Sisinius, who is head of the separate groups of men and women. In order to act as an effective leader for women, he has both rid himself of "masculine desires" (that is, apparently heterosexual desires for women) and has "bridled the feminine traits of the women."[32] Thus, the scriptures have been fulfilled, says Palladius, citing Galatians 3:28—itself a text with a queer history, as Dale Martin has shown.[33] It is, then, the loss of one man's heterosexual desire and his ability to "silence" or "muzzle" the women's (collective) femaleness (which is equated with their inherent sexuality) that leads to there being no male or female.[34] Further, the women's femaleness is muzzled not because they control their own desires but apparently because a man no longer desires them.[35] Thus, in this *adelphotēs* there is a loss of (male) heterosexuality but not of men and women.

Adelphotēs, then, for Palladius has multiple meanings, but he always uses it in reference to monastic situations without heterosexuality: a collective male brotherhood; a collective female sisterhood;[36] or this group of men and women, once (male) desire is checked. The use of this term to describe the monks of Nitria, including Melania, therefore, is significant. Palladius emphasizes Melania's presence by calling her chosen or remarkable among the monks, a position that also makes her particularly notable in being able to testify to the virtues of the deceased male monk Or.[37] She draws attention for being a woman participating in what I argue is in this text a male monastic activity: remembering *other* monks.[38] The implication, however, is also that she can do so because she is not the object of male desire and so is part of the *adelphotēs*. She is queer in her challenge to a normative view of women as sexual beings among male ascetics, *and* she is genderqueer since she has a female masculinity in her ability to remember.

Both her general role in memory and her label as *hē anthrōpos* of God connect Melania to the next figure whom Palladius describes, the monk Pambo. Palladius's memory of Pambo comes from Melania herself. Melania here has two voices: the first voice, of her account, and the second voice, wherewith she records Pambo's memory, including his voice. Thus, here there is a male voice (Pambo) reported by a woman's voice (Melania) preserved through a male writer's pen (Palladius). Once again, Melania stands out—she is not the usual female role, having only the first voice, but she has the second as well; this dual role makes her like Palladius and a select few other male figures. Further, none other than Pambo authorized *her* memory of *him*. As he approaches death, he gives his only possession—the last basket that he was weaving—to Melania, specifically "that you may remember me."[39] The transmission of holy authority at death is a common motif in monastic texts, but the signifier was often clothing, echoing the biblical models of Elijah and Elisha.[40] What happens here is subtly but significantly different: the marker of Pambo's memory is located not in monastic clothing but in a monastic work-product. Social memory theory again helps unpack the meaning of this event: the production of the basket requires a repetitive bodily motion (weaving) that, like writing, creates what Paul Connerton labels a "habit memory" of the social values of this community.[41] The basket thus transmits the social memory of the monastic community that Pambo represents; Melania is the guardian of that memory. Melania's status here is based not only on her wealth or her patronage (the subject of much of the story), but on her connection to the memory of Pambo, whom Melania identifies as *ho anthrōpos* of God: the masculine equivalent to the term Palladius used for Melania in the previous chapter. Pambo's masculinity in this phrase is (to use again Judith Halberstam's argument) made possible by Melania's female masculinity.[42] Both are part of the *adelphotēs* whose memory Melania helps preserve. Melania thus, like Palladius, has particular authority over the memory of the Egyptian desert, something she can transport (like the basket) to Jerusalem.

Melania's memory is her source of authority in these accounts, but only because she is queered through it. Within the narrative framework of the *Lausiac History*, Melania functions in relationship to memory in a manner similar to what the queer-memory theorists Christopher Castiglia and Christopher Reed have argued the character Karen does in the television show *Will and Grace*. This show, which appeared on American television from the late 1990s to the mid-2000s, had four main characters: two gay men, Will and his friend Jack, and two straight women, Grace and her employee, Karen; Castiglia and Reed argue the stronger relationships were between Will and Grace and between Jack and Karen. They further contrast the heteronormative title character, Grace, who has a "strained and anxious" relationship to memory, with Karen, who actively celebrates a memory that connects her to queer culture. One result is that rather than being an isolated figure, Karen participates in the community that is based on this memory.[43] So too Melania has a strong relationship to (male) monastic memory, since she is both subject and object of memory, and she blurs both gender distinction and sexuality in her memory of others.[44] Melania is like Karen in terms of the blend between a heterosexual female self and participation in the memories of a group that is not populated by heterosexual women. Castiglia and Reed write: "Despite her always offstage husband and children, Karen's participation in gay cultural memory 'queers' her in ways that become occasionally explicit," as when she (and not Grace) is invited to gay male-only parties.[45] Likewise, Melania, despite her (dead) husband and absent child (now under the care of a guardian), and her later leadership of a female monastery in Jerusalem, participates in the male aspects of monastic cultural memory in ways that queer her, also occasionally becoming explicit: *hē anthrōpos* of God.[46] In Palladius's *Lausiac History*, some women are remembered as women, some as women equal to men; but Melania's memory is queer.

MELANIA, MARCELLA, AND PAULA: THE GENDERQUEERED VERSUS THE GENDERED MEMORY OF MONASTICISM

Melania's queer memory also shapes how Palladius remembers her, not just how she remembers in his text; it becomes a genderqueered memorial. Each of two other discussions of Melania in the *Lausiac History* stands in contrast to two women associated with Jerome: Marcella and Paula. These juxtapositions reveal how the memory of monastic women is part of the larger argument about Origenism, gender, and monasticism.[47] Writing in the wake of the theological purge of Egyptian monasticism after charges of Origenism, there may have been pressure for Palladius to engage in forgetting, a "willed amnesia,"[48] about the gendered aspects of the monastic past that were now controversial. Instead, he promotes the genderqueerness of Origenist monasticism, as remembered through Melania, over and against Jerome's straight monasticism, evidenced in Palladius's memory of Paula. Both positions are made explicit not just through the language of the body and sexuality but also through memory and community. Melania is not made male with Paula remaining female; rather, both are remembered as Roman matrons[49] who had differing relationships with the larger (male) monastic communities, differences that strengthened and weakened them accordingly. Paula thus serves as a Grace to Melania's Karen; the two figures function as "embodiments of competing attitudes or social positions," with specifically "different attitudes towards memory."[50] Finally, both women have eschatological fates mapped onto them that show the positive and negative outcomes of these competing gendered monasticisms.

My first example requires an extension beyond the *Lausiac History* to contrast a text of Jerome's—his letter to Principia that he "dedicates to the memory of that holy woman Marcella"—with Palladius's account of Melania's trip to Rome.[51] In each account the woman in question appears as a teacher in Rome, and each is remembered in relationship to Egyptian monasticism, Rome, and Jerusalem. Despite these shared points, the differences are vast. Apart from the fact that the two women are associated with opposing positions on the theological dispute in question, each woman teaches quite differently. Marcella, as Andrew Cain has shown, functions as a representative for Jerome.[52] In addition, Jerome suggests her method of teaching, such that she hides her participation, stemmed from Marcella's self-understanding of her gender and scripture; "For she knew that the apostle had said: 'I suffer not a woman to teach' [1 Tim. 2:12], and she would not seem to inflict a wrong upon the male sex."[53] This wrong would be twofold: Marcella's teaching could emasculate those who sought her advice, including priests, and it would put all involved in opposition to Paul's commands. Marcella has a properly gendered relationship to scripture. She teaches, but as a woman, defined by the Bible; her voice is not her words, and so her voice does not connote agency, as voice does for memory in Palladius.

In addition to teaching orthodoxy, Marcella learns monasticism in Rome, not from Jerome but from Egyptian leaders who are there in exile from Arian persecutions. She thus is instructed in the Jerome-approved Egyptian monasticism of Antony and Pachomius, without having to travel to Egypt and possibly be exposed to other forms of monasticism there.[54] As a result of these teachings, Marcella is, in Jerome's account, the first aristocratic woman to embrace monasticism in Rome, and she is so successful in gaining female followers in monastic seclusion on the outskirts of the city that Rome, says Jerome, was "transformed into another Jerusalem." Jerome's claim, however, is somewhat odd, since he has emphasized that only women are part of Marcella's community and that it is not in the city but outside it—yet somehow men also became part of this transformation: not only did "monastic establishments for virgins become numerous," but also "of hermits there were countless numbers."[55] Jerome's need to keep gender fixed, and separate, leads him to elide how Marcella's leadership can include conversions of men to the monastic way of life. Finally, in his account, Marcella saves Rome from heresy (once again not publicly but working behind the scene),[56] only to see it then fall to invasion, an occasion that also leads to her death. Her experience of the invasion is also gendered: she is beaten but not raped (Jerome says because of her age); she also prays on behalf of her companion Principia that she not be raped either, a prayer that is fulfilled.

The relationship between place, monasticism, and gender in this memory of Marcella is complex, showing the import to Jerome of creating a social memory of a monasticism that is both gender-appropriate and theologically correct. Marcella is remembered as the founder of an Egyptian-style (but not Origenist) monasticism in Rome, but on the outskirts—which nevertheless transforms the city itself into Jerusalem, a Rome-turned-Jerusalem that then falls even as Marcella is safe in the church of the apostle Paul (the same apostle who does not permit a woman to teach). The role of the cities, and their relationship with Egyptian monasticism, is particularly significant, since memory theory has shown that places hold memory and are a source of identity.[57] Marcella, in Jerome's account, remains fixed in location, but she transforms the space around her in ways suitable to her gender.[58] Because her gender-fixity is the basis of her strength in this account, it creates a social memory that reinforces gender rather than challenges it. Jerome has used his memory of a past figure to lay claim to the "social power that authority over the past secures."[59]

In contrast, Palladius uses appeals to the past to create a different social memory of monasticism, one wherein gender is not a boundary, a marker of the binary, nor even a hierarchy in which Melania has improved her status from strictly female to male. Rather, Palladius's memory of Melania offers an alternative account of a woman teaching, one that does not fix her gender but again allows fluidity between female and male roles. She, like Marcella, has studied scripture, but rather than through one man (as Marcella through Jerome) through multiple (male) "ancient commentators."[60] Unlike Marcella, Melania "instructs"[61] in her own voice, not as the mouthpiece for a male teacher. She teaches family members, apparently in private, so that they are converted to Christianity and specifically monasticism; but she also holds forth, apparently publicly, to those of "senatorial class and their wives" about the impending fall of Rome, as foretold in scripture.[62] That is, she teaches about scripture to the ruling class of the city. Palladius records a speech by Melania, thereby remembering her as indenpendent.[63] Melania's actions throughout this section position her as clearly female in relation to her family. Here Palladius refers to her only son and her separation from him as well as her concern about her granddaughter. Yet the description also calls to mind the male roles of the monastic abba bringing Egyptian monasticism via Jerusalem to Rome; of scriptural interpreter; and, by invoking senatorial rank, of orator to the Senate. Rather than saving Rome from heresy, she saves her family to monastic life and then attempts to save those in Rome by preparing for its fall. Although no longer in the male monastic setting of Nitria, Palladius's memory of Melania here shows the same qualities of genderqueerness as earlier. Palladius thus continues to use the memory of Melania as a monastic figure, now after she has left Egypt, to shape a social memory of a monasticism in which gender has a distinctly different role than in Jerome.

This contrast is even more evident in Palladius's memories of Melania and Paula, and of their respective relationships with the male monastic leaders Evagrius and Jerome. Melania has a well-known role in Palladius's description of Evagrius, who, he states, deserves to be remembered.[64] In scholarship, this story is often referred to for biographical information about Evagrius: his early connection with the Cappadocians, his problematic love affair, his flight to Jerusalem, his eventual confession to Melania, and his subsequent move to Egypt. If, however, we ask how Melania is being remembered in Palladius's account, specifically in terms of gender, a question arises: Why, and how, does Evagrius confess to Melania rather than any male monastic leader in Jerusalem? Further, after vowing to Melania to take on the monastic life, why does Evagrius go to Egypt rather than stay in Jerusalem, where monasticism is certainly practiced, not least by those figures who themselves have left Egypt? The positivistic answer, "That is what really happened," remains possible as an explanation, particularly to the first question;[65] but at least one element—that Melania puts on Evagrius's habit—is, according to Columba Stewart, contradicted by Evagrius himself in his letters.[66] In Palladius's account, Melania's wealth and status are central to her portrayal and make possible her level of social contact with male monks, thereby raising the possibility that she was head of the double monastery.[67]

From a social memory perspective, however, it is important that Palladius remembers their interaction in the terms that he does, since the confession itself centers on issues of sexuality and because his later description of Melania and Rufinus's monastic communities associates her only with the women. Thus the queer aspects of Melania that stem from her relationship with Evagrius enter into the social memory of the genderqueer monasticism that Palladius promotes. As with her trip to Rome, Melania here takes on both female and male roles. Palladius explicitly identifies her as a "female Roman"[68] whom Evagrius somehow meets, and whom he later describes in relationship to a female community in Jerusalem, whereas Rufinus's relationship to the monastic community is somewhat obscured.[69] Yet Melania is able to discern Evagrius's concealment of sin, like a monastic prophet; she listens to his confession, like a late antique (male) monastic abba to a disciple, which leads to his spiritual healing;[70] she elicits a vow from him, and she makes him a monk by giving him his habit.[71] When he leaves for Egypt shortly thereafter, the implication is that he must go to the Egyptian desert in order to avoid the dangers of the city, to which he has succumbed not just once (in Constantinople) but twice (again in Jerusalem).[72] These dangers are located in Evagrius's flesh, which his illness specifically attacks.[73] It is Melania who brings about the means to curing this flesh, this sexuality, since the vow she gains from him leads him to Egypt.[74] Palladius affirms later in the chapter that Evagrius was particularly plagued by the demon of fornication and that he gained mastery over it only three years before his death.[75]

Melania's gendered actions vis-à-vis Evagrius engage her earlier authority over the memory of Egyptian monasticism in the Pambo story. Because Melania keeps Pambo's basket until her own death in Jerusalem, it serves as a marker of the link between (Origenist) monasticism in Nitria and these monasteries in Jerusalem.[76] Melania's appointment as guardian of that memory allows her to have similar authority over Evagrius. By extension, she is instrumental in the development of Evagrian monasticism in Egypt, precisely what Jerome has now attacked.[77] Because of the link between memory and location, Melania is remembered as head of both female and male spaces, the female monastery in Jerusalem (but also Evagrius and his heterosexual masculinity) and the desert of Egypt. Palladius's genderqueer memory of her links her to the whole monastic community, which strengthens her.

In contrast, Paula, Palladius suggests, is remembered only in relationship to one man, one who does not allow her to be genderqueer despite her ability to be such. Descriptions of Paula, as Demetrios Katos has recently noted, occasion two of Palladius's direct attacks on Jerome.[78] Katos has made the case that what has angered Palladius here is that Jerome has extended his own change of position on Origen to Paula. I emphasize that Jerome has done so to Paula's *memory*. Palladius's response not only criticizes Jerome; it reshapes the memory of Paula to criticize the role of gender in Jerome's monasticism.

Genderqueer memory now extends into an Origenist eschatology, fulfilled by Palladius's form of monasticism but denied by Jerome's. Palladius identifies both Paula and Melania as female Romans, and both women are specifically associated with an ability to learn and with prophecies.[79] As with Marcella and Melania, however, the differences between how these shared characteristics shape memory are significant. Melania's learning connects her with a larger community, the multiple male commentators and other monks, mostly male, who also share in this learning. Further, her learning specifically allows her to be freed both from "knowledge falsely so called" and from the body itself. The books create wings, such that she becomes a "spiritual bird" who flies to Christ.[80] Paula, in contrast, despite "being a genius of a woman" was limited from her full (genderqueer) potential since Jerome's envy led him to stand in her way. Paula, unlike Melania, remains a woman; her individual relationship with one person's memory weakens Paula; or, to use a different term, it closets her. Thus Paula is remembered only in terms of Jerome, who "prevailed upon her to work towards his own end and purpose" and so thwarted her genius.[81] Both figures' association with prophecy sums up this contrast. A monk makes a prophecy that Paula will die and so escape Jerome's meanness or malign influence.[82] Melania's link with the Sibylline prophecy, however, leads everyone in Rome, despite their response to Melania's teaching, to praise God.[83] Melania's connection to prophecy leads to her triumph as a biblical interpreter and teacher; the prophecy about Paula leads to her death, her only way out of the (anti-Origenist) closet that Jerome has put her in.

CONCLUSION: THE GENDERQUEER MEMORY OF MELANIA

The memory of Melania in Palladius's text appears in multiple relationships. Melania is remembered in connection: to several men (Pambo, Rufinus, Evagrius, a governor,[84] male kin, and Palladius himself); to individual and collective women (the immured virgin, Silvania, Olympias, and the entire female monastery in Jerusalem); to the household (when she travels to her family in Rome) and to the public (when she teaches those of "senatorial class and their wives"); to the Egyptian desert, to Jerusalem, and to Rome. Even with the ancient view of women as underdeveloped men, Melania is remembered as outside the binary, not able to be classified as either a woman or a man. Paulinus's rhetorical query about Melania— "if I can call someone with such manly virtues a woman"—makes this clear; he cannot rightly call her a woman, but neither does he call her a man.[85] This is a promiscuous memory, nevertheless rooted in ascetic morality. Its queerness helps explain the association of Evagrius's great letter with Melania.[86] There are multiple options, as queerness demands: perhaps Evagrius wrote her the letter and addressed her as a man, given her mastery of his masculinity and his heterosexuality in their encounter in Jerusalem; perhaps later editors changed the references to male, because they recognized the maleness in the memory of Melania; or perhaps even it is simply that the letter was *remembered* as being written to her, despite the male references within the text, which can remain unaltered within this memory. If the lady threatened to vanish with the linguistic turn and then appeared in materialized form, as David Brakke has argued,[87] with memory theory this lady, at least, comes out as a queer monk.

NOTES

1. Demetrios Katos, *Palladius of Helenopolis: The Origenist Advocate* (Oxford: Oxford University Press, 2011), 100. For a detailed account of Palladius and his relationship with Lausus, see Claudia Rapp,"Palladius, Lausus and the *Historia Lausiaca*," in *Novum Millennium: Studies on Byzantine History and Culture Dedicated to Paul Speck, 19 December 1999*, ed. Claudia Sode and Sarolta A. Takács (Aldershot: Ashgate, 2001), 279–89.

2. Arthur Fisher ("Women and Gender in Palladius' *Lausiac History*," *Studia Monastica* 33 [1991]: 23–50, at 27) has noted that this appeal is "repeated." Palladius, *Historia Lausiaca*, prol. 9. (Greek text: *The Lausiac History of Palladius: A Critical Discussion Together with Notes on Early Egyptian Monachism*, ed. Cuthbert Butler [Cambridge: Cambridge University Press, 1898–1904; reprint, Hildesheim: Georg Olms, 1967], 12. English translation: *Palladius: The Lausiac History*, trans. Robert T. Meyer [Westminster, Md.: Newman Press, 1965], 26; I reference Meyer throughout, but this translation is often misleading at key points. As a result, I have made modifications, minor ones unnoted but significant ones discussed as necessary.)

3. For the argument that Palladius saw Melania as an appropriate model for Lausus, see Katos, *Palladius*, 104. For "gender-bent," see Elizabeth A. Clark, "Holy Women, Holy Words: Early Christian

Women, Social History and the 'Linguistic Turn,'" *Journal of Early Christian Studies* 6 (1998): 413-30.

4. Cf. Gillian Cloke, *"This Female Man of God": Women and Spiritual Power in the Patristic Age, AD 350-450* (New York: Routledge, 1995), 181, 212-14, and esp. 214-15, which focuses on Melania the Elder; and Patricia Cox Miller, "Is There a Harlot in This Text? Hagiography and the Grotesque," in *The Cultural Turn in Late Ancient Studies: Gender, Asceticism, and Historiography*, ed. Dale B. Martin and Patricia Cox Miller (Durham: Duke University Press, 2005), 87-88 and particularly 98 note 7, which references all the primary sources, not just Palladius, that describe Melania the Elder in male terms. Miller draws on the earlier work by Cloke. For a recent full discussion and survey of the scholarship, see Ross Kraemer, "Women and Gender," in *The Oxford Handbook of Early Christian Studies*, ed. Susan Ashbrook Harvey and David Hunter (Oxford: Oxford University Press, 2008), esp. 478.

5. See Verna E. F. Harrison, "Review of Gillian Cloke, 'This Female Man of God,' : *Women and Spiritual Power in the Patristic Age, AD 350-450*," *Journal of Theological Studies*, n.s., 48 (1997): 694-700, at 700. Harrison's position that Palladius, among others, promoted a "positive" view of ascetic women as "human" is also reflected in Fisher's earlier article ("Women and Gender," 1991: above, note 2) and Katos's recent book (*Palladius*, 105). Fisher's argument is for a "holy androgyny" for Melania; for a review and critique of using "androgyny" to imply equality, see Dale Martin, *Sex and the Single Savior: Gender and Sexuality in Biblical Interpretation* (Louisville: Westminster John Knox Press, 2006), 83-85.

6. Elizabeth A. Clark, "Melania the Elder and the Origenist Controversy: The Status of the Body in a Late Ancient Debate," in *Nova et Vetera: Patristic Studies in Honor of Thomas Patrick Halton*, ed. John Petruccione (Washington, D.C.: Catholic University of America Press, 1998), 117-27. Also important was her social status and wealth, cf. E. A. Clark, "Holy Words."

7. Fisher argues that Palladius sees sexuality as of "very secondary importance" and that women in his text are less concerned with bodies than are men ("Women and Gender," 38).

8. Elizabeth A. Castelli, "The Future of Sainthood," this volume.

9. Virginia Burrus, "Queer Father: Gregory of Nyssa and the Subversion of Identity," in *Queer Theology: Rethinking the Western Body*, ed. Gerard Loughlin (Oxford: Blackwell, 2007), 147-62, particularly 147, where she also draws on the work of David Halperin. Amy Hollywood, "Queering the Beguines: Mechthild of Magdeburg, Hadewijch of Anvers, Marguerite Porete," in *Queer Theology*, 163-74, particularly 166 for the point that ideas about queer religiosities "de-naturalize and destabilize normative conceptions of human sexuality." I wish to thank the anonymous reader for the University of California Press, who directed my attention to these two works.

10. Becca Chase and Paula Ressler, "An LBGT/Queer Glossary," *The English Journal* 98 (2009): 23-24. See also Annamarie Jagose, *Queer Theory: An Introduction* (New York: New York University Press, 1996), 3.

11. See Miller, "Is There a Harlot?"

12. As part of her emphasis on the humanity versus gender division, Verna E. F. Harrison argues that "female man," is an overtranslation of the Greek; instead *anthrōpos* means "person" and so equality ("Review," 698-99); *contra*, Cloke, "This Female Man," 226 note 2, arguing that the phrase does not indicate a female human being but "actively convey[s] androgyny of sexual status"; but cf. Dale Martin's point, drawing on Thomas Laqueur, that the ancient body existed on a hierarchical spectrum. Thus, even a female person has, by not being just a woman, moved up the spectrum toward manhood. This view of the body supports the position that masculine ascetic women have left behind at least part of their weaker, female, selves and achieved a higher, male, status (Martin, *Sex and the Single Savior*, 83-84).

13. Judith Halberstam, *Female Masculinity* (Durham: Duke University Press, 1998). Halberstam largely examines female masculinity versus "dominant masculinity" and admittedly spends little time on "female femininity or male femininity" (273). Female masculinity differs from androgyny, because the latter seeks to erase gender distinctions through a blending, whereas the former creates a gender alternative to the binary female/male.

14. Palladius, *Historia Lausiaca*, prol. 2–3 (ed. C. Butler, 9–10; trans. Meyer, 23–24, here altered).
15. This is paraphrase of a sentence in Sue Campbell, "The Second Voice," *Memory Studies* 1 (2008): 41–49, at 42.
16. Palladius, *Historia Lausiaca*, prol. 2 (ed. C. Butler, 9–10; trans. Meyer, 23).
17. For example, Palladius can include monks who died before he came to Egypt (e.g., Nathaniel: ibid. 16) and those about whom he receives reports from others (e.g., Sarapion: ibid. 37, where "the fathers used to tell" [ed. C. Butler, 109; trans. Meyer, 105]). Further, near the end of his work he draws on other written sources (ibid. 65 [ed. C. Butler, 160–61; trans. Meyer, 146]). My approach to understanding the shaping of memory stems from the work of Maurice Halbwachs, for which see his *On Collective Memory*, ed. and trans. Lewis A. Coser (Chicago: University of Chicago Press, 1992).
18. This description is based on an analogous description of the character Jack in the television show *Will and Grace*, in Christopher Castiglia and Christopher Reed, "'Ah, Yes, I Remember It Well': Memory and Queer Culture in *Will and Grace*," *Cultural Critique* 56 (2004): 163.
19. For a discussion of how collective memory does not imply social cohesion but can be part of a social contest, see Campbell, "Second Voice," 44.
20. Campbell, "Second Voice," 43.
21. Cf. William Harmless, S.J., "Remembering Poemen Remembering: The Desert Fathers and the Spirituality of Memory," *Church History* 69 (2000): 483–518, esp. 512–18, examining Poemen as a "man of memory" (514). For Palladius remembering women as practicing monasticism like men, see his description of the female monastery in the Pachomian system (*Historia Lausiaca* 33).
22. Ibid. 41.1 (ed. C. Butler, 128; trans. Meyer, 117, but cf. 203 note 368, acknowledging that the Greek is "manly women" [which I use here] and not actually "courageous women," which he uses in his text). This passage, as noted above, suggests that although Palladius does not believe that these women are no longer female, he does regard them as having moved upward toward masculinity. Similarly, Palladius refers to "fathers, male and female" in his prologue (ed. C. Butler, 10). Meyer (23) takes the Greek to mean "of fathers, of male and female anchorites." But here Katos is correct that "male and female" qualifies the fathers (*Palladius*, 105); presumably, then, ascetic women could be collapsed into the category male. Melania's masculinity, however, is not explicitly linked to ascetic practices, as in the case of these women.
23. E. A. Clark, "Holy Women, Holy Words," 416–17.
24. Burrus, "Queer Father," 147.
25. John the Little also spends thirty years in "confinement" (the Greek differs here) but for unstated reasons. Cf. Palladius, *Historia Lausiaca* 35.2 (ed. C. Butler, 100; trans. Meyer, 99).
26. Ibid. 5.1 (ed. C. Butler, 21; trans. Meyer, 36). Meyer translates μήτε γυναιξὶ μήτε ἀνδράσι συντυγχάνουσα κατ' ὄψιν as "she never looked a man or woman in the face," but the verb carries the sense "meeting with." Cuthbert Butler's critical edition includes variants that emphasize the visual nature of her separation: she does not see others' faces, and none, regardless of gender, sees hers. Likewise, I modify Melania's claim that she did not see Alexandra's face from Meyer's translation.
27. Cf. Virginia Burrus, *Saving Shame: Martyrs, Saints, and Other Abject Subjects* (Philadelphia: University of Pennsylvania Press, 2008), 93.
28. Halberstam, *Female Masculinity*, 175–76.
29. As quoted in Jagose, *Queer Theory*, 5.
30. Palladius, *Historia Lausiaca* 9 (ed. C. Butler, 29; trans. Meyer, 43).
31. Ibid. 49.2 (ed. C. Butler, 144; trans. Meyer, 132). See Daniel F. Stramara, Jr., "*Adelphotēs*: Two Frequently Overlooked Meanings," *Vigiliae Christianae* 51 (1997): 316–20. Palladius also uses the term to refer to a female monastery (*Historia Lausiaca* 33 and 70). Stramara does not include this reference, in *Historia Lausiaca* 9, in his discussion.
32. καὶ τὸ ἑαυτοῦ ἄρρεν τῆς ἐπιθυμίας ἐλάσας καὶ τὸ τῶν γυναικῶν θῆλυ τῇ ἐγκρατείᾳ φιμώσας (Palladius, *Historia Lausiaca* 49.2: ed. C. Butler, 144; trans. Meyer, 132).

33. Dale Martin, *Sex and the Single Savior,* 88–90; of particular importance is his suggestion that the usual English translation "*neither* male *nor* female" should be replaced with a more literal "no male or female" in order to allow queer readings. I have used this alternative translation for the Palladius passage that follows.

34. For the link between femaleness and sexuality see Cloke, *"This Female Man,"* 33, as cited in Miller, "Is There a Harlot?" 92.

35. Similarly, in another monastery, where the female community has a male overseer, Palladius pays attention to the dangers of male heterosexuality, specifically of the monk Elias, who lives in a female community. Because Elias was "tempted by lust," he has a vision in which three angels castrate him, though not "truly." Palladius does not mention the women's sexuality—or their possible desire for Elias—suggesting a lack of female agency in monastic sexuality. Palladius's concerns with heterosexuality in these *other* monastic settings that have both men and women also "queer" Melania, who can be included in this *adelphotēs* at Nitria without any guards against sexual desire, hers or that of the male monks with whom she lives.

36. Cf. Stramara, *"Adelphotēs,"* 318.

37. ἐξαιρέτως: Palladius, *Historia Lausiaca* 9 (ed. C. Butler, 29; trans. Meyer, 43).

38. Thus I am arguing in favor not of an "asexual unity" that is a "completed male" (Martin, 84), but of a loss of heterosexuality that still maintains a gender differentiation. That purpose of gender distinction—heterosexuality—may lead to asexuality but not to genderlessness.

39. Palladius, *Historia Lausiaca* 10.5 (ed. C. Butler, 31; trans. Meyer, 45).

40. Rebecca Krawiec, "'Garments of Salvation': Representations of Monastic Clothing in Late Antiquity," *Journal of Early Christian Studies* 17 (2009): 125–50.

41. Paul Connerton, *How Societies Remember* (Cambridge: Cambridge University Press, 1989).

42. His masculinity here is legible because it had already left the male body in being attached to Melania in the previous chapter (Halberstam, *Female Masculinity,* 2).

43. Castiglia and Reed, "Ah, Yes," 164.

44. In being both subject and object, Melania is here configured much like Poemen in the *Apophthegmata Patrum,* who is associated with monastic remembering and memory, as William Harmless has shown ("Remembering Poemen Remembering," 514).

45. Castiglia and Reed, "Ah, Yes," 166.

46. This would be explicit to a Greek reader, since the use of the feminine article, *hē,* with *anthrōpos* was unusual (Cloke, *"This Female Man,"* 226 note 2). Melania's follower Olympias "walking according to her reverence [ὅπις] and in her very footsteps" (Palladius, *Historia Lausiaca* 56.1; here modified from Meyer 137) also receives this phrase (*hē anthrōpos tou theou*) in another of Palladius's texts (*Dialogue on the Life of St. John Chrysostom* 56). Cf. Harrison, "Review," 699; and see Miller, "Is There a Harlot?" 98 note 7 for these references.

47. Cf. Katos, *Palladius,* esp. 116–18, arguing that the entire *Historia Lausiaca* is written as a defense of the monks whom Jerome had attacked as Origenist or Pelagianist, or both; Katos specifically focuses on Palladius's "homage" (118) to Melania and his attack of Jerome's relationship with Paula. Yet Katos denies that issues of gender are part of these portraits, because Palladius is more interested in creating a "universal" monasticism (105). Katos's argument that Palladius constructs his text as a defense and as an advocacy on behalf of these monks to the imperial court, especially Pulcheria, is strong; and as Katos says, it particularly explains the prominence of Melania. Yet I clearly disagree about the idea of a universal monasticism that elides gender. Palladius is well aware of Melania's queer-gendered aspects (even if he would not conceive of such a theoretical term) and does not hesitate to present her as such, a position that I argue extends the construction of the *Historia Lausiaca* as an Origenist apologetics.

48. Castiglia and Reed, "Ah, Yes," 159, using this term to refer to the "willed amnesia" of the gay male community after the AIDS crisis about queer culture prior to that crisis.

49. Both women are called Ῥωμαίας, which Meyer translates as both "Roman lady" and "Roman matron." Wilkinson has pointed out, however, that Melania is a Spaniard who moved to Rome, and thus her homeland is Spain, not Italy, as Palladius himself notes (Kevin W. Wilkinson, "The Elder Melania's Missing Decade," *Journal of Late Antiquity* 5 (2012): 166-84, at 176). Palladius's reference to Melania as a Roman could be a class reference, making her the equivalent of a Paula.

50. Castiglia and Reed, "Ah, Yes," 162-63.

51. Latin text: *Sancti Eusebii Hieronymi Epistulae*, ed. Isidorus Hilberg, vol. 3 (CSEL 56: 145-56). English translation: *Jerome: Letters and Select Works*, trans. W.H. Fremantle, G. Lewis, and W.G. Martley (NPNF, ser. 2, 6: 253-58). I am not arguing that Palladius, whose text is later, knew of Jerome's letter (dated 412 C.E.) and thus that it shaped his account of Melania, in the way that Katos has made connections between Jerome's letters that read as veiled attacks and the stories of the monks that begin Palladius's history. Cf. note 47 above.

52. Andrew Cain, "Rethinking Jerome's Portraits of Holy Women," in *Jerome of Stridon: His Life, Writing and Legacy*, ed. Andrew Cain and Josef Lössl (Surrey: Ashgate, 2009), 52-56.

53. Jerome describes the audience as "many [of the male sex], including some priests" (*Ep.* 127.7, CSEL 56: 151; NPNF, ser. 2, 6: 255-56).

54. Paula visited Egypt prior to the outbreak of the Origenist controversy; since this portrait, although about earlier events, was written in the early fifth century, Jerome would have been likely to be aware of exposure to Origenism in some forms of Egyptian monasticism, particularly the one that Palladius preserves.

55. *Ep.* 127.8 (CSEL 56: 151-52; NPNF, ser. 2, 6: 256).

56. Ibid. 9-10 (CSEL 56: 152-53; NPNF, ser. 2, 6: 256-57).

57. Campbell, "Second Voice," 42.

58. This is perhaps Jerome's answer to the contradiction of the term "holy *woman*," which he uses to describe Marcella; cf. Miller, "Is There a Harlot?" 90-91.

59. Campbell, "Second Voice," 42.

60. Palladius, *Historia Lausiaca* 55 (ed. C. Butler, 148-49; trans. Meyer, 136-37).

61. The verb is κατηχέω, used repeatedly in this section to describe Melania's activity with various people in Rome (ibid. 54 [ed. C. Butler, 146-48; trans. Meyer, 134-36]).

62. τοὺς συγκλητικοὺς καὶ τὰς ἐλευθέρας (ibid. [ed. C. Butler, 147; trans. Meyer, 135, but modified]).

63. This is not a "prompted" memory, one in which a person recalls his or her vocation to monasticism, or practices, or struggles, as elsewhere in Palladius's history.

64. Palladius, *Historia Lausiaca* 38.1 (ed. C. Butler, 116; trans. Meyer, 110). Katos (*Palladius*, 120-22) argues that Palladius makes this appeal to preserve Evagrius's memory specifically *contra* Jerome. For a recent discussion of the influence of Evagrius Ponticus on Palladius and this work, see Rapp, "Palladius," 285. The classic work remains René Draguet, "L'*Histoire lausiaque*, une œuvre écrite dans l'esprit d'Évagre." *Revue de l'Histoire Ecclésiastique* 41 (1946): 321-64.

65. This, for example, is how Fisher ("Women and Gender," esp. 31 for this tale) reads Palladius.

66. Columba Stewart, "Evagrius Ponticus on Monastic Pedagogy," in *Abba: The Tradition of Orthodoxy in the West: Festschrift for Bishop Kallistos (Ware) of Diokleia*, ed. John Behr, Andrew Louth, and Dimitri E. Conomos (Crestwood, N.Y.: St. Vladimir's Seminary Press, 2003), 241-71, at 244.

67. Stewart's evidence from Evagrius (ibid.) makes clear that Rufinus must have been in Jerusalem at this time. This point, however, remains elusive in scholarship on the relationships among Evagrius, Melania, and Rufinus. Francis X. Murphy has competing descriptions, at one point suggesting that Rufinus must have been in Jerusalem by 379 or 380 ("Melania the Elder: A Biographical Note," *Traditio* 5 [1947]: 59-77, at 70), although later hypothesizing that Evagrius met Rufinus in Egypt, implying that Rufinus was not in Jerusalem when Evagrius confessed to Melania (72). Dysinger's version of these events assumes that Rufinus was in Jerusalem at the time but does not question why Evagrius would confess to Melania and not Rufinus (Luke Dysinger, OSB, *Psalmody and Prayer in the Writings of Evagrius Ponticus* [Oxford:

Oxford University Press, 2005], 12–13, where he also notes (note 25) Gabriel Bunge's view that Rufinus and the whole community were just as important as Melania but that Melania receives prominence because of her "status as superior of the double monastery." For a definition and history of the double monastery, including occasional female leaders (though not Melania), see Daniel F. Stramara, Jr., "Double Monasticism in the Greek East, Fourth through Eighth Centuries," *Journal of Early Christian Studies* 6 (1998): 269–312.

68. Cf. note 49 above.

69. Palladius, *Historia Lausiaca* 46.5–6 (ed. C. Butler, 135–36; trans. Meyer, 124). She built the monastery and lived there while "holding a company of fifty virgins" (modification of Meyer). Rufinus lived with her (συνέζη, which Meyer translates as "dwelt close by") and had the "same habits"(ὁμότροπος), but no men are mentioned in connection with him or the monastery that Melania built. Further, Palladius stresses that both of them then engaged in hospitality of "bishops, solitaries [μονάζοντας], and virgins" and heard monastic vows. If Melania was head of a double monastery, Palladius obscures that in his description here, in contrast to his account of Melania's relationship with Evagrius (where again Rufinus is not mentioned). Cf. Murphy, who describes it as a "double monastery under their mutual guidance" ("Melania," 72).

70. Likewise, Fisher ("Women and Gender," 31) notes that here Melania acts like a medieval abbot. Contrast Murphy's description of Melania's treatment of Evagrius as "hospitality" ("Melania," 72). On her trip to Rome, Melania teaches a male monk about proper asceticism; there Palladius describes her as "like a wise mother approaching her own son." She is a μήτηρ, not an ἀμμά, even as she acts like a monastic elder. Cf. Palladius, *Historia Lausiaca* 55.2 (ed. C. Butler, 149; trans. Meyer, 136).

71. Ibid. 38.9 (ed. C. Butler, 119–20; trans. Meyer, 112–13).

72. Evagrius "goes abroad" (ἐξέρχεται)—a term for entering the monastic life; cf. Kevin Wilkinson's discussion ("Elder Melania's Missing Decade," 175–76) of Palladius's use of this term in relationship to Melania and her move from Spain, to Rome, to the East.

73. In Constantinople, the dangerous love affair was clearly carnal; in Jerusalem, Evagrius's backsliding, which leads to his illness, is first signaled in a return to his previous "clothing" and "speech": two terms that, if less expressly sexual, also implicate the body in terms of its relationship to the city and its values.

74. Although she does not explicitly send him to Egypt, as Stewart points out ("Evagrius Ponticus on Monastic Pedagogy," 244).

75. Palladius, *Historia Lausiaca* 38.13 (ed. C. Butler, 122; trans. Meyer, 114).

76. Ibid. 10.5 (ed. C. Butler, 31; trans. Meyer, 45).

77. For the progression of Jerome's positions about Origen and Origenism, including his antipathy toward Rufinus and Melania the Elder, see Elizabeth A. Clark, *The Origenist Controversy: The Cultural Construction of an Early Christian Debate* (Princeton: Princeton University Press, 1992), 121–51.

78. Katos, *Palladius*, 114–15.

79. Though here the text is corrupted; cf. *The Lausiac History of Palladius: A Critical Discussion*, ed. C. Butler, 128. For a discussion of learning as an important qualification for ascetic women, including Melania the Elder and Marcella, see Elizabeth A. Clark, "Ascetic Renunciation and Feminine Advancement: A Paradox of Late Ancient Christianity," *Anglican Theological Review* 63 (1981): 240–57.

80. Palladius, *Historia Lausiaca* 55.3 (ed. C. Butler, 149; trans. Meyer, 136–37).

81. Ibid. 41.2 (ed. C. Butler, 128; trans. Meyer, 118).

82. βασκανίας: ibid. 36.6 (ed. C. Butler, 108; trans. Meyer, 104).

83. Ibid. 54.7 (ed. C. Butler, 148; trans. Meyer, 135–36).

84. For a discussion of Melania's authority in confronting this governor, see Sigrid Mratschek-Halfmann, "Melania and the Unknown Governor of Palestine," *Journal of Late Antiquity* 5.2 (2012): 250-68, esp. 257-58.

85. For this reference along with others, cf. Miller, "Is There a Harlot?" 98 note 7; see also Catherine Conybeare, *Paulinus Noster: Self and Symbols in the Letters of Paulinus of Nola* (Oxford: Oxford University Press, 2000), 81–82, for a discussion of how his masculine references to Melania fit with his ideas of friendship and a balance between the current gender hierarchy and the eventual attainment of "neither male nor female" as in Gal. 3:28.

86. For a discussion about the state of scholarship on whether the letter was or was not to Melania because of the masculine references, see *Evagrius Ponticus*, ed. Augustine M. Casiday (London: Routledge, 2006), 59–60.

87. David Brakke, "The Lady Appears: Materializations of 'Woman' in Early Monastic Literature," in *The Cultural Turn in Late Ancient Studies: Gender, Asceticism, and Historiography*, ed. Dale B. Martin and Patricia Cox Miller (Durham: Duke University Press, 2005), 25–39.

PART FOUR

Wisdom and Heresy

THE EMERGENCE OF AN IMPERIALLY sanctioned Christian orthodoxy, and of networks of writers, practitioners, and institutions that could define and (to some extent) enforce that orthodoxy, is one of the most dramatic changes in Roman culture to take place during the lifetimes of the two Melanias. Melania the Elder was part of a Christian generation that had been born not long after the death of Constantine in 337, a generation that came of age after the establishment of legal tolerance and imperial favor for Christianity but before the legal or ecclesial status of the Nicene Creed was fully settled, either within the imperial family or in the Roman Empire as a whole. What is perhaps most remarkable about the rise of Christian orthodoxy in those decades is not the specific content of the doctrines upheld but how the idea of a public, enforced, orthodoxy and the related idea of heresy became normal. The lives of Melania the Elder and Melania the Younger, however, show how difficult it was to coordinate orthodox theological content with the concrete lives of the individuals who sought or claimed to be orthodox. The sheer fact that defining orthodoxy was an ongoing process, taking place over long stretches of time and large geographical areas, meant that the system of interactions from which orthodoxy emerged could not also be contained within the limits of any one person. The history of orthodoxy is the history not of an aggregate of orthodox people but of a system that came into being on a scale larger than the human. Individuals could live within this system, but they could never replicate the entire system in themselves. The chapters in this section describe the various ways that the lives of the Melanias participated in the system of orthodoxy but also, in significant ways, failed to conform to it.

Robin Darling Young's chapter uses the writings of Evagrius to reorient the life of Melania the Elder toward an older paradigm of Christian thought and practice, in which Melania is a gnostic teacher and guide, in contrast to her portrait in Palladius and Jerome as someone participating in theological party strife as an anti-Arian and Origenist. This shift in categories is illuminating: although there is certainly theological content to Evagrian gnosticism, in this paradigm there is also an attempt to align that content with the spiritual practice of the individual gnostic. This attempt is, however, incompatible in both content and form with the new and more systemic kind of orthodoxy that was emerging during Melania's lifetime, which presupposed systems of truth that were potent public forces.

In Susanna Drake's chapter, we see the tension between two different albeit overlapping social systems, the family and class network that made up Roman nobility in late antiquity and the religious and ecclesial system that made up orthodoxy, especially in Augustine's North Africa. Although their gifts and support to North African churches, and Pinian's near-conscription into the priesthood, indicate the couple's strong ecclesial ties, Melania the Younger and her husband fit more consistently into the older system of nobility than into the new orthodoxy. Their complex relationship with Augustine is compounded by Gerontius's depiction of Melania the Younger as potentially both Pelagian and Augustinian on doctrinal questions. The apparent lack of clarity in doctrine, Drake argues, can be explained by looking at Melania as part of the late ancient nobility, in a way that precluded an exclusive allegiance to North African orthodoxy.

A similar lack of alignment becomes clear in Christine Shepardson's chapter on Gerontius, Melania, Nestorianism, Miaphysitism, and Chalcedonian orthodoxy. Shepardson describes the complex chronology leading up to the dominance of Chalcedonian thought in the later fifth century, after Melania the Younger's death, and argues that Gerontius's portrait of Melania is anachronistically anti-Chalcedonian, as Gerontius himself became, after the Council of Chalcedon. At the same time, the complicated and relatively quick shifts in definitions of orthodoxy in the fifth century led Gerontius to depict Melania as staunchly orthodox in a way that often left the content of that orthodoxy undefined. Melania herself did not live long enough to continue into the specific system of orthodoxy that Gerontius inhabited, and his posthumous biography attempts to correct this fundamental problem.

The chapters in this section demonstrate the complexities involved in the rise of Christian orthodoxy from the mid-fourth to the mid-fifth century. They invite us to consider these complexities not strictly as theological problems, nor as political conflicts, but as problems in the coexistence of limited individuals with social systems that expand beyond the confines of a single life.

8

A Life in Letters

Robin Darling Young

In an age of silenced women,[1] Melania the Elder (ca. 340–410) spoke forcefully. Celebrated and admired in her own lifetime, she has regained her fame in the late twentieth century, in large part thanks to my beloved teacher, the historian Elizabeth Clark. A grandee of the imperial aristocracy, Melania controlled her own wealth under the Roman civil code;[2] she could provide public benefactions and promote the career of her son in the city of Rome.[3] Her power did not diminish when she left Rome at his maturity, in about 373. As a pilgrim in Egypt and Palestine, she controlled a retinue, distributed largesse, and freely intimidated a Roman provincial official. Melania's dramatic return to Rome twenty-seven years later magnified her fame, and after her death an imperial courtier received her biography, interwoven with those of well-known ascetics, as a composite portrait of desert holy people.[4] Recently Melania has figured in discussions of asceticism, of late ancient women and their images, and of the debates over Origen's theology in the early fifth century. Works by two main admirers, Paulinus of Nola and Palladius of Helenopolis, have been historians' chief sources for her activities.[5] Likewise Melania's main detractor, Jerome, backhandedly confirmed her fame.[6]

But a more obscure source, the Evagrian letter collection, makes available a different aspect of Melania's life. Her friend Evagrius of Pontus knew her not only as a powerful patron and determined ascetic but as a woman who put into practice a refashioned discipline of ascetic philosophy—the arduous and esoteric path of the *gnōstikos*, or Christian sage. According to Palladius, Evagrius became her protégé and disciple in Jerusalem in 382. He cultivated their friendship in his letters from Egypt, and later he made at least one visit to her house in Jerusalem. Although Melania's letters have not survived, his letters to her show her as a full participant

153

in the Christian study circles that still, in the late fourth century, flourished in Egypt and in Palestine.

As Clark has shown, the learned Melania exercised a patronage customary among wealthy Roman women—a practice of patronage that had faded after the Republic only to revive in late antiquity as women's money funded pilgrimages and monastic foundations.[7] Melania was indeed the lady who vanishes from sight once she has served the literary purpose of her male admirers, but nonetheless her own purposes were real.[8] Palladius's *Lausiac History* and Paulinus of Nola's two letters dramatize Melania and fit her image to the purposes of their authors; both are third-person accounts, and in them Melania is, respectively, an admired ascetic leader and a virgin heroine returning to her family in Rome toward the end of her career.[9]

Yet the letters that Evagrius wrote to Melania differ strongly—by content, genre, and intention—from theirs. In this source there are second-person addresses and descriptions—sentences and phrases that supplement those other portraits of Melania. His letters indicate several aspects of Melania's work attested by neither Paulinus nor Palladius: first, that Melania herself wrote or dictated literary works in the form of letters; second, that she was not merely a reader of Origen but a participant in a way of life guided by Origen's work; and third, that she conformed to the portrait of a *gnōstikos* and friend of God that Evagrius and his circle had been cultivating at least since his arrival in Egypt, probably in 382. In addition, Evagrius's *Pros Parthenon* seems to mention her as leader of a group of ascetic women. Finally, these letters—contrary to a recent assertion—help show that Evagrius's famous letter known as *Ad Melaniam* was addressed to her. This correspondence provides convergent evidence not only that Melania participated actively in the revival of Origen's thought at the end of the fourth century but, further, that she was willing to fund the circumstances for the dissemination of that thought.[10]

MELANIA AS A PRESENCE IN EVAGRIUS'S LETTERS

Since Evagrius composed all sixty-four of his extant letters and the *Pros Parthenon* during his seventeen years in Egypt, they probably constitute the first textual witness to Melania's activities—well before Paulinus's letters, and twenty years and more before Palladius made the final edition of his *Lausiac History*. For that reason, and because the letters communicate esoteric teaching to a smaller circle of recipients, they should be a primary witness to Melania's project.

It would be surprising if Melania did not write more than those now-lost letters, for Evagrius can hardly have been her only correspondent. Melania remained involved in the affairs of her family and of her ascetic friends from her residence in Jerusalem. But lacking her own compositions, historians have been forced to depend upon depictions of her in the writings of others. Palladius made her life the centerpiece of his last work, the *Historia Lausiaca,* and thus presented her to an audience at the imperial court in Constantinople through the work's dedication to the courtier Lausus. Evagrius, on the other hand, wrote to Melania as a patron and confidant, and as a fellow teacher, while she was still alive. Although Palladius's work appeared two decades into the fifth century, and thus almost forty years after Evagrius's first encounter with Melania, it was a series of biographical sketches meant to defend the style of asceticism associated with Evagrius, one that had been destroyed in 400, the same year when Melania left Jerusalem for the West. Though her work appears reflected in the letters of her friend, these letters nonetheless transmit her teaching.[11] Previous work on Evagrius's writings lacks specific attention to these particular letters.[12]

How did Melania join the *gnōstikoi* of Egypt and Jerusalem? In a recent article on her lost decade, Kevin Wilkinson records Melania's solicitude toward her surviving son and demonstrates her financial acumen. In 362, mourning the deaths of her husband and two children, she moved to Rome with her son Publicola. Melania provided for his future by installing him in Roman senatorial circles; she saw to his education, found patrons in the Senate, financed the games he was obliged to provide as quaestor and praetor, and finally appointed a legal guardian for him. Wilkinson writes:[13]

> In other words, although Melania was likely committed to almsgiving, financial support of the Church, and other forms of *noblesse oblige* favored by Christian aristocrats in Rome, she was mostly living a life not unlike any other ambitious senatorial mother. This explains why her ascetic biographers [Palladius and Paulinus?] found nothing very edifying to record until, in her early thirties, she finally embarked on the more perfect life of a nun.

This episode demonstrates Melania's expertise already in her twenties in the late Roman patronage system. She was no less a patron when she funded the Nicene monks after their exile from Egypt in 373 or when she returned to Rome to see to the interests of her granddaughter and namesake, Melania the Younger.[14]

Wilkinson does not mention, though, that Palladius highlights the role of Melania—and in fact inserts her at many apparently unnecessary points in the *Lausiac History*—because he recognizes the ongoing power of her name, a name that was surely remembered in Constantinople as well, and probably also by Lausus, Palladius's own patron. Palladius wrote the *Lausiac History* in 419/20, after he had already written a book in support of John Chrysostom, and he wrote as an advocate of the now-destroyed community of intellectual ascetics in Kellia, perhaps hoping to preserve its memory—and its writings—through gaining Lausus's sympathy for this now-disappeared group. His account influenced those of Socrates and Sozomen, both active later in the capital.[15]

Palladius also aimed to preserve the memory of his teacher Evagrius, and of precisely how the life of Evagrius intersected Melania's. If she acted as patron to her own son, and as patron to the monks of Egypt under the hostile Arian bishop, she was also acting as patron to Evagrius when he arrived in Jerusalem. In order to see how this is so, it will be necessary to review the part of Evagrius's life in which Melania acted as an axis around which he made the great turn from ecclesiastical politics to the life of a solitary.[16]

MELANIA AND EVAGRIUS IN JERUSALEM

Antoine Guillaumont describes the relationship between Melania and Evagrius in his posthumously published *Un philosophe au désert*.[17] According to Guillaumont, the departure of Gregory of Nazianzus from Constantinople, and the appointment of Nectarius as his episcopal successor, led Evagrius into difficulty. Nectarius was a disappointment by comparison; a praetor of senatorial rank, trained in the law, he was baptized, consecrated, and quickly established as bishop in Constantinople, but perhaps with little of Gregory's depth or finesse.[18] Evagrius had worked closely with Gregory in theological disputes before the Council of Constantinople and there had proven his intellectual abilities. Among the notables of the city, Evagrius was celebrated. At thirty-six he was a deacon, according to Palladius, and he was an expert rhetorician and dialectician. Like the Cappadocians, he was a man from the provinces, but he had gained a fine education, provided by a wealthy father. He was not a monk before this time, in Cappadocia; rather, he had been a talented student of Basil of Caesarea there, and after Basil's death he joined Gregory in Constantinople to assist him in the controversies before, and during, the Council of Constantinople.[19] The pro-Nicenes Melania and Rufinus may even have heard of Evagrius before he came to Jerusalem; they certainly moved in the same social circles.

Guillaumont conjectured that Evagrius shone in a "high society" of Constantinople "deeply excited over eloquence, dialectic, and even more, theological discussion." Perhaps because Evagrius mingled with the wealthy, Guillaumont remarks, he was thus "led to pursue a worldly life." But there is no real evidence that he had not always lived a worldly life or that his arrival in Constantinople was not prompted by high ambition—an earlier version of the force driving his literary career once he had settled among the lavras of Kellia and the same ambition that probably made him an appealing assistant to Gregory of Nazianzus, with his own "high ambition."[20]

That very retreat to the countryside has often been used as the therapeutic hinge upon which Evagrius's life turns—a conversion from the habits of pride and lust to an ascetic combat with the same. And the propulsion for the movement, according to Guillaumont and other scholars, was provided by a woman from the very high society that had corrupted him. Evagrian scholarship has relied upon this passage from Palladius to get Evagrius from Constantinople to Jerusalem, where he met

Melania, and thence to Egypt, where she sent him to her monastic friends–friends who, clearly, owed her a debt and had (according to Palladius) later recognized this by a gift exchange.

Palladius writes that Evagrius had become involved with the wife of a praetorian prefect. In the year 379/80, this official was Sophronius, a Cappadocian native and a Christian; Guillaumont speculates that Evagrius may have been received by him in the company of Gregory of Nazianzus. The affection between wife and deacon was mutual, according to both versions of Palladius; both either tacitly or explicitly deny any sexual congress.

Perhaps because scholars of Evagrius are also scholars of monasticism, they have customarily accepted with little question Palladius's account. Augustine Casiday, for instance, describes the situation in the following way:[21]

> The up-and-coming controversialist from Pontus must have cut a dashing figure in Nicene circles, with his clerical dignity, handsome appearance and elegant clothing. But Evagrius' time in Constantinople was not entirely about pummeling heretics, and his good looks precipitated his downfall. He initiated an ill-advised, if unconsummated, romance with the wife of a prominent functionary, in consequence of which he had to leave the city very quickly. But where to go next?

Like other scholars, Casiday assumes that this suave Evagrius had already been a monk before serving as Gregory's deacon. Guillaumont portrays Evagrius as a vacillating personality, like Gregory of Nazianzus, so that like the latter he abandoned his duties in the capital. Jerusalem, Guillaumont speculated, would have been more attractive than Cappadocia, even though organized asceticism flourished in the latter. Thus in the spring or summer of 382, when shipping had resumed on the Mediterranean, Evagrius would have departed for Jerusalem. His encounter with Melania allows Palladius to both praise Melania as a discerning healer and to cast Evagrius in the role of repentant sinner healed by her.

Palladius's biographies of monks would continue, in the monastic realm, the tradition of collected biographies found in Philostratus or Suetonius, and the *Lausiac History* as a whole is meant both to teach its readers about the proper witness of an ascetic and gnostic life and to amuse them with a fantastic travelogue of the Egyptian monasteries, which few could see for themselves. More proximately, it was meant for the edification of Lausus, the *praepositus sacri cubiculi*, and as justification for the good work of the monastic philosophers of the late fourth century in Egypt, Jerusalem, and elsewhere. Its reportage on those monks finds an echo in the church historians' treatments, where Sozomen and Socrates speak positively of Evagrius and his group; and it repeats the information that Rufinus planted in his *Historia Monachorum in Aegypto*. These witnesses were confident in the triumph of their approach and function within Christianity, and they considered themselves part of a well-established tradition effective against both heresy and stupidity.

Their cohort could be said to include Gregory of Nazianzus and Gregory of Nyssa, as well as Athanasius and Anthony; their more ancient sources included Philo, Clement, and Origen—but not just Christian teachers; they knew the resources of the ancient learned tradition generally and used it without embarrassment.

Palladius, Sozomen, and Socrates are the main written sources for the work of these scholarly ascetics, and Palladius had been one of those ascetics in the late fourth century before Theophilus's destruction of Kellia scattered its inhabitants.[22] Palladius also provides the only source for the biography of Melania the Elder, whose amazing wealth provided for the study center and ascetic establishments on the Mount of Olives in Jerusalem, and whose intelligence and learning gain her a flattering portrait by Palladius—one that promotes the idea of Melania as a monastic leader and example. Many if not most scholars have repeated Palladius's accounts as if they were entirely trustworthy.

But Palladius repeats certain tropes of earlier stories of monks, emphasizing for his reader Lausus the uncanny powers and superlative virtue of his heroes and heroines. In at least one case—his brief biography of Ephrem the Syrian—he has concocted or repeated an account differing greatly from the actual life of Ephrem known from that author's own works.[23] Likewise, scholars have begun to notice that certain elements of Evagrius's biography do not square with repeated teachings in the genuine works of Evagrius. Ascetic torments characterize his career as a monk, according to Palladius; but these are nowhere mentioned in his own elaborate and lengthy discourses on the moral and mental training of the monk. Palladius, then, appears to have conformed his biographies to the expectations of the 420s and the imperial court, trying perhaps to meld the monastic tales of Athanasius and Jerome with a history and a defense of his former associates in Egypt of the 380s and 390s.[24]

It is for this reason that any consideration of Melania as teacher within the circle of the Mount of Olives benefits from documents dating from closer to her own time, ones that do not conform her biography to the norms of ascetic holiness as envisioned twenty years after the fact. For whereas Paulinus will portray Melania as a prophet, Palladius will imply that Melania was an angel, an ascetic herself and a patron of monks, defying even imperial officials to protect them. Palladius also described her significance for Evagrius—she was a discerning physician and a quasi-angelic presence who could both protect and command him. (See below.) But Palladius is writing to defend Melania against attacks like Jerome's[25]—and after Theophilus's destruction of Kellia. The settlements there were long gone, and likewise their cooperation with the ascetic compound on the Mount of Olives. Melania had from the late 370s to 400 cultivated friends among the monks, and these friends had been scattered; Evagrius had died.

Unlike Evagrius's modern biographers, Palladius, if no doubt leaving out pertinent details, emphasizes, far more than Evagrius's love affair, the element of fear in accounting for Evagrius's involvement and sudden departure from Constantinople. The deacon, Palladius wrote, was "highly honored in the entire city," but "was caught in the trap of a mental image of desire for a woman, as he himself explained to us, after he was freed from the thought." He was rescued by an "angelic vision" appearing

> in the form of the soldiers of the praetorian prefect [hyparch], and he seized him and led as if into the courtroom and threw him into the so-called *custodia*, and bound him with iron collars, put chains on his neck, and tied his hands. They did not tell him the cause. But he was aware in his conscience that it was thanks to what he had done, and he surmised that her husband had brought it about. Now he was exceedingly anxious, because there was another trial occurring, where others were being subjected to torture in order to extract a confession, for some complaint. But the angel who brought the vision changed its form into the presence of a genuine friend, and spoke to him as he was bound together with forty criminals, saying, "Why is my lord the deacon detained here?" He said to him: "In truth, I do not know, but I have a suspicion that a certain one from the hyparchs is struck by an unreasonable jealousy against me. And I am afraid that the archon himself will be bribed with money, and subject me to vengeance."

Palladius continues the story of Evagrius's conversion by relating that the angelic vision revealed itself as a friend who advised flight. Though Palladius does not explain why Evagrius left for Jerusalem as soon as possible, he does record that Evagrius met Melania but continued in his old behavior until he became ill. Melania, however, became Evagrius's rescuer, as the next section of his biography relates:[26]

> When the doctors were helpless and could not find a *therapeia* for him, the blessed Melania said to him: "Son, I am not pleased with your long illness. Tell me what is in your mind [*dianoia*], for your sickness is not without the aid of God [i.e., is caused by God]." Then he confessed to her the entire matter. She said to him: "Give me a promise in the presence of the Lord that you have the single life as your goal, and even though I may be a sinner, I will pray that there be given to you the preservation of life." He agreed. He arose and was well in a few days. He arose, received a change of clothing from her hands, and went abroad to the mountain of Nitria.

This account, which Palladius claims to have heard from Evagrius himself, may already have been reinterpreted before that time. Evagrius places his attraction in the context of his own later teaching about *logismoi*, or tempting thoughts; he also highlights the importance of angelic and demonic intervention. It is notable that Palladius portrays Evagrius's preoccupation in his last days in Constantinople—namely that he would be interrogated and tortured despite his high rank—acknowledged by the angel who salutes him as "my lord the deacon."

In this difficulty, Evagrius needed a patron if he were not to suffer judicial torture. The angel who came to him in prison (cf. Acts 12:5–17, 16:16–40, for the escapes of Peter and Paul, respectively) was a heavenly patron; in Palladius's account, he was anticipating the patronage of Melania connecting Evagrius with two biblical precedents—and apostles, no less; but once Evagrius reached Jerusalem, it appears that Melania, not an angel, was to act as his patron and protector.

It is odd that no scholar, so far as I know, has questioned whether Evagrius escaping from Constantinople would really be safe from the imperial police force—usually the army—when he arrived in another city where there was also an imperial police force and good means of communication among imperial officials. Yet Melania had already acted as a patron—not only in the case of her son but in the case also of the Egyptian ascetics banished by the Arian praetorian prefect there, whom she had protected in 375. Perhaps Evagrius had already heard of her haughty response to the imperial governor of Palestine on that occasion:[27]

> And having arrested her, he threw her into prison, ignorant that she was a lady. But she told him: "For my part, I am So-and-So's daughter and So-and-So's wife, but I am Christ's slave. And do not despise the cheapness of my clothing. For I am able to exalt myself if I like, and you cannot terrify me in this way or take any of my goods. So then I have told you this, lest through ignorance you should incur judicial accusations. For one must in dealing with insensate folk be as audacious as a hawk." Then the judge, recognizing the situation, both made an apology and honored her, and gave orders that she should succor the saints without hindrance.

But there is another possibility, previously overlooked: that Evagrius knew that Melania was in Jerusalem and went there to seek her help. Guillaumont himself has pointed to this possibility without making the connection: Rufinus and Melania were "gens de grande culture, lecteurs, en particulier, des livres d'Origène et de ses successeurs alexandrins," and like the Cappadocians were opponents of Arian doctrines. It is possible that these allies knew each other, or knew of each other, and that one set—perhaps Gregory of Nyssa, still present in Constantinople—guided the endangered deacon to another set, where he could be offered protection. Indeed, Gregory may have known of Melania's presence in Jerusalem and relayed the information to Evagrius with a recommendation; not only did Gregory share Evagrius's teachings,[28] but he had traveled to Jerusalem and "Arabia" after the council and could hardly have failed to know of Melania and Rufinus's presence there.[29]

It is also unclear where Evagrius stayed while in Melania's vicinity in Jerusalem. Although Rufinus and Melania are often described as running a double monastery on the Mount of Olives, exactly how their community worked is not known—nor either is it known whether their pursuit of the monastic life was in any way monastic in the sense that it was organized with a community as well as rules. Certainly Melania was a respected celibate, as was Rufinus; but it is uncertain whether she required Evagrius to undertake the single life. She also gave him a change of clothing; this is usually interpreted to mean the monastic life, but it may well mean that she gave him a distinctive garb not associated with organized monasticism, much as philosophers would wear the cloak as a sign of their profession.

Throughout Palladius's account, the source is stated to be Evagrius himself. But the episode does not appear in any of Evagrius's works; nor does it appear in the letters that he sent to Melania; perhaps his silence derives from his customary reluctance to speak biographically. Nonetheless, these writings to her, preserved only in their Syriac version, indicate both respect for her as a teacher and an acknowledgment that she was a friend of God—in other words, that according to Evagrius she held the highest possible status among Christian teachers.

THE ORACULAR MELANIA

The second section on Melania in the *Lausiac History* is a much more public episode. In chapter 54, Palladius continues Melania's story, taking it up after her departure from Jerusalem. According to Palladius, Melania left Jerusalem for Rome in order to make certain that her granddaughter would not stray into heresy or bad living. But a particularly dramatic episode took place when Melania helped Melania the Younger and her husband, Pinianus, to abandon the use of their marriage for the ascetic life. As she had for Evagrius, Melania "led them away from Rome and brought them to the haven of a holy and calm life."

Palladius writes of her: "When she did this, she was actually fighting beasts [*thēriomachein*]—I mean the members of the Senate and their wives, who would have stood in the way of their renunciation. But she said, "Little children, it was written over four hundred years ago, 'It is the last hour [1 John 2:18].' Why are you fond of the vain things of life? Beware lest the days of the Antichrist overtake you, and you not enjoy your wealth and your ancestral property." Later Palladius wrote that her prophecy had been fulfilled—"When they had all left Rome, a barbarian deluge, mentioned long before in prophecy, fell upon Rome" (*Or. Sibyl.* 4.65). In warning the senatorial aristocracy of Rome, Melania in Palladius's portrayal is doubly oracular as both prophet and Sibyl, since she is made to quote the Oracle—but she also assumes the role of Christ, warning her children about the Antichrist, the agent of the earth's destruction (e.g., Matthew 24–25).

In addition to arranging a work that defends the now-dispersed scholarly monks of Kellia, Palladius has also deployed his portrait of Melania the monastic aristocrat to make those same monks her clients, appealing to his audience of imperial courtiers in Constantinople. Diminished by her near-supernatural powers, though, is Melania's acumen as a scholar and *gnōstikos*. Only Evagrius's letters testify to her efforts in that ascetic labor.

MELANIA IN EVAGRIUS'S LETTERS

Between his arrival in Egypt in 383 and his death in 399, Evagrius had contact with Melania both directly and indirectly. He returned to Jerusalem once from Kellia, and he both wrote to and received letters from Melania and others in the Mount of Olives community during the sixteen years of his life in Egypt. Sometimes these letters accompanied a treatise—as in the case of the *Gnostic Trilogy*, sent to Anatolius in Jerusalem, or the *Antirrhetikos*, sent to Abba Loukios in Egypt. More often, though, he probably sent single letters, delivered by a trusted courier. Most of the letters passed between Evagrius and other ascetics and therefore could be expected to discuss monastic thought and practice.

Beyond the ordinary reason for writing letters, Evagrius may also have had his own reasons for producing them. If Evagrius knew the letters of Antony or Pachomius, he may also have wanted to modify or surpass those letters as instructions in ascetic practice. Furthermore, he may have wanted his letters to provide examples of eloquence, of philosophizing, and a record of his own circumstances of teaching. Since it has been suggested that Evagrius collected the letters before the end of his life, he may have thought of the collection as an important supplement to his other works.

If the letters are meant to complete or add to his other writings, then their main distinguishing mark may be their description of Evagrius's and his correspondents' practice of the ascetic life. Most of Evagrius's other works were either collections of *kephalaia* for diagnosis and cure of obstacles to ascetic practice and the *gnōsis* to which it was designed to lead, but the *Letters* adopt a far more personal tone—in part because they are responses to particular friends or petitioners of Evagrius, and in part because Evagrius really felt what he described. *Letter* 12, possibly a response to a letter from Gregory of Nazianzus, gives one example of his tone:[30]

> No letter did you send us, o man of wonder, but a sweet food that drips down honey in drops, and sweetens our soul [Prov. 16:24]. Just at the moment when you were thinking about us, immediately you wrote, and as if in a mirror you fashioned with a word the love you have for us [Wis. 7:26].

In other letters, Evagrius regrets his lack of progress, corrects his correspondents, or shows his affection; in one letter to an unknown friend, he writes of himself as "your Evagrius."[31]

Thanks to the later condemnations following the Council of Constantinople II of 553, much of Evagrius's work has not survived in Greek, and only fragments of the letters remain in their original language. In the fifth century, perhaps in Jerusalem, Syrians—probably monastics—translated them into Syriac, and possibly in that same century they were translated into Armenian, where a smaller and modified collection survives. In all but two of the Syriac manuscripts preserving the letters, the entire collection has been identified with Melania, and one of them mentions her by name in the superscription: "Letters that were sent by the blessed Mar Evagrius to various people, the first to the servant of Christ Melania." Guillaumont affirms that the first letter was probably written to Melania, and the

German translator of the letters, Gabriel Bunge, has identified from internal evidence six letters to Melania in the Syriac version of Evagrius's surviving letters: 1, 8, 31, 32, 35, and 37.

More controversial is the letter usually called *Ad Melaniam*.[32] Gabriel Bunge, followed by Augustine Casiday, has reassigned the recipient of the letter as Rufinus, since the Syriac translator refers to the recipient as "sir," and there other references to a masculine recipient.[33] But Guillaumont holds out the possibility that the difficulty of continuing to assign the letter to her "is lifted a bit if one supposes a mistake of the [Syriac] translator reading the title *Melanion* and the name being taken [by the translator], by means of its form, for the name of a man."[34] The letters' repeated references to secrecy and esoteric knowledge Guillaumont compares with the secrecy of Plato's *Letters* 2 and 7, and elsewhere he understands Evagrius's esotericism as similar to Clement's, from whom Evagrius borrowed the term *gnōstikos*. Furthermore, Guillaumont's female recipient "is someone, as was Melania, with whom Evagrius had a great intellectual intimacy and to whom he was able to confide his more profound ideas."

Guillaumont's argument does not strain credulity, comparable as it is with the presentation of the contemporary Macrina as a woman who could share the ideas of her brother, or for that matter Hypatia, who was the teacher of Synesius of Cyrene. In the late fourth century, it remained possible for women and men to be part of the same philosophical circle.

A further letter, apparently addressed to both Rufinus and Melania, brings the total of their letters to seven. Most prominent is consistency to the point of repetitiousness. The same ideas that inform his central trilogy—the *Praktikos*, the *Gnostikos*, and the *Kephalaia Gnostika*[35]—can also be found in his biblical scholia and in other works. Evagrius also sorts his works pedagogically into those for solitaries advanced in knowledge and contemplation, those for teachers, and those for beginning solitaries or male and female monks living in community.[36]

Casiday downplays the letters' significance when he writes that "the letters are on the whole occasional pieces that are interesting chiefly for the light that they shed on Evagrius' daily life, his relations with his contemporaries, his use of scripture, his role as a spiritual guide, and so forth."[37] In actuality, however, many of the letters contain coded but distinct references to esoteric teaching, and the ones to Melania are no exception. Evagrius regarded Melania as a teacher and as a friend—and by implication as a *gnōstikos* like himself. But it is clear from the letters apparently directed to her not only that is she one who comforts him in affliction, and a teacher to the male and female members of her community, but also that she is party to the knowledge gained through ascetic training.

The first letter addressed to her, for instance, appears on the surface to be merely an exhortation to patience in temptation, with a closing passage praising Melania's role as an example for men and women alike. Yet the letter also contains phrases that, when compared with other works of Evagrius, indicate a hidden teaching that the two of them shared. For instance, in *Letter* 1.2, Evagrius writes that "if alone in these pains [of temptations] we will reflect, and bless the Lord, and listen patiently to those who are serving us, we will hear words helpful for contemplations." Here he refers, however, to the "*logoi* of providence and judgment," contained in a mind imbued with *gnōsis* of the origin and completion of the world and the rational beings within it.

Another letter apparently written to Melania refers to her possession of *gnōsis* and impassibility (*apatheia*):[38]

> I have delighted greatly in your love; your love of hospitality is perfected for me. And what should I bestow upon you for the rest that I have found in your presence? For the Lord will be in your heart "a great high priest, he who passed through the heavens" [Heb. 4:14] and "fills the universe" [Eph. 1:23]. He will "raise your head above your enemies" [Ps. 26:6]; he will teach you the knowledge of righteousness and reveal to you the wisdom of his mysteries. Your fruit will be abundant, and your root will flourish beside the waters [Ps. 1:3]. Your mind will not dry your ears [of corn], and the dew of heaven will come upon your harvest; your vine will spring up, and your race will be glorious. The Lord will eat from it, and he will reside in your Paradise. For you have done well for us, humble and sinners, as we possess nothing worthy of your love.

In this letter Melania read that she will be taught by Christ himself—a possible recollection of Origen's belief that the most spiritually advanced were taught by the Logos[39]. Elsewhere in Evagrius's writings, waters symbolize *gnōsis*, or the Henad (Trinity); in another letter, ears of corn (Gen. 41:6) are *gnōsis*; the "dew of heaven," Isaac's blessing (Gen. 27:28) is the kingdom of heaven, and the latter is "impassibility of the soul accompanied by true knowledge of beings" and is in yet another letter dispensed by the true gnostic to the "needy"—those still struggling in the life of the *praktikē*. Further, the vine symbolizes the *nous*, in which (Evagrius predicts) Christ will come to dwell.[40]

Throughout his encoded letters to Melania, Evagrius expresses the existence of their friendship, a term and a practice already well articulated in late fourth-century discourse in its social sense as *philia*. But Evagrius viewed friendship not only as a relationship between equals but as a special bond among *gnōstikoi*, and he laid out a series of *kephalaia* on the subject in his *Scholia on Proverbs*, a book that contains a number of references to a friend. In one of those scholia he writes: "Spiritual friendship is virtue and knowledge of God, through which we join ourselves to friendship with the holy powers, if it is true that human beings who repent [*metanoountes*] become causes of joy for the angels. Thus the Savior calls servants friends when he has judged them worthy to receive a better contemplation [*theōria*].[41]

Thus friendship, for Evagrius, was a highly specialized term, representing a distinct accomplishment in the ascetic life. His views on friendship are best articulated in those same *Scholia on Proverbs,* whose author, Solomon, "often recalls the friend and friendship." Building a syllogism with scriptural quotations, Evagrius writes:[42]

> "Truth" and "friendship" are Christ. Therefore all those having the knowledge of Christ are friends of each other. It is thus that the savior has called his disciples friends, and John was a friend of the bridegroom, Moses also and all the saints. And it is only in this kind of friendship that the friends of the same person are also friends of each other.

For Evagrius, the preeminent examples of friendship in scripture are Moses and Job; thus his reference to Job in his first letter to Melania alludes to their friendship through a reference to the meaning of Job as God's friend, because he "saw God and learned from him what was the cause of these temptations he endured."[43]

At the end of the first letter, Evagrius anticipates Palladius's description of her as "that [female] man of God":[44]

> You also, temperate woman, be zealous to become a beautiful image, not to women only, but also to men—to become to everyone like an archetype, a form of patience, for it is suitable for a disciple of Christ to struggle unto blood, and to show to everyone that Our Lord arms women with manliness against demons, and strengthens weakened souls with the gifts of the commandments and of faith.

Letter 8 concerns the proposed travel of another ascetic, the deacon Severa, to visit Evagrius—a visit to which he objected: "Teach your sisters and your children not to undertake a lengthy journey and not to go into deserted places without testing, for this is foreign to every soul that has withdrawn far from the world."[45] Since Evagrius must have known that Melania and other women had earlier traveled to visit Egyptian ascetics, his caution might reflect not only his reluctance to see women but a reasonably cautious desire not to call attention to himself—especially in view of Theophilus of Alexandria's wish to ordain him.[46]

The final three letters of the collection signal—as does the *Ad Melaniam*—continuous correspondence between the two friends. In *Letter* 31, Evagrius praises Melania as a *gnōstikos,* as he also does in *Letter* 37; in the brief *Letter* 35 he refers to her solicitousness, apparently for his health.

In the last two letters to Melania, Evagrius continues undiminished the conversation with his fellow *gnōstikos. Letter* 35 indicates that Melania wrote to ask about his well-being: "For you were solicitous on my behalf," he wrote; "of this I am persuaded, through the love with which you loved me." Evagrius then predicted that she would "'see the good things of Jerusalem all the days of your life [Ps. 127(128):5],' and this is a gift to you—that you will see 'the sons of your sons [Ps. 127(128):6].' And sons like these one will receive when he prays very greatly." Again, Evagrius speaks in code to a knowledgeable friend; the "contemplation of Jerusalem" is not the result of a pilgrimage to the Holy City; rather, it refers (in *Kephalaia Gnostika* 5.6 and 5.21) to the "contemplation of angels," the equivalent of the contemplation of nature, whereby the *logoi*, or structuring words, of created beings reveal themselves to angels and the virtuous.[47] The height of contemplation is the *theōria* of the Trinity, which Evagrius designates Mount Zion. In neither case does he connect *gnōsis* and contemplation to physical objects.

The final letter to Melania is similarly encoded. *Letter 37* refers to Melania's letters to him as "cool waters to a thirsty soul" (Prov. 25:25):

> The letters of your mind beautifully quench the fire that comes about for us from the world, just like those which your Excellency wrote and sent to us previously. For everything which is useful to our honor and our comfort you have provided from your whole soul.

In return, Evagrius promises to ask the Lord to give Melania the "crown of righteousness" (2 Tim. 4:8) and to make her "fellow heir of the holy ones [Rom. 8:17; Eph. 1:19, 3:6], inasmuch as you accomplished love for them, and showed unto us the tenderness of love." Again, *gnōsis* is meant; thus *Kephalaia Gnostika* 1.75 reads: "If the 'crown of righteousness' is holy knowledge, and if, furthermore, the gold containing the gems indicates worlds that have been or that will be, then the crown placed on the head of contestants by the righteous judge is the contemplation of the corporeal nature and the incorporeal"—that is, of God and creation, visible and invisible. "The Lord," Evagrius concludes, "will requite you, and will reveal to you the mysteries of his wisdom [Rom. 11:25] and establish you over the 'ten cities' [Luke 19:17] that you will lead the rational souls from evil to virtue, and from ignorance to knowledge of Christ."[48]

Evagrius's shorter letters to Melania show that he corresponds with her as one gnostic teacher to another. His longer letter to her, the *Ad Melaniam*, cannot be discussed in this chapter—but it is consistent with the evidence of the rest of their correspondence in presenting her as one who shared his understanding of the esoteric dimension of the ascetic life[49]. From these letters, in addition to the *Ad Melaniam*, it is clear that Evagrius regarded Melania as a *gnōstikos* and a teacher who knew the skills of instructing those who were beginning a life of contemplation, as well as the habit of contemplation herself.

And here the two portraits of Melania converge. Palladius knew Melania as a learned "man of God," as a coworker with Rufinus, and as a patron of monastics and of her own granddaughter. We think of Rufinus, Melania, and their friends as the second or third generation of monastics, and of Evagrius as the founder (at least in retrospect) of monastic contemplation. But I argue that such a perspective is distorting. The Jerusalem and Kellian circles of Melania, Evagrius, Rufinus, and their friends, were rather the end of something—the end of esoteric instruction, of the tradition of the Christian *gnōstikos*, the end of a form of life among early Christian groups that had begun in the second century. This life had more in common structurally, and philosophically, with philosophical circles like Plotinus's group in Rome, or perhaps Valentinus's, though its form of training, its texts, and its exegesis were of course different.⁵⁰ An association that had begun in the wake of an imperially sponsored council came to resemble an association much older, even if it flourished in a quasi-monastic settlement. With Evagrius's death and Melania's departure for Rome, this fourth-century gnostic chapter came to a close.

NOTES

1. See Mary Beard, "The Public Voice of Women," *London Review of Books* 36 (20 March 2014): 11–14, http://www.lrb.co.uk/v36/n06/mary-beard/the-public-voice-of-women (accessed April 13, 2014)

2. During this time, Melania may have commissioned a bath in Rome adorned with an epigram by Filocalus. See Alan Cameron, "Filocalus and Melania," *Classical Philology* 87.2 (1992): 140–44.

3. The chronology of Melania's early adulthood as a widow and mother in Rome receives thorough discussion in Kevin Wilkinson, "The Elder Melania's Missing Decade," *Journal of Late Antiquity* 5.1 (2012): 166–84. He seeks to disprove the redating proposed by Nicole Moine, "Melaniana," *Recherches Augustiniennes* 15 (1980): 3–79, roughly returning to the chronology of F. X. Murphy in "Melania the Elder: A Biographical Note," *Traditio* 5 (1947): 59–77.

4. Palladius's *Lausiac History* is most recently discussed in Nathan K. C. Bennett, "Education as Asceticism and the Education of Asceticism in Greco-Roman and Christian Discourse" (Ph.D. dissertation, Claremont Graduate University, 2013). See also *Palladius: The Lausiac History*, ed. and trans. Robert T. Meyer (Westminster, Md.: Newman Press, 1965). The text is found in *The Lausiac History of Palladius: A Critical Discussion Together with Notes on Early Egyptian Monachism*, ed. Cuthbert Butler, vol. 2 (Cambridge: Cambridge University Press, 1904; reprint, Hildesheim: Georg Olms, 1967).

5. Paulinus of Nola describes Melania's public appearance in Italy in his *Epistle* 29. See *Sancti Pontii Meropii Paulini Nolani Epistulae Opera*, part 1, *Epistulae*, ed. Wilhelm Hartel, 2nd ed., (Vienna: Verlag der Österreichischen Akademie der Wissenschaften, 1999). See the discussion of Paulinus's descriptions of Melania in Dennis E. Trout, *Paulinus of Nola: Life, Letters, and Poems* (Berkeley and Los Angeles: University of California Press, 1999), 206–8 and 226–27. See also Joseph T. Lienhard, *Paulinus of Nola and Early Western Monasticism, with a Study of the Chronology of His Works and an Annotated Bibliography, 1879–1976* (Bonn: Peter Hanstein, 1977); and Catherine Conybeare, *Paulinus Noster: Self and Symbols in the Letters of Paulinus of Nola* (Oxford: Oxford University Press, 2000). See also Christine Luckritz Marquis's analysis of Melania the Elder as a financial patron, and on her role in the Origenist controversy, in her chapter "Namesake and Inheritance," also in this volume. Luckritz Marquis also reassesses the evidence of Paulinus and especially Palladius, but with attention to the intersection of asceticism and patronage rather than the focus here on philosophy, education, and political influence.

6. Having previously expressed admiration for Melania (*Ep.* 39.5) Jerome slandered Melania in his *Epistle* 133.3 and erased her name from his *Chronicle*. For a discussion of the disputes in Palestine between Melania and Rufinus, on the one hand, and Jerome (and Epiphanius of Salamis) on the other, see E. D. Hunt, *Holy Land Pilgrimage in the Later Roman Empire, AD 312–460* (Oxford: Clarendon Press, 1982); and idem, "Palladius of Helenopolis: A Party and Its Supporters in the Church of the Late Fourth Century," *Journal of Theological Studies*, n.s., 24.2 (1973): 456–80.

7. Elizabeth A. Clark, "Patrons, Not Priests: Gender and Power in Late Ancient Christianity," *Gender and History* 2.3 (1990) 253–74; eadem, "Ascetic Renunciation and Feminine Advancement: A Paradox of Late Ancient Christianity," *Anglican Theological Review* 63 (1981): 240–57; and for the larger context of Melania in the late-fourth-century battle over Origenism, see eadem, *The Origenist Controversy: The Cultural Construction of an Early Christian Debate* (Princeton: Princeton University Press, 1992).

8. Elizabeth A. Clark, "The Lady Vanishes: Dilemmas of a Feminist Historian after the 'Linguistic Turn,'" *Church History* 67.1 (1998): 1–31.

9. See in particular René Draguet, "*L'Histoire Lausiaque*, une œuvre écrite dans l'ésprit d'Evagre," *Revue de l'Histoire Ecclésiastique* 41 (1946): 321–64, and 42 (1947): 5–49; and Claudia Rapp, "Palladius, Lausus and the *Historia Lausiaca*," in *Novum Millennium: Studies on Byzantine History and Culture Dedicated to Paul Speck, 19 December 1999*, ed. Claudia Sode and Sarolta A. Takács (Aldershot: Ashgate, 2001), 279–89.

10. The letters of Evagrius were edited, translated from the Syriac, and annotated and with a long introduction, by Gabriel Bunge in *Evagrios Pontikos: Briefe aus der Wüste* (Trier: Paulinus-Verlag, 1986). An edition and translation of the letters from Syriac and the surviving Greek fragments is under way for eventual publication in Sources Chrétiennes, under the direction of Paul Géhin; and an English translation by the present author will appear in the series Fathers of the Church, published by the Catholic University of America Press. Paul Géhin, a scholar of Evagrius and the editor of many of Evagrius's works, has announced his forthcoming critical edition of the *Epistles* in "En marge de la constitution d'un Repertorium Evagrianum Syriacum, quelques remarques sur l'organisation en corpus des œuvres d'Evagre," *Parôle de l'Orient* 35 (2010): 285–301, esp. 288.

11. Of Evagrius's preserved letters, five have been assigned to his correspondence with Melania, with an additional one assigned to Rufinus and Melania together. The long letter *Ad Melaniam* is an appropriate missive to a fellow gnostic and need not be reassigned to Rufinus. And furthermore, if Evagrius's *Pros Parthenon* is addressed to Severa the deacon, resident in Jerusalem, then it would very likely have been read by Melania as well, as referring to her. See notes 32–34 below.

12. *Euagrios Ponticus*, ed. Wilhelm Frankenberg, Abhandlungen der königlichen Gesellschaft der Wissenschaften zu Göttingen, Philologisch-historische Klasse, Neue Folge 13.2 (Berlin: Weidmannsche Buchhandlung, 1912): 564–610. A partial Armenian version exists (in Armenian): *The Life and Works of the Holy Father Evagrius Ponticus in an Armenian Version of the Fifth Century, with Introduction and Notes*, ed. Barsegh Sargisean (Venice: Surb Ghazar, 1907). The surviving Greek fragments are discussed in Claire Guillaumont, "Fragments grecs inédits d'Evagre le Pontique," *Texte und Untersuchungen zur Geschichte der Altchristlichen Literatur* 133 (1987): 209–21; and Paul Géhin, "Nouveaux fragments grecs des lettres d'Evagre," *Révue d'Histoire des Textes* 24 (1994): 117–47. See Luke Dysinger's translation of fourteen letters, the *Ad Melaniam* and the *Epistula Fidei* at http://www.ldysinger.com/Evagrius/11_Letters/00a_start.htm; Augustine M. Casiday's translation of six letters (*On the Faith, Letters 7, 8, 19 and 20, the Great Letter*) in *Evagrius Ponticus* (London: Routledge, 2006); Joel Kalvesmaki's translation and discussion of *Epistle* 57 in http://www.ldysinger.com/Evagrius/11_Letters/00a_start.htm; Robin Darling Young in "Cannibalism and Other Family Woes in Letter 55 of Evagrius of Pontus," in *The World of Early Egyptian Christianity: Language, Literature, and Social Context—Essays in Honor of David W. Johnson*, ed. James E. Goehring and Janet A. Timbie (Washington, D.C.: Catholic University of America Press, 2007), 130–39; and the letters accompanying surviving Greek treatises, most recently in *Evagrius of Pontus: The Greek Ascetic Corpus*, ed. and trans. Robert Sinkewicz (Oxford: Oxford University Press, 2003). An earlier translation of the *Ad Melaniam* or Great Letter was made available by Martin Parmentier and is reprinted in *Forms of Devotion: Conversion, Worship, Spirituality, and Asceticism*, ed. Everett Ferguson (New York: Garland Publishing, 1999), 272–309. For Evagrius's relationship with Melania, and his letters to her community, see Susanna Elm, *Virgins of God: The Making of Asceticism in Late Antiquity* (Oxford: Oxford University Press, 1994; reprint: 2000), 77–78.

13. See above, note 3.

14. On Melania's continuing largess, her immense wealth, and her power in the Roman judicial system, see Sigrid Mratschek-Halfmann, "Melania and the Unknown Governor of Palestine," *Journal of Late Antiquity* 5.2 (2012): 250–68; and Michele Renee Salzman, *The Making of a Christian Aristocracy: Social and Religious Change in the Western Roman Empire* (Cambridge, Mass.: Harvard University Press, 2002), 174.

15. See, respectively, Theresa Urbainczyk, *Socrates of Constantinople: Historian of Church and State* (Ann Arbor: University of Michigan Press, 1997); and Hartmut Leppin, "The Church Historians (I): Socrates, Sozomenus, and Theodoretus," in *Greek and Roman Historiography in Late Antiquity: Fourth to Sixth Century A.D.*, ed. Gabriele Marasco (Leiden: Brill, 2003): 219–54.

16. Recent scholarly discussion of Evagrius can be said to date from Antoine Guillaumont's publication of the unexpurgated version of the *Kephalaia Gnostica* and the accompanying historical study, *Les "Képhalaia Gnostica" d'Évagre le Pontique et l'histoire de l'Origénisme chez les grecs et chez les syriens* (Paris: Editions du Seuil, 1962).

17. *Un philosophe au désert: Évagre le Pontique* (Paris: Vrin, 2004), esp. 41–52.

18. Claudia Rapp, *Holy Bishops in Late Antiquity: The Nature of Christian Leadership in an Age of Transition* (Berkeley and Los Angeles: University of California Press, 2005), 182.

19. Joel Kalvesmaki, "The *Epistula Fidei* of Evagrius of Pontus: An Answer to Constantinople," *Journal of Early Christian Studies* 20 (2012): 113–39. Kalvesmaki (115) revives an earlier position in Evagrian scholarship to argue that Evagrius wrote the letter either from Jerusalem or from Egypt, and thus later than 382—and not as a defense but as a pastoral letter continuing the teaching of Gregory of Nazianzus and displaying already Evagrius's familiarity with a "higher epistemology": i.e., Christian gnosis.

20. See now Susanna Elm's convincing demonstration of Gregory's ambitions in her *Sons of Hellenism, Fathers of the Church: Emperor Julian, Gregory of Nazianzus, and the Vision of Rome* (Berkeley and Los Angeles: University of California Press, 2012).

21. *Evagrius Ponticus*, ed. Casiday, 8.

22. For a recent discussion of Palladius's activities in Constantinople, as a defender of John Chrysostom, and later of Kellia and Melania, see Demetrios Katos, *Palladius of Helenopolis: The Origenist Advocate* (Oxford: Oxford University Press, 2011).

23. For the transformation of Ephrem's life into standard hagiography, see *The Syriac Vita Tradition of Ephrem the Syrian*, ed. and trans. Joseph P. Amar (Louvain: Peeters, 2011).

24. Andrew Crislip, *Thorns in the Flesh: Illness and Sanctity in Late Ancient Christianity* (Philadelphia: University of Pennsylvania Press, 2013), 96–100.

25. See most recently Stefan Rebenich, *Jerome* (London: Routledge, 2002), 198.

26. *Lausiac History*, chapter 38. (Translation my own.) See also the Coptic *Life of Evagrius*, translated in Tim Vivian, *Four Desert Fathers: Pambo, Evagrius, Macarius of Egypt, and Macarius of Alexandria: Coptic Texts Relating to the Lausiac History of Palladius.* (Crestwood, N.Y.: St. Vladimir's Seminary Press, 2004).

27. See Sigrid Mratschek-Halfmann, "Melania and the Unknown Governor of Palestine," in *Journal of Late Antiquity* 5.2 (2012): 250–68.

28. See Kevin Corrigan, *Evagrius and Gregory: Mind, Soul and Body in the Fourth Century* (Farnham: Ashgate, 2009).

29. In his second and third letters, Gregory gives an account of his pastoral visits to Jerusalem and "Arabia" after the Council of Constantinople, and so in 381. See *Gregory of Nyssa, The Letters: Introduction, Translation and Commentary*, ed. and trans. Anna Sivas (Leiden: Brill, 2006), 48.

30. *Euagrios Ponticus*, ed. Frankenberg, 576. All translations from Evagrius's letters are based on the Frankenberg edition of one Syriac manuscript, cited above (note 12), and are my own.

31. Ibid., 578.

32. Antoine Guillaumont (*Philosophe*, 140) writes that this letter was written toward the end of Evagrius's life, after the *Kephalaia Gnostica*, and after the Origenist controversy had exploded in Palestine.

33. *Briefe*, ed. Bunge, 176–90; *Evagrius Ponticus*, ed. Casiday, 63. Now see Augustine M. Casiday, *Reconstructing the Theology of Evagrius of Pontus: Beyond Heresy* (Cambridge: Cambridge University Press, 2013).

34. See the discussion in Guillaumont, *Philosophe*, 145–47.

35. These works, which survive entire in Syriac translation and in part in Greek, will be made available in an English translation through Oxford University Press as *The Gnostic Trilogy*, trans. Robin Darling Young et al. (Robin Darling Young, Luke Dysinger, OSB, Joel Kalvesmaki, Charles Stang, Columba Stewart).

36. For a general introduction to his ascetic works, see now *Evagrius of Pontus: The Greek Ascetic Corpus*, ed. and trans. Robert E. Sinkewicz (Oxford: Oxford University Press, 2003).

37. *Evagrius Ponticus*, ed. Casiday, 32; see also 31–32.

38. *Epistle* 19.1.

39. See Joseph W. Trigg, "God's Marvelous *Oikonomia*: Reflections on Origen's Understanding of Divine and Human Pedagogy in the Address Ascribed to Gregory Thaumaturgus," *Journal of Early Christian Studies* 9.1 (2001): 27–52.

40. See, for instance, *Eight Thoughts* 4.8: "A calm sea is a delight to contemplate, but there is nothing more delightful than a state of peace. For dolphins go diving in a sea that is calm; thoughts worthy of God swim in a state of peace," in *Evagrius of Pontus: The Greek Ascetic Corpus*, ed. Sinkewicz, 80. On waters, see *Ep.* 31; on the ears of corn, see *Ep.* 41; on the needy, *Ep.* 37.2.

41. *Scholia on Proverbs* 189, on Prov. 19:4, in *Evagre le Pontique: Scholies aux Proverbes*, ed. and trans. Paul Géhin (Paris: Cerf, 1987).

42. *Scholia on Proverbs* 304, quoting Prov. 25:10a.

43. *Epistle* 1.1: *Euagrios Ponticus*, ed. Frankenberg, 568.

44. The block quotation: *Epistle* 1.1: *Euagrios Ponticus*, ed. Frankenberg.
"that [female] man of God": *Lausiac History* 9.
Praktikos 81: "The observance of the commandments is a support for the practical life; and their guardian is the fear of God, which is a product of upright faith; and faith is an inherent good, which exists naturally in those who do not yet believe in God."

45. See the discussion in *Evagrius Ponticus*, ed. Casiday, 61, 213. Elsewhere Evagrius opposes pilgrimage, specifically pilgrimage to Jerusalem (*Ep.* 25).

46. *Epistle* 13: *Euagrios Ponticus*, ed. Frankenberg, 576. For Theophilus's career, see now Norman F. Russell, *Theophilus of Alexandria* (London: Routledge, 2007).

47. *Les six centuries des "Képhalaia Gnostica" d'Evagre le Pontique: Édition critique de la version syriaque commune et édition d'une nouvelle version syriaque, intégrale, avec une double traduction française*, ed. Antoine Guillaumont (Paris: Firmin-Didot, 1958).

48. *Epistle* 37: *Euagrios Ponticus*, ed. Frankenberg, 584. *Kephalaia Gnostika* 6.24 reads: "If those who will be angels in the world to come are given authority 'over five' or 'over ten cities,' it is obvious that they will also receive the knowledge that can urge rational souls from vice to virtue and from ignorance to the knowledge of God."

49. See most recently Charles M. Stang, "Evagrius of Pontus on 'the Great Gift of Letters,'" in *Syriac Encounters: Papers Presented at the Sixth North American Syriac Symposium*, ed. Maria Doerfler et al. (Maria Doerfler, Emmanuel Fiano, Kyle Smith, and Luk van Rompay [Louvain: Peeters, 2015]), 151–62.

50. See Edward Watts, *City and School in Late Antique Athens and Alexandria* (Berkeley and Los Angeles: University of California Press, 2006), 184, for a discussion of the similarities and differences between Didymus the Blind's classroom in Alexandria and Evagrius's in Kellia.

9

Friends and Heretics

Susanna Drake

Melania the Younger, her husband, Pinianus, and her mother, Albina, arrived in North Africa in the autumn of 410. After spending some time in Thagaste, the aristocratic entourage traveled to Hippo, where they received a strange welcome from the members of Augustine's church. Upon hearing about the money and land that Melania's family had given to the church in Thagaste, Augustine's congregants crowded the church in Hippo and tried to force Pinianus into accepting a position as priest among them, thus ensuring that Pinianus and Melania's wealth would benefit the church in Hippo. According to Augustine, Pinianus so wanted to avoid becoming their priest that he was willing to sign an oath pledging that he would remain in North Africa if the crowds would cease clamoring for his ordination. In a letter to Albina, Augustine relates what happened as he began to cosign this oath.[1] Augustine writes: "When I began to [sign my name], the pious Melania spoke against it. I wondered why she did this so late, as if we could make [Pinianus's] promise and oath void by not signing it; but nevertheless I obeyed, and so my signature remained incomplete."[2]

Melania stops Augustine midscript. In Augustine's narration of this curious case of *scriptus interruptus*, Melania appears on the scene of rowdy congregants right in time to stop his authorization of the oath, thereby safeguarding her family's freedom to leave North Africa. In Augustine's recounting, Melania's protest—her "no"— commands the immediate obedience of the great bishop, so much so that he leaves off signing his full name.[3] What to make of this empty space after Augustine's half signature? This break in the script—this gap—represents one of those marginal moments of a text in which we can explore "its ethical and political agendas."[4] As Elizabeth Clark, building on the work of Gayatri Spivak, has so helpfully taught historians of early Christianity, the "gaps and absences in a text" often expose "another logic haunting its surface." What is absent or "unnatural relates to the social order of power in which the text participates."[5]

The gap in this particular text—the half-signed oath—gestures to a theological rift that developed between Augustine and Melania. Just as Augustine was unable to lure Melania and her family to stay in his North African enclave, he was unable to trust them to be steady purveyors of his truth. We know from Augustine's treatise *De Gratia Christi* (written after the family left North Africa) that Melania and her family remained, in his estimation, insufficiently orthodox.[6] Melania and Pinianus's orthodoxy was also compromised by their family and friends. They were caught in the middle of the theological debates of the day, including the Origenist and Pelagian controversies. In Rome, they ran in circles that included Melania the Elder, her friend Rufinus (both Origenists), and (everybody's friend) Paulinus of Nola, who notoriously played for both teams in the Origenist and Pelagian controversies.[7] It was in these very circles of aristocratic men and women that Pelagius began to develop his ideas.[8] This chapter explores how Gerontius's *Vita Melaniae Iunioris* broaches some of the central theological topics that occupied Augustine in his debates with Pelagius and with Pelagius's later defender, Julian of Eclanum.

In his *Vita*, Gerontius depicts Melania's passion for orthodoxy as "hotter than fire."[9] He reports that she tried to persuade each heretic whom she encountered to the orthodox faith, and if her efforts were unsuccessful, she would refuse to accept gifts from him. The conspicuous silences of the *vita* also attest to Gerontius's efforts to avoid compromising Melania's orthodoxy. As he avoids any mention of Melania's grandmother, Melania the Elder, presumably because of her Origenist leanings, so, too, he steers clear of pitting Melania against the great bishop of Hippo.[10] Gerontius makes no mention of the scene Augustine describes in his letters to Albina and Alypius.[11] Instead, he portrays Melania and Pinianus as eager to accept the excellent counsel of Augustine and his fellow bishops. Melania and Pinianus, he reports, "did just as they had been advised" by the "most saintly and important bishops of Africa."[12] According to Gerontius, it was Augustine who commanded the obedience of Melania, not the other way around.

Despite his insistence on Melania's orthodoxy and her proper submission to Augustine's authority, Gerontius's *vita* contains vestiges of the Pelagian controversy. The link between Melania and her family, on the one hand, and Pelagius and his views, on the other, haunts the surface of Melania's *vita*. I am less interested in portraying Gerontius as a partisan in the Pelagian controversy and more interested in exploring how the questions raised in the course of the debates between Augustine, Pelagius, and Pelagius's followers, which occurred in the second and third decades of the fifth century, persisted into the middle part of that century, when

Gerontius wrote the *vita*, and remained, at least in some corners, unresolved.[13] Gerontius's *Vita Melaniae Iunioris* is a text in which we can trace the continuing attraction of some Pelagian ideas about Christian elitism, the transfer of nobility, human capacities for sinlessness, and the innocence of babies.

Like Gerontius's *vita*, Pelagius's *Letter to Demetrias*, written in 413, also idealizes the life of an aristocratic virgin and weaves together the threads of asceticism, nobility, humility, and perfection. Demetrias was a member of the "greatest Christian family of all"—the daughter of Olybrius and Anicia Juliana, the granddaughter of Petronius Probus and Anicia Faltonia Proba.[14] Like Melania and her family, the *gens Anicia* fled Rome for Africa in 410. They settled in Carthage, where Demetrias was publicly veiled as a virgin by Aurelius, bishop of Carthage. Demetrias's *velatio* was, as Peter Brown has remarked, "the spiritual marriage of a top aristocrat to Christ."[15] Unlike Melania and Pinianus, however, Demetrias and her family returned to Rome (and their wealth) when peace was restored, and she lived out her days as the *Amnia Virgo* in her villa on the Via Latina.[16]

Much of what follows is informed by a reading of Gerontius's *vita* alongside Pelagius's *Letter to Demetrias*, which was commissioned by the Anician women on the occasion of Demetrias's *velatio*. Pelagius's epistolary presentation of the elite virgin shares some of the same concerns with the aristocratic hagiography of Gerontius. Both authors describe (and align) their female subjects' spiritual and worldly riches. And both shed light on the burgeoning ideology of nobility among aristocratic Christians and their spiritual guides and protégés in the early fifth century. It was this ideology of nobility, in particular, that fueled the flames of the Pelagian controversy.

NOBILITY AND HUMILITY

Peter Brown has argued that one of the characteristics of Pelagian theology was a concern for nobility and distinction. Pelagius's writings, Brown observes, reflect a "widespread striving to create an aristocratic *élite*.... The ideal Christian of Pelagian literature was a *prudens*, carefully reared in conformity to the divine law, to be different from the ignorant crowd."[17] For example, Pelagius describes the newly veiled virgin Demetrias in this way: "She remembers—as well she should—the worldly wealth and reputation she left behind, the pleasures she gave up, the attractions of this life she rejected. Consequently, she is not satisfied with the ordinary way.... She demands something singular and outstanding."[18] Gerontius similarly fashions Melania, her renunciation, and her saintly way of life as singular and outstanding. Gerontius's Melania is distinctly elite—a "highborn and magnanimous servant of Christ."[19] Melania is distinguished in the beginning of the *vita* by her worldly nobility and wealth, and her worldly distinction is transferable to the spiritual realm: like Demetrias, Melania is all the more wealthy for her extravagant renunciation of wealth; she is all the more noble for her humble performances of deference.[20]

In narrative vignettes, Gerontius portrays his heroine as simultaneously wealthy and poor, magnanimous and beggarly. He reports that after their seven-year sojourn in North Africa, Melania and her family traveled to Jerusalem, where they distributed yet more gold to the poor. (This was, of course, years after their famous divestment in Rome.) Gerontius writes:[21]

> Since they themselves did not want to distribute with their own hands the gold left to them, they gave it to those who were entrusted with administering charity for the poor. They did not wish for people to see them doing good deeds. They were in such a state of poverty that the holy woman Melania assured us of this: "When we first arrived here we thought of inscribing ourselves on the church's register and of being fed with the poor from alms." Thus they became extremely poor for the sake of the Lord.

In the same breath, Gerontius describes Melania as a noblewoman with gold to spare and as an extremely poor Christian renunciant, begging at the church door. Gerontius's ever-present reminder of Melania's wealth and nobility activates the Pelagian idea that spiritual excellence could derive from earthly nobility.[22]

In another story, Gerontius describes Melania's entrance into Constantinople, where she was fittingly received by the *praepositus* Lausus and ensconced in his palace. In Constantinople, Melania also encounters her uncle, who tearfully recalls "how delicately [Melania] was brought up, more so than the rest of her family."[23] These contextual details of Melania's high status and delicate upbringing provide the occasion for another demonstration of her humility. In a speech aimed at encouraging her uncle to be baptized, Melania describes her own renunciations. She says: "I have despised glory, possessions, and every pleasure of this present life."[24]

The juxtaposition of worldly and spiritual nobility—of great wealth and great repudiation of wealth—recalls Pelagius's counsel to Demetrias. Pelagius celebrates Demetrias's transfer of nobility from the worldly to the otherworldly register when he writes of her: "Already noble in this world, she desires to be even nobler before God and seeks in her moral conduct values as precious as the objects which she spurned in this world."[25] Brown has noted that with these words, Pelagius "had implicitly validated the nobility of her family. He derived the prospective sanctity of Demetrias directly from her Anician descent: the one led to the other."[26] For Pelagius, earthly nobility was a field well suited to cultivate Christian nobility. For Augustine, however, the two registers of nobility could not be farther apart.

In his letter to Demetrias's mother, fired off as a hasty retort to Pelagius's letter, Augustine makes no mention of Demetrias's worldly, highborn status but reminds her instead of the "innate poverty" of her "human heart" and her perilous proximity to "that mass of death and perdition derived from Adam."[27] Remarking on these theologians' interest in writing to Demetrias and her family, Andrew Jacobs notes, "Demetrias's *nobilitas* and her ascetic vocation are reshaped and reconfigured by Pelagius ... and Augustine to fit their own visions of Christian subjectivity and salvation."[28] In regard to Pelagius's letter, "the idiom of worldly status ... is entirely appropriated, translated into a new 'social logic' in which 'rank and honor' are forever transformed into a vision of Christian elitism."[29] For Augustine, by contrast, the notion that spiritual riches could be rooted in (and explained by) worldly status became increasingly abhorrent (and heretical) during the course of the Pelagian controversy. The tension between nobility and humility—in the worldly as well as the spiritual register—haunts not only the famous theologians' correspondence with Demetrias in 413–17 but also Gerontius's *vita*, composed more than thirty years later.

Like Pelagius before Demetrias, Melania's hagiographer was dazzled by the wealth and worldly dignity of his subject and did not want to erase it entirely from view. And as with Pelagius's descriptions of Demetrias, Gerontius constructed Melania as an exemplar of Christian elitism, distinguished and extraordinary in her embrace of the holy life. Despite Gerontius's insistence on Melania's "excess of humility,"[30] he never fully renounced her excess of wealth and human glory.[31] Gerontius's *vita* participated in a celebration of nobility and earthly status that was similar to—if not identical with—the "widespread striving to create an aristocratic *élite*"[32] that lay at the heart of Pelagianism. The second decade of the fifth century was marked, in part, by a momentum that sought to capture the ideology of an aristocratic elitism—which spilled over from a pre-Christian Roman past—and to sweep it into the Christian era. It was the same momentum that inspired male hagiographers to linger on the worldly wealth and high status of their female subjects, and it was the same momentum that began to trouble Augustine around 414 and eventually to repulse him.

PERFECTION AND SIN

Closely linked to Gerontius's discussions of Melania's elite status and humility are his descriptions of Melania's spiritual perfection. Here we can trace the vestiges of Pelagius's challenge to Augustine regarding the human capacity for sinlessness. Gerontius's *vita* reflects a tension between Melania's great spiritual power and her sinfulness. In some passages, Gerontius praises Melania's near-spiritual perfection and, in others, he depicts Melania as quick to acknowledge herself as an impoverished, despicable sinner. Melania, he notes, is "advancing toward perfection,"[33] and she counsels her followers to imitate a statue by nobly submitting "to everything—to insult, reproach, contempt—in order that [they] may inherit the kingdom of Heaven."[34] In her advice to her followers, Melania encourages *apatheia*—a level of self-control and composure that remains "undisturbed by the passions"[35]—a concept that Jerome deemed heretical in the Origenist controversy and that surfaced a few years later in a different guise, namely Pelagian perfectionism.[36]

Pelagius's letter to Demetrias again provides a good comparison insofar as it gives us insight into Pelagius's thoughts on sinlessness and perfection. For Pelagius, humans are condemned not by an innate sinfulness but by an indulgence of bad habits that begin in early childhood.[37] Habit, for Pelagius, was like rust; it was external to the will and thus could be undone. One could scrape off the rust and be restored to an original luster by living a life of virtue and sinlessness.[38] According to Pelagius, Demetrias's youth provided her a greater flexibility for reversing the course of bad habit and practicing a holy life. He writes that her soul "will climb to the very pinnacle of perfection and will exercise a facility in good living which is grounded in well-established custom. The soul will be amazed by its own virtue."[39]

Gerontius, for his part, walks a fine line between portraying his heroine as nearly perfect and passionless and depicting her as one who is cognizant of her own sinfulness. For Gerontius, Melania's speeches provide an occasion for him to have the saint attest to her own sinful nature. Calling herself a useless servant, Melania states that she is unaware "of anything completely good in herself."[40] On her deathbed she attests to her sinfulness, praying to God: "I have given my soul and body to you, who formed me in my mother's womb, and you have taken my right hand to guide me in your counsel. But being human, I have sinned against you many times both in word and in deed, against you who alone are pure and without sin."[41] Yet a few lines later, when Gerontius describes Melania's ascent into heaven, he insinuates that she in fact *had* reached a state akin to angelic perfection while on Earth: "The holy angels joyously received her, for in her corruptible body she had copied their *apatheia*."[42] Gerontius reports that the evil powers were "able to find nothing of their own in her."[43] As in the passages discussed above, Gerontius here attests to Melania's spiritual perfection, her likeness to the angels, her *apatheia*, and lack of evil, but in Melania's speeches about herself she emphasizes her sinful nature and lack of innate goodness. The literary strategy whereby Gerontius describes Melania's perfection and then offers a quotation from Melania herself attesting to her sinfulness enables Gerontius to have his cake and eat it, too. The text here preserves a Pelagian remnant of the human striving for spiritual perfection in the midst of Augustinian testaments to human depravity.

The tensions between humility and nobility, sinfulness and perfection, reach their apex in Gerontius's descriptions of Melania's encounters with the empresses Serena and Eudocia. Gerontius reports that when Melania, still in her early twenties and new to the ascetic life, visited the empress Serena, Melania wore dirty rags and a veil that she refused to take off in the presence of the empress. She was humbler than any beggar at the queen's door, "delivering herself to death daily." Yet Gerontius's Melania was also nobler than any queen, bearing gifts of crystal, silver, and silk, even sitting atop Serena's golden throne.[44] With the humble, shabbily dressed Melania on the imperial throne, Serena delivers the following speech to the palace servants:[45]

Let us learn from [Melania] that pious judgment conquers all the pleasure of the body. Behold, she has trod underfoot the softness of her upbringing, the massiveness of her wealth, the pride of her worth, and quite simply, all the delightful things of this life. She does not fear weakness of the flesh nor voluntary poverty, nor any other things of this sort at which we shudder. She has rather even bridled nature itself and delivered herself to death daily, demonstrating to everyone by her very deeds that before God, woman is not surpassed by man in anything that pertains to virtue, if her decision is strong.

While Serena's speech sounds a few too many notes of Pelagian optimism, Gerontius is careful to report that the more the empress praised Melania, "the more she humbled herself."[46] The juxtaposition of lowliness and nobility—of rags and riches—enables Gerontius to construct Melania as a key figure in the circles of the aristocratic elite and the ascetic elite while not compromising her humility.

A later scene with the empress Eudocia provides another occasion for Gerontius to measure Melania's virtue, humility, and nobility against that of a royal woman. Gerontius reports that Melania, now advanced in years, went out to meet Eudocia at Sidon and stayed in the martyrium of Saint Phocas, the very location where the Canaanite woman replied to Jesus that "even the dogs eat the crumbs that fall from their masters' table."[47] Although she was at first reluctant to travel "through the cities in such humble attire," fearing that she might be reproached, Melania was honored by the empress, who called Melania her true spiritual mother. Eudocia professed that she wished to be worthy of Melania while she "still serve[d] the Lord in the flesh."[48]

The empress then accompanied Melania to deposit the relics of Saint Stephen in a martyrium that Melania had constructed.[49] After hurting her foot in the process, Eudocia offered prayers in the Church of the Anastasis. The Latin version of the *vita* records her prayer: "I thank you, Lord, for deeming me worthy to visit, not because of merit, but because of your benevolence and the intervention of your holy martyrs and your handmaid Melania."[50] The Latin editor here adds an anti-Pelagian touch to Eudocia's prayer, underscoring that her worthiness derives not from human merit but from divine grace and saintly intervention. Yet the narration of the scene with Eudocia also preserves the (Pelagian, Augustinian) tension between Gerontius's depiction of Melania as noble, worthy, and important in worldly circles and his portrayal of her as mindful of her own unworthiness and humble beyond comparison. These accounts of Melania's royal encounters illustrate how Melania competes with the empresses for both prestige and humility.[51]

BABIES

Pelagius himself fades from the scene around 418, but Julian of Eclanum takes up the Pelagian cause and becomes, in Elizabeth Clark's estimation, the sharpest opponent Augustine ever confronted.⁵² The debate between Augustine and Julian concerned babies: whether or not they were born with sin; whether or not they should be baptized as infants; and to what extent baptism erased past sins.⁵³ When Julian defended, at the very least, the innocence of infants and the blamelessness of human reproduction, Augustine replied (with renewed clarity and resolve) that every baby, with the exception of Jesus, is born with the stain of Adam's original sin, transmitted (albeit mysteriously) through conception, an act that itself is sullied by sexual lust.⁵⁴ Julian retorted that, in Augustine's estimation, God was a *nascentium persecutor*—a tormentor of newborns.⁵⁵

Babies also figure, although less prominently, in Gerontius's *vita* of Melania.⁵⁶ We can find in Gerontius's discussion of babies a reminder of the all-too-recent debates between Julian and Augustine. The speedy baptism of Melania and Pinianus's son, born prematurely, suggests that Melania's practice and theology was in line with Augustine's understanding of original sin and infant baptism.⁵⁷ A later scene in the *vita*—a scene astutely analyzed by Maria Doerfler in this volume—suggests that questions about infant sin and mortality remained a thorny issue into the 450s.⁵⁸

When Melania was already advanced in years, she was called to the bed of a woman whose fetus had died in the womb. The woman's life was endangered, and after praying over her and putting a miraculous belt around her waist, Melania was able to heal the woman: the stillborn infant emerged, and the woman's life was saved. In good Augustinian fashion, Melania claims none of the glory of this miracle for herself but attributes the healing instead to a saint, the previous owner of the miraculous belt.⁵⁹ But the Latin translation of the *vita* adds to this healing story by having Melania teach about the relationship of babies to sin. She says: "Indeed, God has made nothing filthy or unclean in humans; he has instead created all members according to reason. Only sin is filthy and abominable; for it is not possible for [bodily] members to be unclean, because God has created these [members], from whom are born the patriarchs, prophets, apostles and other saints."⁶⁰ This little speech plunges the Latin text into the sea of conflict between Augustine and Julian of Eclanum.

One can trace in this speech a defense of the innocence of babies, bodies, and sexual reproduction. Like Julian, Melania insists that God creates nothing unclean. But read alongside Augustine's anti-Pelagian writings, Melania's speech also sounds the notes of an Augustinian defense. According to the Latin editor of the *vita*, Melania, like Augustine, insisted that filth attached to sin alone, not to the body in general nor to the sexual organs in particular, for these too are part of God's creation. In this section, I discuss some of the ways in which arguments about infant sin shaped Augustine's debates with Julian of Eclanum regarding the status of the body, sex, marriage, and reproduction. The Latin editor of Melania's *vita*, I suggest, used the opportunity of Melania's healing of the woman with a stillborn baby to echo Augustine's justification of the goodness of the body and sexual reproduction.

One way in which Augustine defended his position on original sin was by reasoning backwards: If Jesus died to save everyone, babies included, then all are guilty of sin, even at the moment of birth.[61] Each human is, as Augustine put it, a "massa peccati," a lump of sin, undeserving of God's grace.[62] Considered in this way, it is understandable why a certain sentence in Pelagius's *Letter to Demetrias* so enraged Augustine in 417. Pelagius had written in praise of Demetrias's spiritual riches, which derived not from familial inheritance but from herself:[63]

> You have possessions which rightly entitle you to be set above others, indeed even more so; for everyone realizes that your nobility in the physical sense and your wealth belong to your family, not to you, but no one except you yourself will be able to endow you with spiritual riches, and it is for these that you are rightly to be praised, for these that you are deservedly set above others, and they are things which cannot be within you unless they come from you.

The notion that spiritual wealth derived from Demetrias alone—or that anything good could derive from a human—was, in Augustine's view, a poisonous doctrine.[64] Augustine's anger at this remark is evident in his warning letter to Juliana: "So go ahead and let the virgin of Christ read that from which she will believe that her virginal sanctity and all her spiritual riches belong to her only from herself, and thus ... let her learn to be ungrateful to God!"[65] To deny original sin was, for Augustine, to limit the full reach of God's grace.

By 418, Augustine and Julian's debate about original sin had come to encompass a debate about marriage, sex, and reproduction.[66] Julian claimed that Augustine's understanding of original sin reflected a Manichean hatred of the body and a disparagement of human reproduction.[67] He demanded that Augustine account for the exact origin of an infant's sin, for in Julian's reading of Augustine the corollary of original sin is a denigration of sexual reproduction as evil and an understanding of the (sexed) body as a deformity.[68] In *Against Julian*, Augustine responds to these charges by arguing that "no uncleanness of the natures, however great it be, is any crime of marriage, for the proper good of marriage is plainly distinct from many faults of the natures."[69] Nuptial union, Augustine continues, is a good, especially for the purpose of procreation.[70] Furthermore, the condition of bodies is good, not evil. "The condition of the newborn," Augustine writes, "is the work of God operating well from evil men."[71] Augustine considers an extreme case to make his argument for the goodness of the human body at birth:[72]

> If men were subject to the evil of lust to such an extent that if the honesty of marriage were removed, all of them would have intercourse indiscriminately, in the manner of dogs, the condition of the bodies, of which God is the author, would not be a deformity merely because all sexual union happened to be evil. Even now, in evil adulterous union, we see that the work of God in the condition of the bodies is good.

Augustine defends himself against the claims of Julian by upholding not only original sin but also the goodness and divine blessing of marriage, sexual reproduction, and bodies.

In *De Peccato Originali,* Augustine maintains that the filth in which we are born is the filth of sin, and sin alone.[73] The Latin editor of the *Vita Melaniae Iunioris* takes the opportunity of the story of a stillbirth to enter into this debate and clarify Augustine's position. Like Augustine, the Latin editor of Melania's *vita* affirms the cleanness and goodness of the human body and all its members; after all, the apostles, saints, prophets, and patriarchs had bodies such as these. In this story, which describes the bodily parts of the stillborn infant in vivid detail, the Latin editor represents Melania as voicing an Augustinian defense of the simultaneous goodness of human bodies and filthiness of human sin. Melania is thus posthumously conscripted for orthodoxy.

CONCLUSION: MELANIA AND THE CATEGORIES OF ORTHODOXY AND HERESY

The boundaries that Augustine sought to define as those that separated him from Pelagius and his followers—and the Catholic faith from heresy—were not the boundaries that confined Melania, her family, or her hagiographer. Melania and her family were interested and invested in the theological debates, so much so that they pleaded Pelagius's case before Augustine, claiming that he had renounced allegedly Pelagian views. But the stories about Melania, Albina, and Pinianus show that any after-the-fact overlay of the categories of orthodoxy and heresy necessarily obscures our understanding. Like the half-signed oath that Augustine abandoned, Melania's conscription into orthodoxy remains incomplete. As she interrupts Augustine in the middle of signing his name, so she interrupts the neat historical and theological taxonomies that seek to cordon off the orthodox from the heretical.

If we adjust the focus away from theological debates that have become dominant and starkly dichotomous only in hindsight, what other centers of identity formation and intellectual contestation and alliance emerge? Elizabeth Clark has wisely advised students of early Christianity to attend not only to theological issues but also to "nontheological issues [that lie] only slightly beneath the surface of [theological] controversies."[74] Clark observes that relations of "kinship, marriage, hospitality . . . , religious mentorship, gift-giving, and literary and financial patronage illumine the developing antagonisms with less recourse to the theological debate than students of Christian history would have imagined."[75] In the case of Melania and her family, attention to social relations of kinship, hospitality, letter writing, and patronage illuminates not so much developing antagonisms but, rather, Melania and her family's attempts at diplomacy and resolution. Augustine's brief mentions of Melania portray her as a woman who *intervenes*—albeit not always to his liking—to settle, prevent, or smooth over disputes. Melania and her mother, like Juliana (Demetrias's mother), and like Paulinus of Nola, among others, forged strategic ties on both sides of the aisle. These illustrious Christians met or corresponded with Pelagians and Augustinians alike. They were late ancient bipartisans.

Peter Brown has described how aristocratic families such as Melania's and Juliana's offered protection against charges of heresy to their intellectual and spiritual protégés. He writes:[76]

> In their role of patrons of Christian scholars and Christian spiritual guides, great lay families considered themselves to be as much the judges of the limits of orthodoxy in their region as were the bishops and clergy. The protection Melania the Elder and her friends and relatives extended to Rufinus showed the extent to which Christian intellectual activity in Rome remained rooted in the *domus*—in the town houses of the wealthy and in the patronage the owners of these houses exercised—quite as much as in the churches.

We can trace the difficulties of the shift in the arbitration of orthodoxy and heresy from *domus* to church—from lay family to bishop—in, first, the letters of the Church Fathers (Augustine, Jerome, Rufinus, Pelagius) and their aristocratic interlocutors (often women) and, second, the aristocratic hagiography of the late fourth to the mid-fifth century.

In Augustine's first letter to Melania, Pinianus, and Albina, written before his anti-Pelagian tracts, he laments the fact that he cannot pay them a visit. It is 410, and they have recently settled near him, in Thagaste, and he wishes that he could, in his words, "not hasten, but fly" to them, for they are "lights kindled into vehement flame by the Supreme Light, raised aloft by lowliness of spirit, and deriving more glorious luster from the glory which [they] have despised."[77] But winter chill, heavy rains, and an imperiled congregation keep him away. In his final correspondence with them, he writes to them in Jerusalem, where they have recently met with Pelagius. Seven and a half years have passed since his first letter to them, and Augustine is knee-deep in his refutation of Pelagius's heresy. Augustine writes his *De Gratia Christi* to warn Melania, Pinianus, and Albina about their unsuccessful attempt to rehabilitate Pelagius. In the first lines of this book, Augustine inscribes the troubling theological chasm that has opened between himself and Melania, Albina, and Pinianus.[78] They remain for him, as for us, tantalizingly out of reach.

NOTES

1. Augustine, *Ep.* 126.1–3 (ed. K. D. Daur, CCL 31B: 185–87).
2. Ibid. 126.5 (ed. Daur, CCL 31B: 188): "At ubi coepi subscribere, sancta Melania contradixit. Miratus sum quare tam sero, quasi promissionem illam et iurationem nos, non subscribendo, facere possemus infectam: sed tamen obtemperavi; ac sic remansit mea non plena subscriptio."
3. Cf. Peter Brown's narration of this scene in *Through the Eye of a Needle: Wealth, the Fall of Rome, and the Making of Christianity in the West, 350–500 AD* (Princeton: Princeton University Press, 2012),

324: "At the very moment Augustine was holding the pen to append his signature to the oath extracted from Pinianus, Melania simply said: No. That was the end of the matter. Melania's was the voice of the super-rich, whose members felt entitled (as did Paulinus of Nola) to live where they wished and to take their money with them."

4. Elizabeth A. Clark, "The Lady Vanishes: Dilemmas of a Feminist Historian after the 'Linguistic Turn,'" *Church History* 67.1 (1998): 1–31, at 11.

5. Ibid., 11–12.

6. Cf. Augustine, *De Gratia Christi* 1.1–2 (*De Perfectione Iustitiae Hominis, De Gestis Pelagii, De Gratia Christi, De Nuptiis et Concupiscentia*, ed. C. F. Vrba and J. Zycha, CSEL 42: 125).

7. Clark describes Paulinus as follows: "The prime person in the Origenist controversy who exemplifies the importance of 'weak-tied relationships' is perhaps Paulinus of Nola. Paulinus was linked by many ties with partisans of both Jerome's and Rufinus's circles—and with circles of both Pelagians and Augustinians in the debate that later ensued. During the Origenist controversy, Paulinus was doubtless most connected with Rufinus's group: as a relative of Melania the Elder who lauded her ascetic virtues for posterity, Paulinus reached out to her whole circle of relatives and companions (Rufinus, Melania the Younger and Pinianus, Apronianus and Avita). So likewise was he linked both personally and through letters with major disputants on the Pelagian side of the controversy (Pelagius himself, Julian of Eclanum, and the latter's family) as well as with the anti-Pelagians Augustine, Alypius, and Jerome" (Elizabeth A. Clark, *The Origenist Controversy: The Cultural Construction of an Early Christian Debate* [Princeton: Princeton University Press, 1992], 41–42).

8. For more on Pelagius and the Roman aristocracy, see Caroline P. Bammel, "The Last Ten Years of Rufinus' Life and the Date of His Move South from Aquileia," *Journal of Theological Studies*, n.s., 28 (1977): 372–429, at 421; Kate Wilkinson, *Women and Modesty in Late Antiquity* (Cambridge: Cambridge University Press, 2015); and Peter Brown, "The Patrons of Pelagius," *Journal of Theological Studies* 21 (1970): 59 (reprinted in *Religion and Society in the Age of Saint Augustine* [London: Faber and Faber, 1972], 211. See now Brown's observation that "the Pelagian Controversy was also an incident in the history of the Christian aristocracy of Rome" (*Through the Eye of a Needle*, 291). Pinianus's close friend Timasius, who was present at the near-ordination of Pinianus in Augustine's church and served as an emissary between the two (*Ep.* 126.6 [ed. Daur, CCL 31B: 188–89]), was a Pelagian disciple (Bammel, "Last Ten Years," 422).

9. Gerontius, *Vita Melaniae Iunioris*, prol. (*Vie de sainte Mélanie*, ed. and trans. Denys Gorce, SC 90: 126). Unless otherwise noted, I follow the English translation of Elizabeth A. Clark, *Gerontius, The Life of Melania the Younger: Introduction, Translation, and Commentary* (Lewiston, N.Y.: Edwin Mellen Press, 1984). For more on Melania's orthodoxy, see Gerontius, *Vita Melaniae Iunioris* 36, 54 (*Vie de sainte Mélanie*, ed. Gorce, SC 90: 194, 232–34).

10. On Melania the Elder and the Origenist controversy, see Christine Luckritz Marquis, "Namesake and Inheritance," in this volume.

11. Augustine, *Ep.* 125, 126 (ed. Daur, CCL 31B: 180–94).

12. Gerontius, *Vita Melaniae Iunioris* 20 (*Vie de sainte Mélanie*, ed. Gorce, SC 90: 170).

13. For more on the legacy of Pelagianism, especially in the East, see R. A. Markus, "The Legacy of Pelagius: Orthodoxy, Heresy and Conciliation," in *The Making of Orthodoxy: Essays in Honour of Henry Chadwick*, ed. Rowan Williams (Cambridge: Cambridge University Press, 1989), 214–34, at 215.

14. See discussion in Brown, *Through the Eye of a Needle*, 300–303; quotation at 301.

15. Ibid., 302.

16. *Amnia Virgo* is the epitaph on Demetrias's tomb. See *Inscriptiones Christianae Urbis Romae Septimo Saeculo Antiquiores*, n.s., vol. 6, *Coemeteria in Viis Latina Labicana et Praenestina*, ed. Giovanni Battista de Rossi and Antonio Ferrua (Vatican City: Pontificio Instituto di Archeologia Christiana, 1975), no. 15764. Quoted in Brown, *Through the Eye of a Needle*, 307.

17. Peter Brown, "Pelagius and His Supporters: Aims and Environment," in *Religion and Society in the Age of Saint Augustine* (London: Faber and Faber, 1972), 183–207, at 188–89.

18. Pelagius, *Epistula ad Demetriadem* 1 (*PL* 33: 1099). English translation in B. R. Rees, *Pelagius: Life and Letters*, vol. 2 (Rochester, N.Y.: Boydell Press, 1988), 29–70, at 36.

19. Gerontius, *Vita Melaniae Iunioris* 17 (*Vie de sainte Mélanie*, ed. Gorce, SC 90: 160). For a discussion of how Pelagius uses "idioms of aristocratic status" to describe Demetrias's asceticism, see Andrew Jacobs, "Writing Demetrias: Ascetic Logic in Ancient Christianity," *Church History* 69.4 (2000): 719–48, at 726. Jacobs encourages readers to "note the double significance of Demetrias's 'nobility' and 'riches.' Not only do they mark her worldly status as an Anician heiress, they redouble the importance of her ascetic renunciation. She would not be able in so praiseworthy a fashion to spurn her wealth and status had she not possessed them in the first place. In this inverted fashion, secular riches and rank *do*, in fact, allocate higher status to the Christian virgin" (726). A similar dynamic, I suggest, is at play in Gerontius's *Life of Melania*.

20. As Dennis Trout has written of Melania and her noble family members, they "hoped to rest their claims to special status simultaneously on their great wealth and their repudiation of it" (*Paulinus of Nola: Life, Letters, and Poems* [Berkeley and Los Angeles: University of California Press, 1999], 20).

21. Gerontius, *Vita Melaniae Iunioris* 35 (*Vie de sainte Mélanie*, ed. Gorce, SC 90: 194).

22. See discussion in Brown, *Through the Eye of a Needle*, 306–7. My reading of Gerontius's presentation of Melania as simultaneously wealthy and beggarly differs from that of Lynda Coon, who argues that Gerontius is ambivalent about—even critical of—Melania's wealth and public benefaction. See the discussion in Lynda L. Coon, *Sacred Fictions: Holy Women and Hagiography in Late Antiquity* (Philadelphia: University of Pennsylvania Press, 1997), 110–16.

23. Gerontius, *Vita Melaniae Iunioris* 53 (*Vie de sainte Mélanie*, ed. Gorce, SC 90: 230).

24. Ibid.

25. Pelagius, *Epistula ad Demetriadem* 1 (*PL* 33: 1099; trans. Rees, 36).

26. Brown, *Through the Eye of a Needle*, 306.

27. Augustine, *Ep.* 188.5–7 (ed. A. Goldbacher, CSEL 57: 123–25).

28. Jacobs, "Writing Demetrias," 743.

29. Ibid., 727–28.

30. Gerontius, *Vita Melaniae Iunioris* 41 (*Vie de sainte Mélanie*, ed. Gorce, SC 90: 206).

31. Compare Virginia Burrus's analysis of Jerome's presentation of Paula's "excessiveness" in his hagiographical letter to Paula's daughter, Eustochium (*Ep.* 108, ed. I. Hilberg, *Sancti Eusebii Hieronymi Epistulae*, CSEL 55 [Vienna: Verlag der Österreichischen Akademie der Wissenschaften, 1996], 306–51), in Virginia Burrus, *The Sex Lives of Saints: An Erotics of Ancient Hagiography* (Philadelphia: University of Pennsylvania Press, 2004), 60–69.

32. Brown, "Pelagius and His Supporters," 188.

33. Gerontius, *Vita Melaniae Iunioris* 20 (*Vie de sainte Mélanie*, ed. Gorce, SC 90: 170).

34. Ibid. 44 (*Vie de sainte Mélanie*, ed. Gorce, SC 90: 210–12).

35. E. A. Clark, *Origenist Controversy*, 16.

36. See Jerome, *Ep.* 133 (ed. I. Hilberg, *Sancti Eusebii Hieronymi Epistulae*, CSEL 56 [Vienna: Verlag der Österreichischen Akademie der Wissenschaften, 1996], 242–44), for the linkage of Origenist *apatheia* and Pelagian perfectionism. See also E. A. Clark, *Origenist Controversy*, 222–24.

37. Pelagius, *Epistula ad Demetriadem* 8 (*PL* 33: 1104–5; trans. Rees, 44).

38. Ibid. See discussion in Brown, *Through the Eye of a Needle*, 309.

39. Pelagius, *Epistula ad Demetriadem* 13 (*PL* 33: 1108). Here I follow the English translation of J. Patout Burns in his *Theological Anthropology* (Philadelphia: Fortress Press, 1981), 52.

40. Gerontius, *Vita Melaniae Iunioris* 42, 62 (*Vie de sainte Mélanie*, ed. Gorce, SC 90: 208, 250).

41. Ibid. 64 (*Vie de sainte Mélanie*, ed. Gorce, SC 90: 258).

42. Ibid. 70 (*Vie de sainte Mélanie*, ed. Gorce, SC 90: 270).

43. Ibid.

44. Ibid. 12 (*Vie de sainte Mélanie*, ed. Gorce, SC 90: 150).

45. Ibid.

46. Ibid.

47. Ibid. 58 (*Vie de sainte Mélanie*, ed. Gorce, SC 90: 242). The quotation is from Matt. 15:27. Elizabeth Clark has observed that the mere "mention of this biblical episode serves to remind the reader of Melania's characteristic humility and sets the stage for a new manifestation of her self-effacement in her reunion with the Augusta of the East": Elizabeth A. Clark, "Claims on the Bones of Saint Stephen: The Partisans of Melania and Eudocia," *Church History* 51.2 (1982): 141–56, at 149.

48. Gerontius, *Vita Melaniae Iunioris* 58 (*Vie de sainte Mélanie*, ed. Gorce, SC 90: 242).

49. Sources disagree as to whether Melania or Eudocia had constructed the martyrium and organized the deposition of Stephen's bones there. Compare Gerontius's account to that in the *Life of Peter the Iberian* (*Vita Petri Hiberi*, in *Petrus der Iberer: Ein Charakterbild zur Kirchen- und Sittengeschichte des fünften Jahrhunderts—Syrische Übersetzung einer um das Jahr 500 verfassten griechischen Biographie*, ed. and trans. Richard Raabe [Leipzig: J.C. Hinrichs, 1895]). See discussion in E.A. Clark, "Claims," 143–47.

50. Gerontius, *Vita Melaniae Iunioris* (Latin version) 59.2; *La vie latine de sainte Mélanie*, ed. and trans. Patrick Laurence (Jerusalem: Franciscan Printing Press, 2002), 274: "Gratias tibi ago, Domine, quia non secundum meum meritum, sed secundum tuam beneuolentiam et sanctorum tuorum martyrum interuentum et ancillae tuae Melaniae me uisitare dignatus es." This is the first instance in which the Latin editor of the *vita* sounds an anti-Pelagian note. The second (discussed below in the section entitled "Babies") occurs in Gerontius's *Vita Melaniae Iunioris* 61 (ed. Laurence, 278). For more on the differences between the Greek and Latin *vitae* and how they relate to the construction of orthodoxy and heresy, see Tina Shepardson, "Posthumous Orthodoxy," in this volume.

51. Clark writes that Eudocia's "association with Melania here serves the same function as the introduction of Serena earlier in the account, namely, to demonstrate that Melania mingled with royalty and was honored by them as a saintly woman whom even empresses would do well to emulate" (E.A. Clark, "Claims," 150).

52. E.A. Clark, *Origenist Controversy*, 216.

53. Clark remarks, "I doubt that at any time before or after the first three decades of the fifth century were a group of celibate men so concerned with babies. Whether they were discussing 'babies-in-theory,' or flesh-and-blood babies, is difficult to judge: the passion with which they detail the sufferings and death of infants and their shrieks and wails upon receiving the baptismal waters, might suggest the latter. How and why did babies capture the theological imagination of a generation? The answer, I think, lies in the fact that in this *topos* resided the point of greatest tension for those attempting at the same time to champion human freedom that allowed the assignment of praise and blame, to answer the thorny question of the soul's origin, and to uphold both the goodness and the power of God" (E.A. Clark, *Origenist Controversy*, 194).

54. See, e.g., Augustine, *Contra Secundam Juliani Responsionem Opus Imperfectum* 1.3–5, 2.87–98 (CSEL 85: 7–9, 223–30). For a helpful summary of the debates between Augustine and Julian, see Elizabeth A. Clark, "Vitiated Seeds and Holy Vessels: Augustine's Manichean Past," in Karen King, ed. *Images of the Feminine in Gnosticism* (Harrisburg: Trinity Press International, 1988), 367–401.

55. Augustine, *Contra Secundam Juliani Responsionem Opus Imperfectum* 1.48 (CSEL 85: 38). Quoted in Gerald Bonner, "Augustine and Pelagianism," *Augustinian Studies* 24 (1993): 27–47, at 29.

56. For more on the role of babies in the *Vita Melaniae Iunioris*, see Maria Doerfler, "Holy Households," in this volume.

57. Gerontius, *Vita Melaniae Iunioris* 5 (*Vie de sainte Mélanie*, ed. Gorce, SC 90: 136).

58. See Maria Doerfler, "Holy Households," in this volume.

59. Gerontius, *Vita Melaniae Iunioris* (Latin version) 61 (ed. Laurence, 278).

60. Ibid.

61. For discussion of the prenatal transmission of sin, see E.A. Clark, *Origenist Controversy*, 239.

62. Augustine, *Contra Duas Epistolas* 2.7.15 (CSEL 60: 475–78).

63. Pelagius, *Epistula ad Demetriadem* 11 (*PL* 33: 1107; trans. Rees, 48).

64. Cf. Augustine, *Ep.* 188.2.5 (ed. Goldbacher, CSEL 57: 122): "What [Pelagius] wrote, [that spiritual riches] 'come from you alone': that is poison."

65. Ibid. 188.2.4 (ed. Goldbacher, CSEL 57: 122).

66. See discussion in E. A. Clark, *Origenist Controversy*, 236–43.

67. Julian, *Libellus Fidei* 3.15 (*PL* 48: 521). See discussion in E. A. Clark, *Origenist Controversy*, 218–20, 236–37.

68. Augustine quotes Julian as accusing him of the following arguments: "The reason for the existence of the sexes is the union of bodies," and "If the union of bodies is always evil, the condition of bodies in the different sexes is a deformity," in Augustine, *Contra Julianum* 3.16 (*PL* 44: 717; trans. in *St. Augustine on Marriage and Sexuality*, ed. Elizabeth A. Clark [Washington D.C.: The Catholic University of America Press, 1996], 88).

69. Augustine, *Contra Julianum* 2.1 (*PL* 44: 671; E. A. Clark, *St. Augustine on Marriage*, 87).

70. Ibid. 3.16 (*PL* 44: 717; E. A. Clark, *St. Augustine on Marriage*, 88).

71. Ibid. (*PL* 44: 718; E. A. Clark, *St. Augustine on Marriage*, 89).

72. Ibid. (*PL* 44: 717; E. A. Clark, *St. Augustine on Marriage*, 88).

73. Augustine, *De Peccato Originali* 32 (CSEL 42: 195–96). Augustine has in mind Job 14:4–5: "Who can bring a clean thing out of an unclean? No one can. Since their days are determined, and the number of their months is known to you, and you have appointed the bounds that they cannot pass" (NRSV). See also Augustine, *Contra Secundam Juliani Responsionem Opus Imperfectum* 1.5 (CSEL 85: 8–9).

74. E. A. Clark, *Origenist Controversy*, 14.

75. Ibid., 16.

76. Brown, *Through the Eye of a Needle*, 301. See also the conclusion of Robin Darling Young's chapter, "A Life in Letters," in this volume.

77. Augustine, *Ep.* 124.1 (ed. Daur, CCL 31B: 178).

78. Augustine, *De Gratia Christi* 1.1–2 (*De Perfectione Iustitiae Hominis, De Gestis Pelagii, De Gratia Christi, De Nuptiis et Concupiscentia*, ed. Vrba and Zycha, CSEL 42: 125).

10

Posthumous Orthodoxy

Christine Shepardson

Melania the Younger died in 439 C.E., more than a decade before the Council of Chalcedon, in 451, and the bitter conflicts that ensued. Nevertheless, the *Vita Melaniae Iunioris* portrays the saint as actively involved in numerous religious and political controversies that *preceded* her death. In the Greek *vita*, this involvement includes her denunciation of the teachings of Nestorius, which were rejected during his lifetime in 431 at the Council of Ephesus. Elizabeth Clark has built on earlier scholarship to argue persuasively that Greek rather than Latin is more likely to be the original language of the *Vita Melaniae*,[1] and scholars have accepted Carolus De Smedt's late-nineteenth-century identification of the *vita*'s author as Gerontius.[2] A longtime friend and priest of Melania, Gerontius became the staunchly anti-Chalcedonian head of her monasteries on the Mount of Olives in the decades after her death. There is no doubt that Melania, with her extraordinary wealth and high status, lived visibly upon the stage of late antiquity, spending time with Augustine, conversing with imperial leaders, and founding monasteries.[3] The details of her *vita* suggest, however, that even if the sharp anti-Nestorianism that her Greek biography attributes to her is historically plausible, it also served a significant purpose for the anti-Chalcedonian monk-priest Gerontius, who later recorded it. As Susanna Drake has shown above in her chapter in this volume, the *vita*'s particular retelling of the 420s and 430s proved useful to its author in the 450s.[4] Reading the events of Melania's life and the narrative of her subsequent *Life* against an intricate backdrop of shifting doctrinal politics reveals the complexity of interpreting claims of Christian orthodoxy in the middle decades of the fifth century, as it does also the more general difficulty of labeling chronologically contingent lives with such abstract categories as orthodox or heretical.

The Greek *vita* explicitly portrays Melania as saving many from "the polluted doctrine of Nestorius,"[5] a condemnation that is particularly noteworthy in the later context of the *vita*'s production. Clark dates the original (Greek) text to 452/3, when the anti-Chalcedonian leader Theodosius, whom Clark posits as the *vita*'s recipient, was briefly the bishop of Jerusalem. Bishop Juvenal of Jerusalem's unexpected concession to the Council of Chalcedon in 451 led to a revolt in Palestine that sent him into exile and named Theodosius the new, if fleeting, bishop of that episcopal see. At that time, many opposing Christians like Gerontius argued that the creed recently confirmed at the Council of Chalcedon revived what they labeled as a Nestorian doctrine that had been anathematized at the Council of Ephesus twenty years earlier. Thus, akin to the coded correspondence that Robin Darling Young identifies above in her chapter between Evagrius and Melania the Elder, in 452/3 an anti-Nestorian representation of Melania the Younger would have supported Gerontius's critique of the newly distinct Chalcedonian Christians, providing Gerontius and his colleagues with valuable support in the pressing battles that they faced during the decades following Melania the Younger's death.

As Clark wrote in the introduction to her translation of the *vita*: "We may reasonably conclude that the *Vita Melaniae Junioris* is not free of tendentious, indeed propagandistic, qualities."[6] I argue that this includes the representation of Melania as resolutely anti-Nestorian. The history of Gerontius's *Vita Melaniae* highlights the ironies of this complex period. Although most texts authored by Christians who rejected Chalcedon were not preserved in the imperial languages of Greek and Latin and their liturgies, this *vita*—separated from any explicit association with its author—is an exception.[7] Unfortunately for Gerontius, however, although the Christological stance that he attributed to Melania remained orthodox in imperial Christianity, his later anti-Chalcedonian views, which he considered to be the natural extension of Melania's anti-Nestorianism, did not. The result of this tumultuous history is a *vita* of an acceptably orthodox saint with a Greek and Latin manuscript history that was preserved by the very Chalcedonian communities that Gerontius positioned the hagiography to denounce, highlighting the ahistoricity of the terms "orthodoxy" and "heresy" and the capriciousness with which they intersect the historically contingent details of individual lives.

THE FIFTH-CENTURY POLITICS OF CHRISTIAN ORTHODOXY

The shifting allegiances and definitions of imperial orthodoxy in the fifth and sixth centuries rival even the notorious upheavals of the fourth century in their complexity. With the Council of Ephesus in 431, the Council of Chalcedon in 451, and the tangled webs of religious and political affiliations stretching around the empire through the decades, it was no easy task to walk the elusive line of

Christian orthodoxy. Not only did imperial support shift frequently from one doctrinal community to another, but the boundaries of the communities themselves were anything but static. A brief introduction to these Christological controversies and to Gerontius will provide the necessary context for the analysis of the Greek *vita* that follows.

The Council of Ephesus deposed the bishop Nestorius and emphasized the unity of Christ's divine and human aspects. Nestorius, concerned about the implications of God dwelling within Mary's womb, rejected the title *Theotokos* (God-bearer) for Mary the mother of Jesus. Nestorius argued that Mary could instead be called *Christotokos*, Christbearer, but this proposal was unacceptable to Nestorius's powerful critics, particularly Cyril of Alexandria. Cyril wrote: "If anyone separates the *hypostaseis* in the one Christ after the union [i.e., the Incarnation]... let him be anathema. If anyone attributes to two persons [*prosōpois dysin*], that is, to two *hypostaseis*, the sayings ... made by the saints in reference to Christ or those made by him concerning himself, ... let him be anathema."[8] Nestorius was deposed and his teachings censured at the Council of Ephesus, and all Christians who inherit the Late Roman definition of orthodoxy consider his teachings to be heretical to this day.

The Council of Ephesus was not, however, a clear-cut end to the controversies raised between Cyril and Nestorius. Only two decades later, a Christian leader named Eutyches was criticized for teaching that Christ had only a single nature [*physis*] after the Incarnation. Eutyches strongly rejected Nestorius's teachings and agreed with his opponents at Chalcedon that Christ was one person *out of* [*ek*] two natures. Eutyches did not agree, however, that Christ maintained two natures after the Incarnation, or could be described as one person *in* [*en*] two natures. Eutyches argued, rather, that the incarnate Christ had one nature, alongside the one person and one *hypostasis* established by Cyril. As a result, Eutyches did not accept the doctrine ratified at the Council of Chalcedon, which defined Christ as one person *in* two natures: "One and the same Christ, Son, Lord, only-begotten, acknowledged in two natures, ... the difference of natures being in no way destroyed by the union [i.e., Incarnation], but rather the distinctive character of each nature being preserved and coming together into one person and one *hypostasis*."[9] Given the Council of Ephesus's recent emphasis on Christ's single person and single *hypostasis*, it is understandable that Eutyches and his followers were surprised by the Council of Chalcedon's insistence that the incarnate Christ retained *two* natures. Until today, Coptic, Armenian, Syrian, and Ethiopian Orthodox Christians reject the Council of Chalcedon and emphasize Christ's single nature after the Incarnation. Ironically, Chalcedonian Christians and those who rejected Chalcedon each consider themselves to be the sole legitimate heir of Cyril of Alexandria's anti-Nestorian orthodoxy, showing that an individual's claim to orthodoxy depends on timing as well as doctrine.

Gerontius produced the original *Vita Melaniae* while he was deeply entwined in the social and political networks of the controversies surrounding the Council of Chalcedon. John Rufus, an anti-Chalcedonian bishop of Gaza's port city Maiuma, included some stories about Gerontius in his *Life of Peter the Iberian*, from the beginning of the sixth century, and the Chalcedonian leader Cyril of Scythopolis mentioned Gerontius several decades later in his *Lives of the Monks of Palestine*. Both John and Cyril of Scythopolis identify Gerontius as the head of Melania's monasteries on the Mount of Olives, and Cyril specifically mentions that Gerontius held that position for forty-five years after Melania's death.[10] John and Cyril also agree that Gerontius strongly rejected the outcome of the Council of Chalcedon, although as an anti-Chalcedonian Christian himself John praised the very aspects of Gerontius's behavior that the Chalcedonian Cyril criticized.[11]

John Rufus, however, includes further details about Gerontius's life that are otherwise unattested. John mentions that Gerontius was "by family a Jerusalemite," but that as a child he "was accepted for the service of watchman by the holy Melania and her husband."[12] John claims that Melania and her husband, Pinian, took Gerontius with them to Jerusalem to take monastic vows, and that later Gerontius became Melania's priest in addition to being the leader of her monasteries on the Mount of Olives.[13] According to John, Gerontius "would often celebrate three gatherings of the divine service in a single day, and especially on the holy Sunday: one on the holy mountain, and one in the monastery for men, and again one in the monastery for women. On the remaining days, he celebrated daily a gathering and a private service for the blessed Melania according to the custom of the Church of Rome."[14] Although some early scholars accepted John's claims, others have persuasively challenged the historicity of this story of Gerontius's childhood.[15] Nevertheless, John Rufus's description in his *Plerophoriae* of Gerontius as a deacon in Melania's monastery before his rise to the priesthood remains historically plausible.[16] Childhood details aside, it seems reasonable to conclude that Gerontius was a monk and priest who knew Melania personally, oversaw her monasteries after her death, and became a stalwart leader among those who rejected the Council of Chalcedon. A study of the Greek *Vita Melaniae* reveals a heroine who is orthodox in ways that would have been consonant with Gerontius's own anti-Chalcedonian views in the aftermath of 451.

THE ORTHODOX AND ANTI-NESTORIAN MELANIA OF THE GREEK *VITA*

As Elizabeth Clark noted, both the Greek and Latin versions of the *Vita Melaniae* strongly emphasize the orthodoxy of their heroine: "There can be no doubt that Gerontius wished to present Melania as an exemplar of sound doctrine whose 'ardor for the orthodox faith' was 'hotter than fire.'"[17] Yet, as Clark was quick to acknowledge, "what constituted orthodoxy in the fifth century was not so easily ascertained in the midst of the era's doctrinal struggles: those who won the debate were not the only ones who thought themselves correct."[18] Melania the Younger, like her grandmother and namesake, Melania the Elder, consorted with leaders engaged in intense debates over religious orthodoxy and orthopraxy, and not all her close acquaintances escaped accusations of heresy. Nevertheless, Melania's *vita* insists she was a paragon of orthodoxy, even if the details of what defined her as orthodox are sometimes vague in ways that allow her to float unscathed through the accusations of heresy that troubled her hagiographer.

The years 431 and 432 were particularly significant for Melania, as her mother died in 431, the year of the Council of Ephesus, which denounced Nestorius and his teachings, and her husband died in the following year. Melania built a women's monastery on the Mount of Olives soon after her mother's death and a men's monastery in the same region a few years later, in 435. Another year or two after building the second monastery, she seems to have traveled to Constantinople to see her uncle Volusian, who was visiting from Rome for an imperial wedding in the Eastern capital. The *vita* portrays Melania as instructing many in Christian orthodoxy while she is in Constantinople for this visit, including among her pupils (in the Greek *vita*) the emperor Theodosius II, his wife, Eudocia, and his powerful older sister Pulcheria. Melania soon returned to Jerusalem, where she was joined by the empress Eudocia; and the saint died not long after, in 439.

Clark has already detailed many of Melania the Younger's relations with those accused of Origenism, Pelagianism, and perhaps Donatism.[19] Despite these associations, Melania emerges from the *vita* as unassailably (because imprecisely) orthodox. Not only does the Greek *vita* begin with a general insistence that Melania burned with an "ardor for the orthodox faith,"[20] but Gerontius scatters reminders of this claim throughout the narrative. "She had such zeal for the name of our Lord Jesus Christ and the orthodox faith," he writes, "that if she heard that someone was a heretic, even in name, and advised him to make a change for the better, he was persuaded.... But if he was not persuaded, she would in no way accept anything from him."[21] Similarly, Gerontius describes an occasion when Melania chastised him for mentioning in the liturgy the name of a woman whom some considered to be a heretic. Gerontius concluded regarding Melania: "Thus she believed it was a transgression against the orthodox faith to name heretics during the holy Eucharist."[22] Gerontius elsewhere noted: "Only the Lord himself knows ... how many Samaritans, pagans, and heretics she persuaded through money and exhortations to come back to God!"[23] In Jerusalem Melania "was not quick to see anyone except the holy and highly regarded bishops, especially those who stood out for their doctrine, so that she might spend the time of their conferences inquiring about the divine word";[24] and she instructed the women in her monastery: "Before all else, let us guard the holy and orthodox faith without deviation, for this is the groundwork and the foundation of our whole life in the Lord."[25] Given the varieties of religious controversies in these decades, it is perhaps not surprising but nevertheless strategic that the *vita* so often speaks simply of Melania's orthodoxy without offering more detail that might have caused difficulties in the later vicissitudes of these arguments.

One exception to Gerontius's decision to keep the details of Melania's orthodoxy rather vague is in the aggression that she shows in the Greek (though notably not the Latin) *vita* toward the teachings of Nestorius. "Just then," Gerontius wrote, "the Devil threw the souls of the simple people into great trouble through the polluted doctrine of Nestorius. Therefore many of the wives of senators and some of the men illustrious in learning came to our holy mother in order to investigate the orthodox faith with her. And she, who had the Holy Spirit indwelling, did not cease talking theology from dawn to dusk."[26] Again Gerontius describes how Melania "turned many who had been deceived to the orthodox faith and sustained others who doubted."[27] He repeats this claim at the end of the section about her stay in Constantinople, including—in the Greek version—the imperial family, and particularly the empress Eudocia, among her pupils.[28] Eudocia, like Gerontius himself, supported those who rejected Chalcedon in the first years after the council. Both the empress and Gerontius thus serve in the *vita* to provide a narrative bridge between Melania's anti-Nestorian orthodoxy of the 430s and later anti-Chalcedonian Christianity.

THE NEW NESTORIANS OF CHALCEDON: THE RHETORIC OF ANTI-CHALCEDONIAN HERESIOLOGY

It is evidence of the serpentine undulations in the definition of orthodoxy in the fifth century, and of the significance of the timing of its attachment to a historical individual, that Gerontius could present an orthodoxly anti-Nestorian Melania while concurrently being deemed heretical for his own rejection of the Council of Chalcedon. Gerontius, the enemy of Saint Melania's enemy Nestorius, was, in the judgment of later Greek tradition, a heretic. It is easy to understand why those who rejected the outcome of the Council of Chalcedon argued that Chalcedonian orthodoxy revived the teachings of Nestorius. Although it is commonplace to note that Christians who rejected Chalcedon largely considered those who accepted the council to be thinly disguised Nestorians,[29] scholars have not yet observed that the networks surrounding some of the earliest of these accusations are directly related to Gerontius and the empress Eudocia and thus deserve attention in an analysis of the *Vita Melaniae*.

Among the earliest accusations that Chalcedonian Christians taught the heresy of Nestorius are those suggested by the defensive responses of the Chalcedonian empress Pulcheria and her husband, Marcian, to the heads of Jerusalem's monasteries, dated to late 452 or early 453.[30] The monks' letters that prompted the imperial replies do not survive, but the separate letters from Marcian and Pulcheria defend the imperial couple, arguing that the "two natures" language of Chalcedon's creed was not a novelty and did not teach "two Sons." Marcian was the emperor who had convened the Council of Chalcedon in 451; he had become emperor by marrying Pulcheria, the powerful Augusta and sister of Eudocia's husband, the emperor Theodosius II, upon Theodosius's death. Pulcheria and Nestorius had a very public antipathy for each another, and Pulcheria gave her strong support to the councils of Ephesus and of Chalcedon. Marcian and Pulcheria both had clear reasons to remain unswerving defenders of Chalcedonian Christianity throughout their reign.

Another letter from 453, from the emperor Marcian to the bishop Macarius and the monks of Sinai, defended the emperor against claims made by the bishop Theodosius of Jerusalem, who allegedly asserted that the Council of Chalcedon inappropriately taught "two Sons."[31] Such correspondence offers persuasive evidence that Bishop Theodosius and the monks of Jerusalem were accusing those who followed Chalcedon of adhering to teachings that had been condemned in 431. Gerontius was the head of Melania the Younger's monasteries in Jerusalem during these years and a steadfast advocate of his bishop, Theodosius, the subject of the emperor's letter and, according to Clark, the likely recipient of the *Vita Melaniae*. These three imperial letters thus provide significant contextual clues for interpreting Gerontius's contemporaneous presentation of Melania's anti-Nestorian activity.

Decades later, the anti-Chalcedonian leader John Rufus produced his *Plerophoriae*. Evidence suggests that John Rufus first wrote the *Plerophoriae* in Greek, most likely between 512 and 518. Unlike Gerontius's Greek *vita*, however, the explicitly anti-Chalcedonian *Plerophoriae* survives only in Syriac, because of its renunciation by later Greek-speaking Chalcedonian Christians and its acceptance by Syriac-speaking Christians who rejected the council. This text, like the epistles noted above, reveals anew an anti-Chalcedonian claim that those who followed Chalcedon repeated the heresy of Nestorius:[32]

> Now if these who denied [*ṭlam*] God at Chalcedon say to us, "For what reason do you call us transgressors, that is, faithless [*ṭālume*]?" we respond to them, . . . "You, then, who at Ephesus rejected Nestorius, the leader of the two natures [*kyāne*], . . . and who anathematized these who dared or are daring to think or teach thus, how are you not guilty and transgressors, you who restored at Chalcedon those same things that at that time you destroyed?"

John repeats these accusations several times in the passages that follow: "After you destroyed impiety, you restored it again. . . . After you destroyed this wicked doctrine at the Council of Ephesus, . . . you openly restored it at the Council of

Chalcedon."³³ John Rufus, an anti-Chalcedonian monk in the Jerusalem monastery that Melania founded and Gerontius had led, provides further evidence for the initial category confusion that followed Chalcedon and for the concurrent conflation and condemnation of Chalcedonian and Nestorian teachings within Melania's monasteries in the decades after her death.

Cyril of Scythopolis's *Lives of the Monks of Palestine* is even later, being written around 543–58, but it provides additional clues regarding Gerontius's own understanding of the relation between Chalcedonian and Nestorian teachings. Gerontius makes a narrative appearance in Cyril of Scythopolis's *Life of Euthymius* and *Life of Sabas,* and in these stories Gerontius explicitly accuses Chalcedonian Christians of reviving the heresy of Nestorius. The *Life of Euthymius* first describes the friendly relationship with the empress Eudocia, wife of Emperor Theodosius II, and the anti-Chalcedonian bishop Theodosius of Jerusalem: "Coming to Palestine, this man [Bishop Theodosius] beguiled the empress [Eudocia], who was here at that time, and seduced all the monastic population, inveighing against the Council of Chalcedon as having subverted the true faith and approved the doctrine of Nestorius."³⁴ In Cyril's narrative, Bishop Theodosius then sends Gerontius and another anti-Chalcedonian monk to try to convert the ascetic Euthymius, the Chalcedonian hero of this narrative. "When these men arrived," Cyril wrote, "and began their plea, Euthymius said, 'Far be it from me to share in the murderous crimes of [Bishop] Theodosius or be seduced by his heresy.' Elpidius and Gerontius replied, 'But ought we to share the doctrines of Nestorius, which have been approved by the council now assembled at Chalcedon by means of the expression *'in* two natures'?'"³⁵ In keeping with the Chalcedonian imperial letters of Marcian and Pulcheria, and the anti-Chalcedonian writings of John Rufus, this sixth-century Chalcedonian text attributes to Gerontius directly the claim that the Council of Chalcedon championed the heretical doctrines of Nestorius.

A SLIPPERY SLOPE: FROM MELANIA TO ANTI-CHALCEDONIAN CHRISTIANITY

The strong likelihood that Gerontius personally criticized those who followed the Council of Chalcedon as having resurrected the heresy of Nestorius has significant implications for understanding the presentation of Melania in the *Vita Melaniae Iunioris.* As Robin Darling Young has shown for Melania the Elder above in this volume, so too Melania the Younger survives in the writings of a male acquaintance who portrays her as a patron for his endangered community. Given that Melania died before 451, and given the sharp accusations and religious and political turmoil and realignments that followed, and given, too, that the *vita* does not explicitly mention the schism over the Council of Chalcedon, scholars have understandably not read the *vita* as a distinctly anti-Chalcedonian text. Clark noted more generally, however: "The *Vitae* of saints composed in this period ... were notoriously open to doctrinal manipulation by their authors."[36] I propose that in the Greek *Vita Melaniae* Gerontius critiques not only Nestorians but also his Chalcedonian opponents of the mid-fifth century.

The explicitly anti-Nestorian passages of the Greek life discussed above are, of course, also the most explicit and most powerfully anti-Chalcedonian passages when read alongside the rhetoric in the *vita*'s immediate context. For an anti-Chalcedonian author in Jerusalem in the years of Theodosius's episcopacy to portray Melania as strongly against Nestorius was simultaneously to present her as an opponent of Chalcedon. Melania had died fewer than fifteen years earlier and had left her mark on the region. That the *vita* portrays such a politically, financially, and religiously influential saint as so ardently opposed to Nestorius's heretical teachings, unleashed, as the *vita* claims, by the devil himself, implicitly claims a powerful ally for Gerontius's anti-Chalcedonian community.

As Clark has noted, the *vita*'s portrayal of Proclus, bishop of Constantinople (431–46), also complements the text's anti-Nestorian agenda.[37] The *vita* claims that when Melania came to Constantinople to try to turn her uncle Volusian to Christianity, she asked "the holy bishop" Proclus for assistance. Proclus successfully persuaded Volusian, who then said: "If we had three men in Rome like lord Proclus, no one there would be called a pagan."[38] "Proclus's letters and sermons testify ... ," Elizabeth Clark wrote, "to his campaign against Nestorianism."[39] In this passage too, then, the *Vita Melaniae* advocated an anti-Nestorian orthodoxy that aided Gerontius's anti-Chalcedonian efforts in Palestine in 452/3.

In addition to the explicit anti-Nestorian passages and the praise for the strongly anti-Nestorian bishop Proclus, the *Vita Melaniae* also identifies a clear leadership succession that would last beyond Melania's lifetime into the years of the controversy over Chalcedon. Although Clark has pointed out that Cyril of Alexandria's presence in the *vita* is smaller than one may expect,[40] the praise of him as "the most holy bishop" nevertheless places Melania, Gerontius, and the audience in a positive relationship with this bishop, who became the measure of orthodoxy.[41] Cyril was, of course, at the center of the conflict with Nestorius at the Council of Ephesus in 431, and his name became synonymous with religious orthodoxy in the decades that followed. Ironically, his death, in 444—that is, before the Council of Chalcedon in 451—meant that like Melania the Younger he could represent a pillar of Christian orthodoxy to later Chalcedonian and anti-Chalcedonian Christians alike. Thus, Adam Schor has shown how important it was to leaders of both communities to trace their doctrine and ordinations through Cyril of Alexandria in the decades and centuries after his death.[42] Andrew Louth, in fact, concludes that the Syrian bishops rejected Chalcedon because they believed that it betrayed Cyril's orthodox teachings.[43]

The *Vita Melaniae Iunioris* not only claims an orthodox succession through its association with Cyril of Alexandria, but it also makes other distinct efforts to connect Melania's anti-Nestorian orthodoxy with the authority and legitimacy of Gerontius's later leadership. Near death, Melania speaks with many groups of people in the *vita*, including an entreaty to the martyrs whose relics surround her: "Be my ambassadors to the God who loves humankind, so that he may receive my soul in peace and guard the monasteries up to the end in the fear of him."[44] Further, in the *vita* Melania specifically passes her authority to her priest, the text's author, much in the way that Athanasius describes the ascetic Antony bequeathing his sheepskin and thus his authority to his bishop-hagiographer.[45] To the women of her monastery, Melania says in this text: "I entrust you to the lord priest and exhort you not to distress him in anything, but to submit to him in all humility, knowing that he too carried your burden for the sake of God, and that she who resists him and does not submit to him causes grief to God."[46] To a beloved bishop and his clergy, "the blessed woman said, 'I commend to you the priest and the monasteries; oversee all as a good shepherd looks after flocks endowed with reason, imitating your own master.'"[47] To "the monks from her monastery," she said, "I exhort you to give relief to the priest in all ways"; and to the author himself, Melania ostensibly said, "I now entrust the monasteries to you."[48] Reread in a later Palestinian context, these commands to follow Gerontius faithfully as Melania's appointed and orthodox priest take on new meaning in the heat of the controversy after Chalcedon, when Gerontius found himself politically at odds with the imperial definition of orthodoxy.

Last but not least, the *vita*'s praise for the empress Eudocia, and the numerous ways in which the empress submits to Melania's religious authority in the narrative, would likewise have had significant repercussions in the years immediately after the Council of Chalcedon. Eudocia received the title Augusta when she married the emperor Theodosius II in 421, a title that carried weight even when she and her husband did not see eye to eye. From the beginning of their marriage, Eudocia had to compete for her husband's allegiance with the emperor's older sister Pulcheria, an Augusta in her own right and a powerful force in religious and political circles throughout her adulthood.[49] There is no evidence of Eudocia's engagement in the theological debates surrounding the Council of Ephesus—in fact, tradition claims that she was the well-educated daughter of a pagan teacher and adopted Christianity only for her imperial wedding.[50] Nevertheless, after the marriage of her daughter Eudoxia to the young Western emperor Valentinian III in Constantinople, in 437, Eudocia enters more visibly into the historical record.

As noted above, the *Vita Melaniae Iunioris* claims that Melania's uncle Volusian traveled from Rome for the wedding between Eudoxia and Valentinian III, and Melania went to Constantinople to see him. While she was in the capital, she combatted heresy and benefited "most particularly the Christ-loving imperial women" and "the most pious emperor Theodosius."[51] Whether or not Melania actually spoke about Christianity with the imperial family during her time in Constantinople, this visit does appear to be the beginning of a relationship with at least the empress Eudocia.

Gerontius claims that while Melania was visiting Constantinople, Eudocia expressed "a desire to worship at the Holy Places," and Melania persuaded the emperor to make Eudocia's trip possible.[52] The *Vita Melaniae* presents a respectful relationship between the saint and the empress,[53] depicting Melania as "a true spiritual mother" to Eudocia, who showers Melania with praise and honor.[54] Although scholars have good reason to challenge the historical accuracy of the *vita*'s claim that Eudocia left Constantinople to travel to Jerusalem in 438 primarily because of Melania,[55] evidence suggests that Eudocia did in fact visit Melania in Jerusalem before the saint's death in 439 and returned to live in Bethlehem by 443.[56] Regardless of the historicity of Eudocia's deference to Melania, the narrative representation sends a clear message to the *vita*'s audience about Melania's high status and of Eudocia's orthodoxy by virtue of her submission to this quintessentially orthodox saint.[57]

Unlike Melania, however, Eudocia (d. 460) lived through the Council of Chalcedon and the first decade of its aftermath, and she was a firm and active supporter of the anti-Chalcedonian Christians in Palestine at least until 455. Peter the Iberian was a political hostage in Constantinople as a child, and years later, in 452/3, he was ordained as an anti-Chalcedonian bishop by Bishop Theodosius of Jerusalem. Eudocia helped Peter flee from the capital to Melania's monastery around 438, before the saint's death, and continued to protect him from imperial persecution even after his escape.[58] She also supported Theodosius's replacement of Juvenal as bishop of Jerusalem.[59] Although Eudocia seems to have publicly supported the Council of Chalcedon in the last five years of her life, the shift appears to have been due to external pressures.[60] With the loss of her emperor husband in 450, and the loss of her emperor son-in-law in 455, she lost the political stature publicly to reject imperial orthodoxy. Even so, according to Cornelia Horn, "Even after Eudocia entered into communion with Juvenal as ransom for Constantinople's support in rescuing her family in Rome, she still protected Romanus and gave support to other anti-Chalcedonians until her death in 460."[61] Regardless, the Greek *Vita Melaniae* most likely dates from the time of Theodosius's episcopacy in Jerusalem in 452/3, when Eudocia would have been a recognizable ally of Gerontius's Christianity. The close relationship portrayed in the *vita* between Melania and Eudocia is thus one more way in which the *Vita Melaniae* supported Gerontius's anti-Chalcedonian struggle.

THE LATIN *VITA*

The Latin version of the *vita* presents an interesting contrast to the Greek text on the related issues of Melania's anti-Nestorianism and the text's praise of the empress Eudocia.[62] Perhaps most notably, the Latin version does not include any mention of Nestorius or Nestorians. When Melania visits Constantinople in the Latin *vita*, she teaches, and the devil fights against her, but it is not explicitly against Nestorius's teachings and followers. Although the Latin *vita* shows Melania as notably orthodox and fighting heretics, her struggles against Donatists—not surprisingly unique to the Latin text—and against the teachings of Pelagius are brought to the fore, as Susanna Drake discusses in her chapter above.[63]

In addition, the Latin includes a noteworthy story toward the end of the *vita* that is absent from the Greek version and portrays the empress Eudocia in an unflattering light. In both the Greek and the Latin versions, Melania speaks with the women in her monastery as she lies close to death and exhorts them to live well and listen to their priest, Gerontius.[64] In the Latin version, however, this section is expanded to include a warning from Melania that if the women misbehave in the years after her death, she "will return in person and reprimand" whoever is negligent.[65] The Latin narrative interrupts Melania's speech at this point to inform the reader that this indeed came to pass, describing a visit of the saint to Eudocia when the empress inappropriately tried to persuade some of the women in Melania's Jerusalem monastery to travel to Constantinople. Melania appeared and not only reprimanded a woman who planned to leave the monastery and some women who were already en route; she also appeared "to the empress herself, who claimed to have had a vision of the saint" asking the empress not to take the sequestered women away from their Jerusalem monastery.[66] As Clark commented: "Eudocia is here presented as insensitive to the need for the cloistering of nuns, a necessity (it is implied) that any truly devout person would have understood without being chastised by Melania in a vision."[67] This Latin representation of Eudocia is decidedly less flattering than the depiction in the Greek *vita*.

Clearly the textual differences in the Greek and Latin representations of Nestorius and the empress Eudocia are related. The Greek text roundly condemns Nestorianism while praising the empress, who at the very time the text was produced was actively engaged in helping strongly anti-Nestorian (and anti-Chalcedonian) Christians in Jerusalem; the Latin text, on the other hand, removes any explicit reference to Nestorius's teachings and adds a pointed critique of Eudocia. In the Eastern empire between 451 and 455, an anti-Chalcedonian author would have seen an anti-Nestorian Melania and a pro-Eudocia story such as that in the Greek *vita* as productively anti-Chalcedonian.[68]

CONCLUSION

After the Council of Chalcedon, Gerontius participated in a contentious and convoluted struggle. Bishop Juvenal of Jerusalem led the Second Council of Ephesus, in 449, which accepted the teachings of Eutyches that would soon be rejected at the Council of Chalcedon. Juvenal's surprising acceptance two years later of the doctrine of Chalcedon was understood by many of his Palestinian colleagues to be in sharp contrast to his earlier teachings, and a local uprising sent the bishop temporarily into exile. The epistolary exchange that followed between the monks of Jerusalem and the emperor Marcian and the empress Pulcheria was but one manifestation of the betrayal felt by Palestinian monks like Gerontius, who were convinced that Chalcedon had revived the recent Nestorian heresy.

In this context, Gerontius's *Life of Melania the Younger* represents several ironies. The text of a Christian who rejected the Council of Chalcedon, it nevertheless survives in Greek and Latin because it tells the life of a saint who remained untainted by the strong anti-Chalcedonian commitments of her hagiographer. Even if the blunt categories of orthodoxy and heresy are ubiquitous in Christian history, the content of the terms depends entirely on the specific context of their use, with the result that they often sit awkwardly and imperfectly upon the chronologically embedded life of any given individual. Like Cyril of Alexandria's, Melania's anti-Nestorian views and death before 451 provided rich fodder for later Chalcedonian and anti-Chalcedonian Christians alike. It turned out to be to Melania's great advantage that Gerontius highlighted her anti-Nestorianism without his anti-Chalcedonian interests being explicit enough to later readers to cause his supposed heresy to tarnish her orthodoxy or, in other words, that in the post-Chalcedonian contests Gerontius shaped Melania's orthodoxy in the vocabulary of pre-Chalcedonian Christianity. Even though Melania's anti-Nestorianism would have been intelligibly anti-Chalcedonian to its author, the coded condemnations in her *vita* were flexible enough to be interpreted in different ways. In a conflict whose boundaries, categories, and allegiances were shifting so quickly, orthodoxy came to be as much about timing as it was about doctrine. We can imagine Melania's and Gerontius's mutual surprise that so many of the very Christians who later deemed her a saint considered her priest and hagiographer a heretic.

NOTES

1. Gerontius, *The Life of Melania the Younger: Introduction, Translation, and Commentary*, trans. Elizabeth A. Clark (Lewiston, N.Y.: Edwin Mellen Press, 1984), 5–13.

2. Carolus De Smedt, "Vita Sanctae Melaniae Junioris," *Analecta Bollandiana* 8 (1889): 17; Gerontius, *Life*, trans. E. A. Clark, 13–16.

3. On Melania the Younger, patronage, and politics, also see Caroline T. Schroeder, "Exemplary Women," and Christine Luckritz Marquis, "Namesake and Inheritance," in this volume.

4. Susanna Drake, "Friends and Heretics," in this volume.

5. Gerontius, *Vita Melaniae Iunioris* 54 (SC 90: 232). Unless otherwise noted, I have followed the English translation in Gerontius, *Life of Melania the Younger*, trans. E. A. Clark.

6. Ibid., 151–52.

7. For liturgical references, see the evidence collected ibid., 1–2; and in Mariano Rampolla del Tindaro, ed., *Santa Melania giuniore, senatrice romana: Documenti contemporanei e note* (Rome: Tipografia Vaticana, 1905), 291–92.

8. Cyril of Alexandria, *Ep.* 17.19 (*Third Letter to Nestorius*). Unless otherwise noted, I have followed the English translation in, *St. Cyril of Alexandria: Letters 1–50*, trans. John I. McEnerney (Washington, D.C.: Catholic University of America Press, 1987), with consultation of the Greek text in *Acta Concili-*

orum Oecumenicorum, tome 1, *Concilium Universale Ephesenum*, vol. 1, *Acta Graeca*, part 1, *Collectio Vaticana 1-32*, ed. Eduard Schwartz and Johannes Straub (Berlin: de Gruyter, 1927), 33-42.

9. *The Acts of the Council of Chalcedon*, vol. 2, ed. and trans. Richard Price and Michael Gaddis (Liverpool: Liverpool University Press, 2005), 204.

10. Cyril of Scythopolis, *Lives of the Monks of Palestine (Life of Euthymius)* 67.14-17; John Rufus, *Life of Peter Iberian* 44. For Cyril's text, I have followed the English translation in *Cyril of Scythopolis: Lives of the Monks of Palestine*, trans. Richard Price (Kalamazoo: Cistercian Publications, 1991), with consultation of the Greek text in *Kyrillos von Skythopolis*, ed. Eduard Schwartz (Leipzig: J.C. Hinrichs, 1939). For the text of John Rufus, I have followed the English translation in *John Rufus: The "Lives" of Peter the Iberian, Theodosius of Jerusalem, and the Monk Romanus*, ed. and trans. Cornelia Horn and Robert R. Phenix, Jr. (Atlanta: Society of Biblical Literature, 2008), with consultation of the Syriac text in the same volume.

11. John Rufus, *Life of Peter Iberian* 47 (ed. and trans. Horn and Phenix, 62-65); Cyril of Scythopolis, *Lives of the Monks of Palestine (Life of Euthymius)* 48.24-49.13 (trans. Price, 45-46); cf. 115.1-4 (trans. Price, 124).

12. John Rufus, *Life of Peter Iberian* 45 (trans. Horn and Phenix, 60-63).

13. Ibid. 45-46 (trans. Horn and Phenix, 60-63).

14. Ibid. 46 (trans. Horn and Phenix, 62-63).

15. See Gerontius, *Life*, trans. E. A. Clark, 15-17. Cf., Adhémar d'Alès, "Les deux *vies* de sainte Mélanie la Jeune," *Analecta Bollandiana* 25 (1906): 407-8; and *Vie de sainte Mélanie: Texte grec, introduction, traduction et notes*, ed. and trans. Denys Gorce, SC 90 (Paris: Cerf, 1962), 60-62.

16. John Rufus, *Plerophoriae* 41 (PO 8.1: 92). All translations from the *Plerophoriae* are my own, based on the Syriac text in *Jean Rufus, évêque de Maïouma, Plérophories: C'est-á-dire témoignages et révélations contre le Concile de Chalcédoine*, ed. François Nau and trans. Maurice Brière, PO 8.1 (Paris: Firmin-Didot, 1912).

17. Gerontius, *Life*, trans. E. A. Clark, 141; cf. Gerontius, *Vita Melaniae Iunioris*, prol. (SC 90: 126; trans. E. A. Clark, 26).

18. Gerontius, *Life*, trans. E. A. Clark, 141.

19. Ibid., 141-52.

20. Gerontius, *Vita Melaniae Iunioris*, prol. (SC 90: 126; trans. E. A. Clark, 26). The Latin mentions Melania's *fides* without any additional detail. See *La vie latine de sainte Mélanie*, ed. and trans. Patrick Laurence (Jerusalem: Franciscan Printing Press, 2002).

21. Gerontius, *Vita Melaniae Iunioris* 27 (SC 90: 180; trans. E. A. Clark, 46).

22. Ibid. 28 (SC 90: 182; trans. E. A. Clark, 47). Clark suggests that this woman may have been Melania the Elder, Melania the Younger's grandmother, whose friendships with those associated with Origenism raised questions about her own orthodoxy. See Gerontius, *Life*, trans. E. A. Clark, 150.

23. Gerontius, *Vita Melaniae Iunioris* 29 (SC 90: 184; trans. E. A. Clark, 47-48).

24. Ibid. 36 (SC 90: 194; trans. E. A. Clark, 51-52).

25. Ibid. 43 (SC 90: 210; trans. E. A. Clark, 57).

26. Ibid. 54 (SC 90: 232-34; trans. E. A. Clark, 66). The Latin passage is similar but has no specific reference to the teachings of Nestorius (Gerontius, *Vita Melaniae Iunioris* 54 [*Vie*, ed. and trans. Laurence, 260]).

27. Ibid. 54 (SC 90: 234; trans. E. A. Clark, 66).

28. Ibid. 56 (SC 90: 238; trans. E. A. Clark, 68).

29. See, for example, John Behr, *The Case against Diodore and Theodore: Texts and Their Contexts* (Oxford: Oxford University Press, 2011), 100.

30. For the Greek, see *Acta Conciliorum Oecumenicorum*, tome 2, vol. 1, part 3, *Concilium Universale Chalcedonense*, ed. Eduard Schwartz and Johannes Straub (Berlin: de Gruyter, 1935), 483-88. For an English summary of the letters, see *The Acts of the Council of Chalcedon*, vol. 3, ed. and trans. Richard Price and Michael Gaddis (Liverpool: Liverpool University Press, 2005), 182-83.

31. For the Greek, see *Acta Conciliorum Oecumenicorum* 2.1.3, *Concilium Universale Chalcedonense*, ed. Schwartz and Straub, 490–91. For an English summary, see *Acts of the Council of Chalcedon*, ed. and trans. Price and Gaddis, vol. 3, 183.

32. John Rufus, *Plerophoriae* 59 (ed. Nau and trans. Brière, PO 8.1: 114–15).

33. Ibid. 59 (ed. Nau and trans. Brière, PO 8.1: 115).

34. Cyril of Scythopolis, *Lives of the Monks of Palestine (Life of Euthymius)* 41–42 (trans. Price, 38).

35. Ibid., 42 (trans. Price, 38–39).

36. Gerontius, *Life*, trans. E. A. Clark, 141.

37. Ibid., 147. It is noteworthy, however, that the representation of Proclus is similar in the Greek and Latin versions, even though all explicit references to Melania as anti-Nestorian are absent from the Latin text.

38. Gerontius, *Vita Melaniae Iunioris* 53 (SC 90: 232; trans. E. A. Clark, 66).

39. Gerontius, *Life*, trans. E. A. Clark, 147.

40. Ibid., 18–19. Cyril is not mentioned, for example, in Gerontius's description of Melania and Pinian's return trip to Egypt soon after they arrived in Jerusalem (Gerontius, *Vita Melaniae Iunioris* 37–39 [SC 90: 196–202; trans. E. A. Clark, 52–54]). Neither does Gerontius mention Cyril's presence at the dedication of some of Stephen's relics, in contrast to the later *Life of Peter the Iberian* by John Rufus (Gerontius, *Vita Melaniae Iunioris* 58–59 [SC 90: 240–46; trans. E. A. Clark, 70–72]; John Rufus, *Life of Peter the Iberian* 49 [trans. Horn and Phenix, 64–69]). Regarding the complex politics of the translation of Stephen's relics, see Elizabeth A. Clark, "Claims on the Bones of Saint Stephen: The Partisans of Melania and Eudocia," *Church History* 51.2 (1982): 141–56.

41. Gerontius, *Vita Melaniae Iunioris* 34 (SC 90: 190; trans. E. A. Clark, 50).

42. Adam Schor, *Theodoret's People: Social Networks and Religious Conflict in Late Roman Syria* (Berkeley and Los Angeles: University of California Press, 2011), e.g., 1–2, 115, 125.

43. Andrew Louth, "Why Did the Syrians Reject the Council of Chalcedon?" in *Chalcedon in Context: Church Councils, 400–700*, ed. Richard Price and Mary Whitby (Liverpool: Liverpool University Press, 2009), 115.

44. Gerontius, *Vita Melaniae Iunioris* 64 (SC 90: 260; trans. E. A. Clark, 77).

45. David Brakke identified these power dynamics of Athanasius's story about Antony. See his *Athanasius and the Politics of Asceticism* (Oxford: Clarendon Press, 1995 [reissued as *Athanasius and Asceticism* (Baltimore: The Johns Hopkins University Press, 1998)]), 246–47.

46. Gerontius, *Vita Melaniae Iunioris* 65 (SC 90: 262; trans. E. A. Clark, 78).

47. Ibid. 67 (SC 90: 264; trans. E. A. Clark, 79). On the identity of this bishop, see Gerontius, *Life*, trans. E. A. Clark, 19–20.

48. Gerontius, *Vita Melaniae Iunioris* 68 (SC 90: 264; trans. E. A. Clark, 79–80).

49. Pulcheria's powerful influence on her younger brother, Theodosius II, is well documented, particularly in her condemnation of Nestorius during his time as bishop of Constantinople and during the events surrounding the Council of Ephesus. Her influence at church councils continued after the death of her brother when she married Marcian, the emperor who called the Council of Chalcedon. The Council of Chalcedon records numerous acclamations not only for the reigning Augusti, Marcian and Pulcheria, but also specifically for Pulcheria as a beacon of religious orthodoxy (*Acta Conciliorum Oecumenicorum*, tome 2, vol. 1, part 2, *Concilium Universale Chalcedonense*, ed. Schwartz and Straub). Following in the footsteps of her mother, the empress Eudoxia, who was renowned for her rejection of John Chrysostom during his brief time as bishop of Constantinople, Pulcheria was one of the politically and religiously influential Theodosian empresses. For an overview of this history, see Kenneth Holum, *Theodosian Empresses: Women and Imperial Dominion in Late Antiquity* (Berkeley and Los Angeles: University of California Press, 1982). For the relations between Eudocia and Pulcheria in particular, see ibid., 175–216.

50. Holum rejects the traditional story of the choice of Eudocia as Theodosius II's bride, a story recorded, for example, by the sixth-century historian John Malalas, but accepts that she did not become demonstrably involved in Christianity until after her daughter's wedding (ibid., 112-21, 183).

51. Gerontius, *Vita Melaniae Iunioris* 56 (SC 90: 238; trans. E. A. Clark, 68).

52. Ibid.

53. Elizabeth Clark's study of the relics of Saint Stephen reveals a sharp rivalry between Melania and Eudocia. See E. A. Clark, "Claims," 146, 149-56. This realization highlights the benefits that Gerontius would have gained particularly from how he chose to depict Melania and her relation to Stephen's relics and to the empress Eudocia. By portraying Melania as a spiritual mother to Eudocia, and by depicting Melania, rather than Eudocia (as portrayed by John Rufus), as the owner of Stephen's relics and the builder of his martyrium outside Jerusalem, Gerontius strengthened the message of Melania's sanctity and authority that he hoped his *vita* would convey.

54. Gerontius, *Vita Melaniae Iunioris* 58 (SC 90: 242; trans. E. A. Clark, 70).

55. The reasons for Eudocia's departure from the capital appear to have been more complicated than Gerontius's story suggests. Holum provides persuasive evidence that Eudocia may well have left to ease tensions aggravated by Pulcheria's forceful presence and continuing influence over Eudocia's husband and the discord between the two Augustae, made palpable in 438 by the events surrounding the *adventus* of the relics of John Chrysostom. (See Holum, *Theodosian Empresses*, 184-85.) Clark speculates along similar lines after surveying the varied evidence in the ancient sources (E. A. Clark, "Claims," 147-49).

56. Holum, *Theodosian Empresses*, 191-94, 217; E. A. Clark, "Claims," 143, 147, 151.

57. See also Susanna Drake's reading of this story in her chapter above in this volume.

58. E. A. Clark, "Claims," 145; Paul Devos, "Quand Pierre l'Ibère vint-il à Jérusalem?" *Analecta Bollandiana* 86 (1968): 337-50. See also Cornelia Horn, "Empress Eudocia and the Monk Peter the Iberian: Patronage, Pilgrimage, and the Love of a Foster-Mother in Fifth-Century Palestine," *Byzantinische Forschungen* 28 (2004): 197-213.

59. E. A. Clark, "Claims," 145; Holum, *Theodosian Empresses*, 222.

60. Ibid., 224; cf. *Acta Conciliorum Oecumenicorum*, tome 2, vol. 4, part 77, *Concilium Universale Chalcedonense*, ed. Schwartz and Straub; Cyril of Scythopolis, *Lives of the Monks of Palestine (Life of Euthymius)* 47-49, 53-54; E. A. Clark, "Claims," 146.

61. Horn and Phenix, *John Rufus*, liv.

62. Clark notes these differences, among others (Gerontius, *Life*, trans. E. A. Clark, 22-23).

63. For the reference to the Donatist controversy, see Gerontius, *Vita Melaniae Iunioris* 21 (*Vie*, ed. and trans. Laurence, 194). Compare also Gerontius, *Life*, trans. E. A. Clark, 113-14, 145-46. Regarding the Pelagian controversy, see Gerontius, *Vita Melaniae Iunioris* 61 (*Vie*, ed. and trans. Laurence, 278-80). Compare also Gerontius, *Life*, trans. E. A. Clark, 147-48. Regarding Melania's time in North Africa, see Susanna Drake's chapter above in this volume.

64. Gerontius, *Vita Melaniae Iunioris* 65 (SC 90: 160-62; trans. E. A. Clark, 78).

65. Ibid. 65 (*Vie*, ed. and trans. Laurence, 290-92).

66. Ibid. (*Vie*, ed. and trans. Laurence, 292).

67. Gerontius, *Life*, trans. E. A. Clark, 23.

68. If the Latin version dates to sometime after Eudocia removed her public support from the anti-Chalcedonian community, roughly in 455, then an anti-Chalcedonian editor may understandably have reshaped the positive Greek presentation of the empress to criticize her recent withdrawal. Before Valentinian III's death in 455, even a Chalcedonian editor may have hesitated to circulate a Latin text that reprimanded Eudocia, the mother-in-law of the reigning Western emperor; thus 455 may be recommended as a terminus post quem for this Latin *vita*.

PART FIVE

In the Holy Places

ONE WAY TO APPROACH THE DYNAMISM of the age of the Melanias is through consideration of space and place: the Melanias were bodies in motion, enacting the possibilities of Christian identity in multiple ways in multiple locations. To take place, as the theorist of religion Jonathan Z. Smith once noted, marks place not only in geography but in chronology: places not only *are;* they also *occur.* If one place can characterize the varied possibilities of being and becoming Christian in late antiquity, particularly as seen through the lives of Melania the Elder and her namesake granddaughter, it is the charged and ambivalent Holy Land. Constantine the Great resurrected Jerusalem, which had been dramatically changed from its roots in Israelite and Judean history through a series of wars with Rome that spanned the first and second centuries. In the fourth century, Constantine engaged in major building projects there, of imperial churches and memorials of events from biblical narratives, in an effort to make visible the specifically Christian importance of the city. A generation after Constantine, the holy city and its environs became the privileged milieu for a dynamic series of Christian lives. It was there that Melania the Elder set up her monastic centers, on the Mount of Olives; it was there that Melania the Younger founded her own churches and ascetic communities. They were part of a wave of Christians journeying from all parts of the Roman Empire, who saw in this newly Christianized place the opportunity to live in ways that echoed the sacred narratives that had recently become part of imperial identity.

The ancient terms for place signal the richness that we can mine from place's contemplation: *locus* may refer at once to a physical location or a passage in a text, as we see in the deeply layered pilgrimage account of Egeria, the female pilgrim from Spain, whose pilgrimage diary provides us with one of the most vivid sources for early Christian ritual in the Holy Land. *Loca sancta,* holy places, in her vibrant narrative are the sites where she plants her feet in veneration and are also the citations of scripture that she has recited there. *In hoc loco,* in this place, Christians began to enact and reenact an idealized kind of Christian identity. The Greek *topos* also connotes both location and performance: around the same time as Egeria's journey, the bishop and theologian Gregory of Nyssa composes a letter redolent with rhetorical flourishes (known as *topoi,* commonplaces) concerning the dangers of seeking God in the holy places (*topoi*).

In this same period, as Egeria insinuated herself *in hoc loco* and Gregory fretted over his *topoi,* the Holy Land itself—particularly around the holy city of Jerusalem—became a literal site for the creation and mobilization of new Christian identities. In this section, the mobilization of Christianity is engaged from two complementary perspectives. First, Andrew Jacobs asks how we should understand Jerusalem as a particular kind of destination in the age of the Melanias: How and why did so many Western Christians, seeking ascetic perfection, establish themselves in the Holy Land, and what do these serial migrations tell us about early Christian potentialities of power and personhood? Here, Christianity takes place on many spatial scales and in many different places at once: in the broad scale of the Roman Empire, in the local, and to Western eyes exotic, space of the holy places, and also in the intimate spaces of the ascetic body.

Stephen Shoemaker then maps the Christianization of the holy city in finer detail, through the ritual inscription of the city. Through an exploration of a late ancient chantbook from Jerusalem, we see how the Jerusalem of the Melanias was overlaid with new sights and sounds that reveal (perhaps) a surprising figure hovering over the liturgical life of Melanian Jerusalem: the Virgin Mary, taking center stage here long before her controversial rise to prominence after the Council of Ephesus in 431, the council that is usually credited with accelerating the rise of devotion to Mary throughout the empire. This Christian space of Jerusalem—the place that housed both Melania the Elder and Melania the Younger—here emerges as an experimental space, a place that resists fixity, vibrating with possibility.

11

The Lost Generation

Andrew S. Jacobs

LOST GENERATIONS

From the 360s through the 420s—a period roughly framed by the prominence of the two Melanias[1]—a small cadre of ascetically minded wealthy Christians migrated from Rome to Jerusalem.[2] Scholars have viewed these migrant monks from diverse perspectives: as pilgrims, refugees, itinerant philosophers, cosmopolitan gadabouts.[3] In order to think more broadly about the role of place and space in the construction of imperial Christian piety, politics, wealth, and status, I compare these ascetic émigrés to another notable group of migrant virtuosi: the so-called Lost Generation of expatriate American writers and artists living in Paris after World War I.

Like our ascetic émigrés, the Lost Generation were almost immediately mythologized (indeed, they participated vigorously in their own hagiography),[4] and within a very short time these artists abroad came to represent a new kind of postwar American.[5] This mythological force emerged out of the deliberate tension produced between the center at home and the colonized periphery.[6] Taking on the mantle of a lost generation, displaced but never out of place, these migrant virtuosi modeled a new paradigm for identity. In what follows I use the Lost Generation of Americans in Paris as a historical mirror in order to reflect back themes of empire, exile, and elitism that shape the space of the late ancient Christian empire of the Melanias.

LOST IN EMPIRE

The politics of empire frame both lost generations in distinctive but mutually illuminating fashion. Students of U.S. literature chronologically bookend the lost generation in Paris within the political upheavals of the two world wars.[7] Of course, Americans had been going to Paris before 1914 (as Christians had visited Aelia Capitolina before the 360s). In addition, only a very few of the artists who came to Paris in the 1920s had actually served in the war. In a broader sense, though, this American lost generation was liberated by the political displacements of war to seek fulfillment abroad.[8] Similarly, the geopolitical reorientations of the 1930s and the dawn of a new world war foreclosed many of those possibilities.

Significant moments of political crisis also punctuate the ascetic migrations of the fourth and fifth centuries. The earliest Western settlers in the new Constantinian Holy Land probably arrived in the 360s. Palladius in his *Lausiac History* recounts the monastic flight of Innocent, a former dignitary in the palace of the emperor Constantius (*tōn epidoxōn en tōi palatiōi*). Appalled by the fornications of his son Paul, an imperial guard (*domestikon strateuomenon*), Innocent, who was probably Italian,[9] fled his secular life and settled on the Mount of Olives,[10] soon after Julian's reign.[11] Western ascetic resettlers continued to arrive, in fits and starts, through the early 400s.[12] In the late 410s, Melania the Younger arrived, and with her, her chaste husband, Pinian, prompted to move (in part) by the barbarian invasions that penetrated to the Mediterranean Basin.[13] Two moments of sharp political destabilization—the disastrous reign of Julian in the 360s and the barbarian invasions of the 410s and 420s—frame our lost monastic generation.[14] Geopolitical disturbances need not be sufficient to explain the migratory patterns of our protagonists; nonetheless, they provide crucial spatial and political context. These dislocations take place across vast spaces, marked by fissures that stretched across seas and continents; they inscribe these movements in imperial space.[15]

If the physical and ideological space of empire informs the chronological bounds of our lost generations, so too, I contend, does it shape the thematic bounds. At the heart of the Lost Generation identity is a complex relationship between an imperial center—at once disavowed and recuperated—and a provincial periphery, a locus of both generative creativity and stark disorientation. This split sense of dislocation and relocation is captured in Gertrude Stein's famous declaration, delivered to a British audience in 1936: "America is my country and Paris is my hometown."[16] Here, the site of artistic renaissance is absorbed into the imperial center: to be an artist in Paris *is* to be an American—indeed, somehow, in *America*. Notably, Stein is often remembered as saying, "America is my country *but* Paris is my hometown," or something similar, emphasizing the disjunction between imperial center and artistic periphery.[17] Writers throughout the 1930s and following reaffirmed this doubled, split image of the generative, disjunctive Paris of the Lost Generation: a site of refuge and exile, of artistic nourishment and estrangement.[18] Only by disavowing the imperial center and fleeing to the periphery can the artist become a virtuoso; yet that new, virtuoso persona is always reinscribed as a new, idealized, imperial identity.[19] Of course the particular global politics of the early twentieth century, with its fragmentary nation-empires, cannot map precisely onto the sweeping imperialism of the Roman world. My point here, as throughout this chapter, is to use the twentieth century as a heuristic mirror: What can we learn looking back twice, as it were, about the imperial framings of individual ambitions?

EXILE AND EMPIRE: DISAVOWALS AND RECLAMATIONS

Presumably a variety of motives both mundane and spiritual led Western ascetics to move to the East. The mythic texts of this Lost Generation, however—as also of their twentieth-century counterparts—developed a clear narrative of moral insufficiency at the imperial center that inhibited the realization of a full ascetic life. According to her relative Paulinus,[20] Melania the Elder strove to pursue a life of holiness in Rome after the deaths of her husband and two of her three sons.[21] Her own relatives—tools of the "envious dragon,"[22] Paulinus writes—tried to stand in her way. When Melania at least broke free, her liberation was both spiritual and geographic:[23]

> Abandoning worldly life and her own country, she chose to bestow her spiritual gift at Jerusalem, and to dwell there as a foreigner from her body ["a corpore peregrinaretur"]. She became an exile from her fellow citizens, but a citizen among the saints.[23]

Paulinus here condenses the rather long route that Melania took from Rome to Jerusalem in the interests of capturing a particular spatial relationship between center and "abroad."[24] Melania moves directly from Rome to a life of foreignness (*peregrinatio*), an exile (*exsul*) in Jerusalem. Writing about the Lost Generation of the 1920s, Donald Pizer captures the mythic mentality of the expatriate or self-exiled state of mind: "The world one has been bred in is perceived to suffer from intolerable inadequacies and limitations; another world seems to be free of those failings and to offer a more fruitful way of life."[25] For the American artists of the postwar period (at least as they were remembered, or as they themselves recalled years later) the United States could not properly nourish their artistry: the restraints of prohibition, the stifling provincialism of the Red Scare, the wealthy merchant classes that prized capital over genius all worked against their artistic self-realization.[26] Likewise, according to Paulinus, Melania must flee Rome in order to pursue a more fruitful life of renunciation in the Holy Land.

When the monastic biographer Palladius describes Melania's return to the West, Rome and ascetic perfection are once more placed in tension. Melania arrived like a tidal wave of piety, instructing and converting relatives, "and led them out from Rome and brought them into the holy and calm harbor of life. And in this way she did battle against all those 'beasts' [*pros pantas ethēriomachēse*], that is, the senators and their wives, hindering her on account of the renunciation of the remaining households."[27] Bereft of its last saints, the city of Rome at last succumbs to "some barbarian hurricane."[28]

Jerome paints a similar picture of the failure of the imperial center around the time of his own emigration from Rome. As Andrew Cain has detailed, Jerome's successful sojourn in Rome, as an ascetic and scriptural maestro, took a steep downward turn in 384: his own controversial writings, the sudden death of Paula's daughter Blesilla (following Jerome's ascetic counsel),[29] and finally the death of Jerome's patron Bishop Damasus soured the ambitious monk on the capital city.[30] Sensing an imminent move, Jerome in a letter to Marcella from this period ponders retirement from the bustling city to the restorative countryside, a pastoral trope adopted from Roman aristocratic writing.[31]

By the time he leaves the city of Rome, in 385, under the shadow of some indeterminate ecclesiastical condemnation,[32] Jerome has moved from the language of aristocratic retreat to that of biblical condemnation. Rome has become a site of demonic and irreligious scandal, "always persecuting the holy."[33] Jerome begins to call Rome Babylon, from which he prays he may arrive at last "at Jerusalem once more."[34] He longs, he writes, to be "restored to my own country." "I was stupid," he laments, "when I wished to sing a song of the Lord in a strange land."[35] Rome is here the site of exile—the biblical Babylon from which Jerome returns to Zion—yet, in later years, he would remember it as both Babylon and a strange shadow Jerusalem, the home of the Senate of Pharisees who condemned him (like Jesus).[36] Whether the home town rejecting its prophet or the site of alienation, the city of Rome consistently resists ascetic perfection.[37] As a doubled exile (in Rome and from Rome at once), Jerome embraces the role of scandalous expatriate "back home."[38] Once ensconced in Bethlehem, Jerome laments to those back in Rome the impossibility of their pursuing truly pious lives in the squalid, crowded, and impious capital, center of a falling world.[39] Jerome's pessimism about the ascetic possibilities of the imperial city are, of course, made only worse after the barbarian incursions of the early 400s.[40]

For Melania the Younger and Pinian, Rome—particularly as a site of familial and financial interests—symbolizes all that stands in the way of their ascetic dreams. In his chapter on Melania the Younger, Palladius reiterates the inherent opposition of Rome to ascetic pursuits, as Melania's parents "by force" (*biasamenoi*) married her to "one of the first citizens of Rome."[41] Her marital ties are compounded by untold riches, and Palladius's brief account of Melania's disentanglement from Rome details both marital and financial renunciations.[42] These renunciations are amplified in Gerontius's later *Life of Melania the Younger*.[43] Even after she has convinced Pinian that they should embrace chastity, the twin constraints of family and wealth keep them tied to their old lives.[44] Finally, when Melania's father dies, they are freed from parental constraint: right away "they left the great city of Rome."[45] As in earlier accounts of the elder Melania, spiritual liberation and geographic departure from the city of Rome go hand in hand. After a long effort to divest themselves of their wealth (which, as Gerontius makes clear, is imperial in its scope),[46] living first in the Italian suburbs and then in North Africa, "when they had renounced the whole burden of their riches, did they at last start out for Jerusalem."[47] "At last" (*hysteron*) in Jerusalem, they can truly practice asceticism.

THE ARTIST ABROAD

As the specific site from which these ascetic virtuosi must free themselves, the city of Rome remains central to the myth of renunciation. The spatial center therefore forms a site not just of rejection but also of deep affiliation, a powerful site to be renounced, which can therefore never be forgotten. Precisely mirroring this split sense of alienation and affiliation with the imperial center are the ways that the new home abroad is doubly understood. The Lost Generation of the 1920s found Paris uniquely suited to the nourishment of their artistic genius.[48] At the same time, Paris never ceases to be for them a foreign space.[49] These divided spatial loyalties in an analogous manner inform the way that Jerusalem became configured by these Western monastic immigrants in late antiquity.

Jerome vigorously championed the possibilities of ascetic advancement available to the hardy soul willing to relocate to the environs of Jerusalem.[50] In a letter to Marcella from Paula and Eustochium preserved among Jerome's letters—which many scholars presume was written by Jerome himself—the recent monastic transplants implore their friend to join them abroad: "As Judea is exalted [*sublimior*] above all other provinces, so is this city [Jerusalem] exalted above Judea."[51] The language of the provinces highlights the distance from (and relation to) Rome, positing Jerusalem as a new Christian capital in distinctly Roman terms. Later on, the letter returns to the language of provincial identity:[52]

> Certainly if some preeminent orator blames someone or other for having learned Greek letters at Lilybaeum instead of at Athens, and Latin not at Rome but in Sicily (because each and every province has its own certain way, but one can't be equal to another), why should we suppose anyone could achieve the pinnacle of studies away from our own "Athens"?[52]

According to this analogy, the Christian must travel abroad (like a Roman learning Greek or a provincial learning Latin) in order to master Christianity. The spatial analogy wobbles a bit: Marcella is at once the foreigner who must study abroad and the native Christian coming home. Jerusalem is at once home ("our Athens") and abroad, the foreign site where nativeness is mastered.[53]

Of course, seeking perfection in the Holy Land was not for everybody: only an ascetic elite whose souls already strove for perfection. Around 400, Jerome wrote a eulogy for the Roman noblewoman Fabiola, who had given up a life of sin (she had remarried while her first husband was still alive) and embarked on a project of sacred beneficence. But "Rome was too narrow for her kindness," as Jerome writes,[54] and so Fabiola sailed for Jerusalem to perfect her largess.[55] But the sudden rumor of barbarian incursions, along with what Jerome refers to cryptically as "some dissension among us,"[56] prompted Fabiola to return to Rome, her homeland (*ad patriam*). Jerome, by contrast, "was held firm by these Eastern habitations, and an age-old desire for the holy places."[57] The nourishing soil of the Holy Land is not for every Western ascetic: it is the abode of an ascetic elite, migrant virtuosi in training.[58]

The triumphs of the ascetic elites are also highlighted by the failure of other ascetic migrants in the *Life of Melania the Younger*. Gerontius describes "a certain noblewoman who ended her way of life abroad in the holy places [*gynaikos hypatou tinos en xeneteiai katalysasēi ton bion eis tous hagious topous*]," whose name he mentioned at the offering of the Eucharist. Melania, incensed that he should name a heretic at the holy offering, rises on the spot and refuses Communion.[59] Gerontius is coy on the identity of this "certain woman,"[60] but the contrast between Melania the successful monk and the failed woman who came to seek a life of holiness abroad is clear enough to his readers. A similar near-miss ascetic migrant in the *vita* is Paula the Younger, the granddaughter of Jerome's companion Paula, who became Melania the Younger's monastic protégée: upon returning from a sojourn in Egypt, Melania visited with Paula and "brought her back to much humility from great vanity and a Roman disposition [*Rhōmaïkou phronēmatos*]."[61]

These virtuosi demonstrated their dedication, in part, by resisting the allure of home, by toughing it out in a space that was particularly conducive to their ascetic aspirations but, at the end of the day, also resolutely foreign. I have described elsewhere Jerome's particular doubled vision of the Christian Holy Land as native and foreign terrain.[62] In his conflict with Rufinus, he mocks his erstwhile schoolmate for his rusty Latin while (implicitly) praising his own multilingualism.[63] The implication here is that, of the two migrant monks, the one who has retained a sense of his cultural origins is the more successful ascetic émigré.[64] According to Gerontius, Melania the Younger demonstrated a similar multilingual capacity, "codeswitching" with such ease between Latin and Greek that "when she read in Latin, it seemed to everyone that she did not know Greek, and, on the other hand, when she read in Greek, it was thought that she did not know Latin."[65] The bilingual facility of Jerome and Melania embodies perfectly their double-sitedness: ascetic virtuosi nourished by the foreign soil of the Holy Land, yet never fully detached from their Latin roots. The religious lives of Melania the Younger and Jerome reflected this doubledness as well. Jerome, living for decades abroad, preached in Latin.[66] (We may also imagine that he made use of his Latin translations of Greek homilies for pastoral purposes.) According to John Rufus,[67] Melania the Younger kept distinctly Roman liturgical customs that survived even beyond her death in the monasteries that she endowed on the Mount of Olives. Whether or not such claims are strictly accurate,[68] they reflect an ongoing framing of the imperial origins of Melania and other ascetic émigrés. Gerontius refers to her even after her death as "Melania the Roman."[69]

Scholars have noted for decades the logistical and metaphorical intertwining of ascetic migration and religious travel during this period.[70] Jerome's monastic settlement probably functioned as a pilgrimage hostel, amplifying the foreignness of his monastic experience abroad.[71] In one letter, he notes that "from India, Persia, Ethiopia daily we gaze upon crowds of monks."[72] These monks were also pilgrims, and not just in a spiritual sense but a very real, spatial sense. When Palladius writes of Melania that "she was a foreigner [*xeniteusasa*] for thirty-seven years,"[73] it is unclear whether he means for that period of time she practiced asceticism or lived away from home—and, likely, the distinction made little sense to Palladius.[74] For this generation of ascetic virtuosi, the foreignness of the monastic call could be fully embodied and realized in the Holy Land, that site of *peregrinatio* and *xeniteia* that was also "our Athens," the one place in the world most perfectly adapted to engender Christian virtue.

A NEW SELF EMERGES

The mythology of the lost generation of migrant monks in the fifth century placed its ascetic heroes in a spatial tension: at home when abroad but always the most fully realized examples of a Roman Christian virtue. No surprise, then, that our narratives of ascetic migrations in the Theodosian age so often portray the impact of these ascetic virtuosi back home. We have already seen Palladius's account of Melania the Elder's brief and tumultuous return to Rome. Paulinus also contrasts Melania's sanctity with her decidedly nonascetic "silk-clad children and grandchildren" who come to meet her. In Paulinus's telling, though, the contrast is more pedagogical than apocalyptic:[75]

> Up to now the daughter of Zion has possessed her, and longs for her; but now the daughter of Babylon possesses and admires her. For now even Rome herself in the greater number of her population is the daughter of Zion rather than of Babylon. So Rome admires Melania, as she dwells in the shadow of humility and the light of truth.[75]

The brilliant shadow cast by Melania materially transforms Babylon. Again, we note the wobbly analogy between home and exile and Zion and Babylon, made even hazier by the transformation of Rome from Babylon to Zion. Jerome, in his eulogy for Paula, also emphasizes how—even after death—her example in Bethlehem has made her famous in Rome.[76]

Melania the Younger does not return home to the city of Rome, not even as a ghostly image of perfection like Paula, but does nonetheless model her new piety in an imperial capital in the *Life of Melania the Younger*. After Pinian's death and the construction of a new monastery, Melania received letters from her uncle Volusian, "ex-prefect of greater Rome [*tēs megalēs Rhōmēs*]."[77] Volusian, now in Constantinople, was still a pagan, and Melania yearned to convert him.[78] Her trip from Jerusalem to Constantinople moves like an imperial triumph across a newly Christianized empire.[79]

In Constantinople she finds a stubborn pagan uncle and Christian nobles hoodwinked by Nestorian heresy. The shining light of her piety works against both these blights in the new capital.[80] Heretical influences are banished, and Volusian is converted. Volusian's conversion signals the full Christianization of New Rome, which Melania's concluding prayer configures in clear spatial terms: "How great is [the Lord's] concern for even one soul, that in his goodness he arranged for Volusian to come from Rome and moved us to come from Jerusalem."[81] Constantinople is the in-between space in which Rome comes to enjoy the bright light of piety acquired by the ascetic virtuoso in the Holy Land.[82]

The interplay between these multiple spaces—imperial center, provincial periphery—in the production of Christian Romanness shows us that the identity forged abroad is not a unitary identity, a new Christian self that will seamlessly move us from the old world to the new. The spatialized narrative of the lost generation is a narrative of division and separation, of a split self that is at home neither in the center nor abroad. I do not think this split self, mapped across diverse and fractured terrains, is necessarily a Christian innovation; indeed, as I have argued elsewhere, Roman imperial power was always, in some respects, split against itself and its others.[83]

CONCLUSIONS: A LOST GENERATION FOUND

The spatial narrative that I have been tracing—between Rome and Jerusalem—is also not the only spatial narrative of ascetic perfection in late antiquity. We must place this particular spatialized vision alongside the myth of the desert,[84] the closed fountain of the women's cloister,[85] even the bishop's household:[86] all idealized, asceticized Christian spaces in late antiquity. What I have attempted to do here, through the historical intertext of the Lost Generation, is highlight the particular imperializing effects of one of these narratives. The positing of a special place outside the imperial center creates a vantage point from which a select few—an ascetic elite—might critique the values of the center. As we have seen, the possibilities for personhood that arise out of this spatially split matrix are also split and divided. Little surprise, then, that out of this space of critique arise new possibilities of personhood in the Christian Roman Empire: gender, class, status, and even the boundaries of the human body are called into question in this space of ascetic virtuosity in the Holy Land.[87]

Comparison with the Lost Generation in Paris also allows us to raise the very question of *generationality*. Reframing national identity through rhetoric of a generation gave to the Lost Generation in Paris a chronological as well as a spatial component.[88] Not only is the space abroad set apart (geographically, artistically, and morally) from the imperial center, but it is explicitly a site for youthful regeneration. Yet that young generation, thinking new thoughts and dreaming new dreams, will one day (soon) also be the old guard awaiting displacement by a new generation.

This rhetoric of generationality is useful in thinking about this influential cadre of ascetic émigrés, as well. As sociologists have been pointing out since the 1920s, the notion of a generation has little to do with actual demographic progression. (Otherwise, of course, it makes little sense to speak of Melania the Elder and Melania the Younger as members of the same generation.) Generations emerge as markers, spaces of cultural, political, and social innovation. When we think of Christians in the Roman Empire before and after this lost generation of ascetic migrants, it is clear they also mark a watershed: not merely the imperialization of Christianity (and the Christianization of empire) but new ways of thinking about bodies, status, and hierarchy emerge on the other side.[89] In our textbook surveys of the fourth and the early fifth century we routinely call this period the post-Constantinian era. When we think of the transformations of personhood engendered—in part—by a small group of ascetic virtuosi seeking new ways of being on the fringes of empire, we may also begin thinking of it as the age of the Melanias.

NOTES

Many thanks to my research assistant at Scripps College, Beatrice Smith, for her bibliographic work on the Lost Generation, and to my erstwhile colleague, Chris Guzaitis, for her expertise in U.S. imperialism and Steiniana.

1. On the chronology of Melania the Elder's life, see Francis X. Murphy, "Melania the Elder: A Biographical Note," *Traditio* 5 (1947): 59–77; and Kevin W. Wilkinson, "The Elder Melania's Missing Decade," *Journal of Late Antiquity* 5 (2012): 166–84, who argues that Melania did not live in Rome after the deaths of her husband and two of her children (*contra* Nicole Moine, "Melaniana," *Recherches Augustiniennes* 15 [1980]: 3–79).

2. Melania the Elder was not the first of these immigrants. Günter Stemberger, *Jews and Christians in the Holy Land: Palestine in the Fourth Century* (Edinburgh: T. & T. Clark, 2000), 115–16, identifies Innocent of Rome as the earliest settler from the West in Jerusalem (on which see below). Another earlier Western settler may have been Florentinus (see below, note 12).

3. On ascetic travel in late antiquity, see Maribel Dietz, *Wandering Monks, Virgins, and Pilgrims: Ascetic Travel in the Mediterranean Word, A.D. 300–800* (University Park: Pennsylvania State University Press, 2005).

4. Several prominent expatriates produced autobiographies of this period, the most notable being Ernest Hemingway's *A Moveable Feast* (most recently a "restored" version has been edited by Hemingway's grandson Sean: *A Moveable Feast: The Restored Edition* [New York: Scribner's, 2009]), as well as Gertrude Stein, *The Autobiography of Alice B. Toklas* (New York: Harcourt Brace, 1933), and Malcolm Cowley, whose *Exile's Return: A Literary Odyssey of the 1920s* (New York: Norton, 1934)

established many of the common tropes associated with the Lost Generation. See Craig Monk, *Writing the Lost Generation: Expatriate Autobiography and American Modernism* (Iowa City: University of Iowa Press, 2008); and Nancy F. Cott, "Revisiting the Transatlantic 1920s: Vincent Sheean vs. Malcolm Cowley," *American Historical Review* 118 (2013): 46–75.

5. This identity encompassed not only artistic but broader cultural values of politics, personal freedom, and selfhood typically known (in literary contexts) as modernism: see Marc Dolan, *Modern Lives: A Cultural Re-Reading of "The Lost Generation"* (West Lafayette, Ind.: Purdue University Press, 1996).

6. Donald Pizer, *American Expatriate Writing and the Paris Moment: Modernism and Place* (Baton Rouge: Louisiana State University Press, 1996).

7. Dolan, *Modern Lives*, 16 (citing Robert Wohl, *The Generation of 1914* [Cambridge, Mass.: Harvard University Press, 1979], 45), notes that the term "Lost Generation" was coined in Germany ("verlorene Generation") in 1912 to describe prewar political unease and was "used extensively in Britain and France in the first years after World War I to describe the literal age cohort that had been 'lost' forever in the fighting of 1914–18." See also Michael Soto, *The Modernist Nation: Generation, Renaissance, and Twentieth-Century American Literature* (Tuscaloosa: University of Alabama Press, 2004), 33–43. According to Hemingway, *Moveable Feast*, 61, Gertrude Stein applied it to the postwar expatriates. The phrase, with its ascription to Stein ("in conversation"), had already appeared in 1926 as an epigraph to Hemingway's *The Sun Also Rises* balanced neutrally (or even positively) with a long quote from Ecclesiastes. In *A Moveable Feast*, however, the phrase redounds to Stein's discredit: "I thought too of Miss Stein and Sherwood Anderson and egotism and mental laziness versus discipline and I thought who is calling who a lost generation?" (62)

"Lost generation" may be said to encompass U.S. writers and artists settled, for some period of time, in Paris in the decades following World War I: see Monk, *Writing the Lost Generation*, 1–7; and Dolan, *Modern Lives*, 9–47. See also Brooke Lindy Blower, *Becoming Americans in Paris: Transatlantic Politics and Culture between the World Wars* (New York: Oxford University Press, 2011).

8. On attempts to catalogue the lost generation dating back to the 1930s, see Soto, *Modernist Nation*, 43–50.

9. Athanasius (*Epistula ad Palladium Presbyterum*, in *Patrologia Graeca*, edited by J.-P. Migne, 26: 1168 [Paris, 1857]) and Basil (*Ep.* 258.2: Ἰννοκεντῷ τῷ Ἰταλῷ; text in *Basil: Letters*, vol. 4, *Letters 249–368 on Greek Literature*, LCL 270, ed. Roy J. Deferrari [Cambridge, Mass.: Harvard University Press, 1934], 38–40) establish Innocent as an Italian.

10. Palladius, *Historia Lausiaca* 44; text in *La Storia lausiaca*, ed. G. J. M. Bartelink and trans. Marino Barchiesi (Milan: A. Mondadori, 1974), 214–18. See Stemberger, *Jews and Christians*, 115–16; E. D. Hunt, *Holy Land Pilgrimage in the Later Roman Empire, AD 312–460* (Oxford: Clarendon Press, 1982), 167; and Jan Willem Drijvers, *Cyril of Jerusalem: Bishop and City* (Leiden: Brill, 2004), 23.

11. See Hunt, *Holy Land Pilgrimage*; and Stemberger, *Jews and Christians*; and the commentary of Cuthbert Butler, ed., in *The Lausiac History: A Critical Discussion Together with Notes on Early Egyptian Monachism* (Cambridge: Cambridge University Press, 1904; reprint, Hildesheim: Georg Olms, 1967), 219–21, on the suggestion that Innocent is the future bishop of Rome. This suggestion is rejected by Francis X. Murphy, *Rufinus of Aquileia (345–411): His Life and Works* (Washington, D.C.: Catholic University of America Press, 1945), 56, but it persists: see *Palladius: The Lausiac History*, ed. and trans. Robert T. Meyer (Westminster, Md.: Newman Press, 1965), 204; and idem, *Palladius: Dialogue on the Life of St. John Chrysostom* (Mahwah, N.J.: Paulist Press, 1985), 3. Palladius, *Historia Lausiaca* 44.4, mentions that Innocent lives at a shrine containing relics of John the Baptist (λείψανα ... Ἰωάννου τοῦ βαπτίστου [*Storia lausiaca*, ed. Bartelink, 216]); Hunt (*Holy Land Pilgrimage*, 167) connects Innocent's guardianship of John's remains with their dispersal and defilement by Julian. (See Rufinus, *Historia Ecclesiastica* 11.28 [*Tyrannii Rufini Scripta Varia*, ed. Manlio Simonetti (Rome: Città Nuova, 2000), 304–6)].)

12. Melania the Elder and Rufinus settled in Jerusalem in the 370s, although Rufinus may have arrived earlier as a guest of an Italian émigré, Florentinus, in whose care Jerome wrote to Rufinus in 374 or 375: Jerome, *Ep.* 4 and 5 (*Sancti Eusebii Hieronymi Epistulae*, ed. Isidorus Hilberg, CSEL 54: 19–23). Florentinus may be another early ascetic immigrant, if he is the same Florentinus (or Florentius) whom Jerome mentions as one of a few notable monks ("insignes monachi") in his continuation of Eusebius's *Chronicon* s.a. 377 (in *Die Chronik des Hieronymus / Hieronymi Chronicon: Eusebius' Werke 7.1*, 3rd ed., Die Griechischen Christlichen Schriftsteller der Ersten Drei Jahrhunderte 47, edited by Rudolf Helm [Berlin: Akademie-Verlag, 1984], 248): "Among them Florentinus was so merciful toward the needy that he was commonly called 'father of the poor.'" Jerome followed Paula and Eustochium to the Holy Land in the 380s, eventually settling in Bethlehem, where they constructed monasteries. John Cassian and his companion Germanus stayed at Egyptian monasteries in Bethlehem in the 380s. We may also include here such short-term settlers as Egeria, Silvia, and Poemenia, ascetic Western travelers often called pilgrims but whose sojourns, we should recall, often lasted several years. On the Western origins of these women, see Hunt, *Holy Land Pilgrimage*, 160–63.

13. Jerome speaks of refugees to the Holy Land in his *Commentarius in Ezechielem* 3, pref. (ed. F. Glorie, CCL 75: 91). Some scholars suppose, based on John Rufus, *Vita Petri Iberi* 46 (Syriac text and English translation in *John Rufus: The "Lives" of Peter the Iberian, Theodosius of Jerusalem, and the Monk Romanus*, ed. and trans. Cornelia B. Horn and Robert R. Phenix, Jr. [Atlanta: Society of Biblical Literature, 2008], 60–61), that Gerontius, monastic author of the *Vita Melaniae Iunioris*, had been raised in Rome by Melania and Pinian and immigrated with them in the 410s: see the discussion of Elizabeth A. Clark, *The Life of Melania the Younger: Introduction, Translation, and Commentary* (Lewiston, N.Y.: Edwin Mellen Press, 1984), 14–17.

14. On the far-reaching intellectual and political fissures embodied in and left by Julian's reign, see Susanna Elm, *Sons of Hellenism, Fathers of the Church: Emperor Julian, Gregory of Nazianzus, and the Vision of Rome* (Berkeley and Los Angeles: University of California Press, 2012).

15. Cott, "Revisiting the Transatlantic 1920s," 52: "A world-changing catastrophe, the war also unleashed new possibilities for those coming of age in its wake."

16. Gertrude Stein, "An American and France," delivered to the Anglo-French Society in Oxford (1936) and published in *What Are Masterpieces?* (New York: Pitman Publishing, 1970), 61–70.

17. Stein switches between "and" and "but" in her correspondence from this period, signaling the degree to which she internalized and reproduced this doubled vision of the relation between home and abroad: see Edward Burns and Ulla E. Dydo, eds., with William Rice, *The Letters of Gertrude Stein and Thornton Wilder* (New Haven: Yale University Press, 1996), 69; *The Letters of Gertrude Stein and Carl van Vechten, 1913–1946*, volume 2, *1935–1946*, ed. Edward Burns (New York: Columbia University Press, 1986), 538. Carolyn A. Durham, *Literary Globalism: Anglo-American Fiction Set in France* (Lewisburg, Penn.: Bucknell University Press, 2005), 13, produces the hybrid epigraph "America is my country but France is my home and Paris is my home town," citing all versions as possibly "apocryphal in any case" (211 note 1).

18. Martin Halliwell, "Tourists or Exiles? American Modernists in Paris in the 1920s and 1950s," *Nottingham French Studies* 44 (2005): 54–68; Pizer, *American Expatriate Writing*, 10–24.

19. On the colonialist fragmentations that underlie Stein's statement about Paris and America, see Shawn H. Alfrey, "'Oriental Peaceful Penetration': Gertrude Stein and the End of Europe," *The Massachusetts Review* 38 (1997): 405–16.

20. Paulinus, at least, claimed consanguinity with Melania the Elder: see Dennis E. Trout, *Paulinus of Nola: Life, Letters, and Poems* (Berkeley and Los Angeles: University of California Press, 1999), 26 note 19, 41.

21. Paulinus, *Ep.* 29.8–9 (*Sancti Pontii Meropii Paulini Nolani Opera*, part 1, *Epistulae*, ed. Wilhelm von Hartel and Margit Kamptner, CSEL 29: 253–57).

22. Ibid. 10 (ed. Hartel and Kamptner, CSEL 29: 257): "invidum draconem."

23. Ibid.

24. Jerome, *Chronicon* s.a. 374, condenses Melania's story: "Melania, most noble of Roman women... sailed for Jerusalem" (GCS 24: 247); in *Ep.* 39.5 (ed. Hilberg, CSEL 54: 305) he recounts that Melania's children died soon after her husband (her husband was still unburied ["necdum humato"]) and that immediately from the funeral she set sail for Jerusalem. But see Kevin Wilkinson, "Elder Melania's Missing Decade," 173–75.

25. Pizer, *American Expatriate Writing*, 1; and Nancy L. Green, "Expatriation, Expatriates, and Expats: The American Transformation of a Concept," *American Historical Review* 114 (2009): 307–28.

26. Halliwell, "Tourists or Exiles?" 56–57.

27. Palladius, *Historia Lausiaca* 54.4–5 (*Storia lausiaca*, ed. Bartelink, 246–48).

28. Ibid. 54.7 (*Storia lausiaca*, ed. Bartelink, 248).

29. See Kate Cooper, *The Virgin and the Bride: Idealized Womanhood in Late Antiquity* (Cambridge, Mass.: Harvard University Press, 1996), 92–115.

30. Andrew Cain, *The Letters of Jerome: Asceticism, Biblical Exegesis, and the Construction of Christian Authority in Late Antiquity* (Oxford: Oxford University Press, 2009), 99–128.

31. Jerome, *Ep.* 43.2–3 (ed. Hilberg, CSEL 54: 321): "Let Rome keep to itself its noise and bustle, let the cruel shows of the arena go on, let the crowd rave at the circus, let the playgoers revel in the theatres and—for I must not altogether pass over our Christian friends—let the House of Ladies hold its daily sittings." On ascetic adaptation of aristocratic *otium*, see Virginia Burrus, *The Making of a Heretic: Gender, Authority, and the Priscillianist Controversy* (Berkeley and Los Angeles: University of California Press, 1995), 9–13.

32. Cain, *Letters of Jerome*, 114–24, argues that Paula's family led the charge against Jerome in order to prevent him from leading her (and her fortune) away from Rome to the Holy Land and that Jerome was convicted on charges of conduct (financial and amorous) unbecoming a priest.

33. Jerome, *Ep.* 45.4 (ed. Hilberg, CSEL 54: 325–26): "O Envy, first biting yourself! O satanic cunning, always persecuting holy things! No other Roman women supplied drama to the city, except Paula and Melanium, who held property in contempt and left behind their relatives and raised up the Lord's cross as their particular seal of piety."

34. Lucy Grig, "Deconstructing the Symbolic City: Jerome as Guide to Late Antique Rome," *Papers of the British School at Rome* 80 (2012): 125–43, outlines the complex overlays of cultural memory that characterize Jerome's descriptions of Rome throughout his career (building on Karin Sugano, *Das Rombild des Hieronymus* [Frankfurt a.M.: Peter Lang, 1983]); and John Curran, "Jerome and the Sham-Christians of Rome," *Journal of Ecclesiastical History* 48 (1997): 213–29.

35. Jerome, *Ep.* 45.6 (ed. Hilberg, CSEL 54: 327).

36. Jerome, *Interpretatio Libri Didymi de Spiritu Sancto*, prol.: "When I lived in Babylon, and I was a serf of the purple-clad whore, and I lived according to the law of the Quirites.... And the senate of the Pharisees shouted.... And I returned to Jerusalem: and after the house of Romulus and the Lupercalian games, I gazed upon the lodging place of Mary and the Savior's cave" (*Traité du Saint-Esprit*, ed. and trans. Louis Doutreleau, SC 386: 138-40).

37. P. Laurence, "Rome et Jérôme: Des amours contrariées," *Revue Bénédictine* 107 (1997): 227–49, breaks down Jerome's "Janus-faced" attitudes toward the city as a doubled vision of a pagan Rome (rejected) and a Christian Rome (idealized).

38. Green, "Expatriation," 320–21.

39. In his letter to Heliodorus, Jerome bemoans the "calamities of our times," and concludes that the "Roman world is falling" (*Ep.* 60.15, 16 [ed. Hilberg, CSEL 54: 568, 570]). In his letter to Laeta on the education of Paula the Younger, Jerome describes Rome's "squalid" conditions (*Ep.* 107.1 [ed. Hilberg, CSEL 55: 291]) and, after detailing a rigorous program of ascetic education for Paula, admits that such a pedagogical program is impossible in Rome, wherefore Laeta should send Paula to her grandmother and aunt in Bethlehem (*Ep.* 107.13 [ed. Hilberg, CSEL 55: 303]).

40. See Michele Renee Salzman, "Apocalypse Then? Jerome and the Fall of Rome in 410," in *Maxima Debetur Magistro Reverentia: Essays on Rome and the Roman Tradition in Honor of Russell T. Scott,* ed. Paul Harvey, Jr., and Catherine Conybeare (Como: New Press, 2009), 175–92.

41. Palladius, *Historia Lausiaca* 61.1 (*Storia lausiaca,* ed. Bartelink, 264).

42. Ibid. 3–6 (*Storia lausiaca,* ed. Bartelink, 264–68).

43. Gerontius, *Vita Melaniae Iunioris* 1 (*Vie de sainte Mélanie: Texte grec, introduction, traduction et notes,* ed. and trans. Denys Gorce, SC 90: 130), describes her parents as "forcibly uniting her in marriage" (μετὰ πολλῆς βίας συνάπτουσιν αὐτὴν πρὸς γάμον τῷ μακαρίῳ ἀνδρὶ Πινιανῷ), similar to Palladius's description (see above), with which Gerontius was probably familiar. Translations of the *vita* are based on Gerontius, *Life of Melania the Younger,* trans. E. A. Clark, modified for clarity.

44. In despair, they even contemplate running away: "They planned with each other to withdraw [ἀναχωρεῖν] and flee the city [φεύγειν τῆς πόλεως]" (Gerontius, *Vita Melaniae Iunioris* 6 [*Vie de sainte Mélanie,* ed. and trans. Gorce, SC 90: 138]). "Some heavenly perfume" (εὐωδία τις . . . οὐράνιος) intervenes to bring them to their senses; Susan Ashbrook Harvey, *Scenting Salvation: Ancient Christianity and the Olfactory Imagination* (Berkeley and Los Angeles: University of California Press, 2006), 64–65, places this scene in the context of similar olfactory miracles.

45. Gerontius, *Vita Melaniae Iunioris* 7 (*Vie de sainte Mélanie,* ed. and trans. Gorce, SC 90: 140).

46. Ibid. 19 (*Vie de sainte Mélanie,* ed. and trans. Gorce, SC 90: 162–64): "They fearlessly gave away the remainder of their possessions in Rome, . . . possessions that were, so to speak, enough for the whole world."

47. Ibid. 34 (*Vie de sainte Mélanie,* ed. and trans. Gorce, SC 90: 190).

48. Cott, "Revisiting the Transatlantic 1920s."

49. Halliwell, "Tourists or Exiles?" 57–62; Pizer, *American Expatriate Writing,* 10–20. Stein, "An American and France," repeatedly emphasizes the requisite foreignness of Paris (especially in comparison with England): "That is what foreignness is, that it is there but it does not happen. England to an American English writing to an American is not in this sense a foreign thing. And so we go to Paris. That is a great many of us go to Paris" (68).

50. Unlike the generalized, Abraham-inspired *peregrinatio* advocated by other contemporary monastics (among them Jerome himself in his famous [pre-Bethlehem] letter to Eustochium, *Ep.* 22.1 [ed. Hilberg, CSEL 54:144]), Jerome insists on the specific site of relocation. On spiritual and monastic understandings of *peregrinatio* (Greek ἀναχώρησις), see Daniel Caner, *Wandering, Begging Monks: Spiritual Authority and the Promotion of Monasticism in Late Antiquity* (Berkeley and Los Angeles: University of California Press, 2002); and Dietz, *Wandering Monks.*

51. Jerome, *Ep.* 46.3 (ed. Hilberg, CSEL 54: 332). Most scholars assume that Jerome is writing to Marcella, using the conceit of Paula's and Eustochium's voices: see, for instance, Cain, *Letters of Jerome,* 95–98.

52. Jerome, *Ep.* 46.9 (ed. Hilberg, CSEL 54: 339). The "orator" whom Jerome mentions is Cicero, *Divinatio in Caecilium* 39 (*Cicero: The Verrine Orations,* vol. 1, *Against Caecilius, Against Verres,* part 1; part 2, books 1–2, ed. and trans. L. H. G. Greenwood, Loeb Classical Library 221 [Cambridge, Mass.: Harvard University Press, 1928], 36).

53. Many of Jerome's letters throughout the 390s and 400s press his aristocratic allies back West to resettle in the Holy Land, there to pursue true Christianity: Jerome, *Ep.* 53, 71, 122, 139, 145 (ed. Hilberg, CSEL 54: 442–65; 55: 1–7; 56: 56–71, 267–68, 306–7).

54. Jerome, *Ep.* 77.6 (ed. Hilberg, CSEL 55: 44). On Fabiola, see Cain, *Letters of Jerome,* 171–78. As Cain points out, the eulogy to Oceanus served as a cover letter for the dense and detailed exegetical *Epistle* 78 (ed. Hilberg, CSEL 55: 49–87), written (posthumously) to Fabiola.

55. Possibly Jerome had convinced her to endow monastic foundations there (see Jerome, *Ep.* 77.7 [ed. Hilberg, CSEL 55: 44–45]); Jerome, *Ep.* 77.8 (ed. Hilberg, CSEL 55: 45), notes that he was looking for a "little place for her to live" (*habitaculum*), similar to "Mary's inn."

56. Cain, *Letters of Jerome*, 173, assumes based on the dates (394–95) that Fabiola was loath to become embroiled in the burgeoning Origenist controversy. See also Hunt, *Holy Land Pilgrimage*, 191.

57. Jerome, *Ep.* 77.8 (ed. Hilberg, CSEL 55: 46). During his brief sojourn in Syria, Jerome had used similar shaming language for companions who were unable to tough it out in the monastic wilderness. (See *Ep.* 14, to Heliodorus [ed. Hilberg, CSEL 54: 44–62].) What has developed in the meantime is Jerome's explicit contrast between Rome, the *patria*, and the "holy places."

58. Pizer, *American Expatriates*, 22–24, notes the negative models in Hemingway's *Moveable Feast* (such as Scott Fitzgerald and Ezra Pound), who fail to respond appropriately to the *locus amoenus* of Paris. We may read Jerome's sudden change of heart toward Paulinus—encouraging in *Ep.* 53, discouraging in *Ep.* 58 (ed. Hilberg, CSEL 54: 442–65, 527–41)—not only as a political calculation (see Hunt, *Holy Land Pilgrimage*, 192–93) but also a change in Jerome's perception of Paulinus's fitness for Holy Land asceticism.

59. Gerontius, *Vita Melaniae Iunioris* 28 (*Vie de sainte Mélanie*, ed. and trans. Gorce, SC 90: 180–82).

60. Clark, in Gerontius, *Life of Melania the Younger*, trans. E. A. Clark, 150, speculates that the heretic was Melania the Elder herself; T. D. Barnes concurs (*Early Christian Hagiography and Roman History* [Tübingen: Mohr Siebeck, 2010], 251–52).

61. Gerontius, *Vita Melaniae Iunioris* 40 (*Vie de sainte Mélanie*, ed. and trans. Gorce, SC 90: 202–4).

62. See my *Remains of the Jews: The Holy Land and Christian Empire in Late Antiquity* (Stanford: Stanford University Press, 2003), 56–99.

63. Jerome, *Apologia adversus Rufinum* 1.17, 3.6 (*Apologie contre Rufin*, ed. and trans. Pierre Lardet, SC 303: 46–50, 228–32).

64. See my "'What Has Rome to Do With Bethlehem?' Cultural Capital(s) and Religious Imperialism in Late Ancient Christianity," *Classical Receptions Journal* 3 (2011): 29–45.

65. Gerontius, *Vita Melaniae Iunioris* 26 (*Vie de sainte Mélanie*, ed. and trans. Gorce, SC 90: 180).

66. See the recent translations of Sister Marie Liguori Ewald, *The Homilies of Saint Jerome*, 2 vols. (Washington, D.C.: Catholic University of America Press, 1964–66).

67. *Vita Petri Iberi* 46 (ed. and trans. Horn and Phenix, *John Rufus: The "Lives,"* 62–63).

68. The publisher of the Latin version of the *Vita Melaniae Iunioris*, Cardinal Mariano Rampolla, sought to heighten the Roman aspect of Melania's liturgical practices as described in the *vita*; Clark, *Life of Melania the Younger*, 119–28, treats these claims with more skepticism.

69. Gerontius, *Vita Melaniae Iunioris*, prol. (*Vie de sainte Mélanie*, ed. and trans. Gorce, SC 90: 124). So too Palladius refers to her grandmother as "Melania the Roman": *Historia Lausiaca* 38.8 (*Storia lausiaca*, ed. Bartelink, 198).

70. Bruria Bitton-Ashkelony, "*Imitatio Mosis* and Pilgrimage in the *Life of Peter the Iberian*," in *Christian Gaza in Late Antiquity*, ed. eadem and Aryeh Kofsky (Leiden: Brill, 2004), 107–29, at 109: "From the fourth century on an explicit affinity is noticeable in monastic culture between the phenomenon of pilgrimage and the realization of *xeniteia*." See also eadem, *Encountering the Sacred: The Debate on Christian Pilgrimage in Late Antiquity* (Berkeley and Los Angeles: University of California Press, 2005), 140–73.

71. Jerome, *Ep.* 107.2, 108.14 (ed. Hilberg, CSEL 55: 292, 325); *Apologia adversus Rufinum* 3.17 (*Apologie contre Rufin*, ed. and trans. Lardet, SC 303: 258–60). Andrew Cain, "Jerome's *Epitaphium Paulae*: Hagiography, Pilgrimage, and the Cult of Paula," *Journal of Early Christian Studies* 18 (2010): 105–39, at 108–13, details the construction projects of Jerome and Paula, including the *diversorium peregrinorum*; see now also Andrew Cain, *Jerome's Epitaph on Paula: A Commentary on the "Epitaphium Sanctae Paulae"* (Oxford: Oxford University Press, 2013), 311–14.

72. Jerome, *Ep.* 107.2 (ed. Hilberg, CSEL 55: 292).

73. Palladius, *Historia Lausiaca* 54.2 (*Storia lausiaca*, ed. Bartelink, 247). The "thirty-seven years" of this passage has caused much confusion in modern scholarship on Melania: see Kevin Wilkinson, "Elder Melania's Missing Decade."

74. In the same passage Palladius notes that Melania "persevered in her foreignness [ἐγκαρτερήσασα τῇ ξενιτείᾳ]." Meyer, in *Palladius: The Lausiac History*, ed. and trans. Meyer, 134, renders this word in both places as "gave hospitality to," but such a translation seems to be stretching the definition. Bartelink, in Palladius, *Storia lausiaca*, ed. Bartelink, renders it as "perseverato ... nella vita ascetica," but earlier renders ξενιτεύσασα as "visse separate dal mondo." (See also 387 note 8, where he discusses the chronological and translational difficulties of this passage.) See s.vv. ξενετεία and ξενιτεύω in G. W. H. Lampe, ed., *A Patristic Greek Lexicon* (Oxford: Clarendon Press, 1961), 931–32.

75. Paulinus, *Ep.* 29.13 (ed. Hartel and Kamptner, CSEL 29: 260–61).

76. Jerome, *Ep.* 108.3 (ed. Hilberg, CSEL 55: 308).

77. Gerontius, *Vita Melaniae Iunioris* 50 (*Vie de sainte Mélanie*, ed. and trans. Gorce, SC 90: 224).

78. Rufinus Antonius Agrypinus Volusianus, Melania's maternal uncle, may be one of the most sought-after pagans for Christian conversion: the dedicatee of Augustine's *City of God* and recipient of numerous letters from the African bishop, Volusian seemed happy to remain non-Christian until soon before his death. See Gerontius, *Life of Melania the Younger*, trans. E. A. Clark, 129–33.

79. Gerontius, *Vita Melaniae Iunioris* 51 (*Vie de sainte Mélanie*, ed. and trans. Gorce, SC 90: 224–26).

80. Ibid. 54 (*Vie de sainte Mélanie*, ed. and trans. Gorce, SC 90: 232–34).

81. Ibid. 55 (*Vie de sainte Mélanie*, ed. and trans. Gorce, SC 90: 238).

82. The interplay between piety acquired abroad and transformation of the political center is reinforced by the immediately following narrative of the empress Eudoxia's harrowing journey back to Jerusalem with Melania: ibid. 56 (*Vie de sainte Mélanie*, ed. and trans. Gorce, SC 90: 238–40).

83. See my *Christ Circumcised: A Study in Early Christian History and Difference* (Philadelphia: University of Pennsylvania Press, 2012), 6–10, 15–19, and passim.

84. James Goehring, "The Encroaching Desert: Literary Production and Ascetic Space in Early Christian Egypt," in *Ascetics, Society, and the Desert: Studies in Egyptian Monasticism* (Harrisburg, Penn.: Trinity Press International, 1999), 73–88 (reprinted from *Journal of Early Christian Studies* 1 [1993]: 281–96).

85. See Peter Brown, *The Body and Society: Men, Women, and Sexual Renunciation in Early Christianity*, 2nd ed. (New York: Columbia University Press, 2008), 341–65; and David Brakke, *Athanasius and the Politics of Asceticism* (Oxford: Clarendon Press, 1995), 21–57.

86. See Kristina Sessa, *The Formation of Papal Authority in Late Antique Italy: Roman Bishops and the Domestic Sphere* (Cambridge: Cambridge University Press, 2011); and Kate Cooper, *The Fall of the Roman Household* (Cambridge: Cambridge University Press, 2007).

87. We should not forget one of the most significant discourses of moral revaluation to be reimported back from the Holy Land to Rome: the ideas of Origen, translated and transmitted by Rufinus: see Elizabeth A. Clark, *The Origenist Controversy: The Cultural Construction of an Early Christian Debate* (Princeton: Princeton University Press, 1992). Similarly the Lost Generation in Paris, performed by such figures as Djuna Barnes, Josephine Baker, and James Baldwin, was notably more open to racial and sexual diversity and experimentation than U.S. society in general at the time.

88. Dolan, *Modern Lives*, 10–11, and Soto, *Modernist Nation*, 17–46, on generational rhetoric before and after the Lost Generation. Soto draws particular attention (on pp. 23–24) to Karl Mannheim's 1923 essay "The Problem of Generations" (in *From Karl Mannheim*, ed. Kurt H. Wolff, 2nd ed. [New Brunswick: Transaction Publishers, 1993], 351–98), itself an essay written in exile (from Germany).

89. Averil Cameron, "Ascetic Closure and the End of Antiquity," in *Asceticism*, ed. Vincent L. Wimbush and Richard Valantasis (New York: Oxford University Press, 1995), 147–61, approaches similar questions of historical periodization and the rise of asceticism from a different perspective.

12

Sing, O Daughter(s) of Zion

Stephen J. Shoemaker

As the Christianization of civic life rapidly transformed the Roman Empire of the fourth and fifth centuries, one of the most effective means by which Christianity came to inhabit the empire's cities was through the development of public liturgy.[1] Ritual practices that had once been held in private, often in the homes of individual Christians, now emerged into the public sphere, not only in the many new churches that began to spring up but even in the streets of the city itself, with the establishment of stational and processional liturgies. Memories of the apostles and saints were also inscribed onto the urban landscape, as shrines and pilgrimage presented another means of Christianizing this space. Perhaps nowhere are all these elements on better display than in Jerusalem during the lifetimes of Melania the Elder and Melania the Younger, both of whom played active roles in shaping Jerusalem's Christian topography. Indeed, the *Life of Melania the Younger* is an especially important source for understanding the early history of the Jerusalem liturgies, and this same Melania was herself actively involved in promoting the veneration of St. Stephen's relics, both topics that Elizabeth Clark has illuminated for us in the course of her expansive career.[2] Yet the choice to focus on Jerusalem in this regard is not governed entirely by the two Melanias' residence there. Rather, Jerusalem offers an unrivaled test case for investigating the development of Christian liturgies in late antiquity, inasmuch as our sources for the Jerusalem liturgy are extremely rich in comparison with other urban centers, and Jerusalem seems to have "acted as a crossroads for a number of liturgical traditions." The fact that the early Jerusalem liturgy was highly influential in the development of later Byzantine liturgy during the early Middle Ages only serves to heighten its significance.[3]

Jerusalem was of course a major site of pilgrimage in late antiquity, a topic that has been well explored in recent decades. Likewise, the Jerusalem calendar and its daily, weekly, and stational liturgies have also been studied in some detail. Yet remarkable new evidence is beginning to emerge regarding the hymnography of the Jerusalem services during the late fourth and the fifth century from the recently published Jerusalem Georgian Chantbook (*iadgari/tropologion*). Through this invaluable new source, which will be the primary focus of this chapter, we gain unprecedented knowledge of the songs that filled the soundscape of late antiquity's churches. While liturgists and musicologists have already begun to draw important conclusions from this chantbook regarding the structure and format of Jerusalem's public liturgies in late antiquity, I here wish to explore what these hymns may reveal about the development of early Christian piety. In particular, the Sunday hymns from the Jerusalem Chantbook show that by the later fourth and the early fifth century devotion to the Virgin and her intercessions was already embedded in the regular public worship of Jerusalem's churches. The persistence of this motif across Jerusalem's hymnography offers surprisingly early evidence of Marian veneration, which seems to have reached a rather advanced state in the Holy City well in advance of the events of the Third Council (431).

THE JERUSALEM LITURGY IN THE AGE OF THE MELANIAS

Of course, Jerusalem's early pilgrims offer some of the best-known accounts of its public ceremonies, and of all these visitors from abroad none can match the depth with which Egeria recounts her experience of the Jerusalem liturgy during her three-year stay between 381 and 384.[4] Egeria gives a brief account of the daily offices, and she remains our best source for these practices during the period in question. The daily cycle begins and ends in darkness with matins and vespers, and two additional services intervene, one at midday (sext) and another in the afternoon (nones). There is, it would seem, also an additional observance of tierce during Lent and a special matins service for Sunday.[5] Of particular interest is that these observances seem not to have involved readings from the scriptures but focused instead on praise and intercession. Readings from the scriptures entered into the daily office, it would appear, only through the Jerusalemite practice of reading appointed lections at the various sacred sites through the practice of stational liturgy, about which more will be said below.[6]

Egeria also describes the weekly Sunday services, which, she notes, were conducted according to a pattern that is "everywhere the custom on the Lord's Day," with the exception that in Jerusalem all the presbyters are allowed to preach.[7] Here we also have important supplementary information from Cyril of Jerusalem's *Mystagogical Catecheses*, which has engendered much discussion concerning the nature of the Eucharistic prayers in this era.[8] On the whole, it would appear that in the Melanias' Jerusalem this most solemn moment of the liturgy was still evolving in terms of content, and the Anaphora seems to have reached a standard format only during the early fifth century.[9] Nevertheless, the basic structure of the Eucharist is otherwise fairly clear, largely following a pattern witnessed already in Justin Martyr's *First Apology*.[10] The Eucharistic celebration began with the Liturgy of the Word, which included readings from the scriptures, preaching, and intercessory prayers, a program witnessed even more clearly in the Jerusalem Armenian Lectionary from the early fifth century.[11] Cyril's fifth *Mystagogical Catechesis* additionally describes a hand-washing ceremony immediately preceding the mysteries of the Eucharist that would follow in the Liturgy of the Faithful, a practice confirmed by later sources from the sixth and seventh centuries.[12] Following the prayers of consecration, Cyril relates that the congregation recited the Lord's Prayer, after which the priest invited the congregants to receive the Eucharistic elements, concluding then with prayers and a dismissal.[13] On the whole, it is a pattern still recognizable today in Christian communities that maintain a more traditional pattern of worship. At the time of Egeria's visit, the Eucharist was celebrated not only on Sundays in Jerusalem, but also on Wednesdays and Fridays and possibly Saturdays as well, except during Lent, when the Eucharist was reserved for Sundays alone. Nevertheless, these weekday liturgies were soon discontinued in the early fifth century, in accordance with the fourth-century Council of Laodicea (363/4), which forbids the celebration of the Eucharist on fasting days.[14]

The observance of Lent introduces one of the most distinctive and important aspects of the Jerusalem liturgy in the late fourth and early fifth century, namely the observance of a liturgical calendar and the related practice of stational worship and processions. Jerusalem's introduction of a Christian calendar is, as John Baldovin observes, "the most significant contribution of the liturgy in Jerusalem" to both the Christian East and the West.[15] In particular, the Jerusalem calendar was responsible for the introduction and diffusion of a number major Christian feasts, including, for example, the observance of the Dormition and Assumption on 15 August, the Exaltation of the Holy Cross on 14 September, and the Presentation of the Virgin on 21 November.[16] Of these three feasts, only the second is mentioned by Egeria, who at the end of her account notes this annual celebration of the Church of Golgatha's dedication, its Encainia. This feast, which commemorated the discovery of the True Cross, was according to Egeria equal in importance even to Epiphany and Easter.[17] Egeria fails to mention the 15 August Feast of the Virgin Mary, although it appears in the early fifth-century Armenian Lectionary, not yet as a commemoration of the Dormition but instead as a feast celebrating Mary's Divine Maternity.[18] Egeria's silence, however, offers no guarantee that this Marian feast was not observed during the late fourth century, inasmuch as her account is highly selective and does not offer a complete liturgical calendar, instead focusing only on certain major feasts. The Armenian Lectionary indicates twenty-six special feasts that were observed during the year, and their absence from Egeria's description seemingly reflects her focus primarily on dominical feasts rather than sanctoral commemorations, as others have noted. Presumably, many if not most of the Armenian Lectionary's observances were already in place during Egeria's visit.[19] As for the Presentation of the Virgin, this is a more recent feast that originated from the dedication of the sixth-century Nea Church in Jerusalem. It first appears in the Jerusalem Georgian Lectionary, which represents the Jerusalem calendar as it developed in the period between the mid-fifth and the early seventh century. This Georgian Lectionary reflects a considerable expansion of the hagiopolite liturgy during this period, so that nearly every day of the year was marked by a liturgical commemoration, providing an important paradigm for the many other liturgical calendars that would follow.[20]

Egeria's focus, however, lies squarely on the observances of Epiphany, Lent, Holy Week, and Easter, so that she is largely silent concerning other aspects of the liturgical year. At the time of her visit, the church year began with Epiphany on 6 January, which in Jerusalem held the observance of the Nativity, rather than 25 December. At the time, this was no local aberration, and there is widespread evidence for the celebration of Christmas on 6 January in early Christianity, reaching as far back as Clement of Alexandria.[21] Indeed, it was only in the middle of the sixth century, with strong imperial pressure coming from the emperor Justinian himself, that the date of Christmas was finally moved from 6 January to 25 December in Jerusalem, and to the present day in the Armenian Church, Christmas continues to be observed on 6 January, following this ancient custom.[22] The *Life of Melania the Younger*, however, informs us that she celebrated the Nativity in Bethlehem on 25 December 439, which some scholars have adduced as evidence that the date of Jerusalem's Christmas celebration already had shifted by this time.[23] Nevertheless, it seems much more likely that this difference reflects the fact that, as Charles (Athanase) Renoux notes, Melania did not follow the Jerusalem rite strictly in her foundations but instead observed many Roman practices, including the date of Christmas, as one might expect of this Italian aristocrat abroad, whose status as émigrée in Jerusalem was thoughtfully explored in the preceding chapter.[24]

One of the most intriguing aspects of the three main festivals that Egeria describes, Epiphany, Easter, and Encaenia, is that all three were celebrated over eight days at a variety of liturgical stations scattered across the Holy City and in its immediate vicinity.[25] Although her account is again highly selective and incomplete, it is invaluable as the earliest witness to this emerging practice of the Jerusalem church, which brought Christianity out into the streets and the surroundings of the city. Not surprisingly, these liturgical octaves had the complex of churches at Golgatha and the Holy Sepulcher as their focus, making forays during the week to Sion, the Mount of Olives, Bethany, and, in later years, to the Church of St. Stephen. The feast of Epiphany, as might be expected, began with a procession to Bethlehem, a vigil there, followed by a procession back to Jerusalem on the morning of the feast. In the more complete picture offered by the Armenian Lectionary, we find a year filled with liturgical activities scattered throughout the city, and its additional feasts lead to new stations at Bethpage, at the second mile from Bethlehem, at Anatoth, and even as far afield as Kiriath Jearim for the feast of the Ark of the Covenant.[26] In this way the Christians of late ancient Jerusalem took full advantage of their uniquely consecrated terrain, fusing feast with place through ritual commemoration. These were truly movable feasts of a slightly different sort, and through their processions between the city's major shrines and beyond to more remote stations in Bethany and Bethlehem, they visibly wove the Christian faith into the fabric of Jerusalem's urban landscape. These stational movements and memorials make up one of the most distinctive qualities of the early Jerusalem liturgy, and although there is limited evidence for similar practices elsewhere—in Rome and in Constantinople, for instance[27]—nowhere else is the public worship of a late ancient city on such rich display.

THE JERUSALEM GEORGIAN CHANTBOOK AND THE HYMNOGRAPHY OF LATE ANCIENT JERUSALEM

Of course, this general outline of the early Jerusalem liturgy is by now fairly well known and indeed has been since the discovery of Egeria's travelogue at the end of the nineteenth century. Publication of the Jerusalem Armenian and Georgian lectionaries roughly a half-century ago subsequently enabled us to fill in many of the gaps in Egeria's account and to trace the development of the Jerusalem liturgies into the early Islamic period as it expanded to include even more feasts and stations. Nevertheless, the recent publication of the Jerusalem Georgian Chantbook offers a new and largely unexploited resource for further reconstruction of worship in late ancient Jerusalem, giving us for the first time some sense of the sounds that filled its places of worship. Egeria, for instance, mentions the singing of hymns and antiphons over one hundred times, and here we find hymns for virtually every service in the Jerusalem rite, although sadly their tunes remain lost to the ages. It is true that the Armenian Lectionary preserves the early psalmody of Jerusalem, and the *Life of Melania the Younger* occasionally refers to the singing of psalms at the daily office and chanting, although there is no mention of any hymns.[28] Nevertheless, the liturgies described in the *Life of Melania* reflect monastic practices, which already by this time had begun to develop according to a different pattern from the public liturgies that one would have found in the churches of Jerusalem.[29] From a slightly later period, the Georgian Lectionary regularly provides incipits for the hymns to be sung at various feasts,[30] but this earliest Christian hymnal remains unequaled for its witness to the music of the late ancient church. Its pages reveal a rich corpus of sophisticated theological poetry steeped in biblical allusions, such that, as Peter Jeffery observes, "the importance of this material for the history of Christian hymnody and theology... cannot be overstated."[31]

Yet even though a critical edition of the chantbook was published now over thirty years ago, its songs and its liturgical calendar have remained largely ignored by all but a handful of liturgists and musicologists. No doubt this neglect is largely a consequence of the fact that this massive collection of hymns survives only in Old Georgian, a difficult and obscure language known by few scholars of late antiquity. Compounding this problem is the publication of the edition in Georgia late in the Soviet period, so that there are few exemplars available in the West.[32] Moreover, the edition itself is somewhat unwieldy, running to more than five hundred and fifty pages in length and including another four hundred pages of studies and indices. The critical text is also somewhat problematic, inasmuch as it is a composite of several rather different manuscripts, not all of which, it seems, reflect the same liturgical context: some manuscripts preserve more archaic forms than others, and at least one witnesses to the monastic liturgies of Deir Mar Saba in the Judean Desert rather than to the urban rite of late ancient Jerusalem. As they are presented in the critical edition, it requires some effort to distinguish the contents of one manuscript from the others, making it difficult to reconstruct the individual hymns and to understand the history of the collection.

The Jerusalem Georgian Chantbook survives in two major recensions, one of them clearly older than the other, and at present only this earlier version has been edited. As for the more recent version, it has now been discovered in the Greek original among the new finds in the collection of Mount Sinai, and we may hope that before long someone will undertake an edition of this important liturgical manuscript from the eighth or the ninth century.[33] Nevertheless, for the earliest hymnography of Jerusalem and, indeed, of Christianity in general, we remain dependent on this earlier version of the chantbook, which presently survives only in Old Georgian translation. As a collection, this older recension of the Jerusalem Chantbook seemingly dates to before the beginning of the seventh century at the latest, but many of its various components can be dated somewhat earlier. The newer version of the chantbook is distinguished from the older particularly by its inclusion of newer materials, and these added hymns, as Stig Frøyshov explains, locate the point of transition from the old chantbook to the new in the early seventh century.[34] Hélène Métrévéli similarly concludes on the basis of these two collections that the older version of the chantbook was translated from Greek into Georgian sometime toward the end of the sixth or at the beginning of the seventh century, a position also shared by most other specialists on early Georgian liturgical materials.[35] Accordingly, the hymns of the collection must be even earlier.

The earlier Georgian Chantbook itself consists of three major parts. The largest section provides hymns for the evening office, the morning office, and the

Eucharist—in that order—for each of the year's liturgical feasts, following the order of the liturgical calendar.[36] Yet the calendar that governs the organization of this section begins not with the Nativity, as one would expect, but instead with the Annunciation. As Jeffery explains, this feature reflects a more primitive practice of observing the feast of the Annunciation during Advent, which was relatively common during the fifth century. Nevertheless, the observance of the Annunciation on 25 March and the related placement of the Nativity on 25 December reflect Justinian's orders that Jerusalem's calendar should conform to the imperial standard in this regard. Thus, Jeffery concludes, the older chantbook's calendar "appears to straddle the reorganization of the Christmas cycle," which would date the calendar to the mid-sixth century and, presumably, most of its hymns even earlier.[37] A similar calendar also is present in the early Georgian homiliaries, which scholars have dated to the fifth or sixth century, offering important confirmation of this date.[38]

A short collection of hymns follows this major festal cycle, providing what Jeffery describes as supplementary troparia for the major feasts, and again these are arranged according to the liturgical calendar, but without any indication of where the hymns were to be used in the liturgy.[39] After this brief interlude, the edition then continues with another major section devoted to the hymns appointed for ordinary Sundays, entitled the Hymns of the Resurrection, since this topic was the primary focus of the Sunday service.[40] In the various manuscripts, this collection appears sometimes before and sometimes after the festal calendar and its hymns, leading Jeffery to conclude that these Sunday hymns were a more recent collection, most likely from the eighth century, that had been added as an appendix to the older collection of proper chants for the yearly feasts.[41] Nevertheless, these hymns of the Sunday service have since been studied in some detail, and over the last fifteen years their contents have been increasingly brought to light, largely through the remarkable industry of Charles Renoux, who recently has completed a multivolume translation and study of the entire corpus according to each of its manuscripts.[42] Not only has Renoux made this invaluable collection of hymns more widely accessible through their translation in French, but his analysis of the hymns and the structure of the chantbook's services has persuasively identified the bulk of the hymns as compositions from the fourth and the early fifth century. Thus we now have available in these Hymns of the Resurrection a remarkable and unparalleled compendium of Christian hymns from late ancient Jerusalem, revealing for the first time the songs of early Christian worship, presumably as they were sung at the Sunday services of the Melanias' Jerusalem.

As Frøyshov notes, Jeffery's late dating for this collection of Sunday hymns cannot be correct, since they are part of the old version of the chantbook. Inasmuch as this early version was replaced by a newer version during the early seventh century, an update that included a new collection of hymns for the Sunday services, this older Sunday hymnal must be earlier than the beginning of the seventh century.[43]

Frøyshov accordingly dates the collection itself to the sixth century, although certain structural elements appear to date a little earlier, to the fourth or fifth century.[44] The hymns themselves, however, are another matter. One assumes that they were not newly composed for this sixth-century codification, but that rather the bulk of the hymns are almost certainly older than the collection itself. The only question then is, How much older? Here the work of Renoux in particular is invaluable, and his analysis of the hymns has persuasively determined that on the whole they appear to belong to the fourth and the fifth century. Moreover, the weight of his arguments strongly favors their composition before the middle of the fifth century. Renoux convincingly draws a number of parallels to liturgical practices from the later fourth century, to the writings of Cyril and Hesychius of Jerusalem, and generally to the theology of the fourth century. By contrast the issues of Chalcedon and other more recent developments seem notably absent from the hymns. The presence of many of the same hymns in the Armenian hymnography likewise points to an early date for these compositions.[45] Thus, although it is difficult to be certain that every one of the chantbook's Sunday songs belongs to this period, we may take some confidence that the greater part of its hymns are from the fourth and the early fifth century, affording us an unparalleled window into the liturgical chant and the hymnography of public worship in late ancient Christianity.

Renoux's decision to extract the individual manuscripts from the critical edition by translating each one separately may seem like an unnecessary multiplication of labor, but in light of their different qualities and contexts, such a presentation makes the material much more accessible to scholars. Of the seven manuscripts preserving the Old Jerusalem Chantbook, one is lacking all but a small portion of the Resurrection hymns, but since this particular manuscript seems to reflect monastic usage, it is of only limited value for reconstructing the ceremonies of Jerusalem's churches.[46] The remaining six manuscripts all reflect to different degrees the Sunday worship of the Jerusalem Cathedral rite, with some corresponding more directly than others to the actual usage. For instance, several of the manuscripts appear to be more or less anthologies whose compilers have sought to collect as much of Jerusalem's early hymnody as possible without regard to actual liturgical usage, adding additional strophes that perhaps have been taken from different exemplars, or alternatively leaving some out. Of the different manuscripts, Renoux concludes that one, Sinai Georgian 18, is the closest to the actual liturgical practice of late ancient Jerusalem, and accordingly his translation of this manuscript offers an important basis for the study of liturgical chant and poetry during this period. With these hymns we come as close as we possibly may (barring the discovery of the Greek original) to the music of the Sunday services in the Church of the Anastasis during the late fourth and the early fifth century.[47]

Among the most remarkable features of this collection is its organization according to a program of eight musical tones, which were used in a regular, repeating sequence for the music of the Sunday services during the period between Pentecost and Lent. This structure, known as the Oktoechos, still governs the practice of liturgical chant in the Eastern Orthodox, Armenian Orthodox, and Syrian Orthodox churches today, and it was also an important feature of the Western liturgies in the Middle Ages. Perhaps for this reason, the octotonal structure of these Sunday hymns has so far been the predominant focus of scholarship on the Jerusalem Georgian Chantbook. For each of the eight tones, or modes, or melodies, as they are also sometimes called, the chantbook provides a complete sequence of hymns for the services of vespers, matins, and the liturgy, in that order. Although the specific musical elements of these ancient eight tones are unfortunately lost, judging from more recent medieval evidence it would appear that each tone was characterized by a distinctive modality as well as by certain recurring melodic elements—motifs, melodic formulas, and melodic types—that together define a particular tone.[48]

The origins of this popular musical system have long posed something of a mystery, but this early chantbook now appears to confirm its derivation from the public liturgies of late ancient Jerusalem. Earlier scholarship, following the work of Anton Baumstark, long looked to Syria and the so-called Oktoechos of Severus of Antioch as the source of the widespread practice of using eight successive tones to sing the liturgy. Nevertheless, more recent scholarship has shown that this collection is a later production, and the roots of the Oktoechos structure are instead to be found in late ancient Palestine.[49] It is not entirely clear, however, when the Jerusalem liturgies introduced this modal sequence: even if its hymns seemingly belong to the fourth and the fifth century, this in itself offers no guarantee that their arrangement according to an Oktoechos is equally ancient. Aelred Cody and Jeffery accordingly suggested that the octotonal system first arose in Palestine only during the eighth century (although Cody did not know the Georgian Chantbook).[50] Nevertheless, Frøyshov has convincingly established the existence of this practice of using the eight tones to sing the liturgy by the sixth century at the latest, and he argues somewhat more speculatively but persuasively that Jerusalem's public liturgies had begun to use an eight-mode liturgical system already during the fifth century, and possibly even by the later fourth century.[51]

MARIAN VENERATION IN THE HYMNS OF THE JERUSALEM CHANTBOOK

One notable difference, however, between the Sunday Oktoechos of the ancient Jerusalem Chantbook and the traditional Byzantine Oktoechos is the latter's regular inclusion of Theotokia. These hymns in praise of the Virgin Mary regularly appear in the Byzantine Oktoechos as the ninth ode of the canon for matins, a practice that was introduced, according to tradition, by John of Damascus in the eighth century.⁵² Yet although the Jerusalem Georgian Chantbook lacks this particular liturgical feature, its hymns nonetheless reveal unmistakably that Marian piety and belief in the efficacy of her intercessions had already established themselves prominently in late ancient worship and hymnography, at least in late fourth and early fifth-century Jerusalem. The chantbook's hymns offer particularly early evidence of devotion to the Virgin and prayers for her intercessions, and accordingly these hymns appear to offer one of the richest and most overlooked sources for exploring the beginnings of Marian piety.

There is, however, some variation in the level of Marian devotion witnessed in the different manuscripts of the early chantbook. In fact, one of the most important differences among the manuscripts is the presence in four of a collection of Praises of the Holy Theotokos, a remarkable corpus in its own right that surely is the oldest surviving compilation of Marian hymns. These hymns to the Virgin appear at the end of the matins service for each of the eight tones, and they vary in length from thirty to one hundred and fifty lines, with an average of about fifty lines and variant strophes in some of the manuscripts.⁵³ Renoux counts a total of fifty-four strophes in MS Sinai Georg 41, which has best preserved the hymns, and he further notes that a significant number of these strophes appear in different contexts in the five other manuscripts.⁵⁴ Partly on this basis, Renoux concludes that these hymns were not part of the actual matins service, but that rather they reflect a regrouping by early redactors who found the space at the end of matins and before the beginning of the liturgy a convenient place for gathering together hymns to the Virgin for each tone, so that they could easily be found. As Métrévéli and Jeffery similarly suggest, these Marian hymns appear to represent collections of Theotokia for each mode, from which one could pick and choose on a given occasion.⁵⁵

Collectively this element of the chantbook preserves a fairly sizable corpus of Marian hymnography, which affords some of the earliest liturgical evidence for devotion to the Virgin in the regular weekly services. There is of course some question regarding the date of this material, particularly inasmuch as this collection of hymns is lacking in two of the most important manuscripts of the early Oktoechos. Clearly these hymns were composed before the sixth century at the latest, since, like the rest of the ancient chantbook, they antedate its replacement by the newer version of the chantbook in the early seventh century. Nevertheless, Renoux's analysis of the content of these hymns finds them likely to be even earlier. In their theology and imagery of the Virgin's role in the economy of salvation they are broadly reflective of fifth-century Christianity, finding parallels particularly in Hesychius of Jerusalem (d. ca. 451) and other writers of the same period, as Renoux frequently indicates in the abundant notes that accompany his translations.⁵⁶ Indeed, one of the more striking parallels is the final strophe of a hymn that corresponds remarkably with a passage from the opening of Proclus's *First Homily* on the Theotokos,[57] a coincidence that Renoux attributes to the well-known fact that Proclus often borrowed from existing hymns in composing his homilies.[58]

There is, however, a single strophe that shows influence from the Chalcedonian definition, making a brief reference to the unity of Christ's two natures without confusion.[59] On the basis of this isolated passage, Renoux suggests that perhaps these hymns to the Virgin originated only after the Fourth Council (451), leading him to the more general conclusion that the hymns were composed within the context of fifth-century Marian theology.[60] Nevertheless, the exceptional nature of this single reference to Chalcedon certainly raises the possibility that the passage is a late addition to a corpus of hymns that, like the rest of the chantbook's hymns, otherwise had formed before the middle of the fifth century and possibly even earlier, during the fourth. There is certainly little question that many of these Marian hymns, including especially the strophe adopted by Proclus, likely belong to the pre-Ephesian period, although it is unfortunately difficult to be more specific. And given the notable absence of the issues and terminology arising from the Council of Chalcedon (451) in these hymns (with the exception of this one passage), the arguments advanced by Leena Mari Peltomaa for dating the Akathist hymn to the period before Chalcedon would seem to apply equally if not even more to this early collection of Marian hymnography.[61] Thus it would appear that we have in these Praises of the Holy Theotokos from the early chantbook a sizable collection of hymns to the Virgin that is at least as old as the Akathist and quite possibly even earlier.

Nevertheless, as important as this remarkable collection of hymns to the Virgin is for understanding the early history of Marian devotion, they are by no means the limit of the chantbook's witness to a relatively advanced Marian piety already embedded within the hymnography of Sunday worship. There are in fact repeated acclamations to the Virgin and pleas for her intercessions scattered across the hymns of the Oktoechos.[62] This is true in all the manuscripts, and these praises and invocations of the Theotokos are so diffuse and interwoven with the rest of the hymnography that there can be little question that they form an integral part of the ancient Sunday hymnal rather than a more recent addition. Like the rest of these hymns, then, the chantbook's exaltations and petitions to Virgin most likely date to the fourth and fifth centuries, and on the basis of Renoux's arguments, it seems clear that the late fourth and the early fifth century offer more favorable circumstances for the composition of these hymns than the earlier or later decades of that period. And once again, the absence of the themes and terminology issuing from the Fourth Council (451) in the Sunday hymns of the chantbook suggests their composition before the middle of the fifth century.[63]

Thus we have in the Oktoechos of the Jerusalem Georgian Chantbook some surprisingly early evidence of fairly advanced Marian devotion at the heart of the Holy City's public liturgies. Not only is there emphasis on Mary's Divine Maternity and praises of her unsurpassed holiness and purity, as one may expect from such an early source, but there is also ample evidence of prayers for her intercessions and belief in the unequaled efficacy of Mary's supplications with her son, a sign that veneration of the Virgin was already by this time beginning to assume its unique position within the emerging cult of the saints.[64] The fact that many of these same hymns and their repeated invocations of Mary's intercession also appear in the early Armenian hymnography again offers strong confirmation that this theme was already prominent in the Jerusalem liturgies before the early fifth century, at which time much of the Jerusalemite rite, including its early lectionary, was adopted by the Armenian church.[65] Moreover, as Renoux additionally notes, the titles assigned to the Virgin in the hymns of the Oktoechos are "sober and classical," in contrast to what he describes as the "luxuriance of appellations and images" in the special collection of Praises to the Holy Theotokos that follows the matins service in four of the manuscripts.[66] Perhaps the comparative restraint evident in the rest of the Sunday hymns is a symptom of their relative antiquity, indicating that the Marian piety of the Oktoechos itself is quite early and belongs to a stage of the liturgy older than what is reflected in the fifth-century hymns of the Praises to the Holy Theotokos. Indeed, the weight of the evidence seems to favor the conclusion that the Oktoechos's hymns and their Marian piety are in the main older than the Council of Ephesus (431), and accordingly they appear to offer some of the earliest evidence for liturgical devotion to the Virgin Mary.

Altogether then, these hymns from the Jerusalem Georgian Chantbook present important early evidence of Marian veneration and invocation, practices that had entered the Sunday public liturgies of the Holy City seemingly before Chalcedon and even before the controversies of Ephesus. So here yet again, as often seems to be the case with Marian piety, we find indications that the *lex orandi* of late ancient Christianity was a bit ahead of its *lex credendi* with respect to honoring and venerating the Virgin.[67] The early emergence of such devotion to Mary in Jerusalem, rather than in Egypt or Constantinople as one might expect in light of the events of the Third Council (431), is not all that surprising. No doubt this development in the Sunday liturgy corresponds with the celebration of the Memory of Mary on 15 August, a feast that had been celebrated in Jerusalem since the first decades of the fifth century, if not even earlier. Likewise, it was around this same time that the Virgin's tomb began to emerge as a focus of veneration.[68] Thus, although scholarship on early Marian piety has often tended to look elsewhere for the first shoots of devotion to the Virgin, it seems increasingly clear that Jerusalem in the age of the two Melanias stood at the forefront of the emerging cult of the Theotokos, as witnessed especially by its early liturgies and holy shrines.

It is odd, however, that there is no trace of this devotion to Mary in the *Life of Melania*, even though Melania the Younger was an ardent opponent of Nestorius and, according to her *vita*, had met in Constantinople with Proclus, who was among the greatest advocates of Marian piety in this period (as noted also in Christine Shepardson's contribution in this volume).[69] Why this should be the case is admittedly not clear, particularly since Mary had been identified as an important model for female ascetics in the previous century by such authorities as Athanasius and Evagrius Ponticus.[70] It is hard to imagine that Melania and the members of her religious community could have been ignorant of Mary's ascetic stature or her veneration. But so it is: sometimes our sources do not behave as they should. In an earlier text, the omission would perhaps not be so glaring, but by the middle of the fifth century such silence is quite peculiar, especially in light of Melania's personal and theological allegiances.

Of course, Marian veneration is but one of many more topics that remain to be explored across the expanse of the chantbook's hymns, and to be sure here we have merely scratched the surface even of this particular theme. The Jerusalem Georgian Chantbook offers scholars a unique and almost entirely unknown resource for advancing our knowledge of early Christian liturgy and hymnography. This hymnal provides yet another remarkable liturgical manual from late ancient Jerusalem that surely will add much to our already rich knowledge of its sacred ceremonies. One of the chantbook's most important contributions is certainly its calendar, which reveals aspects of Jerusalem's developing stational liturgy in the period between the Armenian and Georgian lectionaries. Likewise its festal hymns offer unprecedented knowledge of the songs that filled the air as Jerusalem's Christians moved throughout the streets of their city, making use of its uniquely sacred landscape to commemorate the holidays and heroes of their faith. But surely one of the chantbook's most invaluable contributions is the insight that it affords into Jerusalem's ordinary Sunday worship, evidenced particularly in the Oktoechos. Of course, we have long known of early Christian hymns from other sources, particularly in the Syriac tradition. Yet here for the first time we encounter the cycle of songs that resounded regularly within the churches of a late ancient city—and Jerusalem no less, allowing us to better imagine the joyful noise that filled ancient Christianity's liturgical soundscape. While Melania the Younger's *Life* tells us about the liturgical practice of her monastery, here we find the hymns that regularly proclaimed the faith through poetry and music in the churches of the Melanias' Jerusalem. And so with this new perspective, we may possibly add another dimension to our understanding of how the Christians of late antiquity sought to Christianize the space—in this case, the acoustic space—of their urban environment.

NOTES

1. See, e.g., Paul F. Bradshaw, *The Search for the Origins of Christian Worship: Sources and Methods for the Study of Early Liturgy*, 2nd ed. (Oxford: Oxford University Press, 2002), 211–30. See also John

Francis Baldovin, *The Urban Character of Christian Worship: The Origins, Development, and Meaning of Stational Liturgy* (Rome: Pontificium Institutum Studiorum Orientalium, 1987), 229–68. By "public liturgy" we mean here what liturgical specialists commonly designate Cathedral Liturgy, as opposed to Monastic Liturgy. Cathedral Liturgy is generally distinguished by the fact that such worship "was presided over by the bishop or his representative": John Francis Baldovin, *Liturgy in Ancient Jerusalem* (Bramcote: Grove Books, 1989), 30. See also Bradshaw, *Search*, 172–75; Stéphane Verhelst, "The Liturgy of Jerusalem in the Byzantine Period," in *Christians and Christianity in the Holy Land: From the Origins to the Latin Kingdoms*, ed. O. Limor and Guy G. Stroumsa (Turnhout: Brepols, 2006), 421–59, 424–26.

2. Gerontius, *The Life of Melania the Younger: Introduction, Translation, and Commentary*, trans. Elizabeth A. Clark (Lewiston, N.Y.: Edwin Mellen Press, 1984), esp. 59–61, 117, 124–26; eadem, "Claims on the Bones of Saint Stephen: The Partisans of Melania and Eudocia," *Church History* 51.2 (1982): 141–56.

3. Baldovin, *Liturgy*, 5–6, 29.

4. *Éthérie: Journal de voyage*, ed. and trans. Hélène Pétré (Paris: Cerf, 1971). On the date, see Paul Devos, "Le date du voyage d'Égérie," *Analecta Bollandiana* 85 (1967): 165–94; idem, "Égérie à Bethléem; Le 40e jour après Paques à Jérusalem, en 383," *Analecta Bollandiana* 86 (1968): 87–108; Baldovin, *Urban Character*, 55–57; John D. Wilkinson, *Egeria's Travels: Newly Translated with Supporting Documents and Notes*, 3rd ed. (Warminster: Aris and Phillips, 1999), 169–71.

5. Egeria, *Itinerarium* 24, 27.4–5 (*Éthérie*, ed. Pétré, 188–99, 210–11); see also Baldovin, *Liturgy*, 30; Verhelst, "Liturgy," 448–52. As Baldovin in particular notes, the terminology for these services is complicated, and above I aim more for familiarity rather than trying to resolve the complex issues of nomenclature. Likewise, it is not entirely clear whether the morning service consists of one service or two.

6. Baldovin, *Liturgy*, 32–33.

7. Egeria, *Itinerarium* 25.1 (*Éthérie*, ed. Pétré, 198–99; trans. J. D. Wilkinson, *Egeria's Travels*, 145).

8. There is some debate as to whether the *Mystagogical Catecheses* was actually by Cyril or instead by his successor John, or whether possibly it was first written by Cyril and then revised by John: see Johannes Quasten, *Patrology*, vol. 3 (Westminister, Md.: Newman Press, 1950): 364–66; Bradshaw, *Search*, 113–14. Nevertheless, for the present purposes it should suffice that they reflect with some certainty the liturgical practices of Jerusalem in the later fourth century.

9. Baldovin, *Liturgy*, 25–28; cf. Cyril of Jerusalem, *Orations* 22 and 23, *PG* 33: 1097A–1128A. For a broader perspective, see also Paul F. Bradshaw, *Eucharistic Origins* (Oxford: Oxford University Press, 2004), 147–52.

10. Justin Martyr, *First Apology* 65–67 (ed. and trans. Denis Minns and P. M. Parvis, *Justin, Philosopher and Martyr: Apologies* [Oxford: Oxford University Press, 2009], 252–62).

11. Baldovin, *Liturgy*, 23. See also Athanase Renoux, *Le codex arménien Jérusalem 121*, 2 vols. (Turnhout: Brepols, 1969–71); concerning the date (between 415 and 439), see vol. 1: 169–81.

12. Baldovin, *Liturgy*, 24–25; cf. Cyril of Jerusalem, *Oration 23 (Mystagogical Catecheses 5)*, 2 (*Catéchèses mystagogiques*, ed. Auguste Piédagnel and trans. Pierre Paris [Paris: Cerf, 1966], 146–51); *Les hymnes de la Résurrection*, ed. and trans. Charles Renoux, vol. 1, *Hymnographie liturgique géorgienne: Textes du Sinaï 18* (Paris: Cerf, 2000), 136; Michel Tarchnischvili, *Le grand lectionnaire de l'église de Jérusalem (Ve–VIIe siècle)*, 2 vols., CSCO 188, 189. 204–5, Scriptores Iberici 9, 10, 13, 14 (Louvain: Secretariat of the CSCO, 1959–60), vol. 1: 8 (Geor.) and 14 (Lat.).

13. Baldovin, *Liturgy*, 28–29

14. Egeria, *Itinerarium* 27 (*Éthérie*, ed. Pétré, 206–15); Bradshaw, *Eucharistic Origins*, 146; Baldovin, *Liturgy*, 31; Verhelst, "Liturgy," 452.

15. Baldovin, *Liturgy*, 34.

16. Ibid., 42–44.; Verhelst, "Liturgy," 442–46.

17. Egeria, *Itinerarium* 48–49 (*Éthérie*, ed. Pétré, 262–67).

18. Athanase Renoux, *Codex arménien*, vol. 2: 354-57. Concerning the nature and history of this early feast, see, e.g., Stephen J. Shoemaker, *Ancient Traditions of the Virgin Mary's Dormition and Assumption* (Oxford: Oxford University Press, 2002), 78-132; Walter D. Ray, "August 15 and the Development of the Jerusalem Calendar" (Ph.D. dissertation, University of Notre Dame, 2000); Bernard Capelle, "La fête de la Vierge à Jérusalem au Ve siècle," *Le Muséon* 56 (1943): 1-33; and Stéphane Verhelst, "Le 15 août, le 9 av. et le kathisme," *Questions Liturgiques* 82 (2001): 161-91.

19. E.g., Baldovin, *Urban Character*, 94; Ray, "August 15," 6.

20. Baldovin, *Liturgy*, 43-44; idem, *Urban Character*, 72-80.

21. Bradshaw, *Search*, 187-89.

22. Baldovin, *Liturgy*, 35. See also Athanase Renoux, "L'Epiphanie à Jérusalem au IVme et au Vme siècle," *Revue des Études Arméniennes* 2 (1965): 343-59; Michel van Esbroeck, "La lettre de l'empereur Justinien sur l'Annonciation et la Noël en 561," *Analecta Bollandiana* 86 (1968): 356-62. According to Verhelst ("Liturgy," 431-34), the patriarch Juvenal attempted to change the date to December 25 around 450, yet the Nativity continued to be widely observed on 6 January, thus necessitating Justinian's imperial intervention; see also idem, "La liturgie de Jérusalem à l'époque byzantine: Genèse et structures de l'année liturgique" (Ph.D. dissertation, Hebrew University of Jerusalem, 1999), 40-65.

23. Gerontius, *Life of Melania the Younger* 63 (*Vie de sainte Mélanie*, ed. Denys Gorce, SC 90 [Paris: Cerf, 1962], 254-55). See Verhelst, "Liturgy," 433; idem, "Liturgie," 49-51.

24. Athanase Renoux, *Codex arménien*, vol. 1: 172; although see also Gerontius, *Life of Melania*, trans. E. A. Clark, 122-29.

25. Egeria, *Itinerarium* 25.6-12; 39, 40, 49 (*Éthérie*, ed. Pétré, 200-206, 240-45, 264-67).

26. Athanase Renoux, *Codex arménien*, vol. 2: 330-31, 348-49, 354-57.

27. See Baldovin, *Urban Character*, 105-226; Michel van Esbroeck, "Le culte de la Vierge de Jérusalem à Constantinople aux 6e-7e siècles," *Revue des Études Byzantines* 46 (1988): 181-90.

28. E.g., Gerontius, *Life of Melania* 36, 41, 42, 46, 47, 49, 57, 64, 68 (*Vie de sainte Mélanie*, ed. Gorce, SC 90: 196, 204, 208, 214, 216, 220, 222, 240, 260, 268); Gerontius, *Life of Melania*, trans. E. A. Clark, 52, 54, 56, 60, 61, 69, 78, 81).

29. E.g., ibid. 125; see also Baldovin, *Liturgy*, 30.

30. The hymns of the Georgian Lectionary were studied in Helmut Leeb, *Die Gesänge im Gemeindegottesdienst von Jerusalem (vom 5. bis 8. Jh.)* (Vienna: Herder, 1970), a work that appeared before the editions of the Georgian Chantbook.

31. Peter Jeffery, "The Sunday Office of Seventh-Century Jerusalem in the Georgian Chantbook (Iadgari): A Preliminary Report," *Studia Liturgica* 21 (1991): 52-75, 54, 58.

32. E. Metreveli, Cʻ. Čankievi, and L. Xevsuriani, უძველესი იადგარი (*Uzvelesi iadgari* [*The Oldest Chantbook*]. Tʻbilisi: Mecʻniereba, 1980). It is of course a great benefit now that this edition has been made available online through the TITUS project: http://titus.uni-frankfurt.de/texte/etcs/cauc/ageo/liturg/udzviad/udzvi.htm. This edition supersedes the earlier edition by Akaki Šaniże, A. Martirosovi, and A. Jišiašvili, ჭილ-ეტრატის იადგარი (*Čil-etratis iadgari* [*The Papyrus-Parchment Iadgari*]. Tʻbilisi: Gamomcʻemloba "Mecʻniereba," 1977).

33. Paul Géhin and Stig Frøyshov, "Nouvelles découvertes sinaïtiques: À propos de la parution de l'inventaire des manuscrits grecs," *Revue des Études Byzantines* 58 (2000): 167-84, 178-79.

34. Stig Frøyshov, "The Early Development of the Liturgical Eight-Mode System in Jerusalem," *St. Vladimir's Theological Quarterly* 51 (2007): 139-78; see now also idem, "The Georgian Witness to the Jerusalem Liturgy: New Sources and Studies," in *Inquiries into Eastern Christian Worship: Selected Papers of the Second International Congress of the Society of Oriental Liturgy, Rome, 17-21 September 2008*, ed. B. Groen, S. Hawkes-Teeples, and S. Alexopoulos (Louvain: Peeters, 2012), 227-67, 233-38; see also Andrew Wade, "The Oldest *Iadgari*: The Jerusalem Tropologion, V-VIII c.," *Orientalia Christiana Periodica* 50 (1984): 451-56, 451.

35. Hélène Métrévéli, "Les manuscrits liturgiques géorgiens des IXe–Xe siècles et leur importance pour l'étude de l'hymnographie byzantine," *Bedi Kartlisa: Revue de Kartvélologie* 36 (1978): 43–48, 47. See also G. Peradzè, "Les monuments liturgiques prébyzantins en langue géorgienne," *Le Muséon* 45 (1932): 255–72; *Hymnes de la Résurrection*, ed. and trans. Renoux, vol. 1: 85–86.

36. Metreveli, Čankievi, and Xevsuriani, უძველესი იადგარი (*Uzvelesi iadgari* [*The Oldest Chantbook*]), 7–333.

37. Jeffery, "Sunday Office," 57. See also idem, "The Earliest Christian Chant Repertory Recovered: The Georgian Witnesses to Jerusalem Chant," *Journal of the American Musicological Society* 47 (1994): 1–38, 14.

38. Métrévéli, "Manuscrits," 46; Michel van Esbroeck, *Les plus anciens homéliaires géorgiens: Étude descriptive et historique* (Louvain-la-Neuve: Université Catholique de Louvain, Institut Orientaliste, 1975), 326–27.

39. Metreveli, Čankievi, and Xevsuriani, უძველესი იადგარი, 334–66; Jeffery, "Sunday Office," 55.

40. Ibid., 367–512.

41. Peter Jeffery, "The Earliest *Oktōēchoi*: The Role of Jerusalem and Palestine in the Beginnings of Modal Ordering," in *The Study of Medieval Chant: Paths and Bridges, East and West—In Honor of Kenneth Levy*, ed. Peter Jeffery (Woodbridge: Boydell Press, 2001), 147–209, 200–201. In earlier articles, however, Jeffery seems to allow that these hymns also date to before the early seventh century.

42. The first and most important of these translations and studies is *Hymnes de la Résurrection*, ed. and trans. Renoux, vol. 1. The project has now been completed with the recent publication of *Les hymnes de la Résurrection*, ed. and trans. Charles Renoux, vol. 2, *Hymnographie liturgique géorgienne: Texte des manuscrits Sinaï 40, 41 et 34*, Patrologia Orientalis 52.1 (Turnhout: Brepols, 2010); and *Les hymnes de la Résurrection*, ed. and trans. Charles Renoux, vol. 3, *Hymnographie liturgique géorgienne: Introduction, traduction, annotation des manuscrits Sinaï 26 et 20 et index analytique des trois volumes*, Patrologia Orientalis 52.2 (Turnhout: Brepols, 2010). Renoux has also translated the festal hymns from Lazarus Saturday through Pentecost from the oldest manuscript (which reflects a monastic setting): idem, *L'hymnaire de Saint-Sabas (Ve–VIIe siècle): Le manuscrit géorgien H 2123*, vol. 1, *Du samedi de Lazare à la Pentecôte*, Patrologia Orientalis 50.3 (Turnhout: Brepols, 2008). Another important set of German translations has been published by Hans-Michael Schneider, which translates hymns from the beginning of the festal collection: those for the Annunciation, the Nativity and its octave, and Epiphany and its octave. See Hans-Michael Schneider, *Lobpreis im rechten Glauben: Die Theologie der Hymnen an den Festen der Menschwerdung der alten Jerusalemer Liturgie im georgischen Udzvelesi Iadgari* (Bonn: Borengässer, 2004).

43. Frøyshov, "Early Development," 165–66.

44. Ibid., 166–68.

45. *Hymnes de la Résurrection*, ed. and trans. Renoux, vol. 1: 30–64; see also the very brief summary of some of these points in Frøyshov, "Early Development," 166; and idem, "Georgian Witness," 237.

46. See *Hymnaire de Saint-Sabas*, trans. Renoux. See also *Hymnes de la Résurrection*, ed. and trans. Renoux, vol. 1: 10–11.

47. See the summary in *Hymnes de la Résurrection*, ed. and trans. Renoux, vol. 3: 325–26, which gives a good summary of the differences. See also *Hymnes de la Résurrection*, ed. and trans. Renoux, vol. 1: 10–13; and see the brief remarks in Jeffery, "Earliest *Octōēchoi*," 200–201, who supposes a developmental typology on the basis of these differences that is not entirely warranted.

48. Miloš Velimirović, "Ēchos," in *The New Grove Dictionary of Music and Musicians*, 2nd ed., ed. Stanley Sadie and John Tyrrell (New York: Grove, 2001); for a more detailed discussion, see Egon Wellesz, *A History of Byzantine Music and Hymnography*, 2nd ed. (Oxford: Clarendon Press, 1961), 326–47. See also the helpful general introduction to the Oktoechos in Job Getcha, *The Typikon Decoded: An Explanation of Byzantine Liturgical Practice*, trans. Paul Meyendorff (Yonkers, N.Y.: St Vladimir's Seminary Press, 2012), 24–31.

49. Frøyshov, "Early Development," 139–40; Aelred Cody, "The Early History of the Octoechos in Syria," in *East of Byzantium: Syria and Armenia in the Formative Period*, ed. Nina G. Garsoïan, Thomas F. Mathews, and Robert W. Thomson (Washington, D.C.: Dumbarton Oaks, 1982), 89–113; Jeffery, "Earliest *Octōēchoi*."

50. Cody, "Early History," 102; Jeffery, "Earliest *Octōēchoi*," 200–209. Nevertheless, Jeffery earlier dates the Oktoechos structure to before the eighth century: idem, "Sunday Office," 60.

51. Frøyshov, "Early Development," 164–69, 171–73.

52. See Wellesz, *History*, 242–43; Hélène Métrévéli, Ts. Tchankieva, and L. Khevsouriani, "Le plus ancien tropologion géorgien," *Bedi Kartlisa: Revue de Kartvélologie* 39 (1981): 54–62, 60; *Hymnes de la Résurrection*, ed. and trans. Renoux, vol. 1: 12, 19–20.

53. Translations of these hymns have been published in *Hymnes de la Résurrection*, ed. and trans. Renoux, vols. 2 and 3.

54. *Hymnes de la Résurrection*, ed. and trans. Renoux, vol. 2: 20

55. Ibid., 20–21.; Métrévéli, Tchankieva, and Khevsouriani, "Plus ancien tropologion," 60–61; Jeffery, "Sunday Office," 58.

56. *Hymnes de la Résurrection*, ed. and trans. Renoux, vol. 2: 21–22.

57. Metreveli, Čankievi, and Xevsuriani, უძველესი იადგარი, 439, lines 27–31; ed. and trans. Renoux in *Hymnes de la Résurrection*, vol. 2: 160; Proclus of Constantinople, *Proclus of Constantinople and the Cult of the Virgin in Late Antiquity: Homilies 1–5, Texts and Translations*, ed. and trans. Nicholas Constas (Leiden: Brill, 2003), 136, lines 18–22. (Cf. *PG* 65: 681B).

58. *Hymnes de la Résurrection*, ed. and trans. Renoux, vol. 2: 22; see also 160 note 1. See also Proclus of Constantinople, *L'homilétique de Proclus de Constantinople*, ed. and trans. François Joseph Leroy, S.J. (Vatican City: Biblioteca Apostolica Vaticana, 1967), 275–76.

59. Metreveli, Čankievi, and Xevsuriani, უძველესი იადგარი, 399, lines 10–13; *Hymnes de la Résurrection*, ed. and trans. Renoux, vol. 2: 122.

60. *Hymnes de la Résurrection*, ed. and trans. Renoux, vol. 2: 22–23.

61. Leena Mari Peltomaa, *The Image of the Virgin Mary in the Akathistos Hymn* (Leiden: Brill, 2001), esp. xiii, 26–27, 50–62, 85–91, 97–101.

62. E.g., *Hymnes de la Résurrection*, ed. and trans. Renoux, vol. 1, passim: e.g., 60–62, 98, 100–101, 104–5, 109.

63. In addition to the passage considered above from the "Praises to the Holy Theotokos," see also one other possible example in Metreveli, Čankievi, and Xevsuriani, უძველესი იადგარი, 479, line 1; *Hymnes de la Résurrection*, ed. and trans. Renoux, vol. 2: 285 note 8. Here the hymn uses the term უქცევალად (ἀτρέπτως), which, as Renoux notes, despite its association with Chalcedon, was used well before the Fourth Council.

64. E.g., ibid., vol. 1, passim: e.g., 54, 62, 109, 111, 116, 117.

65. Ibid., 52–54.

66. Ibid., 60–62.

67. See, e.g., Stephen J. Shoemaker, "Marian Liturgies and Devotion in Early Christianity," in *Mary: The Complete Resource*, ed. Sarah Jane Boss (London: Continuum Press, 2007), 130–45; idem, "Epiphanius of Salamis, the Kollyridians, and the Early Dormition Narratives: The Cult of the Virgin in the Later Fourth Century," *Journal of Early Christian Studies* 16 (2008): 369–99; idem, "The Cult of the Virgin in the Fourth Century: A Fresh Look at Some Old and New Sources," in *The Origins of the Cult of the Virgin Mary*, ed. Chris Maunder (London: Burns and Oates, 2008), 71–87; Stephen J. Shoemaker, "Apocrypha and Liturgy in the Fourth Century: The Case of the 'Six Books' Dormition Apocryphon," in *Jewish and Christian Scriptures: The Function of "Canonical" and "Non-canonical" Religious Texts*, ed. James H. Charlesworth and Lee M. McDonald (London: T. and T. Clark, 2010), 153–63.

68. Shoemaker, *Ancient Traditions*, 78–107.

69. Gerontius, *Life of Melania the Younger* 33 (*Vie de sainte Mélanie*, ed. Gorce, SC 90: 232; *Life of Melania*, trans. E. A. Clark, 65–66). See also E. A. Clark, *Life of Melania*, 147.

70. Athanasius, *Letter to Virgins* 1.11–18, 35, 45 (*Lettres festales et pastorales en copte*, ed. L.-Th. Lefort. 2 vols., CSCO 150, 151, Scriptores Coptici 19, 20 [Louvain: Imprimerie Orientaliste L. Durbecq, 1955], 77–81, 90, 94–95; David Brakke, *Athanasius and the Politics of Asceticism* [Oxford: Clarendon Press, 1995], 277–79, 285–86, 288); Evagrius Ponticus, *Exhortation to a Virgin* 2 (*Nonnenspiegel und Mönchsspiegel des Euagrios Pontikos*, ed. Hugo Gressmann [Leipzig: J. C. Hinrichs, 1913], 143–65; ed. and trans. Robert E. Sinkewicz, *Evagrius of Pontus: The Greek Ascetic Corpus* [Oxford: Oxford University Press, 2003], 131). I thank Robin Darling Young for the latter reference.

PART SIX

Modernities

ANCIENT SOURCES CONSISTENTLY DEPICTED THE Melanias' vast wealth—both monetary and spiritual—as a legacy to support and inspire future generations. In their lifetimes, familial and religious connections embedded the Melanias within extensive social networks. Soon after the Melanias' deaths, the writings of their contemporaries embedded them within an even farther-reaching set of textual networks. These proved to be particularly resilient and long-lasting, connecting the Melanias to ages far removed from their own. Well over a thousand years after their deaths, the Melanias still loomed larger than life.

This does not mean, however, that the Melanias' influence remained constant. Rather, knowledge of the Melanias ebbed and flowed. But the last hundred or so years appear to have been particularly important for the shaping of the Melanias' cultural afterlife. This section, "Modernities," examines three recent rediscoveries of the Melanias. The first essay begins in the early twentieth century with the unexpected discovery of Gerontius's *Life of Melania the Younger* by an "almost-pope." The second essay begins in the 1970s and examines the increasing prominence of the Melanias within modern Coptic Orthodox homilies and devotional literature. The third essay begins in the late twentieth century with Western feminist scholars rediscovering Gerontius's hagiography. In each of these cases, many of the issues so prominent in ancient discussions of the Melanias—wealth, gender, asceticism, orthodoxy, apologetics, and polemics—again come to the fore, though often in radically different contexts and configurations.

Michael Penn's chapter explores early twentieth-century scholarly and popular accounts of Melania the Younger inspired by Cardinal Rampolla's discovery and 1905 publication of Gerontius's *Life of Melania*. Immediately after Rampolla's work,

Melania became the subject of academic reviews, worldwide newspaper articles, and two popular books. In this burst of turn-of-the-century popularity Melania's *vita* took on a life of its own. Nonetheless, regardless of whether the discussion appeared in the *Revue de Philosophie,* the *Washington Post,* or the *Locomotive Engineers Journal,* early twentieth-century accounts of Melania recirculated many of the same themes that made Melania's life so popular in antiquity. They were also particularly invested in emphasizing the reliability of Gerontius's work. As a result, the early twentieth century did not simply rediscover an ancient hagiography; rather, it expanded upon the original text's tropes and represented a further development in the Melanias' hagiographic legacy.

Stephen J. Davis's contribution next shows how the legacies of these two early Christian women have been reclaimed (and reshaped) by Egyptian Christian leaders for different sociocultural aims. During the past four decades, the Melanias have made appearances in Arabic-language homilies and books as part of a collective effort to revive Coptic monasticism in Egypt. This effort has by no means been monolithic. In the writings of Pope Shenouda III (d. 2012), the Melanias are conscripted as part of an effort to encourage young Coptic women to embrace responsibilities of motherhood and the use of wealth to support the church before any decision to commit themselves to the monastic life in older age. But other Coptic leaders have reclaimed the figures of the Melanias for different purposes. In the works of the well-known monk Matthew the Poor (d. 2006) and in modern Copto-Arabic editions of the *Paradise of the Fathers* (or *The Garden of the Monks*), the Melanias are placed within monastic genealogies that effectively subordinate them to their ancient male counterparts, and in this way they are presented as gendered models for modern Coptic nuns, and nuns-in-training, whose vocation involves vows of obedience to their male church leaders.

Elizabeth A. Castelli's chapter asks what happens when the second-wave feminist interest in reconstructing women's history has run its course, and it posits a potentially new theoretical trajectory that focuses on Melania the Younger not as a woman but rather as a saint. Building on the historical theorist Michel de Certeau's observation that hagiography resides at the margins of history as "a corpus of difference," this chapter combs through the *Life of Melania the Younger* anew, lifting up details in the narrative that emphasize tensions between sanctity and materiality, and between competing ideas of excess in the story of Melania's life, in order to suggest that the figure of the saint that emerges from the narrative may serve as a politically productive figure for contemporary debates about economy and domesticity.

Each of these chapters explores dynamics similar to those found in ancient texts concerning the Melanias. But, set in times and places closer to our own, they highlight how even in modernity many continue to use the Melanias to spur the imagination. Their analysis both documents and contributes to the Melanias' ongoing legacy.

13

Afterlives

Michael Penn

Elizabeth A. Clark's *Life of Melania the Younger* helped spark a Melania revival that made the present volume possible. As Elizabeth Castelli explores in her chapter, Clark's translation was part of a larger moment in women's history marked by "'women's voices' and 'women's lives' being lifted up out of the archives and situated in the big story of the past." As Clark herself later reflects, one of the reasons that the *Life of Melania* became so central to this larger project of historical recovery was the acceptance of its authenticity claims. Here, finally, was a source whose narrative details assured its veracity.

Castelli explains that soon, however, "the conversation changed as the theoretical frameworks of semiotics, rhetoric, and poststructuralist critique replaced the certainties of *We Were There*." Here too Melania—and Elizabeth Clark—played a central role in the conversational shift. Now the very narrative details of Melania's *life* that had reassured a previous generation of the *life*'s authenticity were seen as an "effect of the real," markers of effective rhetoric as opposed to guarantors of historical truth. Clark concluded her landmark article "The Lady Vanishes":[1]

> Has, then, "the lady vanished"? If this question means, Can we recover her pure and simple from texts? my answer is no. But that is not the last word: she leaves her traces, through whose exploration, as they are imbedded in a larger social-linguistic framework, she lives on. "Afterlife" comes in different forms—or so we should know from the study of Christian history and theology.

But Elizabeth Clark's 1984 translation of Melania's *vita* was itself already an afterlife. Unbeknownst to most modern scholars, Clark's translation did not simply affect second-wave feminist scholarship. It also represented the second wave of twentieth-century Melania enthusiasm. For, eighty-one years earlier, a surprising turn of events led to an international focus on the life of this fifth-century ascetic. From the halls of the Vatican to a press room in New Zealand, clergy, scholars, and journalists were all writing about Melania. This first wave of twentieth-century Melania fervor constantly focused on issues of veracity, the very topic that lived on to haunt late twentieth-century discussions of Melania's *life*. As seems appropriate for this series of *Nachleben,* it was a long-anticipated death that initially set into motion the widespread interest in Melania the Younger and its truth claims.

AN ALMOST-POPE

When Leo XIII's health began declining in 1899, few expected him to live much longer.[2] But the pope just wouldn't die. One of his archbishops even began calling him "His Eternity, Leo XIII."[3] And so, four years later, when the ninety-three year old pope was pronounced dead at 4:04 P.M., July 20, none of his cardinals were surprised. In fact, they essentially had already chosen his successor.

By July 1903, Cardinal Mariano Rampolla had been the Vatican secretary of state for sixteen years and, when sixty-two cardinals sequestered themselves in the Vatican to choose the next pope, Rampolla appeared to be Leo's natural successor.[4] The conclave's initial votes simply confirmed the expected. The secretary of state was the clear front-runner in the first ballot cast on the morning of August 1 and already had twenty-four of the forty-two votes needed for the pontificate. The afternoon ballot showed him gaining momentum, picking up an additional five ballots and having almost twice as many votes as his closest contender.[5] Everyone anticipated that, in just over a day, Rampolla would be the next pope.[6]

Well, not quite everyone ... The little-known Polish cardinal Jan Puzyna had secretly brought with him a letter that forever changed the history of the papacy. Drawing upon a sixteenth-century tradition that gave particularly powerful European monarchs the right of exclusion, the Austrian emperor Franz Josef had instructed Cardinal Puzyna to veto Rampolla's candidacy.[7] No one knows why the emperor opposed Rampolla. Even today, internet sites continue to speculate about the emperor's motive.[8]

Rampolla's peers were equally puzzled, and the next ballots reflected the cardinals' confusion. The secretary of state maintained a lead, but support began to coalesce around a compromise candidate, Cardinal Giuseppe Melchiore Sarto. The next day Cardinal Sarto took the lead, thirty-five to sixteen. On the morning of August 4, Sarto took the name Pius X, having been elected pope by fifty votes to Rampolla's ten.[9] Pius X wasted no time. Within six months of gaining the papal throne, Pius X had abolished the right of exclusion and also, coincidentally, had got himself a new secretary of state. Cardinal Rampolla was now out of a job and, in the words of one papal historian, "the brilliant Rampolla was consigned to oblivion."[10]

Well, not quite oblivion ... Nineteen years earlier, a much younger Rampolla had visited the Spanish monastery of Escurial, where he discovered a previously unknown Latin biography of Melania the Younger attributed to her confessor Gerontius. Realizing the import of his find, the young Rampolla made himself a handwritten copy of the manuscript. But Rampolla's meteoric rise in the Vatican hierarchy precluded him from publishing his work. The surprising election of Pius X, however, changed all this. A year and a half after what one contemporary euphemistically referred to as Rampolla's "being freed from the cares of statecraft and diplomacy," this almost-pope published a 385-page work on Melania's *life*.[11] It included an edition of the Latin manuscript that he had discovered, editions of other Greek and Latin manuscripts that contained biographical information on Melania, an Italian translation of Melania's Greek *vita*, two hundred pages of notes, and—most influential—Rampolla's own twenty-three page summary of Melania's life and times.

Rampolla's *Santa Melania giuniore, senatrice romana* met with lavish praise in both Catholic and non-Catholic publications. It was lauded as "a sumptuous and stately folio that probably contains all that can be known from extant materials concerning the younger Melania,"[12] "a masterpiece of the highest scholarship,"[13] a "veritable monument of erudition."[14] Rampolla "vient d'élever à sainte Mélanie la Jeune une monument splendide."[15] "Les details en sont meticuleusement soignés et l'ensemble est magistral,"[16] which "den hochinteressanten und wichtigen Inhalt der Vita zur vollen Geltung bringen und nach allen Seiten hin beleuchten."[17]

As one reviewer summarized, "the work was greeted with praise in every quarter."[18] Often, however, praise of Rampolla's volume focused less on its content than the circumstances under which it was written. In these cases, early twenty-century cardinal and early fifth-century *vita* began to merge, as some reviewers began to write a hagiography of Rampolla. For example, one reviewer stated:[19]

> So no one who knows anything of the history of the last Conclave can fail to realize that when Cardinal Rampolla, less than three years after his dignified submission to the veto of a hostile government, published a stately folio attesting his continued allegiance to the studies which had been his first love, he not only set a great example of Christian fortitude, but once more justified the choice which had made him both Prince of the Church and one of its most influential administrators.

A more secular type of hagiography also appeared. In this version, Rampolla was compared with famous statesmen such as the British prime ministers Disraeli and Gladstone, who, once they had finished their service to their country, returned to a service to scholarship.[20]

Even more influential in the early twentieth-century reception of Melania's *life* than the blurring between book review and hagiography was the blurring between the Vatican's former secretary of state and Melania's ancient hagiographer. Although

Rampolla's *Santa Melania* included an edition of the Latin *life* that he had discovered in Escurial, Rampolla did not produce a modern translation of this document. In place of a translation, Rampolla included his own extended paraphrase of Melania's *vita*. This twenty-three page summary of Melania's fifth-century *life* had a narrative arc that not only followed but also frequently amplified the hagiographic agenda of its exemplar.

Rampolla's introduction includes an apologetic defense of Melania's confessor Gerontius, whose simplicity guaranteed the authenticity of his biography of Melania. His writing preserves a "gem of purest water, flashing from the august brow of Christian Rome with the light of Gospel simplicity."[21]

Gerontius's "gem" tells the tale of "such masculine heroism of virtue" that only Providence could bestow upon a young woman.[22] How much more miraculous, given the young Melania's circumstances. According to Rampolla, despite the church's supposed triumph over paganism, fifth-century Roman elites were led astray by women's acquisitive desires and became "wholly devoted to pleasure."[23]

Having set the scene of Roman society infected by "the contagion of sensuality and vice,"[24] Rampolla next combines data from Melania's Latin *life*, Greek *life*, and references to Melania in other patristic authors such as Augustine, Jerome, and Palladius. Rampolla then expands this pastiche through the addition of his own imaginative details to produce a linear, triumphant narrative of Melania's renunciation of worldly wealth and embrace of ascetic purity. In the subsequent pages, Rampolla follows Gerontius's trajectory. But as his summary is longer than its source, Rampolla has plenty of space to expand its themes.[25] The cardinal's version of Melania's biography ends with an extended narrative of Melania's death and her veneration among the Eastern churches. The last sentence concludes: "It is only in her native land that her memory is in oblivion."[26]

Rampolla's *Santa Melania giuniore, senatrice romana* clearly intended to remedy this oblivion, but it did so in a way that is surprisingly difficult to categorize. The book's editions of Greek and Latin and its two hundred pages of footnotes imply a scholarly audience. Nevertheless, this audience is far from a secular one, and Rampolla's additions make his account arguably even more hagiographic than Gerontius's. The influence of Rampolla's new hagiography of Melania quickly eclipsed that of its predecessor. The effect of Rampolla's paraphrase was particularly strong in the English-speaking world, where a translation of Melania's *vita* was not available until 1984.[27] In contrast, an English translation of Rampolla's summary appeared in 1909. As a result, most early twentieth-century readers were not really reading the *Life of Melania* as depicted by the hagiographer Gerontius. Rather, they were reading Gerontius's *Life of Melania* as retold by Cardinal Rampolla. Rampolla, the almost-pope, had become Melania's most recent hagiographer. But this role would soon be usurped by others. For not long after Rampolla published his work, Melania's *vita* quickly took on a life of its own.

MELANIA, "THE RICHEST WOMAN WHO EVER LIVED"

The *Washington Post* broke the story on October 21, 1906: "Saint Melania Richest Woman That Ever Lived."[28] The article begins with Cardinal Rampolla's manuscript discovery and goes on to incorrectly state that Rampolla's recent book included his translation of this manuscript. The introductory paragraph concludes that "what follows is an abridgement of his narrative." In other words, like most early twentieth-century writers on Melania, this author presents a précis of Rampolla's paraphrase of the *vita*. As its headline suggests, the article's summary of Rampolla's summary focuses on Melania's wealth, in particular the extent of Melania's fortune and the difficulties she encountered in trying to donate it to the church. As the author quips: "How hard it was to become poor!" The article ends by estimating Melania's income. Melania's *life* claims that she received an annual income of 120,000 pieces of gold. In his book, Rampolla suggests that this was equivalent to 116,640,000 francs in 1905 terms. The *Post* then translates this to $175 million in 1906 dollars (a sum equal to over four billion dollars a year in 2016, thus surpassing the estimated annual worth of Bill Gates).[29] This focus on the accurate quantification of Melania's wealth would not, however, be limited solely to the early twentieth century. This same detail would also attract substantial scholarly attention in the late twentieth century. Each repetition of this number reinforced its validity. Each conversion into the reader's contemporary currency emphasized the exactitude of the account.

The early twentieth-century American media quickly picked up the *Washington Post* article and its estimate of Melania's wealth. Within a few weeks, reprints of the article began appearing in papers ranging from the *New York Sun* to the *Baltimore American* to the *Salt Lake City Herald* to the *Intermountain Catholic*.[30] These other papers reprinted the *Post* article word for word (often without attribution) but under new headlines, all of them emphasizing Melania's gender and especially her fortune: "The Wealthiest Woman," "The Richest of All Women," and "Richest Woman in History."[31] The *Salt Lake Herald* even moved the $175 million figure of Melania's annual income from the article's conclusion, as it appeared in the *Washington Post*, to the headline.

The *Post* story's popularity led to further reprintings in the unlikeliest of places: for example, the *Locomotive Engineers Journal*, where it followed the poem "Pa and I." It seems, however, that the editors from the Brotherhood of Locomotive Engineers considered Melania's actions a little too radical. Immediately after the article on Melania's asceticism and philanthropy, the editors added a multipage Christian critique of socialism written by one Reverend Stelzle.[32]

Soon after the *Washington Post* article, another version of Rampolla's discovery circulated internationally, appearing in newspapers ranging from New Zealand's *Auckland Star* to Cleveland's *Plain Dealer* to the *Baltimore Sun*.[33] The *Plain Dealer's* recension consists of a full-page spread. The top half of the page is dominated by artistic renderings of a veiled Melania before Queen Serena, a central image of two humble worshippers venerating the saint, an illumination of Melania from the Escurial manuscript, a page of text from the manuscript, and a fairly dashing picture of a young Cardinal Rampolla. The headline reads: "The Richest Woman Who Ever Lived. The amazing history of Saint Melania who had a yearly income of $30,000,000 discovered after many centuries and revealed to the world by Cardinal Rampolla."[34]

The article copy begins by explaining how "one of the greatest scholars in Rome . . . has learned every detail concerning the life of this wonderful woman, the richest woman of her day, one of the Roman nobility, with thousands of slaves at her feet." The remainder consists of a summary of Melania's *life* written by Rampolla himself. This précis distills many of the features of Rampolla's *Santa Melania* into a single page. The article also makes sure to explain why the headline's $30,000,000 figure for Melania's annual income differs from the more commonly cited $175 million. According to Rampolla, gold was six times more valuable in antiquity. So Melania's gold must be assessed at six times the going rate, hence the article copy cites Melania's wealth really to be $180 million per annum. Once again quantification and mathematical conversion continued to add an aura of authenticity and exactitude.

Just over a month later, the *Baltimore Sun* reprinted the entirety of the *Plain Dealer*'s Melania article as part of a larger feature. In this case, the page began not with artistic renditions of Melania and Rampolla but with the headline "Millionaires Who Were Richer than Rockefeller."[35] The article opened: "It is generally assumed that John D. Rockefeller is the richest man in the world today, but that he is the richest man in history is far from certain." The article's subtitle, "Patiomkin, of Russia, and Melania, of Rome, Exceeded John D.," revealed Rockefeller's alleged contenders. What intrigued about the *Sun*'s rendition was not simply the comparison between Melania and Rockefeller. Rather, the *Sun* also made explicit a tendency found throughout early twentieth-century discussions of Melania, the blurring of Gerontius's *vita* and Rampolla's summary of it. In this case, the *Sun* incorrectly stated that Rampolla had translated the Escurial manuscript into Italian. It then quoted excerpts from Rampolla's summary of Melania's *life* but misattributed these as direct quotations from Gerontius's *vita*.

Just as Rampolla took many of his narrative cues from Melania's original hagiographer, Gerontius, so too these more popular presentations of Melania took their cues from her more recent hagiographer Rampolla. In many cases, they even reproduced Rampolla's own summary of Melania's *life* word for word and sometimes even confused this for a direct translation of Gerontius's *vita*. Gerontius's description of Melania's wealth was only one of the many themes found in his *life*. This focus became more concentrated in Rampolla's book as he even more consciously contrasted Melania's "heroic renunciation" with the "insatiable avarice" of her times.³⁶ Ironically, it was one of Rampolla's more technical footnotes on this topic that most influenced Melania's appearance in the popular press, and his quantification of Melania's wealth appeared in almost all subsequent newspaper articles about Melania. Rampolla never published a translation of the Latin *vita* into a modern language. Nevertheless, it was the cardinal's translation of Melania's alleged income into a modern currency that captured the imagination of early twentieth-century readers and resulted in Melania's becoming "the richest woman who ever lived."

SAINTE MÉLANIE, NOT QUITE THAT RICH

Rampolla's colossal figure of Melania's wealth helped popularize this ascetic saint for the early twentieth century, just as Gerontius's original quantification of Melania's wealth was meant to draw in the ancient reader. But there still remained an obstacle for her wider reception in modernity. Rampolla had produced "a sumptuous folio with abundant illustrative matter," but "the Cardinal's eloquent narrative and exhaustive dissertations could not possibly reach more than a narrow circle of specialists."³⁷ Brief newspaper articles reflected Melania's potential appeal. But the former Vatican secretary of state's Italian tome was too inaccessible for the masses. In stepped Georges Goyau, widely published essayist and historian, the son-in-law of a French president and the future secretary of the Académie Française.³⁸

In 1908, Goyau published *Sainte Mélanie*, "a little 'bijou' of historical exposition and right Catholic feeling that will be highly appreciated by all who have not time or occasion to read the larger and more costly 'Santa Melania' of Cardinal Rampolla."³⁹ One could buy Goyau's "jewel" for only two francs.⁴⁰ But with its diminished price tag also came a diminution of Melania's wealth.

Although the popular press widely reported Rampolla's estimate of Melania's income, this figure was more controversial among contemporary scholars. The Latin *life* refers to 120,000 pieces of gold. But does "pieces" here mean 120,000 pounds of gold? or 120,000 gold coins, which were generally 1/72 of a pound?⁴¹ Rampolla's choice of "pounds" helped propel Melania into the popular imagination. But as Goyau and others pointed out, it seemed unrealistic. One scholar estimated that Melania would have needed a million laborers to cultivate enough land to support such a fortune, and another pointed out that Rampolla's figure exceeded the 1904 gross national product of Switzerland.⁴² No one, however, wanted to cut Rampolla's estimate by 71/72. An annual income of 120,000 gold coins (that is, 1,600 pounds) would have made Melania's fortune close to the senatorial minimum, a hefty sum but nowhere near the degree of wealth envisioned by her contemporaries, to say nothing of early twentieth-century newspapers. So Goyau proposed a compromise solution. Rampolla was correct: "pieces" meant pounds. But a later scribe must have inadvertently added a zero. Instead of having an annual income of 120,000 pounds of gold, Melania really had only 12,000. Melania was no longer richer than Rockefeller, but she was still wealthy enough for her ascetic renunciation to reflect the "héroïsme de cette femme."[43] But at the same time as Goyau's calculations decreased Melania's net worth, they increased the historical worth of her *vita*. The beauty of Goyau's solution was not simply that he now had a realistic figure for Melania's income. Rather, it also preserved the veracity of Melania's two previous hagiographers, Gerontius and Rampolla. Gerontius reported the number correctly. Rampolla interpreted it correctly. The only weak link was an accounting error by a careless copyist with poor math skills.

This issue of authenticity became increasingly important in early twentieth-century writings about Melania. Rampolla's book had already referred to Gerontius's veracity.[44] In his preface to *Sainte Mélanie*, Goyau built upon this theme. He reported that "cette biographie de sainte Mélanie est attachante et vivante. Nulle trace, ici, de ces formations légendaires qui souvent mettent en conflit la critique et la piété."[45] Instead, Gerontius presented an authentic biography, an eyewitness testimony without extraneous or invented details.[46] As a result, like the summary in Rampolla's *Santa Melania*, Goyau's *Sainte Mélanie* is mainly a rewording of Gerontius's *life*.

Goyau published his book as part of the series "Les Saints," which sought to popularize specific Catholic saints and whose individual volumes were seen as "commendable for their brevity, good order and proportion, select bibliography, moderate and critical temper—above all for their habitually excellent literary quality and correctness of form."[47] Although meant to appeal to a more popular audience, Goyau's discussion of Melania's biography nevertheless came with greater academic trappings than much of Rampolla's work.

Goyau's preface pays homage to Melania's previous hagiographers, assuring his readers that the book's plot comes from Gerontius and its chronology from Rampolla.[48] But unlike Rampolla's summary of Melania's life and times, the body of Goyau's exposition weaves together direct quotations from a wide range of patristic sources. It also includes numerous footnotes citing modern scholarship. This did not, however, make Goyau's *Sainte Mélanie* particularly critical of its predecessors. Like Rampolla's summary, Goyau's book is mainly an amplified paraphrase of late ancient hagiography. But just as late twentieth-century scholarship would eventually characterize much of Gerontius's account as a piling up of details to create the similitude of absolute veracity, so too Goyau's pastiche of summaries, quotations, and footnotes reinforces its own truth claims, providing yet more authority to the account's authenticity.

Nevertheless, the combination of Gerontius's narrative details and frequent scholarly citation was well received by contemporaries. The *Times Literary Supplement* seemed particularly fond of Goyau's rendition. In its words, Melania had been "reared as carefully as Sleeping Beauty." Nevertheless, just as "a modern philosopher has said, 'Le succès m'ennuie.' The Roman Senatrix might have written, 'L'opulence m'ennuie.' And when the time came to marry her she might have added, 'L'amour m'ennuie.'" Expanding on this image of a French-speaking Melania, the *Times Literary Supplement* plays on the name of this "indomitable little saint": "Mélanie! The sound evokes some kind and canny French-woman of the lower middle class, economical, managing, good-natured, with black eyes (and the faintest shadow of a black moustache) above her keen, bright smile. Nothing could be less like the unworldly heiress of the *gens Valeria*."[49] Other reviews focused less on a Francophile Melania and more on *Sainte Mélanie*'s French author. Goyau was seen as "l'auteur du modèle de biographie."[50] His book was "un livre où tout est rigoureusement authentique," one that almost reached the "high water mark as a scholarly but withal attractive manipulation of a Saint's Life under the Roman Empire."[51]

Goyau's "attractive manipulation" ended, however, with a slightly different theme than had its predecessors. For Rampolla, the most important context for understanding Melania was her early experience of the depravity of late fourth-century Rome. Hence the cardinal's emphasis remained on Melania's material wealth. As with Gerontius before him, for Rampolla, the more money Melania had, the more she could give away, and the better she could serve as a foil to "the loathsome state of that society in whose bosom she first drew breath."[52] For Goyau, the key context for understanding Melania's import was not the decadence of fourth-century Rome but the fifth-century conflicts between Rome and the barbarians. Melania's renunciation of wealth, regardless of its actual sum, illustrated how Christian virtue could ultimately succeed in combining Roman and barbarian society. In the words of one of Goyau's reviewers, it illustrated "the part played by woman in the civilizing and Christianizing of Europe."[53] Goyau himself, however, made a grander claim. According to Goyau, Melania's life modeled a world beyond a clash of Rome and the barbarians, helping form "une seule société, mère de la nôtre."[54] *Sainte Mélanie* ended with Goyau noting Melania's relevance for the contemporary world, one with greater divisions and potential conflicts than that of the fifth century and thus in greater need of the "l'esprit chrétien de détachement," which alone is "capable de réaliser la véritable paix fondée sur la justice."[55] Although no longer the "richest woman who ever lived," Goyau's Mélanie shaped the future of the civilized world and, in the early twentieth century, had the potential to do so again. Goyau quite clearly felt "an almost utopian longing for an unearthed, long-buried narrative about the past that might portend a still different, brighter future"—words that Elizabeth Castelli applies in her chapter to 1980s feminist readings of Melania's *life* but that seem equally applicable to the early twentieth century as well.

MELANIA'S REMARKABLE *VITA*

According to Goyau, "Mélanie évidemment, consolée de l'oubli de la Terre par la quiétude du Ciel, attendit sans impatience."[56] At the turn of the twentieth century, Melania's fourteen hundred years of fortitude had clearly paid off. In 1903 Rampolla first announced his discovery of Melania's Latin *vita;* in 1904 the cardinal unexpectedly lost the papacy; in 1905 the Vatican's now *former* secretary of state published *Santa Melania;* in late 1906 and early 1907 newspapers worldwide proclaimed Melania to be history's richest woman, and in 1908 Goyau published *Sainte Mélanie.* As for the English-speaking world, it too required much less patience than Melania had, needing to wait only until 1909 for an English version of Melania's *life.* But as with its predecessors, this latest installment in Melania's repertoire was not a translation of an ancient document but rather a translation of Rampolla's summary.

In 1906, the Jesuit father Herbert Thurston first published an article extolling Rampolla's "editorial labours."[57] Three years later, he edited an English edition of Rampolla's work that sold for the bargain price of $1.50.[58] The resulting 1909 *Life of St. Melania* presented a translation only of Rampolla's preface and Rampolla's summary of Melania's *life.* But Thurston also supplemented Rampolla's work in two important ways.

First, Thurston interwove Rampolla's summary with numerous quotations, primarily from Gerontius's *life.* As a result, Thurston gave the reader much more direct access to Melania's Latin *vita* than Rampolla had done. Like *Sainte Mélanie,* this intercalation of modern and ancient material also led to a narrative in which the authority of ancient and modern authors reinforced each other. Yet unlike Goyau, Thurston did not use footnotes that occasionally cited disagreement among scholars. Instead Thurston's edition was quite homogeneous, with the authority of the fifth-century confessor and the twentieth-century cardinal blending together to form a seamless account.

Second, Thurston included his own preface to the work, which amplified many of the themes found in earlier discussions of Melania. As Thurston put it:[59]

> There are Saints' Lives and Saints' Lives. . . . The bulk of these documents, especially those belonging to certain specified epochs, are devoid of any touch of human individuality. They are like the portraits of Holy Doctors or Virgins, painted according to the canons of Byzantine art. We might shuffle all the names and almost all the dates, and the new arrangement would be just as near the truth, as much or as little instructive as the old. Miracles abound in such records, together with virtues and moral reflection of the most approved quality, but there is nothing for the memory to lay hold of. To have read one is to have read them all. . . . Still, there are some few remarkable exceptions to be found in this incredibly weary waste of banality and tediousness.

According to Thurston, what distinguishes Gerontius's writings is "how living and real is the personal interest of the narrative."[60] For Thurston it is this "wonderfully delicate and natural" flavor of Melania's *life* that best guarantees its authenticity.[61] The exact same argument would reappear in the late twentieth century as scholars again claimed that Gerontius's exceptionally detailed account made it an exceptional historical source.

Thurston's work had a strong effect upon the English-speaking world. Almost all English reviews of Rampolla's *Santa Melania* are actually reviews of Thurston's version of the work. As a result, despite reviewers' frequent references to "authentic history," what they and most of their Anglophile audience were now reading was Thurston's framing and expansion of Rampolla's summary of Gerontius's hagiography.[62] Nevertheless, Thurston's compilation was seen as "a splendid example of biographical history in its best form, [which] may well serve as a model."[63] What struck reviewers most was the work's immediacy. Its "most trustworthy account . . . is a real source of edification, inasmuch as it describes a genuine conflict between nature and grace in a human soul."[64] These reviews often mirror Thurston's emphasis on authenticity and personal interest. One even refers to Father Thurston's "charming introduction," which would "undoubtedly be read with much pleasure," a description not far removed from Thurston's own characterization of Gerontius's writing.[65]

. . .

Because Pius X had eliminated the right of exclusion, future papal elections were to be solely ecclesiastical decisions. As a result, in the early 1910s many viewed Rampolla as once again a viable papal candidate, believing that the cardinal would become Pius's successor. Such speculation ended on December 17, 1913, when Cardinal Rampolla predeceased the reigning pope. Rampolla's death resulted in a spate of obituaries, which always spoke of his achievements as the Vatican's secretary of state, often cited his close calls at becoming pope, and occasionally mentioned his discovery of Melania's Latin *vita*.[66]

Such reports sometimes included rather surprising discussions of Melania. For example, the *Manchester Guardian* contained perhaps the only popular-press piece that never referred to Melania's wealth. Instead, almost the entire issue was dedicated to the difficulties that fifth-century female ascetics faced as they engaged in their "hunger strikes." It concluded: "The late Cardinal pointed out, what the suffragist prisoners have doubtlessly learned from experience, that Saint Melania declared that the kind of food she found it most difficult to refuse was that containing a portion of fat."[67] Although this author once again used Melania to put forward the theme of women's insatiability, for at least a brief moment the "richest woman in the world" had nevertheless become a suffragette, a surprisingly apt portent of the role she would play decades later in her next afterlife.

After 1913 Melania made only cameo appearances in the popular press. In 1919 a reviewer of Princess Troubetzkoy's spiritualist novel *The Elusive Lady* compared the novel's antagonistic ghost with Melania the Younger.[68] In 1921 a second edition of Goyau's *Sainte Mélanie* was reprinted. But in general, Melania once again had to wait "sans impatience." Her next revival began in 1962 with a new critical edition and French translation of the Greek *vita*.[69] It took off in earnest in the 1980s with Melania becoming a central figure in feminist historiography. It is this second afterlife that has made possible the chapters found in this volume.

Few scholars involved in this most recent wave of Melania scholarship are aware of her early twentieth-century popularity. Nevertheless, there remain intriguing parallels between these two afterlives. The same narrative details that attracted early twentieth-century readers to Melania's *vita* were equally enticing to late twentieth-century scholars. Throughout much of the 1980s and 1990s many scholars assessed the *vita* little differently than their counterparts had done in 1908, when one reviewer claimed that "we have not here the dry bones, but the living and speaking portrait of this patrician lady of the fifth century."[70]

But then these two afterlives began to diverge. Focusing on the narrative elements that so intrigued readers at the turn of the nineteenth to the twentieth century, scholars at the turn of the twentieth to the twenty-first began to reassess Melania's *life*. Particularly influential was Elizabeth Clark's 1998 article "The Lady Vanishes." Clark warned that "the very details that social historians claim give veracity to a text are here repositioned as a creative artist's attempt to create an illusory reality in the minds of readers," having observed that "such details are precisely what literary theorist Ronald Barthes has named 'the effect of the real.'"[71]

Melania's early twentieth-century popularity helps illustrate the strength of this reality effect. Whether presented by an almost-pope, the son-in-law of a French president, a Jesuit priest, or a locomotive engineer, what people found most enticing about Gerontius's narrative was the impression that it represented "a really human document" that stemmed from its author's "strict veracity."[72] Although Melania's early twentieth-century afterlife was sparked by the discovery of a Latin manuscript, the document itself soon dropped from analysis. The alleged immediacy and transparency of Gerontius's account was so great, it did not matter that what people most often read were paraphrases of paraphrases.

Late twentieth-century interest in Melania was sparked not by a manuscript discovery but by an English translation. So too, the political commitments of a turn-of-the-century almost-Pope and second-wave feminist historians differed greatly. Nevertheless both of Melania's *Nachleben* were haunted by a quest for authenticity as, in Castelli's words, modern authors tried "to make late ancient hagiography answer to the imperatives of twentieth-century social-historical commitments." This curious tale of Melania's early twentieth-century revival and its surprising congruence with late twentieth-century scholarship reminds us how Melania and her afterlives do not so easily vanish.

NOTES

1. Elizabeth A. Clark, "The Lady Vanishes: Dilemmas of a Feminist Historian after the 'Linguistic Turn'" *Church History* 67 (1998): 31.

2. Francis A. Burkle-Young, *Papal Elections in the Age of Transition, 1878–1922* (Lanham, Md.: Lexington Books, 2000), 71.

3. Ibid., 79.

4. "Cardinal Rampolla," *The Review of Reviews* 27 (Mar. 1903): 266; "Who Will Be Pope after Leo XIII? Rampolla Regarded as One of the Strongest Possibilities," *The Atlanta Constitution*, July 6, 1903: 5; "Gotti and Rampolla: Traits of Two of the Cardinals Mentioned for the Papal Successorship," *The Washington Post*, July 21, 1903: 15; "Thought to Be for Rampolla," *The Sun*, July 29, 1903: 8.

5. Burkle-Young, *Papal Elections*, 80–82.

6. "Rampolla Given Lead: Said to Have Received 20 Votes on First Ballot; It Is Generally Believed in Rome That a Choice Will Be Made Monday," *The Sun* Aug. 2, 1903: 1; "Rampolla Leading in Race for Crown," *The Atlanta Constitution*, Aug. 2, 1903: 3; "Pope's Election Believed Near: Rampolla Said to Lead," *Chicago Daily Tribune*, Aug. 2, 1903: 1; "Pope's Election Believed Near: Sacred College of Cardinals Is Expected to Name Successor of Leo XIII on Tomorrow's Balloting; Rampolla Said to Lead," *Chicago Daily Tribune* Aug. 2, 1903: 1.

7. Burkle-Young, *Papal Elections*, 83–85.

8. Several suggest that Cardinal Rampolla was secretly a leading member of a "dark swamp of Satanic intrigue and Freemasonic-Kabbalistic anti-Christianity" (http://cfnews.org/ch-ramp.htm.). The "alternate history discussion board" even includes an extended entry on what would have happened had the Austrian emperor not vetoed Rampolla. Apparently, this would eventually have resulted in the electoral defeat of President Woodrow Wilson, issuing in the 1916 presidency of Charles Hughes (http://www.alternatehistory.com/discussion/showthread.php?t = 3708).

9. Burkle-Young, *Papal Elections*, 86–92.

10. Ibid., 93.

11. Mariano Cardinale Rampolla del Tindaro, *Santa Melania giuniore, senatrice romana: Documenti contemporanei e note* (Rome: Tipografia Vaticana, 1905). E. C. Butler, "Review: Cardinal Rampolla's *Melania the Younger*," *Journal of Theological Studies* 7 (1906), 630.

12. E. C. Butler, "Review: Cardinal Rampolla's *Melania*," 630.

13. "New Books," *Catholic World* 89 (May 1909): 246.

14. E. C. Butler, "Review: Cardinal Rampolla's *Melania*," 632.

15. M.-J. Lagrange, "Review: *Santa Melania giuniore, senatrice romana*," *Revue Biblique Internationale* 3 (1906): 300.

16. D. Bède Lebbe, "Review: M. Cardinale Rampolla del Tindaro, *Santa Melania giuniore, senatrice romana*," *Revue Bénédictine* 23 (1906): 459.

17. Fr. Diekamp, "Review: Rampolla del Tindaro, *Santa Melania giuniore, senatrice romana*," *Theologische Revue* 5 (May 22, 1906): 241. Apparently, Cardinal Rampolla did a little self-promotion as well. Upon hearing of her interest in the work, Rampolla sent a copy of his book to the Italian queen Margherita ("Able Disclosures in Rampolla Papers," *Philadelphian Inquirer*, May 17, 1914: 2; "Letters Show Rampolla Was Independent," *El Paso Herald*, May 23, 1914, section "Cable News and Too Late to Classify"). Later, a special apostolic delegate arrived at the United States Library of Congress to donate a ceremonial copy of Rampolla's work to the library's manuscript collection: *Report of the Librarian of Congress and Report of the Superintendent of the Library Building and Grounds* (Washington, D.C.: U.S. Government Printing Office, 1912), 8.

18. Patrick J. Healy, "Review: *The Life of St. Melania*," *Catholic University Bulletin* 15 (1909): 787.

19. Herbert Thurston, "Preface," in Mariano Rampolla del Tindaro, *The Life of St. Melania by His Eminence Cardinal Rampolla*, ed. H. Thurston, trans. E. M. A. Leahy (London: Burns & Oates, 1908), v.

20. Herbert Thurston, "The Editorial Labours of Cardinal Rampolla," *The Month* 108 (1906): 508. A similar comparison appears in "Miscellany," *Manchester Guardian* Dec. 20, 1913: 7.

21. Rampolla del Tindaro, *Santa Melania*, v (trans. Leahy, *Life of St. Melania*, 2).

22. Ibid., vi.
23. Ibid., ix.
24. Ibid., xii.
25. As one of many possible examples, when narrating Melanius's stay in Nola Rampolla begins: "Let us for a moment in imagination join that holy company on a calm night in January" (Ibid., xxxi [trans. Leahy, *Life of St. Melania*, 88]). This "moment in imagination" lasts for pages before returning to the *vita*'s plotline.
26. Ibid., xliii (trans. Leahy, *Life of St. Melania*, 164).
27. Elizabeth A. Clark, *The Life of Melania the Younger: Introduction, Translation, and Commentary* (Lewiston, N.Y.: Edwin Mellen Press, 1984).
28. "Saint Melania Richest Woman That Ever Lived," *The Washington Post*, Oct. 21, 1906: 4. Surprisingly, the bold headline encompassed not simply a report about Melania. Having finished the story with a few column inches to spare, the *Post* included two other pieces under the same headline. The first spoke of the modern world's most "thrifty" hen; having run off from a Tennessee farm, she made a nest in the woods and then set the world record for having twenty-six chicks in one brood. The final two column inches consist of a joke titled "One Woman's Way." A woman enters a bank wanting to cash a check. The bank teller asks her how she can identify herself. The anonymous woman answers, "with the aid of the mirror." Whether intentional or not, the contrast is striking. The ancient world's most famous female ascetic is followed by the modern world's most fecund fowl and a misogynistic joke concerning women's vanity.
29. Adjustment based on consumer price index back to 1913, the earliest date for which standard CPI data is provided by the U.S. Department of Labor Statistics.
30. "The Richest of All Women," *New York Sun*, Oct. 21, 1906, section 3, p. 1; "Richest of All Women," *Baltimore American*, Dec. 16, 1906: 57; "Richest Woman," *Salt Lake Herald* Apr. 7, 1907: 4; "Richest of All Women," *Intermountain Catholic*, Feb. 16, 1907: 1.
31. "The Wealthiest Woman," *Locomotive Engineers Journal* 41 (1907): 207–8.
32. Rev. Charles Stelzle, "Socialism and the Church," ibid.: 208–9.
33. "The Richest Woman Who Ever Lived: The Amazing History of Saint Melania the Younger," *Auckland Star* 1907, 10. "The Richest Woman Who Ever Lived: The Amazing History of Saint Melania, the Younger," *Cleveland Plain Dealer* Nov. 25, 1906: 56.
34. The copy of the article itself, however, slightly exceeds the *Washington Post*'s estimate of Melania's wealth. Rampolla states that since the purchasing power of ancient gold was six times higher than in the early twentieth century, her income was really about $180,000,000 a year.
35. "Millionaires Who Were Richer than Rockefeller: Patiomkin, of Russia, and Melania, of Rome, Exceeded John D.," *Baltimore Sun*, Jan. 6, 1907: 14.
36. Rampolla del Tindaro, *Santa Melania*, ix.
37. "*Sainte Mélanie*," *Dublin Review* 143 (July 1908): 427.
38. For an overview of Goyau's life and works, see Juliette Heuzey-Goyau, *Dieu premier servi: Georges Goyau—Sa vie et son œuvre* (Paris: Bonne Presse, 1947).
39. Georges Goyau, *Sainte Mélanie*, 383–439 (Paris: Lecoffre, 1908); "Book Notices," *Catholic University Bulletin* 14 (1908): 327.
40. "Notes bibliographiques," *Revue Canadienne* 1 (1908): 383.
41. For a brief discussion of this debate, see E. A. Clark, *Life of Melania the Younger*, 95–96.
42. Ibid., 95; Goyau, *Sainte Mélanie*, 12–13.
43. Ibid., 207.
44. Rampolla del Tindaro, *Santa Melania*, lxxiii.
45. Goyau, *Sainte Mélanie*, vii.
46. Ibid.
47. "Book Notices," *Catholic University Bulletin* 14 (1908): 327.

48. Goyau, *Sainte Mélanie*, x.
49. "Sainte Mélanie," *Times Literary Supplement*, Aug. 6, 1908: 253.
50. T. De Visan, "Review: *Sainte Mélanie*," *Revue de Philosophie* 12 (1908): 288.
51. "Notes bibliographiques," *Revue Canadienne* 1 (1908): 383. "Sainte Mélanie," *Dublin Review* 143 (July 1908): 427.
52. Rampolla del Tindaro, *Santa Melania*, vii (trans. Leahy, *Life of St. Melania*, 8).
53. "Sainte Mélanie," *Dublin Review* 143 (July 1908): 428.
54. Goyau, *Sainte Mélanie*, 205.
55. Ibid., 208.
56. Ibid., ii.
57. Herbert Thurston, "Editorial Labours," 508–21.
58. "Book Reviews and Literary Notes," *Catholic Fortnightly Review* 16 (1909): 319.
59. Rampolla del Tindaro, *Life of St. Melania*, ed. Thurston, vii–viii.
60. Ibid., x.
61. Ibid., xii.
62. "New Books," *Catholic World* 89 (May 1909): 247.
63. "Book Reviews," *American Catholic Quarterly Review* 34 (1909): 378.
64. "Criticism and Notes," *The American Ecclesiastical Review* 40 (1909): 771; "New Books," *Catholic World* 89 (May 1909): 247.
65. Healy, "Review: *The Life of St. Melania*," 787.
66. E.g., "The Most Popable of Cardinals," *Current Literature* 50 (1911), 498–501; "Cardinal Rampolla Dead: Former Papal Secretary of State Barred from Tiara by Austria—Lived in Retirement, a Disappointed Man, after Defeat, but Was Regarded as Next Pope," *The Washington Post*, Dec. 17, 1913: 3; "Cardinal Rampolla Dies at Age of 70: Former Papal Secretary of State Was Mentioned as a Possible Successor to Pius X," *The New York Times*, Dec. 17, 1913: 3; "Cardinal Rampolla Passes from Earth: Once Papal Secretary of State—Mentioned as Successor to Pope Pius X," *The Atlanta Constitution*, Dec. 17, 1913: 11; "Cardinal Rampolla," *Chicago Daily Tribune*, Dec. 17, 1913: 2; "Rampolla Passes Away: Mentioned as Successor to Pope Pius X," *Los Angeles Times*, Dec. 17, 1913: 15; "Rampolla Was 'the Gentleman Born,'" *Baltimore Sun*, Dec. 19, 1913: 6; "Pope Shocked by Rampolla Death," *Chicago Daily Tribune*, Dec. 18, 1913: 4; "Rampolla in State," *Los Angeles Times*, Dec. 18, 1913: I6; "Cardinal Rampolla," *Manchester Guardian*, Dec. 18, 1913: 8; "Pope Lauds Rampolla," *Baltimore Sun*, Dec. 18, 1913: 2; "Death of Cardinal Rampolla: A Statesman of the Vatican," *The Times of India*, Dec. 18, 1913: 7.
67. "Miscellany," *Manchester Guardian*, Dec. 20, 1913: 7.
68. "A Virginian Ghost," *The Saturday Review*, Jan. 11, 1919: 39; Amélie Rives (Princess Troubetzkoy), *The Elusive Lady* (London: Hurst & Blackett, 1918).
69. *Vie de sainte Mélanie*, ed. and trans. Denys Gorce, Sources Chrétiennes 90 (Paris: Cerf, 1962).
70. "Sainte Mélanie," *Dublin Review*, 428.
71. Elizabeth A. Clark, "The Lady Vanishes," 20, 19.
72. Rampolla del Tindaro, *Life of St. Melania*, ed. Thurston, viii.

14

Monastic Revivals

Stephen J. Davis

It is well known that Melania the Elder (d. 410) and Melania the Younger (d. 439) both traveled to Egypt and visited monks there before settling in Jerusalem and founding monasteries on the Mount of Olives. But their visits to the Egyptian desert were rather brief: neither stayed more than a year, and both would live out the rest of their lives in Palestine. After their deaths, the Melanias became prominent saints in Western church traditions, but their impact in the Egyptian church's collective memory has been minimal over the centuries.

Melania the Elder was famously commemorated in Palladius's *Lausiac History*, an early fifth-century work about Egyptian monasticism, but this text was written in Asia Minor and largely transmitted outside Egypt in Greek and Latin, and in Syriac as part of a larger composite collection called *The Paradise of the Fathers* (about which I'll say more in due course). In any case, neither Melania is included in the official list of saints and saints' days of the Coptic church. For over fifteen centuries, grandmother and granddaughter were largely forgotten in Egyptian Christian life and liturgy.

This essay is about how they have been reclaimed and remembered in the modern Coptic Orthodox Church. During the past four decades, these two late Roman women have begun making notable cameo appearances in Arabic-language homilies and books produced by male Egyptian church leaders. Here, I try to make sense of the Melanias' return to Egypt by discussing selected examples of how they have been reintroduced as models of piety, as part of a successful effort to revive Coptic monasticism in the late twentieth and the early twenty-first century. Focusing on three Arabic sources as my primary evidence—an audio recording of a homily by Pope Shenouda III, a history of monasticism by the monk Matthew the

Poor (Mattā al-Miskīn), and a modern reworking of the aforementioned *Paradise of the Fathers*—I address how male church leaders have appropriated the Melanias as gendered models for Coptic nuns and female laity.

But first, some crucial context related to the revival of monasticism in modern Egypt. By the late Middle Ages, monasteries in Egypt found themselves significantly reduced in both population and cultural influence. In the sixteenth century, the Muslim historian al-Maqrīzī reported on this dire situation.[1] In his day, he found many monasteries abandoned to the encroaching sands of the desert. The smaller number of communities that survived had only a handful of monks left. This pattern of decline continued into the first half of the twentieth century.

Beginning in the 1940s and 1950s, however, and gaining pace under the patronage of Pope Kyrillos VI (r. 1959–71) and his successor Pope Shenouda III (r. 1971–2012), Coptic monastic communities for both men and women witnessed an unprecedented resurgence. When one visits these communities today, the difference is readily apparent. Where there had previously been deteriorating buildings, there are now new churches of grand scale, extensive agricultural reclamation of desert land, and visitors' centers catering to the consumer appetites of pilgrims and tourists. Where previously there was only a small remnant of the monastics (or none at all), there are now hundreds, many of whom are drawn from the professional and educated classes of society—engineers, doctors, and lawyers who have taken their skills and applied them to the revival of monastic life as a second career for men and women throughout Egypt. It is in the context of this modern monastic revival that we find the two Melanias reentering the picture.

In her landmark article "The Lady Vanishes," Elizabeth A. Clark borrowed the language of Claude Lévi-Strauss to talk about how male Christian writers and other ancient men "used women to 'think with.'"[2] This recognition of the discursive uses to which female figures were put is equally applicable to the construction of gender—and the construction of the patristic past—in modern ecclesiastical contexts. My aim is to ask how these two late Roman women have been used to "think with" in the Coptic Orthodox Church from around 1970 to today. For evidence, I turn to the teachings of Pope Shenouda III and to literature produced by contemporary Coptic monks, including the well-known spiritual theologian Matthew the Poor (Mattā al-Miskīn)—male church leaders who have appropriated the Melanias for the purpose of promoting monasticism as the epitome of Christian faithfulness among both lay and monastic audiences. In retelling the biographies of these late Roman saints to potential recruits on the one hand, and to already consecrated monks and nuns on the other, these leaders had markedly different goals. While Pope Shenouda III used the lives of the Melanias to endorse certain societal values connected with marriage and wealth, Matthew the Poor and other modern monastic authors sought to incorporate them into expanded genealogies of the early Egyptian monastic fathers and mothers. In the process, both the elder and the younger Melania have been reconscripted as adopted daughters of the Egyptian desert.

THROUGH THE EYE OF A NEEDLE: POPE SHENOUDA III ON THE MELANIAS, MARRIAGE, MONEY, AND THE MONASTIC LIFE

Let me turn first to the role that the Melanias played in the teachings of Pope Shenouda III. My primary text in this case is not a written document at all but rather an audio clip downloaded from the Internet in November 2012, about eight months after His Holiness's death.[3] When I first discovered this online audio clip and clicked Play, a familiar voice from beyond the grave began to narrate the stories of the two Melanias in sequence, accompanied by a lilting Middle Eastern instrumental sound track. In the appendix to this article, I provide a full translation of Shenouda III's hagiographical homily, which was probably one installment in a series of summaries on the lives of saints he presented to his congregation in Cairo.[4] The vast majority of that congregation consisted of lay parishioners, with a large number of youths and young families. The original date of this particular Arabic homily is unknown, although I suspect (given the tenor of his voice and the quality of the recording) that it must have been recorded rather early in his reign as pope, perhaps in the 1970s or early 1980s.

The homily is less than five minutes long (4:44, to be exact), and in it Shenouda III presents a biographical synopsis for each Melania. In both cases, what he emphasizes as wonderful (and worth repeating several times) is the fact that these women got married and had children before choosing to enter the monastic life. He tells his audience: "They both possessed something wonderful. Both of these saints, Melania the Elder and Melania the Younger, got married. They got married and had children. And then they entered the monastic life, a type [of life] that is not found often." A second important point of emphasis for Shenouda III is the fact that the two women were wealthy. Thus he emphasizes: "They were very rich. They were very rich. They got married, had children, and then entered the monastic life."

In the case of Melania the Elder, Shenouda III goes on to note that "she married a very rich man and had three sons with him," two of whom died in childhood when she was still a young woman. Then, after highlighting her youth and beauty, Shenouda III notes that "she remained a widow for forty-six years engaged in works of asceticism [*nusk*] and renunciation [*zuhd*]; she left her children with some people who cared for them; she went to the desert of Scetis, and she donated her wealth to the monks and clerics."

In Shenouda III's hands, the Melanias are presented as what I will call controlled, semiascetic models for a predominantly lay audience. They are exemplars to be imitated, although only under certain circumscribed conditions. Young single women in the congregation are not urged to give it all up and enter a convent before they have performed certain social duties incumbent upon them—namely to get married and have children, and thereby help to rear a new generation of the faithful. Then—maybe as a second career choice—they may consider the virtues of sexual renunciation.

The value of the Melanias as models of piety for Shenouda III, therefore, was grounded as much in their preascetic commitments as in their postascetic lives. This is true not only with respect to sexuality and childbirth but also with respect to wealth. Those who have wombs are expected to use them. By the same token, those who have money are expected to donate it. This point is reemphasized in one of Shenouda III's pamphlets, entitled *So Many Years with the Problems of People, Part One: Biblical Questions,* in which he pushes back ever so gently against Jesus's teaching about rich people, camels, and eyes of needles in the Synoptic Gospels (Matt. 19:23–26, Mark 10:24–25, Luke 18:24–25). He comments: "History also gives us other examples of holy rich people who entered the kingdom of God. St. Melania, who was very rich, spent much of her money on monasteries and on building churches. She then chose the monastic life after she was widowed."[5]

To his female lay readers and listeners, he might have concluded by saying, "Go and do likewise." In this way, Shenouda III appropriated the Melanias for a specific dual purpose: first, to endorse a modern, bourgeois vision of Coptic family life as the engine of biological and economic production;[6] and second, to uphold the monastic life as an ideal second career for those who have already generated both offspring and financial capital, and who now aspire to build up their treasure in heaven after fulfilling their earthly duties.[7]

It should be noted that the online availability of Shenouda III's sermon demonstrates how his particular vision for women's roles in Coptic families was subsequently taken up and actively promoted among the faithful via modern media technologies. In their 2013 article "Emerging Christian Media in Egypt," Febe Armanios and Andrew Amstutz have explored how such new technologies have been used to "present traditional gender roles in a new packaging."[8] While the authors focus primarily on the boom of videos and films produced by Copts over the last three decades, they also give a nod to how modern sound media—beginning with cassettes in the 1970s and 1980s and continuing with digital files in the third millennium—have reinforced this same ecclesiastical message emphasizing female subordination to patriarchal authority, whether to fathers and husbands in the home or to bishops and other clerics in churches and monastic settings.[9]

As argued here, Shenouda III's treatment of the Melanias in his hagiographical homily articulates particular concerns related to the management of women's bodies in negotiating social transitions from maternal to monastic vocations. In the audio recording and online dissemination of that sermon, we also see the medial mechanisms through which those same concerns came to reverberate outside the walls of Shenouda III's church and in the private homes and apartments of Coptic families—places where the pope's sermon could be listened to on laptops and cell phones, and where such female virtues were expected to be embodied.

GENDERING (AND ENGENDERING) MONASTIC GENEALOGIES: THE MELANIAS IN MATTHEW THE POOR AND A MODERN PARADISE OF THE FATHERS

Shenouda III's has not been the only voice or perspective on the subject of the Melanias in the modern Coptic Orthodox Church. In the words and writings of other male Egyptian ecclesiastical leaders, the Melanias have been appropriated for purposes related more specifically to the recruitment and training of female monastics. For such writers, what has been at stake is the question of how to situate—and thereby subordinate—the ascetic example of the Melanias not in relation to a modern bourgeois family ethic but in relation to ancient patristic genealogies of Desert Fathers.

As Clark notes when discussing Michel Foucault in her book *History, Theory, Text*, genealogies have long had the communal function of enacting domains of knowledge and power in relation to human bodies and practices.[10] In the late twentieth- and early twenty-first-century revival of Coptic monasticism, such domains of knowledge and power have not been organized around adherence to elaborate rules or canons (as was the case in the late ancient monasteries overseen by Pachomius and Shenoute of Atripe, for instance). Instead, the modern recruitment and training of monks and nuns has been mediated through a particular text and through practices of commentary and devotional reading attendant to it. In Arabic, the text is called *Bustān al-ruhbān* (*The Garden of the Monks*). A modern edition of this *Garden* was published in the 1940s. In 1968, a revised and expanded version edited by Bishop Athanasius of Beni Suef began serving as a standard guidebook for men and women preparing to dedicate themselves to the monastic life, and for monks and nuns already pursuing that life in monasteries and convents.[11] Over the past forty-five years, the text has gone through several editions and expansions.

The Garden in fact belongs to the complex and varied textual history of the *Apophthegmata Patrum*. In late antiquity, different versions of these sayings and stories were disseminated in Greek and Latin. In the seventh century, the east Syrian monk Enanisho combined the *Apophthegmata* with Palladius's *Lausiac History* (as well as material from Jerome) in the aforementioned Syriac text called *The Paradise of the Fathers*.[12] Other language editions followed, often with alternative titles and widely varying contents. One medieval manuscript found at the Monastery of St. Catherine at Mount Sinai, for example, contains a collection of stories under the title *The Garden*, consisting of "accounts of the Old Men and Fathers."[13]

The modern Arabic edition of *The Garden of the Fathers*, however, has been significantly reconceived and does not simply replicate earlier versions. Instead, it incorporates a number of other early monastic sources newly made available to the editors through modern English and French translations. In the 1968 edition, the work's contents are organized into two parts. In the first, the collection of sayings is associated with names of different monks (beginning with Anthony and Macarius the Great and ending with lesser figures). In the second, the collection is organized as a series of exercises designed to train monks and nuns in matters related to the themes of will, spirit, thought, and love.

In her 1995 book *Contemporary Coptic Nuns*, Nelly van Doorn–Harder documents how *The Garden* has been used as a primary tool for spiritual development among young women training for entrance into the convent as well as among nuns already in monastic residence. Through devotional readings of the text under a spiritual director, prospective nuns acquaint themselves with the teachings of the Desert Fathers and prepare themselves for taking their vows of chastity, obedience, and poverty. The monastic models in this *Garden* are almost exclusively male: although a few Desert Mothers (such as Amma Sarah) are mentioned in passing, there is no mention of the Melanias.[14]

The needs of nuns-in-training, however, have prompted the publication of other literature complementary to *The Garden of the Fathers*—books akin to training manuals—and in some of this literature the Melanias make a conspicuous appearance. One example is a 1972 volume entitled *al-Rahbanah al-qibṭīyah fī 'aṣr al-Qiddīs Anbā Maqār* (Coptic Monasticism in the Age of Saint Macarius the Great), written by Matthew the Poor (Mattā al-Miskīn), the famous contemplative monk, abbot of the Monastery of St. Macarius in Wādī al-Naṭrūn, who died in 2006.[15] Another example is a vastly expanded 2008 edition of *The Garden of the Monks*, which includes additional stories and commentary for those interested in deepening their acquaintance with Egyptian monastic history.[16] In both cases, one sees how the Melanias (but especially Melania the Elder) have been incorporated into a renovated monastic genealogy produced for modern Coptic consumption.

Matthew the Poor's appropriation of Melania the Elder in his book *Coptic Monasticism* is conditioned by two factors related to globalization in a postcolonial world: the importation of Western scholarly translations into Egypt and the appropriation of Western saints for the purpose of presenting Egyptian monasticism as a paradigm for ecumenical spirituality.

First, Matthew the Poor notably draws his information about the Melanias not from Coptic or Arabic manuscript traditions but from English and French translations of Palladius's *Lausiac History* and other, analogous literature. He gives an account of Melania's contact with the luminaries of the desert, and especially her interactions with the monk Pambo. (He highlights in particular the story about her gift of silver and her receipt of a basket at his deathbed.) In doing so, Matthew draws directly on the French translation of the stories by René Draguet and on English translations by Helen Waddell and E. A. W. Budge.[17]

Second, Matthew the Poor recounts Melania the Elder's activities under the heading "The Visit of Important Persons to Nitria Had an International Influence." Throughout, Melania is characterized as "the Spanish saint" and "friend of the saints."[18] She is shown seeking out the saints' company, asking them questions, and "serv[ing] them in their exile."[19] And yet, as a privileged recipient of the monks' hospitality, she (along with her fellow foreigner Rufinus) was able to settle in a house and reside there "for a long time."[20] As a result, Melania is cast as both a resident alien and a symbol of Egyptian ecumenicity: she is a Spanish saint who has become, in effect, an adopted daughter of the Egyptian desert. Thus, in the person of Melania the Elder, prospective monks and nuns reading Matthew's work are shown how, through small and large acts of hospitality, Egyptian monasticism embraces (and incorporates within itself) the wider Christian world.

Similar themes surrounding the Melanias are echoed in an expanded 2008 edition of *The Garden of the Monks,* published by a group of anonymous "monks of the desert of Scetis" (most likely Matthew the Poor's monastic disciples at the Monastery of St. Macarius). The edition contains a new introduction and expanded contents. In the introduction, there is a section specifically dedicated to the travels of foreigners who came to Egypt, collected the sayings of the fathers, and transported monasticism back to their countries.[21] Melania the Elder falls into this category (again paired with Rufinus); so does Melania the Younger, who is now given her own subheading.

The body of the text itself is expanded to include not only the teachings of Anthony and Macarius, who are found in the original 1968 edition of *The Garden,* but also the sayings and stories of their most prominent disciples. Melania the Elder is mentioned in sections on Macarius of Alexandria and Pambo, both disciples of Macarius the Great.[22] She is portrayed as a "Roman princess" who receives a fleece from the hand of Macarius of Alexandria as a memento, and who attends to Pambo at his deathbed and receives from him a basket as a gift.[23] The details of her interactions with these Desert Fathers come straight from Palladius's *Lausiac History.* The editors cite Robert T. Meyer's English translation and render selected excerpts in Arabic, although the detail of Melania's role in burying Pambo is edited out in the Arabic translation, perhaps censored for modern Coptic sensibilities regarding what it would entail for a female monk to prepare a male body for burial.[24] In any event, the resultant text is something of a patchwork quilt, with quotes from Palladius interspersed among other passages taken from the *Apophthegmata Patrum* and from Arabic manuscripts in the library at the Monastery of St. Macarius.

What is most striking, however, is the discursive effect of these successive stories: the elder Melania is inserted into an authorized (and authorizing) monastic genealogy, where she assumes a subordinate role. In her case, her place is a matter of two degrees of separation: she is eyewitness and friend to two famous followers and disciples of Macarius the Great himself. She is a beneficiary of holy proximity—of grace by association—and in this capacity she is a benefactor for prospective nuns who would seek to follow her into *The Garden of the Monks*, into *The Paradise of the Fathers*.

CONCLUSION

In this essay, I have sought to show a different way out of late antiquity and into the modern and contemporary world of homiletic exhortation and monastic practice in Egypt. As it turns out, the Melanias have indeed revisited Egypt, and they have played their own small role in the revival of Coptic Orthodox monastic piety. But their role has not been monolithic, nor has it been of their own making. In Shenouda III's homily and its hagioaural reproduction in modern media, we have seen how the two Melanias were co-opted as preascetic models for underwriting lay bourgeois family values.[25] Before considering a second career as a nun, a young Coptic woman should follow these Roman exemplars by first heeding her biological call and fulfilling her economic duties to the community. By contrast, in Matthew the Poor and in a recent edition of *The Garden of the Monks* published by the Monastery of St. Macarius, we have seen how the foreign saint Melania the Elder was domesticated through the construction of monastic genealogies. Linked but also crucially subordinated to her male counterparts, the elder Melania (with her eponymous granddaughter in tow) comes to serve as a model perfectly suited for contemporary Coptic nuns and nuns-in-training whose everyday devotions are designed to cultivate a similar posture of subordination in relation to the lessons imparted by the Desert Fathers. In these different ways, two famous late Roman women of independent means are adopted and co-opted for the purpose of training female Coptic bodies in how to submit to male authority in both marriage and monasticism.

APPENDIX: SHENOUDA III, A BRIEF HOMILY ON THE TWO MELANIAS

I'll tell you about Saint Melania. In truth, there are two saints named Melania—Melania the Elder and Melania the Younger. Melania the Elder was the grandmother of Melania the Younger. The two of them, these two saints, both named Melania, lived in the fourth and fifth centuries. They both possessed something wonderful. Both of these saints, Melania the Elder and Melania the Younger, got married. They got married and had children. And then they entered the monastic life, a type [of life] that is not found often. They were very rich. They were very rich. They got married, had children, and then entered the monastic life. And they founded monasteries for female monastics, and they founded monasteries for men as well, especially in Jerusalem. Melania the Elder was born in Rome in the year 342. And she went to her rest at age sixty-nine. Her grandfather was a consul. She married a very rich man and had three sons with him. Two of them died in childhood. At the time when she was widowed, she was still a young woman, at twenty-three years of age. And she did not marry again even though many people tried to woo her on account of her beauty, her wealth, and all her [fine] attributes. And she was only a young woman, twenty-three years of age. And she did not remarry. She remained a widow for forty-six years engaged in works of asceticism [*nusk*] and renunciation [*zuhd*]; she left her children with some people who cared for them; she went to the desert of Scetis, and she donated her wealth to the monks and clerics. And one time, she was imprisoned, and when the governor realized that she was a Roman woman, he released her, and they established a monastery in Jerusalem. . . . They established a monastery in Jerusalem in which were fifty virgins. And Saint Jerome knew her. And Melania the Elder was the one at whose hands Saint Mār Ūghrīs repented. She was the one who guided him to repentance, and he later entered the monastic life and became Saint Mār Ūghrīs. They call him Saint Evagrius. Her [i.e., Melania's] third son got married and had a child named Melania. This is Melania the Younger, granddaughter of Melania the Elder. She grew up and got married, and then later entered the monastic life and made an agreement with her husband that they would live as brothers. They lived as brothers, and then her husband entered the monastic life in a monastery, and she also entered the monastic life in a monastery. And she also established monasteries for male monks and for female monks. And she concerned herself with hospitals and with the care of churches. And after [experiencing] all her jewelry, clothing, and wealth, and wearing simple clothes like her maidservants, she established a women's monastery and lived in it. She ate once a day in the evening: dry bread. She concerned herself with prayer, reading, contemplation, and the memorization of verses. She visited the holy places, and she visited the deserts of Egypt and was blessed by the anchorites. And she visited the Mount of Olives and established a monastery for women there under her direction. And she received Communion before her death and she and her mother [i.e., her grandmother] are among the great saints of the church.

NOTES

1. al-Maqrīzī, *al-Mawāʿiẓ wa al-iʿtibār fī dhikr al-khiṭaṭ wa al-athār*, ed. Muhammad Zeinahum and Madihat al-Sharqāwa (Cairo: Maktabat Madbūlī, 1998); relevant section ed. and trans. B. T. A. Evetts in al-Maqrīzī, *The Churches and Monasteries of Egypt and Some Neighboring Countries* (Oxford: Clarendon Press, 1895; reprint, Piscataway, N.J.: Gorgias, 2001).

2. Elizabeth A. Clark, "The Lady Vanishes: Dilemmas of a Feminist Historian after the 'Linguistic Turn,'" *Church History* 67 (1998), 1–31, at 27.

3. The file is entitled *Sīrat al-Qiddīsah Mīlānīyā* (*The Life of Saint Melania*). A copy of the clip was uploaded to YouTube (along with a grainy image of the two saints identified with Arabic captions) on

MONASTIC REVIVALS 269

December 29, 2011: http://www.youtube.com/watch?v=pR_zZxj4dts; last accessed on June 23, 2016. The one who posted the recording (Bskska1980) did so in commemoration of Melania the Younger's feast day in the Western liturgical calendar, December 31: see Alban Butler, "December 31: St. Melania the Younger," in *The Lives of the Fathers, Martyrs, and Other Principal Saints: Compiled from Original Monuments and Other Authentick Records*, vol. 12 (Dublin: James Duffy, 1866; http://www.bartleby.com/210/12/313.html, last accessed on June 23, 2016). A number of other Arabic-language Christian Web sites have links (many now no longer active) for downloading the same recording.

4. Other audio clips circulating online include biographical summaries of Anastasia, Augustine, Didymus, Mar Ephrem, and Severus (of Antioch).

5. Pope Shenouda III, *So Many Years with the Problems of People, Part One: Biblical Questions*, trans. St. George Coptic Orthodox Church, 2nd ed. (Cairo: Dar el-Tebaa el-Kawmia, 1993), 74.

6. This is consistent with Shenouda III's fundamental regard for "the Coptic family as the rock on which the community stands": Sana S. Hasan, *Christians versus Muslims in Modern Egypt: The Century-Long Struggle for Coptic Equality* (Oxford: Oxford University Press, 2003), 127.

7. It should be noted that the use of the Melanias for such hortatory purposes has been echoed in Coptic Orthodox Church online blogs. One example comes from the Coptic Orthodox Diocese of Los Angeles, which published a short online essay entitled "The Role of Women in the Church" (April 9, 2009, http://lacopts.org/2009/04/09/the-role-of-women-in-the-church; last accessed June 23, 2016). The essay lists "examples of saintly women" from "the patristic era," and mentions Melania the Elder as among "women who had great wealth, [who] used their wealth to build monasteries."

8. Febe Armanios and Andrew Amstutz, "Emerging Christian Media in Egypt: Clerical Authority and the Visualization of Women in Coptic Video Films," *International Journal of Middle East Studies* 45 (2013), 513-33, at 513. Here they draw a parallel to trends in "American evangelical entertainment media" and quote from the work of Kelsy Burke and Amy McDowell, "Superstars and Misfits: Two Pop-Trends in the Gender Culture of Contemporary Evangelicalism," *Journal of Religion and Popular Culture* 24 (2012), 72.

9. Armanios and Amstutz, "Emerging Christian Media," 517.

10. Elizabeth A. Clark, *History, Theory, Text: Historians and the Linguistic Turn* (Cambridge, Mass.: Harvard University Press, 2004), 117-18.

11. *Bustān al-ruhbān li-ābā' al-kinīsah al-qibṭīyah*, ed. Bishop Athanasius of Beni Suef, 2nd ed. (Beni Suef: Lagnat al-taḥrīr wa al-nashr, 1976); Pieternella van Doorn-Harder, *Contemporary Coptic Nuns* (Columbia: University of South Carolina Press, 1995), 54-55.

12. H. G. B. Teule, "Paradise of the Fathers, Book of," in *The Gorgias Encyclopedic Dictionary of the Syriac Heritage*, ed. S. P. Brock, A. M. Butts, G. A. Kiraz, and L. van Rompay (Beth Mardutho: The Syriac Institute; and Piscataway, N.J.: Gorgias Press, 2011), 322.

13. Joseph-Marie Sauget, "Un nouveau témoin de collection d'Apophthegmata Patrum: Le Paterikon du Sinaï arabe 547," *Le Muséon* 86 (1973), 5-35, at 10; see also Sauget, *Une traduction arabe de la collection d'Apophthegmata Patrum de 'Enānīšo': Étude du MS. Paris arabe 253 et des témoins parallèles*, CSCO 495 (Louvain: Peeters, 1987), 10; Lucien Regnault, "Apophthegmata Patrum," in *The Coptic Encyclopedia*, vol. 1 (New York: Macmillan, 1991), 177-78; and Georg Graf, *Geschichte der christlichen arabischen Literatur*, vol.1, *Die Übersetzungen* (Vatican City: Biblioteca Apostolica Vaticana, 1944), 381-83.

14. Van Doorn-Harder (*Contemporary Coptic Nuns*, 132, 221 note 11) counts a mere three Desert Mothers among a chorus of 130 Fathers.

15. Mattā al-Miskīn, *al-Rahbanah al-qibṭīyah fī 'aṣr al-Qiddīs Anbā Maqār*, 4th ed. (Wādī al-Naṭrūn: Dayr al-Qiddīs Anbā Maqār, 2006).

16. Monks of the Desert of Scetis, *Firdaws al-Ābā' (Bustān al-ruhbān al-muwassa')* [*Paradise of the Fathers* (The Expanded *Garden of the Monks*)], 3rd ed., 3 vols. (Wādī al-Naṭrūn: Maṭba'at al-Daltā, 2008).

17. al-Miskīn, *al-Rahbanah al-qibṭīyah*, 184–85; cf. 873–74. Elsewhere, relying on other sources Matthew relates a separate tale about how Melania the Elder traveled to Scetis and built a church there for the monk and priest Isidore (Mattā al-Miskīn, *al-Rahbanah al-qibṭīyah*, 185, 222).

18. Ibid., 184–85, 197.
19. Ibid., 184–85, 238 note 2.
20. Ibid., 317.
21. Monks of the Desert of Scetis, *Firdaws al-Ābā'*, 11–16.
22. Ibid., 373–93 at 386, 420–30 at 429.
23. Ibid., 386, 429.
24. Ibid., 10.
25. My use of the term "hagioaural" is meant as a play on the term "hagiopics," coined by Pamela Grace (*The Religious Film: Christianity and the Hagiopic* [Chichester: Wiley-Blackwell, 2009], 1–2) and redeployed in the study of modern Coptic visual media by Febe Armanios and Andrew Amstutz ("Emerging Christian Media").

15

The Future of Sainthood

Elizabeth A. Castelli

This essay began as an homage to Elizabeth Clark, written for a conference held in April 2013 to honor her countless contributions as colleague, mentor, and friend—a true pioneer in the study of early Christianity and the religious worlds of late antiquity. Having undertaken to write a paper that somehow concerns one of the Melanias, I found myself feeling rather daunted. Rereading Clark's scholarship, I had a growing and foreboding sense of myself as merely adding a minor footnote to a magnum opus. How, indeed, to say more when Clark has done her work with such erudition, scrupulous attention to detail, and indeed comprehensiveness? The experience was not so much one of *déjà lu* as *déjà écrit*. Anything one may write has already been written . . . by Clark herself.[1]

But, in returning to the *Life of Melania the Younger* after the two decades or more since I last read it, I found myself thinking above all about the intellectual context in which Clark first produced her translation and commentary—a context in which women's history was just emerging as a field of academic inquiry. Back in the late 1970s and early 1980s, there was a kind of exhilaration that emerged out of the experience of discovery—women's voices and women's lives being lifted up out of the archives and situated in the big story of the past. At the time, there was something radical and subversive about the restorative practice of expanding history's repertoire. Emblematic of such intellectual commitments, one of the earliest second-wave books of women's history published during these heady years of intellectual insurrection by feminist historians bore the declarative and insistent title *We Were There*.[2] The title itself signaled the then-radical assertion that the conventional erasures of the experiences and historical contributions of half the human race left accounts of the past wanting and partial. At the same time, it also enacted a kind of representational politics, seeking to answer an unabashedly activist question: But where are the women?

For people interested in things premodern and religious, the project of answering the activist question became an academic imperative as well as a challenging activity of patchwork and inference, demanding a flexible methodology that attended to fragments of testimony drawn from archives whose histories were themselves products of complex transmissions and omissions. These obstacles notwithstanding, feminist scholars mined the literary sources, lining up details from ancient historians next to passing comments in letters and lives, and bit by bit a new (and more inclusive) version of the story emerged, and certain things came into view: political and theological conflicts, networks of affiliation and patronage, institutions founded and sustained. Yet there remained an uncannily hagiographical echo reverberating amid (at least some of the reception of) this intellectual labor, historical women morphing into exemplars, their life stories heard as responses to an almost utopian longing for an unearthed, long-buried narrative about the past that might portend a still different, brighter future. This is not to dismiss altogether the notion of the utopian, which has contributed richly to feminist theory and activism, but to recognize its sometimes vexed relationship to the project of feminist critique.[3]

Then two things happened more or less at the same time: first, women's history seemed to have run its course, giving way to the history of gender, or the history of sexuality, or both. Second, history itself took a turn, variously characterized as the linguistic turn, the literary turn, or the cultural turn. The conversation changed as the theoretical frameworks of semiotics, rhetoric, and poststructuralist critique replaced the certainties of *We Were There* with the seductive instabilities of *différance*. There was no single watershed moment, but surely at least one critical turning point was the publication of Joan Wallach Scott's now-canonical essay "Gender: A Useful Category of Historical Analysis" in the *American Historical Review* in 1986. In this essay, Scott formulated a twofold definition of gender (as a mode for expressing cultural meanings associated with perceived sexual difference and as a way of codifying and signifying power).[4] Even though Scott herself had originally written the title of her essay as a question—"Is Gender a Useful Category of Historical Analysis?"—and then had seen her question turned into a declaration by the editors of the *AHR*, who insisted that the titles of articles in the journal could not end in a question mark, her essay nevertheless signaled a critical turn.[5] Attention pivoted away from women's history as a subset of social history and toward a cultural or ideological history, attentive to how language and other processes of signification produce certain historical effects. Women did not fully disappear as historical actors, but the self-evidence of the category itself was called thoroughly into question. Increasingly scholars began to focus their attention on how talk about and cultural representations of women serve political and theological ends, regardless of the presence or absence of women as historical actors in the contestations in question. Clark herself documented some of the impact of these changes for the field of early Christian studies in her 1998 essay "The Lady Vanishes."[6] This move was not without controversy: whereas some critics of the literary turn worried over the erasure or effacement of historical women, others insisted that the writing of history cannot be held captive to an untheorized or undertheorized identity politics. As Joan Scott put it in her most recent book, *The Fantasy of Feminist History,* "identities don't preexist their strategic political invocations."[7]

The older question of Where are the women? was a question, then, posed by and for social history. Ironically, for the history of early Christianity, hagiography answered the question, but answered it slant, as Emily Dickinson might have put it. That is, social history is precisely the sort of history that hagiography is ill-equipped to address in the first place, since it answers to a different set of imperatives and logics and operates at a different register. In order to make late ancient hagiography answer to the imperatives of twentieth-century social-historical commitments, one would have had to contain the wild excesses of hagiography within a kind of reductive framework. Meanwhile, the hagiographical tradition also happened to muddle the purportedly transparent identity categories presupposed by the question Where are the women? Christian hagiography put the spotlight on exemplary women but then immediately and delightfully called their stable identities *as women* into question. We know this now to be a commonplace in early Christian sources, including the *Life of Melania the Younger,* where, in the prologue, her biographer commits himself to narrating "the manly deeds of this blessed woman."[8] Later, he testifies to her reception by the monks at Nitria "as if she were a man," when "in truth, she had been detached from the female nature and had acquired a masculine disposition, or rather a heavenly one."[9] Old-school hagiography was an occasion of gender trouble *avant la lettre.* In this sense, Melania is the kind of saint that even Judith Butler could love.

What exactly are we to do with hagiographical literature like *The Life of Melania the Younger,* having passed through the age of *We Were There* and through the time of the linguistic (or literary or cultural) turn? Now that even Judith Butler and Joan Scott have been heard in public uttering an exasperated and near-heretical "Enough already with gender!"[10]—where are we to turn? What is the feminist future of the past?

To think this question through, I find myself putting three different theoretical fragments together—fragments concerning the genre of hagiography, figurations of sanctity, and a recent turn in political philosophy: not a linguistic turn, but a religious one.

Fragment one: Michel de Certeau's theoretical reflection on the genre of hagiography as a variant of historiography, a variant he seeks to rescue from expulsion from the professional practice of thinking about and reconstructing the past.[11] Certeau opens his essay on the question with an evocation of hagiography's marginality, transgressiveness, and otherness: "On the outer edge of historiography," he announces, "as its temptation and betrayal, there exists another discourse . . . a corpus of difference."[12] It is a discourse that violates norms, speaks the language of the body and narratively thematizes whole "systems of representation."[13] So—hagiography as a marginal, excessive, morally charged discourse of difference, uncannily akin to feminist theory's own intervention into historiography and academic writing as a whole, via the notion of *différance*.

Fragment two: the recent religious turn in certain political-theory circles on the left and the consequent emergence of the figure of the saint as a privileged signifier for resistance and critique. For example, in "Politics, Psychoanalysis, and Religion in the Age of Terror," a chapter of his recent book on Marxism and psychoanalysis in Latin America, the literary critic Bruno Bosteels observes how philosophers on the left in recent years have not merely turned toward religion and political theology as resources for theoretical renewal but specifically have sought "to model new forms of militantism upon the figure of the saint."[14] Bosteels cites Badiou's and Žižek's Saint Paul, Hardt and Negri's Saint Francis, and alongside them Derrida's engagement with Saint Augustine (and Hélène Cixous's portrait of Jacques Derrida as a Young Jewish Saint). Bosteels writes: "The saint confronts us with a tangle of references at the intersection between politics, religion, and psychoanalysis. In fact, insofar as saints seem to come marching in at an almost unstoppable speed, few tasks could be more urgent today than to begin unraveling this dense tangle of references."[15] The remainder of the chapter engages in a close reading of the Argentine theorist León Rozitchner's *La cosa y la cruz: Cristianismo y capitalismo (en torno a las Confesiones de san Agustín)*.[16] Rozitchner's book is a subject for a different day, but Bosteels's provocation is nevertheless compelling, and as confounding as I can find the likes of Badiou and Žižek (among others) in their attempts to make Paul the patron saint of their own minds,[17] I nevertheless find myself wondering how this turn to sanctity among political philosophers relates to the project of understanding how late ancient sources are renewed by new theoretical framings at different moments in scholarly history.

Fragment three: taking up Joan Scott's insistence that identities do not preexist their strategic political invocations, what would it mean to think now about the identity, not of woman or women, but of the saint as an identity currently invoked strategically and politically in so many venues? And what would it mean to read the *Life of Melania the Younger* in such terms—not as an empirical history of a particular early Christian woman, which we have already concluded is a dead end, but as an instantiation of the very category of saintliness—and a saintliness that not only addresses political and theological conflicts in her own time or its immediate aftermath but also offers a critique for other times as well? And may thinking about Melania in these terms offer an opportunity for a feminist intervention into the new hagiography of the political left, which seems to be reinscribing a particular masculinist genealogy of Christian sainthood in its exuberance for its own religious turn? What may such a reading look like?

Rereading *The Life of Melania the Younger* with these questions in mind produced a renewed sense of its remarkable strangeness, its radical inversions of conventional values, its peculiar attention to unresolved details, its "holy zones of weirdness," to invoke Kathleen Skerrett's evocative turn of phrase.[18] If the saint has come in recent years to stand for a disruption of the dominant paradigms and a possible resource for critique, can Melania be reread—not as a straightforward exemplar of early Christian womanhood but as a saintly if ambivalent avatar for a hypermaterialist age?

On one reading, *The Life of Melania the Younger* may seem to be just one more example of the genre of the saint's *life*, trafficking in familiar tropes: noble birth (blood as "a metaphor for grace," as Certeau puts it),[19] a series of encounters with obstacles and opponents (wealth, parental authority, the weather, heresy, the devil himself), numerous opportunities to display virtue through ascetical rigors, various accounts of miraculous interventions and wise teachings, and a narrative arc that culminates in the rewards of eternal life. Articulated in a genre akin to the ancient romance, the saint's *life* performs what Certeau calls "a 'vacation' function."[20] It offers itself up as a delicious, even forbidden treat—as Melania herself is said, having finished her more sober meal of scripture and homilies, to have gobbled up the *lives* of the Fathers as if she were eating dessert.[21] A brief aside on the sweet delectability of saintly stories: One begins to wonder about the archetypical possibilities of the reception of saints' *lives* in their forbidden deliciousness when, a millennium and a half later, the classicist, translator, and poet Anne Carson confesses in an essay on women mystics that, at age five, she needed to be restrained from her own exuberantly readerly response to a book of saints' *lives*, whose words and images were so luscious that she wanted to eat the pages.[22]

So, on one reading, *The Life of Melania the Younger* merely presents itself as another example of a familiar (if delicious) genre. But the *Life* is also filled with so many curious details, excesses that complicate the path from renunciation to reward considerably, details that invite us to a rereading focusing less on gender than on saintliness. In their 2011 edited volume, *Saints: Faith without Borders*, the medievalist Françoise Meltzer and the late ancient art historian Jaś Elsner begin by reflecting on modernity's fascination with "excess, marginality, transgression, porous subjectivity—terms that also define the curious category of the saint."[23] Saints, they argue, are aligned with rhetorical forms that are by definition exorbitant. Their bodies are sites of surplus, their worlds filled with endless antinomies.[24]

Their very existence *as* saints refuses domestication and, more broadly, the underlying structures that govern the household: *oikonomia* itself.

The refusal of domestication and of *oikonomia* lies at the heart of Melania's story, even as it is a story of longing for a different kind of home. The narrative is framed by this opposition: her biographer opens the narrative by telling his readers that Melania is from a senatorial family, "foremost among Romans of senatorial rank."[25] Seventy chapters later, as he narrates her afterlife, she is welcomed into eternity by heavenly royalty: angels, prophets, apostles, and martyrs—one elite social formation exchanged for another, one familial framework for another, an earthly home abandoned in search of a heavenly one.

But this exchange takes place through a relentless lifetime of smaller material transactions. Indeed, the *Life* stages the refusal of *oikonomia* most notably through a seemingly endless series of entanglements with property, problems of ownership, and the power of money. Melania does not struggle for a moment against the corrupting diversions of sexual desire (at least not against her own)—indeed, she is described from the start as wounded by divine love and filled with hatred for the world after having had the experience of marriage.[26] But as she tries to extricate herself from the conventional demands of her marital circumstances, she sets herself to remaking her own subjectivity in other terms. In the process, she turns the tables on the relationship between sex and money. Moreover, the inconvenient children she has borne are meanwhile dispatched with remarkable narrative economy, and Melania is left to bask in her mystical and quasi-erotic woundedness. But in this whole narrative process, Melania introduces an alternative economy, domesticity, and sexuality into the mix. As the story unfolds, she is not above manipulation, subterfuge, or shady side deals to get her way, and even at one point stages a dramatic hunger strike to resist her parents' authority.

Melania emerges early on in the narrative as a precocious ascetic, wounded by divine love, yearning for Christ from her earliest youth, longing for bodily chastity. But her drive toward sexual purity appears rather remarkably in the terms of monetary exchange. Having "had the experience of marriage and totally despising the world," in desperation ("begging ... with much piteous wailing"), she comes up with an ingenious quid pro quo, an inverted prostitution: in place of the conventional prostitutional exchange—sex for money—she offers her husband instead all her property in exchange for no-sex. If this is not a parody of the transactions of prostitution, then it is certainly an inversionary send-up of the conventional marriage contract. For she proposes to her young husband—she is fourteen; he is seventeen—an explicit exchange, a pact: "If, my lord, you consent to practice chastity along with me and live with me according to the law of continence, I contract with you as the lord and master of my life. If, however, this seems burdensome to you, and if you do not have the strength to bear the burning passion of youth, just look: I place before you all my possessions; hereafter you are master of them and may use them as you wish, if only you will leave my body free so that I may present it spotless, with my soul, to Christ on that fearsome day. For it is in this way that I shall fulfill my desire for God [tēn kata Theon mou epithymian]."²⁷ This proposed property exchange, this inverted marriage contract, opens up the prospect that she might pursue with unreserved fervor her true love-object: God.

Melania's relationship to money and property continues to dominate the entire narrative. Born into unfathomable wealth, she becomes both a disobedient daughter and a class traitor in her relentless desire to divest herself of her property. The *Life* devotes several chapters to Melania's project of divestment, part of her and her husband's larger project of making themselves "enemies to the confusions of secular life."²⁸ The chapters about property, though polemically devoted to a broader narrative arc about Melania's single-minded commitment to ascetic renunciation, inadvertently introduce a more complicated story about the problematic adhesiveness of private ownership. It is easier, it seems, for a camel to pass through the eye of a needle than for even the most determined Roman aristocrat to dispose of her obscene surplus of wealth.

Weighted down by houses and estates and slaves in Rome, its suburbs, and several imperial provinces, Melania and her husband encounter multiple obstacles to divestment. Where other saints' *lives* typically dispatch worldly possessions in a few short sentences, here the narrator lingers over the problems associated with getting rid of all the property. So, Pinian's house in Rome is unsalable because no one—not a single senator nor even the empress Serena herself—has enough money to buy it for what it is worth, and ultimately "they let it go for less than nothing since it was burned [after the barbarian invasion of Rome]."²⁹ There are other properties around Rome, Italy, Spain, Campania, and beyond that need all to be sold. When these are finally disposed of just in advance of Alaric's invasion, people say how lucky they were to sell before the arrival of the barbarians.³⁰ And yet, still more properties remain to be dispatched—in Sicily, Africa, Mauretania, Britain, and beyond.³¹

Real estate is not Melania's only vexing problem when it comes to her property. Perhaps the most curious episodes in the *Life* concern the disposition of the slaves on her and Pinian's estate outside Rome. Upon learning of their plans to sell their slaves, Pinian's brother Severus reportedly stirs up the slaves, who say: "If we are forced to be sold, rather than to be put on the open market, we prefer to have your brother Severus as our master and buy us."³² Although clearly an opportunistic and self-serving effort on the part of Severus to benefit from his brother's impulse toward divestment, the upheaval it represents is attributed by the narrator to a cosmic opponent: "the devil, the enemy of truth." Within a few sentences, the slaves' request (whatever its proximate cause) becomes transformed into an occasion "when their slaves in the suburbs revolted."³³ It is too much to expect that a narrative from this period would contain the seeds of an abolitionist impulse. Yet it is noteworthy that, at the level of the narrative's logic, the enslaved multitude of Melania's domestic and agricultural workforce remains cast either still as (actual or potential) property or as pawns in a cosmic drama, pitting the saint against the forces of perdition. Indeed, it is this conflict that causes Melania to manipulate her network and to appeal directly to the empress Serena for help to resolve the situation. So much for simple divestment–divestment that might, theoretically at least, have included manumission of the enslaved workers. Melania stays uneasily embedded in the economic networks and spheres of influence that come to her as her birthright, even as she seeks to get out from under them.

The overarching goal of the various proposed transactions scattered throughout the narrative is the divestment of property, but every narrative instance ends up emphasizing the near-impossibility of Melania's making a definitive deal. Her proposed antimarriage contract is neither accepted nor rejected. Rather her virtue is put in spiritual escrow by Pinian, who insists that they must have two children before entertaining a life of married chastity. In the case of Melania's slaves, the property itself—the enslaved workers on Melania's estate outside Rome—refuses to perform its assigned role as the object to be exchanged in the service of Melania's progressive spiritual journey. Indeed, as the narrative unfolds, one has a sense of all elements of the material world and the materialization of wealth itself as embodiments or instantiations of excess, wildness, noncooperation with sanctity—sanctity's twin and opposite: the house that is too expensive to find a buyer and ends up in ashes following the barbarian invasions, the slaves whose audacity to express a preference regarding to whom they might be sold framed as demonically inspired—and later, gifts and tips refused, the gold coins hidden in hermits' caves but theatrically rejected by their recipients, and so on. No transaction is ever straightforwardly resolved in this *life;* money and property adhere uneasily to the saint, possessions themselves stubbornly and sometimes demonically seeking to possess her.

The devil himself intervenes explicitly in chapters 17 and 18 of the *Life,* taunting Melania by suggesting that she is trying to buy her way into heaven—"What sort of place is this Kingdom of Heaven, that it can be bought with so much money?"[34]—and by emphasizing the value and beauty of her estate, an argument that she must fight off with thoughts of the vulnerability of these riches "that today exist and tomorrow will be destroyed by the barbarians, or by fire, or by time, or by some other circumstance"—though even here, there is no complete disruption of *oikonomia* possible, only the substitution of "these corruptible things" by "eternal goods that exist forever."[35] And virtue itself and religious devotions are pursued not for their own sake but to assure an advantageous place in the future divine economy: pieties and rigors point toward "reward . . . in the age to come."[36]

There are many other places in the text where the paradoxes of Melania's wealth and property, where monetary transactions that serve the larger project emerge in quirky details: on the verge of the birth of her second doomed child, Melania keeps vigil all night—the Feast of St. Lawrence—and, according to the Latin version of the *Life*, bribes the eunuchs sent by her father to surveil her not to betray her to him.[37] Later, the *Life* informs us that "by money and admonitions she persuaded many young men and women to stay clear of licentiousness and an impure manner of life,"[38] another occasion of the exchange of money for no-sex. Despite her reportedly complete divestment of property, she nevertheless buys islands for monks and builds and endows monasteries.[39] These transactions can withstand closer analysis, but for the purposes of this essay I simply want to emphasize the remarkable way in which money and property keep reappearing as the centerpiece of Melania's sanctity—but in a paradoxical yet inescapable fashion.

There is more to be said about materiality and the paradoxical role of property in the *Life of Melania*, but this short exercise in reading for the identity of the saint in this text—an identity produced out of strategic political invocation, as Joan Scott would have it—draws our attention to the enigmatic places in the text, the odd narrative circlings-back, the attention to material details: the holy zones of weirdness that may make a productive sort of imaginative intervention into our own peculiar historical moment when *oikonomia* (as both economy and the household) is both the source and the subject of such complicated contestation.

Melania's struggles to extract herself from the system of wealth and exchange that entangled her, her desire for a different set of entanglements, mark her with the sign of saintliness—an excessive refusal of the prevailing systems of value. But what of the contemporary embrace of the saint in our own time? Likely it is no accident but rather an acknowledgment of the saint as a potentially productive figure for the refusal of our own prevailing systems of value—in particular the market. Taking the matter a step further, does not *the study of the saint* (such study as a synecdoche for humanistic inquiry as a whole) also perform a similar refusal of the ubiquity of market forces?

In a recent essay, Adi Ophir briefly traces the history of *Geisteswissenschaften*, arguing that the radical challenge of the humanities ("the sciences of the spirit") resides "not in their subject matter but rather the way men and women of spirit spend their time.... This activity involves a labor of the mind detached from any necessity, in which the product cannot be dissociated from the process and cannot be imagined or modeled beforehand; the product's value cannot be estimated in advance, and often not in retrospect."[40] There is of course a limit to the analogy I am sketching: the humanities are not a religious or theological project, and scholars are not, generally speaking, exactly saintly. But there remains something suggestive in the attention that the saint receives at the moment, invested with a mix of resistance and hopefulness. When Ophir writes of the history of *Geisteswissenschaften*, he emphasizes how the spirit figures simultaneously as an effect of subtraction and as a supplement.[41] In this frame, one finds a reflection of the hagiographical figurations of the saint (Melania) in scholarly efforts to retrieve from an ancient life a story worthy of historical analysis, both hagiography and scholarly reconstruction indifferent to the logics of exchange and use value, committed rather to an alternative living-out of a different set of values. This is not to romanticize the figure of either Melania or the scholar who spends time reconstructing the history of the text that once celebrated her existence or translating that text for an audience of modern readers. But it is to notice that both projects—Melania's exhausting and imperfectly achieved project of separating herself from her material possessions and the scholar's attention to long-past religious impulses, activities, and affinities—(both projects) resist the dominant economic logics of their own moments, the tendencies of their social worlds to define value solely in terms of use and exchange and to reduce all other forms of activity to incoherence and waste.

As the production of knowledge has moved from the reconstruction of women's history through a feminist history of *différance* and the cultural turn, and now on to the rereading of saintly histories in the service of recuperating the figure of the saint as a political resource for cultural critique and even for a defense of the life of the mind, perhaps the *Life of Melania the Younger* may offer up a small supplement—in all its enigmatic peculiarity—to the broader project of theorizing saintliness in our own moment of vexed political economy.

NOTES

1. Gerontius, *The Life of Melania the Younger*, trans. Elizabeth A. Clark, *The Life of Melania the Younger: Introduction, Translation, and Commentary* (Lewiston, N.Y.: Edwin Mellen Press, 1984). For the broader impact of Clark's work in the field of late ancient Christianity, see Dale B. Martin and Patricia Cox Miller, eds., *The Cultural Turn in Late Ancient Studies: Gender, Asceticism, and Historiography* (Durham: Duke University Press, 2005).

2. Barbara Mayer Wertheimer, *We Were There: The Story of Working Women in America* (New York: Pantheon Books, 1977).

3. The literature on feminist utopian thought is wide-ranging. See Angelika Bammer, *Partial Visions: Feminism and Utopianism in the 1970s* (New York: Routledge, 1991); Jennifer Burwell, *Notes on Nowhere: Feminism, Utopian Logic, and Social Transformation* (Minneapolis: University of Minneapolis Press, 1997); and José Esteban Muñoz, *Cruising Utopia: The Then and There of Queer Futurity* (New York: New York University Press, 2009). See also the 2013 Scholar and Feminist Conference at the Barnard Center for Research on Women in New York City: http://bcrw.barnard.edu/event/utopia/.

4. This essay has a complex reception history, even in Joan Scott's own writing and thought. It was reprinted in the first edition of her *Gender and Politics of History* (New York: Columbia University Press, 1988) and then again in the revised edition of that collection published in 1999. The revised edition includes a preface in which Scott ponders rather pessimistically the ongoing usefulness of the category gender, which in her view has been domesticated and eviscerated of its political power. For a full discussion of the problematics involved, see Judith Butler and Elizabeth Weed, eds., *The Question of Gender: Joan W. Scott's Critical Feminism* (Bloomington: Indiana University Press, 2011).

5. Judith Butler and Elizabeth Weed, "Introduction," in *The Question of Gender*, 1.
6. Elizabeth A. Clark, "The Lady Vanishes: Dilemmas of a Feminist Historian after the 'Linguistic Turn,'" *Church History* 67 (1998): 1–31.
7. Joan Wallach Scott, *The Fantasy of Feminist History* (Durham: Duke University Press, 2011), 46.
8. Gerontius, *Life of Melania the Younger*, prol. (trans. E. A. Clark, 25). Note that throughout I cite Clark's English translation of the Greek text (hereafter *Life*). See also *Vie de sainte Mélanie: Texte grec, introduction, traduction et notes*, ed. and trans. Denys Gorce, Sources Chrétiennes 90 (Paris: Cerf, 1962), quote at 126.
9. Gerontius, *Life* 39 (ed. Gorce, SC 90: 200–202; trans. E. A. Clark, 54).
10. Judith Butler, "Speaking Up, Talking Back: Joan Scott's Critical Feminism," in *The Question of Gender*, ed. Judith Butler and Elizabeth Weed, 11–28, quotation at 21. See also Judith Butler, Éric Fassin, and Joan Wallach Scott, "Pour ne pas finir avec le 'genre' . . . : Table ronde," *Sociétés et Répresentations* 24 (2007): 285–306.
11. Michel de Certeau, "A Variant: Hagio-Graphical Edification," in *The Writing of History*, trans. Tom Conley (New York: Columbia University Press, 1988), 269–83.
12. Ibid., 269.
13. Ibid., 275, 279.
14. Bruno Bosteels, *Marx and Freud in Latin America: Politics, Psychoanalysis, and Religion in Times of Terror* (London: Verso, 2012), 129–57, quotation at 129.
15. Ibid., 129–30.
16. Buenos Aires: Editorial Losada, 1997.
17. Elizabeth A. Castelli, "The Philosophers' Paul in the Frame of the Global: Some Reflections," *South Atlantic Quarterly* 109 (2010): 653–76; reprinted, with minor changes, in *Paul and the Philosophers*, ed. Ward Blanton and Hent de Vries (New York: Fordham University Press, 2013), 143–58.
18. Kathleen Roberts Skerrett, "Sex, Law, and Other Reasonable Endeavors," *differences: A Journal of Feminist Cultural Studies* 18 (2007): 81–96, quotation at 94.
19. Certeau, "Variant," 276.
20. Ibid., 272–73.
21. Gerontius, *Life* 23 (ed. Gorce, SC 90: 174; trans. E. A. Clark, 45).
22. Anne Carson, "Decreation: How Women Like Sappho, Marguerite Porete and Simone Weil Tell God," in *Decreation: Poetry, Essays, Opera* (New York: Knopf, 2005), 155–83, episode at 175.
23. Françoise Meltzer and Jaś Elsner, "Introduction," in *Saints: Faith without Borders*, ed. Françoise Meltzer and Jaś Elsner (Chicago: University of Chicago Press, 2011), ix.
24. Ibid., xii.
25. Gerontius, *Life*, prol. 1 (ed. Gorce, SC 90: 130; trans. E. A. Clark, 25, 27).
26. Ibid. 1 (ed. Gorce, SC 90: 130; trans. E. A. Clark, 27).
27. Ibid. 1 (ed. Gorce, SC 90: 130–32; trans. E. A. Clark, 28).
28. Ibid. 7 (ed. Gorce, SC 90: 140; trans. E. A. Clark, 31).
29. Ibid. 14 (ed. Gorce, SC 90: 156; trans. E. A. Clark, 38).
30. Ibid. 19 (ed. Gorce, SC 90: 162–64; trans. E. A. Clark, 41–42).
31. Ibid. 11 (ed. Gorce, SC 90: 144–46; trans. E. A. Clark, 34).
32. Ibid. 10 (ed. Gorce, SC 90: 144–46; trans. E. A. Clark, 33).
33. Ibid. 10–11 (ed. Gorce, SC 90: 144–46; trans. E. A. Clark, 33–34).
34. Ibid. 17 (ed. Gorce, SC 90: 160; trans. E. A. Clark, 40).
35. Ibid. 18 (ed. Gorce, SC 90: 162; trans. E. A. Clark, 40–41).
36. Ibid. 46 (ed. Gorce, SC 90: 214; trans. E. A. Clark, 59).
37. Ibid. 5 (ed. Gorce, SC 90: 134; trans. E. A. Clark, 29). On the Latin version, see ibid., trans. E. A. Clark, 189 note 6.

38. Ibid. 29 (ed. Gorce, SC 90: 182; trans. E. A. Clark, 47).
39. Ibid. 19 (ed. Gorce, SC 90: 162–64; trans. E. A. Clark, 41).
40. Adi Ophir, "The Sciences of Spirit," *differences: A Journal of Feminist Cultural Studies* 24 (2014): 160–74, quotation at 164.
41. Ibid., 168.

Afterword

Randall Styers

In *The Pasteurization of France,* the philosopher and historian of science Bruno Latour masterfully dispels the notion that the phenomenon we know by the name Louis Pasteur was an autonomous and self-sufficient thinker single-handedly unlocking the secrets of the microbe.[1] Despite the pervasive mystique surrounding Pasteur, Latour is intent on demonstrating that this figure is better understood as one node in a wide-ranging web of social agents and material forces, a web that included broad networks of medical researchers and social reformers, global political and colonial interests, emerging mechanisms for the dissemination of scientific discovery, specific items of medical apparatus, and even the microbes themselves, which could be identified, cultivated, and mobilized to establish new forms of scientific truth. Pasteur's discoveries and their impact, together with the individual agency of the figure himself, were not the product of a singular genius but a development of that complex web. As Latour explains: "A crowd may move a mountain; a single man cannot. If, therefore, we say of a man that he has moved a mountain, it is because he has been credited with (or has appropriated) the work of the crowd that he claimed to command but that he also followed."[2]

The essays collected in this volume bear ample witness to Latour's argument. Just as the nineteenth-century Louis Pasteur can best be understood by considering his place within the broad network that constituted his conditions of possibility, so also Melania the Elder and Melania the Younger, these intriguing aristocratic Roman women, can best be understood by exploring their positions with much broader social and material structures. The authors of the essays compiled here demonstrate the centrality of expansive systems in constituting these women—systems of late ancient property ownership and economic exchange, social class, household and gender regulation, religious difference and conflict, geographic and material environments, even modern cultural and scholarly appropriation. What we can see of the personal agency of the Melanias unfolds within that network, and that agency itself is, in turn, a product of the workings of the network. Extending the narration of the lives of these women to include the range of agents, institutions, and forces that gave them shape provides invaluable new insights on these women and their significance in early Christian history.

At the same time, as the essays in this volume also attest, renarrating the lives of these women also opens a rich window onto the current state of the scholarly study of the late ancient Christian world. The very structure of this volume demonstrates the vitality and breadth of contemporary early Christian studies. The authors of these essays ask compelling new questions—many without definitive answers—as they use the lives of the Melanias to move the scholarly conversation in provocative new directions.

In this regard, these authors demonstrate the deep influence of their mentor, Elizabeth A. Clark. As the introduction to this volume explains, Clark's work has revolutionized early Christian studies. In a series of groundbreaking texts since the late 1970s, she has expanded the canon, challenged entrenched scholarly categories, introduced invaluable new methodological tools, and taught by example the value of historicizing and contextualizing every aspect of the historian's craft.

Bruno Latour warns us against simplistic hagiography, a caution we should surely heed here. Elizabeth Clark's career reflects the dramatic theoretical revolution that has spread throughout the humanities since the 1960s. By the 1980s the field of patristics itself was evolving in ways that could receive her insights (despite some hard-worn growing pains). Surely the crop of emerging young scholars who gravitated to study with Clark demonstrates the receptivity to her work in the most fertile academic quarters. Liz Clark did not move a mountain single-handedly, but at the same time she was in the vanguard, exerting enormous energy, creativity, and methodological innovation as she worked to remake the craft of late ancient history.[3]

Early Christian studies has changed dramatically under Clark's tutelage, but her influence has also spread far beyond that specific field of inquiry. Throughout her career, Clark's work has both reflected and inspired enormous transformation within the discipline of religious studies more broadly. Over the past six decades, the academic study of religion has expanded dramatically, moving from its earlier home in denominational schools and seminaries and into new university settings, particularly public research universities. These new departments came to house an extraordinary array of scholars trained in fields as varied as textual studies and literary theory, history, ethnography, sociology, psychology, philosophy, art, archaeology, and critical cultural theory. As Mark C. Taylor has underscored, this expansion in institutional context, together with the growing cultural emphasis over recent decades on multiculturalism and pluralism, has prompted major changes in the discipline.⁴ Religious dogmatism is no longer so dominant in teaching or research in these new contexts, and the distinction between religious studies and theological studies has become far more pronounced in many quarters. At the same time, the confluence of divergent methods in these new settings has provided an opening for new forms of critical social analysis of the operations of religion.

Other changes have also taken root. Religion, the concept at the heart of this discipline, has always proved notoriously difficult to define.⁵ But that difficulty assumed a different tone in light of Wilfred Cantwell Smith's recognition of the specifically Western (and Christian) origins of the modern notion of religion.⁶ A generation of recent scholars has worked to excavate the concrete genealogy of the concept—the deep level at which it is shaped by Christian, and specifically Protestant, theological norms.

Even as the discipline's central concept has been historicized in new ways, so also a host of related disciplinary vocabulary (foundational terms such as myth, mysticism, ritual, and so on) has been subjected to similar critical, historical analysis. At the same time, a range of other scholars—using the tools of Marxism, postcolonial theory, and other critical methods—has moved to interrogate the concrete ideological foundations on which the discipline of religious studies itself rests. The cultural history of the study of religion has become a major source of critical self-reflection for the discipline, and this inquiry has, in turn, shed invaluable light on the constitution of Western modernity more broadly.

Elizabeth Clark has been a central figure in the critical turn that has characterized religious studies over recent decades. Her work is permeated with deep critical insight, and her writing has modeled the application of tools drawn from contemporary literary and critical social theory to late ancient studies. Clark has utilized—and honed—conceptual resources drawn from critical methods ranging from feminist theory to social-network theory. In her 2004 *History, Theory, Text: Historians and the Linguistic Turn*, for example, she worked to demonstrate to a new generation of historians the bounty to be found in literary and cultural theory for the study of historical texts.⁷ In that book, she offered a masterful survey of an enormous range of contemporary critical theory, but her primary objective was to contextualize these new approaches within an expansive intellectual history, showing their deep links to long-standing epistemological issues central to the historical method. And in this context, Clark also offered concrete case studies to demonstrate the value of these theoretical tools for the study of premodernity.

In addition, over her career Clark has worked to offer invaluable critical interrogation of concepts such as orthodoxy, heterodoxy, and other terms central to the vocabulary of modern scholarship on religion. In her most recent publications, Clark has turned explicitly to explore the cultural history of the study of religion, as she has worked to excavate the cultural dynamics within which early church history was institutionalized in American higher education through the nineteenth and the early twentieth century.[8] This recent research has focused on the ideological and social interests—and unexpected preoccupations—that shaped the study of Christian history in these new institutional settings.

One of the great testaments to Clark's vision has been the array of scholars from wide-ranging fields of study who have benefited from her insights and her example. Clark's work is deeply grounded in the methods of history, and that grounding has allowed her not simply to utilize static theoretical tools but instead to test and modify—and often sharpen—those tools as she engages her source materials and historical contexts. Clark's methodological prowess, her intellectual rigor, and her theoretical sophistication have given her an authority to assess the value of critical methods and concepts that few contemporary scholars can equal. Her work is invaluable to an enormous range of historians (of the late ancient world, of premodernity, and of Western culture more broadly), religious studies scholars of every variety, critical theorists, and creative thinkers throughout the humanities.

Elizabeth Clark's scholarly career has exemplified a range of intellectual virtues, beginning with her boundless energy, deep curiosity, and meticulous attention to detail. But Clark has also shown a deep recognition that she cannot work alone—her efforts have turned on her ability to mobilize a broad cadre of students, colleagues, and intellectual companions toward common scholarly passions. Through her boundless hospitality and deep generosity, her diligent mentoring and promotion of a new generation of scholars and colleagues, and her graceful leadership within the institutions of her scholarly disciplines, Clark has mobilized and inspired a broad network of compatriots and institutional structures, all in an effort to challenge the status quo in unexpected ways, to invigorate the imagination of what is possible, to help make the world anew.

NOTES

1. Bruno Latour, *The Pasteurization of France*, trans. Alan Sheridan and John Law (Cambridge, Mass.: Harvard University Press, 1988).

2. Ibid., 22.

3. See in this regard Elizabeth A. Castelli, "The Future of Sainthood," in this volume.

4. Mark C. Taylor, "Introduction," in Taylor, ed., *Critical Terms for Religious Studies* (Chicago: University of Chicago Press, 1998), 12–13.

5. See, for example, James H. Leuba, "Appendix," in *A Psychological Study of Religion: Its Origin, Function, and Future* (New York: AMS Press, 1912), 339–61, listing almost fifty definitions of "religion" from various major thinkers beyond the set of definitions Leuba addresses in the body of his text.

6. See Wilfred Cantwell Smith, *The Meaning and End of Religion: A New Approach to the Religious Traditions of Mankind* (New York: Macmillan, 1963).

7. See Elizabeth A. Clark, *History, Theory, Text: Historians and the Linguistic Turn* (Cambridge, Mass.: Harvard University Press, 2004).

8. See Elizabeth A. Clark, *Founding the Fathers: Early Church History and Protestant Professors in Nineteenth-Century America* (Philadelphia: University of Pennsylvania Press, 2011).

CONTRIBUTORS

ELIZABETH A. CASTELLI is Ann Whitney Olin Professor of Religion at Barnard College. She is the author of *Martyrdom and Memory: Early Christian Culture-Making* (New York: Columbia University Press, 2004) and the translator of Pier Paolo Pasolini's *Saint Paul* (London: Verso, 2012). She is the editorial director of *The Marginalia Review of Books* and the founding editor of *Postscripts: The Journal of Sacred Texts and Contemporary Worlds*.

CATHERINE M. CHIN is Associate Professor of Classics at the University of California at Davis. She is the author of *Grammar and Christianity in the Late Roman World* (Philadelphia: University of Pennsylvania Press, 2008), and co-editor, with Moulie Vidas, of *Late Ancient Knowing: Explorations in Intellectual History* (Berkeley and Los Angeles: University of California Press, 2015).

L. STEPHANIE COBB is the George and Sallie Cutchin Camp Professor of Bible at the University of Richmond. She is the author of numerous articles on gender and sexuality in early Christian history and the author of *Dying to Be Men: Gender and Language in Early Christian Martyr Texts* (New York: Columbia University Press, 2008). She is currently working on a monograph examining discourses of the body and pain in early Christian martyr texts.

STEPHEN J. DAVIS is Professor of Religious Studies at Yale University. He has authored several books, including *The Cult of St. Thecla* (Oxford: Oxford University Press, 2001), *The Early Coptic Papacy* (Cairo and New York: AUC Press, 2004), *Coptic Christology in Practice* (Oxford: Oxford University Press, 2008), and *Christ Child: Cultural Memories of a Young Jesus* (New Haven: Yale University Press, 2014). He is also the founder and executive director of the Yale Monastic Archaeology Project (YMAP).

MARIA DOERFLER is Assistant Professor of Religious Studies at Yale University. Her work has been published in the *Journal of Early Christian Studies*, the *Journal of Ecclesiastical History*, *Church History*, and *Le Muséon*. She is currently working on her first book project, on Roman law, monasticism, and the development of clerical identity in the early fifth century.

SUSANNA DRAKE is Associate Professor of Religious Studies at Macalester College. She is the author of *Slandering the Jew: Sexuality and Difference in Early Christian Texts* (Philadelphia: University of Pennsylvania Press, 2013), and is currently working on a monograph on veiling in late antiquity.

ANDREW S. JACOBS is Professor of Religious Studies and Mary W. and J. Stanley Johnson Professor of Humanities at Scripps College. He is the author of *Remains of the Jews: The Holy Land and Christian Empire in Late Antiquity* (Stanford: Stanford University Press, 2004), *Christ Circumcised: A Study in Early Christian History and Difference* (Philadelphia: University of Pennsylvania Press, 2012), and *Epiphanius of Cyprus: A Cultural Biography of Late Antiquity* (Berkeley and Los Angeles: University of California Press, forthcoming [2016]).

REBECCA KRAWIEC is Professor and Chair of Religious Studies and Theology at Canisius College. She is the author of numerous articles on asceticism and gender that have appeared in the *Journal of Early Christian Studies* and *Church History*. and is the author of *Shenoute and the Women of the White Monastery: Egyptian Monasticism in Late Antiquity* (Oxford: Oxford University Press, 2002).

CHRISTINE LUCKRITZ MARQUIS is Assistant Professor of Church History at Union Presbyterian Seminary. She is the translator and co-editor of *The History of the Great Deeds of Bishop Paul of Quentos and Priest John of Edessa* (Piscataway, N.J.: Gorgias Press, 2010) and is currently working on a monograph on space, memory, and violence in Egyptian asceticism.

MICHAEL PENN is William R. Kenan, Jr., Professor of Religion at Mount Holyoke College. He is the author of *Kissing Christians: Ritual and Community in the Late Ancient Church* (Philadelphia: University of Pennsylvania Press, 2005), *Envisioning Islam: Syriac Christians in the Early Muslim World* (Philadelphia: University of Pennsylvania Press, 2015), and *When Christians First Met Muslims: A Source Book of the Earliest Syriac Writings on Islam* (Berkeley and Los Angeles: University of California Press, 2015).

CAROLINE T. SCHROEDER is Professor of Religious Studies at the University of the Pacific. She is the author of *Monastic Bodies: Discipline and Salvation in Shenoute of Atripe* (Philadelphia: University of Pennsylvania Press, 2007), and co-creator of *Coptic SCRIPTORIUM*, an interdisciplinary and computational research platform for work in Coptic texts. She is currently working on a book entitled *Children and Family in Late Antique Egyptian Monasticism*, under contract with Cambridge University Press.

CHRISTINE SHEPARDSON is Lindsay Young Professor of Religious Studies at the University of Tennessee at Knoxville. She is the author of *Anti-Judaism and Christian Orthodoxy: Ephrem's Hymns in Fourth-Century Syria* (Washington, D.C.: Catholic University Press, 2008) and *Controlling Contested Places: Late Antique Antioch and the Spatial Politics of Religious Controversy* (Berkeley and Los Angeles: University of California Press, 2014).

STEPHEN J. SHOEMAKER is Professor of Religious Studies at the University of Oregon and is the editor of the *Journal of Early Christian Studies*. His numerous publications include: *Ancient Traditions of the Virgin Mary's Dormition and Assumption* (Oxford: Oxford University Press, 2002), *The Death of a Prophet: The End of Muhammad's Life and the Beginnings of Islam* (Philadelphia: University of Pennsylvania Press, 2012), and *Saint Mary: Early Christian Devotion to the Mother of Jesus* (New Haven: Yale University Press, forthcoming [2016]).

RANDALL STYERS is Associate Professor and Chair of Religious Studies at the University of North Carolina at Chapel Hill. He is the author of *Making Magic: Religion, Magic, and Science in the Modern World* (Oxford: Oxford University Press, 2004) and co-editor of *Light against Darkness: Dualism in Ancient Mediterranean Religion and the Contemporary World* (Göttingen: Vandenhoeck and Ruprecht, 2011). He is currently working on a book on the politics of religious studies in contemporary university settings.

KRISTI UPSON-SAIA is Associate Professor of Religious Studies at Occidental College. She is the author of *Early Christian Dress: Gender, Virtue, and Authority* (New York: Routledge, 2011) and is the co-editor of *Dressing Judeans and Christians in Antiquity* (Aldershot: Ashgate, 2014). She is also the co-founder and co-chair of the Working Group on Religion, Medicine, Disability, and Health in Late Antiquity.

ROBIN DARLING YOUNG is Associate Professor of Spirituality at The Catholic University of America. She is the author of *"In Procession before the World": Martyrs' Sacrifices as Public Liturgy in Early Christianity* (Milwaukee: Marquette University Press, 2001) and is co-editor of numerous volumes, including *To Train His Soul in Books: Essays on Syrian Asceticism in Honor of Sidney H. Griffith* (Washington, D.C.: Catholic University of America Press, 2007) and *Ascetic Culture: Essays in Honor of Philip Rousseau* (Notre Dame: University of Notre Dame Press, 2013).

ACKNOWLEDGMENTS

We thank first Elizabeth A. Clark, to whom we dedicate this volume. Early in her career, Clark published an English translation and commentary on the *Life of Melania the Younger*, restoring Melania the Younger and her grandmother to the pantheon of early Christian luminaries after centuries of being overlooked. Clark has modeled sophisticated scholarship for an entire field, influencing research trajectories well beyond her immediate students'. As just one part of her long and distinguished career, her mentorship and instruction have created the intellectual community that has produced this book.

Most of the chapters published here were first presented at the symposium "Late Antiquity Made New," held at Duke University in April 2013. We owe the success of both the symposium and the book to program-committee members Maria Doerfler, Laura S. Lieber, Jeremy Schott, Caroline T. Schroeder, and Annabel Wharton. Maria and Laura provided fierce leadership on the ground at Duke during the planning for the event and since then have generously given their continued support for the book. The consultations leading up to the symposium and the conversations among the contributors at the event were invaluable. We also appreciate the labor of Serena Bazemore, Marissa Lane, and Tammy Thornton at Duke. In addition, Jeremy Schott helped develop the theme and overall vision for the book.

During the process of publication, the guidance and care of a number of people has helped to ensure that this book will reach its audience. We thank University of California Press editor Eric Schmidt for his advice on improving the book and for his unwavering confidence in our work. Christopher Beeley and the editorial board of the series Christianity in Late Antiquity offered important counsel as we shaped the volume. Tyler Schwaller has aided us immensely by creating and editing the bibliography. We especially appreciate the comments of the anonymous readers during the review process; their insights and suggestions have greatly improved this volume. The editors also wish to acknowledge contributor Andrew Jacobs for providing further editorial advice at key moments during the project.

This book is the product of many friendships. We are deeply grateful to the people and institutions that have allowed these friendships to flourish.

BIBLIOGRAPHY

PRIMARY SOURCES

Acta Conciliorum Oecumenicorum. Volume 1, *Concilium Universale Ephesenum*. Edited by Eduard Schwartz and Johannes Straub. Berlin: de Gruyter, 1925.

Acta Conciliorum Oecumenicorum. Volume 2, *Concilium Universale Chalcedonense*. Edited by Eduard Schwartz and Johannes Straub. Berlin: de Gruyter, 1935.

The Acts of the Christian Martyrs. Edited and translated by Herbert Musurillo. Oxford Early Christian Texts. Oxford: Clarendon Press, 1972.

The Acts of the Council of Chalcedon. Edited and translated by Richard Price and Michael Gaddis. 3 vols. Translated Texts for Historians 45. Liverpool: Liverpool University Press, 2005.

Ambrose. *De Fide*. Edited by O. Faller. Corpus Scriptorum Ecclesiasticorum Latinorum 78. Berlin: de Gruyter, 1962.

———. *De Officiis Ministrorum*. Edited by M. Testard. Corpus Christianorum, Series Latina 15. Turnhout: Brepols, 2000.

———. *De Poenitentia*. Edited by Roger Gryson. Sources Chrétiennes 179. Paris: Cerf, 1971.

———. *Epistulae et Acta*. Edited by O. Faller and M. Zelzer. Corpus Scriptorum Ecclesiasticorum Latinorum 82.1–4. Berlin: de Gruyter, 1968–96.

Anonymous. *Treatise against Novatian*. In *Novatiani Opera Quae Supersunt*, edited by G. F. Diercks. Corpus Christianorum, Series Latina 4. Turnhout: Brepols, 1972.

Aphrahat. *Demonstrationes I–XXII*. Edited by D. J. Parisot. Volume 1 of Patrologia Syriaca, edited by R. Graffin. Paris: Firmin-Didot, 1894.

———. *Demonstratio XXIII*. Edited by D. J. Parisot. In Patrologia Syriaca, vol. 2, edited by R. Graffin. Paris: Firmin-Didot, 1907.

Athanasius [of Alexandria]. *Athanasius: The Life of Antony and the Letter to Marcellinus*. Translated by Robert C. Gregg. Classics of Western Spirituality. New York: Paulist Press, 1980.

———. *Epistola ad Episcopos Aegypti et Libyae*. In *Athanasius: Werke* 1.1.1. Edited by K. Metzler. Berlin: de Gruyter, 1996.

———. *Epistola ad Palladium Presbyterum*. In *Patrologia Graeca*, edited by J.-P. Migne, 26: 1168. Paris, 1857.

———. *Lettres festales et pastorales en copte*. Edited and translated by L.-Th. Lefort. Corpus Scriptorum Christianorum Orientalium 150, 151. Louvain: Imprimerie Orientaliste L. Durbecq, 1955.

———. *Vie d'Antoine*. Edited and translated by G. J. M Bartelink. Sources Chrétiennes 400. Paris: Cerf, 1994.

Athanasius of Beni Suef, ed. *Bustān al-ruhbān li-ābā' al-kinīsa al-qibṭīya*. 2nd ed. Beni Suef: Lagnat al-taḥrīr wa al-nashr, 1976.

Augustine. *The Confessions*. Translated by Maria Boulding. Part 1, vol. 1 of *The Works of Saint Augustine: A Translation for the Twenty-First Century*. Hyde Park, N.Y.: New City Press, 1997.

———. *Confessiones*. In *Patrologia Latina*, edited by J.-P. Migne, 32: 657–868. Paris, 1841.

———. *The Confessions and Letters of St. Augustine*. Translated by J. G. Pilkington and J. G. Cunningham. Nicene and Post-Nicene Fathers, First Series, vol. 1. Buffalo: Christian Literature Publishing, 1888.

———. *Contra Secundam Iuliani Responsionem Opus Imperfectum, Libri 1–3*. Edited by M. Zelzer. Corpus Scriptorum Ecclesiasticorum Latinorum 85.1. Berlin: de Gruyter, 1974.

———. *De Civitate Dei*. Edited by Bernhard Dombart and Alphons Kalb. Corpus Christianorum, Series Latina 47, 48. Turnhout: Brepols, 1955.

———. *De Natura et Origine Animae*. Library of Latin Texts. Turnhout: Brepols, 2010.

———. *De Peccatorum Meritis et Remissione et De Baptismo Parvulorum, De Spiritu et Littera, De Natura et Gratia, De Natura et Origine Animae, Contra Duas Epistulas Pelagianorum*. Edited by C. F. Vrba and J. Zycha. Corpus Scriptorum Ecclesiasticorum Latinorum 60. Vienna: Tempsky, 1913.

———. *De Perfectione Iustitiae Hominis, De Gestis Pelagii, De Gratia Christi, De Nuptiis et Concupiscentia*. Edited by C. F. Vrba and J. Zycha. Corpus Scriptorum Ecclesiasticorum Latinorum 42. Vienna: Tempsky, 1902.

———. *Epistolae*. Edited by A. Goldbacher. Corpus Scriptorum Ecclesiasticorum Latinorum 34.1, 34.2, 44, 57, 58. Vienna: Tempsky, 1895–1923.

———. *Epistulae CI–CXXXIX*. Edited by K. D. Daur. Corpus Christianorum, Series Latina 31B. Turnhout: Brepols, 2009.

———. *In Epistolam Joannis ad Parthos Tractatus X*. Edited by P. Agaësse. Sources Chrétiennes 75. Paris: Cerf, 1961.

———. *St. Augustine: Homilies on the Gospel of John, Homilies on the First Epistle of John, Soliloquies*. Translated by John Gibb, H. Browne, and C. C. Starbuck. Nicene and Post-Nicene Fathers, First Series, vol. 7. Buffalo: Christian Literature Publishing, 1888.

———. *St. Augustine on Marriage and Sexuality*. Edited by Elizabeth A. Clark. Washington, D.C.: Catholic University of America Press, 1996.

———. *Sancti Aurelii Augustini in Iohannis Evangelium Tractatus CXXIV*. Edited by Radbodus Willems. Corpus Christianorum, Series Latina 36. Turnhout: Brepols, 1954.

———. *Sermones de Novo Testamento (51–70A)*. Corpus Christianorum, Series Latina 41Aa. Edited by P.-P. Verbraken et al. Turnhout: Brepols, 2008.

———. *Sermones de Novo Testamento (151–56)*. Edited by G. Partoens. Corpus Christianorum, Series Latina 41Ba. Turnhout: Brepols, 2008.
———. *Sermones de Sanctis*. In *Patrologia Latina*, edited by J.-P. Migne, 38: 1247–484. Paris, 1865.
———. *Sermones de Scripturis*. In *Patrologia Latina*, edited by J.-P. Migne, 38: 23–994. Paris, 1865.
———. *Sermones de Vetere Testamento (1–50)*. Edited by C. Lambot. Corpus Christianorum, Series Latina 41. Turnhout: Brepols, 1961.
———. *Sermons*. Edited by John E. Rotelle. Translated by Edmund Hill. 11 vols. Works of Saint Augustine. Brooklyn: New City Press, 1990.
———. *Sermons III/8 (273–305A)*. Trans. Edmund Hill. Hyde Park, N.Y.: New City Press, 1994.
———. *Soliloquia*. Edited by W. Hörman. Corpus Scriptorum Ecclesiasticorum Latinorum 89. Berlin: de Gruyter, 1986.
Basil of Caesarea. *Ascetica*. In *Patrologia Graeca*, edited by J.-P. Migne, 31: 600–652. Paris, 1857.
———. *The Asketikon of St Basil the Great*. Translated by Anna Silvas. Oxford Early Christian Studies. Oxford: Oxford University Press, 2005.
———. *Epistolae*. In *Basil: Letters*. 4 vols. Loeb Classical Library 190, 215, 243, 270. Edited and translated by Roy J. Deferrari. Cambridge, Mass.: Harvard University Press, 1926–34.
———. *Homilia Quod Deus Non Est Auctor Malorum*. In *Patrologia Graeca*, edited by J.-P. Migne, 31: 329–54. Paris, 1857.
———. *Moralia*. In *Patrologia Graeca*, edited by J.-P. Migne, 31: 699–888. Paris, 1857.
———. *On the Human Condition*. Translated by Verna Harrison. Crestwood, N.Y.: St. Vladimir's Seminary Press, 2005.
———. *Regulae Brevius Tractatae*. In *Patrologia Graeca*, edited by J.-P. Migne, 31: 1079–1306. Paris, 1857.
———. *Regulae Fusius Tractatae*. In *Patrologia Graeca*, edited by J.-P. Migne, 31: 889–1052. Paris, 1857.
The Book of Pontiffs (Liber Pontificalis): The Ancient Biographies of the First Ninety Roman Bishops, to AD 715. Translated by Raymond Davis. 2nd ed., rev. Translated Texts for Historians 6. Liverpool: Liverpool University Press, 2000. [See also *Le Liber Pontificalis*.]
Celsus. *On Medicine*. Translated by Walter George Spencer. 3 vols. Loeb Classical Library 292, 304, 336. Cambridge, Mass.: Harvard University Press, 1935–38.
Cicero. *Divinatio in Caecilium*. In *Cicero: The Verrine Orations*, vol. 1, *Against Caecilius, Against Verres*, part 1; part 2, books 1–2, translated by L. H. G. Greenwood, Loeb Classical Library 221. Cambridge, Mass: Harvard University Press, 1928.
———. *Tusculan Disputations*. Translated by J. E. King. Loeb Classical Library 141. London: Heinemann, 1927.
Clement of Alexandria. *Paedagogus*. Edited by M. Marcovich. Supplements to Vigiliae Christianae 61. Leiden: Brill, 2002.
Conciliorum Oecumenicorum Generaliumque Decreta: Editio Critica. Volume 1, *The Oecumenical Councils from Nicaea I to Nicaea II (325–787)*. Edited by Antonio García y García et al. Corpus Christianorum. Turnhout: Brepols, 2006.

Cyprian. *Ad Quirinum, Ad Fortunatum, De Lapsis, De Ecclesiae Catholicae Unitate.* Volume 1 of *Opera.* Edited by R. Weber and M. Bévenot. Corpus Christianorum, Series Latina 3. Turnhout: Brepols, 1972.

———. *Epistulae 1–57.* Edited by G. Diercks. Corpus Christianorum, Series Latina 3B. Turnhout: Brepols, 1994.

Cyril of Alexandria. *St. Cyril of Alexandria: Letters 1–50.* Translated by John I. McEnerney. Fathers of the Church 76. Washington, D.C.: Catholic University of America Press, 1987. [Greek text in *Concilium Universale Ephesenum,* edited by Eduard Schwartz and Johannes Straub, tome 1, vol. 1 of *Acta Conciliorum Oecumenicorum.* Berlin: de Gruyter, 1925.]

Cyril of Jerusalem. *Catéchèses mystagogiques.* Edited by Auguste Piédagnel. Translated by Pierre Paris. Sources Chrétiennes 126. Paris: Cerf, 1966.

Cyril of Scythopolis. *Kyrillos von Skythopolis.* Edited by Eduard Schwartz. Texte und Untersuchungen zur Geschichte der Altchristlichen Literatur 49. Leipzig: J. C. Hinrichs, 1939.

———. *Lives of the Monks of Palestine.* Translated by Richard Price. Cistercian Studies Series 114. Kalamazoo: Cistercian Publications, 1991.

The Didascalia Apostolorum in Syriac. Edited and translated by Arthur Vööbus. 2 vols. Corpus Scriptorum Christianorum Orientalium, Scriptores Syri, 401, 402, 407, 408. Louvain: Secretariat of the CSCO, 1979.

Egeria. *Egeria's Travels.* Edited and translated by John Wilkinson. 3rd ed. Warminster: Aris & Phillips, 1999.

———. *Éthérie: Journal de voyage.* Edited and translated by Hélène Pétré. Sources Chrétiennes 21. Paris: Cerf, 1948.

Ephrem the Syrian. *Des heiligen Ephraem des Syrers Hymnen de Fide.* Edited and translated by Edmund Beck. Corpus Scriptorum Christianorum Orientalium 154, 155. Louvain: Secretariat of the CSCO, 1955.

———. *Des heiligen Ephraem des Syrers Hymnen de Nativitate (Epiphania).* Edited and translated by Edmund Beck. Corpus Scriptorum Christianorum Orientalium 186, 187. Louvain: Secretariat of the CSCO, 1959.

———. *Des heiligen Ephraem des Syrers Hymnen de Paradiso und contra Julianum.* Edited and translated by Edmund Beck. Corpus Scriptorum Christianorum Orientalium 174, 175. Louvain: Secretariat of the CSCO, 1957.

———. *Des heiligen Ephraem des Syrers Hymnen de Virginitate.* Edited and translated by Edmund Beck. Corpus Scriptorum Christianorum Orientalium 223, 224. Louvain: Secretariat of the CSCO, 1962.

———. *Des heiligen Ephraem des Syrers Sermones.* Edited and translated by Edmund Beck. 4 vols. Corpus Scriptorum Christianorum Orientalium, Scriptores Syri, 305–6, 311–12, 320–21, 334–35. Louvain: Secretariat of the CSCO, 1970.

———. *The Syriac* Vita *Tradition of Ephrem the Syrian.* Edited and translated by Joseph P. Amar. 2 vols. Corpus Scriptorum Christianorum Orientalium 629, 630. Louvain: Peeters, 2011.

Epiphanius. *Panarion.* Edited by K. Holl. Die Griechischen Christlichen Schriftsteller der Ersten Drei Jahrhunderte 25. Leipzig: J. C. Hinrichs, 1915.

Evagrius of Pontus. *Briefe aus der Wüste.* Edited and translated by Gabriel Bunge. Sophia 24. Trier: Paulinus-Verlag, 1986.

———. *Évagre le Pontique: Scholies aux Proverbes*. Edited and translated by Paul Géhin. Sources Chrétiennes 340. Paris: Cerf, 1987.

———. "Evagrius: Letters." Translated by Luke Dysinger, OSB: http://www.ldysinger.com /Evagrius/11_Letters/00a_start.htm.

———. *Evagrius of Pontus: The Gnostic Trilogy*. Translated by Robin Darling Young et al. [Robin Darling Young, Luke Dysinger, OSB, Joel Kalvesmaki, Charles Stang, and Columba Stewart]. Oxford: Oxford University Press, forthcoming.

———. *Evagrius of Pontus: The Greek Ascetic Corpus*. Edited and translated by Robert E. Sinkewicz. Oxford Early Christian Studies. Oxford: Oxford University Press, 2003.

———. "Evagrius of Pontus' 'Letter to Melania,' I." Translated by Martin Parmentier. In *Forms of Devotion: Conversion, Worship, Spirituality, and Asceticism*, Recent Studies in Early Christianity 5, edited by Everett Ferguson, 272–309. New York: Garland Publishing, 1999.

———. *Euagrius Ponticus*. Edited by Wilhelm Frankenberg. Abhandlungen der Königlichen Gesellschaft der Wissenschaften zu Göttingen, Philologisch-Historische Klasse, neue Folge, 13.2. Berlin: Weidmannsche Buchhandlung, 1912.

———. *The Life and Works of the Holy Father Evagrius Ponticus in an Armenian Version of the Fifth Century, with Introduction and Notes*. Edited by Barsegh Sargisean. Venice: Surb Ghazar, 1907.

———. *Nonnenspiegel und Mönchsspiegel des Euagrios Pontikos*. Edited by Hugo Gressmann. Texte und Untersuchungen 39.4. Leipzig: J. C. Hinrichs, 1913.

———. *On the Faith, Letters 7, 8, 19 and 20, the Great Letter*. In *Evagrius Ponticus*, The Early Church Fathers, edited by Augustine M. Casiday. London: Routledge, 2006.

———. *Les six centuries des "Kephalaia gnostica" d'Évagre le Pontique: Édition critique de la version syriaque commune et édition d'une nouvelle version syriaque, intégrale, avec une double traduction française*. Edited by Antoine Guillaumont. Patrologia Orientalis 28. Paris: Firmin-Didot, 1958.

———. *Talking Back: A Monastic Handbook for Combating Demons*. Translated by David Brakke. Cistercian Studies Series 229. Trappist, Ky.: Cistercian Publications, 2009.

Galen. *De Tumoribus praeter Naturam*. In Jeremiah Reedy, "Galen, *De Tumoribus praeter Naturam*: A Critical Edition with Translation and Indices." Ph.D. dissertation, University of Michigan, 1968.

Gerontius. *The Life of Melania the Younger*. [*Vita Melaniae Iunioris; Vita Sanctae Melaniae Iunioris*] Translated by Elizabeth A. Clark, *The Life of Melania the Younger: Introduction, Translation, and Commentary*, Studies in Women and Religion 14. Lewiston, N.Y.: Edwin Mellen Press, 1984.

———. *Vie de sainte Mélanie: Texte grec, introduction, traduction et notes*. Edited and translated by Denys Gorce. Sources Chrétiennes 90. Paris: Cerf, 1962.

———. *La vie latine de sainte Mélanie*. Edited and translated by Patrick Laurence. Studium Biblicum Franciscanum 41. Jerusalem: Franciscan Printing Press, 2002.

Le grand lectionnaire de l'Église de Jérusalem (Ve–VIIe siècle). Edited and translated by Michel Tarchnischvili. 2 vols. Corpus Scriptorum Christianorum Orientalium 188–89, 204–5, Scriptores Iberici 9–10, 13–14. Louvain: Secretariat of the CSCO, 1959–60.

Gregory the Great. *Dialogues*. 3 vols. Edited by Adalbert de Vogüé. Sources Chrétiennes 251, 260, 265. Paris: Cerf, 1978–80.

———. *Leo the Great, Letters and Sermons; Gregory the Great, The Book of Pastoral Rule and Selected Epistles*. Translated by Charles Lett Feltoe and James Barmby. Nicene and Post-Nicene Fathers, Second Series, vol. 12. Buffalo: Christian Literature Publishing, 1895.

———. *Règle pastorale*. Edited by Bruno Judic and Floribert Rommel. Translated by Charles Morel. 2 vols. Sources Chrétiennes 381, 382. Paris: Cerf, 1992.

Gregory of Nazianzus. *Discours 1–3*. Edited by Jean Bernardi. Sources Chrétiennes 247. Paris: Cerf, 1978.

———. *Discours 32–37*. Edited by Paul Gallay. Sources Chrétiennes 318. Paris: Cerf, 1985.

Gregory of Nyssa. *Ascetical Works*. Translated by Virginia Woods Callahan. Fathers of the Church 58. Washington, D.C.: Catholic University of America Press, 1967.

———. *Gregorii Nysseni Opera Ascetica*. Edited by Werner Wilhelm Jaeger, John Peter Cavarnos, and Virginia Woods Callahan. Leiden: Brill, 1952.

———. *Gregory of Nyssa, The Letters: Introduction, Translation and Commentary*. Edited and translated by Anna Silvas. Supplements to Vigiliae Christianae 83. Leiden: Brill, 2007.

———. *Lettres*. Edited by Pierre Maraval. Sources Chrétiennes 363. Paris: Cerf, 1990.

———. *St. Gregory of Nyssa: The Life of St. Macrina*. Translated by W.K. Lowther Clarke. Early Church Classics. London: Society for Promoting Christian Knowledge, 1916. [http://catalog.hathitrust.org/Record/001406402.]

———. *Vie de sainte Macrine*. Edited by Pierre Maraval. Sources Chrétiennes 178. Paris: Cerf, 1971.

Hippocrates. *Hippocrates*. Translated by W.H.S. Jones et al. 10 vols. Loeb Classical Library 147–50, 472, 473, 477, 482, 509, 520. Cambridge, Mass.: Harvard University Press, 1923–2012.

Hippolytus. *In Susannam*. In *Patrologia Graeca*, edited by J.-P. Migne, 10: 689–98. Paris, 1857.

———. *Omnium Haeresium Refutatio*. In *Patrologia Graeca*, edited by J.-P. Migne, 16: 3009–3454. Paris, 1860.

L'hymnaire de Saint-Sabas (Ve–VIIe siècle): Le manuscrit géorgien H 2123. Volume 1, *Du samedi de Lazare à la Pentecôte*. Translated by Charles Renoux. Patrologia Orientalis 50.3. Turnhout: Brepols, 2008.

Les hymnes de la Résurrection. Volume 1, *Hymnographie liturgique géorgienne: Textes du Sinaï 18*. Edited and translated by Charles Renoux. Sources Liturgiques 3. Paris: Cerf, 2000.

Les hymnes de la Résurrection. Volume 2, *Hymnographie liturgique géorgienne: Texte des manuscrits Sinaï 40, 41 et 34*. Edited and translated by Charles Renoux. Patrologia Orientalis 52.1. Turnhout: Brepols, 2010.

Les hymnes de la Résurrection. Volume 3, *Hymnographie liturgique géorgienne: Introduction, traduction, annotation des manuscrits Sinaï 26 et 20 et index analytique des trois volumes*. Edited and translated by Charles Renoux. Patrologia Orientalis 52.2. Turnhout: Brepols, 2010.

Inscriptiones Christianae Urbis Romae Septimo Saeculo Antiquiores. Nova Series, vol. 6, *Coemeteria in Viis Latina Labicana et Praenestina*. Ed. Giovanni Battista de Rossi and Antonio Ferrua. Vatican City: Pontificio Instituto di Archeologia Cristiana, 1975.

Irenaeus. *Adversus Haereses, Book 4*. Edited by A. Rousseau et al. [A. Rousseau, B. Hemmerdinger, C. Mercier, and L. Doutreleau.] Sources Chrétiennes 100.1–2. Paris: Cerf, 1965.

Jerome. *Apologie contre Rufin.* Edited and translated by Pierre Lardet. Sources Chrétiennes 303. Paris: Cerf, 1983.

———. *Die Chronik des Hieronymus / Hieronymi Chronicon.* In *Eusebius' Werke* 7.1, 3rd ed., Die Griechischen Christlichen Schriftsteller der Ersten Drei Jahrhunderte 47, edited by Rudolf Helm. Berlin: Akademie-Verlag, 1984.

———. *Commentarii in Prophetas Minores.* Edited by M. Adriaen. Corpus Christianorum, Series Latina 76, 76A. Turnhout: Brepols, 1969.

———. *Commentariorum in Hiezechielem Libri XIV.* Edited by F. Glorie. Corpus Christianorum, Series Latina 75. Turnhout: Brepols, 1964.

———. *Dialogus adversus Pelagianos.* Edited by C. Moreschini. Corpus Christianorum, Series Latina 80. Turnhout: Brepols, 1990.

———. *Sancti Eusebii Hieronymi Epistulae.* Edited by Isidorus Hilberg and Margit Kamptner. 2nd ed. CSEL 54–56. Vienna: Verlag der Österreichischen Akademie der Wissenschaften, 1996.

———. *The Homilies of Saint Jerome.* Translated by Sister Marie Liguori Ewald. 2 vols. Fathers of the Church 48, 57. Washington, D.C.: Catholic University of America Press, 1964–66.

———. *Interpretatio Libri Didymi de Spiritu Sancto.* Edited by L. Doutreleau. Sources Chrétiennes 386. Paris: Cerf, 1992.

———. *Jerome: Letters and Select Works.* Translated by W. H. Fremantle, G. Lewis, and W. G. Martley. Nicene and Post-Nicene Fathers, Second Series, vol. 6. Buffalo: Christian Literature Publishing, 1893.

———. *Jerome's Epitaph on Paula: A Commentary on the Epitaphium Sanctae Paulae.* Edited and translated by Andrew Cain. Oxford Early Christian Texts. Oxford: Oxford University Press, 2013.

———. *Sancti Eusebii Hieronymi Epistulae.* Edited by Isidorus Hilberg. 3 vols. Corpus Scriptorum Ecclesiasticorum Latinorum 54–56. Vienna and Leipzig: F. Tempsky and G. Freytag, 1910–18.

John Chrysostom. *Ad Eos Qui Scandalizati Sunt.* Edited by A.-M. Malingrey. Sources Chrétiennes 79. Paris: Cerf, 2000.

———. *Ad Theodorum Lapsum 1.* Edited by J. DuMortier. Sources Chrétiennes 117. Paris: Cerf, 1966.

———. *Commentarius in Epistolam ad Galatas.* In *Patrologia Graeca*, edited by J.-P. Migne, 61: 611–82. Paris, 1862.

———. *De diabolo tentatore.* Edited by A. Peleanu. Sources Chrétiennes 560. Paris: Cerf, 2013.

———. *De Sacerdotio.* Edited by A.-M. Malingrey. Sources Chrétiennes 272. Paris: Cerf 1980.

———. *Homiliae de Statuis ad Populum Antiochenum Habitae.* In *Patrologia Graeca*, edited by J.-P. Migne, 49: 15–222. Paris, 1862.

———. *Homiliae in Acta Apostolorum.* In *Patrologia Graeca*, edited by J.-P. Migne, 60: 13–384. Paris, 1862.

———. *Homiliae in Epistolam ad Hebraeos.* In *Patrologia Graeca*, edited by J.-P. Migne, 63: 9–236. Paris, 1862.

———. *Homiliae in Epistolam Primam ad Corinthios.* In *Patrologia Graeca*, edited by J.-P. Migne, 61: 9–382. Paris, 1862.

———. *Homiliae in Epistolam Primam ad Timotheum.* In *Patrologia Graeca*, edited by J.-P. Migne, 62: 501–600. Paris, 1862.

———. *Homiliae in Epistolam Secundam ad Corinthios*. In *Patrologia Graeca*, edited by J.-P. Migne, 61: 381–610. Paris, 1862.

———. *Homiliae in Epistolam Secundam ad Timotheum*. In *Patrologia Graeca*, edited by J.-P. Migne, 62: 599–662. Paris, 1862.

———. *In Eutropium*. In *Patrologia Graeca*, edited by J.-P. Migne, 52: 391–96. Paris, 1862.

———. *St. Chrysostom: Homilies on Galatians, Ephesians, Philippians, Colossians, Thessalonians, Timothy, Titus, and Philemon*. Translated by Gross Alexander and John A. Broadus. Nicene and Post-Nicene Fathers, First Series, vol. 13. Buffalo: Christian Literature Publishing, 1889.

———. *St. Chrysostom: Homilies on the Gospel of St. John and the Epistle to the Hebrews*. Translated by Frederic Gardiner. Nicene and Post-Nicene Fathers, First Series, vol. 14. Buffalo: Christian Literature Publishing, 1889.

———. *St. Chrysostom: On the Priesthood, Ascetic Treatises, Select Homilies and Letters, Homilies on the Statues*. Translated by W. R. W. Stephens, R. Blackburn, and T. P. Brandram. Nicene and Post-Nicene Fathers, First Series, vol. 9. Buffalo: Christian Literature Publishing, 1889.

John Moschos. *Pratum Spirituale*. Edited by M.-J. Roüet de Journel. Sources Chrétiennes 12. Paris: Cerf, 1946.

———. *The Spiritual Meadow*. Translated by John Wortley. Cistercian Studies Series 139. Kalamazoo: Cistercian Publications, 1992.

John of Ephesus. *Lives of the Eastern Saints*. Edited and translated by E. W. Brooks. 3 vols. Patrologia Orientalis 17–19. Paris: Firmin-Didot, 1923–25.

John Rufus. *Jean Rufus, évêque de Maïouma: Plérophories—C'est-á-dire témoignages et révélations contre le Concile de Chalcédoine*. Edited by François Nau and translated by Maurice Brière. Patrologia Orientalis 8.1. Paris: Firmin-Didot, 1912.

———. *The "Lives" of Peter the Iberian, Theodosius of Jerusalem, and the Monk Romanus*. Edited and translated by Cornelia B. Horn and Robert R. Phenix, Jr. Writings from the Greco-Roman World 24. Atlanta: Society of Biblical Literature, 2008.

Julian of Eclanum. *Libellus Fidei*. In *Patrologia Latina*, edited by J.-P. Migne, 48: 508–36. Paris, 1846.

Justin Martyr. *Justin, Philosopher and Martyr: Apologies*. Edited and translated by Denis Minns and P. M. Parvis. Oxford Early Christian Texts. Oxford: Oxford University Press, 2009.

Leo the Great. *Tractatus*. Edited by Antoine Chavasse. Corpus Christianorum, Series Latina 138, 138A. Turnhout: Brepols, 1987.

Le Liber Pontificalis: Texte, introduction et commentaire. Edited by Louis Duchesne and Cyrille Vogel. 3 vols. 2nd ed. Bibliothèque des Écoles Françaises d'Athènes et de Rome, series 2, vol. 3. Paris: Boccard, 1955. [See also *The Book of Pontiffs*.]

al-Maqrīzī. *The Churches and Monasteries of Egypt and Some Neighboring Countries*. Edited and translated by B. T. A. Evetts. Oxford: Clarendon Press, 1895. [Reprint, Piscataway, N.J.: Gorgias, 2001.]

———. *al-Mawāʿiẓ wa al-iʿtibār fī dhikr al-khiṭaṭ wa al-athār*. Edited by Muhammad Zeinahum and Madihat al-Sharqāwa. 3 vols. Ṣafaḥāt min tārīkh Miṣr 39. Cairo: Maktabat Madbūlī, 1998.

Marcus Aurelius. *Meditations: M. Antonius Imperator ad Se Ipsum*. Edited by Jan Hendrik Leopold. Leipzig: Teubner, 1908.
Martial. *Epigrams*. Edited and translated by D.R. Shackleton Bailey. 3 vols. Loeb Classical Library 94, 95, 480. Cambridge, Mass.: Harvard University Press, 1993.
Monks of the Desert of Scetis. *Firdaws al-Ābā' (Bustān al-ruhbān al-muwassaʻ)*. [*Paradise of the Fathers* (The Expanded *Garden of the Monks*).] 3rd ed. 3 vols. Wādī al-Naṭrūn: Maṭbaʻat al-Deltā, 2008.
Origen. *Contra Celsum*. Edited by Marcel Borret. 5 vols. Sources Chrétiennes 132, 136, 147, 150, 227. Paris: Cerf, 1969–76.
———. *De Principiis*. Edited by Henri Crouzel and Manlio Simonetti. 5 vols. Sources Chrétiennes 252, 253, 268, 269, 312. Paris: Cerf, 1978–84.
———. *Homilies on Numbers*. Edited by Christopher A. Hall. Translated by Thomas P. Scheck. Ancient Christian Texts. Downers Grove, Ill.: InterVarsity Press, 2009.
———. *In Numeros Homiliae*. Edited by L. Doutreleau. 3 vols. Sources Chrétiennes 415, 442, 461. Paris: Cerf, 1996–2001.
———. *On First Principles*. Translated by G.W. Butterworth. Gloucester, Mass.: Peter Smith, 1973.
Palladius. *Dialogue on the Life of St. John Chrysostom*. Edited and translated by Robert T. Meyer. Ancient Christian Writers 45. Mahwah, N.J.: Paulist Press, 1985.
———. *Dialogue sur la vie de Jean Chrysostome*. Edited and translated by Anne-Marie Malingrey. 2 vols. Sources Chrétiennes 341, 342. Paris: Cerf, 1988.
———. *The Lausiac History of Palladius: A Critical Discussion Together with Notes on Early Egyptian Monachism*. Edited by Cuthbert Butler. Texts and Studies vol. 6, parts 1 and 2. Cambridge: Cambridge University Press, 1898–1904. [Reprint, Hildesheim: Georg Olms, 1967.]
———. *Palladius: The Lausiac History*. Edited and translated by Robert T. Meyer. Ancient Christian Writers 34. Westminster, Md.: Newman Press, 1965.
———. *Quatre ermites égyptiens: D'après les fragments coptes de l'Histoire lausiaque*. Edited by Gabriel Bunge. Translated by Adalbert de Vogüé. Spiritualité Orientale 60. Bégrolles-en-Mauges: Abbaye de Bellefontaine, 1994.
———. *La Storia lausiaca*. Edited by G.J.M. Bartelink. Translated by Marino Barchiesi. Vite dei Santi 2. Milan: Mondadori, 1974.
Passion de Perpétue et de Félicité suivi des Actes. Edited and translated by Jacqueline Amat. Sources Chrétiennes 417. Paris: Cerf, 1996.
The Passion of Perpetua and Felicity. Edited and translated by Thomas J. Heffernan. New York: Oxford University Press, 2012.
The Passion of S. Perpetua, Newly Edited from the Mss. with an Introduction and Notes: Together with an Appendix Containing the Original Latin Text of the Scillitan Martydom. Edited by J. Armitage Robinson. Texts and Studies 1, no. 2. Cambridge: Cambridge University Press, 1891.
Paul of Aegina. *Paulus Aegineta*. Edited by I.L. Heiberg. 2 vols. Corpus Medicorum Graecorum vol. 9, parts 1 and 2. Berlin: Akademie-Verlag, 1921–24.
Paulinus of Nola. *Epistulae*. Edited and translated by Matthias Skeb. 3 vols. Fontes Christiani 25.1–3. Freiburg: Herder, 1998.

———. *The Letters of St. Paulinus of Nola*. Translated by P. G. Walsh. 2 vols. Ancient Christian Writers 35, 36. Westminster, Md.: Newman Press, 1966–67.

———. *Sancti Pontii Meropii Paulini Nolani Opera*. Part 1, *Epistulae*. Edited by Wilhelm von Hartel and Margit Kamptner. 2nd ed. Corpus Scriptorum Ecclesiasticorum Latinorum 29. Vienna: Verlag der Österreichischen Akademie der Wissenschaften, 1999.

Pelagius. *Pelagius: Life and Letters*. Translated by B. R. Rees. Rochester: Boydell Press, 1998.

Peter the Iberian. *Petrus der Iberer: Ein Charakterbild zur Kirchen- und Sittengeschichte des fünften Jahrhunderts—Syrische Übersetzung einer um das Jahr 500 verfassten griechischen Biographie*. Edited and translated by Richard Raabe. Leipzig: J. C. Hinrichs, 1895.

Plutarch. *Lives*. Translated by Bernadotte Perrin. 11 vols. Loeb Classical Library 46, 47, 65, 80, 87, 98–103. Cambridge, Mass.: Harvard University Press, 1914–26.

———. *Moralia*. Translated by Frank Cole Babbitt et al. 17 vols. Loeb Classical Library 197, 222, 245, 305, 306, 321, 337, 405, 406, 424–29, 470, 499. Cambridge, Mass.: Harvard University Press, 1927–76.

———. *Plutarchos: Tiberius und Gaius Gracchus*. Edited by Konrat Ziegler. Heidelberg: Winter, 1911.

Proclus of Constantinople. *L'homilétique de Proclus de Constantinople*. Edited and translated by François Joseph Leroy, S.J. Studi e Testi 247. Vatican City: Biblioteca Apostolica Vaticana, 1967.

Proclus of Constantinople and the Cult of the Virgin in Late Antiquity: Homilies 1–5, Texts and Translations. Edited and translated by Nicholas Constas. Supplements to Vigiliae Christianae 66. Leiden: Brill, 2003.

Pseudo-Athanasius. *The Life and Activity of the Holy and Blessed Teacher Syncletica*. Translated by Elizabeth Castelli in *Ascetic Behavior in Greco-Roman Antiquity: A Sourcebook*, Studies in Antiquity and Christianity, edited by Vincent L. Wimbush, 265–311. Minneapolis: Fortress Press, 1990.

———. *Vita Syncleticae*. In *Patrologia Graeca*, edited by J.-P. Migne, 28: 1485–1558. Paris, 1857.

Quintus Curtius. *History of Alexander*. Edited and translated by John C. Rolfe. 2 vols. Loeb Classical Library 368, 369. Cambridge, Mass.: Harvard University Press, 1946.

Rufinus. *Historia Ecclesiastica*. In *Tyrannii Rufini Scripta Varia*, Corpus Scriptorum Ecclesiae Aquileiensis 5.2, edited by Manlio Simonetti. Rome: Città Nuova, 2000.

The Seven Ecumenical Councils. Edited and translated by Henry R. Percival. Nicene and Post-Nicene Fathers, Second Series, vol. 14. Buffalo: Christian Literature Publishing, 1900.

Simon of Ṭaibūtheh. *Medico-Mystical Work*. In *Early Christian Mystics*, Woodbrooke Studies 7, edited and translated by Alphonse Mingana, 1–69. Cambridge: W. Heffer and Sons, 1934.

Soranus. *Soranus' Gynecology*. Translated by Owsei Temkin. Baltimore: The Johns Hopkins University Press, 1991.

Sozomen. *Historia Ecclesiastica*. In *Patrologia Graeca*, edited by J.-P. Migne, 67: 843–1630. Paris, 1864.

Sulpicius Severus. *Vie de Saint Martin*. Edited by Jacques Fontaine. 3 vols. Sources Chrétiennes 133–35. Paris: Cerf, 1967–69.

Tertullian. *Adversus Marcionem*. In *Opera*, vol. 1. Corpus Christianorum, Series Latina 1. Turnhout: Brepols, 1954.

———. *De Anima*. See below, Waszink, under "Secondary Sources."
———. *De Paenitentia*. In *Opera*, vol. 1. Corpus Christianorum, Series Latina 1. Turnhout: Brepols, 1954.
———. *Scorpiace*. In *Opera*, vol. 2, *Opera Montanistica*. Corpus Christianorum, Series Latina 2. Turnhout: Brepols, 1954.
———. *Scorpiace*. In *Tertullian*, Early Church Fathers, edited and translated by Geoffrey D. Dunn. New York: Routledge, 2004.
Theodoret. *Histoire des moines de Syrie: Histoire Philothée*. Edited and translated by Pierre Canivet and Alice Leroy-Molinghen. 2 vols. Sources Chrétiennes 234, 257. Paris: Cerf, 1977–79.
Victor Vitensis. *Historia Persecutionis Africanae Provinciae sub Geiserico et Hunirico Regibus Wandalorum*. Monumenta Germaniae Historica: Scriptores, Auctores Antiquissimi 3.1. Edited by Karl Felix von Halm. Berlin: Weidmann, 1879. [Reprinted 1981. See also http://bardcollege.worldcat.org/title/historia-persecutionis-africanae-provinciae/oclc /771381298?ht=edition&referer=di.]

SECONDARY SOURCES

d'Alès, Adhémar. "Les deux *vies* de sainte Mélanie la Jeune." *Analecta Bollandiana* 25 (1906): 401–50.
Alexandre, Monique. "Les nouveaux martyrs: Motifs martyrologiques dans la vie des saints et thèmes hagiographiques dans l'éloge des martyrs chez Grégoire de Nysse." In *The Biographical Works of Gregory of Nyssa: Proceedings of the Fifth International Colloquium on Gregory of Nyssa, Mainz, 6–10 September 1982*, Patristic Monograph Series 12, edited by Andreas Spira, 33–70. Cambridge, Mass.: Philadelphia Patristic Foundation, 1984.
Alfrey, Shawn H. "'Oriental Peaceful Penetration': Gertrude Stein and the End of Europe." *The Massachusetts Review* 38.3 (1997): 405–16.
Amélineau, Émile, ed. "De *Historia Lausiaca* Quaenam Sit Huius ad Monachorum Aegyptiorum Historiam Scribendam Utilitas." Ph.D. dissertation, University of Paris. Paris: E. Leroux, 1887.
Arjava, Antti. *Women and Law in Late Antiquity*. Oxford: Clarendon Press, 1996.
Armanios, Febe, and Andrew Amstutz. "Emerging Christian Media in Egypt: Clerical Authority and the Visualization of Women in Coptic Video Films." *International Journal of Middle East Studies* 45.3 (2013): 513–33.
Balberg, Mira. "Rabbinic Authority, Medical Rhetoric, and Body Hermeneutics in Mishnah Nega'im." *AJS Review* 35.2 (2011): 323–46.
Baldovin, John Francis. *Liturgy in Ancient Jerusalem*. Grove Liturgical Study 57. Bramcote: Grove Books, 1989.
———. *The Urban Character of Christian Worship: The Origins, Development, and Meaning of Stational Liturgy*. Orientalia Christiana Analecta 228. Rome: Pontificium Institutum Studiorum Orientalium, 1987.
Bammel, Caroline P. "The Last Ten Years of Rufinus' Life and the Date of His Move South from Aquileia." *Journal of Theological Studies*, n.s., 28.2 (1977): 372–429.
Bammer, Angelika. *Partial Visions: Feminism and Utopianism in the 1970s*. New York: Routledge, 1991.

Barbera, Mariarosaria, Sergio Palladino, and Claudia Paterna. "La domus dei Valerii sul Celio alla luce delle recenti scoperte." *Papers of the British School at Rome* 76 (2008): 75–354.

Barnes, Timothy David. *Early Christian Hagiography and Roman History*. Tria Corda 5. Tübingen: Mohr Siebeck, 2010.

———. *Tertullian: A Historical and Literary Study*. Oxford: Clarendon Press, 1971.

Barnish, S. J. B. "Transformation and Survival in the Western Senatorial Aristocracy, c. A.D. 400–700." *Papers of the British School at Rome* 56 (1988): 120–55.

Beard, Mary. "The Public Voice of Women." *London Review of Books* 36.6 (20 March 2014): 11–14.

Behr, John. *The Case against Diodore and Theodore: Texts and Their Contexts*. Oxford Early Christian Texts. Oxford: Oxford University Press, 2011.

Bennett, Jane. *Vibrant Matter: A Political Ecology of Things*. Durham: Duke University Press, 2010.

Bennett, Nathan. "Education as Asceticism and the Education of Asceticism in Greco-Roman and Christian Discourse." Ph.D. dissertation, Claremont Graduate University, 2013.

Bitton-Ashkelony, Bruria. *Encountering the Sacred: The Debate on Christian Pilgrimage in Late Antiquity*. Transformation of the Classical Heritage 38. Berkeley and Los Angeles: University of California Press, 2005.

———. "*Imitatio Mosis* and Pilgrimage in the *Life of Peter the Iberian*." In *Christian Gaza in Late Antiquity*, Jerusalem Studies in Religion and Culture 3, edited by Bruria Bitton-Ashkelony and Arieh Kofsky, 107–29. Leiden: Brill, 2004.

de Blaauw, Sible. *Cultus et decor: Liturgia e architettura nella Roma tardoantica e medievale—Basilica Salvatoris, Sanctae Mariae, Sancti Petri*. 2 vols. Studi e Testi 355, 356. Vatican City: Biblioteca Apostolica Vaticana, 1994.

Blower, Brooke Lindy. *Becoming Americans in Paris: Transatlantic Politics and Culture between the World Wars*. New York: Oxford University Press, 2011.

Bogost, Ian. *Alien Phenomenology; or, What It's Like to Be a Thing*. Posthumanities 20. Minneapolis: University of Minnesota Press, 2012.

Bonner, Gerald. "Augustine and Pelagianism." *Augustinian Studies* 24 (1993): 27–47.

Booth, Alan D. "Quelques dates hagiographiques: Mélanie l'Ancienne, saint Martin, Mélanie la Jeune." *Phoenix* 37.2 (1983): 144–51.

Bosteels, Bruno. *Marx and Freud in Latin America: Politics, Psychoanalysis, and Religion in Times of Terror*. London: Verso, 2012.

Bowden, William, and John Mitchell. "The Triconch Palace at Butrint: The Life and Death of a Late Roman Domus." In *Housing in Late Antiquity: From Palaces to Shops*, Late Antique Archaeology 3.2, edited by Luke Lavan, Lale Özgenel, and Alexander Sarantis, 455–74. Leiden: Brill, 2007.

Bowes, Kimberly Diane. *Houses and Society in the Later Roman Empire*. Duckworth Debates in Archaeology. London: Duckworth, 2010.

———. *Private Worship, Public Values, and Religious Change in Late Antiquity*. Cambridge: Cambridge University Press, 2008.

Bradley, Keith. "The Roman Child in Sickness and Health." In *The Roman Family in the Empire: Rome, Italy, and Beyond*, edited by Michele George, 67–92. Oxford: Oxford University Press, 2005.

Bradshaw, Paul F. *Eucharistic Origins*. Oxford: Oxford University Press, 2004.
———. *The Search for the Origins of Christian Worship: Sources and Methods for the Study of Early Liturgy*. 2nd ed. Oxford: Oxford University Press, 2002.
Brakke, David. *Athanasius and the Politics of Asceticism*. Oxford Early Christian Studies. Oxford: Clarendon Press, 1995. [Reissued as *Athanasius and Asceticism*. Baltimore: The Johns Hopkins University Press, 1998.]
———. *Demons and the Making of the Monk: Spiritual Combat in Early Christianity*. Cambridge, Mass.: Harvard University Press, 2006.
———. "The Lady Appears: Materializations of 'Woman' in Early Monastic Literature." In *The Cultural Turn in Late Ancient Studies: Gender, Asceticism, and Historiography*, edited by Dale B. Martin and Patricia Cox Miller, 25–39. Durham: Duke University Press, 2005.
Brandenburg, Hugo. *Ancient Churches of Rome from the Fourth to the Seventh Century: The Dawn of Christian Architecture in the West*. Translated by Andreas Kropp. Bibliothèque de l'Antiquité Tardive 8. Turnhout: Brepols, 2005.
Bremmer, Jan N., and Marco Formisano, eds. *Perpetua's Passions: Multidisciplinary Approaches to the Passio Perpetuae et Felicitatis*. Oxford: Oxford University Press, 2012.
Brenk, Beat. "Spolia from Constantine to Charlemagne: Aesthetics versus Ideology." *Dumbarton Oaks Papers* 41 (1987): 103–9.
Brilliant, Richard, and Dale Kinney, eds. *Reuse Value: Spolia and Appropriation in Art and Architecture from Constantine to Sherrie Levine*. Farnham: Ashgate, 2011.
Brock, Sebastian P. "Early Syrian Asceticism." *Numen* 20.1 (1973): 1–19.
———. "Saints in Syriac: A Little-Tapped Resource." *Journal of Early Christian Studies* 16.2 (2008): 181–96.
Brock, Sebastian P., and Susan Ashbrook Harvey. *Holy Women of the Syrian Orient*. Transformation of the Classical Heritage 13. Berkeley and Los Angeles: University of California Press, 1998.
Brown, Peter R. L. "Aspects of the Christianization of the Roman Aristocracy." *Journal of Roman Studies* 51 (1961): 1–11.
———. *The Body and Society: Men, Women, and Sexual Renunciation in Early Christianity*. Lectures on the History of Religions, n.s., 13. New York: Columbia University Press, 1988. [2nd ed. 2008.]
———. *The Cult of the Saints: Its Rise and Function in Latin Christianity*. Chicago: University of Chicago Press, 1981.
———. "The Patrons of Pelagius." *Journal of Theological Studies* 21 (1970): 56–72. [Reprinted in *Religion and Society in the Age of Saint Augustine* (London: Faber and Faber, 1972), 208–26.]
———. "Pelagius and His Supporters: Aims and Environment." In *Religion and Society in the Age of Saint Augustine*, 183–207. London: Faber and Faber, 1972.
———. *Through the Eye of a Needle: Wealth, the Fall of Rome, and the Making of Christianity in the West, 350–550 A.D*. Princeton: Princeton University Press, 2012.
Bryant, Levi R. *Onto-Cartography: An Ontology of Machines and Media*. Speculative Realism. Edinburgh: Edinburgh University Press, 2013.
Burke, Kelsy, and Amy McDowell. "Superstars and Misfits: Two Pop-Trends in the Gender Culture of Contemporary Evangelicalism." *Journal of Religion and Popular Culture* 24.1 (2012): 67–79.

Burkle-Young, Francis A. *Papal Elections in the Age of Transition, 1878–1922.* Lanham, Md.: Lexington Books, 2000.

Burns, Edward, ed. *The Letters of Gertrude Stein and Carl Van Vechten, 1913–1946.* 2 vols. New York: Columbia University Press, 1986.

Burns, Edward, and Ulla E. Dydo, eds. *The Letters of Gertrude Stein and Thornton Wilder.* With the assistance of William Rice. New Haven: Yale University Press, 1996.

Burns, J. Patout, ed. *Theological Anthropology.* Translated by J. Patout Burns. Sources of Early Christian Thought. Philadelphia: Fortress Press, 1981.

Burrus, Virginia. *"Begotten, Not Made": Conceiving Manhood in Late Antiquity.* Stanford: Stanford University Press, 2000.

———. *The Making of a Heretic: Gender, Authority, and the Priscillianist Controversy.* Transformation of the Classical Heritage 24. Berkeley and Los Angeles: University of California Press, 1995.

———. "Queer Father: Gregory of Nyssa and the Subversion of Identity." In *Queer Theology: Rethinking the Western Body,* edited by Gerard Loughlin, 147–62. Oxford: Blackwell, 2007.

———. *Saving Shame: Martyrs, Saints, and Other Abject Subjects.* Divinations. Philadelphia: University of Pennsylvania Press, 2008.

———. *The Sex Lives of Saints: An Erotics of Ancient Hagiography.* Divinations. Philadelphia: University of Pennsylvania Press, 2004.

Burwell, Jennifer. *Notes on Nowhere: Feminism, Utopian Logic, and Social Transformation.* American Culture 13. Minneapolis: University of Minnesota Press, 1997.

Butler, Alban. "December 31: St. Melania the Younger." In *The Lives of the Fathers, Martyrs, and Other Principal Saints, Compiled from Original Monuments and Other Authentick Records,* vol. 12. Dublin: James Duffy, 1866. http://www.bartleby.com/210/12/313.html.

Butler, Edward Cuthbert. "Review: Cardinal Rampolla's *Melania the Younger.*" *Journal of Theological Studies* 7.28 (1906): 630–32.

Butler, Judith. "Speaking Up, Talking Back: Joan Scott's Critical Feminism." In *The Question of Gender: Joan W. Scott's Critical Feminism,* 21st Century Studies 4, edited by Judith Butler and Elizabeth Weed, 11–28. Bloomington: Indiana University Press, 2011.

Butler, Judith, Éric Fassin, and Joan Wallach Scott. "Pour ne pas en finir avec le 'genre' . . . : Table ronde." *Sociétés et Représentations* 24.2 (2007): 285–306.

Butler, Judith, and Elizabeth Weed, eds. *The Question of Gender: Joan W. Scott's Critical Feminism.* 21st Century Studies 4. Bloomington: Indiana University Press, 2011.

Butler, Rex D. *The New Prophecy and "New Visions": Evidence of Montanism in the Passion of Perpetua and Felicitas.* Patristic Monograph Series 18. Washington, D.C.: Catholic University of America Press, 2006.

Cain, Andrew. "Jerome's *Epitaphium Paulae*: Hagiography, Pilgrimage, and the Cult of Saint Paula." *Journal of Early Christian Studies* 18.1 (2010): 105–39.

———. *Jerome's Epitaph on Paula: A Commentary on the "Epitaphium Sanctae Paulae."* Oxford Early Christian Texts. Oxford: Oxford University Press, 2013.

———. *The Letters of Jerome: Asceticism, Biblical Exegesis, and the Construction of Christian Authority in Late Antiquity.* Oxford Early Christian Studies. Oxford: Oxford University Press, 2009.

Cain, Andrew, and Josef Lössl, eds. *Jerome of Stridon: His Life, Writings and Legacy.* Farnham: Ashgate, 2009.

Cameron, Alan. "The Antiquity of the Symmachi." *Historia: Zeitschrift für Alte Geschichte* 48.4 (1999): 477–505.
———. "Filocalus and Melania." *Classical Philology* 87.2 (1992): 140–44.
———. "The Roman Friends of Ammianus." *Journal of Roman Studies* 54 (1964): 15–28.
Cameron, Averil. "Ascetic Closure and the End of Antiquity." In *Asceticism*, edited by Vincent L. Wimbush and Richard Valantasis, 147–61. New York: Oxford University Press, 1995.
———. "Virginity as Metaphor: Women and the Rhetoric of Early Christianity." In *History as Text: The Writing of Ancient History*, edited by Averil Cameron, 181–205. London: Duckworth, 1989.
Cameron, Lynne, and Graham Low, eds. *Researching and Applying Metaphor*. Cambridge Applied Linguistics Series. Cambridge: Cambridge University Press, 1999.
Campbell, Sue. "The Second Voice." *Memory Studies* 1.1 (2008): 41–48.
Caner, Daniel. *Wandering, Begging Monks: Spiritual Authority and the Promotion of Monasticism in Late Antiquity*. Transformation of the Classical Heritage 33. Berkeley and Los Angeles: University of California Press, 2002.
Capelle, Bernard. "La fête de la Vierge à Jérusalem au Ve siècle." *Le Muséon* 56 (1943): 1–33.
Carson, Anne. "Decreation: How Women like Sappho, Marguerite Porete and Simone Weil Tell God." In *Decreation: Opera, Essays, Poetry*, 155–83. New York: Knopf, 2005.
Casiday, Augustine M. *Reconstructing the Theology of Evagrius Ponticus: Beyond Heresy*. Cambridge: Cambridge University Press, 2013.
Castelli, Elizabeth A. "The Life and Activity of the Holy and Blessed Teacher Syncletica." In *Ascetic Behavior in Greco-Roman Antiquity: A Sourcebook*, edited by Vincent L. Wimbush, 265–311. Minneapolis: Fortress Press, 1990.
———. "The Philosophers' Paul in the Frame of the Global: Some Reflections." *South Atlantic Quarterly* 109.4 (2010): 653–76. [Reprinted with minor changes in *Paul and the Philosophers*, edited by Ward Blanton and Hent de Vries, 143–58. New York: Fordham University Press, 2013.]
———. "Virginity and Its Meaning for Women's Sexuality in Early Christianity." *Journal of Feminist Studies in Religion* 2.1 (1986): 61–88.
Castiglia, Christopher, and Christopher Reed. "'Ah, Yes, I Remember It Well': Memory and Queer Culture in *Will and Grace*." *Cultural Critique* 56.1 (2004): 158–88.
de Certeau, Michel. "A Variant: Hagio-Graphical Edification." In *The Writing of History*, translated by Tom Conley, 269–83. New York: Columbia University Press, 1988.
———. *The Writing of History*. Translated by Tom Conley. European Perspectives. New York: Columbia University Press, 1988.
Chase, Becca, and Paula Ressler. "An LGBT/Queer Glossary." *English Journal* 98.4 (2009): 23–24.
Clark, Elizabeth A. "1990 Presidential Address: Sex, Shame, and Rhetoric: En-Gendering Early Christian Ethics." *Journal of the American Academy of Religion* 59.2 (1991): 221–45.
———. "Antifamilial Tendencies in Ancient Christianity." *Journal of the History of Sexuality* 5.3 (1995): 356–80.
———. *Ascetic Piety and Women's Faith: Essays on Late Ancient Christianity*. Studies in Women and Religion 20. Lewiston, N.Y.: Edwin Mellen Press, 1986.

———. "Ascetic Renunciation and Feminine Advancement: A Paradox of Late Ancient Christianity." *Anglican Theological Review* 63 (1981): 240–57.
———. "The Celibate Bridegroom and His Virginal Brides: Metaphor and the Marriage of Jesus in Early Christian Ascetic Exegesis." *Church History* 77.1 (2008): 1–25.
———. "Claims on the Bones of Saint Stephen: The Partisans of Melania and Eudocia." *Church History* 51.2 (1982): 141–56.
———. *Clement's Use of Aristotle: The Aristotelian Contribution to Clement of Alexandria's Refutation of Gnosticism.* Lewiston, N.Y.: Edwin Mellen Press, 1977.
———. "The Devil's Gateway and the Brides of Christ: Women in the Early Christian World." In *Ascetic Piety and Women's Faith: Essays on Late Ancient Christianity*, 23–60. Lewiston, N.Y.: Edwin Mellen Press, 1986.
———. "Foucault, the Fathers, and Sex." *Journal of the American Academy of Religion* 56.4 (1988): 619–41.
———. *Founding the Fathers: Early Church History and Protestant Professors in Nineteenth-Century America.* Philadelphia: University of Pennsylvania Press, 2011.
———. *History, Theory, Text: Historians and the Linguistic Turn.* Cambridge, Mass.: Harvard University Press, 2004.
———. "Holy Women, Holy Words: Early Christian Women, Social History, and the 'Linguistic Turn.'" *Journal of Early Christian Studies* 6.3 (1998): 413–30.
———. *Jerome, Chrysostom, and Friends: Essays and Translations.* 2nd ed. Studies in Women and Religion 2. Lewiston, N.Y.: Edwin Mellen Press, 1982.
———. "Jerome for the Non-Specialist." *The Classical Review*, n.s., 54.1 (2004): 126–27.
———. "John Chrysostom and the 'Subintroductae.'" *Church History* 46.2 (1977): 171–85.
———. "The Lady Vanishes: Dilemmas of a Feminist Historian after the 'Linguistic Turn.'" *Church History* 67.1 (1998): 1–31.
———. "Melania the Elder and the Origenist Controversy: The Status of the Body in a Late Ancient Debate." In *Nova et Vetera: Patristic Studies in Honor of Thomas Patrick Halton*, edited by John Petruccione, 117–27. Washington, D.C.: Catholic University of America Press, 1998.
———. "New Perspectives on the Origenist Controversy: Human Embodiment and Ascetic Strategies." *Church History* 59.2 (1990): 145–62.
———. *The Origenist Controversy: The Cultural Construction of an Early Christian Debate.* Princeton: Princeton University Press, 1992.
———. "Patrons, Not Priests: Gender and Power in Late Ancient Christianity." *Gender and History* 2.3 (1990): 253–74.
———. "Piety, Propaganda, and Politics in the Life of Melania the Younger." *Studia Patristica* 18.2 (1989): 167–83.
———. "The Place of Jerome's Commentary on Ephesians in the Origenist Controversy: The Apokatastasis and Ascetic Ideals." *Vigiliae Christianae* 41.2 (1987): 154–71.
———. *Reading Renunciation: Asceticism and Scripture in Early Christianity.* Princeton: Princeton University Press, 1999.
———. "Sane Insanity: Women and Asceticism in Late Ancient Christianity." *Medieval Encounters* 3.3 (1997): 211–30.
———. "Theory and Practice in Late Ancient Asceticism: Jerome, Chrysostom, and Augustine." *Journal of Feminist Studies in Religion* 5.2 (1989): 25–46.

———. "Vitiated Seeds and Holy Vessels: Augustine's Manichean Past." In *Images of the Feminine in Gnosticism*, Studies in Antiquity and Christianity, edited by Karen L. King, 367–401. Philadelphia: Fortress Press, 1988.

———. *Women and Religion: The Original Sourcebook of Women in Christian Thought.* Rev. ed. San Francisco: HarperSanFrancisco, 1996.

———. "Women, Gender, and the Study of Christian History." *Church History* 70.3 (2001): 395–426.

———. *Women in the Early Church.* Message of the Fathers of the Church 13. Collegeville, Minn.: Liturgical Press, 1990.

Clark, Elizabeth A., and Diane F. Hatch. *The Golden Bough, the Oaken Cross: The Virgilian Cento of Faltonia Betitia Proba.* Texts and Translations 5. Chico, Calif.: Scholars Press, 1981.

Clark, Gillian. "Women and Asceticism in Late Antiquity: The Refusal of Status and Gender." In *Asceticism*, edited by Vincent L. Wimbush and Richard Valantasis, 33–48. New York: Oxford University Press, 1995.

Click, Melissa A., Hyunji Lee, and Holly Willson Holladay. "Making Monsters: Lady Gaga, Fan Identification, and Social Media." *Popular Music and Society* 36.3 (2013): 360–79.

Cloke, Gillian. *This Female Man of God: Women and Spiritual Power in the Patristic Age, AD 350–450.* New York: Routledge, 1995.

Cobb, L. Stephanie. *Dying to Be Men: Gender and Language in Early Christian Martyr Texts.* Gender, Theory, and Religion. New York: Columbia University Press, 2008.

Cody, Aelred. "The Early History of the Octoechos in Syria." In *East of Byzantium: Syria and Armenia in the Formative Period*, edited by Nina G. Garsoïan, Thomas F. Mathews, and Robert W. Thomson, 89–113. Washington, D.C.: Dumbarton Oaks, 1982.

Connerton, Paul. *How Societies Remember.* Themes in the Social Sciences. Cambridge: Cambridge University Press, 1989.

Conybeare, Catherine. *Paulinus Noster: Self and Symbols in the Letters of Paulinus of Nola.* Oxford Early Christian Studies. Oxford: Oxford University Press, 2000.

Coole, Diana H., and Samantha Frost, eds. *New Materialisms: Ontology, Agency, and Politics.* Durham: Duke University Press, 2010.

Coon, Lynda L. *Sacred Fictions: Holy Women and Hagiography in Late Antiquity.* Philadelphia: University of Pennsylvania Press, 1997.

Cooper, Kate. *The Fall of the Roman Household.* Cambridge: Cambridge University Press, 2007.

———. "A Father, a Daughter and a Procurator: Authority and Resistance in the Prison Memoir of Perpetua of Carthage." *Gender and History* 23.3 (2011): 685–702.

———. "The Household and the Desert: Monastic and Biological Communities in the *Lives of Melania the Younger*." In *Household, Women, and Christianities in Late Antiquity and the Middle Ages*, edited by Anneke B. Mulder-Bakker and Jocelyn Wogan-Browne, 11–35. Turnhout: Brepols, 2005.

———. "Poverty, Obligation, and Inheritance: Roman Heiresses and the Varieties of Senatorial Christianity in Fifth-Century Rome." In *Religion, Dynasty, and Patronage in Early Christian Rome, 300–900*, edited by Kate Cooper and Julia Hillner, 165–89. Cambridge: Cambridge University Press, 2007.

———. *The Virgin and the Bride: Idealized Womanhood in Late Antiquity.* Cambridge, Mass.: Harvard University Press, 1996.

Coptic Orthodox Diocese of Los Angeles. "The Role of Women in the Church (Part II)." Blog, April 9, 2009. http://lacopts.org/story/the-role-of-women-in-the-church.

Corrigan, Kevin. *Evagrius and Gregory: Mind, Soul and Body in the Fourth Century*. Farnham: Ashgate, 2009.

Coster, Charles Henry. "Christianity and the Invasions: Two Sketches." *The Classical Journal* 54.4 (1959): 146–59.

Cott, Nancy F. "Revisiting the Transatlantic 1920s: Vincent Sheean vs. Malcolm Cowley." *American Historical Review* 118.1 (2013): 46–75.

Cowley, Malcolm. *Exile's Return: A Literary Odyssey of the 1920s*. New York: Norton, 1934.

Crenshaw, Kimberlé. "Mapping the Margins: Intersectionality, Identity Politics, and Violence against Women of Color." *Stanford Law Review* 43.6 (1991): 1241–99.

Crislip, Andrew T. *Thorns in the Flesh: Illness and Sanctity in Late Ancient Christianity*. Divinations. Philadelphia: University of Pennsylvania Press, 2013.

Curran, John R. "Jerome and the Sham-Christians of Rome." *Journal of Ecclesiastical History* 48.2 (1997): 213–29.

———. *Pagan City and Christian Capital: Rome in the Fourth Century*. Oxford Classical Monographs. Oxford: Oxford University Press, 2000.

Dalton, Ormonde Maddock. *Byzantine Art and Archaeology*. Oxford: Clarendon Press, 1911.

Deleuze, Gilles. *Difference and Repetition*. Translated by Paul Patton. New York: Columbia University Press, 1994.

Deliyannis, Deborah Mauskopf. *Ravenna in Late Antiquity*. Cambridge: Cambridge University Press, 2010.

Denzey, Nicola. "Facing the Beast: Justin, Christian Martyrdom, and Freedom of the Will." In *Stoicism in Early Christianity*, edited by Tuomas Rasimus, Troels Engberg-Pedersen, and Ismo Dunderberg, 176–98. Peabody, Mass.: Hendrickson Publishers, 2010.

De Smedt, Carolus. "Vita Sanctae Melaniae Junioris." *Analecta Bollandiana* 8 (1889): 16–63.

De Visan, T. "Review: *Sainte Mélanie*." *Revue de Philosophie* 12 (1908): 288.

Devos, Paul. "Le date du voyage d'Égérie." *Analecta Bollandiana* 85 (1967): 165–94.

———. "Égérie à Bethléem: Le 40e jour après Paques à Jérusalem, en 383." *Analecta Bollandiana* 86 (1968): 87–108.

———. "Quand Pierre l'Ibère vint-il à Jérusalem?" *Analecta Bollandiana* 86 (1968): 337–50.

Diekamp, Fr. "Review: Rampolla del Tindaro, *Santa Melania giuniore, senatrice romana*." *Theologische Revue* 5 (May 22, 1906): 241.

Dietz, Maribel. *Wandering Monks, Virgins, and Pilgrims: Ascetic Travel in the Mediterranean World, A.D. 300–800*. University Park: Pennsylvania State University Press, 2005.

Dolan, Marc. *Modern Lives: A Cultural Re-Reading of the "Lost Generation."* West Lafayette, Ind.: Purdue University Press, 1996.

van Doorn-Harder, Pieternella. *Contemporary Coptic Nuns*. Studies in Comparative Religion. Columbia: University of South Carolina Press, 1995.

Draguet, René. "*L'Histoire lausiaque*, une œuvre écrite dans l'esprit d'Évagre." *Revue de l'Histoire Ecclésiastique* 41 (1946): 321–64.

———. "*L'Histoire lausiaque*, une œuvre écrite dans l'esprit d'Évagre." *Revue de l'Histoire Ecclésiastique* 42 (1947): 5–49.

Drijvers, Jan Willem. *Cyril of Jerusalem: Bishop and City*. Supplements to Vigiliae Christianae 72. Leiden: Brill, 2004.

Durham, Carolyn A. *Literary Globalism: Anglo-American Fiction Set in France*. Lewisburg, Penn.: Bucknell University Press, 2005.
Dysinger, Luke, OSB. *Psalmody and Prayer in the Writings of Evagrius Ponticus*. Oxford Theological Monographs. Oxford: Oxford University Press, 2005.
Edwards, Catharine. *Death in Ancient Rome*. New Haven: Yale University Press, 2007.
Elm, Susanna. "Evagrius Ponticus' 'Sententiae ad Virginem.'" *Dumbarton Oaks Papers* 45 (1991): 97–120.
———. *Sons of Hellenism, Fathers of the Church: Emperor Julian, Gregory of Nazianzus, and the Vision of Rome*. Transformation of the Classical Heritage 49. Berkeley and Los Angeles: University of California Press, 2012.
———. *Virgins of God: The Making of Asceticism in Late Antiquity*. Oxford Classical Monographs. Oxford: Oxford University Press, 1994. [Reprint: 2000.]
Elm von der Osten, Dorothee. "Perpetua Felicitas: Die Predigten des Augustinus zur Passio Perpetuae et Felicitatis (s. 280–282)." In *Die christlich-philosophischen Diskurse der Spätantike: Texte, Personen, Institutionen—Akten der Tagung vom 22.–25. Februar 2006 am Zentrum für Antike und Moderne der Albert-Ludwigs-Universität Freiburg*, Philosophie der Antike 28, edited by Therese Fuhrer, 275–98. Stuttgart: Franz Steiner, 2008.
Esch, Arnold. "On the Reuse of Antiquity: The Perspectives of the Archaeologist and of the Historian." In *Reuse Value: Spolia and Appropriation in Art and Architecture from Constantine to Sherrie Levine*, edited by Richard Brilliant and Dale Kinney, 13–31. Farnham: Ashgate, 2011.
Étienne, R. "La démographie des familles impériales et sénatoriales au IVe siècle après J.-C." In *Transformation et conflits au quatrième siècle après J.-C.*, edited by A. Alföldi and J. Straub, 133–68. Bonn: R. Habelt, 1978.
Fisher, Arthur L. "Women and Gender in Palladius' *Lausiac History*." *Studia Monastica* 33 (1991): 23–50.
Flower, Harriet I. *Ancestor Masks and Aristocratic Power in Roman Culture*. Oxford: Oxford University Press, 1996.
Frøyshov, Stig. "The Early Development of the Liturgical Eight-Mode System in Jerusalem." *St. Vladimir's Theological Quarterly* 51.2–3 (2007): 139–78.
———. "The Georgian Witness to the Jerusalem Liturgy: New Sources and Studies." In *Inquiries into Eastern Christian Worship: Selected Papers of the Second International Congress of the Society of Oriental Liturgy, Rome, 17–21 September 2008*, Eastern Christian Studies 12, edited by Bert Groen, Steven Hawkes-Teeples, and Stefanos Alexopoulos, 227–67. Louvain: Peeters, 2012.
Garland, Robert. *The Eye of the Beholder: Deformity and Disability in the Graeco-Roman World*. 2nd ed. London: Bristol Classical Press, 2010.
Geertman, Herman. "Il fastigium Lateranense e l'arredo presbiteriale: Una lunga storia." In Herman Geertman, Sible de Blaauw, and Christina van der Laan, *Hic fecit basilicam: Studi sul Liber Pontificalis e gli edifici ecclesiastici di Roma da Silvestro a Silverio*, 133–48. Louvain: Peeters, 2004.
Géhin, Paul. "En marge de la constitution d'un Repertorium Evagrianum Syriacum, quelques remarques sur l'organisation en corpus des œuvres d'Evagre." *Parole de l'Orient* 35 (2010): 285–301.

———. "Nouveaux fragments grecs des lettres d'Évagre." *Revue d'Histoire des Textes* 24 (1994): 117–47.

Géhin, Paul, and Stig Frøyshov. "Nouvelles découvertes sinaïtiques: À propos de la parution de l'inventaire des manuscrits grecs." *Revue des Études Byzantines* 58.1 (2000): 167–84.

Gell, Alfred. *Art and Agency: An Anthropological Theory.* Oxford: Clarendon Press, 1998.

Getcha, Job. *The Typikon Decoded: An Explanation of Byzantine Liturgical Practice.* Translated by Paul Meyendorff. Orthodox Liturgy Series 3. Yonkers, N.Y.: St. Vladimir's Seminary Press, 2012.

Gibbs, Raymond W. "Embodied Experience and Linguistic Meaning." *Brain and Language* 84.1 (2003): 1–15.

———. *The Poetics of Mind: Figurative Thought, Language, and Understanding.* Cambridge: Cambridge University Press, 1994.

Gibbs, Raymond W., Paula Lenz Costa Lima, and Edson Francozo. "Metaphor Is Grounded in Embodied Experience." *Journal of Pragmatics* 36.7 (2004): 1189–1210.

Gibbs, Raymond W., and Gerard Steen, eds. *Metaphor in Cognitive Linguistics: Selected Papers from the Fifth International Cognitive Linguistics Conference, Amsterdam, July 1997.* Amsterdam: John Benjamins, 1999.

Gleason, Maud W. *Making Men: Sophists and Self-Presentation in Ancient Rome.* Princeton: Princeton University Press, 1995.

Goehring, James E. *Ascetics, Society, and the Desert: Studies in Egyptian Monasticism.* Studies in Antiquity and Christianity. Harrisburg, Penn.: Trinity Press International, 1999.

———. "The Encroaching Desert: Literary Production and Ascetic Space in Early Christian Egypt." *Journal of Early Christian Studies* 1.3 (1993): 281–96.

Goyau, Georges. *Sainte Mélanie, 383–439.* Paris: J. Gabalda, 1908.

Grace, Pamela. *The Religious Film: Christianity and the Hagiopic.* New Approaches to Film Genre 4. Chichester: Wiley-Blackwell, 2009.

Graf, Georg. *Die Übersetzungen.* Volume 1 of *Geschichte der christlichen arabischen Literatur.* Studi e Testi 118. Vatican City: Biblioteca Apostolica Vaticana, 1944.

Graver, Margaret. *Stoicism and Emotion.* Chicago: University of Chicago Press, 2007.

Green, Nancy L. "Expatriation, Expatriates, and Expats: The American Transformation of a Concept." *American Historical Review* 114.2 (2009): 307–28.

Griffith, Susan B. "*Iatros* and *Medicus:* The Physician in Gregory Nazianzen and Augustine." In *Orientalia: Clement, Origen, Athanasius, the Cappadocians, Chrysostom,* Studia Patristica 41, edited by F. Young, M. Edwards, and P. Parvis, 319–25. Louvain: Peeters, 2006.

Grig, Lucy. "Deconstructing the Symbolic City: Jerome as Guide to Late Antique Rome." *Papers of the British School at Rome* 80 (2012): 125–43.

Grubbs, Judith Evans. "Church, State, and Children: Christian and Imperial Attitudes toward Infant Exposure in Late Antiquity." In *The Power of Religion in Late Antiquity,* edited by Andrew Cain and Noel Lenski, 119–31. Farnham: Ashgate, 2009.

Guillaumont, Antoine. *Les "Képhalaia Gnostica" d'Évagre le Pontique et l'histoire de l'Origénisme chez les grecs et chez les syriens.* Patristica Sorbonensia 5. Paris: Editions du Seuil, 1962.

———. *Un philosophe au désert: Évagre le Pontique.* Textes et Traditions 8. Paris: Vrin, 2004.

Guillaumont, Claire. "Fragments grecs inédits d'Évagre le Pontique." *Texte und Untersuchungen zur Geschichte der Altchristlichen Literatur* 133 (1987): 209–21.

Haines-Eitzen, Kim. "'Girls Trained in Beautiful Writing': Female Scribes in Roman Antiquity and Early Christianity." *Journal of Early Christian Studies* 6.4 (1998): 629–46.
Halberstam, Judith. *Female Masculinity*. Durham: Duke University Press, 1998.
Halbwachs, Maurice. *On Collective Memory*. Edited and translated by Lewis A. Coser. The Heritage of Sociology. Chicago: University of Chicago Press, 1992.
Hall, Stuart. "Women among the Early Martyrs." In *Martyrs and Martyrologies: Papers Read at the 1992 Summer Meeting and the 1993 Winter Meeting of the Ecclesiastical History Society*, Studies in Church History 30, edited by Diana Wood, 1–21. Oxford: Blackwell, 1993.
Halliwell, Martin. "Tourists or Exiles? American Modernists in Paris in the 1920s and 1950s." *Nottingham French Studies* 44.3 (2005): 54–68.
Halporn, J. W. "Literary History and Generic Expectations in the *Passio* and *Acta Perpetuae*." *Vigiliae Christianae* 45.3 (1991): 223–41.
Hansen, Maria Fabricius. *The Eloquence of Appropriation: Prolegomena to an Understanding of Spolia in Early Christian Rome*. Analecta Romana Instituti Danici, Supplementum 33. Rome: L'Erma di Bretschneider, 2003.
Harmless, William, S.J. "Remembering Poemen Remembering: The Desert Fathers and the Spirituality of Memory." *Church History* 69.3 (2000): 483–518.
Harrison, Verna E. F. "Review of Gillian Cloke, '*This Female Man of God*': *Women and Spiritual Power in the Patristic Age, AD 350–450*." *Journal of Theological Studies* n.s., 48.2 (1997): 694–700.
———. "Women, Human Identity, and the Image of God: Antiochene Interpretations." *Journal of Early Christian Studies* 9.2 (2001): 205–49.
Harvey, Susan Ashbrook. "Sacred Bonding: Mothers and Daughters in Early Syriac Hagiography." *Journal of Early Christian Studies* 4.1 (1996): 27–56.
———. *Scenting Salvation: Ancient Christianity and the Olfactory Imagination*. Berkeley and Los Angeles: University of California Press, 2006.
Harvey, Susan Ashbrook, and David G. Hunter, eds. *The Oxford Handbook of Early Christian Studies*. Oxford Handbooks in Religion and Theology. Oxford: Oxford University Press, 2008.
Hasan, Sana S. *Christians versus Muslims in Modern Egypt: The Century-Long Struggle for Coptic Equality*. Oxford: Oxford University Press, 2003.
Healy, Patrick J. "Review: *The Life of St. Melania*." *Catholic University Bulletin* 15 (1909): 786–87.
Hemingway, Ernest. *A Moveable Feast: The Restored Edition*. Edited by Séan A. Hemingway. New York: Scribner, 2009. [First published by Scribner, 1964.]
Heuzey-Goyau, Juliette. *Dieu premier servi: Georges Goyau—Sa vie et son œuvre*. Paris: Bonne Presse, 1947.
Hill, L. "The First Wave of Feminism: Were the Stoics Feminists?" *History of Political Thought* 22.1 (2001): 13–40.
Hillner, Julia. "Domus, Family, and Inheritance: The Senatorial Family House in Late Antique Rome." *Journal of Roman Studies* 93 (2003): 129–45.
Hollywood, Amy. "Queering the Beguines: Mechthild of Magdeburg, Hadewijch of Anvers, Marguerite Porete." In *Queer Theology: Rethinking the Western Body*, edited by Gerard Loughlin, 163–74. Oxford: Blackwell, 2007.

Holman, Susan R. "Martyr Saints and the Demon of Infant Mortality: Folk Healing in Early Christian Pediatric Medicine." In *Children and Family in Late Antiquity: Life, Death and Interaction,* Interdisciplinary Studies in Ancient Culture and Religion 15, edited by Christian Laes, Katariina Mustakallio, and Ville Vuolanto, 235–56. Louvain: Peeters, 2015.

Holst-Warhaft, Gail. *Dangerous Voices: Women's Laments and Greek Literature.* New York: Routledge, 1992.

Holum, Kenneth G. *Theodosian Empresses: Women and Imperial Dominion in Late Antiquity.* Transformation of the Classical Heritage 3. Berkeley and Los Angeles: University of California Press, 1982.

Hope, Valerie M. *Roman Death: The Dying and the Dead in Ancient Rome.* London: Continuum Press, 2009.

Horn, Cornelia B. "Empress Eudocia and the Monk Peter the Iberian: Patronage, Pilgrimage, and the Love of a Foster-Mother in Fifth-Century Palestine." *Byzantinische Forschungen* 28 (2004): 197–213.

———. "Raising Martyrs and Ascetics: A Diachronic Comparison of Educational Role-Models for Early Christian Children." In *Children in Late Ancient Christianity,* Studien und Texte zu Antike und Christentum 58, edited by Cornelia B. Horn and Robert R. Phenix, Jr., 293–316. Tübingen: Mohr Siebeck, 2009.

Horn, Cornelia B., and John W. Martens. *"Let the Little Children Come to Me": Childhood and Children in Early Christianity.* Washington, D.C.: Catholic University of America Press, 2009.

Horn, Cornelia B., and Robert R. Phenix, Jr., eds. *Children in Late Ancient Christianity.* Studien und Texte zu Antike und Christentum 58. Tübingen: Mohr Siebeck, 2009.

Hunt, E. D. *Holy Land Pilgrimage in the Later Roman Empire, AD 312–460.* Oxford: Clarendon Press, 1982.

———. "Palladius of Helenopolis: A Party and Its Supporters in the Church of the Late Fourth Century." *Journal of Theological Studies,* n.s., 24.2 (1973): 456–80.

Jackson, Ralph. *Doctors and Diseases in the Roman Empire.* Norman: University of Oklahoma Press, 1988.

Jacobs, Andrew S. *Christ Circumcised: A Study in Early Christian History and Difference.* Divinations. Philadelphia: University of Pennsylvania Press, 2012.

———. *Remains of the Jews: The Holy Land and Christian Empire in Late Antiquity.* Divinations. Stanford: Stanford University Press, 2003.

———. "'What Has Rome to Do with Bethlehem?' Cultural Capital(s) and Religious Imperialism in Late Ancient Christianity." *Classical Receptions Journal* 3.1 (2011): 29–45.

———. "Writing Demetrias: Ascetic Logic in Ancient Christianity." *Church History* 69.4 (2000): 719–48.

Jagose, Annamarie. *Queer Theory: An Introduction.* New York: New York University Press, 1996.

Jeffery, Peter. "The Earliest Christian Chant Repertory Recovered: The Georgian Witnesses to Jerusalem Chant." *Journal of the American Musicological Society* 47.1 (1994): 1–38.

———. "The Earliest *Oktōēchoi*: The Role of Jerusalem and Palestine in the Beginnings of Modal Ordering." In *The Study of Medieval Chant: Paths and Bridges, East and West—In Honor of Kenneth Levy,* edited by Peter Jeffery, 147–209. Woodbridge: Boydell Press, 2001.

———. "The Sunday Office of Seventh-Century Jerusalem in the Georgian Chantbook (Iadgari): A Preliminary Report." *Studia Liturgica* 21 (1991): 52–75.
Johnson, Mark. *The Body in the Mind: The Bodily Basis of Meaning, Imagination, and Reason*. Chicago: University of Chicago Press, 1987.
Jonsson, Terese. "Some Thoughts on Intersectionality and Class." *Between the Lines* (blog). https://researchingbetweenthelines.wordpress.com/2012/05/26/some-thoughts-on-intersectionality-and-class/.
Kalkman, Richard G. "Two Sermons: *De Tempore Barbarico* Attributed to St. Quodvultdeus, Bishop of Carthage—A Study of Text and Attribution with Translation and Commentary." Ph.D. dissertation, Catholic University of America, 1963.
Kalvesmaki, Joel. "The *Epistula Fidei* of Evagrius of Pontus: An Answer to Constantinople." *Journal of Early Christian Studies* 20.1 (2012): 113–39.
Katos, Demetrios S. *Palladius of Helenopolis: The Origenist Advocate*. Oxford Early Christian Studies. Oxford: Oxford University Press, 2011.
Kinnard, Isabelle. "*Imitatio Christi* in Christian Martyrdom and Asceticism: A Critical Dialogue." In *Asceticism and Its Critics: Historical Accounts and Comparative Perspectives*, edited by Oliver Freiberger, 131–50. Oxford: Oxford University Press, 2006.
Kinney, Dale. "'Spolia. Damnatio' and 'Renovatio Memoriae.'" *Memoirs of the American Academy in Rome* 42 (1997): 117–48.
Kirmayer, Laurence J. "The Body's Insistence on Meaning: Metaphor as Presentation and Representation in Illness Experience." *Medical Anthropology Quarterly* 6.4 (1992): 323–46.
Kövecses, Zoltán. *Metaphor and Emotion: Language, Culture, and Body in Human Feeling*. Cambridge: Cambridge University Press, 2000.
Kraemer, Ross Shepard. "Women and Gender." In *The Oxford Handbook of Early Christian Studies*, Oxford Handbooks in Religion and Theology, edited by Susan Ashbrook Harvey and David G. Hunter, 465–92. Oxford: Oxford University Press, 2008.
Kraemer, Ross Shepard, and Shira Lander. "Perpetua and Felicitas." In *The Early Christian World*, edited by Philip Francis Esler, vol. 2: 1048–68. London: Routledge, 2000.
Krautheimer, Richard. *Three Christian Capitals: Topography and Politics*. Una's Lectures 4. Berkeley and Los Angeles: University of California Press, 1983.
Krautheimer, Richard, Spencer Corbett, and Alfred K. Frazer, eds. *Corpus Basilicarum Christianarum Romae: The Early Christian Basilicas of Rome (IV–IX Cent.)*. 5 vols. Monumenti di Antichità Cristiana, ser. 2. Vatican City: Pontificio Istituto di Archeologia Cristiana, 1937–80.
Krawiec, Rebecca. "Asceticism." In *The Oxford Handbook of Early Christian Studies*, Oxford Handbooks in Religion and Theology, edited by Susan Ashbrook Harvey and David G. Hunter, 764–85. Oxford: Oxford University Press, 2008.
———. "'From the Womb of the Church': Monastic Families." *Journal of Early Christian Studies* 11.3 (2003): 283–307.
———. "'Garments of Salvation': Representations of Monastic Clothing in Late Antiquity." *Journal of Early Christian Studies* 17.1 (2009): 125–50.
Kuefler, Mathew. *The Manly Eunuch: Masculinity, Gender Ambiguity, and Christian Ideology in Late Antiquity*. Chicago Series on Sexuality, History, and Society. Chicago: University of Chicago Press, 2001.

Lagrange, M.-J. "Review: *Santa Melania giuniore, senatrice romana.*" *Revue Biblique Internationale* 3 (1906): 300–303.

Lakoff, George, and Mark Johnson. *Metaphors We Live By.* Chicago: University of Chicago Press, 1980.

Lampe, G. W. H., ed. *A Patristic Greek Lexicon.* Oxford: Clarendon Press, 1961.

Latour, Bruno. *The Pasteurization of France.* Translated by Alan Sheridan and John Law. Cambridge, Mass.: Harvard University Press, 1988.

———. *Reassembling the Social: An Introduction to Actor-Network-Theory.* Clarendon Lectures in Management Studies. Oxford: Oxford University Press, 2005.

Laurence, P. "Rome et Jérôme: Des amours contrariées." *Revue Bénédictine* 107 (1997): 227–49.

Layton, Richard A. "Plagiarism and Lay Patronage of Ascetic Scholarship: Jerome, Ambrose and Rufinus." *Journal of Early Christian Studies* 10.4 (2002): 489–522.

Lebbe, D. Bède. "Review: M. Cardinale Rampolla del Tindaro, *Santa Melania giuniore, senatrice romana.*" *Revue Bénédictine* 23 (1906): 459.

Leeb, Helmut. *Die Gesänge im Gemeindegottesdienst von Jerusalem (vom 5. bis 8. Jh.).* Wiener Beiträge zur Theologie 28. Vienna: Herder, 1970.

Lepelley, Claude. "Mélanie la Jeune entre Rome, la Sicile et l'Afrique: Les effets socialement pernicieux d'une forme extrême de l'ascétisme." *Kōkalos* 43–44.1 (1997–98): 15–32.

Leppin, Hartmut. "The Church Historians (I): Socrates, Sozomenus, and Theodoretus." In *Greek and Roman Historiography in Late Antiquity: Fourth to Sixth Century A.D.*, edited by Gabriele Marasco, 219–54. Leiden: Brill, 2003.

Leuba, James H. *A Psychological Study of Religion: Its Origin, Function, and Future.* New York: Macmillan, 1912.

Lienhard, Joseph T. *Paulinus of Nola and Early Western Monasticism, with a Study of the Chronology of His Works and an Annotated Bibliography, 1879-1976.* Theophaneia 28. Bonn: Peter Hanstein, 1977.

Lieu, Samuel N. C. "Constantine in Legendary Literature." In *The Cambridge Companion to the Age of Constantine*, edited by Noel Lenski, rev. ed., 298–321. Cambridge: Cambridge University Press, 2012.

Liverani, Paolo. "Reading Spolia in Late Antiquity and Contemporary Perception." In *Reuse Value: Spolia and Appropriation in Art and Architecture from Constantine to Sherrie Levine*, edited by Richard Brilliant and Dale Kinney, 33–51. Farnham: Ashgate, 2011.

———. "Saint Peter's, Leo the Great and the Leprosy of Constantine." *Papers of the British School at Rome* 76 (2008): 155–72.

Loughlin, Gerard, ed. *Queer Theology: Rethinking the Western Body.* Oxford: Blackwell, 2007.

Louth, Andrew. "Why Did the Syrians Reject the Council of Chalcedon?" In *Chalcedon in Context: Church Councils, 400–700*, edited by Richard Price and Mary Whitby, 107–16. Liverpool: Liverpool University Press, 2009.

Luce, Stephen B. "Archaeological News and Discussions." *American Journal of Archaeology* 47.1 (1943): 102–24.

MacMullen, Ramsay. *The Second Church: Popular Christianity A.D. 200-400.* Writings from the Greco-Roman World, Supplement Series, 1. Atlanta: Society of Biblical Literature, 2009.

MacWhinney, Brian. "The Emergence of Language from Embodiment." In *The Emergence of Language*, edited by Brian MacWhinney, 213–56. Mahwah, N.J.: Lawrence Erlbaum Associates, 1999.
Mannheim, Karl. "The Problem of Generations." In *From Karl Mannheim*, edited by Kurt H. Wolff, 2nd ed., 351–98. New Brunswick: Transaction Publishers, 1993.
Markus, R. A. "The Legacy of Pelagius: Orthodoxy, Heresy and Conciliation." In *The Making of Orthodoxy: Essays in Honour of Henry Chadwick*, edited by Rowan Williams, 214–34. Cambridge: Cambridge University Press, 1989.
Marlowe, Elizabeth. "Framing the Sun: The Arch of Constantine and the Roman Cityscape." *Art Bulletin* 88.2 (2006): 223–42.
Martin, Dale B. *Sex and the Single Savior: Gender and Sexuality in Biblical Interpretation*. Louisville: Westminster John Knox Press, 2006.
Martin, Dale B., and Patricia Cox Miller, eds. *The Cultural Turn in Late Ancient Studies: Gender, Asceticism, and Historiography*. Durham: Duke University Press, 2005.
Marx-Wolf, Heidi, and Kristi Upson-Saia. "State of the Question: Religion, Medicine, Disability, and Health in Late Antiquity." *Journal of Late Antiquity* 8.2 (2015): 257–72.
McNamara, Jo Ann. "Sexual Equality and the Cult of Virginity in Early Christian Thought." *Feminist Studies* 3.3–4 (1976): 145–58.
Meltzer, Françoise, and Jaś Elsner, eds. *Saints: Faith without Borders*. Chicago: University of Chicago Press, 2011.
Métrévéli, Hélène. "Les manuscrits liturgiques géorgiens des IXe–Xe siècles et leur importance pour l'étude de l'hymnographie byzantine." *Bedi Kartlisa: Revue de Kartvélologie* 36 (1978): 43–48.
Metreveli, E., C'. Čankievi, and L. Xevsuriani. უძველესი იადგარი. (*Uzvelesi iadgari*. [*The Oldest Chantbook*].) Żveli K'art'uli Mcerlobis Żeglebi 2. Tbilisi: Mec'niereba, 1980.
Métrévéli, Hélène, Ts. Tchankieva, and L. Khevsouriani. "Le plus ancien tropologion géorgien." *Bedi Kartlisa: Revue de Kartvélologie* 39 (1981): 54–62.
Miller, Patricia Cox. *The Corporeal Imagination: Signifying the Holy in Late Ancient Christianity*. Divinations. Philadelphia: University of Pennsylvania Press, 2009.
———. "Is There a Harlot in This Text? Hagiography and the Grotesque." In *The Cultural Turn in Late Ancient Studies: Gender, Asceticism, and Historiography*, edited by Dale B. Martin and Patricia Cox Miller, 87–102. Durham: Duke University Press, 2005.
al-Miskīn, Mattā. *al-Rahbanah al-qibṭīyah fī 'aṣr al-Qiddīs Anbā Maqār*. 4th ed. Wādī al-Naṭrūn: Dayr al-Qiddīs Anbā Maqār, 2006.
Moine, Nicole. "Melaniana." *Recherches Augustiniennes* 15 (1980): 3–79.
Monk, Craig. *Writing the Lost Generation: Expatriate Autobiography and American Modernism*. Iowa City: University of Iowa Press, 2008.
Morton, Timothy. *Hyperobjects: Philosophy and Ecology after the End of the World*. Posthumanities 27. Minneapolis: University of Minnesota Press, 2013.
Moss, Candida R. *Ancient Christian Martyrdom: Diverse Practices, Theologies, and Traditions*. New Haven: Yale University Press, 2012.
Mratschek-Halfmann, Sigrid. "Melania and the Unknown Governor of Palestine." *Journal of Late Antiquity* 5.2 (2012): 250–68.
———. "*Multis enim notissima est sanctitas loci*: Paulinus and the Gradual Rise of Nola as a Center of Christian Hospitality." *Journal of Early Christian Studies* 9.4 (2001): 511–53.

Muñoz, José Esteban. *Cruising Utopia: The Then and There of Queer Futurity.* Sexual Cultures. New York: New York University Press, 2009.
Murphy, Francis X. "Melania the Elder: A Biographical Note." *Traditio* 5 (1947): 59–77.
———. *Rufinus of Aquileia (345–411): His Life and Works.* Washington, D.C.: Catholic University of America Press, 1945.
Nathan, Geoffrey S. *The Family in Late Antiquity: The Rise of Christianity and the Endurance of Tradition.* New York: Routledge, 2000.
Niquet, Heike. *Monumenta virtutum titulique: Senatorische Selbstdarstellung im spätantiken Rom im Spiegel der epigraphischen Denkmäler.* Heidelberger Althistorische Beiträge und Epigraphische Studien 34. Stuttgart: Steiner, 2000.
Nussbaum, Martha Craven. "The Incomplete Feminism of Musonius Rufus: Platonist, Stoic, and Roman." In *The Sleep of Reason: Erotic Experience and Sexual Ethics in Ancient Greece and Rome,* by Martha C. Nussbaum and Juha Sihvola, 283–326. Chicago: University of Chicago Press, 2002.
———. *The Therapy of Desire: Theory and Practice in Hellenistic Ethics.* 2nd ed. Princeton: Princeton University Press, 2009.
———. *Upheavals of Thought: The Intelligence of Emotions.* Cambridge: Cambridge University Press, 2001.
Ophir, Adi. "The Sciences of the Spirit." *differences: A Journal of Feminist Cultural Studies* 24.3 (2014): 160–74.
Osiek, Carolyn. "Perpetua's Husband." *Journal of Early Christian Studies* 10.2 (2002): 287–90.
Parkin, Tim G. *Demography and Roman Society.* Ancient Society and History. Baltimore: The Johns Hopkins University Press, 1992.
Peltomaa, Leena Mari. *The Image of the Virgin Mary in the Akathistos Hymn.* The Medieval Mediterranean 35. Leiden: Brill, 2001.
Peradzè, G. "Les monuments liturgiques prébyzantins en langue géorgienne." *Le Muséon* 45 (1932): 255–72.
Pizer, Donald. *American Expatriate Writing and the Paris Moment: Modernism and Place.* Modernist Studies. Baton Rouge: Louisiana State University Press, 1996.
Praet, Danny. "'*Meliore cupiditate detentus*': Christian Self-Definition and the Rejection of Marriage in the Early Acts of the Martyrs." *Euphrosyne* 31 (2003): 457–73.
Princess Troubetzkoy. *See* Rives, Amélie.
Quasten, Johannes. *Patrology.* 4 vols. Westminster, Md.: Newman Press, 1950–86.
Rampolla del Tindaro, Mariano. *The Life of St. Melania by His Eminence Cardinal Rampolla.* Edited by Herbert Thurston. Translated by Ellen Mary Agnes Leahy. London: Burns & Oates, 1908.
———. *Santa Melania giuniore, senatrice romana: Documenti contemporanei e note.* Rome: Tipografia Vaticana, 1905.
Rapp, Claudia. "Figures of Female Sanctity: Byzantine Edifying Manuscripts and Their Audience." *Dumbarton Oaks Papers* 50 (1996): 313–44.
———. *Holy Bishops in Late Antiquity: The Nature of Christian Leadership in an Age of Transition.* Transformation of the Classical Heritage 37. Berkeley and Los Angeles: University of California Press, 2005.

———. "Palladius, Lausus and the *Historia Lausiaca*." In *Novum Millennium: Studies on Byzantine History and Culture: Dedicated to Paul Speck, 19 December 1999*, edited by Claudia Sode and Sarolta A. Takács, 279–89. Aldershot: Ashgate, 2001.

———. "Storytelling as Spiritual Communication in Early Greek Hagiography: The Use of Diegesis." *Journal of Early Christian Studies* 6.3 (1998): 431–48.

Rasimus, Tuomas, Troels Engberg-Pedersen, and Ismo Dunderberg, eds. *Stoicism in Early Christianity*. Peabody, Mass.: Hendrickson Publishers, 2010.

Ray, Walter Dean. "August 15 and the Development of the Jerusalem Calendar." Ph.D. dissertation, University of Notre Dame, 2000.

Rebenich, Stefan. *Jerome*. The Early Church Fathers. London: Routledge, 2002.

Regnault, Lucien. "Apophthegmata Patrum." In *The Coptic Encyclopedia*, edited by Aziz S. Atiya, vol. 1: 177–78. New York: Macmillan, 1991.

Renoux, Athanase (Charles). *Le codex arménien Jérusalem 121*. 2 vols. Patrologia Orientalis 35.1, 36.2. Turnhout: Brepols, 1969–71.

———. "L'Epiphanie à Jérusalem au IVme et au Vme siècle." *Revue des Études Arméniennes* 2 (1965): 343–59.

Reydams-Schils, Gretchen. *The Roman Stoics: Self, Responsibility, and Affection*. Chicago: University of Chicago Press, 2005.

Rives, Amélie. [Princess Troubetzkoy.] *The Elusive Lady*. London: Hurst & Blackett, 1918.

Rozitchner, León. *La cosa y la cruz: Cristianismo y capitalismo (en torno a las Confesiones de san Agustín)*. Biblioteca Filosófica. Buenos Aires: Editorial Losada, 1997.

Rubenson, Samuel. *The Letters of St. Antony: Monasticism and the Making of a Saint*. Studies in Antiquity and Christianity. Minneapolis: Fortress Press, 1995.

Russell, Norman F.. *Theophilus of Alexandria*. The Early Church Fathers. London: Routledge, 2007.

Salazar, Christine F. "Fragments of Lost Hippocratic Writings in Galen's Glossary." *Classical Quarterly* 47.2 (1997): 543–47.

———. *The Treatment of War Wounds in Graeco-Roman Antiquity*. Studies in Ancient Medicine 21. Leiden: Brill, 2000.

Salisbury, Joyce E. *Perpetua's Passion: The Death and Memory of a Young Roman Woman*. New York: Routledge, 1997.

Saller, Richard P. *Patriarchy, Property, and Death in the Roman Family*. Cambridge: Cambridge University Press, 1994.

Salzman, Michele Renee. "Apocalypse Then? Jerome and the Fall of Rome in 410." In *Maxima Debetur Magistro Reverentia: Essays on Rome and the Roman Tradition in Honor of Russel T. Scott*, Biblioteca di Athenaeum 54, edited by Paul B. Harvey, Jr., and Catherine Conybeare, 175–92. Como: New Press, 2009.

———. "Aristocratic Women: Conductors of Christianity in the Fourth Century." *Helios* 16 (1989): 207–20.

———. "Elite Realities and Mentalities: The Making of a Western Christian Aristocracy." *Arethusa* 33.3 (2000): 347–62.

———. *The Making of a Christian Aristocracy: Social and Religious Change in the Western Roman Empire*. Cambridge, Mass.: Harvard University Press, 2002.

———. *On Roman Time: The Codex-Calendar of 354 and the Rhythms of Urban Life in Late Antiquity*. Transformation of the Classical Heritage 17. Berkeley and Los Angeles: University of California Press, 1990.

Samellas, Antigone. *Death in the Eastern Mediterranean (50–600 A.D.): The Christianization of the East—An Interpretation*. Studien und Texte zu Antike und Christentum 12. Tübingen: Mohr Siebeck, 2002.

Šaniże, Akaki, A. Martirosovi, and A. Jišiašvili. ძველ-ეგრისულის იადგარი (*Čil-Etratis Iadgari*. [*The Papyrus-Parchment Iadgari*.]) Żveli k'art'uli enis żeglebi 15. T'bilisi: Gamomc'emloba "Mec'niereba," 1977.

Sauget, Joseph-Marie. "Un nouveau témoin de collection d'Apophthegmata Patrum: Le Paterikon du Sinaï arabe 547." *Le Muséon* 86 (1973): 5–35.

———. *Une traduction arabe de la collection d'Apophthegmata Patrum de 'Enānīšō': Étude du MS. Paris arabe 253 et des témoins parallèles*. Corpus Scriptorum Christianorum Orientalium 495. Louvain: Peeters, 1987.

Schneider, Hans-Michael. *Lobpreis im rechten Glauben: Die Theologie der Hymnen an den Festen der Menschwerdung der alten jerusalemer Liturgie im georgischen Udzvelesi Iadgari*. Hereditas: Studien zur alten Kirchengeschichte 23. Bonn: Borengässer, 2004.

Schor, Adam M. *Theodoret's People: Social Networks and Religious Conflict in Late Roman Syria*. Berkeley and Los Angeles: University of California Press, 2011.

Schwartz, E. "Palladiana." *Zeitschrift für die Neutestamentliche Wissenschaft und die Kunde der Älteren Kirche* 36.2 (1937): 161–204.

Scott, Joan Wallach. *The Fantasy of Feminist History*. Next Wave Provocations. Durham: Duke University Press, 2011.

———. *Gender and the Politics of History*. 2nd ed., rev. Gender and Culture. New York: Columbia University Press, 1999. [1st ed. 1988.]

Sessa, Kristina. *The Formation of Papal Authority in Late Antique Italy: Roman Bishops and the Domestic Sphere*. Cambridge: Cambridge University Press, 2011.

———. "Ursa's Return: Captivity, Remarriage, and the Domestic Authority of Roman Bishops in Fifth-Century Italy." *Journal of Early Christian Studies* 19.3 (2011): 401–32.

Shaw, Brent D. "The Family in Late Antiquity: The Experience of Augustine." *Past and Present* 115 (1987): 3–51.

———. "The Passion of Perpetua." *Past and Present* 139 (1993): 3–45.

Shenouda III. *Sīrat al-Qiddīsah Mīlānīyā*. [*The Life of Saint Melania*.] http://www.youtube.com/watch?v=pR_zZxj4dts.

———. *So Many Years with the Problems of People, Part One: Biblical Questions*. Translated by St. George Coptic Orthodox Church. 2nd ed. Cairo: Dar el-Tebaa el-Kawmia, 1993.

Shoemaker, Stephen J. *Ancient Traditions of the Virgin Mary's Dormition and Assumption*. Oxford Early Christian Studies. Oxford: Oxford University Press, 2002.

———. "Apocrypha and Liturgy in the Fourth Century: The Case of the 'Six Books' Dormition Apocryphon." In *Jewish and Christian Scriptures: The Function of "Canonical" and "Non-Canonical" Religious Texts*, Jewish and Christian Texts in Contexts and Related Studies 7, edited by James H. Charlesworth and Lee M. McDonald, 153–63. London: T. & T. Clark, 2010.

———. "The Cult of the Virgin in the Fourth Century: A Fresh Look at Some Old and New Sources." In *The Origins of the Cult of the Virgin Mary*, edited by Chris Maunder, 71–87. London: Burns & Oates, 2008.

———. "Epiphanius of Salamis, the Kollyridians, and the Early Dormition Narratives: The Cult of the Virgin in the Fourth Century." *Journal of Early Christian Studies* 16.3 (2008): 371–401.

———. "Marian Liturgies and Devotion in Early Christianity." In *Mary: The Complete Resource*, edited by Sarah Jane Boss, 130–45. London: Continuum Press, 2007.

Silvas, Anna M. "Edessa to Cassino: The Passage of Basil's 'Asketikon' to the West." *Vigiliae Christianae* 56.3 (2002): 247–59.

Skerrett, Kathleen Roberts. "Sex, Law, and Other Reasonable Endeavors." *differences: A Journal of Feminist Cultural Studies* 18.3 (2007): 81–96.

Smith, Wilfred Cantwell. *The Meaning and End of Religion: A New Approach to the Religious Traditions of Mankind*. New York: Macmillan, 1963.

Snelders, Bas. "The *Traditio Legis* on Early Christian Sarcophagi." *Antiquité Tardive* 13 (2005): 321–33.

Soto, Michael. *The Modernist Nation: Generation, Renaissance, and Twentieth-Century American Literature*. Tuscaloosa: University of Alabama Press, 2004.

Spiegel, Gabrielle M. "History, Historicism, and the Social Logic of the Text in the Middle Ages." *Speculum* 65.1 (1990): 59–86.

Spieser, J.-M. "The Representation of Christ in the Apses of Early Christian Churches." *Gesta* 37.1 (1998): 63–73.

Stacey, Jackie. *Star Gazing: Hollywood Cinema and Female Spectatorship*. New York: Routledge, 1994.

Stang, Charles. "Evagrius of Pontus on 'the Great Gift of Letters.'" In *Syriac Encounters: Papers Presented at the Sixth North American Syriac Symposium, Duke University, 26–29 June 2011*, edited by Maria Doerfler et al. [Maria Doerfler, Emmanuel Fiano, Kyle Smith, and Luk van Rompay]. Louvain: Peeters, 2015.

Stasia, Cristina. "Butch-Femme Interrupted." *Journal of Bisexuality* 3.3–4 (2003): 181–201.

Stein, Gertrude. "An American and France." In *What Are Masterpieces?* 61–70. New York: Pitman Publishing, 1970.

———. *The Autobiography of Alice B. Toklas*. New York: Harcourt, Brace and Company, 1933.

Stelzle, Charles. "Socialism and the Church." *Locomotive Engineers Journal* 41 (1907): 208–9.

Stemberger, Günter. *Jews and Christians in the Holy Land: Palestine in the Fourth Century*. Edinburgh: T. & T. Clark, 2000.

Stewart, Columba. "Evagrius Ponticus on Monastic Pedagogy." In *Abba: The Tradition of Orthodoxy in the West: Festschrift for Bishop Kallistos (Ware) of Diokleia*, edited by John Behr, Andrew Louth, and Dimitri E. Conomos, 241–71. Crestwood, N.Y.: St. Vladimir's Seminary Press, 2003.

Stramara, Daniel F., Jr. "*Adelphotēs*: Two Frequently Overlooked Meanings." *Vigiliae Christianae* 51.3 (1997): 316–20.

———. "Double Monasticism in the Greek East, Fourth through Eighth Century." *Journal of Early Christian Studies* 6.2 (1998): 269–312.

Streete, Gail P. C. *Redeemed Bodies: Women Martyrs in Early Christianity.* Louisville: Westminster John Knox Press, 2009.

Sugano, Karin. *Das Rombild des Hieronymus.* Frankfurt a.M.: Peter Lang, 1983.

Sweetser, Eve. *From Etymology to Pragmatics: Metaphorical and Cultural Aspects of Semantic Structure.* Cambridge Studies in Linguistics 54. Cambridge: Cambridge University Press, 1990.

Taylor, Laramie D., and Tiffany Setters. "Watching Aggressive, Attractive, Female Protagonists Shapes Gender Roles for Women among Male and Female Undergraduate Viewers." *Sex Roles* 65.1–2 (2011): 35–46.

Taylor, Mark C., ed. *Critical Terms for Religious Studies.* Chicago: University of Chicago Press, 1998.

Teule, H. G. B. "Paradise of the Fathers, Book of." In *The Gorgias Encyclopedic Dictionary of the Syriac Heritage,* edited by Sebastian P. Brock et al. [Sebastian P. Brock, Aaron M. Butts, George A. Kiraz, and Lucas van Rompay], 322. Beth Mardutho: The Syriac Institute; and Piscataway: Gorgias Press, 2011.

Thomas, Edmund. *Monumentality and the Roman Empire: Architecture in the Antonine Age.* Oxford: Oxford University Press, 2007.

Thorsteinsson, Runar M. "Stoicism as a Key to Pauline Ethics in Romans." In *Stoicism in Early Christianity,* edited by Tuomas Rasimus, Troels Engberg-Pedersen, and Ismo Dunderberg, 15–38. Peabody, Mass.: Hendrickson Publishers, 2010.

Thurston, Herbert. "The Editorial Labours of Cardinal Rampolla." *The Month* 108 (1906): 508–21.

Tilley, Maureen A. *Donatist Martyr Stories: The Church in Conflict in Roman North Africa.* Translated Texts for Historians 24. Liverpool: Liverpool University Press, 1996.

Treggiari, Susan. *Terentia, Tullia and Publilia: The Women of Cicero's Family.* Women of the Ancient World. New York: Routledge, 2007.

Trigg, Joseph Wilson. "God's Marvelous *Oikonomia*: Reflections on Origen's Understanding of Divine and Human Pedagogy in the Address Ascribed to Gregory Thaumaturgus." *Journal of Early Christian Studies* 9.1 (2001): 27–52.

Trout, Dennis E. *Paulinus of Nola: Life, Letters, and Poems.* Transformation of the Classical Heritage 27. Berkeley and Los Angeles: University of California Press, 1999.

Upson-Saia, Kristi. *Early Christian Dress: Gender, Virtue, and Authority.* Routledge Studies in Ancient History 3. New York: Routledge, 2011.

Urbainczyk, Theresa. *Socrates of Constantinople: Historian of Church and State.* Ann Arbor: University of Michigan Press, 1997.

Van Esbroeck, Michel. "Le culte de la Vierge de Jérusalem à Constantinople aux 6e–7e siècles." *Revue des Études Byzantines* 46 (1988): 181–90.

———. "La lettre de l'empereur Justinien sur l'Annonciation et la Noël en 561." *Analecta Bollandiana* 86 (1968): 351–71.

———. *Les plus anciens homéliaires géorgiens: Étude descriptive et historique.* Publications de l'Institut Orientaliste de Louvain 10. Louvain-la-Neuve: Université Catholique de Louvain, Institut Orientaliste, 1975.

Velimirović, Miloš. "Ēchos." In *The New Grove Dictionary of Music and Musicians,* edited by Stanley Sadie and John Tyrrell. 2nd ed. New York: Grove, 2001.

Verhelst, Stéphane. "La liturgie de Jérusalem à l'époque byzantine: Genèse et structures de l'année liturgique." Ph.D. dissertation, Hebrew University of Jerusalem, 1999.

———. "The Liturgy of Jerusalem in the Byzantine Period." In *Christians and Christianity in the Holy Land: From the Origins to the Latin Kingdoms*, Cultural Encounters in Late Antiquity and the Middle Ages 5, edited by Ora Limor and Guy G. Stroumsa, 421–62. Turnhout: Brepols, 2006.

———. "Le 15 août, le 9 av. et le kathisme." *Questions Liturgiques* 82.3 (2001): 161–91.

Vivian, Tim. *Four Desert Fathers: Pambo, Evagrius, Macarius of Egypt, and Macarius of Alexandria: Coptic Texts Relating to the* Lausiac History *of Palladius*. Crestwood, N.Y.: St. Vladimir's Seminary Press, 2004.

Vuolanto, Ville. "Choosing Asceticism: Children and Parents, Vows and Conflicts." In *Children in Late Ancient Christianity*, Studien und Texte zu Antike und Christentum 58, edited by Cornelia B. Horn and Robert R. Phenix, Jr., 255–91. Tübingen: Mohr Siebeck, 2009.

Wade, Andrew. "The Oldest *Iadgari*: The Jerusalem Tropologion, V–VIII c." *Orientalia Christiana Periodica* 50 (1984): 451–56.

Ward, Benedicta. *Harlots of the Desert: A Study of Repentance in Early Monastic Sources*. Cistercian Studies Series 106. Kalamazoo: Cistercian Publications, 1987.

Ward-Perkins, Bryan. *From Classical Antiquity to the Middle Ages: Urban Public Building in Northern and Central Italy, AD 300–850*. Oxford Historical Monographs. Oxford: Oxford University Press, 1984.

Waszink, J. H. *Quinti Septimi Florentis Tertulliani De Anima*. Leiden: Brill, 2010.

Watts, Edward Jay. *City and School in Late Antique Athens and Alexandria*. Berkeley and Los Angeles: University of California Press, 2006.

Wellesz, Egon. *A History of Byzantine Music and Hymnography*. 2nd ed. Oxford: Clarendon Press, 1961.

Wertheimer, Barbara M. *We Were There: The Story of Working Women in America*. New York: Pantheon Books, 1977.

Wharton, Annabel J. "The Tribune Tower: Spolia as Despoliation." In *Reuse Value: Spolia and Appropriation in Art and Architecture from Constantine to Sherrie Levine*, edited by Richard Brilliant and Dale Kinney, 179–97. Farnham: Ashgate, 2011.

Wiedemann, Thomas E. J. *Adults and Children in the Roman Empire*. New Haven: Yale University Press, 1989.

Wilkinson, John D. *Egeria's Travels, Newly Translated with Supporting Documents and Notes*. 3rd ed. Warminster: Aris and Phillips, 1999.

Wilkinson, Kate. *Women and Modesty in Late Antiquity*. Cambridge: Cambridge University Press, 2015.

Wilkinson, Kevin W. "The Elder Melania's Missing Decade." *Journal of Late Antiquity* 5.1 (2012): 166–84.

Wimbush, Vincent L., and Richard Valantasis, eds. *Asceticism*. New York: Oxford University Press, 1995.

Wiseman, T. P. "Legendary Genealogies in Late-Republican Rome." *Greece and Rome* 21.2 (1974): 153–64.

Wohl, Robert. *The Generation of 1914*. Cambridge, Mass.: Harvard University Press, 1979.

Yarbrough, Anne. "Christianization in the Fourth Century: The Example of Roman Women." *Church History* 45.2 (1976): 149–65.

Young, Robin Darling. "Cannibalism and Other Family Woes in *Letter* 55 of Evagrius of Pontus." In *The World of Early Egyptian Christianity: Language, Literature, and Social Context—Essays in Honor of David W. Johnson,* edited by James E. Goehring and Janet A. Timbie, 130–39. Washington, D.C.: Catholic University of America Press, 2007.

INDEX

Acta Perpetuae et Felicitatis, 114–25. See also *Passion of Perpetua and Felicitas*
Aphrahat, 95
apostolic succession, 26–30
aristocracy, 6–7, 18; Christianity and, 173, 181; genealogical thought, 26–27; homes of, 23, 45; Melania the Elder's relationship to, 39–43. *See also* nobility
asceticism: aristocrats and, 35, 46; and martyrdom, 112, 114, 124–25; and migration, 211–13, 215; and motherhood, 72–81. *See also* nobility. *See also under* gender; Melania the Elder; Melania the Younger; women; wounds
Augustine of Hippo: on babies and original sin, 178–80; interaction with Melania the Younger and Pinian, 171–72, 181; on nobility, 174–75; on the pain and wounds of sin, 92, 94; on Perpetua and Felicitas, 123–25

Basil of Caesarea, 93, 95
Basilica Constantiniana, 24–29. See also *fastigium*
Blesilla, 73, 75
body, 121–22, 178–80; (desirable) female body, 133–34. *See also* wounds
buildings. *See* property

Chalcedon: anti-Chalcedonian, 39, 187, 189, 191–94, 196–98; Chalcedonian, 187–88, 191–92, 197, 232

childbirth, 72
Christology, 188
Clark, Elizabeth A.: on the discursive uses of women, 261; on gender, 51; on history/historiography, 8–9, 111–13, 171–72, 180, 245–46, 256; influence, 8, 284–86; intellectual context, 271–73; on knowledge and power, 264; on metaphor, 87; on orthodoxy/heresy, 189–90, 193–94
clothing, 34–35, 38
cognitive linguistic theory, 87–89. *See also* metaphor
community, 118–20, 124
Constantine, 24–29, 205
Coptic Orthodox Church, 260–61
Council of Chalcedon, 2, 187–88, 191–93, 196
Council of Constantinople, 2, 156, 162
Council of Ephesus, 2, 186–88
cult of the saints, 112–13, 233
Cyprian, 112, 122–23
Cyril of Alexandria, 2, 188, 194
Cyril of Scythopolis, 189, 193

death, noble, 54
domesticity, refusal of, 276

early Christianity, 1–3, 8–9, 27
education, 77–78

Egeria, 205–6, 223–26
Egypt, 137–39, 260–61, 264–67
emotion, 52, 55–58, 74; in Platonism, 57; in Stoicism, 55–56, 58
empire. *See* imperial space
Eudocia, 44, 76, 177, 190–91, 193, 195–97, 201n68
Eudoxia, 53
Eusebius, 24
Eutyches, 188, 197
Evagrius of Pontus, 4, 96, 138–41, 153–66
exile, 209–10, 213

fall, the. *See* reversal of the fall
family, 35–37, 118–19. *See also* community; renunciation
fan culture, 61–63
fastigium, 25, 27–28
Felicitas, 115, 117–19, 121–25. See also *Acta Perpetuae et Felicitatis*; *Passion of Perpetua and Felicitas*
friendship, 55, 164–65

Garden of Monks, The, 264–67
gender, 18, 51, 62, 109, 130, 142n12, 272–73; and asceticism, 51, 109–10, 117–18, 132–33; and emotion, 56–57; and martyrdom, 116, 124; and (monastic) memory, 132–35, 137–38. *See also* death, noble; intersectionality; masculinity. *See also under* Melania the Elder; Melania the Younger
genealogy, 22, 25–28, 266–67; ascetic, 78–79
Georgian Chantbook, 223, 226–31
Gerontius, 4–5, 30, 38–39, 41, 43–45, 112–13, 172–78, 186–87, 189–98; in the eyes of Rampolla, 248
Gregory the Great, 94, 112
Gregory Nazianzus, 94, 156, 158, 162
Gregory of Nyssa, 72, 133, 158, 160, 206

hagiography, 458–59, 247–48, 255, 272–73, 280
health. *See* wounds
heresy, 172, 175, 180–81, 187, 191. *See also* orthodoxy
Hippocrates, 99n19
historiography, 3–8, 11–12, 272–74. *See also under* Clark, Elizabeth A.
Holy Land, 205–6, 211–14
homilies, 262, 267–68, 275
household, 75, 77–81
humility, 174–77

hymns, 223, 226–27, 229–31; of Marian devotion, 230–34. *See also* Georgian Chantbook

imperial space, 207–9, 211–14. *See also* exile
inheritance, 21–23, 35, 43, 46. *See also* property
intersectionality, 51

Jerome, 4, 73–75, 77–79, 136–37, 140, 210–13
Jerusalem: building program, 29–30, 205–6; liturgy and ritual, 222–26; migration to, 207, 209; monasticism in, 137–39, 211; pilgrimage to, 223. *See also* Georgian Chantbook
John Chrysostom, 42, 93–95, 155
John Rufus, 44, 189, 192–93
Julian of Eclanum, 177–79

late antiquity, 1–2, 20
Lausiac History, 4, 35, 130–33, 135, 155, 260. *See also* Palladius
legacy, 35, 39, 42, 46
letters, 153–55, 161–67
Liber Pontificalis, 24–30, 32n34
Life of Anthony, 53
Life of Euthymius, 193
Life of Martin of Tours. *See* Severus
Life of Melania the Younger, 19–24, 29–30, 111–12, 275. *See also* Gerontius; *Vita Melaniae Iunioris*
Life of Peter the Iberian, 44, 189
lineage, 36, 41
liturgy, 222–26
Lives of the Monks of Palestine, 189, 193
lost generation, 207–9, 213–15

Macrina, 60–61, 76, 163
masculinity, 52–54, 56, 109, 130, 134. *See also* emotion. *See also* gender *under* Melania the Elder; Melania the Younger
medicine. *See* wounds
Marcella, 77, 137
Marcian, 191–92, 198
martyrdom, 112–14. See also *Passion of Perpetua and Felicitas*. *See also under* asceticism; gender
martyrs, 111–14, 120
Mary of Egypt, 59
Matthew the Poor, 265–66
memory, 131–34, 140. *See also under* gender
memory theory, 132–33, 135, 138–39
Melania the Elder: agency of, 7–8; asceticism, 4, 35, 37, 40, 42, 74, 161, 163, 209–10; emotions, 74; family, 34–35, 36–37, 40, 43, 138, 155, 161;

INDEX 327

gender, 53, 130, 138–41, 165; *gnōstikos*, 153–54, 161, 163–66; letters, 154; life of, 1, 4, 36, 153–54, 158, 161; memory, 133–36, 138–39, 141; as modern model, 262–67; motherhood, 74–75, 79, 83n16; Origenist leanings, 38, 41–42, 130, 154, 164, 172; patronage, 154–56, 159–60; perfection, spiritual, 176; as queer, 131, 133–36, 138–41; travel, 209, 213, 260; wealth, 35–36, 39–40, 43–44, 139, 153–54, 168n14. *See also* namesake
Melania the Younger: asceticism, 5, 20–21, 35, 37–39, 41–42, 52–53, 57, 97, 112–13, 117, 173–74, 210–11, 276–77; benefaction, 29–30, 44; death, 54–55; emotions, 56–60; family, 41, 171, 210; gender, 52–56, 59; life of, 1, 4–5, 38, 171, 189, 208; and martyrdom, 113–14; miracles, 71, 113, 178; in modern media, 249–53; as modern model, 262–67; motherhood, 74; motherhood, spiritual, 76, 80, 196; orthodoxy/heresy, 172, 180, 189–91, 194–95, 197–98; patronage, 193–94; ritual, 225; senatorial rank, 23; travel, 213–14, 260; wealth, 52, 54, 173–75, 210, 277–79
metaphor, 87–88
migration, 207–8
monasticism, 136–40; and gender/sexuality, 134–35; household, 77; and memory, 132
mortality, 72, 82n5
motherhood, 72–73, 75–76, 78–81, 84n28; spiritual, 76–78. *See also under* asceticism

namesake, 35, 37–39, 43
Nestorianism: anti-, 39, 186–87, 191, 194, 197–98; Nestorian controversy, 2
Nestorius, 2, 186, 188, 192, 197
nobility, 173–76, 179. *See also* aristocracy
North Africa, 116, 122–24, 171–72

Origen, 2, 92–93, 164
Origenism, 38, 41–42, 130, 132, 136, 140; anti-, 4, 42, 45, 132, 140; Origenist controversy, 2, 4, 111, 131–32, 172, 175
original sin, 178–80. *See also* sin
orthodoxy, 150, 172, 180–81, 187–91, 194, 198. *See also* heresy

pain, 90–94
Palladius, 4, 35–45, 130–36, 138–40, 153–55, 157–60, 208–9. *See also Lausiac History*
Paradise of the Fathers, The, 260, 264
Passion of Perpetua and Felicitas (Passio), 114–25; and Melania the Younger, 122–24. *See also Acta Perpetuae et Felicitatis*

Paula, 22, 73, 75, 79–80, 136, 138–40
Paulinus of Nola, 4, 34–38, 75, 154, 158, 172, 182n7
Pelagia, 59
Pelagianism, 173–76, 178; Pelagian controversy, 2, 172–73, 180–81
Pelagius, 172–76, 179
perfection, spiritual, 175–76
Perpetua, 115–25. *See also Acta Perpetuae et Felicitatis*; *Passion of Perpetua and Felicitas*
Pinian, 20–21, 27, 29–30, 53, 171
Proclus, 194
property, 20–21, 31n9, 45; agency of, 21–22, 29–30; genealogical claims of, 22–23, 25–27; inheritance of, 23, 45; patronage, 25–26; reuse of, 23–24; temporal claims of, 22–24, 25–26. *See also* inheritance
Publicola, 36–37, 40, 48n53
pudicitia, 56–57
Pulcheria, 191–92, 195, 198, 200n49

queer theory, 131, 134–36, 142n9
Quodvultdeus, 123–25, 129n60

Rampolla, Mariano (cardinal), 246–49, 250–51, 253, 255
reception history, 247
renunciation, 115–18, 124
reversal of the fall, 121–22, 124–25
ritual, 222, 226
Rome, 23–24; apostolic history, 19–20, 24; as Babylon, 210; Melania the Elder's flight from, 209–10; Melania the Elder's return to, 213; monasticism in, 137–38; in myth of renunciation, 211–14
Rufinus of Aquileia, 4, 40, 74, 139, 145n67, 157, 160

sainthood, 274–76, 279–80
Satan, 121–22, 128n41
Serena (empress), 21, 112, 176–77
Severus, 34–35, 38
Shenouda III, 261–64, 267–68, 268n3
sin, 176, 178
social memory. *See* memory theory
Song of Songs, 86
Stoic theory of emotion, 55–56, 58
Sulpicius Severus, 34
Sylvester, 25, 26, 28

Tertullian, 92, 123
travel, 211–13. *See also* migration

Vita Melaniae Iunioris, 173, 186–87, 194–96. See also Gerontius; *Life of Melania the Younger*

wealth, 13n10, 17–18, 21, 31n9, 35, 43
women, 9, 50–51, 54, 56, 59, 80, 116, 133, 163; asceticism, 82n7, 84n27, 109–10, 117–18; agency, 110; in history, 111, 271–73; and masculinity, 130, 142n12; social roles, 263
worship, 223–26, 228–29
wounds, 86–88, 93–94; and asceticism, 96–98, 104n83, 117; bodily, 96; healthful, 93, 96–97; of heresy, 91–96, 101n38; of sin, 91–98, 101n38; treatment, 89–91, 94–95

www.ingramcontent.com/pod-product-compliance
Lightning Source LLC
Chambersburg PA
CBHW030521230426
43665CB00010B/711